ALSO BY KAREN ARMSTRONG

Fields of Blood

Fields of Blood

Religion and the History of Violence

KAREN ARMSTRONG

ALFRED A. KNOPF   *New York Toronto*
2014

THIS IS A BORZOI BOOK
PUBLISHED BY ALFRED A. KNOPF
AND ALFRED A. KNOPF CANADA

All rights reserved. Published in the United States by Alfred A. Knopf,
a division of Random House LLC, New York, and in Canada by
Alfred A. Knopf Canada, a division of Random House of Canada Limited,
Toronto, Penguin Random House companies. Originally published in
Great Britain by The Bodley Head, an imprint of the
Random House Group Limited, London.

www.aaknopf.com   www.randomhouse.ca

Library of Congress Cataloging-in-Publication Data
Armstrong, Karen, [date]
Fields of blood : religion and the history of violence / Karen Armstrong.
pages   cm
ISBN 978-0-307-95704-7 (hardcover)   ISBN 978-0-385-35310-6 (eBook)
1. Violence—Religious aspects.   I. Title.
BL65.V55A76 2014
201'.72—dc23   2014011057

Library and Archives Canada Cataloguing in Publication
Armstrong, Karen, [date], author
Fields of blood : religion and the history of violence / Karen Armstrong.
Includes bibliographical references and index.
Issued in print and electronic formats.
ISBN 978-0-307-40196-0
eBook ISBN 978-0-307-40198-4
1. Violence—Religious aspects—History.   2. Religion—Social aspects—
History.   I. Title.
BL65.V55A76 2014   201'.76332   C2014-902471-1

Jacket design by Oliver Munday

Manufactured in the United States of America
First Edition

For Jane Garrett

Now Hevel became a shepherd of flocks, and Kayin became
    a worker of the soil

. . .

But then it was, when they were out in the field
that Kayin rose up against Hevel his brother
and he killed him.
Yнwн said to Kayin:
Where is Hevel your brother?
He said:
I do not know. Am I the watcher of my brother?
Now he said:
What have you done!
Hark—your brother's blood cries out to me from the soil!

—GENESIS 4:2, 8–10, *translated by Everett Fox*

Contents

Fields of Blood

Introduction

E very year in ancient Israel the high priest brought two goats into the Jerusalem temple on the Day of Atonement. He sacrificed one to expiate the sins of the community and then laid his hands on the other, transferring all the people's misdeeds onto its head, and sent the sin-laden animal out of the city, literally placing the blame elsewhere. In this way, Moses explained, "the goat will bear all their faults away with it into a desert place."[1] In his classic study of religion and violence, René Girard argued that the scapegoat ritual defused rivalries among groups within the community.[2] In a similar way, I believe, modern society has made a scapegoat of faith.

In the West the idea that religion is inherently violent is now taken for granted and seems self-evident. As one who speaks on religion, I constantly hear how cruel and aggressive it has been, a view that, eerily, is expressed in the same way almost every time: "Religion has been the cause of all the major wars in history." I have heard this sentence recited like a mantra by American commentators and psychiatrists, London taxi drivers and Oxford academics. It is an odd remark. Obviously the two world wars were not fought on account of religion. When they discuss the reasons people go to war, military historians acknowledge that many interrelated social, material, and ideological factors are involved, one of the chief being competition for scarce resources. Experts on political violence or terrorism also insist that people commit atrocities for a complex range of reasons.[3] Yet so indelible is the aggressive image of religious faith in our secular consciousness that we routinely load the violent sins of the twentieth century onto the back of "religion" and drive it out into the political wilderness.

Even those who admit that religion has not been responsible for all the violence and warfare of the human race still take its essential belligerence for granted. They claim that "monotheism" is especially intolerant and that once people believe that "God" is on their side, compromise becomes impossible. They cite the Crusades, the Inquisition, and the Wars of Religion of the sixteenth and seventeenth centuries. They also point to the recent spate of terrorism committed in the name of religion to prove that Islam is particularly aggressive. If I mention Buddhist non-violence, they retort that Buddhism is a secular philosophy, not a religion. Here we come to the heart of the problem. Buddhism is certainly not a *religion* as this word has been understood in the West since the seventeenth and eighteenth centuries. But our modern Western conception of "religion" is idiosyncratic and eccentric. No other cultural tradition has anything like it, and even premodern European Christians would have found it reductive and alien. In fact, it complicates any attempt to pronounce on religion's propensity to violence.

To complicate things still further, for about fifty years now it has been clear in the academy that there is no universal way to define religion.[4] In the West we see "religion" as a coherent system of obligatory beliefs, institutions, and rituals, centering on a supernatural God, whose practice is essentially private and hermetically sealed off from all "secular" activities. But words in other languages that we translate as "religion" almost invariably refer to something larger, vaguer, and more encompassing. The Arabic *din* signifies an entire way of life. The Sanskrit *dharma* is also "a 'total' concept, untranslatable, which covers law, justice, morals, and social life."[5] *The Oxford Classical Dictionary* firmly states: "No word in either Greek or Latin corresponds to the English 'religion' or 'religious.'"[6] The idea of religion as an essentially personal and systematic pursuit was entirely absent from classical Greece, Japan, Egypt, Mesopotamia, Iran, China, and India.[7] Nor does the Hebrew Bible have any abstract concept of religion; and the Talmudic rabbis would have found it impossible to express what they meant by faith in a single word or even in a formula, since the Talmud was expressly designed to bring the whole of human life into the ambit of the sacred.[8]

The origins of the Latin *religio* are obscure. It was not "a great objective something" but had imprecise connotations of obligation and taboo; to say that a cultic observance, a family propriety, or keeping an oath was *religio* for you meant that it was incumbent on you to do it. The word acquired an important new meaning among early Christian theologians: an attitude of reverence toward God and the universe as a whole. For Saint Augustine (c. 354–430 CE), *religio* was neither a system of rituals and doctrines nor a historical institutionalized tradition but a personal encounter with the transcendence that we call God as well as the bond that unites us to the divine and to one another. In medieval Europe, *religio* came to refer to the monastic life and distinguished the monk from the "secular" priest, someone who lived and worked in the world (*saeculum*).[9]

The only faith tradition that does fit the modern Western notion of religion as something codified and private is Protestant Christianity, which, like *religion* in this sense of the word, is also a product of the early modern period. At this time Europeans and Americans had begun to separate religion and politics, because they assumed, not altogether accurately, that the theological squabbles of the Reformation had been entirely responsible for the Thirty Years' War. The conviction that religion must be rigorously excluded from political life has been called the charter myth of the sovereign nation-state.[10] The philosophers and statesmen who pioneered this dogma believed that they were returning to a more satisfactory state of affairs that had existed before ambitious Catholic clerics had confused two utterly distinct realms. But in fact their secular ideology was as radical an innovation as the modern market economy that the West was concurrently devising. To non-Westerners, who had not been through this particular modernizing process, both these innovations would seem unnatural and even incomprehensible. The habit of separating religion and politics is now so routine in the West that it is difficult for us to appreciate how thoroughly the two co-inhered in the past. It was never simply a question of the state "using" religion; the two were indivisible. Dissociating them would have seemed like trying to extract the gin from a cocktail.

In the premodern world, religion permeated all aspects of life. We shall see that a host of activities now considered mundane were experienced as deeply sacred: forest clearing, hunting, football matches, dice games, astronomy, farming, state building, tugs-of-war, town planning, commerce, imbibing strong drink, and, most particularly, warfare. Ancient peoples would have found it impossible to see where "religion" ended and "politics" began. This was not because they were too stupid to understand the distinction but because they wanted to invest everything they did with ultimate value. We are meaning-seeking creatures and, unlike other animals, fall very easily into despair if we fail to make sense of our lives. We find the prospect of our inevitable extinction hard to bear. We are troubled by natural disasters and human cruelty and are acutely aware of our physical and psychological frailty. We find it astonishing that we are here at all and want to know why. We also have a great capacity for wonder. Ancient philosophies were entranced by the order of the cosmos; they marveled at the mysterious power that kept the heavenly bodies in their orbits and the seas within bounds and that ensured that the earth regularly came to life again after the dearth of winter, and they longed to participate in this richer and more permanent existence.

They expressed this yearning in terms of what is known as the perennial philosophy, so called because it was present, in some form, in most premodern cultures.[11] Every single person, object, or experience was seen as a replica, a pale shadow, of a reality that was stronger and more enduring than anything in their ordinary experience but that they only glimpsed in visionary moments or in dreams. By ritually imitating what they understood to be the gestures and actions of their celestial alter egos—whether gods, ancestors, or culture heroes—premodern folk felt themselves to be caught up in their larger dimension of being. We humans are profoundly artificial and tend naturally toward archetypes and paradigms.[12] We constantly strive to improve on nature or approximate to an ideal that transcends the day-to-day. Even our contemporary cult of celebrity can be understood as an expression of our reverence for and yearning to emulate models of "superhumanity." Feeling ourselves connected to such extraordinary realities satisfies an essential craving. It touches us within, lifts us momentarily beyond ourselves, so that we seem to inhabit our humanity more fully than usual and feel in touch with the deeper currents of life. If we no longer find this experience in a church or temple, we seek it in art, a musical concert, sex, drugs—or warfare. What this last may have to do with these other moments of transport may not be so obvious, but it is one of the oldest triggers of ecstatic experience. To understand why, it will be helpful to consider the development of our neuroanatomy.

Each of us has not one but three brains that coexist uneasily. In the deepest recess of our gray matter we have an "old brain" that we inherited from the reptiles that struggled out of the primal slime 500 million years ago. Intent on their own survival, with absolutely no altruistic impulses, these creatures were solely motivated by mechanisms urging them to feed, fight, flee (when necessary), and reproduce. Those best equipped to compete mercilessly for food, ward off any threat, dominate territory, and seek safety naturally passed along their genes, so these self-centered impulses could only intensify.[13] But sometime after mammals appeared, they evolved what neuroscientists call the limbic system, perhaps about 120 million years ago.[14] Formed over the core brain derived from the reptiles, the limbic system motivated all sorts of new behaviors, including the protection and nurture of young as well as the formation of alliances with other individuals that were invaluable in the struggle to survive. And so, for the first time, sentient beings possessed the capacity to cherish and care for creatures other than themselves.[15]

Although these limbic emotions would never be as strong as the "me first" drives still issuing from our reptilian core, we humans have evolved a substantial hard-wiring for empathy for other creatures, and especially for our fellow humans. Eventually, the Chinese philosopher Mencius (c. 371–288 BCE) would insist that nobody was wholly without such sympathy. If a man sees a child teetering on the brink of a well, about to fall in, he would feel her predicament in his own body and would reflexively, without thought for himself, lunge forward to save her. There would be something radically wrong with anyone who could walk past such a scene without a flicker of disquiet. For most, these sentiments were essential, though, Mencius thought, somewhat subject to individual will. You could stamp on these shoots of benevolence just as you could cripple or deform yourself physically. On the other hand, if you cultivated them, they would acquire a strength and dynamism of their own.[16]

We cannot entirely understand Mencius's argument without considering the third part of our brain. About twenty thousand years ago, during the Paleolithic Age, human beings evolved a "new brain," the neocortex, home of the reasoning powers and self-awareness that enable us to stand back from the instinctive, primitive passions. Humans thus became roughly as they are today, subject to the conflicting impulses of their three distinct brains. Paleolithic men were proficient killers. Before the invention of agriculture, they were dependent on the slaughter of ani-

mals and used their big brains to develop a technology that enabled them
to kill creatures much larger and more powerful than themselves. But
their empathy may have made them uneasy. Or so we might conclude
from modern hunting societies. Anthropologists observe that tribesmen
feel acute anxiety about having to slay the beasts they consider their
friends and patrons and try to assuage this distress by ritual purification.
In the Kalahari Desert, where wood is scarce, bushmen are forced to
rely on light weapons that can only graze the skin. So they anoint their
arrows with a poison that kills the animal—only very slowly. Out of
ineffable solidarity, the hunter stays with his dying victim, crying when
it cries, and participating symbolically in its death throes. Other tribes
don animal costumes or smear the kill's blood and excrement on cavern
walls, ceremonially returning the creature to the underworld from which
it came.[17]

Paleolithic hunters may have had a similar understanding.[18] The cave
paintings in northern Spain and southwestern France are among the
earliest extant documents of our species. These decorated caves almost
certainly had a liturgical function, so from the very beginning art and
ritual were inseparable. Our neocortex makes us intensely aware of the
tragedy and perplexity of our existence, and in art, as in some forms of
religious expression, we find a means of letting go and encouraging the
softer, limbic emotions to predominate. The frescoes and engravings in
the labyrinth of Lascaux in the Dordogne, the earliest of which are seventeen thousand years old, still evoke awe in visitors. In their numinous
depiction of the animals, the artists have captured the hunters' essential
ambivalence. Intent as they were to acquire food, their ferocity was tem-
pered by respectful sympathy for the beasts they were obliged to kill,
whose blood and fat they mixed with their paints. Ritual and art helped
hunters express their empathy with and reverence (religio) for their fellow creatures—just as Mencius would describe some seventeen millennia later—and helped them live with their need to kill them.

In Lascaux there are no pictures of the reindeer that featured so
largely in the diet of these hunters.[19] But not far away, in Montastruc, a
small sculpture has been found, carved from a mammoth tusk in about
11,000 BCE, at about the same time as the later Lascaux paintings. Now
lodged in the British Museum, it depicts two swimming reindeer.[20] The
artist must have watched his prey intently as they swam across lakes and
rivers in search of new pastures, making themselves particularly vulner-

able to the hunters. He also felt a tenderness toward his victims, conveying the unmistakable poignancy of their facial expressions without a hint of sentimentality. As Neil MacGregor, director of the British Museum, has noted, the anatomical accuracy of this sculpture shows that it "was clearly made not just with the knowledge of a hunter but also with the insight of a butcher, someone who had not only looked at his animals but had cut them up." Rowan Williams, the former archbishop of Canterbury, has also reflected insightfully on the "huge and imaginative generosity" of these Paleolithic artists: "In the art of this period, you see human beings trying to enter fully into the flow of life, so that they become part of the whole process of animal life that's going on all around them . . . and this is actually a very religious impulse."[21] From the first, then, one of the major preoccupations of both religion and art (the two being inseparable) was to cultivate a sense of community—with nature, the animal world, and our fellow humans.

We would never wholly forget our hunter-gatherer past, which was the longest period in human history. Everything that we think of as most human—our brains, bodies, faces, speech, emotions, and thoughts—bears the stamp of this heritage.[22] Some of the rituals and myths devised by our prehistoric ancestors appear to have survived in the practices of later, literate cultures. In this way, animal sacrifice, the central rite of nearly every ancient society, preserved prehistoric hunting ceremonies and the honor accorded the beast that gave its life for the community.[23] Much of what we now call "religion" was originally rooted in an acknowledgment of the tragic fact that life depended on the destruction of other creatures; rituals were addressed to helping human beings face up to this insoluble dilemma. Despite their real respect, reverence, and even affection for their prey, however, ancient huntsmen remained dedicated killers. Millennia of fighting large aggressive animals meant that these hunting parties became tightly bonded teams that were the seeds of our modern armies, ready to risk everything for the common good and to protect their fellows in moments of danger.[24] And there was one more conflicting emotion to be reconciled: they probably loved the excitement and intensity of the hunt.

Here again the limbic system comes into play. The prospect of killing may stir our empathy, but in the very acts of hunting, raiding, and battling, this same seat of emotions is awash in serotonin, the neurotransmitter responsible for the sensation of ecstasy that we associate with some forms of spiritual experience. So it happened that these violent pursuits came to be perceived as sacred activities, however bizarre that may seem to our understanding of religion. People, especially men, experienced a strong bond with their fellow warriors, a heady feeling of altruism at putting their lives at risk for others and of being more fully alive. This response to violence persists in our nature. The *New York Times* war correspondent Chris Hedges has aptly described war as "a force that gives us meaning":

> War makes the world understandable, a black and white tableau of them and us. It suspends thought, especially self-critical thought. All bow before the supreme effort. We are one. Most of us willingly accept war as long as we can fold it into a belief system that paints the ensuing suffering as necessary for a higher good, for human beings seek not only happiness but meaning. And tragically war is sometimes the most powerful way in human society to achieve meaning.[25]

It may be too that as they give free rein to the aggressive impulses from the deepest region of their brains, warriors feel in tune with the most elemental and inexorable dynamics of existence, those of life and death. Put another way, war is a means of surrender to reptilian ruthlessness, one of the strongest of human drives, without being troubled by the self-critical nudges of the neocortex.

The warrior, therefore, experiences in battle the transcendence that others find in ritual, sometimes to pathological effect. Psychiatrists who treat war veterans for post-traumatic stress disorder (PTSD) have noted that in the destruction of other people, soldiers can experience a self-affirmation that is almost erotic. Yet afterward, as they struggle to disentangle their emotions of pity and ruthlessness, PTSD sufferers may find themselves unable to function as coherent human beings. One Vietnam veteran described a photograph of himself holding two severed heads by the hair; the war, he said, was "hell," a place where "crazy was natural" and everything "out of control," but, he concluded:

> The worst thing I can say about myself is that while I was there I was so alive. I loved it the way you can like an adrenaline high, the way you can love your friends, your tight buddies. So unreal and the realest thing that ever happened. . . . And maybe the worst thing for me

now is living in peacetime without a possibility of that high again. I hate what that high was about but I loved that high.[26]

"Only when we are in the midst of conflict does the shallowness and vapidness of much of our lives become apparent," Hedges explains. "Trivia dominates our conversation and increasingly our airwaves. And war is an enticing elixir. It gives us a resolve, a cause. It allows us to be noble."[27] One of the many, intertwined motives driving men to the battlefield has been the tedium and pointlessness of ordinary domestic existence. The same hunger for intensity would compel others to become monks and ascetics.

The warrior in battle may feel connected with the cosmos, but afterward he cannot always resolve these inner contradictions. It is fairly well established that there is a strong taboo against killing our own kind—an evolutionary stratagem that helped our species to survive.[28] Still, we fight. But to bring ourselves to do so, we envelop the effort in a mythology—often a "religious" mythology—that puts distance between us and the enemy. We exaggerate his differences, be they racial, religious, or ideological. We develop narratives to convince ourselves that he is not really human but monstrous, the antithesis of order and goodness. Today we may tell ourselves that we are fighting for God and country or that a particular war is "just" or "legal." But this encouragement doesn't always take hold. During the Second World War, for instance, Brigadier General S. L. A. Marshall of the U.S. Army and a team of historians interviewed thousands of soldiers from more than four hundred infantry companies that had seen close combat in Europe and the Pacific. Their findings were startling: only 15 to 20 percent of infantrymen had been able to fire at the enemy directly; the rest tried to avoid it and had developed complex methods of misfiring or reloading their weapons so as to escape detection.[29]

It is hard to overcome one's nature. To become efficient soldiers, recruits must go through a grueling initiation, not unlike what monks or yogins undergo, to subdue their emotions. As the cultural historian Joanna Bourke explains the process:

Individuals had to be broken down to be rebuilt into efficient fighting men. The basic tenets included depersonalization, uniforms, lack of privacy, forced social relationships, tight schedules, lack of sleep, disorientation followed by rites of reorganization according to military codes, arbitrary rules, and strict punishment. The methods of brutalization were similar to those carried out by regimes where men were taught to torture prisoners.[30]

So, we might say, the soldier has to become as inhuman as the "enemy" he has created in his mind. Indeed, we shall find that in some cultures, even (or perhaps especially) those that glorify warfare, the warrior is somehow tainted, polluted, and an object of fear—both an heroic figure and a necessary evil, to be dreaded, set apart.

Our relationship to warfare is therefore complex, possibly because it is a relatively recent human development. Hunter-gatherers could not afford the organized violence that we call war, because warfare requires large armies, sustained leadership, and economic resources that were far beyond their reach.[31] Archaeologists have found mass graves from this period that suggest some kind of massacre,[32] yet there is little evidence that early humans regularly fought one another.[33] But human life changed forever in about 9000 BCE, when pioneering farmers in the Levant learned to grow and store wild grain. They produced harvests that were able to support larger populations than ever before and eventually they grew more food than they needed.[34] As a result, the human population increased so dramatically that in some regions a return to hunter-gatherer life became impossible. Between about 8500 BCE and the first century of the Common Era—a remarkably short period given the four million years of our history—all around the world, quite independently, the great majority of humans made the transition to agrarian life. And with agriculture came civilization; and with civilization, warfare.

In our industrialized societies, we often look back to the agrarian age with nostalgia, imagining that people lived more wholesomely then, close to the land and in harmony with nature. Initially, however, agriculture was experienced as traumatic. These early settlements were vulnerable to wild swings in productivity that could wipe out the entire population, and their mythology describes the first farmers fighting a desperate battle against sterility, drought, and famine.[35] For the first time, backbreaking drudgery became a fact of human life. Skeletal remains show that plant-fed humans were a head shorter than meat-eating hunters, prone to anemia, infectious diseases, rotten teeth, and bone disorders.[36] The earth was revered as the Mother Goddess and her fecundity experienced as an epiphany; she was called Ishtar in Mesopotamia, Demeter in Greece, Isis in Egypt, and Anat in Syria. Yet she was not a comforting presence but extremely violent. The Earth Mother regularly dismembered consorts and enemies alike—just as corn was ground to powder and grapes crushed to unrecognizable pulp. Farming implements were depicted as weapons that wounded the earth, so farming plots became fields of blood. When Anat slew Mot, god of sterility, she cut him in two with a ritual sickle, winnowed him in a sieve, ground him in a mill, and scattered his scraps of bleeding flesh over the fields. After she slaughtered the enemies of Baal, god of life-giving rain, she adorned herself with rouge and henna, made a necklace of the hands and heads of her victims, and waded knee-deep in blood to attend the triumphal banquet.[37]

These violent myths reflected the political realities of agrarian life. By the beginning of the ninth millennium BCE, the settlement in the oasis of Jericho in the Jordan valley had a population of three thousand people, which would have been impossible before the advent of agriculture. Jericho was a fortified stronghold protected by a massive wall that must have consumed tens of thousands of hours of manpower to construct.[38] In this arid region, Jericho's ample food stores would have been a magnet for hungry nomads. Intensified agriculture, therefore, created conditions that that could endanger everyone in this wealthy colony and transform its arable land into fields of blood. Jericho was unusual, however—a portent of the future. Warfare would not become endemic in the region for another five thousand years, but it was already a possibility, and from the first, it seems, large-scale organized violence was linked not with religion but with organized theft.[39]

Agriculture had also introduced another type of aggression: an institutional or structural violence in which a society compels people to live in such wretchedness and subjection that they are unable to better their lot. This systemic oppression has been described as possibly "the most subtle form of violence,"[40] and, according to the World Council of Churches, it is present whenever "resources and powers are unequally distributed, concentrated in the hands of the few, who do not use them to achieve the possible self-realization of all members, but use parts of them for self-satisfaction or for purposes of dominance, oppression, and control of other societies or of the underprivileged in the same society."[41] Agrarian civilization made this systemic violence a reality for the first time in human history.

Paleolithic communities had probably been egalitarian because hunter-gatherers could not support a privileged class that did not share the hardship and danger of the hunt.[42] Because these small communities lived at near-subsistence level and produced no economic surplus, inequity of wealth was impossible. The tribe could survive only if everybody shared what food they had. Government by coercion was not feasible because all able-bodied males had exactly the same weapons and fighting skills. Anthropologists have noted that modern hunter-gatherer societies are classless, that their economy is "a sort of communism," and that people are honored for skills and qualities, such as generosity, kindness, and even-temperedness, that benefit the community as a whole.[43] But in societies that produce more than they need, it is possible for a small group to exploit this surplus for its own enrichment, gain a monopoly of violence, and dominate the rest of the population.

As we shall see in Part One, this systemic violence would prevail in all agrarian civilizations. In the empires of the Middle East, China, India, and Europe, which were economically dependent on agriculture, a small elite, comprising not more than 2 percent of the population, with the help of a small band of retainers, systematically robbed the masses of the produce they had grown in order to support their aristocratic lifestyle. Yet, social historians argue, without this iniquitous arrangement, human beings would probably never have advanced beyond subsistence level, because it created a nobility with the leisure to develop the civilized arts and sciences that made progress possible. All premodern civilizations adopted this oppressive system; there seemed to be no alternative. This inevitably had implications for religion, which permeated all human activities, including state building and government. Indeed, we shall see that premodern politics was inseparable from religion. And if a ruling elite adopted an ethical tradition, such as Buddhism, Christianity, or Islam, the aristocratic clergy usually adapted their ideology so that it could support the structural violence of the state.[44]

In Parts One and Two we shall explore this dilemma. Established by force and maintained by military aggression, warfare was essential to the agrarian state. When land and the peasants who farmed it were the chief sources of wealth, territorial conquest was the only way such a kingdom could increase its revenues. Warfare was, therefore, indispensable to any premodern economy. The ruling class had to maintain its control of the peasant villages, defend its arable land against aggressors, conquer more land, and ruthlessly suppress any hint of insubordination. A key figure in this story will be the Indian emperor Ashoka (c. 268–232 BCE). Appalled by the suffering his army had inflicted on a rebellious city, he tirelessly promoted an ethic of compassion and tolerance but could not in the end disband his army. No state can survive without its soldiers. And once states grew and warfare had become a fact of human life, an even greater force—the military might of empire—often seemed the only way to keep the peace.

So necessary to the rise of states and ultimately empires is military force that historians regard militarism as a mark of civilization. Without disciplined, obedient, and law-abiding armies, human society, it is claimed, would probably have remained at a primitive level or have degenerated into ceaselessly warring hordes.[45] But like our inner conflict between violent and compassionate impulses, the incoherence between peaceful ends and violent means would remain unresolved. Ashoka's dilemma is the dilemma of civilization itself. And into this tug-of-war religion would enter too. Since all premodern state ideology was inseparable from religion, warfare inevitably acquired a sacral element. Indeed, every major faith tradition has tracked that political entity in which it arose; none has become a "world religion" without the patronage of a militarily powerful empire, and, therefore, each would have to develop an imperial ideology.[46] But to what degree did religion contribute to the violence of the states with which it was inextricably linked? How much blame for the history of human violence can we ascribe to religion itself? The answer is not as simple as much of our popular discourse would suggest.

◆   ◆   ◆

Our world is dangerously polarized at a time when humanity is more closely interconnected—politically, economically, and electronically—than ever before. If we are to meet the challenge of our time and create a global society where all peoples can live together in peace and mutual respect, we need to assess our situation accurately. We cannot afford oversimplified assumptions about the nature of religion or its role in the world. What the American scholar William T. Cavanaugh calls "the myth of religious violence"[47] served Western people well at an early stage of their modernization, but in our global village we need a more nuanced view in order to understand our predicament fully.

This book focuses mainly on the Abrahamic traditions of Judaism, Christianity, and Islam because they are the ones most in the spotlight at the moment. Yet because there is such a widespread conviction that monotheism, the belief in a single God, is especially prone to violence and intolerance, the first section of the book will examine it in comparative perspective. In traditions preceding the Abrahamic faiths, we will see not only how military force and an ideology imbued with the sacred were both essential to the state but also how from earliest times there were those who agonized about the dilemma of necessary violence and proposed "religious" ways to counter aggressive urges and channel them toward more compassionate ends.

Time would fail me were I to attempt to cover all instances of religiously articulated violence, but we will explore some of the most prominent in the long history of the three Abrahamic religions, such as Joshua's holy wars, the call to jihad, the Crusades, the Inquisition, and the European Wars of Religion. It will become clear that when premodern people engaged in politics, they thought in religious terms and that faith permeated their struggle to make sense of the world in a way that seems strange to us today. But that is not the whole story. To paraphrase a British commercial: "The weather does lots of different things—and so does religion." In religious history, the struggle for peace has been just as important as the holy war. Religious people have found all kinds of ingenious methods of dealing with the assertive machismo of the reptilian brain, curbing violence, and building respectful, life-enhancing communities. But as with Ashoka, who came up against the systemic militancy of the state, they could not radically change their societies; the most they could do was propose a different path to demonstrate kinder and more empathic ways for people to live together.

When we come to the modern period, in Part Three, we will, of course, explore the wave of violence claiming religious justification that erupted during the 1980s and culminated in the atrocity of September 11, 2001. But we will also examine the nature of secularism, which, despite its manifold benefits, has not always offered a wholly irenic alternative to a religious state ideology. The early modern philosophies that tried to pacify Europe after the Thirty Years' War in fact had a ruthless streak of their own, particularly when dealing with casualties of secular modernity who found it alienating rather than empowering and liberating. This is because secularism did not so much displace religion as create new religious enthusiasms. So ingrained is our desire for ultimate meaning that our secular institutions, most especially the nation-state, almost immediately acquired a "religious" aura, though they have been less adept than the ancient mythologies at helping people face up to the grimmer realities of human existence for which there are no easy answers. Yet secularism has by no means been the end of the story. In some societies attempting to find their way to modernity, it has succeeded only in damaging religion and wounding psyches of people unprepared to be wrenched from ways of living and understanding that had always supported them. Licking its wounds in the desert, the scapegoat, with its festering resentment, has rebounded on the city that drove it out.

Part One

BEGINNINGS

1

Farmers and Herdsmen

Gilgamesh, named in the ancient king lists as the fifth ruler of Uruk, was remembered as "the strongest of men—huge, handsome, radiant, perfect."[1] He may well have existed but soon acquired a legendary aura. It was said that he had seen everything, traveled to the ends of the earth, visited the underworld, and achieved great wisdom. By the early third millennium BCE, Uruk, in what is now southern Iraq, was the largest city-state in the federation of Sumer, the world's first civilization. The poet Sin-leqi-unninni, who wrote his version of Gilgamesh's remarkable life in about 1200 BCE, was still bursting with pride in its temples, palaces, gardens, and shops. He began and ended his epic with an exuberant description of the magnificent city wall, six miles long, that Gilgamesh had restored for his people. "Walk on the wall of Uruk!" he urged his readers excitedly. "Follow its course around the city, inspect its mighty foundations, examine its brickwork, how masterfully it is built!"[2] This splendid fortification showed that warfare had become a fact of human life. Yet this had not been an inevitable development. For hundreds of years, Sumer had felt no need to protect its cities from outside attack. Gilgamesh, however, who probably ruled around 2750 BCE, was a new kind of Sumerian king, "a wild bull of a man, unvanquished leader, hero on the front lines, beloved by his soldiers—*fortress* they called him, *protector of the people, raging flood that destroys all defenses*."[3]

Despite his passion for Uruk, Sin-leqi had to admit that civilization had its discontents. Poets had begun to tell Gilgamesh's story soon after his death because it is an archetypal tale, one of the first literate accounts of the hero's journey.[4] But it also wrestles with the inescapable structural violence of civilized life. Oppressed, impoverished, and miserable, the people of Uruk begged the gods to grant them some relief from Gilgamesh's tyranny:

> The city is his possession, he struts
> Through it, arrogant, his head raised high,
> Trampling its citizens like a wild bull.
> He is king, he does whatever he wants
> The young men of Uruk he harries without a warrant,
> Gilgamesh lets no son go free to his father.[5]

These young men may have been conscripted into the labor bands that rebuilt the city wall.[6] Urban living would not have been possible without the unscrupulous exploitation of the vast majority of the population. Gilgamesh and the Sumerian aristocracy lived in unprecedented splendor, but for the peasant masses civilization brought only misery and subjugation.

The Sumerians seem to have been the first people to commandeer the agricultural surplus grown by the community and create a privileged ruling class. This could only have been achieved by force. Enterprising settlers had first been drawn to the fertile plain between the Tigris and the Euphrates in about 5000 BCE.[7] It was too dry for farming, so they designed an irrigation system to control and distribute the snowmelt from the mountains that flooded the plain each year. This was an extraordinary achievement. Canals and ditches had to be planned, designed, and maintained in a cooperative effort and the water allocated fairly between competing communities. The new system probably began on a small scale, but would have soon led to a dramatic increase in agricultural yield and thus to a population explosion.[8] By 3500, Sumer numbered a hitherto unachievable half-million souls. Strong leadership would have been essential, but what actually transformed these simple farmers into city dwellers is a topic of endless debate. Probably a number of interlocking and mutually reinforcing factors were involved: population growth, unprecedented agricultural fecundity, and the intensive labor required by irrigation—not to mention sheer human ambition—all contributed to a new kind of society.[9]

All that we know for certain is that by 3000 BCE there were twelve cities in the Mesopotamian plain, each supported by produce grown by peasants in the surrounding countryside. Theirs was subsistence-level living. Each village had to bring its entire crop to the city it served; officials allocated a portion to feed the local peasants, and the rest was stored for the aristocracy in the city temples. In this way, a few great families with the help of a class of retainers—bureaucrats, soldiers, merchants, and household servants—appropriated between half and two-thirds of the revenue.[10] They used this surplus to live a different sort of life altogether, freed for various pursuits that depend on leisure and wealth. In return, they maintained the irrigation system and preserved a degree of law and order. All premodern states feared anarchy: a single crop failure caused by drought or social unrest could lead to thousands of deaths, so the elite could tell themselves that this system benefited the population as a whole. But robbed of the fruits of their labors, the peasants were little better than slaves: plowing, harvesting, digging irrigation canals, being forced into degradation and penury, their hard labor in the fields draining their lifeblood. If they failed to satisfy their overseers, their oxen were kneecapped and their olive trees chopped down.[11] They left fragmentary records of their distress. "The poor man is better dead than alive," one peasant lamented. "I am a thoroughbred steed," complained another, "but I am hitched to a mule and must draw a cart and carry weeds and stubble."[12]

Sumer had devised the system of structural violence that would prevail in every single agrarian state until the modern period, when agriculture ceased to be the economic basis of civilization.[13] Its rigid hierarchy was symbolized by the ziggurats, the giant stepped temple-towers that were the hallmark of Mesopotamian civilization: Sumerian society too was stacked in narrowing layers culminating in an exalted aristocratic pinnacle, each individual locked inexorably into place.[14] Yet, historians argue, without this cruel arrangement that did violence to the vast majority of the population, humans would not have developed the arts and sciences that made progress possible. Civilization itself required a leisured class to cultivate it, and so our finest achievements were for thousands of years built on the backs of an exploited peasantry. By no coincidence, when the Sumerians invented writing, it was for the purpose of social control.

What role did religion play in this damaging oppression? All political communities develop ideologies that ground their institutions in the natural order as they perceive it.[15] The Sumerians knew how fragile their groundbreaking urban experiment was. Their mud-brick buildings needed constant maintenance; the Tigris and Euphrates frequently broke their banks and ruined the crops; torrential rains turned the soil into a sea of mud; and terrifying storms damaged property and killed livestock. But the aristocrats had begun to study astronomy and discovered regular patterns in the movements of the heavenly bodies. They marveled at the way the different elements of the natural world worked together to create a stable universe, and they concluded that the cosmos itself must be a kind of state in which everything had its allotted function. They decided that if they modeled their cities on this celestial order, their experimental society would be in tune with the way the world worked and would therefore thrive and endure.[16]

The cosmic state, they believed, was managed by gods who were inseparable from the natural forces and nothing like the "God" worshipped by Jews, Christians, and Muslims today. These deities could not control events but were bound by the same laws as humans, animals, and plants. There was also no vast ontological gap between human and divine; Gilgamesh, for example, was one-third human, two-thirds divine.[17] The Anunnaki, the higher gods, were the aristocrats' celestial alter egos, their most complete and effective selves, differing from humans only in that they were immortal. The Sumerians imagined these gods as preoccupied with town planning, irrigation, and government, just as they were. Anu, the Sky, ruled this archetypal state from his palace in the heavens, but his presence was also felt in all earthly authority. Enlil, Lord Storm, was revealed not only in the cataclysmic thunderstorms of Mesopotamia but also in any kind of human force and violence. He was Anu's chief counselor in the Divine Council (on which the Sumerian Assembly was modeled), and Enki, who had imparted the arts of civilization to human beings, was its minister of agriculture. ·

Every polity—even our secular nation-state—relies on a mythology that defines its special character and mission. The word *myth* has lost its force in modern times and tends to mean something that is not true, that never happened. But in the premodern world, mythology expressed a timeless rather than a historical reality and provided a blueprint for action in the present.[18] At this very early point in history, when the archaeological and historical record is so scanty, the mythology that the Sumerians preserved in writing is the only way we can enter their minds. For these pioneers of civilization, the myth of the cosmic state was an exercise in political science. The Sumerians knew that their stratified society was a shocking departure from the egalitarian norm that had prevailed from time immemorial, but they were convinced that it was somehow enshrined in the very nature of things and that even the gods were bound by it. Long before humans existed, it was said, the gods had lived in the Mesopotamian cities, growing their own food and managing the irrigation system.[19] After the Great Flood, they had withdrawn from earth to heaven and appointed the Sumerian aristocracy to govern the cities in their stead. Answerable to their divine masters, the ruling class had had no choice in the matter.

Following the logic of the perennial philosophy, the Sumerians' political arrangements imitated those of their gods; this, they believed, enabled their fragile cities to participate in the strength of the divine realm. Each city had its own patronal deity and was run as this god's personal estate.[20] Represented by a life-sized statue, the ruling god lived in the chief temple with his family and household of divine retainers and servants, each one of whom was also depicted in effigy and dwelled in a suite of rooms. The gods were fed, clothed, and entertained in elaborate rituals, and each temple owned huge holdings of farmland and herds of livestock in their name. Everybody in the city-state, no matter how menial his or her task, was engaged in divine service—officiating at the deities' rites; working in their breweries, factories, and workshops; sweeping their shrines; pasturing and butchering their animals; baking their bread; and clothing their statues. There was nothing secular about the Mesopotamian state and nothing personal about their religion. This was a theocracy in which everybody—from the highest aristocrat to the lowliest artisan— performed a sacred activity.

Mesopotamian religion was essentially communal; men and women did not seek to encounter the divine only in the privacy of their hearts but primarily in a godly community. Premodern religion had no separate institutional existence; it was embedded in the political, social, and domestic arrangements of a society, providing it with an overarching system of meaning. Its goals, language, and rituals were conditioned by these mundane considerations. Providing the template for society, Mesopotamian religious practice seems to have been the direct opposite of our modern notion of "religion" as a private spiritual experience: it was essentially a political pursuit, and we have no record of any personal devotions.[21] The gods' temples were not simply places of worship but were central to the economy, because the agricultural surplus was stored there. The Sumerians had no word for *priest:* aristocrats who were also the city's bureaucrats, poets, and astronomers officiated at the city cult. This was only fitting, since for them all activity—and especially politics—was holy.

This elaborate system was not simply a disingenuous justification of the structural violence of the state but was primarily an attempt to invest this audacious and problematic human experiment with meaning. The city was humanity's greatest artifact: artificial, vulnerable, and dependent on institutionalized coercion. Civilization demands sacrifice, and the Sumerians had to convince themselves that the price they were exacting from the peasantry was necessary and ultimately worth it. In claiming that their inequitable system was in tune with the fundamental laws of the cosmos, the Sumerians were therefore expressing an inexorable political reality in mythical terms.

It seemed like an iron law because no society ever found an alternative. By the end of the fifteenth century CE, agrarian civilizations would be established in the Middle East, South and East Asia, North Africa, and Europe, and in every one—whether in India, Russia, Turkey, Mongolia, the Levant, China, Greece, or Scandinavia—aristocrats would exploit their peasants as the Sumerians did. Without the coercion of the ruling class, it would have been impossible to force peasants to produce an economic surplus, because population growth would have kept pace with advances in productivity. Unpalatable as this may seem, by forcing the masses to live at subsistence level, the aristocracy kept population growth in check and made human progress feasible. Had their surplus not been taken from the peasants, there would have been no economic resource to support the technicians, scientists, inventors, artists, and philosophers who eventually brought our modern civilization into being.[22] As the American Trappist monk Thomas Merton pointed out, all of us who have benefited from this systemic violence are implicated in the suffering inflicted for over five thousand years on the vast majority of men and women.[23] Or as the philosopher Walter Benjamin put it: "There is no document of civilization that is not at the same time a document of barbarism."[24]

◆ ◆ ◆

Agrarian rulers saw the state as their private property and felt free to exploit it for their own enrichment. There is nothing in the historical record to suggest that they felt any responsibility for their peasants.[25] As Gilgamesh's people complain in the *Epic:* "The city is his possession. . . . He is king, he does whatever he wants." Yet Sumerian religion did not entirely endorse this inequity. When the gods hear these anguished complaints, they exclaim to Anu: "Gilgamesh, noble as he is, splendid as he is, has exceeded all bounds. The people suffer from his tyranny. . . . Is this how you want your king to rule? Should a shepherd savage his own flock?"[26] Anu shakes his head but cannot change the system.

The narrative poem *Atrahasis* (c. 1700 BCE) is set in the mythical period when the deities were still living in Mesopotamia and "gods instead of man did the work" on which civilization depends. The poet explains that the Anunnaki, the divine aristocracy, have forced the Igigi, the lower gods, to carry too great a load: for three thousand years they have plowed and harvested the fields and dug the irrigation canals—they even had to excavate the riverbeds of the Tigris and Euphrates. "Night and day, they groaned and blamed each other," but the Anunnaki take no heed.[27] Finally an angry mob gathers outside Enlil's palace. "Every single one of us gods has declared war. We have put a stop to the digging!" they cry. "The load is excessive. It is killing us!"[28] Enki, minister of agriculture, agrees. The system is cruel and unsustainable, and the Anunnaki are wrong to ignore the Igigis' plight: "Their work was too hard, their trouble too much! Every day the earth resounded. The warning signal was loud enough!"[29] But if nobody does any productive work, civilization will collapse, so Enki orders the Mother Goddess to create human beings to take the Igigis' place. For the plight of their human laborers too, the gods feel no responsibility. The toiling masses are not allowed to impinge on their privileged existence, so when humans become so numerous that their noise keeps their divine masters awake, the gods simply decide to cull the population with a plague. The poet graphically depicts their suffering:

> Their faces covered in scabs, like malt,
> Their faces looked sallow,
> They went out in public hunched,
> Their well-set shoulders slouched,
> Their upstanding bearing slouched.[30]

Yet again aristocratic cruelty does not go uncriticized. Enki, whom the poet calls "far sighted," bravely defies his fellow gods, reminding them that their lives depend on their human slaves.[31] The Anunnaki grudgingly agree to spare them and withdraw to the peace and quiet of heaven. This was a mythical expression of a harsh social reality: the gulf separating the nobility from the peasants had become so great that they effectively occupied different worlds.

The *Atrahasis* may have been intended for public recitation, and the story seems also to have been preserved orally.[32] Fragments of the text have been found spanning a thousand years, so it seems that this tale was widely known.[33] Thus writing, originally invented to serve the structural violence of Sumer, began to record the disquiet of the more thoughtful members of the ruling class, who could find no solution to civilization's dilemma but tried at least to look squarely at the problem. We shall see that others—prophets, sages, and mystics—would also raise their voices in protest and try to devise a more equitable way for human beings to live together.

◆ ◆ ◆

The *Epic of Gilgamesh,* set toward the mid-third millennium, when Sumer was militarizing, presents martial violence as the hallmark of civilization.[34] When the people beg the gods for help, Anu attempts to alleviate their suffering by giving Gilgamesh someone of his own size to fight with and siphon off some of his excessive aggression. So the Mother Goddess creates Enkidu, primeval man. He is huge, hairy, and has prodigious strength but is a gentle, kindly soul, wandering happily with the herbivores and protecting them from predators. But to fulfill Anu's plan, Enkidu has to make the transition from peaceable barbarian to aggressive civilized man. The priestess Shamhat is given the task of educating him, and under her tutelage, Enkidu learns to reason, understand speech, and eat human food; his hair is cut, sweet oil is rubbed into his skin, and finally "he turned into a man. He put on a garment, became like a warrior."[35] Civilized man was essentially a man of war, full of testosterone. When Shamhat mentions Gilgamesh's military prowess, Enkidu becomes pale with anger. "Take me to Gilgamesh!" he cries, pounding his chest. "I will shout in his face: I am the mightiest! I am the man who can make the world tremble! I am supreme!"[36] No sooner do these two alpha males set eyes on each other than they begin wrestling, careening through the streets of Uruk, thrashing limbs entwined in a near-erotic embrace, until finally, satiated, they "kissed each other and formed a friendship."[37]

By this period, the Mesopotamian aristocracy had begun to supplement its income with warfare, so in the very next episode Gilgamesh announces that he is about to lead a military expedition of fifty men to the Cedar Forest, guarded by the fearsome dragon Humbaba, to bring this precious wood back to Sumer. It was probably by such acquisition raids that the Mesopotamian cities came to dominate the northern highlands, which were rich in the luxury goods favored by the aristocracy.[38] Merchants had long been dispatched to Afghanistan, the Indus Valley, and Turkey to bring back timber, rare and base metals, and precious and semiprecious stones.[39] But for an aristocrat like Gilgamesh, the only noble way to acquire these scarce resources was by force. In all future agrarian states, aristocrats would be distinguished from the rest of the population by their ability to live without working.[40] The cultural historian Thorstein Veblen has explained that in such societies, "labor comes to be associated . . . with weakness and subjection." Work, even trade, was not only "disreputable . . . but *morally* impossible to the noble freeborn man." Because an aristocrat owed his privilege to the forcible expropriation of the peasants' surplus, "the obtaining of goods by other methods than seizure comes to be accounted unworthy."[41]

For Gilgamesh, therefore, the organized theft of warfare is not only noble but moral, undertaken not just for his personal enrichment but for the benefit of humanity. "Now we must travel to the Cedar Forest, where the fierce monster Humbaba lives," he announces self-importantly: "We must kill him and drive out evil from the world."[42] For the warrior, the enemy is always monstrous, the antithesis of everything good. But significantly, the poet refuses to give this military expedition any religious or ethical sanction. The gods are solidly against it. Enlil has specifically appointed Humbaba to guard the forest against any such predatory attack; Gilgamesh's mother, the goddess Ninsun, is horrified by the plan and at first blames Shamash, the sun god and Gilgamesh's patron, for

planting this appalling idea in her son's mind. When questioned, however, Shamash seems to know nothing about it.

Even Enkidu initially opposes the war. Humbaba, he argues, is not
evil; he is doing an ecologically sound task for Enlil and being frightening is part of his job description. But Gilgamesh is blinded by the aristocratic code of honor.[43] "Why, dear friend, do you speak like a coward?"
he taunts Enkidu: "If I die in the forest on this great adventure, won't you
be ashamed when people say, 'Gilgamesh met a hero's death battling the
monster Humbaba. And where was Enkidu? He was safe at home!' "[44] It
is not the gods nor even simply greed but pride, an obsession with martial
glory and the desire for a posthumous reputation for courage and dar-
ing, that drives Gilgamesh to battle. "We are mortal men," he reminds
Enkidu:

> Only the gods live forever. *Our* days
> are few in number, and whatever we achieve
> is a puff of wind. Why be afraid then,
> since sooner or later death must come? . . .
> But whether you come along or not,
> I will cut down the tree, I will kill Humbaba,
> I will make a lasting name for myself,
> I will stamp my fame on men's minds forever.[45]

Gilgamesh's mother blames his "restless heart" for this harebrained project.[46] A leisured class has a lot of time on its hands; collecting rents and
supervising the irrigation system is tame work for a species bred to be
intrepid hunters. The poem indicates that already young men were chaf-
ing against the triviality of civilian life that, as Chris Hedges explained,
would lead so many of them to seek meaning on the battlefield.[47]

The outcome was tragic. There is always a moment in warfare when
the horrifying reality breaks through the glamour. Humbaba turns
out to be a very reasonable monster, who pleads for his life and offers
Gilgamesh and Enkidu all the wood they want, but still they hack him
brutally to pieces. Afterward a gentle rain falls from heaven, as though
nature itself grieves for this pointless death.[48] The gods show their displeasure with the expedition by striking Enkidu down with a fatal illness,
and Gilgamesh is forced to come to terms with his own mortality. Unable
to assimilate the consequences of warfare, he turns his back on civiliza-

tion, roaming unshaven through the wilderness and even descending into the underworld to find an antidote to death. Finally, weary but resigned, he is forced to accept the limitations of his humanity and return to Uruk. On reaching the suburbs, he draws his companion's attention to the great wall surrounding the city: "Observe the land it encloses, the palm trees, the gardens, the orchards, the glorious palaces and temples, the shops and market-places, the houses, the public squares."[49] He personally will die, but he will achieve an immortality of sorts by cultivating the civilized arts and pleasures that are enabling humans to explore new dimensions of existence.

Gilgamesh's famous wall was now essential for the survival of Uruk, though, because after centuries of peaceful cooperation, the Sumerian city-states had begun to fight one another. What caused this tragic development?

◆ ◆ ◆

Not everybody in the Middle East aspired to civilization: nomadic herdsmen preferred to roam freely in the mountains with their livestock. They had once been part of the agricultural community, living at the edge of the farmland so that their sheep and cattle did not damage the crops. But gradually they moved farther and farther away until they finally abandoned the constraints of settled life and took to the open road.[50] The pastoralists of the Middle East had probably become an entirely separate community as early as 6000 BCE, though they continued to trade their hides and milk products with the cities in return for grain.[51] They soon discovered that the easiest way to replace lost animals was to steal the cattle of nearby villages and rival tribes. Fighting, therefore, became essential to the pastoralist economy. Once they domesticated the horse and acquired wheeled vehicles, these herdsmen spread all over the Inner Asian Plateau, and by the early third millennium, some had reached China.[52] By this time they were formidable warriors, equipped with bronze weaponry, war chariots, and the deadly composite bow, which could shoot with devastating accuracy at long range.[53]

The pastoralists who settled in the Caucasian steppes of southern Russia in about 4500 BCE shared a common culture. They called themselves Arya ("noble; honorable"), but we know them as Indo-Europeans because their language became the basis of several Asiatic and European tongues.[54] In about 2500 BCE some of the Aryans left the steppes and conquered large areas of Asia and Europe, becoming the ancestors of the Hittites, Celts, Greeks, Romans, Germans, Scandinavians, and Anglo-Saxons we shall meet later in our story. Meanwhile, those tribes who had remained in the Caucasus drifted apart. They continued to live side by side—not always amicably—speaking different dialects of the proto-Indo-European tongue until about 1500 BCE, when they too migrated from the steppes, the Avestan speakers settling in what is now Iran and the Sanskrit speakers colonizing the Indian subcontinent.

Aryans saw the warrior's life as infinitely superior to the tedium and steady industry of agrarian existence. The Roman historian Tacitus (c. 55–120 CE) would later note that the German tribes he encountered far preferred "to challenge the enemy and earn the honour of wounds" to the drudgery of ploughing and the tedium of waiting for the crops to appear: "Nay, they actually think it tame and stupid to acquire by the sweat of toil what they might win by their blood."[55] Like urban aristocrats, they too despised labor, saw it as a mark of inferiority, and incompatible with the "noble" life.[56] Moreover, they knew that the cosmic order (*rita*) was possible only because chaos was kept in check by the great gods (*devas*)*—Mithra, Varuna, and Mazda—who compelled the seasons to rotate regularly, kept the heavenly bodies in their proper places, and made the earth habitable. Human beings too could live together in an orderly, productive way only if they were forced to sacrifice their own interests to those of the group.

Violence and coercion therefore lay at the heart of social existence, and in most ancient cultures this truth was expressed in the ritualized bloodshed of animal sacrifice. Like the prehistoric hunters, Aryans had absorbed the tragic fact that life depends upon the destruction of other beings. They expressed this conviction in the mythical story of a king who altruistically allows himself to be slain by his brother, a priest, and thus brings the ordered world into being.[57] A myth is never simply the story of an historical event; rather, it expresses a timeless truth underlying a people's daily existence. A myth is always about *now*. The Aryans reenacted the tale of the sacrificed king every day by ritually slaying an animal to remind themselves of the sacrifice demanded of every single warrior, who daily put his life at risk for his people.

It has been argued that Aryan society was originally peaceful and did

* In Avestan, the Sanskrit *devas* became *daevas*.

not resort to aggressive raiding until the end of the second millennium.[58] But other scholars note that weapons and warriors figure in the very earliest texts.[59] The mythical stories of the Aryan war gods—Indra in India, Verethragna in Persia, Hercules in Greece, and Thor in Scandinavia—follow a similar pattern, so this martial ideal must have developed in the steppes before the tribes went their different ways. It was based on the hero Trito, who conducts the very first cattle raid against the three-headed Serpent, one of the indigenous inhabitants of a land recently conquered by the Aryans. Serpent had the temerity to steal the Aryans' cattle. Not only does Trito kill him and recover the livestock, but this raid becomes a cosmic battle that, like the death of the sacrificed king, restores the cosmic order.[60]

Aryan religion, therefore, gave supreme sanction to what was essentially organized violence and theft. Every time they set out on a raid, warriors drank a ritual draft of the intoxicating liquor pressed from soma, a sacred plant that filled them with frenzied rapture, just as Trito did before pursuing Serpent; they thus felt at one with their hero. The Trito myth implied that all cattle, the measure of wealth in pastoral society, belonged to the Aryans and that other peoples had no right to these resources. The Trito story has been called "the imperialist's myth par excellence" because it provided sacred justification for the Indo-European military campaigns in Europe and Asia.[61] The figure of Serpent presented those native peoples who dared to resist the Aryan onslaught as inhuman, misshapen monsters. But cattle and wealth were not the only prizes worth fighting for: like Gilgamesh, Aryans would always also seek honor, glory, prestige, and posthumous fame in battle.[62] People rarely go to war for one reason only; rather, they are driven by interlocking motivations—material, social, and ideological. In Homer's *Iliad,* when the Trojan warrior Sarpedon urges his friend Glaukos to make a highly dangerous assault on the Greek camp, he quite unselfconsciously lists all the material perks of a heroic reputation—special seating, the best cuts of meat, booty, and "a great piece of land"—as an integral part of a warrior's nobility.[63] It is significant that the English words *value* and *valor* both have a common Indo-European root, as do *virtue* and *virility.*

But while Aryan religion glorified warfare, it also acknowledged that this violence was problematic. Any military campaign involves activities that would be abhorrent and unethical in civilian life.[64] In Aryan mythology, therefore, the war god is often called a "sinner" because a soldier is forced to act in a way that calls his integrity into question. The warrior always carries a taint.[65] Even Achilles, one of the greatest Aryan warriors, does not escape this stain. Here is Homer's description of the *aristeia* ("triumphal rampage") in which Achilles frenziedly slaughters one Trojan soldier after another:

> As inhuman fire sweeps on in fury through the deep angles
> Of drywood mountain and sets ablaze the depth of the timber
> And the blustering wind lashes the flame along, so Achilleus
> Swept everywhere with his spear, like something more than a
>   mortal.[66]

Achilles has become an inhuman force of purely destructive power. Homer compares him to a thresher crushing barley on the threshing floor, but instead of producing nourishing food, he is "trampling alike dead men and shields" as if the two were indistinguishable, his "invincible hands . . . spattered with bloody filth."[67] Warriors would never attain the first rank in Indo-European society.[68] They always had to struggle "to be the best" (Greek: *aristos*); yet they were still relegated below the priests to the second class. Herdsmen could not survive without raiding; their violence was essential to the pastoralist economy, but the hero's aggression often repelled the very people who revered him.[69]

The *Iliad* is certainly not an antiwar poem, but at the same time as it celebrates the feats of its heroes, it reminds us of the tragedy of war. As in the *Epic of Gilgamesh*, the sorrow of mortality sometimes breaks through the excitement and idealism. The third person to be killed in the poem is the Trojan Simoeisios, a beautiful young man who, Homer says, should have known the tenderness of family life but is beaten down by the Greek warrior Ajax:

> He dropped then to the ground in the dust, like some black poplar
> Which in the land low-lying about a great marsh grows
> Smooth trimmed yet with branches growing at the uttermost tree-
>   top:
> One whom a man, a maker of chariots, fells with the shining
> Iron, to bend it into a wheel for a fine-wrought chariot,
> And the tree lies hardening by the banks of a river.[70]

In the *Odyssey,* Homer goes even further, undermining the entire aristocratic ideal. When Odysseus visits the underworld, he is horrified by the
swarming crowds of gibbering dead, whose humanity has so obscenely
degenerated. Coming upon the disconsolate shade of Achilles, he tries
to console him: Was he not honored like a god before he died, and does
he not now rule the dead? But Achilles will have none of it. "Don't gloss
over death to me in order to console me," he replies. "I would rather be
above the ground still and labouring for some poor peasant man than
be the lord over the lifeless dead."[71]

◆ ◆ ◆

We have no firm evidence, but it was probably pastoralists living in the
mountainous regions surrounding the Fertile Crescent who introduced
warfare to Sumer.[72] The herdsmen would have found the cities' wealth
irresistible, and they had perfected the art of the surprise attack, their
speed and mobility terrifying the city dwellers, who had not yet mastered
the art of horsemanship. After a few such lightning raids, the Sumerians would have taken steps to protect their people and storehouses. But
these assaults probably gave them the idea of using similar techniques
to seize loot and arable land from a neighboring Sumerian city.[73] By the
middle of the third millennium BCE, the Sumerian plain was mobilized
for warfare: archaeologists have discovered a marked increase in walled
fortifications and bronze weaponry in this stratum. This had not been
unavoidable; there was no such escalation of armed conflict in Egypt,
which had also developed a sophisticated civilization but was a far more
peaceful agrarian state.[74] The Nile flooded the fields with almost unfail-
ing regularity, and Egypt was not exposed to the tumultuous climate
of Mesopotamia; nor was it encircled by mountains full of predatory
herdsmen.[75] The Egyptian kingdoms probably had an ad hoc militia to
repel an occasional nomadic attack from the desert, but the weapons
unearthed by archaeologists are crude and rudimentary. Most ancient
Egyptian art celebrates the joy and elegance of civilian life, and there is
little glorification of warfare in early Egyptian literature.[76]

We can only piece together the progress of Sumerian militarization
from fragmentary archaeological evidence. Between 2340 and 2284 BCE,
the Sumerian king lists record thirty-four intercity wars.[77] The first kings
of Sumer had been priestly specialists in astronomy and ritual; now

increasingly they were warriors like Gilgamesh. They discovered that warfare was an invaluable source of revenue that brought them booty and prisoners who could be put to work in the fields. Instead of waiting for the next breakthrough in productivity, war yielded quicker and more ample returns. The Stele of Vultures (c. 2500 BCE), now in the Louvre, depicts Eannatum, king of Lagash, leading a tightly knit and heavily armed phalanx of troops into battle against the city of Umma; this was clearly a society equipped and trained for warfare. The stele records that even though they begged for mercy, three thousand Ummaite soldiers were killed that day.[78] Once the plain had become militarized, each king had to be prepared to defend and if possible extend his territory, the source of his wealth. Most of these Sumerian conflicts were tit-for-tat campaigns for booty and territory. None seem to have been decisive, and there are signs that some people saw the whole business as futile. "You go and carry off the enemy's land," reads one inscription; "the enemy comes and carries off your land." Yet disputes were still settled by force rather than by diplomacy and no state could afford to be militarily unprepared. "The state weak in armaments," commented another inscription, "the enemy will not be driven from its gates."[79]

During these inconclusive wars, Sumerian aristocrats and retainers were wounded, killed, and enslaved, but the peasants suffered far more. Because they were the basis of any aristocrat's wealth, they and their livestock were regularly slaughtered by an invading army, their barns and homes demolished, and their fields soaked with blood. The countryside and peasant villages would become a wasteland, and the destruction of harvests, herds, and agricultural equipment often meant severe famine.[80] The inconclusive nature of these wars meant that everybody suffered and that there would be no permanent gain for anybody, since today's winner was likely to be tomorrow's loser. This would become the besetting problem of civilization, since equally matched aristocracies would always compete aggressively for scarce resources. Paradoxically, warfare that was supposed to enrich the aristocracy often damaged productivity. Already at this very early date it had become apparent that to prevent this pointless and self-destructive suffering, it was essential to hold these competing aristocracies in check. A higher authority had to have the military muscle to impose the peace.

In 2330 a new type of ruler emerged in Mesopotamia when Sargon, a common soldier of Semitic origins, staged a successful coup in the city of Kish, marched to Uruk, and deposed its king. He then repeated this process in one city after another until, for the very first time, Sumer was ruled by a single monarch. Sargon had created the world's first agrarian empire.[81] It was said that with his massive standing army of 5,400 men, he conquered territory in what is now Iran, Syria, and Lebanon. He built Akkad, an entirely new capital city, which may have stood near modern Baghdad. In his inscriptions, Sargon—his name meaning "True and Rightful King"—claimed to have ruled "the totality of lands under heaven," and later generations would revere him as a model hero, not unlike Charlemagne or King Arthur. For millennia, in his memory, Mesopotamian rulers would style themselves "lord of Akkad." Yet we know very little about either the man or his empire. Akkad was remembered as an exotic, cosmopolitan city and an important trade center, but its site has never been discovered. The empire has left little archaeological trace, and what we know of Sargon's life is largely legendary.

Yet his empire was a watershed. The world's first supraregional polity, it became the model for all future agrarian imperialism, not simply because of Sargon's prestige but because there seemed to be no viable alternative. Warfare and taxation would be essential to the economy of every future agrarian empire. The Akkadian Empire was achieved by the conquest of foreign territory: subject peoples were reduced to vassals, and kings and tribal chieftains became regional governors, their task to extort taxes in kind from their people—silver, grain, frankincense, metals, timber, and animals—and send them to Akkad. Sargon's inscriptions claim that he fought thirty-four wars during his exceptionally long reign of fifty-six years. In all later agrarian empires, warfare was not an unusual crisis but became the norm; it was not simply the "sport of kings" but an economic and social necessity.[82] Besides gaining plunder and loot, the chief goal of any imperial campaign was to conquer and tax more peasants. As the British historian Perry Anderson explains, "war was possibly the most *rational* and *rapid* single mode of economic expansion, of surplus extraction, available for any given ruling class."[83] Fighting and obtaining wealth were inseparable and interconnected: freed from the need to engage in productive work, the nobility had the leisure to cultivate their martial skills.[84] They certainly fought for honor, glory, and the sheer pleasure of battle, but warfare was, "perhaps above all, a source of profit, the nobleman's chief industry."[85] It needed no justification, because its necessity seemed self-evident.

We know so little about Sargon that it is hard to be precise about the role of religion in his imperial wars. In one of his inscriptions he claimed that after he defeated the cities of Ur, Lagash, and Umma, "the god Enlil [did] not let him have a rival, gave him the Lower and the Upper Sea and the citizens of Akkad held [posts of] government." Religion had always been inseparable from Mesopotamian politics. The city was viable because it fed and served its deities; doubtless, the oracles of these gods endorsed Sargon's campaigns. His son and successor Naram-Sin (c. 2260–2223), who further extended the Akkadian Empire, was actually known as the "god of Akkad." As a new city, Akkad could not claim to have been founded by one of the Anunnaki, so Naram-Sin declared that he had become the mediator between the divine aristocracy and his subjects. As we shall see, agrarian emperors would often be deified in this way, and it gave them a useful propaganda device that justified major administrative and economic reforms.[86] As ever, religion and politics co-inhered, the gods serving not only as the alter ego of the monarch but also sanctifying the structural violence that was essential to the survival of civilization.

The agrarian empire made no attempt to represent the people or serve their interests. The ruling class regarded the peasant population as virtually a different species. The ruler saw his empire as his personal possession and his army as his own private militia. As long as their subjects produced and relinquished the surplus, the ruling class left them to their own devices, so peasants policed and governed their own communities; premodern communications did not permit the imperial ruling class to impose its religion or culture on the subject peoples. A successful empire supposedly prevented the destructive tit-for-tat warfare that had plagued Sumer, but even so Sargon died suppressing a revolt, and besides constantly subduing would-be usurpers, Naram-Sin also had to defend his borders against pastoralists who had founded their own states in Anatolia, Syria, and Palestine.

After the decline of the Akkadian Empire, there were other imperial experiments in Mesopotamia. From 2113 to 2029, Ur ruled the whole of Sumer and Akkad from the Persian Gulf to the southern Jezirah as well as large parts of western Iran. Then, in the nineteenth century BCE, Sumu-abum, a Semitic-Amorite chieftain, founded a dynasty in the small town of Babylon. King Hammurabi (c. 1792–1750), the sixth in line, gradually gained control of southern Mesopotamia and the western regions of the middle Euphrates. In a famous stele, he is shown standing before Marduk, the sun god, receiving the laws of his kingdom. In his law code, Hammurabi announced that he had been appointed by the gods "to cause justice to prevail in the land, to destroy the wicked and the evil, that the strong might not oppress the weak."[87] Despite the structural violence of the agrarian state, Middle Eastern rulers would regularly make this claim. Promulgating such laws was little more than a political exercise in which the king claimed that he was powerful enough to bypass the lower aristocrats and become a supreme court of appeal to the oppressed masses.[88] His benevolent laws, his code concluded, were the "laws of righteousness, which Hammurabi, *the strong king,* established."[89] Significantly, he published this code at the end of his career, after he had forcefully oppressed any opposition and established a system of taxation throughout his domains that enriched his capital in Babylon.

But no agrarian civilization could advance beyond a certain limit. An expanding empire always outran its resources, once its requirements exceeded what nature, peasants, and animals could produce. And despite the lofty talk about justice for the poor, prosperity had to be confined to an elite. While modernity has institutionalized change, radical innovation was rare in premodern times: civilization seemed so fragile that it was deemed more important to preserve what had been achieved rather than risk something entirely new. Originality was not encouraged, because any new idea that required too great an economic outlay would not be implemented and this frustration could cause social unrest. Hence novelty was suspect, not out of timidity but because it was economically and politically hazardous. The past remained the supreme authority.[90]

Continuity was therefore politically essential. Thus the Akitu festival, inaugurated by the Sumerians in the mid-third millennium, was celebrated each year by every Mesopotamian ruler for over two thousand years. Originally performed in Ur in honor of Enlil when Sumer had become militarized, in Babylon these rituals centered on the city's patron, Marduk.[91] As always in Mesopotamia, this act of worship had an important political function and was essential to the regime's legitimacy. We shall see in Chapter 4 that a king could be deposed for failing to perform these ceremonies, which marked the start of the New Year, when the old year was dying and the king's power also waning.[92] By ritually rehearsing cosmic battles that had ordered the universe at the beginning of time, the ruling aristocracy hoped to make this powerful surge of sacred energy a reality in their state for another twelve months.

On the fifth day of the festival, the presiding priest would ceremonially humiliate the king in Marduk's shrine, evoking the terrifying specter of social anarchy by confiscating the royal regalia, striking the king on the cheek, and throwing him roughly onto the ground.[93] The bruised and abject king would plead with Marduk that he had not behaved like an evil ruler:

> I did not destroy Babylon; I did not command its overthrow; I did not destroy the temple. . . . Esagil. I did not forget its rites; I did not rain blows on the cheeks of the protected citizen. I did not humiliate them. I watched out for Babylon. I did not smash its walls.[94]

The priest then slapped the king again, so hard that tears rose to his eyes—a sign of repentance that satisfied Marduk. Thus reinstated, the king now clasped the hands of Marduk's effigy, the regalia were returned, and his rule was secure for the coming year. The statues of all the patronal gods and goddesses of all the cities in Mesopotamia had to be brought to Babylon for the festival as an expression of cultic and political loyalty. If they were not all present, the Akitu could not be celebrated and the realm would be endangered. The liturgy, therefore, was as crucial for a city's security as its fortifications, and it had reminded the people, only the day before, of the city's fragility.

On the fourth day of the festival, priests and choristers filed into Marduk's shrine for the recitation of *Enuma Elish,* the creation hymn that recounted Marduk's victory over cosmic and political chaos. The first gods to emerge from the slimy primal matter (similar to Mesopotamia's alluvial soil) were "nameless, natureless, futureless,"[95] virtually inseparable from the natural world and seen as enemies of progress. The next gods to emerge from the sludge became progressively more distinct until the divine evolution culminated in Marduk, the most splendid of the Anunnaki. In the same way, Mesopotamian culture had developed from rural communities immersed in the natural rhythms of the countryside that were now regarded as sluggish, static, and inert. But the old times could return: this hymn expressed the fear of civilization lapsing back into abysmal nothingness. The most dangerous of the primitive gods was

Tiamat, whose name means "Void"; she was the salty sea, which, in the Middle East, symbolized not only primeval chaos but the social anarchy that could bring starvation, disease, and death to the entire population. She represented an ever-present threat that every civilization, no matter how powerful, had to be ready to confront.

The hymn also gave sacred sanction to the structural violence of Babylonian society. Tiamat creates a horde of monsters to fight the Anunnaki, a "growling roaring rout, ready for battle," suggestive of the danger the lower classes presented to the state. Their monstrous forms represent the perverse defiance of normal categories and the confusion of identity associated with social and cosmic disorder. Their leader is Tiamat's spouse Kingu, a "clumsy laborer," one of the Igigi, whose name means "Toil." The narrative of the hymn is repeatedly punctuated with this pounding refrain: "She has made the Worm, the Dragon, the Female Monster, the Great Lion, the Mad Dog, the Mad Scorpion and the Howling Storm, the Fish-Man, the Centaur."[96] But Marduk defeats them all, casting them into prison and creating an ordered universe by splitting Tiamat's corpse in two and separating heaven and earth. He then commands the gods to build the city of *bab-ilani,* "gate of the gods," as their earthly home and creates the first man by mixing Kingu's blood with a handful of dust to perform the labor on which civilization depends. "Sons of toil," the masses are sentenced for life to menial labor and are held in subjection. Liberated from work, the gods sing a hymn of praise and thanksgiving. The myth and its accompanying rituals reminded the Sumerian aristocracy of the reality on which their civilization and privilege depended; they must be perpetually primed for war to keep down rebellious peasants, ambitious aristocrats, and foreign enemies who threatened civilized society. Religion was therefore deeply implicated in this imperial violence and could not be separated from the economic and political realities that sustained any agrarian state.

◆ ◆ ◆

The fragility of civilization became clear during the seventeenth century BCE, when Indo-European hordes repeatedly attacked the cities of Mesopotamia. Even Egypt now became militarized, when Bedouin tribesmen, whom the Egyptians called Hyksos ("chieftains from foreign lands"), managed to establish their own dynasty in the delta area during the sixteenth century.[97] The Egyptians expelled them in 1567, but ever afterward the ruling pharaoh was depicted as a warrior at the head of a powerful army. Empire seemed the best defense, so Egypt secured its frontier by subjugating Nubia in the south and coastal Palestine in the north. But by the middle of the second millennium, the ancient Near East was dominated by foreign conquerors; Kassite tribes from the Caucasus took over the Babylonian Empire (c. 1600–1155); an Indo-European aristocracy created the Hittite Empire in Anatolia (1420–1200); and the Mitanni, another Aryan tribe, controlled Greater Mesopotamia from about 1500 until they were conquered by the Hittites in the mid-fourteenth century. Ashur-uballit I, ruler of the city of Ashur in the eastern Tigris region, who was able to exploit the turbulence that followed the collapse of the Mitanni, made Assyria a new power in the Middle East.

Assyria was not a traditional agrarian state.[98] Situated in an area that was not agriculturally productive, since the nineteenth century BCE, Ashur had relied more than other cities on commerce, setting up trading colonies in Cappadocia and planting mercantile representatives in several Babylonian cities. For about a century Ashur was a trading hub, importing tin (crucial for the manufacture of bronze) from Afghanistan and exporting it together with Mesopotamian textiles to Anatolia and the Black Sea. The historical record is so slight, however, that we do not know how this affected the farmers of Ashur or whether commerce mitigated the structural violence of the state. Nor do we know much about Ashur's religious practices. Its kings built impressive temples to the gods, but we know nothing about the personality and exploits of Ashur, its patronal deity, whose mythology has not survived.

The Assyrians began to dominate the region when their king Adad-nirari I (1307–1275) conquered the old Mitanni territories from the Hittites as well as land in southern Babylonia. The economic incentive was always prominent in Assyrian warfare. The inscriptions of Shalmaneser I (1274–45) stressed his martial prowess: he was a "valiant hero, capable of battle with his enemies, whose aggressive battle flashes like a flame and whose weapons attack like a merciless death-trap."[99] It was he who began the Assyrian practice of forcibly moving people around his empire not simply, as was once thought, to demoralize the conquered peoples but principally to stimulate the agricultural economy by replenishing underpopulated regions.[100]

The reign of his son Tukulti-Ninurta I (1244–1208), who made Assyria the most formidable military and economic power of the day, is better documented. He turned Ashur into the ritual capital of his empire and instituted the Akitu festival there, with the god Ashur in the starring role; it appears that the Assyrians introduced a mock battle reenacting Ashur's war with Tiamat. In his inscriptions, Tukulti-Ninurta was careful to credit his victories to the gods: "Trusting in Ashur and the great gods, my lord, I struck and brought about their defeat." But he also makes it clear that warfare was never simply an act of piety:

> I made them swear by the great gods of heaven [and] underworld,
> I imposed upon them the yoke of my lordship, [and then] released
> them to return to their lands. . . . Fortified cities I subdued at my feet
> and imposed corvée. Annually I receive with ceremony their valuable
> tribute in my city Ashur.[101]

Assyrian kings too were plagued by internal dissent, intrigue, and rebellion, yet Tiglath-pileser I (c. 1115–1093) managed to expand the empire, maintaining his domination of the region by perpetual campaigning and large-scale deportations, so that his reign was in effect one continuous war. Punctilious as he was in his devotion to the gods and an energetic builder of temples, his strategy was always dictated by economic imperatives. His chief motive for expanding northward into Iran, for instance, was the acquisition of booty, metal, and animals, which he sent home to boost productivity in Syria at a time of chronic crop failure.[102]

Warfare had become a fact of human life, central to the political, social, and economic dynamics of the agrarian empire, and like every other human activity, it always had a religious dimension. These states would not have survived without constant military effort, and the gods, the alter egos of the ruling class, represented a yearning for a strength that could transcend human instability. Yet the Mesopotamians were not credulous fanatics. Religious mythology may have endorsed their structural and martial violence, but it also regularly called it into question. There was a strong vein of skepticism in Mesopotamian literature. One aristocrat complains that he has always been righteous, joyfully followed the gods' processions, taught all the people on his estate to worship the Mother Goddess, and instructed his soldiers to revere the king as the gods' representative. Yet he has been afflicted with disease, insomnia, and terror, and "no god came to my aid or grasped my hand."[103] Gilgamesh too gets no help from the gods as he struggles to accept Enkidu's death. When he meets Ishtar, the Mother Goddess, he denounces her savagely for her inability to protect men from the grim realities of life: she is like a water-skin that soaks its carrier, a shoe that pinches its wearer, and a door that fails to keep out the wind. In the end, as we have seen, Gilgamesh finds resignation, but the *Epic* as a whole suggests that mortals have no choice but to rely on themselves rather than the gods. Urban living was beginning to change the way people thought about the divine, but one of the most momentous religious developments of the period occurred at about the same time as Sin-leqi wrote his version of Gilgamesh's life. It did not happen in a sophisticated city, however, but was a response to the escalation of violence in an Aryan pastoral community.

◆ ◆ ◆

Early one morning in about 1200 BCE, an Avestan-speaking priest in the Caucasian steppes went to the river to collect water for the morning sacrifice. There he had a vision of Ahura Mazda, "Lord Wisdom," one of the greatest gods in the Aryan pantheon. Zoroaster had been horrified by the cruelty of the Sanskrit-speaking cattle raiders, who had vandalized one Avestan community after another. As he meditated on this crisis, the logic of the perennial philosophy led him to conclude that these earthly battles must have a heavenly counterpart. The most important *daevas*—Varuna, Mithra, and Mazda, who had the honorary title *ahura* ("Lord")—were guardians of cosmic order and stood for truth, justice, and respect for life and property. But the cattle raiders' hero was the war-god Indra, a second-ranking daeva. Perhaps, Zoroaster reflected, the peace-loving ahuras were being attacked in the heavenly world by the wicked daevas. In his vision, Ahura Mazda told him that he was correct and must mobilize his people in a holy war against terror. Good men and women must no longer sacrifice to Indra and the lower daevas but worship the Wise Lord and his fellow ahuras instead; the daevas and the cattle raiders, their earthly henchmen, must be destroyed.[104]

We shall see again and again that the experience of an unusual level of violence would often shock its victims into a dualistic vision that splits the world into two irreconcilable camps. Zoroaster concluded that there must be a malevolent deity, Angra Mainyu, the "Hostile Spirit," who was equal in power to the Wise Lord but was his polar opposite. Every single man, woman, and child, therefore, must choose between absolute

Good and absolute Evil.[105] The Wise Lord's followers must live patient, disciplined lives, bravely defending all good creatures from the assault of evildoers, caring for the poor and weak, and tending their cattle kindly instead of driving them from their pastures like the cruel raiders. They must pray five times a day and meditate on the menace of evil in order to weaken its power.[106] Society must not be dominated by these fighters (*nar-*) but by men (*viras*) who were kind and dedicated to the supreme virtue of truth.[107]

So traumatized was Zoroaster by the ferocity of the raiders' attacks, though, that this gentle, ethical vision was itself permeated with violence. He was convinced that the whole world was rushing toward a final cataclysm in which the Wise Lord would annihilate the wicked daevas and incinerate the Hostile Spirit in a river of fire. There would be a Great Judgment, and the daevas' earthly followers would be exterminated. The earth would then be restored to its original perfection. There would be no more death and disease, and the mountains and valleys would be leveled to form a great plain where gods and humans could live together in peace.[108]

Zoroaster's apocalyptic thinking was unique and unprecedented. As we have seen, traditional Aryan ideology had long acknowledged the disturbing ambiguity of the violence that lay at the heart of human society. Indra may have been a "sinner," but his struggles against the forces of chaos—however tainted by the lies and deceitful practices to which he had to resort—had contributed as much to the cosmic order as the work of the great ahuras. Yet by projecting all the cruelty of his time onto Indra, Zoroaster demonized violence and made him a figure of absolute evil.[109] Zoroaster made few converts in his lifetime: no community could survive in the steppes without the fighters whom he had rejected. The early history of Zoroastrianism remains obscure, but we do know that when the Avestan Aryans migrated to Iran, they took their faith with them. Suitably adapted to the needs of the aristocracy, Zoroastrianism would become the ideology of the Persian ruling class, and Zoroastrian ideals would infiltrate the religion of Jews and Christians living under Persian rule. But that lay in the distant future. In the meantime, the Sanskrit-speaking Aryans began to bring the cult of Indra to the Indian subcontinent.

2

India: The Noble Path

For the Aryans who migrated to the Indian subcontinent, springtime was the season of yoga. After a winter of "settled peace" (*ksema*) in the encampment, it was time to summon Indra to lead them on the warpath into battle once again, and the priests performed a ceremony that reenacted the god's miraculous birth.[1] They also chanted a hymn celebrating his cosmic victory over the chaos dragon Vritra, who had imprisoned the life-giving waters in the primal mountain so that the world was no longer habitable. During this heroic battle, Indra had been strengthened by hymns sung by the Maruts, the storm gods.[2] Now priests chanted these same hymns to fortify the Aryan warriors, who like Indra before his battles drank a draught of soma. At one now with Indra, exalted by the intoxicating liquor, they harnessed their horses to their war chariots in the formalized *yug* ("yoking") ritual and set off to raid the villages of their neighbors, firm now in their conviction that they too were setting the world to rights. The Aryans regarded themselves as "noble," and yoga marked the start of the raiding season, when they really lived up to their name.

As for the pastoralists of the Near East, Indian Aryan ritual and mythology glorified organized theft and violence. For the Indo-Aryans too, cattle rustling needed no justification; like any aristocrats, they regarded forcible seizure as the only noble way to obtain goods, so raiding was per se a sacred activity. In their battles they experienced an ecstasy that gave meaning and intensity to their lives, performing thus a "religious" as well as an economic and political function. But the word *yoga*, which has such different connotations for us today, alerts us to a curious dynamic: in India, Aryan priests, sages, and mystics would frequently use the mythology and rhetoric of warfare to subvert the warrior ethos. No myth ever had a single, definitive meaning; rather, it was constantly recast and its meaning changed. The same stories, rituals, and set of symbols that could be used to advocate an ethic of war could also advocate an ethic of peace. By meditating on the violent mythology and rituals that shaped their worldview, the people of India would work as energetically to create a noble path of nonviolence (*ahimsa*) as their ancestors had promoted the sanctity of the warpath.

But that dramatic reversal would not begin until almost a millennium after the first Aryan settlers arrived in the Punjab during the nineteenth century BCE. There was no dramatic invasion; they arrived in small groups, gradually infiltrating the region over a very long period.[3] During their travels, they would have seen the ruins of a great civilization in the Indus Valley, which at the height of its power (c. 2300–2000 BCE) had been larger than either Egypt or Sumer, but they made no attempt to rebuild these cities, because like all pastoralists, they despised the security of settled life. A rough, hard-drinking people, Aryans earned their living by stealing the herds of rival Aryan tribes and fighting the indigenous peoples, the *dasas* ("barbarians").[4] Because their agricultural skills were rudimentary, they could support themselves only by cattle raiding and plunder. They owned no territory but let their animals graze on other people's lands. Driving relentlessly eastward in search of new pastures, they would not wholly abandon this peripatetic life until the sixth century BCE. Continually on the move, living in temporary encampments, they left no archaeological record. For this early period, therefore, we are entirely dependent on ritual texts that were transmitted orally and that allude, in veiled, riddling fashion, to the mythology that the Aryans used to give shape and significance to their lives.

In c. 1200 a group of learned Aryan families began the monumental task of collecting the hymns that had been revealed to the great seers (*rishis*) of old, adding new poems of their own. This anthology of more than a thousand poems, divided into ten books, would become the Rig Veda, the most sacred of four Sanskrit texts known collectively as Veda ("knowledge"). Some of these hymns were sung during the Aryans' sacrificial rituals to the accompaniment of traditional mimes and gestures. Sound would always have sacred significance in India, and as the musical chant and the enigmatic words stole into their minds, Aryans felt in touch with the mysterious potency that held the disparate elements of the universe together in a cosmic coherence. The Rig Veda was *rita*, divine order, translated into human speech.[5] But to a modern reader these texts do not seem at all "religious." Instead of personal devotion, they celebrate the glory of battle, the joy of killing, the exhilaration of strong drink, and the nobility of stealing other people's cattle.

Sacrifice was essential to any ancient economy. The wealth of society was thought to depend on gifts bestowed by the gods who were its patrons. Humans responded to this divine generosity by giving thanks, thus enhancing the gods' honor and ensuring further benefaction. So Vedic ritual was based on the principle of reciprocal exchange: *do ut des*—"I give to make you give." The priests would offer the choicest portions of the sacrificial animal to the gods, which were transferred to the heavenly world by Agni, the sacred fire, while the leftover meat was the gods' gift to the community. After a successful raid, warriors would distribute their spoils in the *vidatha* ritual, which resembled the potlatch of the northwestern Native Americans.[6] This too was not what we would call a spiritual affair. The chieftain (*raja*) hosting the sacrifice proudly exhibited the cattle, horses, soma, and crops he had seized to the elders of his own clan and to neighboring rajas. Some of these goods were sacrificed to the gods, others were presented to the visiting chieftains, and the rest were consumed in a riotous banquet. Participants were either drunk or pleasantly mellow; there was casual sex with slave girls and aggressively competitive chariot races, shooting matches, and tugs-of-war; there were dice games for high stakes and mock battles. This was not just a glorified party, however. It was essential to the Aryan economy: a ritualized way of redistributing newly acquired resources with reasonable equity and imposing an obligation on other clans to reciprocate. These sacred contests also trained young men in military skills and helped rajas identify talent, so that an aristocracy of the best warriors could emerge.

It was not easy to train a warrior to put himself in harm's way day after day. Ritual gave meaning to an essentially grim and dangerous struggle. The soma dulled inhibitions, and the hymns reminded warriors that by fighting indigenous peoples, they were continuing Indra's mighty battles for cosmic order. It was said that Vritra had been "the worst of the Vratras," the native warrior tribes who lurked menacingly on the fringes of Vedic society.[7] The Aryans of India shared Zoroaster's belief that an immense struggle was raging in heaven between the war-like devas and the peace-loving *asuras*.[*] But unlike Zoroaster, they rather despised the sedentary asuras and were staunchly on the side of the noble devas, "who drove their chariots, while the asuras stayed at home in their halls."[8] Such was their hatred of the tedium and triviality of settled life that only in their marauding did they feel fully alive. They were, so to speak, spiritually programmed: the constantly repeated ritual gestures imprinted in their bodies and minds an instinctive knowledge of how an alpha male should comport himself; and the emotive hymns implanted a deep-rooted sense of entitlement, an entrenched belief that Aryans were born to dominate.[9] All this gave them the courage, tenacity, and energy to traverse the vast distances of northwestern India, eliminating every obstacle in their path.[10]

We know practically nothing about Aryan life during this period, yet because mythology is not wholly about the heavenly world but essentially about the here and now, in these Vedic texts we catch glimpses of a community fighting for its life. The mythical battles—between devas and asuras and Indra and his cosmic dragons—reflected the wars between Aryans and dasas.[11] The Aryans experienced the Punjab as confinement and the dasas as perverse adversaries who were preventing them from attaining the wealth and open spaces that were their due.[12] This emotion ran through many of their stories. They imagined Vritra as a huge snake, coiled around the cosmic mountain and squeezing it so tightly that the waters·could not escape.[13] Another story spoke of the demon Vala, who had incarcerated the sun together with a herd of cows in a cave so that without light, warmth, or food, the world was unviable. But after chanting a hymn beside the sacred fire, Indra had smashed into the mountain, liberated the cows, and set the sun high in the sky.[14] The names Vritra and Vala both derived from the Indo-European root *vr, "to obstruct, enclose, encircle," and one of Indra's titles was Vrtrahan ("beating the resistance").[15] It was for the Aryans to fight their way through their encircling enemies as Indra had done. Liberation (*moksha*) would be another symbol that later generations would reinterpret; its opposite was *amhas* ("captivity"), cognate with the English *anxiety* and the German *Angst*,

---

[*] *Asura* is the Sanskrit version of the Avestan *ahura* ("lord").

evoking a claustrophobic distress.[16] Later sages would conclude that the path to moksha lay in the realization that less is more.

By the tenth century, the Aryans had reached the Doab, between the Yamuna and the Ganges Rivers. There they established two small kingdoms, one founded by the confederation of the Kuru and Panchala clans, the other by the Yadava. Every year when the weather was cooler, the Kuru-Panchala dispatched warriors to establish a new Aryan outpost a little farther to the east, where they would subjugate the local populations, raid their farms, and seize their cattle.[17] Before they could settle in this region, the dense tropical forests had to be cleared by fire, so Agni became the colonists' divine alter ego in this incremental drive eastward and the inspiration of the Agnicayana, the ritualized battle that consecrated the new colony. First, the fully armed warriors processed to the riverbank to collect clay to build a brick fire-altar, a provocative assertion of their right to this territory, fighting any locals who stood in their way. The colony became a reality only when Agni leaped forth on the new altar.[18] These blazing altars distinguished Aryan encampments from the darkness of the barbarian villages. The settlers also used Agni to lure away their neighbors' cattle, which would follow the flames. "He should take brightly burning fire to the settlement of his rival," says a later text. "He thereby takes his wealth, his property."[19] Agni symbolized the warrior's courage and dominance, his most fundamental and divine "self" (atman).[20]

Yet like Indra, his other alter ego, the warrior was tainted. It was said that Indra had committed three sins that had fatally weakened him: he had killed a Brahmin priest, broken a pact of friendship with Vritra, and seduced another man's wife by disguising himself as her husband; he had thus, progressively, forfeited his spiritual majesty (tejas), his physical strength (bala), and his beauty.[21] This mythical disintegration now paralleled a profound change in Aryan society during which Indra and Agni would become inadequate expressions of divinity to some of the rishis. It was the first step in a long process that would undermine the Aryans' addiction to violence.

◆　◆　◆

We do not know exactly how the Aryans established their two kingdoms in the Doab, the "Land of the Arya," but they can only have done so by force. Events may well have conformed to what social historians call the "conquest theory" of state establishment.[22] Peasants have much to lose from warfare, which destroys their crops and kills their livestock. When the economically poorer but militarily superior Aryans attacked them, it is possible that, rather than suffer this devastation, some of the more pragmatic peasants decided to submit to the raiders and offer them part of their surplus instead. For their part, the raiders learned not to kill the goose that lays the golden egg, since they could acquire a steady income by returning to the village to demand more goods. Over time this robbery may have been institutionalized to become regular tribute. Once the Yadavas and Kuru-Panchalas subjugated enough villages in the Doab in this way, they had become in effect aristocratic rulers of agrarian kingdoms, though they still dispatched annual raiding parties to the east.

This transition to agrarian life meant major social change. We can only speculate, of course, but up to this point it seems that Aryan society had not been rigidly stratified: the lesser clansmen fought alongside their chieftains, and priests often took part in the raiding.[23] But with agriculture came specialization. The Aryans found that they now had to integrate the dasas, the native farmers with agricultural knowhow, into their community, so the Vritra myths demonizing the dasas were becoming obsolete, since without their labor and expertise, the agrarian economy would fail. The demands of production also meant that Aryans themselves had to toil in the fields, while others became carpenters, metalsmiths, potters, tanners, and weavers. They would now stay at home, while the best warriors were dispatched to fight in the east. There were probably power struggles between the rajas, who wielded power, and the priests, who gave it legitimacy. Breaking with centuries of tradition, all these innovations had to be grafted onto the Vedic mythos.

Their new wealth and leisure gave the priests more time for contemplation, and they began to refine their concept of divinity. They had always seen the gods as participating in a loftier, more encompassing reality that was Being itself, which by the tenth century they had started to call *Brahman* ("The All").[24] Brahman was the power that held the cosmos together and enabled it to grow and develop. It was nameless, indefinable, and utterly transcendent. Devas were simply different manifestations of the Brahman: "They call him Indra, Mitra, Naruna, Agni, and he is heavenly noble-winged Garatman. To what is One, sages give many a title."[25] With almost forensic determination, the new breed of rishis were intent on discovering this mysterious unifying principle;

the all-too-human devas were not only a distraction but were becoming an embarrassment: they concealed rather than revealed the Brahman. Nobody, one rishi insisted, not even the highest of the gods, knows how our world came into being.[26] The old stories of Indra slaying a monster to order the cosmos now seemed positively infantile.[27] Gradually the gods' personalities began to shrink.[28]

One of these later hymns also gave sacred endorsement to the new stratification of Aryan society.[29] Another rishi meditated on the ancient myth of the king whose sacrificial death had given birth to the cosmos and whom the rishi called Purusha, the primordial "Person." He described Purusha lying down on the freshly mown grass of the ritual arena and allowing the gods to kill him. His corpse was then dismembered and became the components of the universe: birds, animals, horses, cattle, heaven and earth, sun and moon, and even the great devas Agni and Indra, all emerged from different parts of his body. Yet only 25 percent of Purusha's being formed the finite world; the other 75 percent was unaffected by time and mortality, transcendent and illimitable. There would always be something in the human experience of the natural world that would elude our comprehension. In Purusha's self-surrender, the old cosmic battles and agonistic sacred contests were replaced by a myth in which there was no fighting: the king gave himself away without a struggle.

The new social classes of the Aryan kingdom also sprouted from Purusha's body:

> When they divided Purusha, how many portions did they make?
> What did they call his mouth, his arms?
> What do they call his thighs and feet?
> The priest [Brahmin] was his mouth; of both of his arms was the warrior [rajanya] made.
> His thighs became the commoner [vaishya], from his feet the servant [shudra] was produced.[30]

Thus the newly stratified society, the hymn claimed, was not a dangerous break with the egalitarian past but was as old as the universe itself. Aryan society was now divided into four social classes—the seed of the elaborate caste system that would develop later. Each class (varna) had its own sacred "duty" (dharma). Nobody could perform the task allotted to another class, any more than a star could leave its path and encroach on a planet's circuit.

Sacrifice was still fundamental; members of each varna had to give up their own preferences for the sake of the whole. It was the dharma of the Brahmins, who came from Purusha's mouth, to preside over the rituals of society.[31] For the first time in Aryan history, the warriors now formed a distinct class called the rajanya, a new term in the Rig Veda; later they would be known as Kshatriya ("the empowered ones"). They came from Purusha's arms, chest, and heart, the seat of strength, courage, and energy, and their dharma was daily to put their lives at risk. This was a significant development, because it limited violence in the Aryan community. Hitherto all able-bodied men had been fighters and aggression the raison d'être of the entire tribe. The hymn acknowledged that the rajanya was indispensable, because the kingdom could not survive without force and coercion. But henceforth *only* the rajanya could bear arms. Members of the other three classes—Brahmins, vaishyas, and shudras—now had to relinquish violence and were no longer allowed to take part in raids nor fight in their kingdom's wars.

In the two lower classes we see the systemic violence of this new society. They came from Purusha's legs and feet, the lower and largest part of the body; their dharma was to serve, to run errands for the nobility, and bear the weight of the entire social frame, performing the productive labor on which the agrarian kingdom depended.[32] The dharma of the vaishya, the ordinary clansman, now forbidden to fight, was food production; the Kshatriya aristocracy would now confiscate his surplus. The vaishya was thus associated with fertility and productivity but also, being taken from a place close to Purusha's genitals, with carnal appetite, which, according to the two upper classes, made him unreliable. But the most significant development was the introduction of the shudra: the dasa at the base of the social body was now defined as a "slave," one who labors for others, performing the most menial tasks and therefore stigmatized as impure. In Vedic law, the vaishya was to be oppressed; however, the shudra could be removed or slain at will.[33]

The Purusha Hymn thus acknowledged the structural violence that lay at the heart of the new Aryan civilization. The new system may have limited fighting and raiding to one of the privileged classes, but it implied that the forcible subjugation of vaishya and shudra was part of the sacred order of the universe. For the Brahmins and Kshatriyas, the new Aryan aristocracy, productive work was not their dharma, so they had the leisure to explore the arts and sciences. While sacrifice was expected of everybody, the greatest sacrifice was demanded of the lower classes, condemned to a life of servitude and stigmatized as inferior, base, and impure.[34]

•   •   •

The Aryan conversion to agriculture continued. By about 900 BCE, there were several rudimentary kingdoms in the Land of the Arya. Thanks to the switch from wheat cultivation to wet rice production, the kingdoms enjoyed a larger surplus. Our knowledge of life in these emerging states is limited, but again, mythology and ritual can throw some light on the developing political organization. In these embryonic kingdoms, the raja, though still elected by his Kshatriya peers like a tribal chieftain, was well on his way to becoming a powerful agrarian ruler and was now invested with divine attributes during his yearlong royal consecration, the *rajasuya*. During this ceremony, another Kshatriya challenged the new king, who had to win his realm back in a ritualized game of dice. If he lost, he was forced into exile but would return with an army to unseat his rival. If he won, he downed a draught of soma and led a raid into the neighboring territories, and when he returned laden with plunder, the Brahmins acknowledged his kingship: "Thou, O King, art Brahman." The raja was now "The All," the hub of the wheel that pulled his kingdom together and enabled it to prosper and expand.

A king's chief duty was to conquer new arable land, a duty sacralized by the horse sacrifice (*ashvameda*), in which a white stallion was consecrated, set free, and allowed to roam unmolested for a year, accompanied by the king's army who were supposed to protect it. A stabled horse will always make straight for home, however, so the army was in fact driving the horse into territory that the king was intent on conquering.[35] Thus in India, as in any agrarian civilization, violence was woven into the texture of aristocratic life.[36] Nothing was nobler than death in battle. To die in his bed was a sin against the Kshatriya's dharma, and if he felt that he was losing his strength, he was expected to seek out death in the field.[37] A commoner had no right to fight, however, so if he died on the battlefield, his death was regarded as a monstrous departure from the norm—or even a joke.[38]

Yet during the ninth century, some of the Brahmins in the Kuru kingdom began yet another major reinterpretation of ancient Aryan tradition and embarked on a reform that not only systematically extracted all violence from religious ritual but even persuaded the Kshatriyas to change their ways. Their ideas were recorded in the scriptures known as the Brahmanas, which date from the ninth to the seventh centuries BCE. There would be no more crowded potlatches or rowdy, drunken contests. In this entirely new ritual, the patron (who paid for the sacrifice) was now the only layman present and was guided through the elaborate ceremony by four priests. Ritualized raids and mock battles were replaced by anodyne chants and symbolic gestures, although traces of the old violence remained: a gentle hymn bore the incongruous title "The Chariot of the Devas," and a stately antiphon was compared to Indra's deadly mace, which the singers were hurling back and forth "with loud voices."[39] Finally, in the reformed Agnicayana ritual, instead of fighting for new territory, the patron simply picked up the fire pot, took three steps to the east, and put it down again.[40]

We know very little about the motivation that lay behind this reform movement. According to one scholar, it sprang from the insoluble conundrum that the sacrificial ritual, which was designed to give life, actually involved death and destruction. The rishis could not eliminate military violence from society, but they could strip it of religious legitimacy.[41] There was also a new concern about cruelty to animals. In one of the later poems of the Rig Veda, a rishi tenderly soothes the horse about to be slaughtered in the ashvameda:

> Let not thy dear soul burn thee as thou comest, let not the hatchet linger in thy body
> Let not a greedy, clumsy immolator, missing the joints, mangle thy limbs unduly.
> No, here thou diest not, thou art not injured: by easy paths unto the Gods thou goest.[42]

The Brahmanas described animal sacrifice as cruel, recommending that the beast be spared and given as a gift to an officiating priest.[43] If it had to be killed, the animal should be dispatched as painlessly as possible. In the old days the victim's decapitation had been the dramatic climax of the sacrifice; now the animal was suffocated in a shed at a distance from the sacrificial area.[44] Some scholars, however, contend that the reform was driven not by a revulsion from violence per se; rather, violence was now experienced as polluting, and anxious to avoid defilement, priests preferred to delegate the task to assistants who killed the victim outside the sacred ground.[45] Whatever their motivation, the reformers were beginning to create a climate of opinion that looked askance at violence.

They also directed the patron's attention toward his inner world. Instead of inflicting death on the hapless animal, he was now instructed to assimilate death, experiencing it internally in a symbolic rite.[46] During the ceremony, his death was enacted ritually and enabled him for a time to enter the world of the immortal gods. A more internal spirituality was beginning to emerge, one closer to what we call "religion"; and it was rooted in a desire to avoid violence. Instead of mindlessly going through the motions of external rituals, participants were required to become aware of the hidden significance of the rites, making themselves conscious of the connections that, in the logic of the perennial philosophy, linked every single action, liturgical utensil, and mantra to a divine reality. Gods were assimilated with humans, humans with animals and plants, the transcendent with the immanent, and the visible with the invisible.[47]

This was not simply self-indulgent make-believe but part of the endless human endeavor to endow the smallest details of life with meaning. Ritual, it has been said, creates a controlled environment in which, for a while, we lay aside the inescapable flaws of our mundane existence. Yet by so doing we paradoxically become acutely aware of them. After the ceremony, when we return to daily life, we can recall our experience of the way things ought to be. Ritual is, therefore, the creation of fallible human beings who can never fully realize their ideals.[48] So while the day-to-day world of the Aryans was inherently violent, cruel, and unjust, in these new rites participants had the chance to inhabit—if only temporarily—a world from which aggression was rigorously excluded. Kshatriyas could not abandon the violence of their dharma, because society depended on it. But as we will see, some began to become painfully aware of the taint that the warrior had always carried in Aryan society, ever since Indra had been called a "sinner." Some would build on the experience of the new rituals to create an alternative spirituality that would undermine the aggressive martial ethos.

But in the new segmented society, very few people now took part in the Vedic rites, which had become the preserve of the aristocracy. Most lower-class Aryans made simpler offerings to their favorite devas in their own home and worshipped a variety of gods—some adopted from the indigenous population—which would form the multifarious Hindu pantheon that would finally emerge during the Gupta period (320–540 CE). But the most spectacular rituals, such as the royal consecration, would make an impression on the public, and people would talk about them for a long time. They also helped to support the class system. The priest who performed the rites was able to assert his superiority over the raja or Kshatriya patron and thus maintain his place at the head of the body politic. In turn, the raja, who paid for the sacrifice, could invoke divine authority to extract more of the surplus from the vaishyas.

If these infant kingdoms were to become mature states, the king's authority could no longer depend on a sacrificial system based on reciprocal exchange. In the Punjab all the booty and captured cattle had been ritually redistributed and consumed, so the raja had been unable to accumulate wealth independently. But a more developed state required resources of its own to pay for its bureaucracy and institutions. Now, thanks to the massive increase of agricultural productivity in the Doab, the rajas were becoming rich. They controlled the agrarian surplus and were no longer dependent on booty acquired in a raid and ceremonially distributed among the community. They were, therefore, becoming not only economically but politically independent of the Brahmins, who had once presided over and regulated the distribution of resources.

◆ ◆ ◆

By the sixth century BCE, the Aryans had reached the eastern Gangetic basin, a region with higher rainfall and even greater agricultural yield. They were now able to grow rice, fruit, cereal, sesame, millet, wheat, grains, barley, and with this enhanced surplus, support more elaborate states.[49] As more powerful rajas conquered smaller chiefdoms, sixteen large kingdoms emerged, including Magadha in the northeast of the Gangetic plain and Koshala in the southwest, all competing with one another for scarce resources. The priests still insisted that it was their rituals and sacrifices that preserved the cosmic and social order,[50] but the religious texts acknowledged that in reality the political system depended on coercion:

The whole world is kept in order by punishment. . . . If the king did not, without tiring, inflict punishment on those worthy to be punished, the stronger would roast the weaker like fish on a spit. The crow would eat the sacrificial cake and the dog would lick the sacrificial viands, and ownership would not remain with anyone, and the lower ones would usurp the place of the higher ones. . . . Punishment alone governs all created beings, punishment alone protects them, punishment watches over them while they sleep. . . . Punishment is . . . the king.[51]

We lack the archaeological evidence to know much about the organization of these kingdoms, however; here too we have to rely on religious texts, especially the Buddhist scriptures, which were composed and preserved orally and not committed to writing until the first century CE.

An entirely different polity, however, had emerged in the foothills of the Himalayas and on the edge of the Ganges plain: the *gana-sanghas* or "tribal republics" that rejected monarchy and were ruled by assemblies of clan chieftains. They may have been founded by independent-minded aristocrats, who were unhappy with the autocracy of the kingdoms and wanted to live in a more egalitarian community. The tribal republics rejected Vedic orthodoxy and had no interest in paying for expensive sacrifices; instead they invested in trade, agriculture, and warfare, and power was wielded not by a king but by a small ruling class.[52] Because they had no priestly caste, there were only two classes: a Kshatriya aristocracy and the *dasa-karmakaru,* "slaves and laborers," who had no rights or access to resources, although it was possible for enterprising merchants and artisans to achieve higher social status. With their large standing armies, the tribal republics were a significant challenge to the Aryan kingdoms and proved to be remarkably resilient, surviving well into the middle of the first millennium CE.[53] Clearly their independence and at least nominal egalitarianism appealed to something fundamental in the Indian psyche.

The kingdoms and sanghas were both still mainly reliant on agriculture, but the Ganges region was also experiencing a commercial revolution, which produced a merchant class and a money economy. Cities linked by new roads and canals—Savatthi, Saketa, Kosambi, Varanasi, Rajagaha, and Changa—were becoming centers of industry and business. This challenged the structural violence of the class system, since most of the nouveau riche merchants and bankers were vaishyas, and some were even shudras.[54] A new class of "untouchables" (*chandalas*), who had been thrown off their land by the incoming Aryans, now took the place of these aspiring workers at the bottom of the social hierarchy.[55] City life was exciting. The streets were crowded with brightly painted carriages and huge elephants carrying merchandise from distant lands. People of all classes and ethnicities mingled freely in the marketplace, and new ideas began to challenge the traditional Vedic system. The Brahmins, therefore, whose roots were in the countryside, began to seem irrelevant.[56]

As often in times of flux, a new spirituality emerged, and it had three interrelated themes: *dukkha, moksha,* and *karma.* Surprisingly, despite this prosperity and progress, pessimism was deep and widespread. People were experiencing life as *dukkha*—"unsatisfactory," "flawed," and "awry." From the trauma of birth to the agony of death, human existence seemed fraught with suffering, and even death brought no relief because everything and everybody was caught up in an inescapable cycle (*samsara*) of rebirth, so the whole distressing scenario had to be endured again and again. The great eastward migration had been fueled by the Aryans' experience of claustrophobic confinement in the Punjab; now they felt imprisoned in their overcrowded cities. It was not just a feeling: rapid urbanization typically leads to epidemics, particularly when the population rises above 300,000, a sort of tipping point for contagion.[57] No wonder the Aryans were obsessed by sickness, suffering, and death and longed to find a way out.

Rapid change of circumstance also made people more conscious of cause and effect. They could now see how the actions of one generation affected the next, and they began to believe that their deeds (*karma*) would also determine their next existence: if they were guilty of bad karma in this life, they would be reborn as slaves or animals, but with good karma, they might become kings or even gods next time. Merit was something that could be earned, accumulated, and finally "realized" in the same way as mercantile wealth.[58] But even if you were reborn as a god, there was no real escape from life's dukkha, because even gods had to die and would be reborn to lower status. In an attempt to shore up the now-vulnerable class system, perhaps, the Brahmins tried to reconfigure the concepts of karma and samsara: you could enjoy a good rebirth only if you strictly observed the dharma of your class.[59]

Others would draw upon these new ideas to challenge the social system. In the Punjab, the Aryans had tried to fight their way to "liberation" (*moksha*); now some, building on the internalized spirituality of the Brahmanas, were looking for a more spiritual freedom and would investigate their inner world as vigorously as the Aryan warriors had once explored the untamed forests. The new wealth gave the nobility the time and leisure that was essential for such introspective contemplation. The new spirituality was, therefore, strictly for the aristocracy; it was one of the civilized arts that relied on the state's structural violence. No shudra or chandala would be permitted to spend hours in the meditations and metaphysical discussions that between the sixth and second centuries BCE produced the texts known as the Upanishads.

These new teachings may have originally been formulated by Brahmins who lived in the towns and understood the problems arising from urban living.[60] But significantly many new practices were attributed to Kshatriya warriors, and the discussions reported in the Upanishads often took place in the raja's court. They drew on the more interior spirituality of the Brahmanas and took it a step further. The Brhadaranyaka Upanishad, one of the earliest of these texts, was almost certainly composed in the kingdom of Videha, a frontier state on the easternmost point of Aryan expansion.[61] Videha was scorned by the conservative Brahmins in the Doab, but there was a great admixture of peoples in these easterly territories, including Indo-Aryan settlers from earlier waves of migration and tribes from Iran, as well as peoples indigenous to India. Some of these foreigners assimilated to the varna classes but brought their own traditions with them—including, perhaps, a skepticism about Vedic orthodoxy. These new encounters were intellectually stimulating, and the early Upanishads reflect this excitement.

The social and political developments in these new states inspired some of the warrior class to imagine a new world free of priestly ascendency. Thus the Upanishads denied the necessity of the Vedic sacrifices and completed the devas' downgrading by simply assimilating the gods into the contemplative's psyche: " 'Sacrifice to this god. Sacrifice to that god.' People do say these things, but in reality each of these gods is his own creation, for he himself is all these gods."[62] The worshipper now turned within. The focus of the Upanishads was the atman, the "self," which, like the devas, was also a manifestation of the Brahman. So if the sage could discover the inner core of his own being, he would automatically enter into the ultimate reality. Only by the ecstatic knowledge of the self, which would free him of the desire for ephemeral things here below, would a person be liberated from the ceaseless cycle of rebirth and redeath. This was a discovery of immense importance. The idea that the ultimate reality, which was "All" that is, was an immanent presence in every single human being would become a central insight in every major religious tradition. There was therefore no need to perform the elaborate rituals that had upheld the structural violence of the varna system, because once they encountered the deepest part of themselves, practitioners were one with "the All": "If a man knows 'I am *brahman*' in this way, he becomes this whole world. Not even the gods are able to prevent it, for he becomes their very self (*atman*)."[63] It was a defiant declaration of independence, a political as well as a spiritual revolution. The Kshatriya could now cast aside his dependence on the priest who dominated the ritual arena. At the same time as vaishyas and shudras were climbing the social ladder, the warrior aristocracy was making a bid for the first place in society.

Yet the Upanishads also challenged the Kshatriya martial ethos. The atman had originally been Agni, the deepest, divine "self" of the warrior that he had attained by fighting and stealing. The heroic Aryan drive eastward had been motivated by desire for earthly things—cows, plunder, land, honor, and prestige. Now the Upanishad sages urged their disciples to renounce such desire. Anyone who remained fixated on mundane wealth could never be liberated from the cycle of suffering and rebirth, but "a man who does not desire—who is without desires, who is freed from desires, whose only desire is his self (*atman*)—his vital functions do not depart. *Brahman* he is and to *brahman* he goes."[64] New meditative techniques induced a state of mind that was "calm, composed, cool, patient and collected": in short, the very opposite of the old agitated Aryan mentality.[65] One of the Upanishads actually described Indra, no less, living peacefully as a humble student in the forest with his teacher and relinquishing violence in order to find perfect tranquillity.[66]

Aryans had always considered themselves inherently superior to others; their rituals had bred within them a deep sense of entitlement that had fueled their raids and conquests. But the Upanishads taught that because the atman, the essence of every single creature, was identical with the Brahman, all beings shared the same sacred core. The Brahman was the subtle kernel of the banyan seed from which a great tree grows.[67] It was the sap that gave life to every part of the tree; it was also the most fundamental reality of every single human being.[68] Brahman was like a chunk of salt left overnight to dissolve in a beaker of water; even though it could not be seen the next morning, it was still present in every sip.[69] Instead of repudiating this basic kinship with all beings, as the warrior did when he demonized his enemy, these sages were deliberately cultivating an awareness of it. Everyone liked to imagine that he was unique, but in reality his special distinguishing features were no more permanent than rivers that all flowed into the same sea. Once they left the riverbed, they became "just the ocean," no longer proclaiming their individuality, crying "I am that river," "I am this river." Such strident assertion of the ego was a delusion that could only lead to pain and confusion. Release (*moksha*) from such suffering was dependent on the profound acknowledgment that at base everybody was Brahman and should therefore be treated with absolute reverence. The Upanishads bequeathed to India a sense of the fundamental unity of all beings, so that your so-called enemy was no longer the heinous other but inseparable from you.[70]

◆ ◆ ◆

Indian religion had always endorsed and informed the structural and martial violence of society. But as early as the eighth century BCE, the "renouncers" (*samnyasin*) mounted a disciplined and devastating critique of this inherent aggression, withdrawing from settled society to adopt an independent lifestyle. Renunciation was not, as is often thought in the West, simply life negating. Throughout Indian history, asceticism has nearly always had a political dimension and has often inspired a radical reappraisal of society. That certainly happened in the Gangetic plain.[71] Aryans had always possessed the "restless heart" that had made Gilgamesh weary of settled life, but instead of leaving home to fight and steal, the renouncers eschewed aggression, owned no property, and begged for their food.[72] By about 500 BCE, they had become the chief agents of spiritual change and a direct challenge to the values of the agrarian kingdoms.[73] This movement was in part an offshoot of *brahmacharya,* the "holy life" led by the Brahmin student, who would spend years with his guru, studying the Vedas, begging humbly for his bread, and living alone in the tropical forests for a given period. In other parts of the world too, Aryan youths lived in the wild as part of their military training, hunting for food and learning the arts of self-sufficiency and survival. But because the Brahmin's dharma did not include violence, the *brahmacharin* was forbidden to hunt, to harm animals, or ride in a war chariot.[74]

Moreover, most of the renouncers were adult Brahmins when they embarked on their solitary existence, their apprenticeship long past.[75] A renouncer made a deliberate choice. He repudiated the ritual sacrifices that symbolized the Aryan political community and rejected the family household, the institutional mainstay of settled life. He had in effect stepped right outside the systemic violence of the varna system and extracted himself from the economic nexus of society in order to become a "beggar" (*bhiksu*).[76] Some renouncers returned home, only to become social and religious irritants within the community, while others remained in the forest and challenged the culture from without. They condemned the aristocratic preoccupation with status, honor, and glory, yearned for insults "as if they were nectar," and deliberately courted contempt by behaving like madmen or animals.[77] Like so many Indian reformers, the renouncers drew upon the ancient mythology of warfare to model a different kind of nobility. They evoked the heroic days in the Punjab, when men had proved their valor and virility by braving the untamed forest. Many saw the bhiksu as a new kind of pioneer.[78] When a famous renouncer came to town, people of all classes flocked to listen to him.

Perhaps the most important martial ritual revised by the renouncers was yoga, which became the hallmark of renouncer spirituality. Originally, as we have seen, the term had referred to the tethering of the draft animals to the war chariots before a raid; now it became a contemplative discipline that "yoked" the yogin's mental powers in a raid on the unconscious impulses (*vrittis*) of passion, egotism, hatred, and greed that had fueled the warrior ethos and were so deeply entrenched in the psyche that they could be extirpated only by sheer mental force. Yoga may have been rooted in the indigenous traditions of India, but by the sixth century BCE it had become central to the Aryan spiritual landscape. A systematic assault on the ego, it expunged the "I" from the yogin's mind, nullifying the warrior's proud self-assertion: "I am the mightiest! I am supreme!" The ancient warriors of the Punjab had been like the devas, perpetually on the move and constantly engaged in martial activity. Now the new man of yoga sat for hours in one place, holding himself in such unnatural stillness that he seemed more like a statue or a plant than a human being. If he persevered, a skilled yogin had intimations of a final liberation (*moksha*) from the confines of egotism that bore no relation to ordinary experience.

Before he was allowed even to sit in the yogic position, an aspirant had to complete an arduous ethical program, observing five "prohibitions" (*yamas*).[79] The first of these was *ahimsa,* nonviolence: not only was he forbidden to kill or injure another creature, but he could not even speak unkindly or make an irritable gesture. Second, he was forbidden to steal: instead of seizing other people's property like the raiders, the yogin had to cultivate an indifference to material possessions. Lying was also prohibited. Truth-telling had always been central to the Aryan warrior ethos, but the exigencies of war had occasionally forced even Indra into deceit; the aspirant, however, was not permitted to be economical with the truth, even to save his own life. He also abstained from sex and intoxicating substances that could enervate the mental and physical energies that he would need in this spiritual expedition. Finally, he must study the teaching (*dharma*) of his guru and cultivate habitual serenity, behaving kindly and courteously to everybody without exception. This was an initiation into a new way of being human, one that eschewed the greed, self-preoccupation, and aggression of the warrior. By dint of practice, these ethical disciplines would become second nature to the yogin, and when that happened, the texts explained, he would experience "indescribable joy."[80]

• • •

Some renouncers broke even more completely with the Vedic system and were denounced as heretics by the Brahmins. Two in particular made a lasting impact, and significantly, both came from the gana-sanghas. Destined for a military career, Vardhamana Jnatraputra (c. 599–527) was the son of a Kshatriya chieftain of the Jnatra clan of Kundagrama, north of modern Patna. At the age of thirty, however, he changed course and became a renouncer. After a long, difficult apprenticeship, he achieved enlightenment and became a *jina* ("conqueror"); his followers became known as Jains. Even though he went further than anybody else in his renunciation of violence, it was natural for him, as a former warrior, to express his insights in military imagery. His followers called him Mahavira ("Great Champion"), the title of an intrepid warrior in the Rig Veda.

Yet his regime was based wholly on nonviolence, one that vanquished every impulse to harm others. For Mahavira, the only way to achieve liberation (*moksha*) was to cultivate an attitude of friendliness toward everyone and everything.[81] Here, as in the Upanishads, we encounter the requirement found in many great world traditions that it is not enough to confine our benevolence to our own people or to those we find congenial; this partiality must be replaced by a practically expressed empathy for everybody, without exception. If this was practiced consistently, violence of any kind—verbal, martial, or systemic—becomes impossible.

Mahavira taught his male and female disciples to develop a sympathy that had no bounds, to realize their profound kinship with all beings. Every single creature—even plants, water, fire, air, and rocks—had a *jiva,* a living "soul," and must be treated with the respect that we wish to receive ourselves.[82] Most of his followers were Kshatriyas seeking an alternative to the warfare and structural segmentation of society. As warriors, they would have routinely distanced themselves from the enemy, carefully stifling their innate reluctance to kill their own kind. Jains, like the Upanishadic sages, taught their disciples to recognize their community with all others and relinquish the preoccupation with "us" and "them" that made fighting and structural oppression impossible, because a true "conqueror" did not inflict harm of any kind.

Later, Jains would develop a complex mythology and cosmology, but in the early period nonviolence was their only precept: "All breathing, existing, living, sentient creatures should not be slain, nor treated with violence, nor abused, nor tormented, nor driven away. This is the pure, unchangeable law, which the enlightened ones who know have proclaimed."[83] Unlike warriors who trained themselves to become impervious to the agony they inflicted, Jains deliberately attuned themselves to the pain of the world. They learned to move with consummate caution lest they squash an insect or trample on a blade of grass; they did not pluck fruit from a tree but waited till it fell to the ground. Like all renouncers, they had to eat what they were given, even meat, but must never ask for any creature to be killed on their behalf.[84] Jain meditation consisted simply of a rigorous suppression of all antagonistic thoughts and a conscious effort to fill the mind with affection for all creatures. The result was *samayika* ("equanimity"), a profound, life-changing realization that all creatures were equal. Twice a day Jains stood before their guru and repented of any distress they might, even inadvertently, have caused: "I ask pardon of all living creatures. May all creatures pardon me. May I have friendship for all creatures and enmity toward none."[85]

• • •

Toward the end of the fifth century, a Kshatriya from the tribal republic of Sakka in the foothills of the Himalayas shaved his head and donned the renouncer's yellow robe.[86] After an arduous spiritual quest during which he studied with many of the leading gurus of the day, Siddhatta Gotama, later known as the Buddha ("awakened one"), achieved enlightenment by a form of yoga based on the suppression of antagonistic feelings and the careful cultivation of kindly, positive emotions.[87] Like Mahavira, his near contemporary, the Buddha's teaching was based on nonviolence. He achieved a state that he called *nibbana*,* because the greed and aggression that had limited his humanity had been extinguished like a flame.[88] Later the Buddha devised a meditation that taught his monks to direct feelings of friendship and affection to the ends of the earth, desiring that all creatures be free of pain, and finally freeing themselves of any personal attachment or partiality by loving all sentient beings with the "even-mindedness" of *upeksha*. Not a single creature was to be excluded from this radius of concern.[89]

It was summed up in the early prayer, attributed to the Buddha, recited daily by his monks and lay disciples.

> Let all beings be happy! Weak or strong, of high, middle or low
> estate
> Small or great, visible or invisible, near or far away,
> Alive or still to be born—may they all be perfectly happy!
> Let nobody lie to anybody or despise any single being anywhere.
> May nobody wish harm to any single creature, out of anger or
> hatred!
> Let us cherish all creatures as a mother her only child!
> May our loving thoughts fill the whole world, above, below,
> across,—
> Without limit; a boundless goodwill toward the whole world,
> Unrestricted, free of hatred and enmity![90]

---

* *Nibbana* is the equivalent of the Sanskrit *nirvana* in the Pali dialect that may have been spoken by the Buddha. Its literal meaning is "blowing out."

The Buddha's enlightenment had been based on the principle that to live morally was to live for others. Unlike the other renouncers, who retreated from human society, Buddhist monks were commanded to return to the world to help others find release from pain. "Go now," he told his first disciples, "and travel for the welfare, and happiness of the people, out of compassion for the world, for the benefit, welfare, and happiness of gods and men."[91] Instead of simply eschewing violence, Buddhism demanded a positive campaign to assuage the suffering and increase the happiness of "the whole world."

The Buddha summed up his teaching in four "Noble Truths": that existence was dukkha; that the cause of our pain was selfishness and greed; that nirvana released us from this suffering; and that the way to achieve this state was to follow the program of meditation, morality, and resolution that he called the "Noble Path," which was designed to produce an alternative aristocracy. The Buddha was a realist and did not imagine that he could single-handedly abolish the oppression inherent in the varna system, but he insisted that even a vaishya or a shudra would be ennobled if he or she behaved in a selfless, compassionate manner and "abstained from the killing of creatures."[92] By the same token, a man or woman became a "commoner" (*pathujjana*) by behaving cruelly, greedily, and violently.[93]

His sangha, or order of monks and nuns, modeled a different kind of society, an alternative to the aggression of the royal court. As in the tribal republics, there was no autocratic rule, but decisions were made in common. King Pasenedi of Koshala was greatly impressed by the "smiling and courteous" demeanor of the monks, "alert, calm and unflustered, living on alms, their minds remaining as gentle as wild deer." At court, he said wryly, everybody competed acrimoniously for wealth and status, whereas in the sangha he saw monks "living together as uncontentiously as milk with water, looking at one another with kind eyes."[94] The sangha was not perfect—it could never entirely transcend class distinctions— but it became a powerful influence in India. Instead of melting away into the forests like other renouncers, the Buddhists were highly visible. The Buddha used to travel with an entourage of hundreds of monks, their yellow robes and shaven heads demonstrating their dissent from the mainstream, walking along the trade routes beside the merchants. And behind them, in wagons and chariots laden with provisions, rode their lay supporters, many of them Kshatriyas.

The Buddhists and Jains made an impact on mainstream society because they were sensitive to the difficulties of social change in the newly urbanized society of northern India. They enabled individuals to declare their independence of the big agrarian kingdoms, as the tribal republics had done. Like the ambitious vaishyas and shudras, Buddhists and Jains were self-made men, reconstructing themselves at a profound psychological level to model a more empathic humanity. Both were also in tune with the new commercial ethos. Because of their absolute rejection of violence, Jains could not engage in agriculture, which involved the killing of creatures, so they turned to trade and became popular in the new merchant communities. Buddhism did not demand complex metaphysics or elaborate, arcane rituals but was based on principles of reason, logic, and empirical experience that were congenial to the merchant class. Moreover, Buddhists and Jains were pragmatists and realists: they did not expect everybody to become a monk but encouraged lay disciples to follow their teachings insofar as they could. Thus these spiritualties not only entered the mainstream but even began to influence the ruling class.

◆ ◆ ◆

Already during the Buddha's lifetime, there were signs of empire building in the Gangetic plain. In 493 BCE Ajatashatru became king of Magadha; it was said that, impatient for the throne, he had murdered his father, King Bimbisara, the Buddha's friend. Ajatashatru continued his father's policy of military conquest and built a small fort on the Ganges, which the Buddha visited shortly before his death; it later became the famous metropolis of Pataliputra. Ajatashatru also annexed Koshala and Kashi and defeated a confederacy of tribal republics, so that when he died in 461, the Kingdom of Magadha dominated the Gangetic plain. He was succeeded by five unsatisfactory kings, all parricides, until the usurper Mahapadma Nanda, a shudra, founded the first non-Kshatriya dynasty and further extended the borders of the kingdom. The wealth of the Nandas, based on a highly efficient taxation system, became proverbial and the idea of creating an imperial state began to take root. When the young adventurer Chandragupta Maurya, another shudra, usurped the Nanda throne in 321 BCE, the Kingdom of Magadha became the Mauryan Empire.

In the premodern period, no empire could create a unified culture; it existed solely to extract resources from the subject peoples, who would inevitably rise up from time to time in revolt. Thus an emperor was usually engaged in almost constant warfare against rebellious subjects or against aristocrats who sought to usurp him. Chandragupta and his successors ruled from Pataliputra, conquering neighboring regions that had strategic and economic potential by force of arms. These areas were incorporated into the Mauryan state and administered by governors who answered to the emperor. On the fringes of the empire, peripheral areas rich in timber, elephants, and semiprecious stones, served as buffer zones; the imperial state did not attempt direct rule in these areas but used local people as agents to tap their resources; periodically these "forest peoples" resisted Mauryan dominance. The main task of the imperial administration was to collect taxes in kind. In India, the rate of taxation varied from region to region, ranging from one-sixth to one-quarter of agricultural output. Pastoralists were taxed according to the size and productivity of their herds, and commerce was subject to taxes, tolls, and custom dues. The crown claimed ownership of all uncultivated land, and once an area had been cleared, shudras living in overpopulated regions of the Mauryan Empire were forcibly resettled there.[95]

The empire, therefore, depended entirely on extortion and force. Not only did military campaigns increase the wealth of the state by acquiring more arable land, but plunder was an important supplementary revenue, and prisoners of war provided valuable manpower. It may therefore seem strange that the first three Mauryan emperors were patrons of nonviolent sects. Chandragupta abdicated in 297 BCE to become a Jain ascetic; his son Bindusara courted the strictly ascetical Ajivaka school; and Ashoka, who succeeded to the throne in about 268 after murdering two of his brothers, favored the Buddhists. As shudras, they had never been permitted to take part in the Vedic rituals and probably regarded them as alien and oppressive. The independent, egalitarian spirit of these unorthodox sects, on the other hand, would have been highly congenial. But Chandragupta realized that Jainism was incompatible with royal rule, and Ashoka did not become even a lay Buddhist until the end of his reign. Yet alongside Mahavira and the Buddha, Ashoka would become the most central political and cultural figure of ancient India.[96]

On his accession, he took the title Devanampiya, "Beloved of the Gods," and continued to expand the empire, which now extended from Bengal to Afghanistan. In the early years of his reign, Ashoka had lived a somewhat dissolute life and acquired a reputation for cruelty. But that changed in about 260, when he accompanied the imperial army to put down a rebellion in Kalinga in modern Odisha and had an extraordinary conversion experience. During the campaign, 100,000 Kalingan soldiers were killed in battle, many times more had perished from wounds and disease afterward, and 150,000 were deported to the peripheral territories. Ashoka was profoundly shocked by the suffering he witnessed. He had what we might call a "Gilgamesh moment," when the sensory realities of warfare broke through the carapace of cultivated heartlessness that makes warfare possible. He recorded his remorse in an edict inscribed on a massive rock face. Instead of jubilantly listing the numbers of enemy casualties, like most kings, Ashoka confessed that "the slaughter, death and deportation is extremely grievous to Devanampiya and weighs heavily on his mind."[97] He warned other kings that military conquest, the glory of victory, and the trappings of royalty were fleeting. If they had to dispatch an army, they should fight as humanely as possible and enforce their victory "with patience and light punishment."[98] The only true conquest was personal submission to what Ashoka called *dhamma:* a moral code of compassion, mercy, honesty, and consideration for all living creatures.

Ashoka inscribed similar edicts outlining his new policy of military restraint and moral reform on cliff faces and colossal cylindrical pillars throughout the length and breadth of his empire.[99] These edicts were intensely personal messages but could also have been an attempt to give the far-flung empire ideological unity; they may have even been read aloud to the populace on state occasions. Ashoka urged his people to curb their greed and extravagance; promised that, as far as possible, he would refrain from using martial force; preached kindness to animals; and vowed to replace the violent sport of hunting, the traditional pastime of kings, with royal pilgrimages to Buddhist shrines. He also announced that he had dug wells, founded hospitals and rest houses, and planted banyan trees "which will give shade to beasts and men."[100] He insisted on the importance of respect for teachers, obedience to parents, consideration for slaves and servants, and reverence for all sects—for the orthodox Brahmins as well as for Buddhists, Jains, and other "heretical" schools. "Concord is to be commended," he declared, "so that men may hear one another's principles."[101]

It is unlikely that Ashoka's dhamma was Buddhist. This was a broader ethic, an attempt to find a benevolent model of governance based on the recognition of human dignity, a sentiment shared by many contemporary Indian schools. In Ashoka's inscriptions, we hear the perennial voice of those repelled by killing and cruelty who have, throughout history, tried to resist the call to violence. But even though he preached "abstention from killing living beings,"[102] he had tacitly to acknowledge that, as emperor and for the sake of the region's stability, he could not renounce force; nor in these times could he abolish capital punishment or legislate against the killing and eating of animals (although he listed species that should be protected). Moreover, despite his distress about the plight of the Kalingans who had been deported after the battle, there was no question of repatriating them since they were essential to the imperial economy. And as head of state, he could certainly not abjure warfare or disband his army. He realized that even if he abdicated and became a Buddhist monk, others would fight to succeed him and unleash more havoc, and as always, the peasants and the poor would suffer most.

Ashoka's dilemma is the dilemma of civilization itself. As society developed and weaponry became more deadly, the empire, founded on and maintained by violence, would paradoxically become the most effective means of keeping the peace. Despite its violence and exploitation, people looked for an absolute imperial monarchy as eagerly as we search for signs of a flourishing democracy today.

◆ ◆ ◆

Ashoka's dilemma may lie behind the story of the *Mahabharata,* India's great epic. This massive work—eight times the length of Homer's *Iliad* and *Odyssey* combined—is an anthology of many strands of tradition transmitted orally from about 300 BCE but not committed to writing until the early Common Era. The *Mahabharata* is more than a narrative poem, however. It remains the Indian national saga and is the most popular of all India's sacred texts, familiar in every home. It contains the *Bhagavad-Gita,* which has been called India's "national gospel."[103] In the twentieth century, during the buildup to independence, the *Gita* would play a central role in the discussions about the legitimacy of waging war against Britain.[104] Its influence in forming attitudes toward violence and its relation to religion has therefore been unparalleled in India. Long after Ashoka was forgotten, it compelled people of all ranks to grapple with his dilemma, which thus became central to the collective memory of India.

Even though the text was finally redacted by Brahmins, at its heart the epic depicts the pathos of the Kshatriya who could not achieve enlightenment because he was obliged by the dharma of his class to be a man of war. The story is set in the Kuru-Panchala region before the rise of the large sixth-century kingdoms. Yudishthira, eldest son of King Pandu, has lost his kingdom to his cousins, the Kauravas, who rigged the ritual game of dice during his consecration, so that he, his four brothers, and Draupadi, their common wife, had to go into exile. Twelve years later the Pandavas regain the throne in a catastrophic war in which nearly everyone on both sides is killed. The final battle brings the Heroic Age of history to an end and ushers in what the epic calls the Kali Yuga—our own deeply flawed era. It should have been a simple war of good versus evil. The Pandava brothers were all fathered by gods: Yudishthira by Dharma, guardian of cosmic order; Bhīma by Vayu, god of physical force; Arjuna by Indra; and the twins Nakula and Sahadeva by the Ashvins, patrons of fertility and productivity. The Kauravas, however, are incarnations of the asuras, and their struggle therefore replicates on earth the war between devas and asuras in heaven. But even though the Pandavas, with the help of their cousin Krishna, chieftain of the Yadava clan, finally defeat the Kauravas, they have to resort to dubious tactics, and when they contemplate the devastated world at the end of the war, their victory seems tainted. The Kauravas, on the other hand, although they are fighting on the "wrong" side, often act in an exemplary manner. When their leader, Duryodhana, is killed, devas sing his praises and cover his body with a shower of petals.

The *Mahabharata* is not an antiwar epic: innumerable passages glorify warfare and describe battles enthusiastically and in gory detail. Even though it is set in an earlier time, the epic probably reflects the period after Ashoka's death in 232 BCE, when the Mauryan Empire began its decline and India entered a dark age of political instability that lasted until the rise of the Gupta dynasty in 320 CE.[105] There is, therefore, an implicit assumption that empire—or in the poem's terms, "world rule"—is essential to peace. And while the poem is unsparing about the ferocity of empire, it poignantly recognizes that nonviolence in a violent world is not only impossible but can actually cause *himsa* ("harm"). Brahmin law insisted that the king's chief duty was to prevent the fearful chaos that would ensue if monarchical authority failed, and for this, military coercion (*danda*) was indispensable.[106] Yet while Yudishthira is divinely destined to be king, he hates war. He explains to Krishna that even though he knows that it is his duty to regain the throne, warfare brings only misery. True, the Kauravas usurped his kingdom, but to kill his cousins and friends—many of them good and noble men—would be "a most evil thing."[107] He knows that every Vedic class has its particular duty—"The shudra obeys, the vaishya lives by trade. . . . The Brahmin prefers the begging bowl"—but the Kshatriyas "live off killing," and "any other way of life is forbidden to us." The Kshatriya is therefore doomed to misery. If defeated, he will be reviled, but if he achieves victory by ruthless methods, he incurs the taint of the warrior, is "deprived of glory and reaps eternal infamy." "For heroism is a powerful disease that eats up the heart, and peace is found only by giving it up or by serenity of mind," Yudishthira tells Krishna. "On the other hand if final tranquillity were ignited by the total eradication of the enemy that would be even crueler."[108]

To win the war, the Pandavas have to kill four Kaurava leaders who are inflicting grave casualties on their army. One of them is the general Drona, whom the Pandavas love dearly because he was their teacher and initiated them in the art of warfare. In a council of war, Krishna argues that if the Pandavas want to save the world from total destruction by establishing their rule, they must cast virtue aside. A warrior is obliged to be absolutely truthful and keep his word, but Krishna tells Yudishthira that he can kill Drona only by lying to him. In the midst of the battle, he must tell him that his son Ashwatthaman has died so that, overcome with grief, Drona will lay down his weapons.[109] Most reluctantly, Yudishthira agrees, and when he delivers this terrible news, Drona never imagines that Yudishthira, the son of Dharma, would lie. So Drona stops fighting and sits down in his chariot in the yogic position, falls into a trance, and ascends peacefully to heaven. In terrible counterpoint, the chariot of Yudishthira, which has always floated a few inches above the ground, comes crashing down to earth.

Krishna is no Satan, tempting the Pandavas to sin. This is the end of the Heroic Age, and his dark stratagems have become essential because, as he tells the desolate Pandavas, the Kauravas "could not have been slain by you on the battlefield in a fair fight." Had not Indra lied and broken his oath to Vritra in order to save the cosmic order? "Not even the world-guardian gods themselves could have killed by fair means those four noble warriors," Krishna explains. "When enemies become too numerous and powerful, they should be slain by deceit and stratagems. This was the path formerly trodden by the devas to slay the asuras; and a path trodden by the virtuous may be trodden by all."[110] The Pandavas feel reassured and acknowledge that their victory has at least brought peace to the world. But bad karma can only have a bad outcome, and Krishna's scheme has appalling consequences that resonate horribly with us today.

Crazed with sorrow, Ashwatthaman, Drona's son, vows to avenge his father and offers himself to Shiva, the ancient god of the indigenous peoples of India, as a self-sacrifice. Entering the Pandava camp by night, he slaughters the sleeping women, children, and warriors who are "exhausted and weaponless" and hacks horses and elephants to pieces. In his divine frenzy, "his every limb doused in blood, he seemed like Death himself, unloosed by fate . . . inhuman and utterly terrifying."[111] The Pandavas themselves escape, having been warned by Krishna to sleep outside the camp, but most of their family are killed. When they finally catch up with Ashwatthaman, they find him sitting serenely with a group of renouncers beside the Ganges. He fires off a magical weapon of mass destruction, and Arjuna retaliates with a weapon of his own. Had not two of the renouncers, "desiring the welfare of all creatures," positioned themselves between the contending weapons, the world would have been destroyed. Instead Ashwatthaman's weapon is diverted into the wombs of the Pandava women, who will bear no more children.[112] So Yudishthira is proven right: a destructive cycle of violence, betrayal, and lies has rebounded on the perpetrators, resulting in destruction for both sides.

Yudishthira reigns for fifteen years, but he has incurred the ancient stain of the warrior. The light has gone out of his life, and after the war he would have become a renouncer had not his brothers and Krishna strongly opposed it. The king's rod of force is essential for the welfare of the world, Arjuna argued. No king has ever attained glory without slaying his enemies; indeed, it is impossible to exist without harming other creatures: "I don't see anyone living in the world with nonviolence. Even ascetics cannot stay alive without killing."[113] Like Ashoka, who was also unable to stem the violence of imperial warfare, Yudishthira focuses on kindness to animals, the only form of ahimsa that he is able realistically to practice. At the end of his life, he refuses to enter heaven without his devoted dog and is congratulated for his compassion by his father, Dharma.[114] For centuries, the Indian national epic has compelled its audience to appreciate the moral ambiguity and tragedy of warfare; whatever the warrior's heroic code maintained, it was never a wholly glorious activity. Yet it was essential not only to the survival of the state but also for civilization and progress and, as such, had become an unavoidable fact of human life.

Even Arjuna, who is often irritated by his brother's yearning for nonviolence, has an "Ashoka moment." In the *Bhagavad-Gita* he and Krishna debate these problems before the final battle with the Kauravas. As he stands in his chariot beside Krishna in the front line, Arjuna is suddenly horrified to see his cousins and beloved friends and teachers in the enemy ranks. "I see no good in killing my kinsmen in battle," he tells Krishna, "I do not want to kill them, even if I am killed."[115] Krishna tries to hearten him by citing all the traditional arguments, but Arjuna is not impressed: "I will not fight!" he cries.[116] So Krishna introduces an entirely novel idea: a warrior must simply dissociate himself from the effects of his actions and perform his duty without any personal animus or agenda of his own. Like a yogin, he must take the "I" out of his deeds, so that he acts impersonally—indeed, *he* will not be acting at all.[117] Instead, like a sage, even in the frenzy of battle, he will remain fearless and without desire.

We do not know whether this would have convinced Arjuna, because he is suddenly blasted by a terrifying epiphany. Krishna reveals that he is really an incarnation of the god Vishnu, who descends to earth whenever the cosmic order is in jeopardy. As Lord of the World, Vishnu is ipso facto involved in the violence that is an inescapable part of human life, but he is not damaged by it, "since I remain detached in all my actions, Arjuna, as if I stood apart from them."[118] As he gazes at Krishna, Arjuna sees that everything—gods, humans, and the natural order—is somehow present in Krishna's body, and although the battle has not even begun, he sees that the Pandava and Kaurava warriors are already hurtling into the god's blazing mouth. Krishna/Vishnu has therefore already annihilated both armies, and it makes no difference whether Arjuna fights or not. "Even without you," Krishna tells him, "all these warriors . . . will cease to exist."[119] Many politicians and generals have similarly argued that they are only instruments of destiny when they commit atrocities—though few have emptied themselves of egotism and become "free from attachment, hostile to no creature."[120]

The *Bhagavad-Gita* has probably been more influential than any other Indian scripture. Yet both the *Gita* and the *Mahabharata* remind us that there are no easy answers to the problems of war and peace. True, Indian mythology and ritual often glorified greed and warfare but it also helped people to confront tragedy and even devised ways of extirpating aggression from the psyche, pioneering ways for people to live together without any violence at all. We are flawed creatures with violent hearts that long for peace. At the same time as the *Gita* was being composed, the people of China were coming to a similar conclusion.

3

China: Warriors and Gentlemen

The Chinese believed that at the beginning of time, human beings had been indistinguishable from animals. Creatures that would eventually become human had "snake bodies with human faces or the heads of oxen with tiger noses," while future animals could speak and had human skills. These creatures lived together in caves, naked or clad in skins, eating raw meat and wild plants. Humans did not develop differently because of their biological makeup but because they were taken in hand by five great kings, who had discerned the order of the universe and taught men and women to live in harmony with it. These sage kings drove the other beasts away and forced humans to live separately. They developed the tools and technology essential to organized society and instructed their people in a code of values that aligned them with the cosmic forces. Thus for the Chinese, humanity was not a given; nor did it evolve naturally—it was shaped and crafted by the rulers of states. Those who did not live in civilized Chinese society therefore were not really human; and if the Chinese succumbed to social disorder, they too could lapse into bestial savagery.[1]

Some two thousand years after the dawn of their civilization, however, the Chinese were wrestling with some profound social and political dilemmas. For guidance, they turned to their history—or what they imagined it to be in the absence of the scientific and linguistic techniques we employ today. The myths about the sage kings were formed during the turbulent Warring States period (c. 485–221 BCE), when the Chinese were making a traumatic transformation from a multistate system to a united empire, but they may have originated from the mythology of the shamans of hunter-gatherer times. These tales also reflected the Chinese view of themselves in the intervening millennia.

This mythology makes it clear that civilization could not survive without violence. The first sage king, Shen Nung, the "Divine Farmer," was the inventor of agriculture on which progress and culture depended. He could summon rain at will and conjure grain from the sky; he created the plow, taught his people how to plant and till the soil, and liberated them from the need to hunt and kill their fellow creatures. A man of peace, he refused to punish disobedience and outlawed violence in his kingdom. Instead of creating a ruling class, he decreed that everyone should grow his own food, so Shen Nung would become the hero of those who repudiated the exploitation of the agrarian state. But no state could abjure violence. Because the Divine Farmer's successors had had no military training, they were unable to deal adequately with the natural aggression of their subjects, which, unchecked, grew to such monstrous proportions that humans seemed about to slide back into animality.[2] Fortunately, however, a second sage king appeared. He was called Huang Di, the "Yellow Emperor," because he recognized the potential of China's ochre-colored soil.

To farm successfully, people must organize their lives around the seasons; they are dependent on the sun, winds, and storms located in Heaven (*Tian*),[*] the transcendent realm of the sky. So the Yellow Emperor established human society in the "Way" (*Dao*) of Heaven by processing annually across the world, visiting each of the four compass points in turn—a ritual that maintained the regular cycle of the seasons and would be imitated by all future Chinese kings.[3] Associated with storm and rain, the Yellow Emperor, like other storm gods, was a great warrior. When he came to power, the arable land was desolate, rebels were fighting one another, and there was drought and famine. He also had two external enemies: the animal-warrior Chi You, who was harassing his subjects, and the Fiery Emperor, who was scorching the cultivated land. The Yellow Emperor, therefore, drew on his great spiritual "potency" (*de*) and

---

[*] In this chapter, I have used the Pinyin method of Romanizing the Chinese script; I have given the Wade-Giles version as an alternative in cases when this form may be more familiar to a Western audience.

trained an army of animals—bears, wolves, and tigers—that managed to defeat the Fiery Emperor but could make no headway against the brutality of Chi You and his eighty brothers: "They had the bodies of beasts, the speech of men, bronze heads, and iron brows. They ate sand and stones, and created weapons such as staves, knives, lances, and bows. They terrorized all under Heaven and slaughtered barbarically; they loved nothing and nurtured nothing."[4]

The Yellow Emperor tried to help his suffering people, but because "he practiced love and virtuous potency [*de*]," he could not overpower Chi You with force. So he cast up his eyes to Heaven in silent appeal, and a celestial woman descended bearing a sacred text that revealed the secret art of warfare. The Yellow Emperor could now instruct his animal soldiers in the proper use of weaponry and military conduct, and as a result they defeated Chi You and conquered the entire world. While Chi You's savage violence turned men into beasts, the Yellow Emperor transformed his army of bears, wolves, and tigers into human beings by teaching them to fight according to the rhythms of Heaven.[5] A civilization founded on the twin pillars of agriculture and the organized violence of warfare could now begin.

By the twenty-third century BCE, two other sage kings, Yao and Shun, had established a golden age in the Yellow River Plain, which was known forever after as "the Great Peace." But during Shun's reign, the land was devastated by floods, so the king commissioned Yu, his chief of public works, to build canals, drain the marshes, and lead the rivers safely to the sea. Because of Yu's heroic labors, the people could grow rice and millet. Shun was so grateful that he arranged for Yu to succeed him, and he became the founder of the Xia dynasty.[6] Chinese history records three successive ruling dynasties before the establishment of the empire in 221 BCE: Xia, Shang, and Zhou. It seems, however, that the three coexisted throughout antiquity and although the dominant ruling clan of the kingdom changed, the other lineages remained in charge of their own domains.[7] We have no documentary or archaeological evidence for the Xia period (c. 2200–1600 BCE), but it is likely that there was an agrarian kingdom in the great plain by the end of the third millennium.[8]

The Shang, a nomadic hunting people from northern Iran, seized control of the great plain from the Huai Valley to modern Shantung in about 1600 BCE.[9] The first Shang cities may have been founded by the masters of the guilds that pioneered the manufacture of the bronze weapons, war

chariots, and the magnificent vessels that the Shang used in their sacrifices. The Shang were men of war. They developed a typical agrarian
system, but their economy was still heavily subsidized by hunting and
plunder, and they did not establish a centralized state. Their kingdom
consisted of a series of small towns, each governed by a representative
of the royal family and surrounded by massive ramparts of packed earth
to guard against flooding and attack. Each town was designed as a replica of the cosmos, its four walls oriented to the compass directions. The
local lord and his warrior aristocracy lived in the royal palace, served
by retainers—craftsmen, chariot builders, makers of bows and arrows,
blacksmiths, metalworkers, potters, and scribes—who dwelled in the
south of the city. This was a rigorously segmented society. The king was
at the apex of the social pyramid; next in rank were the princes who
ruled the cities, and the barons who lived on revenues from the rural territories; the *shi*, the ordinary warriors, were the lowest-ranking members
of the nobility.

Religion pervaded Shang political life and endorsed its oppressive system. Because they were not part of their culture, the aristocrats regarded
their peasants as an inferior species that was scarcely human. The sage
kings had created civilization by driving the animals away from human
habitations; the peasants therefore never set foot in the Shang towns and
lived quite separately from the nobility in subterranean dwelling pits in
the countryside. Meriting no more regard than the Yellow Emperor had
shown toward Chi You's horde, they led brutally miserable lives. In the
spring the men moved out of the village and took up permanent residence
in huts in the fields. During this season of work, they had no contact
with their wives and daughters, except when the women brought out
their meals. After the harvest, the men moved back home, sealed up their
dwellings, and stayed indoors for the whole of the winter. This was their
period of rest, but now the women began their season of labor—weaving,
spinning, and wine making. The peasants had their own religious rites
and festivals, traces of which have been preserved in the Confucian classic *The Book of Songs*.[10] They could be conscripted in the military campaigns of the aristocracy and are described lamenting so loudly when
they were dragged away from their fields that they were gagged during
the march. They did not take part in the actual fighting—that was the
privilege of the aristocracy—but acted as valets, servants, and carriers

and looked after the horses; still, they were strictly segregated from the nobility, marching and camping separately.[11]

The Shang aristocracy appropriated the surplus produce from the peasants but otherwise took only a ceremonial interest in agriculture. They offered sacrifices to the earth and to the spirits of the mountains, rivers, and winds to obtain a good harvest, and one of the king's tasks was to perform rituals to maintain the agricultural cycle on which the economy depended.[12] But apart from these liturgical rites, the aristocracy left agriculture entirely to the *min,* the "common people." At this date, however, very little of the region was given over to cultivation. Most of the Yellow River Valley was still covered by dense woods and marshes. Elephants, rhinoceroses, buffaloes, panthers, and leopards roamed through the forests, together with deer, tigers, wild oxen, bears, monkeys, and game. The Shang state continued to depend on the surplus produced by the peasants, but like all agrarian aristocracies, the nobility regarded productive work as a mark of inferiority.

Only the Shang king was permitted to approach Di Shang Di, the sky god, who was so exalted that he had no dealings with other human beings. This placed the king in a position similar to Di's, a state of exception that consigned the rest of the nobility to a subordinate place.[13] It invested one man with such absolute privilege that he had no rivals and no need to compete with others. In his presence, a nobleman was as vulnerable as a peasant; the king was above all factions or conflicts of interest and was therefore free to embrace the concerns of the entire social body.[14] He alone could impose peace by offering sacrifice to Di, consulting him about the advisability of a military expedition or the founding of a new settlement. The aristocracy supported him by devoting themselves to three sacred activities that all involved the taking of life: sacrifice, warfare, and hunting.[15] The min took no part in any of these pursuits, so violence was the raison d'être and distinguishing characteristic of the nobility.

These three duties were intricately interconnected in a way that shows how impossible it was to separate religion from other spheres of life in agrarian society. Sacrifice to the ancestors was deemed essential to the kingdom, because the fate of the dynasty depended on the goodwill of their deceased kings who could intercede with Di on its behalf. So the Shang held lavish "hosting" (*bin*) ceremonies at which vast quantities of animals and game were slaughtered—sometimes as many as a hundred beasts in a single ritual—and gods, ancestors, and humans shared a feast.[16] Meat eating was another privilege strictly reserved for the nobility. The sacrificial meat was cooked in exquisite bronze vessels that, like the bronze weapons that had subjugated the min, could be used only by the nobility and symbolized their exalted position.[17] The meat for the bin ceremony was supplied by the hunting expeditions, which, as in other cultures, were virtually indistinguishable from military campaigns.[18] Wild animals could endanger the crops, and the Shang killed them with reckless abandon. Their hunt was not simply a sport but a ritual that imitated the sage kings, who, by driving the animals away, had created the first civilization.

A considerable part of the year was devoted to military campaigning. The Shang had no great territorial ambitions but made war simply to enforce their authority: extorting tribute from peasants, fighting invaders from the mountains, and punishing rebellious cities by carrying off crops, cattle, slaves, and craftsmen. Sometimes they fought the "barbarians," the peoples who surrounded the Shang settlements and had not yet assimilated to Chinese civilization.[19] These militant circuits around the kingdom were a ritualized imitation of the sage kings' annual processions to maintain cosmic and political order.

The Shang attributed their victories to Di, the war god. Yet there also seems to have been considerable anxiety, because it was impossible to rely on him.[20] As we can see from the surviving oracle bones and turtle shells on which the royal diviners inscribed questions for Di, he often sent drought, flooding, and disaster and was an undependable military ally. Indeed, he could "confer assistance" on the Shang but just as easily support their enemies. "The Fang are harming or attacking us," mourned one oracle. "It is Di who orders them to make disaster for us."[21] These scattered pieces of evidence suggest a regime constantly poised for attack, surviving only by ceaseless martial vigilance. There are also references to human sacrifice: prisoners of war and rebels were routinely executed and, although the evidence is not conclusive, may have been offered up to the gods.[22] Later generations certainly associated the Shang with ritual murder. The philosopher Mozi (c. 480–390 BCE) was clearly revolted by the elaborate funerals of a Shang aristocrat: "As for the men who are sacrificed in order to follow him, if he should be a [king], they will be counted in hundreds or tens. If he is a great officer or a baron, they will be counted in tens or units."[23] Shang rituals were violent because martial aggression was essential to the state. And even though the kings implored Di for help in their wars, in reality they owed their success to their military skills and bronze weapons.

• • •

In 1045 BCE the Shang were defeated by the Zhou, a less sophisticated clan from the Wei Valley in the west of the great plain. The Zhou established a feudal system: the king ruled from his western capital but also maintained a presence in a new royal city in the east; the other cities were parceled out to Zhou princes and allies who ruled as his vassals and bequeathed these fiefs to their descendants; and the Shang retained a domain in Song. Continuity was always important in premodern civilization, so the Zhou were anxious to continue the Shang ancestral cult to uphold their regime. But how could they plausibly do so when they had executed the last Shang king? The Duke of Zhou, regent for his nephew, the young King Cheng, found a solution that he announced at the consecration of the new eastern capital. Di, whom the Zhou called "Heaven" (*Tian*), had made the Zhou his instrument to punish the Shang, whose last kings had been cruel and corrupt. Filled with pity for the suffering people, Heaven had revoked the Shang's mandate to rule and appointed the Zhou to succeed them, making King Cheng the new Son of Heaven. This was also a warning for Cheng, who must learn to be "reverently careful" of "the little people," because Heaven would take its mandate away from any ruler who oppressed his subjects. Heaven had chosen the Zhou because of their deep commitment to justice, so King Cheng must not inflict harsh punishments on the min.[24] Even though this did little to reduce the systemic violence of the Chinese state in practice, the mandate of Heaven was an important religious and political development, because, if only in theory, it made the ruler morally accountable to his people and instructed him to feel responsible for them. This would remain an important ideal in China.

Heaven was obviously a very different kind of deity from Di of the Shang, who had had no interest in human behavior. Heaven would never issue commandments or intervene directly in human affairs, however, for Heaven was not supernatural but inseparable from the forces of nature and active also in the royal potency (*de*) of the king and princes who ruled as Heaven's Sons. Heaven was also not omnipotent, because it could not exist without Earth, its divine counterpart. Unlike the Shang, the Zhou exploited the agricultural potential of the great plain on a grand scale, and because Heaven's influence could be implemented on Earth only through the work of human beings, farming, forest clearance, and road building became sacred tasks that completed the creation Heaven had begun. The Chinese were clearly more interested in sanctifying the world they lived in than finding a transcendent holiness beyond.

The Zhou king was supported by a four-tier aristocracy of "gentlemen" (*junzi*); Western scholars have translated their titles as "duke," "marquis," "earl," and "baron." The *shi,* children of younger sons and second-class wives, served as men-at-arms but also as scribes and ritual experts, forming an early "civil" wing of government. The Zhou confederacy of more than a hundred small principalities survived until 771, when their western capital was overrun by the Qong Rang barbarians. The Zhou fled to the east but never fully recovered. Yet the succeeding period witnessed not merely the decline of a dynasty but also the decay of the feudal system. The kings remained nominal rulers but were increasingly challenged by the more aggressive "gentlemen" in the principalities, who were casting aside the deference on which feudalism depended.[25] The boundaries of the Chinese states were also shifting. By this time, the Chinese had absorbed several "barbarian" populations, all with very different cultural traditions that challenged the old Zhou ethos. Cities located far away from the traditional centers of Chinese civilization were becoming locally prominent, and by the end of the eighth century, when Chinese history starts to emerge from the mists of legend, they had become capitals of kingdoms: Jin in the north, Qi in the northwest, and Chu in the south. These states ruled thousands of barbarian subjects, whose grasp of Chinese custom was at best superficial. The small principalities in the center of the great plain had now become extremely vulnerable, because these peripheral states were determined to expand. During the seventh century, they broke with tradition and began to mobilize peasants as fighting foot soldiers; Jin and Chu even brought barbarians into the army, offering them land in return for military service.

Deeply threatened by these aggressive kingdoms, some of the traditional principalities were also riven by internal conflict. With the decline of the Zhou, public order had deteriorated, and increasingly, brute force was becoming the norm. It was not uncommon for princes to kill ministers who dared to challenge their policies; ambassadors could be murdered and rulers assassinated during visits to another principality. To add to the tension, it seems that there was also an environmental crisis.[26] Centuries of aggressive hunting and land clearance that destroyed animal habitats meant that huntsmen were returning empty-handed and there was far less meat at the bin banquets, so the old carefree extravagance was no longer possible. In this climate of uncertainty, people wanted clear directives, so the *shi* ritual experts of the principality of Lu recodified the traditional Chinese custumal law to provide guidance.[27]

The Chinese had an aristocratic code, known as the *li* ("rituals"), that ruled the behavior of the individual but also of the state, and that functioned in a way similar to our international law. The *ru* ("ritualists") now based their reform of this code on the conduct of the sage kings Yao and Shun, whom they presented as models of restraint, altruism, forbearance, and kindness.[28] This new ideology was clearly critical of regimes guided by violent, arrogant, or selfish policies. Yao, it claimed, had been so "reverent, intelligent, accomplished, sincere, and mild" that the potency (*de*) of these qualities had radiated from him to all Chinese families and created the Great Peace.[29] In an extraordinary act of self-abnegation, Yao had bequeathed the empire to the lowborn Shun, passing over his own son because he was deceitful and quarrelsome. Shun even behaved with courtesy and respect to his father, who had tried to murder him. The reformed li were designed to help the gentlemen cultivate these same qualities. A junzi's demeanor should be "sweet and calm."[30] Instead of asserting himself aggressively, he should "yield" (*rang*) to others, and far from stifling him, this would perfect his humanity (*ren*). The reformed li were therefore expressly designed to curb belligerence and chauvinism.[31] Political life should instead be dominated by restraint and yielding.[32] "The li teach us that to give free rein to one's feelings and let them follow their bent is the way of barbarians," explained the ritualists; "the ceremonial fixes degrees and limits."[33] In the family, the eldest son should minister to his father's every need, addressing him in a low, humble voice, never expressing anger or resentment; in return, a father must treat all his children fairly, kindly, and courteously. The system was so designed that each family member received a measure of reverence.[34] We do not know exactly how all this worked out in practice; certainly many Chinese continued to strive aggressively for power, but it seems that by the end of the seventh century, a significant number of those living in the traditional principalities were beginning to value moderation and self-control and even the peripheral states of Qi, Jin, Chu, and Qin accepted these ritualized imperatives.[35]

The li tried to control the violence of warfare by turning it into a courtly game.[36] Killing large numbers of enemies was considered vulgar—it was the "way of barbarians." When an officer boasted that he had slaughtered six of the enemy, his prince had gravely replied: "You will bring great dishonour on your country."[37] It was not proper to slay more than three fugitives after a battle, and a true junzi would fight with his eyes shut so that he would fail to shoot his enemy. During a battle, if the defeated driver of a war chariot paid a ransom on the spot, his opponents would always let him escape. There should be no unseemly triumphalism. A victorious prince once refused to build a monument to commemorate a victory. "I was the cause that two countries exposed the bones of their warriors to the sun! It is cruel!" he cried. "There are no guilty here, only vassals who have been faithful to the end."[38] A commander should also never take unfair advantage of the enemy's weakness. In 638 the Duke of Song was anxiously waiting for the army of the Chu principality, which greatly outnumbered his own. When they heard that Chu troops were crossing a nearby river, his commander urged him to attack at once: "They are many: we are few: let us attack them before they get across!" The duke was horrified and refused to follow this advice. When the Chu had crossed but still not drawn up their battle lines, his commander again urged that they should attack. But again the duke demurred. Even though Song was soundly defeated in the ensuing battle, the duke was unrepentant: "A junzi worthy of the name does not seek to overcome the enemy in misfortune. He does not beat his drum before the ranks are formed."[39]

Warfare was legitimate only if it restored the Way of Heaven by repelling a barbarian invasion or quashing a revolt. This "punitive warfare" was a penal exercise to rectify behavior. A military campaign against a rebellious Chinese city was therefore a highly ritualized affair, which began and ended with sacrifices at the Earth altar. When battle commenced, each side bullied the other with acts of outrageous kindness to prove its superior nobility. Boasting loudly of their prowess, warriors threw pots of wine over the enemy's wall. When a Chu archer used his last arrow to shoot a stag that was blocking his chariot's path, his driver immediately presented it to the enemy team that was bearing down upon them. They at once conceded defeat, exclaiming: "Here is a worthy

archer and well-spoken warrior! These are gentlemen!"[40] But there were
no such limitations in a campaign against barbarians, who could be pursued and slaughtered like wild animals.[41] When the Marquis of Jin and
his army came by chance upon the local Rong peaceably minding their
own business, he ordered his troops to massacre the entire tribe.[42] In a
war of civilized "us" against bestial "them," any form of treachery or
deceit was permitted.[43]

◆ ◆ ◆

Despite the ritualists' best efforts, toward the end of the seventh century
violence escalated on the Chinese plain. Barbarian tribes attacked from
the north, and the southern state of Chu increasingly ignored the rules of
courtly warfare and posed a real threat to the principalities. The Zhou
kings were too weak to provide effective leadership, so Prince Huan of
Qi, by now the most powerful Chinese state, formed a league of states
that bound themselves by oath not to attack each other. But this attempt
would fail, because the nobles, addicted to personal prestige, still wanted
to preserve their independence. After Chu destroyed the league in 597,
the region became engulfed in an entirely new kind of warfare. Other
large peripheral states also began to cast aside traditional constraints,
determined to expand and conquer more territory even if this meant the
enemy's annihilation. In 593, for example, after a prolonged siege, the
people of Song were reduced to eating their children. Small principalities were drawn into the conflict against their will when their territories
became battlefields of competing armies. Qi, for example, encroached
so frequently on the tiny dukedom of Lu that it was forced to appeal to
Chu for help. But by the end of the sixth century, Chu had been defeated
and Qi had become so dominant that the Duke of Lu managed to retain
a modicum of independence only with the help of the western state of
Qin. There was also civil strife: Qin, Jin, and Chu were all fatally weakened by chronic infighting, and in Lu three baronial families effectively
created their own substates and reduced the legitimate duke to a mere
puppet.

Archaeologists have noted a growing contempt for ritual observance
at that time: people were placing profane objects in their relatives' tombs
instead of the prescribed vessels. The spirit of moderation was also in
decline. Many Chinese had developed a taste for luxury that put an
unbearable strain on the economy, as demand outstripped resources, and

some of the lower-ranking nobility tried to ape the lifestyle of the great families. As a result many of the *shi* at the bottom of the aristocratic hierarchy became impoverished and were forced to leave the cities to scrape a living as teachers among the min.

• • •

One *shi,* who held a minor administrative post in Lu, was horrified by the greed, pride, and ostentation of the usurping families. Kong Qiu (c. 551–479) was convinced that the li alone could curb this destructive violence. His disciples would call him Kongfuzi ("our Master Kong"), so in the West we call him Confucius. He never achieved the political career he hoped for and died believing that he was a failure, but he would define Chinese culture until the 1911 Revolution. With his little band of followers, most of them from the warrior aristocracy, Confucius traveled from one principality to another, hoping to find a ruler who would implement his ideas. In the West he is often regarded as a secular rather than a religious philosopher, but he would not have understood this distinction: in ancient China, as the philosopher Herbert Fingarette has reminded us, the secular *was* sacred.[44]

Confucius's teachings were anthologized long after his death, but scholars believe that the *Analects,* a collection of short unconnected maxims, is a reasonably reliable source.[45] His ideology, which sought to revive the virtues of Yao and Shun, was deeply traditional, but his ideal of equality based on a cultivated perception of our shared humanity was a radical challenge to the systemic violence of agrarian China. Like the Buddha, Confucius redefined the concept of nobility.[46] The hero of the *Analects* is the junzi who is no longer a warrior but a profoundly humane scholar and somewhat deficient in the martial arts. For Confucius, a junzi's chief quality was *ren,* a word that he consistently refused to define because its meaning transcended any of the concepts of his day, but later Confucians would describe it as "benevolence."[47] The junzi was required to treat all others at all times with reverence and compassion, a program of action that Confucius summed up in what is called the Golden Rule: "Do not impose upon others what you yourself do not desire."[48] It was, Confucius said, the "single thread" that ran through all his teaching and should be practiced "all day and every day."[49] A true junzi had to look into his heart, discover what gave him pain, and then refuse under any circumstances to inflict that pain on anybody else.

This was not simply a personal ethic but a political ideal. If they practiced ren, rulers would not invade another prince's territory, because they would not like this to happen to their own. They would hate to be exploited, reviled, and reduced to poverty, so they must not oppress others. What would you make of a man who could "extend this benevolence to the common people and bring succor to the multitudes?" asked Confucius's disciple Zigong.[50] Such a man would be a sage! his master exclaimed:

> Yao and Shun would have found such a task daunting! You yourself desire rank and standing; then help others to get rank and standing. You want to turn your merits to account; then help others to turn theirs to account—in fact, the ability to take one's feelings as a guide—that is the sort of thing that lies in the direction of ren.[51]

If a prince ruled solely by force, he might control his subjects' external behavior but not their inner disposition.[52] No government, Confucius insisted, could truly succeed unless it was based on an adequate conception of what it meant to be a fulfilled human being. Confucianism was never a private pursuit for the individual; it always had a political orientation and sought nothing less than a major reformation of public life. Its goal, quite simply, was to bring peace to the world.[53]

All too often the li had been used to enhance a nobleman's prestige, as had been the case in the aggressive courtesy of ritualized warfare. But properly understood, Confucius believed, the li taught people "all day and every day" to put themselves in somebody else's shoes and see a situation from another perspective. If such an attitude became habitual, a junzi would transcend the egotism, greed, and selfishness that were tearing China apart. How can I achieve ren? asked his beloved disciple, Yan Hui. It was quite simple, Confucius replied: "Curb your ego and surrender to the li."[54] A junzi must submit every detail of his life to the rituals of consideration and respect for others. "If for one day, you managed to restrain yourself and return to the rites," Confucius continued, "you could lead the entire world back to ren."[55] But to achieve this, a junzi had to work on his humanity, as a sculptor crafted a rough stone to make it a ritual vessel, a bearer of holiness.[56] He could thus replace the current greed, violence, and vulgarity and restore dignity and grace to human intercourse, transforming the whole of China.[57] The practice of ren was difficult because it required the junzi to dethrone himself from the center of his world,[58] although the ideal of ren was deeply rooted in our humanity.[59]

Confucius emphasized the importance of "yielding." Instead of asserting themselves belligerently and fighting for power, sons should yield to their fathers, warriors to their enemies, noblemen to their ruler, and rulers to their retainers. Instead of seeing family life as an impediment to enlightenment, like the renouncers of India, Confucius saw it as the school of the spiritual quest because it taught every family member to live for others.[60] Later philosophers criticized Confucius for concentrating too exclusively upon the family, but Confucius saw each person as the center of a constantly growing series of concentric circles to which he or she must relate, cultivating a sympathy that went beyond the claims of family, class, state, or race.[61] Each of us begins life in the family, so the family li starts our education in self-transcendence, but it does not end there. A junzi's horizons would gradually expand. The lessons he had learned by caring for his parents, spouse, and siblings would enable him to feel empathy for more and more people: first with his immediate community, then with the state in which he lived, and finally with the entire world.

Confucius was too much of a realist to imagine that human beings could ever abandon warfare; he deplored its waste of life and resources[62] but understood that no state could survive without its armies.[63] When asked to list the priorities of government, he replied: "Simply make sure there is sufficient food and sufficient armaments and make sure you have the support of the common people," although he added that if one of these had to go, it should be weaponry.[64] In the past only the Zhou king had been able to declare war, but now his vassals had usurped this royal prerogative and were fighting one another. If this continued, Confucius feared, violence would proliferate throughout society.[65] "Punitive expeditions" against barbarians, invaders, and rebels were essential, because the government's chief task was to preserve the social order.[66] This, he believed, was why the structural violence of society was necessary. While Confucius always spoke of the min with genuine concern and urged rulers to appeal to their sense of self-respect instead of seeking to control them by force and fear, he knew that if they were not punished when they transgressed, civilization would collapse.[67]

The fourth-century Confucian philosopher Mencius could also only regard the min as born to be ruled: "There are those who use their minds and there are those who use their muscle. The former rule; the latter are ruled. Those who rule are supported by those who are ruled."[68] The min could never join the ruling class because they lacked "teaching" (*jaio*), which in China always implied a degree of force: the pictograph jaio showed a hand wielding a rod to discipline a child.[69] Warfare too was a mode of instruction, essential to civilization. "To wage a punitive war," Mencius wrote, "is to rectify."[70] Indeed, Mencius had even convinced himself that the masses yearned for such correction and that the barbarians vied with one another to be conquered by the Chinese.[71] But it was never permissible to fight equals: "A punitive expedition is waged by one in authority against his subordinates. It is not for peers to punish one another by war."[72] The current interstate warfare between rulers of equal status, therefore, was perverse, illegal, and a form of tyranny. China desperately needed wise rulers like Yao and Shun, whose moral charisma could restore the Great Peace. "The appearance of a true King has never been longer overdue than today," wrote Mencius; "and the people have never suffered more under tyrannical government than today." If a militarily powerful state were to govern benevolently, "the people would rejoice as if they had been released from hanging by the heels."[73]

Despite their convictions about equality, the Confucians were aristocrats who could not transcend the assumptions of the ruling class. In the writings of Mozi (c. 480–390), however, we hear the voice of the commoner. Mozi headed a brotherhood of 180 men, who dressed like peasants and craftsmen and traveled from one state to another, instructing rulers in the new military technology for defending a city when it was besieged by the enemy.[74] Mozi was almost certainly an artisan, and he regarded the elaborate rituals of the nobility as a waste of time and money. But he too was convinced that ren was China's only hope and emphasized the danger of political sympathy extending no further than one's own kingdom even more strongly than Confucius. "Others must be regarded like the self," he insisted. This "concern" (*ai*) must be "all-embracing and exclude nobody."[75] The only way to stop the Chinese from destroying one another was to persuade them to practice *jian ai* ("concern for everybody"). Instead of simply worrying about their own kingdom, Mozi urged each prince to "regard another's state as your own"; for if rulers truly had such solicitous regard for one another, they would not go to war. Indeed, the root cause of all the "world's calamities, dispossessions, resentments, and hatreds is lack of *jian ai*."[76]

Unlike the Confucians, Mozi had nothing positive to say about war. From a poor man's perspective, it made no sense at all. Warfare ruined harvests, killed multitudes of civilians, and wasted weapons and horses. Rulers claimed that the conquest of more territory enriched the state and made it more secure, but in fact only a tiny proportion of the population benefited, and the capture of a small town could result in such heavy casualties that there was nobody left to farm the land.[77] Mozi believed that a policy could be called virtuous only if it enriched the poor, prevented pointless death, and contributed to public order. But humans were egotists: they would adopt jian ai only if they were convinced by irrefutable arguments that their own well-being depended on the welfare of the entire human race, so that jian ai was essential to their *own* prosperity, peace, and security.[78] Hence *The Book of Mozi* included the first Chinese exercises in logic, all dedicated to proving that warfare was not in a ruler's best interests. In words that still ring true today, Mozi insisted that the only way out of the destructive cycle of warfare was for rulers "not to be concerned for themselves alone."[79]

◆ ◆ ◆

In ancient China, Mozi was revered more than Confucius, because he spoke so directly to the problems of this violent time. By the fifth century, the small principalities were surrounded by seven large Warring States—Jin, which had split into the three kingdoms of Han, Wei, and Zhao; Qi, Qin, and its neighbor Shu in the west; and Chu in the south. Their huge armies, iron weaponry, and lethal crossbows were so formidable that any state that could not match them was doomed.[80] Their engineers built defensive walls and fortresses manned by professional garrisons along their frontiers. Supported by strong economies, their armies fought with a deadly efficiency based on unified command, skillful strategy, and trained troops. Brutally pragmatic, they had no time for ren or ritual, and in battle they spared no one: "all who have or keep any strength are our enemies, even if they are old men," one commander maintained.[81] Yet on purely pragmatic grounds, their new military experts advised against excessive plunder and violence,[82] and in their campaigns they were careful not to endanger agricultural output, the state's primary resource.[83] Warfare was no longer a courtly game governed by li to curb aggression; instead it had become a science, governed by logic, reason, and cold calculation.[84]

To Mozi and his contemporaries, it seemed that the Chinese were about to destroy one another, but with hindsight, we can see that in fact they were moving painfully toward a centralized empire that would impose a measure of peace. The chronic warfare of the Warring States period revealed one of the ubiquitous dilemmas of the agrarian state. Unless they were held in check, aristocrats who were bred to fight and had developed a prickly sense of honor would always compete aggressively for land, wealth, property, prestige, and power. In the fifth century, the Warring States began to annihilate the traditional principalities and battle compulsively against each other until in 221 BCE only one of them was left. Its victorious ruler would become the first emperor of China.

We find in this period of Chinese history a fascinating pattern that shows how mistaken it is to imagine that a given set of "religious" beliefs and practices will lead inexorably to violence. Instead, we find people drawing on the same pool of mythology, contemplative disciplines, and ideas but embarking on radically different courses of action. Even though the Warring States were moving toward an ethos that approached modern secularism, their hardheaded strategists regarded themselves as sages and saw their warfare as a species of religion. Their hero was the Yellow Emperor and these commanders were convinced that, like his textbook of military strategy, their own treatises were divinely revealed.

The sage kings had discovered an orderly design in the cosmos that showed them how to organize society; similarly the military commander could discern a pattern in the chaos of the battlefield that enabled him to find the most efficient way to achieve victory. "The one with many strategic factors in his favor wins, the one with few strategic factors in his favor loses," explained Sunzi, a contemporary of Mencius. "Observing the matter in this way, I can see who will win and who will lose."[85] A good commander could even defeat the enemy without any fighting at all. If the odds were stacked against him, the best policy was to wait until the enemy, believing that you were weak, became overconfident and made a fatal mistake. The commander should regard his troops as mere extensions of his will and control them as the mind directs the body. Even though he was of noble birth, an able commander would live among his peasant soldiers, sharing their hardships and becoming the model to which they must conform. He would inflict terrible punishments on his men to make them fear him more than death on the battlefield; indeed, a good strategist would deliberately put his troops into such danger that they had no option but to fight their way out. A soldier could have no mind of his own but should be as subservient and passive in relation to his commander as a woman. Warfare had been "feminized." Indeed, feminine weakness could be more effective than masculine belligerence: the best armies might seem to be as weak as water—but water could be extremely destructive.[86]

"The military is a Way [*dao*] of Deception," said Sunzi. The name of the game was to deceive the enemy:

> Thus when able, manifest inability. When active, manifest
>   inactivity.
> When near, manifest as far. When far, manifest as near.
> When he seeks advantage, lure him.
> When he is in chaos, take him.
> When he is substantial, prepare against him.
> When he is strong, avoid him.
> Attack where he is unprepared. Emerge where he does not expect.[87]

Sunzi knew that civilians would look askance at this martial ethic, but their state could not survive without its troops.[88] The army should therefore be kept apart from mainstream society and be governed by its own laws, because its modus operandi was the "extraordinary" (*qi*), the counterintuitive, doing exactly what did *not* come naturally. This would be disastrous in all other affairs of state,[89] but if a commander learned how to exploit the qi, he could achieve a sagelike alignment with the Way of Heaven:

> Thus one skilled at giving rise to the extraordinary is as boundless
> as Heaven and Earth, as inexhaustible as the Yellow River and the
> ocean.
>   Ending and beginning again, like the sun and moon. Dying and
> then being born, like the four seasons.[90]

The dilemma of even the most benign state was that it was obliged to maintain at its heart an institution committed to treachery and violence.

The cult of the "extraordinary" was not new but was widespread among the population, especially among the lower classes, and might even date back to the Neolithic period. It had strong connections with the mystical school that we call Daoism (or Taoism) in the West, which was far more popular among the masses than the elite.[91] Daoists opposed any form of government and were convinced that when rulers interfered in their subjects' lives, they invariably made matters worse—an attitude similar to the strategists' preference for "doing nothing" and refraining from rushing into action. Forcing people to obey man-made laws and perform unnatural rituals was simply perverse, argued the ebullient hermit Zhuangzi (c. 369–286). It was better to "do nothing," practicing "action by inaction [*wu wei*]." It was deep within yourself, at a level far below the reasoning powers, that you would encounter the Way (*dao*) things really were.[92]

In the West we tend to read the mid-third-century treatise known as the *Daodejing** ("Classic of the Way and Its Potency") as a devotional text for a personal spirituality, but it was actually a manual of statecraft, written for the prince of one of the vulnerable principalities.[93] Its anonymous author wrote under the pseudonym Laozi, or Lao-Tzu—"Old Master." Rulers should imitate Heaven, he taught, which did not interfere with the Ways of men; so if they abandoned their meddlesome policies, political "potency" (*de*) would emerge spontaneously: "If I cease to desire and remain still, the empire will be at peace of its own accord."[94] The Daoist king should practice meditative techniques that rid his mind of busy theorizing so that it became "empty" and "still." Then the Dao of Heaven could act through him, and "to the end of one's days one will meet with no danger."[95] Laozi offered the beleaguered principalities a stratagem for survival. Statesmen usually preferred frenzied activity and shows of strength when they should be doing the exact opposite. Instead of posturing aggressively, they should present themselves as weak and small. Like the military strategists, Laozi used the analogy of water, which seemed "submissive and weak" yet could be far more powerful than "that which is hard and strong."[96] The Daoist ruler should abandon masculine self-assertion and embrace the softness of the "mysterious female."[97] What goes up must come down, so when you strengthened your enemy by appearing to submit, you were actually hastening his

---

* *Tao Te Ching* in the Wade-Giles system.

decline. Laozi agreed with the strategists that military action should always be the last resort: weapons were "ill-omened instruments," he argued, which a sage king used only "when he cannot do otherwise."[98]

> The good leader is not warlike
> The good fighter is not impetuous
> The best conqueror of the enemy is he who never takes the
> offensive.[99]

The wise leader should not even retaliate to an atrocity because this would simply provoke a counterattack. By practicing wu wei instead, he would acquire the potency of Heaven itself: "Because he does not contend, there is no one in the world who can contend with him."[100]

This, alas, proved not to be the case. The victor in the long struggle of the Warring States was not a Daoist sage king but the ruler of Qin, who was successful simply because he had the most territory, manpower, and resources. Instead of relying on ritual, as previous Chinese states had done, Qin had developed a materialistic ideology based solely on the economic realities of warfare and agriculture, shaped by a new philosophy known as Fajia ("School of the Law") or Legalism.[101] *Fa* did not mean "law" in the modern sense; rather, it was a "standard" like the carpenter's square that made raw materials conform to a fixed pattern.[102] It was the Legalist reforms of Lord Shang (c. 390–338) that had put Qin ahead of its rivals.[103] Shang believed that the people must be forced by strict punishments to submit to their subordinate role in a state designed solely to enhance the ruler's power.[104] He eliminated the aristocracy and replaced it with a hand-picked administration wholly dependent on the king. The country was now divided into thirty-one districts, each ruled by a magistrate who answered directly to the capital and conscripted recruits for the army. To boost productivity and free enterprise, peasants were encouraged to buy their land. The nobility of the junzi was irrelevant: honor was achieved only by a brilliant performance on the battlefield. Anyone who commanded a victorious unit was given land, houses, and slaves.

Qin had arguably developed the first secular state ideology, but Shang separated religion from politics, not because of its inherent violence but because religion was impracticably humane. Religious sentiment would make a ruler too benign, which ran counter to the state's best interests.

"A State that uses good people to govern the wicked will be plagued by disorder and be destroyed," Shang insisted. "A state that uses the wicked to govern the good always enjoys peace and becomes strong."[105] Instead of practicing the Golden Rule, a military commander should inflict on the enemy exactly what he did *not* wish for his own troops.[106] Unsurprisingly, Qin's success was deeply troubling to the Confucians. Xunzi (c. 310–219), for example, believed that a ruler who governed by ren would be an irresistible force for good and his compassion would transform the world. He would take up arms only "to put an end to violence, and to do away with harm, not in order to compete with others for spoil. Therefore when the soldiers of the benevolent man encamp they command a godlike respect; and where they pass, they transform the people."[107] But his pupil Li Si laughed at him: Qin was the most powerful state in China, because it had the strongest army and economy; it owed its success not to ren but to its opportunism.[108] During Xunzi's visit to Qin, King Zhao told him bluntly: "The Confucians [*ru*] are no use in running a state."[109] Shortly afterward Qin conquered Xunzi's native state of Zhao, and even though the Zhao king surrendered, Qin troops buried 400,000 of his soldiers alive. How could a junzi exert any restraining influence over such a regime? Xunzi's pupil Li Si now emigrated to Qin, became its prime minister, and masterminded the lightning campaign that resulted in Qin's final victory and the establishment of the Chinese Empire in 221 BCE.

Paradoxically, the Legalists drew on the same pool of ideas and spoke the same language as the Daoists. They also believed that the king should "do nothing" (*wu wei*) to interfere with the Dao of the Law, which should run like a well-oiled machine. The people would suffer if the laws kept changing, maintained the Legalist Han Feizi (c. 280–233), so a truly enlightened ruler "waits in stillness and emptiness" and "lets the tasks of themselves be fixed."[110] He did not need morality or knowledge but was simply the Prime Mover, who remained immobile but set his ministers and subjects in motion:

> Having courage, he does not use it to rage
> He draws out all the warlike in his ministers
> Hence by doing without knowledge he possesses clear-sightedness
> By doing without worthiness he gets results
> By doing without courage, he achieves strength.[111]

There was, of course, a world of difference between the two: Daoists deplored rulers who forced their subjects to conform to an unnatural fa; their sage king meditated to achieve selflessness, not to "get results."[112] But the same ideas and imagery informed the thinking of political scientists, military strategists, and mystics. People could have the same beliefs yet act upon them very differently. Military strategists believed that their brutally pragmatic writings came to them by divine revelation, and contemplatives gave strategic advice to kings. Even the Confucians now drew on these notions: Xunzi believed that the Way could be comprehended only by a mind that was "empty, unified, and still."[113]

• • •

Many people must have been relieved when Qin's victory put a stop to the endless fighting and hoped that the empire would keep the peace. But they had a shocking introduction to imperial rule. Acting on the advice of Prime Minister Li Si, the First Emperor became an absolute ruler. The Zhou aristocracy—120,000 families—were forcibly moved to the capital and their weapons confiscated. The emperor divided his vast territory into thirty-six commanderies, each headed by a civil administrator, a military commander, and an overseer; each commandery was in turn divided into counties governed by magistrates, and all officials answered directly to the central government.[114] The old rituals that had presented the Zhou king as head of a family of feudal lords were replaced by a rite that focused on the emperor alone.[115] When the court historian criticized this innovation, Li Si told the emperor that he could no longer tolerate such divisive ideologies: any school that opposed the Legalist program must be abolished and its writings publicly burned.[116] There was a massive book burning, and 460 teachers were executed. One of the first inquisitions in history had therefore been mandated by a protosecular state.

Xunzi had been convinced that Qin would never rule China because its draconian methods would alienate the people. He was proved right when they rose up in rebellion after the death of the First Emperor in 210 BCE. After three years of anarchy, Liu Bang, one of the local magistrates, founded the Han dynasty. His chief military strategist, Zhang Liang, who had studied Confucian ritual in his youth, embodied Han ideals. It was said that a military text was revealed to him after he had behaved with exemplary respect toward an elderly man, and even though he had no military experience, he led Bang to victory. Zhang was not a bellicose man. He was a Daoist warrior: "not warlike," weak as water, frequently ill, and unable to command on the field. He treated people with humility, practiced Daoist meditation and breath control, abstained from grains, and at one point seriously considered retiring from politics for a life of contemplation.[117]

The Han had learned from Qin's mistakes. But Bang wanted to preserve the centralized state and knew that the empire needed Legalist realism because no state could function without coercion and the threat of violence. "Weapons are the means by which the sage makes obedient the powerful and savage, and brings stability in times of chaos," wrote the Han historian Sima Qian. "Instruction and corporal punishment cannot be abandoned in a household, mutilating punishments cannot be halted under Heaven. It is simply that in using them some are skillful and some clumsy, in carrying them out some are in accord [with Heaven] and some against it."[118] But Bang knew that the state also needed a more inspiring ideology. His solution was a synthesis of Legalism and Daoism.[119] Still reeling from the Qin inquisition, people yearned for "empty," open-minded governance. Han emperors would maintain absolute control over the commanderies but would refrain from arbitrary interventions; there would be strict penal law but no draconian punishments.

The patron of the new regime was the Yellow Emperor. All empires need theater and pageantry, and the Han rituals gave a new twist to the ancient Shang complex of sacrifice, hunting, and warfare.[120] In autumn, the season for military campaigning, the emperor held a ceremonial hunt in the royal parks, which teemed with every kind of animal, to provide meat for the temple sacrifice. A few weeks later there were military reviews in the capital to show off the skills of elite troops and help maintain the martial competence of the min, who manned the imperial armies. At the end of winter there were hunting contests in the parks. These rituals, designed to impress visiting dignitaries, all recalled the Yellow Emperor and his animal troops. Men and animals fought as equal combatants, just as they had at the beginning of time before the sage kings separated them. There were football matches in which players kicked the ball from one side of the field to the other, to reproduce the alternation of *yin* and *yang* in the seasonal cycle. "Kickball deals with the power of circumstances in the military. It is a means to train warriors and recognize who have talent," explained the historian Liu Xiang (77–6 BCE). "It is said that it was created by the Yellow Emperor."[121] Like the Yellow Emperor,

Han rulers would use religious rituals in an attempt to take the bestial savagery out of warfare so that it became humane.

At the start of his reign, Liu Bang had commissioned the Confucian ritualists (ru) to devise a court ceremonial, and when it was performed for the first time, the emperor exclaimed: "Now I realize the nobility of being a Son of Heaven!"[122] The ru slowly gained ground at court, and as the memory of the Qin trauma faded, there was a growing desire for more solid moral guidance.[123] In 136 BCE the court scholar Dong Zhongshu (179–104) suggested to Emperor Wu (r. 140–87) that there were too many competing schools and recommended that the six classical Confucian texts become the official state teaching. The emperor agreed: Confucianism supported the family; its emphasis on cultural history would forge a cultural identity; and state education would create an elite class that could counter the enduring appeal of the old aristocracy. But Wu did not make the mistake of the First Emperor. In the Chinese Empire there would be no sectarian intolerance: the Chinese would continue to see merit in all the schools that could supplement one another. Thus, however diametrically opposed the two schools might be, there would be a Legalist-Confucian coalition: the state still needed Legalist pragmatism, but the ru would temper Fajia despotism.

In 124 BCE Wu founded the Imperial Academy, and for over two thousand years all Chinese state officials would be trained in a predominantly Confucian ideology, which presented the rulers as Sons of Heaven governing by moral charisma. This gave the regime spiritual legitimacy and became the ethos of the civil administration. Like all agrarian rulers, however, the Han controlled their empire by systemic and martial violence, exploiting the peasantry, killing rebels, and conquering new territory. The emperors depended on the army (wu), and in the newly conquered territories the magistrates summarily expropriated the land, deposed existing landlords, and seized between 50 and 100 percent of the peasants' surplus. Like any premodern ruler, the emperor had to maintain himself in a state of exception as the "one man" to whom ordinary rules did not apply. At a moment's notice, therefore, he could order an execution, and nobody dared object. Such irrational and spontaneous acts of violence were an essential part of the mystique that held his subjects in thrall.[124]

Thus while the ruler and the military lived by the "extraordinary," the Confucians promoted the predictable, routinized orthodoxy of wen, the civil order based on benevolence (*ren*), culture, and rational per-suasion. They performed the invaluable task of convincing the public that the emperor really had their interests at heart. They were not mere lackeys—many of the ru were executed for reminding the emperor too forcibly of his moral duty—but their power was limited. When Dong Zhongshu objected that the imperial usurpation of land caused immense misery, Emperor Wu seemed to agree, but ultimately Dong had to com-promise, settling for a moderate limitation of land tenure.[125] The fact was that while the administrators and bureaucrats championed Confu-cianism, the rulers themselves preferred the Legalists, who despised the Confucians as impractical idealists; in their view, King Zhao of Qin had said it all: "The *ru* are no use in running a state."

In 81 BCE, in a series of debates about the monopoly of salt and iron, the Legalists argued that the uncontrolled, private "free enterprise" advo-cated by the ru was wholly impractical.[126] The Confucians were nothing but a bunch of impoverished losers:

> See them now present us with nothing and consider it substance, with "emptiness" and call it plenty! In their coarse gowns and cheap sandals they walk gravely along, sunk in meditation as though they had lost something. These are not men who can do great deeds and win fame. They do not even rise above the vulgar masses.[127]

The ru could therefore only bear witness to an alternative society. The word *ru* is related etymologically to *ruo* ("mild"), but some modern scholars argue that it meant "weakling" and was first used in the sixth century to describe the impoverished shi who had eked out a meager liv-ing by teaching.[128] In imperial China, Confucians were political "softies," economically and institutionally weak.[129] They could keep the benevo-lent Confucian alternative alive and make it a presence in the heart of government, but they would always lack the "teeth" to push their policies through.

That was the Confucian dilemma—similar to the impasse that Ashoka had encountered on the Indian subcontinent. Empire depended on force and intimidation, because the aristocrats and the masses had to be held in check. Even if he had wanted to, Emperor Wu could not afford to rule entirely by ren. The Chinese Empire had been achieved by war-fare, wholesale slaughter, and the annihilation of one state after another;

it retained its power by military expansion and internal oppression and developed religious mythologies and rituals to sacralize these arrangements. Was there a realistic alternative? The Warring States period had shown what happened when ambitious rulers with new weapons and large armies competed against one another pitilessly for dominance, devastating the countryside and terrorizing the population in the process. Contemplating this chronic warfare, Mencius had longed for a king who would rule "all under Heaven" and bring peace to the great plain of China. The ruler who had been powerful enough to achieve this was the First Emperor.

4

The Hebrew Dilemma

When Adam and Eve were expelled from the Garden of Eden, they probably did not fall into a state of original sin, as Saint Augustine believed, but into an agrarian economy.[1] Man (*adam*) had been created from the soil (*adamah*), which in the Garden of Eden was watered by a simple spring. Adam and his wife were free agents, living a life of idyllic liberty, cultivating the garden at their leisure, and enjoying the companionship of their god, Yahweh. But because of a single act of disobedience, Yahweh condemned them both to a life sentence of hard agricultural labor:

> Accursed be the soil because of you! With suffering shall you get your food from it every day of your life. It shall yield you brambles and thistles, and you shall eat wild plants. With sweat on your brow shall you eat your bread, until you return to the soil as you were taken from it. For dust you are, and to dust you shall return.[2]

Instead of peacefully nurturing the soil as its master, Adam had become its slave. From the very beginning, the Hebrew Bible strikes a different note from most of the texts we have considered so far. Its heroes were not members of an aristocratic elite; Adam and Eve had been relegated to mere field hands, scratching a miserable subsistence from the blighted land.

Adam had two sons: Cain, the farmer, and Abel, the herdsman—
the traditional enemy of the agrarian state. Both dutifully brought offerings to Yahweh, who somewhat perversely rejected Cain's sacrifice but
accepted Abel's. Baffled and furious, Cain lured his brother into the family plot and killed him, his arable land becoming a field of blood that
cried out to Yahweh for vengeance. "Damned be you from the soil, which
opened up its mouth to receive your brother's blood!"[3] Yahweh cried.
Henceforth Cain would wander in the land of Nod as an outcast and
fugitive. From the start, the Hebrew Bible condemns the violence at the
heart of the agrarian state. It is Cain, the first murderer, who builds the
world's first city, and one of his descendants is Tubal the Smith (*Kayin*),
"ancestor of all metal-workers in bronze and iron," who crafts its weapons.[4] Immediately after the murder, when Yahweh asks Cain, "Where is
your brother, Abel?" he replies, "Am I my brother's guardian?"[5] Urban
civilization denied that relationship with and responsibility for all other
human beings that is embedded in human nature.

The Pentateuch, the first five books of the Bible, did not reach its
final form until about the fourth century BCE. For the historians, poets,
prophets, priests, and lawyers of Israel, it became the organizing narrative around which they constructed their worldview. Over the centuries,
they would change that story and embroider it, adding or reinterpreting
events in order to address the particular challenges of their own time.
This story began in about 1750 BCE, when Yahweh commanded Abraham, Israel's ancestor, to turn his back on the agrarian society and culture of Mesopotamia and settle in Canaan, where he, his son Isaac, and
his grandson Jacob would live as simple herdsmen. Yahweh promised
that their descendants would one day possess this land and become a
nation as numerous as the sands on the seashore.[6] But Jacob and his
twelve sons (founders of the tribes of Israel) were forced by famine to
leave Canaan and migrate to Egypt. At first they prospered, but eventually the Egyptians enslaved them, and they languished in serfdom
until about 1250 BCE, when Yahweh brought them out of Egypt under
Moses's leadership. For forty years the Israelites wandered in the Sinai
wilderness before reaching the Canaanite border, where Moses died, but
his lieutenant, Joshua, led the Israelites to victory in the Promised Land,
destroying all the Canaanite cities and killing their inhabitants.

The archaeological record, however, does not confirm this story.
There is no evidence of the mass destruction described in the book of

Joshua and no indication of a powerful foreign invasion.[7] But this narrative was not written to satisfy a modern historian; it is a national epic that helped Israel create a cultural identity distinct from her neighbors. When we first hear of Israel in a nonbiblical source, coastal Canaan was still a province of the Egyptian Empire. A stele dating from c. 1201 mentions "Israel" as one of the rebellious peoples defeated by Pharaoh Merneptah's army in the Canaanite highlands, where a network of simple villages stretched from lower Galilee in the north to Beersheba in the south. Many scholars believe that their inhabitants were the first Israelites.[8]

During the twelfth century, a crisis that had long been brewing in the Mediterranean accelerated, perhaps occasioned by sudden climate change. We have no record of what happened to wipe out the region's empires and destroy the local economies. But by 1130 BCE, it was all over: the Hittite capital in Mitanni was in ruins, the Canaanite ports of Ugarit, Megiddo, and Hazor had been destroyed; and desperate, dispossessed peoples roamed through the region. It had taken Egypt over a century to relinquish its hold over its foreign provinces. The fact that Pharaoh Merneptah himself had been forced to fight a campaign in the highlands at the turn of the century suggests that even by this early date the Egyptian governors of the Canaanite city-states were no longer able to control the countryside and needed reinforcements from home. During this lengthy, turbulent process, one city-state after another collapsed.[9] There is nothing in the archaeological record to suggest that these cities were destroyed by a single conqueror. After the Egyptians had left, there may have been conflict between the city elites and the villages or rivalries among the urban nobility. But it was during this period of decline that settlements began to appear in the highlands, pioneered perhaps by refugees fleeing the chaos of the disintegrating cities. One of the very few ways in which peasants could act to better their lot was simply to decamp when circumstances became intolerable, leave their land, and become fiscal fugitives.[10] At a time of such political chaos, the Israelite peasants had a rare opportunity to make an exodus from these failing cities and establish an independent society, without fear of aristocratic retaliation. Advances in technology had only recently made it possible to settle in this difficult terrain, but by the early twelfth century, it seems that the highland villages already housed some eighty thousand people.

If these settlers were indeed the first Israelites, some must have been native to Canaan, though they may have been joined by migrants from the south who brought Yahweh, a god of the Sinai region, with them. Others—notably the tribe of Joseph—may even have come from Egypt. But those Canaanites who had lived under Egyptian rule in the coastal city-states of Palestine would also have felt that in a very real sense they had "come out of Egypt." The Bible acknowledges that Israel was made up of diverse peoples bound together in a covenant agreement,[11] and its epic story suggests that the early Israelites had made a principled decision to turn their backs on the oppressive agrarian state. Their houses in the highland villages were modest and uniform, and there were no palaces or public buildings: this seems to have been an egalitarian society that may have reverted to tribal organization to create a social alternative to the conventionally stratified state.[12]

◆ ◆ ◆

The final redaction of the Pentateuch occurred after the Israelites had suffered the destruction of their own kingdom by Nebuchadnezzar in 587 BCE and had been deported to Babylonia. The biblical epic is not simply a religious document but also an essay in political philosophy: how could a small nation retain its freedom and integrity in a world dominated by ruthless imperial powers?[13] When they defected from the Canaanite city-states, Israelites had developed an ideology that directly countered the systemic violence of agrarian society. Israel must not be "like the other nations." Their hostility to "Canaanites" was, therefore, every bit as much political as it was religious.[14] The settlers seem to have devised laws to ensure that instead of being appropriated by an aristocracy, land remained in the possession of the extended family; that interest-free loans to needy Israelites were obligatory; that wages were paid promptly; that contract servitude was restricted; and that there was special provision for the socially vulnerable—orphans, widows, and foreigners.[15]

Later, Jews, Christians, and Muslims would all make the biblical god a symbol of absolute transcendence, similar to Brahman or Nirvana.[16] In the Pentateuch, however, Yahweh is a war god, not unlike Indra or Marduk but with one important difference. Like Indra, Yahweh had once fought chaos dragons to order the universe, notably a sea monster called Leviathan,[17] but in the Pentateuch he fights earthly empires to establish a people rather than a cosmos. Moreover, Yahweh is the intransigent enemy of agrarian civilization. The story of the tower of Babel is a thinly veiled critique of Babylon.[18] Intoxicated by fantasies of world conquest, its rulers were determined that the whole of humanity live in a single state with a common language; they believed that their ziggurat could reach heaven itself. Incensed by this imperial hubris, Yahweh reduced the entire political edifice to "confusion" (*babel*).[19] Immediately after this incident, he ordered Abraham to leave Ur, at this date one of the most important Mesopotamian city-states.[20] Yahweh insisted that the three patriarchs—Abraham, Isaac, and Jacob—exchange the stratified tyranny of urban living for the freedom and equality of the herdsman's life. But the plan was flawed: again and again the land that Yahweh had selected for the patriarchs failed to sustain them.[21]

This was the Hebrew dilemma: Yahweh insisted that his people abandon the agrarian state, but time and again they found that they could not live without it.[22] To escape starvation, Abraham had to take temporary refuge in Egypt.[23] His son Isaac had to abandon pastoral life and take up farming during a famine but became so successful that he was attacked by predatory neighboring kings.[24] Finally, when "famine had grown severe throughout the world," Jacob was forced to send ten of his sons to Egypt to buy grain. To their astonishment, they met their long-lost brother Joseph in Pharaoh's court.[25]

As a boy, Joseph—Jacob's favorite son—had dreams of agrarian tyranny that he foolishly described to his brothers: "We were binding sheaves in the countryside, and my sheaf, it seemed, stood upright; then I saw your sheaves gather round and bow to my sheaf."[26] The brothers were so incensed that they stuttered in fury: "Would you be king, yes, king over us?"[27] Such fantasies of monarchy violated everything the family stood for, and Jacob took the boy to task: "Are all of us, then, myself, your mother and your brothers to come and bow to the ground before you?"[28] But he continued to indulge Joseph, until, driven beyond endurance, his brothers had him sold into slavery in Egypt, telling their father he had been killed by a wild beast. Yet after a traumatic beginning, Joseph, a natural agrarian, cheerfully abandoned the pastoral ethos and assimilated to aristocratic life with spectacular success. He got a job in Pharaoh's court, took an Egyptian wife, and even called his first son Manasseh—"He-Who-Makes-Me-Forget," meaning "God has made-me-forget . . . my entire father's house."[29] As vizier of Egypt, Joseph saved the country from starvation: warned by a dream of impending agricultural blight, he commandeered the harvest for seven years, sending fixed rations to the cities and storing the surplus, so that when the famine struck, Egypt had grain to spare.[30] But Joseph had also turned Egypt into a house of bondage, because all the hard-pressed Egyptians who had been forced to sell their estates to Pharaoh in return for grain were reduced to serfdom.[31] Joseph saved the lives of his family when hunger forced them to seek refuge in Egypt, but they too would lose their freedom since Pharaoh would forbid them to leave.[32]

Readers of the Pentateuch are often confused by the patriarchs' ethics. None of them are particularly admirable characters: Abraham sold his wife to Pharaoh to save his own skin; Joseph was arrogant and self-centered; and Jacob was shockingly indifferent to the rape of his daughter Dinah. But these are not morality tales. If we read them as political philosophy, things become clearer. Doomed to marginality, Israel would always be vulnerable to more powerful states. Ordered to leave civilization yet unable to survive without it, the patriarchs were in an impossible position. Yet despite his flaws, Abraham still compares favorably with the rulers in this story, who appropriate their subjects' wives, steal their wells, and rape their daughters with impunity.[33] While kings routinely confiscated other people's possessions, Abraham was always meticulously respectful of property rights. He would not even keep the booty he acquired in a raid he had fought simply to rescue his nephew Lot, who had been kidnapped by four marauding kings.[34] His kindness and hospitality to three passing strangers stand in stark contrast to the violence they experienced in civilized Sodom.[35] When Yahweh told Abraham that he planned to destroy Sodom, Abraham begged him to spare the city, because unlike rulers who had scant respect for human life, he had a horror of shedding innocent blood.[36]

When the biblical authors tell us about Jacob on his deathbed blessing his twelve sons and prophesying their future, they are asking what kind of leader is needed to create a viable egalitarian society in such a ruthless world. Jacob rejected Simeon and Levi, whose reckless violence meant that they should never control territory, populations, and armies.[37] He predicted that Judah, who could admit and correct his mistakes, would make an ideal ruler.[38] But no state could survive without Joseph's political savvy, so when the Israelites finally escaped from Egypt, they took Joseph's bones with them to the Promised Land. Then there were occasions when a nation might need Levi's radicalism, because without the aggressive determination of the Levite Moses, Israel would never have left Egypt.

The book of Exodus depicts Egyptian imperialism as an extreme example of systemic oppression. The pharaohs made the Israelites' lives "unbearable," compelling them to "work with clay and with brick, all kinds of work in the fields; [forcing] on them every kind of labour."[39] To stem their rising birthrate, Pharaoh even ordered the midwives to kill all Israelite male babies, but the infant Moses was rescued by Pharaoh's daughter and brought up as an Egyptian aristocrat. One day in instinctive revulsion from state tyranny, Moses, a true son of Levi, killed an Egyptian who was beating a Hebrew slave.[40] He had to flee the country, and Yahweh, who had not revealed himself to Moses the Egyptian aristocrat, first spoke to him when he was working as a shepherd in Midian.[41] During the Exodus, Yahweh could liberate Israel only by using the same brutal tactics as any imperial power: terrorizing the population, slaughtering their children, and drowning the entire Egyptian army. Peaceful tactics were of no avail against the martial might of the state. Yahweh divided the Sea of Reeds in two so that the Israelites could cross dry shod as effortlessly as Marduk had slit Tiamat, the primal ocean, in half to create heaven and earth; but instead of an ordered universe, he had brought into being a new nation that would provide an alternative to the aggression of imperial rule.

Yahweh sealed his pact with Israel on Mount Sinai. The earliest sources, dating from the eighth century BCE, do not mention the Ten Commandments being given to Moses on this occasion. Instead, they depict Moses and the elders of Israel experiencing a theophany on the summit of Sinai during which they "gazed upon God" and shared a sacred meal.[42] The stone tablets that Moses received, "written with the finger of God,"[43] were probably inscribed with Yahweh's instructions for the construction and accoutrements of the tent-shrine in which he would dwell with Israel in the wilderness.[44] The Ten Commandments would be inserted into the story later by seventh-century reformers, who, as we shall see, were also responsible for some of the most violent passages in the Hebrew Bible.

◆　◆　◆

After Moses's death, it fell to Joshua to conquer the Promised Land. The biblical book of Joshua still contains some ancient material, but this was radically revised by these same reformers, who interpreted it in the light of their peculiarly xenophobic theology. They give the impression that,

acting under Yahweh's orders, Joshua massacred the entire population of
Canaan and destroyed their cities. Yet not only is there no archaeological
evidence for this wholesale destruction, but the biblical text itself admits
that for centuries Israelites coexisted with Canaanites and intermarried
with them, and that large swaths of the country remained in Canaanite hands.[45] On the basis of the reformers' work, it is often claimed that
monotheism, the belief in a single god, made Israel especially prone to
violence. It is assumed that its denial of other gods reveals a rabid intolerance not found in the generous pluralism of paganism.[46] But the Israelites
were not monotheists at this date and would not begin to be so until
the sixth century BCE. Indeed, both the biblical and the archaeological
evidence suggests that the beliefs and practices of most early Israelites
differed little from those of their Canaanite neighbors.[47] There are in fact
very few unequivocally monotheistic statements in the Hebrew Bible.[48]
Even the first of the reformers' Ten Commandments takes the existence
of rival deities for granted and simply forbids Israel to worship them:
"You are not to have any other gods before my presence."[49]

In the earliest strand of the conquest narratives, Joshua's violence was
associated with an ancient Canaanite custom called the "ban" (herem).[50]
Before a battle, a military leader would strike a deal with his god: if
this deity undertook to give him the city, the commander promised to
"devote" (HRM) all valuable loot to his temple and offer the conquered
people to him in a human sacrifice.[51] Joshua had made such a pact with
Yahweh before attacking Jericho, and Yahweh responded by deliver-
ing the town to Israel in a spectacular miracle, causing its famous walls
to collapse when the priests blew their rams' horns. Before allowing
his troops to storm the city, Joshua explained the terms of the ban and
stipulated that no one in the city should be spared, since everybody and
everything in the town had been "devoted" to Yahweh. Accordingly, the
Israelites "enforced the ban on everything in the town, men and women,
young and old, even the oxen and sheep and donkeys, massacring them
all."[52] But the ban had been violated when one of the soldiers kept booty
for himself, and consequently the Israelites failed to take the town of Ai
the following day. After the culprit had been found and executed, the
Israelites attacked Ai again, this time successfully, setting fire to the city
so that it became a sacrificial pyre and slaughtering anybody who tried
to escape: "The number of those who fell that day, men and women
together, were twelve thousand, all [the] people of Ai."[53] Finally Joshua

hanged the king from a tree, built a monumental cairn over his body, and reduced the city to "a ruin for ever more, a desolate place, even today."[54]

Ninth-century inscriptions discovered in Jordan and southern Arabia record conquests that follow this pattern to the letter. They recount the burning of the town, the massacre of its citizens, the hanging of the ruler, and the erection of a cultic memorial claiming that the enemy had been entirely eliminated and the town never rebuilt.[55] The ban was not, therefore, the invention of "monotheistic" Israel but was a local pagan practice. One of these inscriptions explains that King Mesha of Moab was commanded by his god Kemosh to take Nebo from King Omri of Israel (r. 885–874). "I seized it and killed every one of [it]," Mesha proclaimed, "seven thousand foreign men, native women, foreign women, concubines—for I devoted it [*HRM*] to destruction to Ashtur Kemosh."[56] Israel had "utterly perished forever."[57] This was wishful thinking, however, because the Kingdom of Israel would survive for another 150 years. In the same vein, the biblical authors record Yahweh's decree that Jericho remain a ruin forever, even though it would become a thriving Israelite city. New nations in the Middle East seem to have cultivated the fiction of a conquest that made the land tabula rasa for them.[58] The narrative of the "ban," therefore, was a literary trope that could not be read literally. Secular as well as religious conquerors would later develop similar fictions claiming that the territory they occupied was "unused" and "empty" until they took possession of it.

• • •

True to their mandate to create an alternative society, Israelites were reluctant at first to establish a regular state "like the other nations" but seem to have lived in independent chiefdoms without a central government. If they were attacked by their neighbors, a leader or "judge" would rise up and mobilize the entire population against an attack. This is the arrangement we find in the book of Judges, which was also heavily revised by the seventh-century reformers. But over time, without strong rule, Israelites succumbed to moral depravity. One sentence recurs throughout the book: "In those days there was no king in Israel, and every man did as he pleased."[59] We read of a judge who made a human sacrifice of his own daughter;[60] a tribe that exterminated an innocent people instead of the enemy assigned them by Yahweh;[61] a group of Israelites who gang-raped a woman to death;[62] and a civil war in which the tribe of Benjamin was almost exterminated.[63] These tales are not held up for our edification; rather, they explore a political and religious quandary. Can our natural proclivity for violence be controlled in a community without a degree of coercion? It appears that the Israelites had won their freedom but lost their souls, and monarchy seemed the only way to restore order. Moreover, the Philistines, who had established a kingdom on the southern coast of Canaan, had become a grave military threat to the tribes. Eventually, the Israelite elders approached their judge Samuel with a shocking request: "Give us a king to rule over us like the other nations."[64]

Samuel responded with a remarkable critique of agrarian oppression, which listed the regular exploitation of every premodern civilization:

> These will be the rights of the king who is to reign over you. He will take your sons and assign them to his chariotry and cavalry, and they will run in front of his chariot. He will use them as leaders of a thousand and leaders of fifty; he will make them plough his ploughland and harvest his harvest and make his weapons of war and the gear for his chariots. He will also take your daughters as perfumers, cooks and bakers. He will take the best of your fields, of your vineyards and olive groves, and give them to his officials. . . . He will take the best of your manservants and maidservants, of your cattle and your donkeys, and make them work for him. He will tithe your flocks, and you yourselves will become his slaves. When that day comes, you will cry out on account of the king you have chosen for yourselves, but on that day Yahweh will not answer you.[65]

Unlike most religious traditions that endorsed this system, albeit reluctantly, Israel had utterly rejected its structural violence but failed to establish a viable alternative. Despite their dreams of freedom and equity, Israelites had discovered, time and again, that they could not survive without a strong state.

Saul, Israel's first king, still ruled as judge and chieftain. But David, who deposed him, would be remembered as Israel's ideal king, even though he was clearly no paragon. The biblical authors did not express themselves as bluntly as Lord Shang, but they probably understood that saints were not likely to be good rulers. David expanded Israelite territory on the east bank of the Jordan, united the separate regions of Israel in the north and Judah in the south, and conquered the city-state of Jerusalem from the Hittite-Jebusites, which became the capital of his united kingdom. There was no question of putting the Jebusites "under the ban," however: David adopted the existing Jebusite administration, employed Jebusites in his bureaucracy, and took over the Jebusite standing army—a pragmatism that may have been more typical in Israel than Joshua's alleged zealotry. David probably did not set up a regular tributary system, however, but taxed only the conquered populations and supplemented his income with booty.[66]

In this young, hopeful kingdom we find a heroic ethos that has nothing "religious" about it.[67] We see it first in the famous account of the young David's duel with the Philistine giant Goliath. Single combat was one of the hallmarks of chivalric war.[68] It gave the warrior a chance to show off his martial skills, and both armies enjoyed watching the clash of champions. Moreover, in Israel's chivalric code, warriors formed a caste of champions, respected for their valor and expertise even if they were fighting for the enemy.[69] Every morning, Goliath would appear before the Israelite lines, challenging one of them to fight him, and when nobody came forward, taunted them for their cowardice. One day the shepherd boy David, armed only with a sling, called Goliath's bluff, knocked him out with a pebble, and decapitated him. But the heroic champion could also be utterly pitiless in battle. When David's army arrived outside the walls of Jerusalem, the Jebusites taunted him: "You will not get in here. The blind and lame will hold you off."[70] So in their hearing David ordered his men to kill *only* "the blind and lame," a ruthlessness designed to terrify the enemy. The biblical text here is fragmentary and obscure, however, and may have been edited by a redactor who was uncomfortable with this story. One later tradition even claimed that David was forbidden by Yahweh to build a temple in Jerusalem, "since you have shed so much blood on the earth in my presence." That honor would be reserved for David's son and successor Solomon, whose name was said to derive from the Hebrew *shalom,* "peace."[71] But Solomon's mother, Bathsheba, was a Jebusite, and his name could also have derived from Shalem, the ancient deity of Jerusalem.[72]

Solomon's temple was built on the regional model and its furniture showed how thoroughly the cult of Yahweh had accommodated itself to the pagan landscape of the Near East. There was clearly no sectarian intolerance in Israelite Jerusalem. At the temple's entrance were two Canaanite standing stones (*matzevoth*) and a massive bronze basin, representing Yam, the sea monster fought by Baal, supported by twelve brazen oxen, common symbols of divinity and fertility.[73] The temple rituals too seem to have been influenced by Baal's cult in neighboring Ugarit.[74] The temple was supposed to symbolize Yahweh's approval of Solomon's rule.[75] There is no reference to his short-lived empire in other sources, but the biblical authors tell us that it extended from the Euphrates to the Mediterranean and was achieved and maintained by force of arms. Solomon had replaced David's infantry with a chariot army, engaged in lucrative arms deals with neighboring kings, and restored the ancient fortresses of Hazor, Megiddo, and Arad.[76] In purely material terms, everything seemed perfect: "Judah and Israel lived in security: each man under his vine and fig tree!"[77] Yet this kind of state, maintained by war and taxes, was exactly what Yahweh had always abhorred. Unlike David, Solomon even taxed his Israelite subjects, and his building projects required massive forced labor.[78] As well as farming their own plots to produce the surplus that supported the state, peasants also had to serve in the army or the corvée for one month in every three.[79]

Some biblical redactors tried to argue that Solomon's empire failed because he had built shrines for the pagan gods of his foreign wives.[80] But it is clear that the real problem was its structural violence, which offended deep-rooted Israelite principles. After Solomon's death a delegation begged his son Rehoboam not to replicate his father's "harsh tyranny."[81] When Rehoboam contemptuously refused, a mob attacked the manager of the corvée, and ten of the twelve tribes broke away from the empire to form the independent Kingdom of Israel.[82]

◆ ◆ ◆

Henceforth the two kingdoms went their separate ways. Situated near important trade routes, the northern Kingdom of Israel prospered, with royal shrines in Bethel and Dan and an elegant capital in Samaria. We know very little about its ideology, because the biblical editors favored the smaller and more isolated Kingdom of Judah. But both probably conformed to local traditions. Like most Middle Eastern kings, the king of Judah was raised to a semidivine "state of exception" during the coronation ritual, when he became Yahweh's adopted son and a member of the Divine Assembly of gods.[83] Like Baal, Yahweh was celebrated as a warrior god who defended his people from their enemies: "When he grows angry he shatters kings, he gives the nations their deserts; smashing their skulls, he heaps the world with corpses."[84] The chief responsibility of the king was to secure and extend his territory, the source of the kingdom's revenues. He was therefore in a perpetual state of conflict with neighboring monarchs, who had exactly the same goals. Israel and Judah were thus drawn inexorably into the local network of trade, diplomacy, and warfare.

The two kingdoms had emerged when the imperial powers of the region were in eclipse, but during the early eighth century, Assyria was in the ascendant again, its military might forcing weaker kings into vassal status. Yet some of these conquered kingdoms flourished. King Jeroboam II (786–746 BCE) became a trusted Assyrian vassal, and the Kingdom of Israel enjoyed an economic boom. But because the rich became richer and the poor even more impoverished, the king was castigated by the prophet Amos.[85] The prophets of Israel kept the old egalitarian ideals of Israel alive. Amos chastised the aristocracy for trampling on the heads of ordinary people, pushing the poor out of their path,[86] and cramming their palaces with the fruits of their extortion.[87] Yahweh, he warned, was no longer unconditionally on Israel's side but would use Assyria as his instrument of punishment.[88] The Assyrians would invade the kingdom, loot and destroy its palaces and temples.[89] Amos imagined Yahweh roaring in rage from his sanctuary at the war crimes committed by the local kingdoms, Israel included.[90] In Judah too, the prophet Isaiah inveighed against the exploitation of the poor and the expropriation of peasant land: "Cease to do evil. Learn to do good, search for justice, help the oppressed, be just to the orphan, and plead for the widow."[91] The dilemma was that this callowness was essential to the agrarian economy and had the kings of Israel and Judah fully implemented these compassionate policies, they would have been easy prey for Assyria.[92]

In 745 Tiglath-pileser III abolished the system of vassalage and incorporated all the conquered peoples directly into the Assyrian state. At the merest hint of dissent, the entire ruling class would be deported and replaced by people from other parts of his empire. The army left a trail of desolation in its wake, and the countryside was deserted as peasants took refuge in the towns. When King Hosea refused to pay tribute in 722, Shalmeneser III simply wiped the Kingdom of Israel off the map and deported its aristocracy. Because of its isolated position, Judah survived until the turn of the century, when Sennacherib's army besieged Jerusalem. The Assyrian army was finally forced to withdraw, possibly because it was smitten by disease, but Lachish, Judah's second city, was razed to the ground and the countryside devastated.[93] King Manasseh (r. 687–642) was determined to keep on the right side of Assyria, and Judah enjoyed peace and prosperity during his long reign.[94] Manasseh rebuilt rural shrines to Baal and brought an effigy of Asherah, the Canaanite mother goddess, into Yahweh's temple; he also set up statues of the divine horses of the sun in the temple, which may have been emblems of Ashur.[95] Few of Manasseh's subjects objected since, as archaeologists have discovered, many of them had similar effigies in their own homes.[96]

• • •

During the reign of Manasseh's grandson Josiah (640–609), however, a group of prophets, priests, and scribes attempted a far-reaching reform. By this time, Assyria was in decline: Pharaoh Psammetichus had forced the Assyrian army to withdraw from the Levant, and Josiah technically became his vassal. But Egypt was occupied elsewhere, and Judah enjoyed a brief period of de facto independence. In 622 Josiah began extensive repairs in Solomon's temple, emblem of Judah's golden age, perhaps as an assertion of national pride. Yet Judeans could not forget the fate of the Kingdom of Israel. Surrounded by huge predatory empires, with Babylon now becoming the dominant power in Mesopotamia, how could Judah hope to survive? Fear of annihilation and the experience of state violence often radicalize a religious tradition. Zoroaster had been a victim of excessive aggression, and this violence had introduced an apocalyptic ferocity into his initially peaceable alternative to the belligerent cult of Indra. Now, in seventh-century Judah, reformers who dreamed of independence but were terrified by the aggression of the great imperial powers brought a wholly new intransigence into the cult of Yahweh.[97]

During the construction work in the temple, the high priest, one of the leading reformers, made a momentous discovery: "I have found the book of the law [*sefer torah*] in the temple of Yahweh," he announced.[98] Until this point, there was no tradition of a written text given on Mount Sinai; in fact, until the eighth century reading and writing had little place in the religious life of Israel. In the early biblical traditions Moses imparted Yahweh's teachings orally.[99] Yet the reformers claimed that the scroll they had discovered had been dictated to Moses by Yahweh himself.[100] Tragically, this precious document had been lost, but now that they had recovered this "second law" (Greek: *deuteronomion*) that supplemented

Yahweh's verbal teaching on Mount Sinai, the people of Judah could make a new start and perhaps save their nation from total destruction. So authoritative was the past in an agrarian state that it was quite customary for people who were promoting an innovative idea to attribute it to an iconic historical figure. The reformers believed that at this time of grave danger, they were speaking for Moses and put forward their own teachings in the speech they make Moses deliver, shortly before his death, in the book of Deuteronomy.

For the very first time, these reformers insisted that Yahweh demanded exclusive devotion. "Listen, Israel," Moses tells his people, "Yahweh is our god, Yahweh alone!"[101] He had not only emphatically forbidden Israelites to worship any other god but had also commanded them to wipe out the indigenous peoples of the Promised Land:

> You must lay them under ban. You must make no covenant with them nor show them any pity. You must not marry with them . . . for this would turn away your son from following me to serving other gods and the anger of Yahweh would blaze out against you and soon destroy you. Instead, deal with them like this: tear down their altars, smash their standing-stones, cut down their sacred poles, and set fire to their idols.[102]

Because they had lost this "second law" recorded by Moses, Israelites had been ignorant of his command; they had condoned the cult of other gods, married Canaanites, and made treaties with them. No wonder Yahweh's anger had "blazed out" against the northern kingdom. Moses, the reformers insisted, had warned the Israelites what would happen. "Yahweh will scatter you among the peoples, from one end of the earth to the other. . . . In the morning you will say, 'how I wish it were evening!' and in the evening, 'how I wish it were morning!' Such terror will grip your heart, such sights your eyes will see."[103] When the scroll was read aloud to Josiah, its teachings were so startling that the king burst into tears, crying: "Great indeed must be the anger of Yahweh, blazing out against us."[104]

It is difficult for us today to realize how strange this insistence on cultic exclusivity would have been in the seventh century BCE. Our reading of the Hebrew Bible has been influenced by two and a half thousand years of monotheistic teaching. But Josiah, of course, had never heard of the First Commandment—"Thou shalt not have strange gods before my presence"—which the reformers would place at the top of the Decalogue. It pointedly condemned Manasseh's introduction of the effigies of "strange gods" into the temple where Yahweh's "presence" (*shechinah*) was enthroned in the Holy of Holies. But pagan icons had been perfectly acceptable there since Solomon's time. Despite the campaigns of such prophets as Elijah, who had urged the people to worship Yahweh alone, most of the population of the two kingdoms had never doubted the efficacy of such gods as Baal, Anat, or Asherah. The prophet Hosea's oracles showed how popular the cult of Baal had been in the northern kingdom during the eighth century, and the reformers themselves knew that Israelites "offered sacrifice to Baal, to the sun, the moon, the constellations and the whole array of heaven."[105] There would be great resistance to monotheism. Thirty years after Josiah's death, Israelites were still devotees of the Mesopotamian goddess Ishtar, and Yahweh's temple was once again full of "the idols of the house of Israel."[106] For many it seemed unnatural and perverse to ignore such a divine resource. The reformers knew that they were asking Judeans to relinquish beloved and familiar sanctities and embark on a lonely, painful severance from the mythical and cultural consciousness of the Middle East.

Josiah was completely convinced by the sefer torah and at once inaugurated a violent orgy of destruction, eradicating the cultic paraphernalia introduced by Manasseh, burning the effigies of Baal and Asherah, abolishing the rural shrines, pulling down the house of sacred male prostitutes and the Assyrian horses. In the old territories of the Kingdom of Israel, he was even more ruthless, not only demolishing the ancient temples of Yahweh in Bethel and Samaria but slaughtering the priests of the rural shrines and contaminating their altars.[107] This fanatical aggression was a new and tragic development, which excoriated sacred symbols that had been central to both the temple cult and the piety of individual Israelites.[108] A tradition often develops a violent strain in a symbiotic relationship with an aggressive imperialism; fearing annihilation by an external foe, people attack an "enemy within." The reformers now regarded the Canaanite cults that Israelites had long enjoyed as "detestable" and "loathsome"; they insisted that any Israelite who participated in them must be hunted down mercilessly.[109] "You must not give way to him, nor listen to him, you must show him no pity," Moses had commanded; "You must not spare him, and you must not conceal his guilt. No, you must kill him."[110] An Israelite town guilty of this idolatry must be put under the "ban," burned to the ground, and its inhabitants slaughtered.[111]

This was all so novel that in order to justify these innovations, the Deuteronomists literally had to rewrite history. They began a massive editorial revision of the texts in the royal archives that would one day become the Hebrew Bible, changing the wording and import of earlier law codes and introducing new legislation that endorsed their proposals. They recast the history of Israel, adding fresh material to the older narratives of the Pentateuch and giving Moses a prominence that he may not have had in some of the earlier traditions. The climax of the Exodus story was no longer a theophany but the gift of the Ten Commandments and the *sefer torah*. Drawing on earlier sagas, now lost to us, the reformers put together a history of the two kingdoms of Israel and Judah that became the books of Joshua, Judges, Samuel, and Kings, which "proved" that the idolatrous iniquity of the northern kingdom had been the cause of its destruction. When they described Joshua's conquests, they depicted him slaughtering the local population of the Promised Land and devastating their cities like an Assyrian general. They transformed the ancient myth of the ban so that it became an expression of God's justice and a literal rather than a fictional story of attempted genocide. Their history culminated in the reign of Josiah, the new Moses who would liberate Israel from Pharaoh once again, a king who was even greater than David.[112] This strident theology left an indelible trace on the Hebrew Bible; many of the writings so frequently quoted to prove the ineradicable aggression and intolerance of "monotheism" were either composed or recast by these reformers.

Yet the Deuteronomist reform was never implemented. Josiah's bid for independence ended in 609 BCE, when he was killed in a skirmish with Pharaoh Neco. The new Babylonian empire replaced Assyria and competed with Egypt for control of the Middle East. For a few years Judah dodged between these great powers, but eventually, after an uprising in Judah in 597, Nebuchadnezzar, king of Babylon, deported eight thousand Judean aristocrats, soldiers, and skilled artisans.[113] Ten years later he destroyed the temple, razed Jerusalem to the ground, and deported five thousand more Judeans, leaving only the lower classes in the devastated land. In Babylonia the Judean exiles were reasonably well treated. Some lived in the capital; others were housed in undeveloped areas near the new canals and could, to an extent, manage their own affairs.[114] But exile is a spiritual as well as a physical dislocation. In Judah the deportees had been the elite class; now they had no political rights, and some even had to work in the corvée.[115] But then it seemed that Yahweh was about to liberate his people again. This time the exodus would not be led by a prophet but would be instigated by a new imperial power.

◆ ◆ ◆

In 559 BCE Cyrus, a minor member of the Persian Achaemenid family, became king of Anshan in southern Iran.[116] Twenty years later, after a series of spectacular victories in Media, Anatolia, and Asia Minor, he invaded the Babylonian empire and astonishingly, without fighting a single battle, was greeted by the population as a liberator. Cyrus was now the master of the largest empire the world had yet seen. At its fullest extent, it would control the whole of the eastern Mediterranean, from what is now Libya and Turkey in the west to Afghanistan in the east. For centuries to come, any ruler who aspired to world rule would try to replicate Cyrus's achievement.[117] But he was not only a pivotal figure in the politics of the region: he also modeled a more benign form of empire.

Cyrus's victory proclamation claimed that when he arrived in Babylonia, "all the people . . . of Sumer and Akkad, nobles and governors, bowed down before him and kissed his feet, rejoicing over his kingship, and their faces shone."[118] Why such enthusiasm for a foreign invader? Ten years earlier, shortly after Cyrus had conquered Media, the Babylonian author of the poem "The Dream of Nabonidus" had given him a divine role.[119] Media had been a threat to Babylon, and Marduk, the poet said, had appeared in a dream to Nabonidus (r. 556–539), the last Babylonian king, to assure him that he was still controlling events and had chosen Cyrus to solve the Median problem. But ten years later the Babylonian Empire was in decline. Nabonidus, engaged in conquests abroad, had been absent from Babylon for several years and had incurred the wrath of the priesthood by failing to perform the Akitu ritual. During this ceremony all Babylonian kings had to swear not "to rain blows on the cheeks of the protected citizen," but Nabonidus had imposed forced labor on the freemen of the empire. Disaffected priests announced that the gods had abrogated his rule and abandoned the city. When Cyrus marched on Babylonia, these priests almost certainly helped him to write his victory speech, which explained that when the people of Babylon had cried out in anguish to Marduk, the god had chosen Cyrus as their champion:

> He took the hand of Cyrus, king of the city of Anshan, and called him by name, proclaiming him aloud for the kingship over all of everything. . . . He ordered that he should go to Babylon. He had him take the road to [Babylon], and like a friend and companion, he walked at his side. . . . He had him enter without fighting or battle, right into Shuanna; he saved his city Babylon from hardship. He handed over to him Nabonidus, the king who did not fear him.[120]

Ritual and mythology, crucial as they were to kingship, did not always endorse state tyranny. Nabonidus was in effect deposed by the priestly establishment for his excessive violence and oppression.

Cyrus's vast multilingual and multicultural empire needed a different mode of government, one that respected the traditional rights of the conquered peoples and their religious and cultural traditions. Instead of humiliating and deporting his new subjects, and tearing down their temples and desecrating the effigies of their gods as the Assyrians and Babylonians had done, Cyrus announced a wholly new policy, preserved in the Cyrus Cylinder, now in the British Museum. Cyrus, it claimed, had arrived in Babylonia as the harbinger of peace rather than of war; he had abolished the corvée, repatriated all the peoples who had been deported by Nebuchadnezzar, and promised to rebuild their national temples. An anonymous Judean exile in Babylonia therefore hailed Cyrus as the *messhiah,* the man "anointed" by Yahweh to end Israel's exile.[121] This prophet, of course, was convinced that it was not Marduk but Yahweh who had taken Cyrus by the hand and shattered the bronze gates of Babylon. "It is for the sake of my servant Jacob, of Israel, my chosen one, that I have called you by your name, conferring a title, though you do not know me," Yahweh had told Cyrus.[122] A new era was at hand, in which the earth would be restored to its primal perfection. "Let every valley be filled in, every mountain laid low," cried the prophet, clearly influenced by the Zoroastrian traditions of his Persian messiah, "let every cliff become a plain, and the ridges a valley."[123]

Most of the Judean exiles chose to stay in Babylonia, and many acculturated successfully.[124] According to the Bible, more than forty thousand of them chose to return to Judea with the liturgical utensils confiscated by Nebuchadnezzar, determined to rebuild Yahweh's temple in the devastated city of Jerusalem. The Persians' decision to allow the deportees to return home and rebuild their temples was enlightened and sensible: they believed it would strengthen their empire, since gods ought to be worshipped in their own countries, and it would win the gratitude of the subject peoples. As a result of this benign policy, the Middle East enjoyed a period of relative stability for some two hundred years.

But the Pax Persiana still depended on military force and taxes extorted from the subject races. Cyrus made a point of mentioning the unparalleled might of his army; as he and Marduk marched on Babylon, "his vast troops whose number, like the water in the river, could not be counted, were marching fully armed at his side."[125] His victory proclamation also noted the tributary system that Cyrus had enforced: at Marduk's "exalted command, all kings who sit on thrones, from every quarter, from the Upper Sea to the Lower Sea, those who inhabit remote districts and the kings of the land of Amurru who live in tents, all of them, brought their weighty tribute into Shuanna and kissed my feet."[126] Even the most peaceable empire required sustained military aggression and massive expropriation of resources from the populations it conquered. If imperial officials and soldiers felt any moral qualms about this, it would sap the empire's energy; but if they could be convinced that these policies would ultimately benefit everyone, they would find them more palatable.[127]

In the inscriptions of Darius I, who came to the Persian throne after the death of Cyrus's son Cambyses in 522 BCE, we find a combination of three themes that would recur in the ideology of all successful empires: a dualistic worldview that pits the good of empire against evildoers who oppose it; a doctrine of election that sees the ruler as a divine agent; and a mission to save the world.[128] Darius's political philosophy was strongly influenced by Zoroastrianism, skillfully adapted to sacralize the imperial project.[129] A large number of the royal inscriptions that have survived in the Persian heartland of the empire referred to the Zoroastrian creation myth.[130] They describe Ahura Mazda, the Wise Lord who had appeared to Zoroaster, ordering the cosmos in four stages, creating successively earth, sky, humanity, and finally "happiness" (*shiyati*), which consisted of peace, security, truth, and abundant food.[131] At first there had been only one ruler, one people, and one language.[132] But after the assault of the Hostile Spirit ("the Lie"), humanity split into competing groups, governed by people who called themselves kings. There was war, bloodshed, and disorder for centuries. Then, on September 29, 522, Darius ascended the throne, and the Wise Lord inaugurated the fifth and final stage of creation: Darius would unite the world and restore the original happiness of mankind by creating a worldwide empire.[133]

Here we see the difficulty of adapting a predominantly peaceful tradition to the realities of imperial rule. Darius shared Zoroaster's horror of lawless violence. After Cambyses's death, he had had to suppress rebellions all over the empire. Like any emperor, he had to quash ambitious aristocrats who sought to unseat him. In his inscriptions Darius associated these rebels with the illegitimate kings who had brought war and suffering to the world after the Lie's assault. But to restore peace and happiness, the "fighting men" whom Zoroaster had wanted to exclude from society were indispensable. The apocalyptic restoration of the world that Zoroaster had predicted at the end of time had been transposed to the present, and Zoroastrian dualism was employed to divide the political world into warring camps. The empire's structural and martial violence had become the final, absolute good, while everything beyond its borders was barbaric, chaotic, and immoral.[134] Darius's mission was to subdue the rest of the world and purloin its resources in order to make other people "good." Once all lands had been subjugated, there would be universal peace and an era of *frasha*, "wonder."[135]

Darius's inscriptions remind us that a religious tradition is never a single, unchanging essence that impels people to act in a uniform way. It is a template that can be modified and altered radically to serve a variety of ends. For Darius, frasha was no longer spiritual harmony but material wealth; he described his palace in Susa as frasha, a foretaste of the redeemed, reunited world.[136] Inscriptions listed the gold, silver, precious woods, ivory, and marble brought in tribute from every region of the empire, explaining that after the Lie's assault, these riches had been scattered all over the world but had now been reassembled in one place, as the Wise Lord had originally intended. The magnificent Apadama relief in Persepolis depicted a procession of the delegates of conquered peoples from far-flung lands duly bringing their tribute to Susa. The ethical vision of Zoroaster, victim of violence and theft on the Caucasian steppes, had been originally inspired by the shocking aggression of the Sanskrit raiders; now that vision had been used to sacralize organized martial violence and imperial extortion.

• • •

The Judeans who returned from Babylon in 539 BCE found their home-land a desolate place and had to contend with the hostility of the for-eigners who had been drafted into the country by the Babylonians. They also faced the resentment of those Judeans who had not been deported and were now strangers to the returnees who had been born into an entirely different culture. When they finally rebuilt their temple, Persian Judea became a temple state governed by a Jewish priestly aristocracy in the name of Persia. The writings of these priestly aristocrats have been preserved in parts of the Pentateuch and the two books of Chronicles, which rewrote the strident history of the Deuteronomists and attempted to adapt ancient Israelite traditions to these new circumstances.[137] These scriptures reflect the exiles' concern that everything stay in its proper place. In Babylon the Judeans had preserved their national identity by liv-ing apart from the local people; now the priests insisted that to be "holy" (*qaddosh*) was to be "separate; other."

Yet unlike the Deuteronomist scriptures, which had demonized the foreigner and yearned to eliminate him, these priestly texts, drawing on exactly the same stories and legends, had developed a remarkably inclu-sive vision. Again, we see the impossibility of describing any religious tradition as a single unchanging essence that will always inspire violence. The priests insisted that the "otherness" of every single creature was sacred and must be respected and honored. In the priestly Law of Free-dom, therefore, nothing could be enslaved or owned, not even the land.[138] Instead of seeking to exterminate the *ger*, the "resident alien," as the Deu-teronomists had insisted, the true Israelite must learn to love him: "If a stranger lives with you in your land do not molest him. You must treat him as one of your own people and love him as yourselves. For you were strangers in Egypt."[139] These priests had arrived at the Golden Rule: the experience of living as a minority in Egypt and Babylonia should teach Israelites to appreciate the pain that these uprooted foreigners might be feeling in Judah. The command to "love" was not about sentiment: *hesed* meant "loyalty" and was used in Middle Eastern treaties when former enemies agreed to be helpful and trustworthy and give each other practical support.[140] This was not an unrealistically utopian ideal but an ethic within everybody's reach.

To temper the harsh rejectionism of the Deuteronomists, the priestly historians included moving stories of reconciliation. The estranged brothers Jacob and Esau finally see the "face of God" in each other.[141] The Chroniclers show Moses refraining from retaliation when the king of Edom refused to grant the Israelites safe passage through his territory during their journey to the Promised Land.[142] The most famous of these priestly writings is the creation story that opens the Hebrew Bible. The biblical redactors placed this priestly creation story before the earlier eighth-century tale of Yahweh's creating a garden for Adam and Eve and their fall from grace. This priestly version extracted all the violence from the traditional Middle Eastern cosmogony. Instead of fighting a battle and slaying a monster, the god of Israel simply uttered words of command when he ordered the cosmos. On the last day of creation, he "saw everything that he had made, and indeed it was very good."[143] This god had no enemies: he blessed every one of his creatures, even his old enemy Leviathan.

This principled benevolence is all the more remarkable when we consider that the community of exiles was under almost constant attack by hostile groups in Judea. When Nehemiah, dispatched from the Persian court to supervise the rebuilding of Jerusalem, was overseeing the restoration of the city wall, each of the laborers "did his work with one hand while gripping his weapon with the other."[144] The priestly writers could not afford to be antiwar but they seem troubled by military violence. They deleted some of the most belligerent episodes in the Deuteronomist history and brushed over Joshua's conquests. They told the stories of David's chivalric warfare but omitted his grim order to kill the blind and lame in Jerusalem, and it was the Chronicler who explained that David was forbidden to build the temple because he had shed too much blood. They also recorded a story about a military campaign against the Midianites, who had enticed the Israelites into idolatry.[145] There was no doubt that it was a just cause, and the Israelite armies behaved in perfect accordance with Deuteronomist law: the priests led the troops into battle, and the soldiers killed the Midianite kings, set fire to their town, and condemned to death both the married women who had tempted the Israelites and the boys who would grow up to be warriors. But even though they had "cleansed" Israel, they had been tainted by this righteous bloodshed. "You must camp for seven days outside the camp," Moses told the returning warriors: "Purify yourselves, you and your prisoners."[146]

In one remarkable story, the Chronicler condemned the savagery of the Kingdom of Israel in a war against an idolatrous Judean king, even though Yahweh himself had sanctioned the campaign. Israelite troops had killed 120,000 Judean soldiers and marched 200,000 Judean prisoners back to Samaria in triumph. Yet the prophet Oded greeted these conquering heroes with a blistering rebuke:

> You have slaughtered with such fury as reaches to heaven. And now you propose to reduce these children of Judah and Jerusalem to being your serving men and women! And are you not all the while the ones who are guilty before Yahweh your God? Now listen to me—release the prisoners you have taken of your brothers, for the fierce anger of Yahweh hangs over you.[147]

The troops immediately released the captives and relinquished all their booty; specially appointed officials "saw to the relief of the prisoners. From the booty, they clothed all those of them who were naked; they gave them clothing and sandals, and provided them with food, drink and shelter. They mounted all those who were infirm on donkeys, and took them back to their kinsmen in Jericho."[148] These priests were probably monotheists; in Babylonia, paganism had lost its allure for the exiles. The prophet who had hailed Cyrus as the messiah also uttered the first fully monotheistic statement in the Bible: "Am I not Yahweh?" he makes the God of Israel demand repeatedly. "There is no other god beside me."[149] Yet the monotheism of these priests had not made them intolerant, bloodthirsty, or cruel; rather, the reverse is true.

Other postexilic prophets were more aggressive. Inspired by Darius's ideology, they looked forward to a "day of wonder" when Yahweh would rule the entire world and there would be no mercy for nations who resisted: "Their flesh will moulder while they are still standing on their feet; their eyes will rot in their sockets; their tongues will rot in their mouths."[150] They imagined Israel's former enemies processing meekly each year to Jerusalem, the new Susa, bearing rich gifts and tribute.[151] Others had fantasies of the Israelites who had been deported by Assyria being carried tenderly home,[152] while their former oppressors prostrated themselves before them and kissed their feet.[153] One prophet had a vision of Yahweh's glory shining over Jerusalem, the center of a redeemed world and a haven of peace—yet a peace achieved only by ruthless repression.

These prophets may have been inspired by the new monotheism. It seems that a strong monarchy often generates the cult of a supreme deity, creator of the political and natural order. A century or more of experiencing the strong rule of such monarchs as Nebuchadnezzar and Darius may have led to the desire to make Yahweh as powerful as they. It is a fine example of the "embeddedness" of religion and politics, which works two ways: not only does religion affect policy, but politics can shape theology. Yet these prophets were also surely motivated by that all-too-human desire to see their enemies suffer as they had—an impulse that the Golden Rule had been designed to modify. They would not be the last to adapt the aggressive ideology of the ruling power to their own traditions and, in so doing, distort them. In this case Yahweh, originally the fierce opponent of the violence and cruelty of empire, had been transformed into an arch imperialist.

Part Two

KEEPING THE PEACE

5

Jesus: Not of This World?

Jesus of Nazareth was born in the reign of the Roman emperor Cae- sar Augustus (r. 30 BCE–14 CE), when all the world was at peace.[1] Under Roman rule, a large group of nations, some of them former impe- rial powers, were able for a significant period to coexist without fight- ing one another for resources and territory—a remarkable achievement.[2] Romans made the three claims that characterize any successful imperial ideology: they had been specially blessed by the gods; in their dualist vision, all other peoples were "barbarians" with whom it was impossible to deal on equal terms; and their mission was to bring the benefits of civilization and peace to the rest of the world. But the Pax Romana was enforced pitilessly.[3] Rome's fully professional army became the most effi- cient killing machine the world had ever seen.[4] Any resistance at all justi- fied wholesale massacre. When they took a city, said the Greek historian Polybius, their policy was "to kill everyone they met and spare no one"— not even the animals.[5] After the Roman conquest of Britain, the Scot- tish leader Calgacus reported that the island had become a wasteland: "The uttermost parts of Britain are laid bare; there are no other tribes to come; nothing but sea and cliffs and more deadly Romans . . . To plun- der, butcher and ravage—these things they falsely name empire."[6]

Polybius understood that the purpose of this savagery was "to strike terror" in the subject nations.[7] It usually worked, but it took the Romans nearly two hundred years to tame the Jews of Palestine, who had ousted an imperial power before and believed they could do it again. After Alexander the Great had defeated the Persian Empire in 333 BCE, Judea had been absorbed into the Ptolemid and Seleucid Empires of his "successors" (*diadochoi*). Most of these rulers did not interfere in the personal lives of their subjects. But in 175 BCE the Seleucid emperor Antiochus IV attempted a drastic reform of the temple cult and banned Jewish dietary laws, circumcision, and Sabbath observance. The Hasmonean priestly family, led by Judas Maccabeus, had led a rebellion and managed not only to wrest Judea and Jerusalem from Seleucid control but even to establish a small empire by conquering Idumaea, Samaria, and Galilee.[8]

These events inspired a new apocalyptic spirituality without which it is impossible to understand the early Christian movement. Crucial to this mind-set was the perennial philosophy: events on earth were an *apokalupsis,* an "unveiling" that revealed what was simultaneously happening in the heavenly world. As they struggled to make sense of current events, the authors of these new scriptures believed that while the Maccabees were fighting the Seleucids, Michael and his angels were battling the demonic powers that supported Antiochus.[9] The book of Daniel, a historical novella composed during the Maccabean wars, was set in Babylonia during the Jewish exile. At its center was the Judean prophet Daniel's vision of four terrifying beasts, representing the empires of Assyria, Babylon, Persia, and finally, Antiochus's Seleucid Empire, the most destructive of all. But then, "coming on the clouds of heaven," Daniel saw "one like the son of man" representing the Maccabees. Unlike the four bestial empires, their rule would be just and humane, and God would give them "an eternal sovereignty which shall never pass away."[10]

Once they had achieved imperial rule, alas, the Hasmoneans' piety was unable to sustain the brute realities of political dominance, and they became as cruel and tyrannical as the Seleucids. At the end of the second century BCE, a number of new sects sought a more authentically Jewish alternative; Christianity would later share some of their enthusiasms. To initiate their disciples, all these sects set up systems of instruction that became the closest thing to an educational establishment in Jewish society. Both the Qumran sect and the Essenes—two distinct groups that are often erroneously identified—were attracted toward an ethical community life: meals were eaten together, ritual purity and cleanliness were stressed, and goods were held in common. Both were critical of the Jerusalem temple cult, which, they believed, the Hasmoneans had corrupted.

Indeed, the Qumran commune beside the Dead Sea regarded itself as an alternative temple: on the cosmic plane, the children of light would soon defeat the sons of darkness, and God would build another temple and inaugurate a new world order. The Pharisees were also committed to an exact and punctilious observance of the biblical law. We know very little about them at this date, however, even though they would become the most influential of these new groups. Some Pharisees led armed revolts against the Hasmoneans but finally concluded that the people would be better off under foreign rule. In 64 BCE, therefore, as the Hasmonean excesses had become intolerable, the Pharisees sent a delegation to Rome requesting that the empire depose the regime.

The following year the Roman warlord Pompey invaded Jerusalem, killing twelve thousand Jews and enslaving thousands more. Not surprisingly, most Jews hated Roman rule, but no empire can survive unless it is able to co-opt at least some of the local population. The Romans ruled Palestine through the priestly aristocracy in Jerusalem, but they also created a puppet king, Herod, a prince of Idumea and a recent convert to Judaism. Herod built magnificent fortifications, palaces, and theaters throughout the country in the Hellenistic style and on the coast constructed Caesarea, an entirely new city, in honor of Augustus. His masterpiece, however, was a magnificent new temple for Yahweh in Jerusalem, flanked significantly by the Antonia fortress, manned by Roman troops. A cruel ruler, with his own army and secret police, Herod was extremely unpopular. The Jews of Palestine were therefore ruled by two aristocracies: the Herodians and the Sadducees, the Jewish priestly nobility. Both collected taxes, so Jews bore a double tax burden.[11]

Like all agrarian ruling classes, both aristocracies employed an order of dependent retainers, who in return for extending their masters' influence among the common people enjoyed higher social status and a share in the surplus.[12] They included the publicans, or tax farmers, who in the Roman Empire were obliged to pass on a fixed sum to the colonial government but were allowed to retain the difference between that and what they managed to extort from the peasants. As a result, they gained a certain independence, but as is apparent in the gospels, they were hated by the common people.[13] The "scribes and Pharisees" of the gospels were another group of retainers who interpreted the Torah, Jewish custumal law, in a way that supported the regime.[14] Not all Pharisees assumed this role, however. Most concentrated on the stringent observance of the

Torah and the development of what would become rabbinic exegesis, and did not ally themselves too closely with the nobility. Had they done so, they would not have retained their popularity with the people. Indeed, so great was the esteem in which they were held that any Jew who hoped for a political career had to study civil law with the Pharisees. Josephus, the first-century-CE Jewish historian, for example, probably became a disciple of the Pharisees to acquire the legal education that qualified him for public life, although he may never have become a full member of the sect.[15]

Once colonized, a people often depends heavily on their religious practices, over which they still have some control and which recall a time when they had the dignity of freedom. In the Jewish case, hostility toward their rulers tended to reach new heights during the important temple festivals, which spoke explosively to the Jews' political subjugation: Passover commemorated Israel's liberation from Egypt's imperial control; Pentecost celebrated the revelation of the Torah, a divine law that superseded all imperial edicts; and the harvest festival of Weeks was a reminder that the land and its produce belonged to Yahweh and not the Romans. This simmering discontent erupted in 4 BCE, when Herod was on his deathbed. He had recently installed in the temple a large golden eagle, symbol of imperial Rome, and Judas and Matthias, two of the most respected Torah teachers, denounced it as an offensive challenge to Yahweh's kingship.[16] In a well-planned protest, forty of their students climbed onto the temple roof, hacked the eagle to pieces, and then courageously awaited the attack of Herod's soldiers.[17] Galvanized by fury, Herod rose from his bed and sentenced the students and their teachers to death, before dying in agony himself two days later.[18]

It is important to note that most of the protests against imperial rule in Roman Palestine were nonviolent; far from being fanatically driven to suicidal aggression by their faith, as Josephus would later suggest, Jews conducted principled demonstrations that resorted to armed force only under extreme pressure. When angry crowds protested against the cruel death of their beloved teachers, Archelaus, Herod's eldest son, asked them what he could do for them. The response reveals that their hostility to Rome was not solely inspired by religious intransigence: "Some clamoured for a lightening of direct taxation, some for the abolition of purchase-tax, others for the release of prisoners."[19] Even though Jerusalem still rang with lamentation, there was no violence against the authorities until Archelaus panicked and sent troops into the temple. Even then the crowds merely pelted them with stones before returning to their devotions. The situation could have been contained, had not Archelaus sent in the army, which killed three thousand worshippers.[20] Protests then spread to the countryside, where popular leaders, acclaimed as "kings," waged guerrilla warfare against Roman and Herodian troops. Again, taxation rather than religion was the main issue. Mobs attacked the estates of the nobility and raided local fortresses, storehouses, and Roman baggage trains to "take back the goods that had been seized from the people."[21] It took P. Quintilius Varus, governor of neighboring Syria, three years to restore the Pax Romana, during which he burned the Galilean city of Sepphoris to the ground, sacked the surrounding villages, and crucified two thousand rebels outside Jerusalem.[22]

Rome now decided that Herod's realm should be divided among his three sons: Archelaus was given Idumaea, Judea, and Samaria; Antipas Galilee and Peraea; and Philip the Transjordan. But Archelaus's rule was so cruel that Rome soon deposed him, and for the first time Judea was governed by a Roman prefect, supported by the Jewish priestly aristocracy, from his residence in Caesarea. When Coponius, the first governor, arranged for a census as a prelude to tax assessment, a Galilean named Judas urged the people to resist. His religious commitment was inseparable from his political protest:[23] paying Roman taxes, Judas insisted, "amounted to slavery, pure and simple," because God was "the only leader and master" of the Jewish people. If they remained steadfast in their opposition and did not shrink "from the slaughter that might come upon them," God would intervene and act on their behalf. [24]

Typically peasants did not resort to violence. Their chief weapon was noncooperation: working slowly or even refraining from work altogether, making their point economically and often cannily. Most Roman governors were careful to avoid offending Jewish sensibilities, but in 26 CE Pontius Pilate ordered the troops in the Antonia fortress to raise military standards displaying the emperor's portrait right next to the temple. At once a mob of peasants and townsfolk marched to Caesarea, and when Pilate refused to remove the standards, they simply lay motionless outside his residence for five days. When Pilate summoned them to the stadium, they found that they were surrounded by soldiers with drawn swords and fell to the ground again, crying that they would rather die than break their laws. They may have relied on divine intervention, but they also knew that Pilate would risk massive reprisals had he slaughtered them all. And they were right: the Roman governor had to admit defeat and take down the standards.[25] The chances of such a bloodless outcome were much slimmer when, fourteen years later, Emperor Gaius Caligula would order his statue to be erected in the Jerusalem temple. Once again the peasants took to the road, "as if at a single signal . . . leaving their houses and villages empty."[26] When the legate Petronius arrived at the port of Ptolemais with the offending statue, he found "tens of thousands of Jews" with their wives and children massed on the plain in front of the city. Again, this was not a violent protest. "On no account would we fight," they told Petronius, but they were prepared to remain in Ptolemais until after the planting season.[27] This was a politically savvy peasants' strike: Petronius had to explain to the emperor "that since the land was unsown, there would be a harvest of banditry, because the requirements of the tribute would not be met."[28] Caligula was rarely moved by rational considerations, however, and the episode could have ended tragically had he not been assassinated the following year.

These peasant communities may have voiced their opposition to Roman rule in terms of their egalitarian Jewish traditions, but they were neither crazed by their fervor nor violent or suicidal. Later popular movements failed because their leaders were less astute. During the 50s CE a prophet called Theudas would lead four hundred people into the Judean desert in a new exodus, convinced that if the people took the initiative, God would send deliverance.[29] Another rebel leader marched a crowd of thirty thousand through the desert to the Mount of Olives, "ready to force an entry into Jerusalem, overwhelm the Roman garrison, and seize supreme power."[30] These movements had no political leverage and were ruthlessly put down. Both these protests were inspired by the apocalyptic and perennial belief that activity on earth could influence events on the cosmic plane. This was the political context of Jesus's mission in the villages of Galilee.

◆　◆　◆

Jesus was born into a society traumatized by violence. His life was framed by revolts. The uprisings after Herod's death occurred in the year of his birth, and he was brought up in the hamlet of Nazareth, only a few miles from Sepphoris, which Varus had razed to the ground; the peasants' strike against Caligula would occur just ten years after his death. During his lifetime, Galilee was governed by Herod Antipas, who financed an expensive building program by imposing heavy taxes on his Galilean subjects. Failure to pay was punished by foreclosure and confiscation of land, and this revenue swelled the huge estates of the Herodian aristocrats.[31] When they lost their land, some peasants were forced into banditry, while others—Jesus's father, the carpenter Joseph, perhaps, among them—turned to menial labor: artisans were often failed peasants.[32] The crowds who thronged around Jesus in Galilee were hungry, distressed, and sick. In his parables we see a society split between the very rich and the very poor: people who are desperate for loans; peasants who are heavily indebted; and the dispossessed who have to hire themselves out as day laborers.[33]

Even though the gospels were written in an urban milieu decades after the events they describe, they still reflect the political aggression and cruelty of Roman Palestine. After Jesus's birth, King Herod slaughtered all the male infants of Bethlehem, recalling Pharaoh, the archetypal evil imperialist.[34] John the Baptist, Jesus's cousin, was executed by Herod Antipas.[35] Jesus predicted that his disciples would be pursued, flogged, and killed by the Jewish authorities,[36] and he himself was arrested by the high-priestly aristocracy and tortured and crucified by Pontius Pilate. From the start, the gospels present Jesus as an alternative to the structural violence of imperial rule. Roman coins, inscriptions, and temples extolled Augustus, who had brought peace to the world after a century of brutal warfare, as "Son of God," "lord," and "savior" and announced the "good news" (*euaggelia*) of his birth. Thus when the angel announced the birth of Jesus to the shepherds, he proclaimed: "Listen, I bring you *euaggelion* of great joy! Today a Savior has been born to you." Yet this "son of God" was born homeless and would soon become a refugee.[37]

One sign of the acute distress of the population was the large number of people afflicted with neurological and psychological symptoms attributed to demons who came to Jesus for healing. He and his disciples seem to have had the skill to "exorcise" these disorders.[38] When they cast out demons, Jesus explained, they were replicating God's victory over Satan in the cosmic sphere. "I watched Satan fall like lightning from Heaven," he told his disciples when they returned from a successful healing tour.[39] So-called spirit possession seems often linked with economic, sexual, or colonial oppression, when people feel taken over by an alien power they cannot control.[40] In one telling incident, when Jesus cast out a host of demons from a possessed man, these satanic forces told him that their name was "legion," identifying themselves with the Roman troops that were the most blatant symbol of the occupation. Jesus did what many colonized people would like to do: he cast "legion" into a herd of swine, the most polluted of animals, which rushed headlong into the sea.[41] The ruling class seems to have regarded Jesus's exorcisms as politically provocative: they were the reason Antipas decided to take action against him.[42]

In Jesus's mission, therefore, politics and religion were inextricable. The event that may have led to his death was his provocative entrance into Jerusalem at Passover, when he was hailed by the crowds as "Son of David" and "king of Israel."[43] He then staged a demonstration in the temple itself, turning over the money changers' tables and declaring that God's house was a "den of thieves."[44] This was not, as is sometimes assumed, a plea for a more spiritual style of worship. Judea had been a temple state since the Persian period, so the temple had long been an instrument of imperial control, and the tribute was stored there—although the high priests' collaboration with Rome had recently brought the institution into such disrepute that peasants were refusing to pay the temple tithes.[45] But neither did Jesus's preoccupation with imperial misrule mean that he was "confusing" religion with politics. As he upturned the tables, he quoted the prophets who had severely castigated those who ignored the plight of the poor but whose religious observance was punctilious. Oppression, injustice, and exploitation had always been religiously charged issues in Israel. The idea that faith should not involve itself in such politics would have been as alien to Jesus as it had been to Confucius.

It is not easy to assess Jesus's attitude to violence, but there is no evidence that he was planning military insurrection. He forbade his disciples to injure others and to retaliate aggressively.[46] He did not resist his arrest and rebuked the disciple who cut off the ear of the high priest's servant.[47] But he could be verbally abusive: he fulminated against the rich;[48] cruelly lambasted those "scribes and Pharisees" who served as retainers;[49] and called down God's vengeance on villages that rejected his disciples.[50] As we have seen, the Jewish peasants of Palestine had a tradition of nonviolent opposition to imperial rule, and Jesus knew that any confrontation with either the Jewish or the Roman ruling class—he did not distinguish the two—would be dangerous. Any disciple, he warned, must be ready to "take up his cross."[51] It seems that, like Judas of Galilee, Jesus may have relied on God to intervene. While she was pregnant with him, his mother had predicted that God had already begun to create a more just world order:

> He has shown the power of his arm
> He has routed the proud of heart.
> He has pulled down princes from their thrones and exalted the
>   lowly.
> The hungry he has filled with good things; the rich sent empty
>   away.
> He has come to the help of Israel his servant.[52]

Like Judas the Galilean, Jesus may have believed that if his disciples did not shrink "from the slaughter that would come upon them" and took the first step, God would overthrow the rich and powerful.

One day the Pharisees and Herodian retainers asked Jesus a trick question: "Is it permissible to pay taxes to Caesar or not? Should we pay, yes or no?" Taxation was always an inflammable issue in Roman Palestine, and if Jesus said no, he risked arrest. Pointing to Caesar's name and image on the denarius, the coin of tribute, Jesus replied: "Give back [*apodote*] to Caesar what belongs to Caesar and to God what belongs to God."[53] In a purely imperial context, Caesar's claim was legitimate: the Greek verb was used for a rendition made when one recognized a rightful claim.[54] But as all Jews knew that God was their king and that everything belonged to him, there was in fact little to "give back" to Caesar. In Mark's gospel, Jesus followed this incident with a warning to the retainers who helped to implement Roman rule and trampled on the poor and vulnerable: "Beware of the scribes who like to walk about in long robes, to be greeted obsequiously in the market squares, to take the front seats in the synagogues and the places of honor at banquets; these are the men who swallow the property of widows, while making a show of lengthy prayers."[55] When God finally established his kingdom, their sentence would be severe.

That Kingdom of God was at the heart of Jesus's teaching.[56] Setting up an alternative to the violence and oppression of imperial rule could hasten the moment when God's power would finally transform the human condition. So his followers must behave *as if* the kingdom had already arrived.[57] Jesus could not drive the Romans from the country, but the "kingdom" he proclaimed, based on justice and equity, was open to everybody—especially those whom the current regime had failed. You should not merely invite your friends and rich neighbors to a festivity, he told his host: "No, when you have a party, invite the poor, the crippled, the lame, and the blind." Invitations should be issued in "the streets and alleys of the town" and "the open roads and hedgerows."[58] "How happy are you who are destitute [ptochos]," Jesus exclaimed; "yours is the kingdom of God!"[59] The poor were the only people who could be "blessed," because anybody who benefited in any way from the systemic violence of imperial rule was implicated in their plight.[60] "Alas for you who are rich, you are having your consolation now," Jesus continued. "Alas for you who have your fill now; you shall go hungry."[61] In God's Kingdom, the first would be last and the last first.[62] The Lord's Prayer is for people who were terrified of falling into debt and could hope only for bare subsistence, one day at a time: "Give us today our daily bread. And forgive us our debts, as we forgive those who are in debt to us. And do not put us to the test, but save us from the evil one."[63] Jesus and his closest companions threw in their lot with the most indigent peasants; they lived rough, itinerant lives, had nowhere to lay their heads, and depended on the support of Jesus's more affluent disciples, such as Lazarus and his sisters Martha and Mary. [64]

Yet the kingdom was not a utopia that would be established at some distant date. At the very beginning of his mission, Jesus had announced: "The time has come and the Kingdom of God has already arrived."[65] The active presence of God was evident in Jesus's miracles of healing. Everywhere he looked, he saw people pushed to the limit, abused, crushed, and desperate: "He felt sorry for them because they were harassed [eskulmenoi] and dejected [errimmenoi], like a sheep without a shepherd."[66] The Greek verbs have political connotations of being "beaten down" by imperial predation.[67] These people would have been suffering from the hard labor, poor sanitation, overcrowding, indebtedness, and anxiety commonly endured by the masses in agrarian society.[68] Jesus's kingdom challenged the cruelty of Roman Judea and Herodian Galilee by approximating more closely to God's will—"on earth as it is in heaven."[69] Those who feared indebtedness must release others from debts; they had to "love" even their enemies, giving them practical and moral support. Instead of taking violent reprisals, like the Romans, people in God's kingdom would live according to the Golden Rule: "To the man who slaps you on one cheek, present the other cheek too; to the man who takes your cloak from you, do not refuse your tunic. Give to everyone who asks you, and do not ask for your property back from the man who robs you. Treat others as you would like them to treat you."[70] Jesus's followers must live as compassionately as God himself, giving generously to all and refraining from judgment and condemnation.[71]

·   ·   ·

After his crucifixion, Jesus's disciples had visions that convinced them that he had been raised to the right hand of God and would shortly return to inaugurate the kingdom definitively.[72] Jesus had worked in rural Roman Palestine and had generally avoided the towns and cities.[73] But Paul, a diaspora Jew from Tarsus in Cilicia, who had not known Jesus, believed that he had been commissioned by God to bring the "good news" of the gospel to the gentile world, so he preached in the Greco-Roman cities along the major trade routes in Asia Minor, Greece, and Macedonia. This was a very different milieu: Paul's converts could not beg for their bread but had to work for their living, as he did, and a significant number of his converts may have been men and women of means. Writing in the 50s CE, Paul is the earliest extant Christian author, and his teachings influenced the accounts of Jesus's life in the gospels of Mark, Matthew, and Luke (known as the Synoptics), written in the 70s and 80s. And while the Synoptics drew upon the earliest Palestinian traditions about Jesus, they were writing in an urban environment permeated by Greco-Roman religion.

Neither the Greeks nor the Romans had ever separated religion from secular life. They would not have understood our modern understanding of "religion." They had no authoritative scriptures, no compulsory beliefs, no distinct clergy, and no obligatory ethical rules. There was no ontological gulf separating the gods from men and women; each human being had a *numen* or *genius* that was divine, and gods regularly took human form. Gods were part of the citizen body so the Greco-Roman city was essentially a religious community. Each city had its own divine patron, and civic pride, financial interest, and piety were intertwined in a way that would seem strange in our secularized world. Participation in the religious festivals in honor of the city's gods was essential to city life: there were no public holidays or weekends, so the Lupercalia in

Rome and the Panathenaea in Athens were rare opportunities for relaxation and celebration. These rituals defined what it meant to be a Roman or an Athenian, put the city on show, invested civic life with transcendent meaning, presented the community at its best, and gave citizens a sense of belonging to a civic family. Participating in these rituals was just as important as any personal devotion to the gods. To belong to a city, therefore, was to worship its gods—though it was perfectly acceptable to worship other deities too.[74]

This was potentially problematic for Paul's Jewish and gentile converts in Antioch, Corinth, Philippi, and Ephesus, who, as monotheists, regarded Roman religion as idolatrous. Judaism was respected as a tradition of great antiquity, and Jews' avoidance of the public cult was accepted in the Roman Empire. At this point, Judaism and Christianity were not yet distinct traditions:[75] Paul's gentile converts saw themselves as part of a new Israel.[76] But in the crowded Greco-Roman cities, Christians often came into conflict with the local synagogue and, when they proudly claimed to belong to a "new Israel," seemed to be behaving with impiety toward the parent faith—an attitude that Romans deplored.[77] Paul's letters show that he was concerned that his converts were becoming conspicuous in a society where difference and novelty could be dangerous. He urged them to observe the customary dress codes,[78] to behave with the decorum and self-control expected of Roman citizens, and to avoid excessively ecstatic demonstrations of piety.[79] Instead of defying the Roman authorities, Paul preached obedience and respect: "You must all obey the governing authorities. Since all government comes from God, the civil authorities are appointed by God, and so anyone who resists authority is rebelling against God's decisions."[80] Rome was not an evil empire but the guarantor of order and stability, so Christians must pay their taxes, "since all government officials are God's officers. They serve God by collecting taxes."[81] But Paul knew that this was only a temporary state of affairs, because Jesus's kingdom would be established on earth in his own lifetime: "The world as we know it is passing away."[82]

While waiting for Jesus's triumphant return, members of his community (ekklesia) should live as Jesus had taught them—kindly, supportively, and generously. They would create an alternative to the structural violence of imperial rule and the self-serving policies of the aristocracy. When they celebrated the Lord's Supper, the communal meal in Jesus's memory, rich and poor should sit at the same table and share the same food. Early Christianity was not a private affair between the individual and God: people derived their faith in Jesus from the experience of living together in a close-knit, minority community that challenged the unequal distribution of wealth and power in stratified Roman society. No doubt the author of the Acts of the Apostles gives an idealized picture of the early ekklesia in Jerusalem, but it reflected a Christian ideal:

> The whole group of believers was united, heart and soul; no one claimed for his own use anything that he had, as everything they owned was held in common . . . None of their members was ever in want, as all those who owned land or houses would sell them, and bring the money from them, to present it to the apostles; it was then distributed to any members who might be in need.[83]

Living in this way gave Christians intimations of new possibilities in humanity epitomized in the man Jesus, whose self-abnegation had raised him to God's right hand. All former social divisions, Paul insisted, had become irrelevant: "In the one Spirit we were all baptized, Jews as well as Greeks, slaves as well as citizens." This sacred community of people who previously had nothing in common made up the body of the risen Christ.[84] In one memorable story, Luke, the evangelist who was closest to Paul, showed that Christians would come to know the risen Jesus not by a solitary mystical experience but by opening their hearts to the stranger, reading their scriptures together, and eating at the same table.[85]

Despite Paul's best efforts, however, the early Christians would never fit easily into Greco-Roman society. They held aloof from the public celebrations and civic sacrifices that bound the city together and revered a man who had been executed by a Roman governor. They called Jesus "lord" (*kyrios*), but this had nothing in common with the conventional aristocracy, which clung to status and regarded the poor with disdain.[86] Paul quoted an early Christian hymn to the Philippian ekklesia, to remind them that God had bestowed the title of kyrios on Jesus because he had "emptied himself [*heauton ekenosen*] to assume the condition of a slave . . . and was humbler yet, even to accepting death, death on a cross."[87] The ideal of *kenosis,* "emptying," would become crucial to Christian spirituality. "In your minds, you must be the same as Christ Jesus," Paul told the Philippians. "There must be no competition among you, no conceit; but everybody is to be self-effacing. Always consider the other person to be better than yourself, so that nobody thinks of his own interests first, but everybody thinks of other people's interests instead."[88] Like the followers of Confucius and Buddha, Christians were cultivating ideals of reverence and selflessness that countered the aggressive self-assertion of the warrior aristocracy.

A tightly knit and isolated community, however, can develop an exclusivity that ostracizes others. In Asia Minor a number of Jewish-Christian communities, who traced their origins to the ministry of Jesus's apostle John, had developed a different view of Jesus. Paul and the Synoptics had never regarded Jesus as God; the very idea would have horrified Paul who, before his conversion, had been an exceptionally punctilious Pharisee. They all used the term "Son of God" in the conventional Jewish sense: Jesus had been an ordinary human being commissioned by God with a special task. Even in his exalted state, there was, for Paul, always a clear distinction between Jesus *kyrios Christos* and God, his Father. The author of the Fourth Gospel, however, depicted Jesus as a cosmic being, God's eternal "Word" (*logos*) who had existed with God before the beginning of time.[89] This high Christology seems to have separated this group from other Jewish-Christian communities. Their writings were composed for an "in-group" with a private symbolism that was incomprehensible to outsiders. In the Fourth Gospel, Jesus frequently baffles his audience by his enigmatic remarks. For these so-called Johannine Christians, having the correct view of Jesus seemed more important than working for the coming of the kingdom. They too had an ethic of love, but it was reserved only for loyal members of the group; they turned their backs on "the world,"[90] condemning defectors as "anti-Christs" and "children of the devil."[91] Spurned and misunderstood, they had developed a dualistic vision of a world polarized into light and darkness, good and evil, life and death. Their most extreme scripture was the book of Revelation, probably written while the Jews of Palestine were fighting a desperate war against the Roman Empire.[92] The author, John of Patmos, was convinced that the days of the Beast, the evil empire, were numbered. Jesus was about to return, ride into battle, slay the Beast, fling him into a pit of fire, and establish his kingdom for a thousand years. Paul had taught his converts that Jesus, the victim of imperial violence, had achieved a spiritual and cosmic victory over sin and death. John, however, depicted Jesus, who had taught his followers not to retaliate violently, as a ruthless warrior who would defeat

Rome with massive slaughter and bloodshed. Revelation was admitted to the Christian canon only with great difficulty, but it would be scanned eagerly in times of social unrest when people were yearning for a more just and equitable world.

◆ ◆ ◆

The Jewish revolt had broken out in Jerusalem in 66 after the Roman governor had commandeered money from the temple treasury. Not everybody supported it. The Pharisees in particular feared that it would make trouble for diaspora Jews, but the new party of Zealots (*kanaim*) thought that they had a good chance of success because the empire was currently split by internal dissension. They managed to drive out the Roman garrison and set up a provisional government, but the emperor Nero responded by dispatching a massive army to Judea led by Vespasian, his most gifted general. Hostilities were suspended during the disturbances that followed Nero's death in 68, but after Vespasian became emperor, his son Titus took over the siege of Jerusalem, forced the Zealots to capitulate, and on August 28, 70, burned city and temple to the ground.

In the Middle East, a temple carried such symbolic weight that an ethnic tradition could barely sustain its loss.[93] Judaism owed its survival to a group of scholars led by Yohanan ben Zakkai, leader of the Pharisees, who transformed a faith based on temple worship into a religion of the book.[94] In the coastal town of Yavneh, they began to compile three new scriptures: the Mishnah, completed around 200, and the Jerusalem and Babylonian Talmuds, which reached their final form in the fifth and sixth centuries respectively. At first, most of the rabbis probably assumed that the temple would be rebuilt, but those hopes were quashed when the emperor Hadrian visited Judea in 130 and announced that he would build a new city called Aelia Capitolina on the ruins of Jerusalem. The following year, as part of his policy of uniting the empire culturally, he outlawed circumcision, the ordination of rabbis, the teaching of the Torah, and public Jewish gatherings. Inevitably, perhaps, there was another revolt, and the tough Jewish soldier Simon bar Koseba planned his guerrilla campaign so skillfully that he held Rome at bay for three years. Rabbi Akiva, a leading Yavneh scholar, hailed him as the messiah, calling him Bar Kokhba ("Son of the Star").[95] But Rome finally gained control, systematically destroying almost a thousand Jewish villages and killing 580,000 Jewish rebels, while countless civilians were either burned to death or died of hunger and disease.[96] After the war, Jews were expelled from Judea and would not be permitted to return for over five hundred years.

The violence of this imperial assault profoundly affected Rabbinic Judaism. Instead of allowing Jews to bring their more aggressive traditions to the fore, they deliberately marginalized them, determined to prevent any more catastrophic military adventures.[97] In their new academies in Babylonia and Galilee, they therefore evolved a method of exegesis that excised any adulation of chauvinism or belligerence. They were not particularly peaceable men—they fought their scholarly battles fiercely—but they were pragmatists.[98] They had learned that Jewish tradition could survive only if Jews learned to rely on spiritual rather than physical strength.[99] They could not afford any more heroic messiahs.[100] They recalled Rabbi Yohanan's advice: "If there is a seedling in your hand and you are informed 'King Messiah has arrived,' first plant your seedling and then go forth to greet him."[101] Other rabbis went further: "Let him come, but let me not see him!"[102] Rome was a fact of life, and Jews must come to terms with it.[103] The rabbis scoured their biblical and oral traditions to show that God had decreed Rome's imperial power.[104] They praised Roman technology and instructed Jews to make a blessing whenever they saw a gentile king.[105] They devised new rules forbidding Jews to bear arms on the Sabbath or to bring weapons into the House of Studies, because violence was incompatible with Torah scholarship.

The rabbis made it clear that instead of being an inflammatory force, religious activity could be used to quell violence. They either ignored the bellicose passages of the Hebrew Bible or gave them a radically new interpretation. They called their exegetical method *midrash*—a word derived from *darash:* "to investigate; go in search of something." The meaning of scripture was not, therefore, self-evident; it had to be ferreted out by diligent study, and because it was God's word, it was infinite and could not be confined to a single interpretation. Indeed, every time a Jew confronted the sacred text, it should mean something different.[106] The rabbis felt free to argue with God, defy him, and even change the words of scripture to introduce a more compassionate reading.[107] Yes, God was often described as a divine warrior in the Bible, but Jews must imitate only his compassionate behavior.[108] The true hero was no longer a warrior but a man of peace. "Who is the hero of heroes?" asked the rabbis. "He who turns an enemy into a friend."[109] A "mighty" man did not prove his mettle on the battlefield but was one "who subdues his passions."[110] When the prophet Isaiah had seemed to praise a soldier "who thrusts back his attacker to the gate," he was really speaking of "those who thrust a parry in the way of Torah."[111] The rabbis described Joshua and David as pious Torah scholars and even argued that David had had no interest in warfare at all.[112] When the Egyptian army drowned in the Sea of Reeds, some of the angels had wanted to sing Yahweh's praises, but he had rebuked them: "My children lie drowned in the sea, and you would sing?"[113]

The rabbis acknowledged that there were divinely ordained wars in their scriptures. They concluded that the campaigns against the Canaanites had been "obligatory" wars, but the Babylonian rabbis ruled that because these peoples no longer existed, warfare could no longer be compulsory.[114] The Palestinian rabbis, however, whose position in Roman Palestine was more precarious, argued that Jews were still obliged to fight sometimes—but only in self-defense.[115] David's territorial wars had been "discretionary," but the rabbis pointed out that even kings had to ask permission of the Sanhedrin, the Jewish governing body, before taking the field. Yet they concluded that because the monarchy and Sanhedrin were no more, discretionary wars were no longer legitimate. They also interpreted a verse in the Song of Songs in such a way as to discourage mass uprisings that could lead to gentile reprisals: "I charge you, daughters of Jerusalem, by the gazelles, by the hinds of the field, not to stir my love, nor rouse it, till it please to awake."[116] Israelites must not take provocative action ("to stir love"); there must be no mass migrations to the Land of Israel and no more rebellions against gentile rule until God issued a directive ("till it please to awake"). If they remained quiet, God would not permit persecution, but if they disobeyed, they would, "like the hinds of the field," be fair game for gentile violence.[117] This abstruse piece of exegesis effectively put a brake on Jewish political action for over a millennium.[118]

· · ·

By the middle of the third century CE, the Roman Empire was in crisis. The new Sassanian dynasty in Persia had conquered Roman territory in Cilicia, Syria, and Cappadocia; the Gothic tribes in the Danube basin continuously attacked the frontier; and Germanic warrior bands harried Roman garrisons in the Rhine Valley. In a short span of sixteen years (268–84), eight emperors were assassinated by their own troops. The economy was in ruins, and local aristocracies fought for power in the cities.[119] Rome was eventually saved by a military revolution, led by professional soldiers from the frontier region, which transformed the Roman army.[120] Aristocrats no longer filled the top positions, the army doubled in size, and legions were broken up into smaller, more flexible detachments. A mobile cavalry force, the *comitatus,* supported the garrisons on the borders, and for the first time Roman citizens were taxed to finance the army. By the end of the third century, the barbarians in the Balkans and northern Italy had been repulsed, the Persian advance had been halted, and Rome had recovered its lost territory. The new Roman emperors were no longer of noble birth: Diocletian (r. 284–305) was the son of a freedman of Dalmatia, Galerius (r. 305–11) a former cattle herder in Carpathia, and Constantius Chlorus (r. 305–06) an undistinguished country gentleman from Nis. They centralized the empire, taking direct control of taxation instead of leaving it to the local nobility, and most significantly, Diocletian shared power with three co-emperors by creating the *tetrarchy* ("rule of four"): Maximian and Constantius Chlorus governed the western provinces, and Diocletian ruled in the east with Galerius.[121]

The third-century crisis brought Christianity to the attention of the imperial authorities. Christians had never been popular; by refusing to take part in the civic cult, they seemed suspicious and easily became scapegoats at times of social tension. According to Tacitus, Nero had blamed Christians for the great fire of Rome and put many to death— these people may be the martyrs seated near God's throne in the book of Revelation.[122] The North African theologian Tertullian (c. 160–220) complained: "If the Tiber rises to the walls, if the Nile fails to rise and flood the fields, if the sky withholds its rain, if there is earthquake or famine or plague, straightway the cry arises: 'The Christians to the lions!' "[123] But it was not customary for an agrarian ruling class to interfere with the religious lives of its subjects, and the empire had no standard policy of persecution. In 112, when Pliny, governor of Bithynia, asked the emperor Trajan how he should treat Christians who were brought before him, Trajan replied that there was no official procedure. Christians should not be actively hunted out, he advised, but if they came before the courts for some reason and refused to sacrifice to the Roman gods, they should be executed for defying the imperial government. Christians who did die in this way were venerated in their communities, and the Acts of the Martyrs, which told the stories of their deaths in lurid detail, were read aloud in the liturgy.

Yet against all odds, by the third century Christianity had become a force to be reckoned with. We still do not really understand how this came about.[124] It has been suggested that the rise of other new religious movements in the empire had made Christianity appear less bizarre. People were now seeking the divine in a human being who was a "friend of God" rather than in a holy place; secret societies, not unlike the Church, were mushrooming throughout the empire. Like Christianity, many of these had originated in the eastern provinces, and they too required a special initiation, offered a new revelation, and demanded a conversion of life.[125] Christianity was also beginning to appeal to merchants and artisans like Paul, who had left their hometowns and taken advantage of the Pax Romana to travel and settle elsewhere; many had lost touch with their roots and were open to new ideas. The egalitarian ethic of Christianity made it popular with the lower classes and slaves. Women found the Church attractive, because the Christian scriptures instructed husbands to treat their wives considerately. Like Stoicism and Epicureanism, Christianity promised inner tranquillity, but its way of life could be followed by the poor and illiterate as well as by members of the aristocracy. The Church had also begun to appeal to some highly intelligent men, such as the Alexandrian Platonist Origen (185–254), who interpreted the faith in a way that interested the educated public. As a result of all this, the Church had become a significant organization. It was not *religio licita,* one of the approved traditions of the empire, so could not own property, but it had ejected some of its wilder elements, and like the empire itself, it claimed to have a single rule of faith; it was multiracial, international, and administered by efficient bureaucrats.[126]

One of the most cogent reasons for the Church's success was its charitable work, which made it a strong presence in the cities. By 250, the church in Rome was feeding fifteen hundred poor people and widows every day, and during a plague or a riot, its clergy were often the only group able to organize food supplies and bury the dead. At a time when the emperors were so preoccupied with defending the frontier that they seemed to have forgotten the cities, the Church had become firmly established there.[127] But in this time of social tension, its prominence could be threatening to the authorities, who now began more systematically to seek Christians out for execution.

It is important to explore the ideal of martyrdom, which has surfaced alarmingly in our own time and is now associated with violence and extremism. Christian martyrs, however, were victims of imperial persecution and did not kill anybody else. The memory of this harassment would loom large in the consciousness of the early Church and shape the Christian worldview. However, until the third-century crisis, there had been no official empire-wide persecution, only sporadic local outbreaks of hostility; even in the third century, there were only about ten years when the Roman authorities intensively pursued Christians.[128] In an agrarian empire the ruling aristocracy expected its religion to be different from that of their subjects, but ever since Augustus, the worship of the gods of Rome was deemed essential to the empire's survival. The Pax Romana was thought to rely on the Pax Deorum, the peace imposed by the gods, who in return for regular sacrifice would guarantee the empire's security and prosperity.

So when Rome's northern frontier was threatened by the barbarian tribes in 250, the emperor Decius ordered all his subjects to sacrifice to his genius to procure the gods' aid on pain of death. This decree was not directed specifically against Christians; moreover, it was difficult to implement, and the authorities do not seem to have hunted down anybody who failed to turn up to the official sacrifice.[129] When Decius was killed in action the following year, the edict was rescinded. In 258, however, Valerian was the first emperor to target the Church specifically, ordering that its clergy be executed and the property of high-ranking Christians confiscated. Once again, not many people seem to have been killed, and two years later Valerian was taken prisoner by the Persians and died in captivity. His successor, Galienus, revoked the legislation, and Christians enjoyed forty years of peace.

Clearly Valerian had been troubled by the Church's organizational strength rather than by its beliefs and rituals. The Church was a new phenomenon. Christians had exploited the empire's improved communications to create an institution with a unity of structure that none of the traditions we have discussed so far had attempted. Each local church was headed by a bishop, the "overseer" who was said to derive his authority from Jesus's apostles, and was supported by presbyters and deacons. The network of such near-identical communities seemed almost to have become an empire within the empire. Irenaeus, the bishop of Lyons (c. 130–200), who was anxious to create an orthodoxy that excluded aggressive sectarians, had claimed that the Great Church had a single Rule of Faith, because the bishops had inherited their teaching directly from the apostles. This was not only a novel idea but a total fantasy. Paul's letters show that there had been considerable tension between him and Jesus's disciples, and his teachings bore little relation to those of Jesus. Each of the Synoptics had his own take on Jesus, and the Johannines were different again; there were also a host of other gospels in circulation. When Christians finally established a scriptural canon— between the fourth and sixth centuries—diverse visions were included side by side.

Unfortunately, however, Christianity would develop a peculiar yearning for intellectual conformity that would not only prove to be unsustainable but that set it apart from other faith traditions. The rabbis would never attempt to create a single central authority; not even God, much less another rabbi, could tell another Jew what to think.[130] The Buddha had adamantly rejected the idea of religious authority; the notion of a single rule of faith and a structured hierarchy was entirely alien to the multifarious traditions of India; and the Chinese were encouraged to see merit in all the great teachers, despite their disagreements.

Christian leaders would make the Church even more threatening to the authorities during the forty peaceful years after Valerian's death. When Diocletian finally established his palace in Nicomedia in 287, a Christian basilica was clearly visible on the opposite hill, seeming to confront the imperial palace as an equal. He made no move against the Church for sixteen years, but as a firm believer in the Pax Deorum at a time when the fate of the empire hung in the balance, Diocletian would find the Christians' stubborn refusal to honor the gods increasingly intolerable.[131] On February 23, 303, he demanded that the presumptuous basilica be demolished; the next day he outlawed Christian meetings and ordered the destruction of churches and the confiscation of Christian scriptures. All men, women, and children were required on pain of execution to gather in the empire's public squares to sacrifice to the gods of Rome. Yet the legislation was implemented in only a few regions and in the West, where there were few Christian communities, hardly any at all. It is difficult to know how many people died as a result. Christians were rarely pursued if they failed to show up for the sacrifice; many apostatized, and others found loopholes.[132] Most of those who were put to death had defiantly presented themselves to the authorities as voluntary martyrs, a practice the bishops condemned.[133] When Diocletian abdicated in 305, these edicts expired, though they were renewed for a period of two years (311–13) by Emperor Maximianus Daia.

The cult of the martyrs, however, became central to Christian piety because they proved that Jesus had not been unique: the Church had "friends of God" with divine powers in its very midst. The martyrs were "other Christs," and their imitation of Christ even unto death had brought him into the present.[134] The Acts of the Martyrs claimed that these heroic deaths were miracles that manifested God's presence because the martyrs seemed impervious to pain. "Let not a day pass when we do not dwell on these tales," Victricius, the fifth-century bishop of Rouen, urged his congregation. "This martyr did not blench under torturers; this martyr hurried up the slow work of the execution; this one eagerly swallowed the flames; this one was cut about but stood up still."[135] "They suffered more than is possible for human beings to bear, and did not endure this by their own strength but by the grace of God," explained Pope Gelasius (r. 492–96).[136] When the Christian slave girl Blandina was executed in Lyons in 177, her companions "looked with their eyes through their sister to the One who was crucified for them."[137]

When the young wife and mother Vibia Perpetua was imprisoned in Carthage in 203, she had a series of remarkable dreams that proved even to her persecutors that she enjoyed special intimacy with the divine. The prison governor himself perceived "that there was a rare power in us," her biographer recalled.[138] Through these "friends of God," Christians could claim respect and even superiority over pagan communities. Yet there would always be more than a hint of aggression in the martyr's "witness" to Christ. On the night before her execution, Perpetua dreamed that she had been turned into a man and wrestled with an Egyptian in the stadium, a man huge and "foul" of aspect, but with an infusion of divine strength, she was able to throw him to the ground. When she woke, she knew that she would not be fighting wild beasts that day but "the Fiend" himself and that "the victory would be mine."[139]

Martyrdom would always be the protest of a minority, yet the violent deaths of the martyrs became a graphic demonstration of the structural violence and cruelty of the state. Martyrdom was and would always be a political as well as a religious choice. Targeted as enemies of the empire and in a relationship of starkly asymmetrical power with the authorities, these Christians' deaths were a defiant assertion of a different allegiance. They had already achieved an eminence that was intrinsically superior to Rome's, and by laying their deaths at the door of the oppressors, the martyrs effectively demonized them. But these Christians were beginning to develop a history of grievance that gave their faith a newly aggressive edge. They were convinced that, like Jesus in the book of Revelation, they were engaged in an ongoing eschatological battle; when they fought, like gladiators, with wild beasts in the stadium, they were battling with demonic powers (embodied in the imperial authorities) that would expedite Jesus's triumphant return.[140] Those who voluntarily presented themselves to the authorities were committing what would later be called "revolutionary suicide." By forcing the authorities to put them to death, they laid bare for all to see the intrinsic violence of the so-called Pax Romana, and their suffering, they firmly believed, would hasten its end.

Other Christians, however, did not regard the empire as satanic; rather, they experienced a remarkable conversion to Rome.[141] Again, this shows that it is impossible to point to an "essential" Christianity that promoted identical courses of action. Origen, for instance, believed that Christianity was the culmination of the classical culture of antiquity; like the Hebrew Scriptures, Greek philosophy had also been an expression of the Logos, the Word of God. The Pax Romana had been providentially ordained. "It would have hindered Jesus' teaching from being spread through the whole world," Origen believed, "if there had been many kingdoms."[142] The statesmanship and wise decision making of the bishops of the Mediterranean cities gained them a reputation for being the "friends of God."[143] Cyprian, bishop of Carthage (200–258), claimed that he presided over a privileged society that was invested with a majesty every bit as powerful as Rome.[144]

In 306 Valerius Aurelius Constantinus, who had distinguished himself as a soldier under Diocletian, succeeded his father Constantius Chlorus as one of the two rulers of the empire's western provinces. Determined to achieve sole supremacy, he campaigned against his coemperor Maxentius. On the night before their final battle at the Milvian Bridge near Rome in 312, Constantine had a vision of a flaming cross in the sky embellished with the motto: "In this conquer!" A dreamer and visionary, Constantine also saw himself as a "friend of God" and would always attribute his subsequent victory to this miraculous omen. That year he declared Christianity to be *religio licita*.

Constantine employed the philosopher Lucius Caecilius Lactantius (c. 260–325) as a tutor for his son Crispus. Lactantius had been converted to Christianity by the courage of the martyrs who had suffered under Maximianus Daia. The state was, he believed, inherently aggressive and predatory. Romans might talk loftily about virtue and respect for humanity but did not practice what they preached. The goals of any political power, Rome included, were always "to extend the boundaries which are violently taken from others, to increase the power of the state, to improve the revenues," and this could only be achieved by *latrocinium,* "violence and robbery."[145] There was no such thing as a "just" war, because it was never permissible to take human life.[146] If Romans really wanted to be virtuous, Lactantius concluded, they should "restore the possessions of others" and abandon their wealth and power.[147] That might have been what Jesus would have done, but it was not likely to happen in Christian Rome.

6

Byzantium:
The Tragedy of Empire

In 323 Constantine defeated Licinius, emperor of the eastern provinces, and became sole ruler of the Roman Empire. His ultimate ambition, however, was to command the civilized world from the shores of the Mediterranean to the Iranian Plateau, as Cyrus had done.[1] As a first step, he moved his capital from Rome to the city of Byzantium at the Bosporus, the juncture of Europe and Asia, which he renamed Constantinople. Here he was greeted by Eusebius (c. 264–340), the bishop of Caesarea: "Let the friend of the All-Ruling God be proclaimed our sole sovereign . . . who has modeled himself after the archetypal form of the Supreme Sovereign, whose thoughts mirror the virtuous rays by which he has been made perfectly wise, good, just, pious, courageous and God-loving."[2] This was a far cry from Jesus's criticism of such worldly authority, but in antiquity, the rhetoric of kingship had always been virtually interchangeable with the language of divinity.[3] Eusebius regarded monarchy, the rule of "one" (*monos*), as a natural consequence of monotheism.[4] There was now one God, one empire, and one emperor.[5] By his military victories, Constantine had finally established Jesus's kingdom, which would soon spread to the entire world. Eusebius understood Constantine's Iranian ambitions perfectly and argued that the emperor was not only the Caesar of Roman Christians but also the rightful sovereign of the Christians of Persia.[6] By crafting and articulating an imperial Christianity and baptizing the latrocinium of Rome, Eusebius entirely subverted the original message of Jesus.

Constantine's conversion was clearly a coup. Christianity was not yet the official religion of the Roman Empire, but it had at last been recognized in Roman law. The Church could now own property, build basilicas and churches, and make a distinctive contribution to public life. Yet those Christians who had accepted imperial patronage so joyfully failed to notice some glaring incongruities. Jesus had told his followers to give all they had to the poor, but the Christian emperor enjoyed immense wealth. In the Kingdom of God, rich and poor were supposed to sit at the same table, but Constantine lived in an exalted state of exception, and Christianity would inevitably be tainted by its connection with the oppressive agrarian state. Eusebius believed that Constantine's conquests were the culmination of sacred history:[7] Jesus had given his disciples all power in heaven and earth, and the Christian emperor had made this a political reality.[8] Eusebius chose to ignore that he had achieved this with the Roman legions that Jesus had condemned as demonic. The close union of church and empire that began in 312 meant that warfare inevitably acquired a sacral character—though Byzantines would always be reluctant to call war "holy."[9] Neither Jesus nor the first Christians could have imagined so great an oxymoron as the notion of a Christian emperor.

Yet again, we see that a tradition that had once challenged state aggression was unable to sustain this ethical stance when it became identified with aristocratic rule. The Christian Empire would inevitably be tainted by the "robbery and violence" (latrocinium) that, Lactantius believed, characterized all imperialism. As in Darius's imperial Zoroastrianism, eschatological fulfillment had been projected onto a political system that was inevitably flawed. Eusebius maintained that Constantine had established the kingdom that Christ was supposed to inaugurate at his Second Coming. He taught the Christians of Byzantium to believe that the ruthless militarism and systemic injustice of the Roman Empire would be transformed by the Christian ideal. But Constantine was a soldier, with very little knowledge of his new faith. It was more likely that Christianity would be converted to imperial violence.

Constantine may have felt the ambiguity of his position, because he delayed his baptism until he was on his deathbed.[10] In the very last year of his life, he was planning an expedition against Persia, but when he fell sick, Eusebius reported, "he perceived that this was the time to purify himself from the offences which he had at any time committed, trusting that whatever sins it had been his lot as a mortal to commit, he could wash them from his soul."[11] He told the bishops: "I shall now set for myself rules of life which befit God," tacitly admitting, perhaps, that for the last twenty-five years he had been unable to do so.[12]

The emperor had experienced these contradictions before he arrived in the East when he had to deal with a case of Christian heresy in North Africa.[13] Constantine felt quite entitled to intervene in such matters because, as he famously said: "I have been established by God as the supervisor of the external affairs of the church."[14] Heresy (*airesis*) was not simply a dogmatic issue but also a political one: the word meant "to choose another path." Because religion and politics were inseparable in Rome, lack of consensus in the Church threatened the Pax Romana. In matters of state, no Roman emperor could permit his subjects to "go their own way." Once he had become sole emperor of the western provinces, Constantine had been bombarded with appeals from the Donatist separatists and was concerned that "such disputes and altercations . . . might perhaps arouse the highest deity not only against the human race, but also against myself, to whose care he has . . . committed the regulation of all things earthly."[15] A significant number of North African Christians had refused to accept the episcopal consecration of Caecilian, the new bishop of Carthage, and had set up their own church with Donatus as their bishop.[16] Because Caecilian's orders were accepted as valid by all the other African churches, the Donatists were destroying the consensus of the Church. Constantine decided that he had to act.

Like any Roman emperor, his first instinct was to crush dissent militarily, but he settled instead for the confiscation of Donatist property. Tragically, however, when the imperial troops marched into a Donatist basilica to carry out the edict, the unarmed congregation resisted, and a massacre followed. At once the Donatists loudly complained that the Christian emperor was persecuting his fellow Christians and that despite Constantine's conversion, nothing had changed since the days of Diocletian.[17] Constantine was forced to revoke the edict, left the Donatists in peace, and instructed orthodox bishops to turn the other cheek.[18] He would have been uneasily aware that the Donatists had gotten away with it. Henceforth he and his successors would be wary of any theological or ecclesiastical discourse that threatened the Pax Christiana on which the security of the empire, they believed, now depended.[19]

Constantine was reluctant to promote his Christianity in the sparsely Christianized West, but his arrival in the East marked his political conversion to the faith. There could as yet be no question of making Christianity the official religion of the empire, and pagans still held public office, but Constantine closed down some pagan temples and expressed his disapproval of sacrificial worship.[20] Christianity's universal claims seemed ideally suited to Constantine's ambition to achieve world rule, and he believed that its ethos of peace and reconciliation were in perfect alignment with the Pax Romana. But to Constantine's horror, the eastern churches, far from being united in brotherly love, were bitterly divided by an obscure—and to Constantine, incomprehensible—theological dispute.

In 318 Arius, presbyter of Alexandria, had put forward the idea that Jesus, the Word of God, had not been divine by nature. Quoting an impressive array of biblical texts, he contended that God had simply conferred divinity upon the man Jesus as a reward for his perfect obedience and humility. At this point there was no orthodox position about the nature of Christ, and many of the bishops felt quite at home with Arius's theology. Like their pagan neighbors, they did not experience the divine as an impossibly distant reality; in the Greco-Roman world, it was taken for granted that men and women regularly became fully fledged gods.[21] Eusebius, the leading Christian intellectual of his day, taught his congregations that God had revealed himself in human form before, first to Abraham, who had entertained three strangers at Mamre and discovered that Yahweh was participating in the conversation; later Moses and Joshua had similar theophanies.[22] For Eusebius, God's Word, or Logos—the divine element in a human being[23]—had simply returned to earth once more, this time in the person of Jesus of Nazareth.[24]

But Arius was vehemently opposed by Athanasius, his bishop's young, combative assistant, who argued that God's descent to earth was not a repetition of previous epiphanies but a unique, unprecedented, and unrepeatable act of love. This resonated in some quarters, where there had been a major shift in the perception of the divine; many Christians no longer felt that they could ascend to God by their own efforts as, Arius claimed, Jesus had done. There seemed an impassable gulf between the God that was life itself and the material world, which now appeared chronically fragile and moribund. Dependent on God for their every breath, humans were powerless to save themselves. But paradoxically, Christians still found that when they contemplated the man Jesus, they saw a new divine potential in humanity, which moved them to look upon themselves and their neighbors differently. There was also a new appreciation of the human body. Christian spirituality had been strongly influenced by Platonism, which sought to liberate the soul from the body, but in some circles in the early fourth century, people were beginning to hope that their hitherto despised bodies could bring men and women to the divine—or at least that it was not a reality separate from the physical, as the Platonists held.[25]

Athanasius's doctrine of incarnation spoke directly to this changed mood. In the person of Jesus, he claimed, God had leaned across the dividing chasm and, in an astounding act of *kenosis* ("self-emptying"), had taken mortal flesh, shared our weakness, and utterly transformed fragile, perishable human nature. "The Logos became human that we might become divine," Athanasius insisted. "He revealed himself through a body that we might receive an idea of the invisible Father."[26] The good news of the gospel was the coming of new life, human because it was divine.[27] Nobody was compelled to "believe" this doctrine; people embraced it because it reflected their personal experience. Athanasius's doctrine of the "deification" (*theosis*) of humanity made perfect sense to those Christians who had become convinced that in some mysterious way they had already been transformed and that their humanity had acquired a new divine dimension. But theosis seemed nonsensical to those who had not experienced it.

Two new "Christianities" had therefore emerged in response to a shift in the intellectual environment, both of which could claim support from past scriptures and luminaries. With quiet and sustained reflection, this dispute could easily have been settled peaceably. Instead it became entangled with imperial politics. Constantine, of course, had no understanding of these theological issues but was determined nevertheless to repair this breach of ecclesiastical consensus. In May 325 he summoned the bishops to a council in Nicaea to settle the matter once and for all. Here Athanasius managed to get the emperor's ear and forced his position through. Most of the bishops, anxious not to incur Constantine's displeasure, signed Athanasius's creed but continued to preach as they had before. Nicaea solved nothing, and the Arian controversy dragged on for another sixty years. Constantine, out of his depth theologically, would eventually veer to the other side and take the Arian position that was promoted by the more cultured, aristocratic bishops.[28] Athanasius, no aristocrat himself, was reviled by his enemies as an upstart "from the lowest depths of society" who was "no different from a common artisan." For all his talk of kenosis, Athanasius never lost his pointy elbows or his theological certainty, which was inspired in no small part by the new monastic movement that had emerged in the deserts around Alexandria.

◆   ◆   ◆

In 270, the year of Constantine's birth, a young Egyptian peasant had walked to church lost in thought. Antony had just inherited a sizable piece of land from his parents but found this good fortune an intolerable burden. He was only eighteen years old, yet now he had to provide for his sister, take a wife, have children, and toil on the farm for the rest of his life to support them all. In Egypt, where famine loomed whenever the Nile failed to flood, starvation was always a real threat, and most people accepted this relentless struggle as inevitable.[29] But Jesus had said: "I am telling you not to worry about your life and what you are to eat and about your body and how to clothe it."[30] Antony also remembered that the first Christians had sold all their possessions and given the proceeds to the poor.[31] Still musing on these texts, he entered the church only to hear the priest reading Jesus's words to a rich young man: "If you wish to be perfect, go and sell what you own and give the money to the poor, and you will have treasure in heaven."[32] Immediately Antony sold his property and embarked on a quest for freedom and holiness that would become a countercultural challenge to both the Christianized Roman state and the new worldly, imperial Christianity. Like other monastic communities we have considered, Antony's followers would try to model a more egalitarian and compassionate way for people to live together.

For the first fifteen years, like other "renouncers" (apotaktikoi), Antony lived at the very edge of his village; then he moved to the tombs on the periphery of the desert and finally ventured farther into the wilderness than any other monk, living for years in an abandoned fortress beside the Red Sea until, in 301 he began to attract disciples.[33] In the immensity of the desert, Antony discovered a tranquillity (hesychia) that put worldly care into perspective.[34] Saint Paul had insisted that Christians must support themselves,[35] so Egyptian monks either worked as day laborers or sold their produce in the market. Antony grew vegetables so that he could offer hospitality to passing travelers, because learning to live kindly with others and sharing your wealth was essential to his monastic program.[36]

For some time, Egyptian peasants had engaged in this type of disengagement (*anchoresis*) to escape economic or social tension. During the third century, there had been a crisis of human relations in the villages. These farmers were prosperous but acerbic and quick with their fists, yet the village's tax burden and the need for cooperation to control the floodwaters of the Nile obliged them to live in unwelcome proximity with uncongenial neighbors.[37] Success was often resented. "Although I possess a good deal of land and am occupied with its cultivation," one farmer explained, "I am not involved with any person in the village but keep to myself."[38] When neighborly relationships became unendurable, therefore, people would sometimes retire to the very edge of the settlement.[39] But once Christianity reached the Egyptian countryside in the late third century, anchoresis was no longer a disgruntled withdrawal but had become a positive choice to live according to the gospel in a way that offered a welcome and challenging alternative to the acrimony and tedium of settled life. The monk (*monachos*) lived alone (*monos*), seeking the "freedom from care" (*amerimmia*) that Jesus had prescribed.[40]

Like the renouncers of previous times, the monks set up a counterculture, casting off their functional role in the agrarian economy and rejecting its inherent violence. A monk's struggle began as soon as he left his village.[41] At first, explained one of the greatest of these anchorites, he was plagued by terrifying thoughts "of lengthy old age, inability to perform manual labor, fear of the starvation that will ensue, of the sickness that follows undernourishment, and the deep shame of having to accept the necessities of life from the hands of others."[42] Their greatest task, however, was to still the violent impulses that lurk in the depths of the human psyche. The monks often described their struggles as a battle with demons, which we moderns usually understand as sexual temptations. But they were less preoccupied by sex than we are: Egyptian monks usually avoided women because they symbolized the economic burden they wanted to escape.[43] Far more threatening than sex to these sharp-tongued Egyptian peasants was the "demon" of anger.[44] However provocative the circumstances, monks must never respond aggressively to any attack. One abbot ruled that there was no excuse for violent speech, even if your brother "plucks out your right eye and cuts off your right hand."[45] A monk must not even look angry or make an impatient gesture.[46] These monks meditated constantly on Jesus's command to "love your enemies" because most of them *did* have enemies in the community.[47] Evagrius of Pontus (d. 399), one of the most influential monastic teachers, drew on Paul's doctrine of kenosis and instructed monks to empty their minds of the rage, avarice, pride, and vainglory that tore the soul apart and made them close their hearts to others. By following these precepts, some learned to transcend their innate belligerence and achieved an interior peace that they experienced as a return to the Garden of Eden, when human beings had lived in harmony with one another and with God.

The monastic movement spread more rapidly, demonstrating a widespread hunger for an alternative to a Christianity that was increasingly tainted by imperial associations. By the end of the fifth century, tens of thousands of monks were living beside the Nile and in the deserts of Syria, Egypt, Mesopotamia, and Armenia.[48] They had, wrote Athanasius, created a spiritual city in the wilderness that was the antithesis of the worldly city, supported by taxation, oppression, and military aggression.[49] Instead of creating an aristocracy that lived off the labor of others, monks were self-sufficient and existed at subsistence level, and whatever surplus they produced, they gave to the poor. Instead of the Pax Romana enforced by martial violence, they cultivated hesychia and systematically rid their minds of anger, violence, and hatred. Like Constantine, Antony was venerated by many as *epigeios theos,* a "god on earth," but he ruled with kindness rather than coercion.[50] The monks were the new "friends of God" whose power had been achieved by a self-effacing lifestyle that had no earthly profit.[51]

◆　◆　◆

After the Council of Nicaea, some Christians began to fall out of love with their emperors. They had expected Christian Rome to become a utopia that would somehow eliminate the cruelty and violence of the imperial state, but they found instead that Roman belligerence had infiltrated the Church. Constantine, his son Constantius II (r. 337–61), and their successors continued the struggle for consensus, using force when necessary, and their victims called them "persecutors." First, it was Athanasius's "Nicenes" who suffered, but after the Council of Constantinople (381), which made Athanasius's creed the official faith of the empire, it was the Arians' turn. There were no formal executions, but people were massacred when soldiers invaded a church to break up a heretical gathering, and increasingly both sides complained far more about their opponents' violence than about their theology. In the early years, while Athanasius still enjoyed Constantine's favor, Arians complained of his "greed, aggression, and boundless ambition"[52] and accused him of "force," "murder," and the "killing of bishops."[53] For their part, the Nicenes vividly described the rattling weapons and flashing swords of the imperial troops, who thrashed their deacons and trampled worshippers underfoot.[54] Both sides dwelled obsessively on their enemies' vicious treatment of the consecrated virgins,[55] and both revered their dead as "martyrs." Christians were developing a history of grievance that intensified during the brief but dramatic reign of the emperor Julian (361–63), known as "the Apostate."

Despite his Christian upbringing, Julian had come to detest the new faith, convinced it would ruin the empire. Many of his subjects felt the same. Those who still loved the old rites feared that this violation of the Pax Deorum would result in political catastrophe. Throughout the imperial domains, Julian appointed pagan priests to sacrifice to the One God worshipped under many names—as Zeus, Jupiter, Helios, or in the Hebrew Bible, "God Most High."[56] He removed Christians from public office, gave special privileges to towns that had never adopted Christianity, and announced that he would rebuild the Jewish temple in Jerusalem. Julian was careful to avoid outright persecution but merely boosted pagan sacrifice, refurbished pagan shrines, and covertly encouraged anti-Christian violence.[57] Over the years a great deal of pent-up resentment had accumulated against the Church, and when Julian's edicts were published, in some towns pagans rioted against Christians, who now discovered how vulnerable they really were.

Once again, some Christians responded to the state that had suddenly turned against them with the defiant gesture of martyrdom. Most of the martyrs who died during these two years were either killed by pagan mobs or put to death by local officials for their provocative attacks on pagan religion.[58] As Jews began work on their new temple and pagans gleefully refurbished their shrines, conflict throughout the empire centered on iconic buildings. Ever since Constantine, Christians had become accustomed to seeing the decline of Judaism as the essential concomitant to the triumph of the Church. Now as they watched the purposeful activity of the Jewish workmen on the temple site in Jerusalem, they felt as if the fabric of their own faith had been undermined. At Merum in Phrygia, there was a more ominous development. While the local pagan temple was being repaired and the statues of the gods polished, three Christians, "unable to endure the indignity put upon their religion and impelled by a fervent zeal for virtue, rushed by night into the temple and broke the images in pieces." This amounted to a suicide attack on a building that seemed to epitomize their new humiliation. Even though the governor urged them to repent, they refused, "declaring their readiness to undergo any sufferings, rather than pollute themselves by sacrificing." Consequently, they were tortured and roasted to death on a gridiron.[59] A new spate of martyr stories appeared, even more sensational than the original *Acta*.

In this aggressive form of martyrdom, the martyrs were no longer the innocent victims of imperial violence: their battles now took the form of a symbolic—and sometimes suicidal—assault upon the enemies of the faith. Like some modern religious extremists, Christians felt that they had suffered a sudden loss of power and prestige—all the more acute in their case because the memory of their days as a despised minority were so recent.[60] Christians courted martyrdom by smashing the pagan gods' effigies, disrupting rituals and defacing the temples that symbolized their degradation, and loudly praising those who had defied Julian's "tyranny." When Julian was killed in a military expedition against Persia and Jovian, a Christian, was proclaimed emperor in his place, it seemed like a divine deliverance. But Julian's reign, which had so rudely shattered the Christians' newfound security and entitlement, had created a polarized religious climate and, at least among the lower classes, had exacerbated hostility between Christians and pagans. "Never again!" would be the Christian watchword as they contemplated renewed attacks on the pagan establishment in the coming years.[61] State repression creates a history of grievance that often radicalizes a religious tradition and can even push an originally irenic vision into a campaign of violence.

· · ·

Christian and pagan aristocrats, however, still shared a common culture that did much to mitigate this aggression among the upper classes. Throughout the empire, young noblemen and talented individuals of humble birth were inducted in a "formation" (*paedeia*) dating from ancient times.[62] It was not a purely academic program, though it was intellectually rigorous, but was primarily an initiation that shaped the behavior of the ruling class and profoundly molded their attitudes. As a result, wherever they traveled in the empire, they found that they could relate to their peers. Paedeia was an important antidote to the violence of late Roman society, where slaves were regularly beaten to death, where the flogging of social inferiors was perfectly acceptable, and where councilors were publicly thrashed for tax arrears. A truly cultivated Roman was unfailingly courteous and self-controlled, since anger, vituperative speech, and irascible gestures were unbecoming to a gentleman, who was expected to yield graciously to others and behave at all times with restraint, calm, and gravitas.

Because of paedeia, the old religion remained an integral part of late Roman culture, and its ethos was also absorbed into the life of the Church, where young men brought these attitudes with them to the baptismal font; some even saw paedeia as an indispensable preparation for Christianity.[63] "With measured words, I learn to bridle rage," the Cappadocian bishop Gregory of Nazianzus (329–90) told his congregation.[64] His friends Basil, bishop of Caesarea (c. 330–79), and Gregory, bishop of Nyssa (331–95), Basil's younger brother, were not baptized until after they had completed this traditional training.[65] The dispassion of paedeia also informed the doctrine of the Trinity, which these three men, often known as the Cappadocian Fathers, developed toward the end of the Arian crisis. They had been uneasy about these disputes, strident on both sides, each of which had cultivated a hardened certainty about these ineffable matters. The Cappadocians practiced the silent, reticent prayer designed by Evagrius of Pontus, in part to strip the mind of such angry dogmatism. They knew that it was impossible to speak about God as we speak about ordinary matters, and the Trinity was designed first to help Christians realize that what we call God lay beyond the reach of words and concepts. They would also introduce Christians to a meditation on the Trinity that would help them to develop attitudes of restraint in their own lives, enabling them to counter aggressive and bellicose intolerance.

Many Christians had been confused by the creed of Nicaea. If there was only one God, how could Jesus be divine? Did that mean that there were two gods? And was there a third: What was the "holy spirit," which had been dealt with so perfunctorily in Athanasius's creed? In the New

Testament this Jewish term had referred to the human experience of the power and presence of the divine, which could never measure up to the divine reality itself. The Trinity was an attempt to translate this Jewish insight into a Hellenistic idiom. God, the Cappadocians explained, had one divine, inaccessible essence (*ousia*) that was totally beyond the reach of the human mind, but it had been made known to us by three manifestations (*hypostases*): the Father (source of being), the Logos (in the man Jesus), and the Spirit that we encounter within ourselves. Each "person" (from the Latin *persona*, meaning "mask") of the Trinity was merely a partial glimpse of the divine *ousia* that we could never comprehend. The Cappadocians introduced converts to the Trinity in a meditation, which reminded them that the divine could never be encapsulated in a dogmatic formula. Constantly repeated, this meditation taught Christians that there was a kenosis at the heart of the Trinity, because the Father ceaselessly emptied itself, transmitting everything to the Logos. Once that Word had been spoken, the Father no longer had an "I" but remained forever silent and unknowable. The Logos likewise had no self of its own but was simply the "Thou" of the Father, while the Spirit was the "We" of Father and Son.[66] The Trinity expressed the paedeia's values of restraint, deference, and self-abnegation, with which the more aristocratic bishops countered the current Christian stridency. Other bishops, alas, were all too ready to embrace it.

• • •

Constantine had given the bishops new authority for the exercise of imperial power, and some, especially those of humble birth, strove for the episcopate as pugnaciously as politicians compete for parliamentary seats today.[67] Some even staged coups, taking over a church by night and barricading the doors during their illegal consecration.[68] "At present we have men who claim to be bishops—a lowly breed who are bogged down in acquiring money and military operations and striving for honorable positions," complained the historian Palladius.[69] They became known as "tyrant-bishops." In ancient Greece, a *tyrannos* was a strongman who seized power by unlawful violence; in the later Roman Empire, the word had general connotations of misrule, cruelty, and unrestrained anger.[70] When Athanasius became a bishop, his opponents regularly called him a tyrant because, they claimed, he was motivated not by the desire to defend the faith but by personal ambition. He was described as "raging like a tyrant" when he sentenced Arians to prison, flogging, and torture, and it was noted that his entourage included "the military and officials of the imperial government."[71] It was clearly easier to imperialize the faith than to Christianize the empire.

During the late fourth century, rioting had become a regular feature of city life. Barbarian tribes were ceaselessly attacking the frontiers, brigandage was rife in the countryside, and refugees poured into the towns.[72] Overcrowding, disease, unemployment, and increased taxes created a tension that often exploded violently, but because the army was needed to defend the borders, governors had no military forces to quell these uprisings and passed the responsibility for crowd control to the bishops.[73] "It is the duty of a bishop like you to cut short and restrain any unregulated movements of the mob," wrote the patriarch of Antioch to a colleague.[74] The bishops of Syria already relied on local monks to man their soup kitchens and serve as stretcher-bearers, hospital porters, and gravediggers. They were greatly loved by the people, especially the urban poor, who enjoyed their ferocious denunciations of the rich. Now they began to police the riots and in the process acquired martial skills.

Unlike Antony's Egyptian monks, the monks of Syria had no interest in fighting the demon of anger. Known as *boskoi,* "grazers," they had no fixed abode but roamed through the mountains at will, feeding on wild plants.[75] One of the most famous boskoi was Alexander the Sleepless, who had left a regular community of monks because he disapproved of its property ownership. He had wholly imbibed the post-Julian ethos of "Never again," and his first act, on emerging from seven solitary years in the desert, was to burn down the largest temple in a pagan village. There could be zero tolerance for the icons of the old religion, which were a standing threat to the security of the Church. Alexander lost out on the palm of martyrdom, however, because he preached so eloquently to the mob that came to kill him that it converted to Christianity on the spot. He founded an order dedicated to "freedom from care," so instead of working for their living, like Antony, his monks lived on alms, refusing to engage in productive labor. And instead of trying to control their anger, they gave it free rein.[76] During the 380s, four hundred of them formed a massive prayer-gang and began a twenty-year trek along the Persian border, singing in shifts all around the clock in obedience to Paul's instructions to "pray without ceasing."[77] The hapless inhabitants of the villages on either side of the frontier were terrorized as the monks chanted the

psalmists' bloodcurdling denunciations of idolatry. Their insistent begging made them an intolerable burden to these rural communities that
could barely support themselves. When they arrived in a city, they squatted in a public space in the center, attracting huge crowds of urban poor
who flocked to hear their fiery condemnation of the rich.

Those who did not feel badgered by them respected the monks for
expressing the values of Christianity in an absolute way. For them, Alexander's virulent intolerance of paganism showed that he really believed
that Christianity was the one true faith. After Julian, some Christians
increasingly defined themselves as a beleaguered community. They gathered around the tombs of local martyrs, listened avidly to the stories of
their suffering, and piously preserved the memory of Julian's persecution,
keeping alive their sense of injury. Many had no time for the courteous
tolerance of the more aristocratic bishops.[78] The pagan temples, which
had symbolized the brief pagan revival, now seemed a standing threat
that became increasingly intolerable. To add fuel to these flames, the
emperors were now ready to exploit the monks' popularity and let these
zealots loose on the pagan world. They would enforce the Pax Christiana as aggressively as they had previously imposed the Pax Romana.

Theodosius I (r. 346–95) was a recent convert and a man of humble
Spanish origins. A brilliant soldier, he had pacified the Danube region and
arrived in Constantinople in 380 determined to implement his bellicose
form of Christianity in the East. It was he who summoned the Council of
Constantinople that made Nicene orthodoxy the official religion of the
empire in 381. He patronized the Roman aristocracy when it suited him,
but his sympathies really lay with the man in the street, and he decided
to create a power base by wooing the disaffected townsfolk through their
beloved monks. He could see the point of destroying the pagan temples;
his empress, Aelia Flacilla, had already distinguished herself in Rome by
leading a crowd of noblewomen to attack pagan shrines. In 388 Theodosius gave the monks the go-ahead, and they fell on the village shrines
of Syria like a plague; with the connivance of the local bishop, they also
destroyed a synagogue at Callinicum on the Euphrates. The pagan ora-
tor Libanius urged the emperor to prosecute this "black-robed tribe"
who were guilty of latrocinium ("robbery and violence"), describing
the "utter desolation" that followed their vicious attacks on the temples
"with sticks and stones and bars of iron, and in some cases, disdain-
ing these, with hands and feet." The pagan priests had no option but

to "keep quiet or die."[79] The monks became the symbolic vanguard of violent Christianization. The mere sound of their chanting was enough to make the governor of Antioch adjourn his court and flee the city. Even though there were no boskoi on Minorca, the leader of the Jewish community there dreamed in 418 that his synagogue was in ruins and its site occupied by psalm-singing monks. A few weeks later the synagogue was in fact destroyed—though not by monks but by fanatic local Christians.[80]

Some bishops opposed this vandalism, but not consistently. Because Roman law protected Jewish property, Theodosius ordered the bishop who had instigated the burning of the Callinicum synagogue to pay for its repair. But Ambrose (339–97), bishop of Milan, forced him to rescind this decree, since rebuilding the synagogue would be as humiliating to the true faith as Julian's attempt to restore the Jewish temple.[81] The Christianization of the empire was now, increasingly, equated with the destruction of these iconic buildings. In 391, after Theodosius had permitted Theophilus, bishop of Alexandria, to occupy the temple of Dionysius, the bishop pillaged all the temples in the city and paraded the looted treasure in an insulting display.[82] In response, the pagans of Alexandria barricaded themselves into the magnificent temple of Serapis with some Christian hostages, whom they forced to reenact the trauma of Diocletian's persecution:

> These they forced to offer sacrifice on the altars where fire was kindled; those who refused they put to death with new and refined tortures, fastening some to gibbets and breaking the legs of others and pitching them into the caverns which a careworn antiquity had built to receive the blood of sacrifices and the other impurities of the temple.[83]

When the pagan leader thought he heard monks singing in some distant part of the shrine, he knew they were doomed. In fact, the Serapaeum was destroyed by imperial soldiers acting on the bishop's orders, but the monks who turned up afterward carrying relics of John the Baptist and squatted in the ruins became the symbols of this Christian triumph.[84] It was reported that many pagans were so shocked by these events that they converted on the spot.

The success of these attacks convinced Theodosius that the best way of achieving ideological consensus in the empire was to ban sacrificial worship and close down all the old shrines and temples. His son and successor, Arcadius (r. 395–408), expressed this policy succinctly: "When [the temples] are overthrown and obliterated, the material foundations for all superstition will have been done away with."[85] He urged local aristocracies throughout the empire to let their zealots loose on the temples to prove that the pagan gods could not even defend their own homes. As one modern historian notes: "Silencing, burning, and destruction were all forms of theological demonstration; and when the lesson was over, monks and bishops, generals and emperors had driven the enemy from the field."[86]

It was Aurelius Augustine, bishop of Hippo in North Africa, who gave the most authoritative blessing to this Christian state violence. He had found by experience that militancy brought in new converts.[87] Writing twenty-five years after agents of the Western emperor Honorius had torn down the temples and idolatrous shrines of Carthage in 399, he asked: "Who does not see how much the worship of the name of Christ has increased!"[88] When Donatist monks had raged through the African countryside in the 390s, destroying the temples and attacking the estates of the nobility, Augustine had at first forbidden the use of force against them, but he soon noticed that the stern imperial edicts terrified the Donatists and made them return to the Church. It is no coincidence, therefore, that it was Augustine who would develop the "just war" theory, the foundation of all future Christian thinking on the subject.[89] When Jesus told his disciples to turn the other cheek when attacked, Augustine argued, he had not asked them to be passive in the face of wrongdoing.[90] What made violence evil was not the act of killing but the passions of greed, hatred, and ambition that had prompted it.[91] Violence was legitimate, however, if inspired by charity—by a sincere concern for the enemy's welfare— and should be administered in the same way as a schoolmaster beat his pupils for their own good.[92] But force must always be authorized by the proper authority.[93] An individual, even if acting in self-defense, would inevitably feel an inordinate desire (*libido*) to inflict pain on his assailant, whereas a professional soldier, who was simply obeying orders, could act dispassionately. In putting violence beyond the reach of the individual, Augustine had given the state almost unlimited powers.

When Augustine died in 430, the Vandals were besieging Hippo. During the last years of his life, one western province after another had fallen to the barbarian tribes, who had set up their own kingdoms in Germany and Gaul, and in 410 Alaric and his Gothic horsemen had sacked the city of Rome itself. In response, Theodosius II (r. 401–50) built a massive fortifying wall around Constantinople, but the Byzantines had long been oriented to the east, were still dreaming of replicating Cyrus's empire, and were able to survive the loss of old Rome without undue repining.[94] Lacking imperial supervision, Western Europe became a primitive backwater, its civilization lost, and for a while it looked as though Christianity itself would perish there. But the Western bishops stepped into the shoes of the departing Roman officials, maintaining a semblance of order in some regions, and the pope, the bishop of Rome, inherited the imperial aura. The popes sent missionaries out to the new barbarian kingdoms who converted the Anglo-Saxons in Britain and the Franks in the old province of Gaul. Over the coming centuries, the Byzantines would look with increasing disdain on these "barbarian" Christians. They would never accept the popes' claim that, as the successors of Saint Peter, they were the true leaders of the Christian world.

•   •   •

In Byzantium the debates on the nature of Christ resumed even more aggressively than before. It might seem that this conflict, which had always expressed itself violently, was caused wholly by religious zeal for correct dogma. The bishops were still searching for a way to express their vision of humanity, vulnerable and moribund as it was, as somehow sacred and divine. But the discussions were fueled in equal measure by the internal politics of the empire. The leading protagonists were "tyrant-bishops," men with worldly ambitions and huge egos, and the emperors continued to muddy the waters. Theodosius II patronized the lawless monks even more assiduously than his grandfather. One of his protégés was Nestorius, patriarch of Constantinople, who argued that Christ had two natures, one human and one divine.[95] Where the Nicene Creed saw humanity and divinity as entirely compatible, however, Nestorius insisted that they could not coexist. His argument was thoughtful and nuanced, and if the debate had been conducted in a peaceable, open-hearted manner, the issue could have been resolved. However, anxious to curb Nestorius's rising star, Cyril, patriarch of Alexandria, vehemently accused him of outright heresy, arguing that when God stooped to save us, he did not go halfway, as Nestorius seemed to suggest, but embraced our humanity in all its physicality and mortality. At the Council of Ephesus (431) that met to decide the issue, each side accused the other of "tyranny." Nestorius claimed that Cyril had sent a horde of "fanatical monks" to attack him and that he had been compelled to surround his house with an armed guard.[96] Contemporary historians had no respect for either side, dismissing Nestorius as a "firebrand" and Cyril as "power-hungry."[97] There was no serious doctrinal conflict, argued Palladius; these men "tore the church asunder" simply "to satisfy their desire for the episcopal office or even the primacy of the episcopate."[98]

In 449 Eutyches, a revered monastic leader in Constantinople, maintained that Jesus had only one nature (*mono physis*), since his humanity had been so thoroughly deified that it was no longer like our own. He accused his opponents—quite inaccurately—of "Nestorianism." Flavian, his bishop, tried to settle the matter quietly but Eutyches was a favorite of the emperor and insisted on making a legal case of it.[99] The result was a virtual civil war over doctrine, in which emperor and monks formed an unholy alliance against the more moderate bishops. A second council was convened at Ephesus in 449 to settle the "Monophysite" problem, headed by the "tyrant-bishop" Dioscorus, patriarch of Alexandria, who was determined to use the council to establish himself as primate of the Eastern Church. To make matters worse, Theodosius brought the monk Barsauma and his crew to Ephesus, ostensibly to represent "all the monks and pious people of the east" but actually to be his storm troopers.[100] Twenty years earlier Barsauma and his monastic thugs had ritually reenacted Joshua's campaign in Palestine and Transjordan, systematically destroying synagogues and temples at all the holy places along the route, and in 438 they had killed Jewish pilgrims on the Temple Mount in Jerusalem. "He has sent thousands of monks against us," his victims complained later; "he has devastated all of Syria; he is a murderer and a slayer of bishops."[101]

When the delegates arrived at Ephesus, they were met by hordes of monks wielding clubs and attacking Eutyches's opponents:

> They were carrying off men, some of them from the ships and others of them from the streets and others from the houses and others from the churches where they were praying and were pursuing others of them that fled; and with all zeal they were searching out and digging even those who were hiding in caves and in holes of the earth.[102]

Hilary of Poitiers, the pope's envoy, thought he was lucky to get out alive, and Bishop Flavian was beaten so badly that he died shortly afterward. Dioscorus refused to allow any dissenting voice to be heard, doctored the minutes, and called in the imperial troops when it came to the vote.

The following year, however, Theodosius died, and the monks lost their imperial support. A new council met at Chalcedon in 451 to reverse Second Ephesus and create a neutral theological middle ground.[103] The "Tome" of Pope Leo, which declared diplomatically that Jesus was fully God and fully man, now became the touchstone of orthodoxy.[104] Dioscorus was deposed, and the roaming Syrian boskoi reined in. Henceforth all monks were required to live and remain in their monastery, forbidden to participate in both worldly and ecclesiastical affairs, and were to be financially dependent on and controlled by the local bishop. But Chalcedon, hailed as the triumph of law and order, was actually an imperial coup. At the beginning of the fourth century, Christians had denounced the presence of imperial troops in their churches as sacrilegious; but after the horror of Second Ephesus, the moderate bishops begged the emperor to take control. Consequently a committee of nineteen of the highest military and civil officials of the empire presided over Chalcedon, set the agenda, silenced dissenting voices, and enforced correct procedure. Henceforth in the Syrian-speaking world, the Chalcedonian Church was known as Melkite—"the emperor's church." In any previous empire the religion of the ruling class had always been distinct from the faith of the subjugated masses, so the Christian emperors' attempt to impose their theology on their subjects was a shocking break with precedent and was experienced as an outrage. Opponents of this imperialized Christianity espoused Eutyches's Monophysitism in protest. In fact, the theological difference between Monophysites and Nicenes was minimal, but the Monophysites could point to other Christian traditions—not least Jesus's stance against Rome—to claim that the Melkites had made an unholy alliance with earthly power.

The debates about the nature of Christ had been an attempt to build a holistic view of reality, one with no impregnable division between the physical and the spiritual realms or the divine and the human. In human society too, the emperor Justinian (r. 527–65) believed, there should be a *symphonia* of church and state, a harmony and concord based on the incarnation of the Logos in the man Jesus.[105] Just as the two natures—

human and divine—were found in a single person, there could be no separation of church and empire; together they formed the Kingdom of God, which would soon spread to the entire world. But there was, of course, a massive difference between Jesus's kingdom and the Byzantine state.

As the barbarians crept ever closer to the walls of Constantinople, Justinian became even more zealous to restore the divine unity by vigorously enforcing the supremacy of "the emperor's church." His attempts to suppress the Monophysite party permanently alienated the people of Palestine, Syria, and Egypt. He declared that Judaism was no longer religio licita: Jews were now debarred from public office, and the use of Hebrew was prohibited in the synagogue. In 528 Justinian gave all pagans three months to be baptized, and the following year he closed the Academy in Athens that had been founded by Plato. In every province from Morocco to the Euphrates, he commissioned churches, built after the style of Constantinople, to symbolize the unity of the empire. Instead of providing a challenging alternative to imperial violence, the tradition that had begun in part as a protest against the systemic oppression of empire had become the tool of Rome's aggressive coercion.

• • •

In 540 Khosrow I of Persia began to transform his ailing kingdom into the economic giant of the region in a reform based on a classic definition of the agrarian state:

> The monarchy depends on the army, the army on money; money comes from the land tax; the land tax comes from agriculture. Agriculture depends on justice; justice on the integrity of officials, and integrity and reliability on the ever-watchfulness of the king.[106]

Khosrow devised a more efficient method of tax collection and invested heavily in the irrigation of Mesopotamia, which previous Persian kings had neglected. With the proceeds he was able to create a professional army to replace the traditional aristocratic levies. War with Christian Rome was now inevitable, since both powers aspired to dominate the region. Khosrow employed Arab tribesmen to police his southern border, and the Byzantines reciprocated by hiring the Banu Ghassan, even though they had converted to Monophysite Christianity, to patrol the frontier from their winter camp near Damascus.

In Khosrow's Persia there was zero tolerance for rebellion but no religious discrimination: on the eve of a revolt, the king warned that he would "kill every man who persists in insubordination against me—be he a good Zoroastrian, a Jew, or a Christian."[107] Like most traditional agrarian rulers, the Persian kings had no interest in imposing their faith on their subjects; even Darius's imperial version of Zoroastrianism had been strictly confined to the aristocracy. Their subjects worshipped as they chose, living in communities of Christians, Jews, and pagans, governed by their own laws and customs, and ruled by religious officials who were agents of the state—an arrangement that determined the social organization of Middle Eastern society for over a millennium. After Khosrow's death, there was a civil war in Persia, and the Byzantine emperor Maurice intervened to put the young Khosrow II (r. 591–628) on the throne. Alienated from the Persian nobility, Khosrow II surrounded himself with Christians, but the splendors of his court set the tone for Middle Eastern monarchy for centuries to come. He continued his father's reforms, making Mesopotamia a vibrant, rich, and creative region. The Jewish community at Ctesiphon (near modern Baghdad) became the intellectual and spiritual capital of world Jewry, and Nisibis, dedicated to the study of Christian scripture, another great intellectual center.[108] While Byzantine horizons were shrinking, Persians were broadening their outlook.

When his ally Maurice was assassinated in a coup in 610, Khosrow seized the opportunity to conduct massive raids for slaves and booty in Byzantium. And when Heraclius, governor of Roman North Africa, gained the imperial throne in another coup, Khosrow embarked on a huge offensive, conquering Antioch (613), large areas of Syria and Palestine (614), and Egypt (619); in 626 the Persian army even besieged Constantinople. But in an extraordinary riposte, Heraclius and his small disciplined army defeated the Persian forces in Asia Minor and invaded the Iranian Plateau, attacking the unprotected estates of the Zoroastrian nobility and destroying their shrines before he was forced to withdraw. Utterly discredited, Khosrow was assassinated by his ministers in 628. Heraclius's campaign had been more overtly religious than any previous war of Christian Rome. Indeed, so intertwined were church and empire by now that Christianity itself had seemed under attack during the siege of Constantinople. When the city was saved, the victory was attributed to Mary, mother of God, whose icon had been paraded to deter the enemy from the city walls.

During the Persian wars a monk finally brought the Christological disputes to an end. Maximus (580–662) insisted that these issues could not be settled simply by a theological formulation: "deification" was rooted in the experience of the Eucharist, contemplation, and the practice of charity. It was these communal rites and disciplines that taught Christians to see that it was impossible to think "God" without thinking "man." If human beings emptied their minds of the jealousy and animosity that ruin their relations with one another, they could, even in this life, become divine: "The whole human being could become God, deified by the grace of God become man—whole man, soul and body, by nature and becoming whole God, soul and body by grace."[109] Every single person, therefore, had sacred value. Our love of God was inseparable from our love of one another.[110] Indeed, Jesus had taught that the iron test of our love of God was that we love our enemies:

> Why did he command this? To free you from hatred, anger and resentment, and to make you worthy of the supreme gift of perfect love. And you cannot attain such love if you do not imitate God and love all men equally. For God loves all men equally and wishes them to "to be saved and to come to the knowledge of the truth."[111]

Unlike the tyrant-bishops who vied for the emperor's backing, Maximus became a victim, not a perpetrator, of imperial violence. Having fled to North Africa during the Persian wars, in 661 he was forcibly brought to Constantinople, where he was imprisoned, condemned as a heretic, and mutilated; he died shortly afterward in exile. But he was vindicated at the third Council of Constantinople in 680 and would become known as the father of Byzantine theology.

The doctrine of deification celebrates the transfiguration of the entire human being in the here and now, not merely in a future state, and this has indeed been the living experience of individual Christians. But this spiritual triumph hardly resembles the "realized eschatology" promoted by emperors and tyrant bishops. After Constantine's conversion, they had convinced themselves that the empire was the Kingdom of God and a second manifestation of Christ. Not even the catastrophe of the

Second Council of Ephesus or the military vulnerability of their empire could shake their belief that Rome would become intrinsically Christian and win the world for Christ. In other traditions people had tried to create a challenging alternative to the systemic violence of the state, but right up to the fall of Constantinople to the Turks in 1453, Byzantines continued to believe that the Pax Romana was compatible with the Pax Christiana. The enthusiasm with which they had greeted imperial patronage was never accompanied by a sustained critique of the role and nature of the state, or its ineluctable violence and oppression.[112]

By the early seventh century, both Persia and Byzantium had been ruined by their wars for imperial dominance. Syria, already weakened by a devastating plague, had become an impoverished region, and Persia had succumbed to anarchy, its frontier fatally compromised. Yet while Persians and Byzantines eyed each other nervously, real danger emerged elsewhere. Both empires had forgotten their Arab clients and failed to notice that the Arabian Peninsula had experienced a commercial revolution. Arabs had been watching the wars between the great powers very closely and knew that both empires were fatally weakened; they were about to undergo an astonishing spiritual and political awakening.

7

The Muslim Dilemma

In 610, the year that saw the outbreak of the Persian-Byzantine war, a merchant from Mecca in the Arabian Hejaz experienced a dramatic revelation during the sacred month of Ramadan. For some years, Muhammad ibn Abdullah had made an annual retreat on Mount Hira, just outside the city.[1] There he fasted, performed spiritual exercises, and gave alms to the poor while he meditated deeply on the problems of his people, the tribe of Quraysh. Only a few generations earlier, their ancestors had been living a desperate life in the intractable deserts of northern Arabia. Now they were rich beyond their wildest dreams, and since farming was virtually impossible in this arid land, their wealth had been entirely created by commerce. For centuries the local nomads (*badawin*) had scratched out a meagre living by herding sheep and breeding horses and camels, but during the sixth century, they had invented a saddle that enabled camels to carry heavier loads than before. As a result, merchants from India, East Africa, Yemen, and Bahrain began to take their caravans through the Arabian steppes to Byzantium and Syria, using the Bedouin to guide them from one watering hole to another. Mecca had become a station for these caravans, and the Quraysh started their own trade missions to Syria and Yemen, while the Bedouin exchanged goods in an annual circuit of regular *suqs* ("markets") around Arabia.[2]

Mecca's prosperity also depended on its status as a pilgrimage center. At the end of the suq season, Arabs came from all over Mecca during the month of Hajj to perform the ancient rituals around the Kabah, the ancient cube-shaped shrine in the heart of the city. Cult and commerce were inseparable: the climax of the hajj was the *tawaf,* the seven circum-ambulations around the Kabah that mirrored the suq circuit, giving the Arabs' mercantile activities a spiritual dimension. Yet despite its extraordinary success, Mecca was in the grip of a social and moral crisis. The old tribal spirit had succumbed to the ethos of an infant market economy and families now vied with one another for wealth and prestige. Instead of sharing their goods, as had been essential for the tribe's survival in the desert, families were building private fortunes, and this emerging commercial aristocracy ignored the plight of the poorer Qurayshis and seized the inheritances of orphans and widows. The rich were delighted with their new security, but those who fell behind felt lost and disoriented.

Poets exalted Bedouin life, but in reality it was a grim, relentless struggle in which too many people competed for too few resources. Perpetually on the brink of starvation, tribes fought endless battles for pastureland, water, and grazing. The *ghazu,* or "acquisition raid," was essential to the Bedouin economy. In times of scarcity tribesmen would invade their neighbors' territory and carry off camels, cattle, food, or slaves, taking care to avoid killing anybody, since this would lead to a vendetta. Like most pastoralists, they saw nothing reprehensible in raiding. The ghazu was a kind of national sport, conducted with skill and panache according to clearly defined rules, which the Bedouin would have thoroughly enjoyed. It was a brutal yet simple way of redistributing wealth in a region where there was simply not enough to go round.

Although the tribesmen had little interest in the supernatural, they gave meaning to their lives with a code of virtue and honor. They called it *muruwah,* a term that is difficult to translate: it encompasses courage, patience, and endurance. Muruwah had a violent core. Tribesmen had to avenge any wrong done to the group, protect its weaker members, and defy its enemies. Each member had to be ready to leap to the defense of his kinsmen if the tribe's honor was impugned. But above all, he had to share his resources. Tribal life on the steppes would be impossible if individuals hoarded their wealth while others went hungry; nobody would help you in a lean period if you had been miserly in your good days. But by the sixth century, the limitations of muruwah were becoming tragically apparent, as the Bedouin got caught up in an escalating cycle of intertribal warfare. They began to regard those outside their kin group as worthless and expendable and felt no moral anguish about killing in defense of the tribe, right or wrong.[3] Even their ideal of courage was now essentially combative, since it lay not in self-defense but in the preemptive strike. Muslims traditionally call the pre-Islamic period *jahiliyyah,* which is usually translated as "the time of ignorance." But the primary meaning of the root *JHL* is "irascibility"—an acute sensitivity to honor and prestige, excessive arrogance, and, above all, a chronic tendency to violence and retaliation.[4]

Muhammad had become intensely aware of both the oppression and injustice in Mecca and the martial danger of jahiliyyah. Mecca had to be a place where merchants from any tribe could gather freely to do business without fear of attack, so in the interests of commerce, the Quraysh had abjured warfare, maintaining a position of aloof neutrality. With consummate skill and diplomacy, they had established the "sanctuary" (*haram*), a twenty-mile zone around the Kabah where all violence was forbidden.[5] Yet it would take more than that to subdue the jahili spirit. Meccan grandees were still chauvinistic, touchy, and liable to explosions of ungovernable fury. When Muhammad, the pious merchant, began to preach to his fellow Meccans in 612, he was well aware of the precariousness of this volatile society. Gathering a small community of followers, many from the weaker, disadvantaged clans, his message was based on the Quran ("Recitation"), a new revelation for the people of Arabia. The ideas of the civilized peoples of the ancient world had traveled down the trade routes and had been avidly discussed among the Arabs. Their own local lore had it that they themselves were descended from Ishmael, Abraham's eldest son,[6] and many believed that their high god Allah, whose name simply meant "God," was identical with the god of the Jews and Christians. But the Arabs had no concept of an exclusive revelation or of their own special election. The Quran was to them simply the latest in the unfolding revelation of Allah to the descendants of Abraham, a "reminder" of what everybody knew already.[7] Indeed, in one remarkable passage of what would become the written Quran, Allah made it clear that he made no distinction between the revelations of any of the prophets.[8]

The bedrock message of the Quran was not a new abstruse doctrine, such as had riven Byzantium, but simply a "reminder" of what constituted a just society that challenged the structural violence emerging in Mecca: that it was wrong to build a private fortune but good to share your wealth with the poor and vulnerable, who must be treated with equity and respect. The Muslims formed an *ummah,* a "community" that provided an alternative to the greed and systemic injustice of Meccan capitalism. Eventually the religion of Muhammad's followers would be called *islam,* because it demanded that individuals "surrender" their whole being to Allah; a *muslim* was simply a man or woman who had made that surrender. At first, though, the new faith was called *tazakka,* which can be roughly translated as "refinement."[9] Instead of hoarding their wealth and ignoring the plight of the poor, Muslims were exhorted to take responsibility for one another and feed the destitute, even when they were hungry themselves.[10] They traded the irascibility of jahiliyyah for the traditional Arab virtue of *hilm*—forbearance, patience, and mercy.[11] By caring for the vulnerable, freeing slaves, and performing small acts of kindness on a daily, even hourly basis, they believed that they would gradually acquire a responsible, compassionate spirit and purge themselves of selfishness. Unlike the tribesmen, who retaliated violently at the slightest provocation, Muslims must not strike back but leave revenge to Allah,[12] consistently treating all others with gentleness and courtesy.[13] Socially, the surrender of islam would be realized by learning to live in a community: believers would discover their deep bond with other human beings, whom they would strive to treat as they would wish to be treated themselves. "Not one of you can be a believer," Muhammad is reported to have said, "unless he desires for his neighbor what he desires for himself."

At first the Meccan establishment took little notice of the ummah, but when Muhammad began to emphasize the monotheism of his message, they became alarmed, for commercial rather than theological reasons. An outright rejection of the local deities would be bad for business and alienate the tribes who kept their totems around the Kabah and came specifically to visit them during the hajj. A serious rift now developed: Muslims were attacked; the ummah, still only a small segment of the Quraysh, was economically and socially ostracized; and Muhammad's life was in jeopardy. When Arabs from Yathrib, an agrarian colony some 250 miles to the north, invited the ummah to settle with them, it seemed the only solution. In 622, therefore, some seventy Muslim families left their homes for the oasis that would become known as al-Madinat, or Medina, the City of the Prophet.

This *hijrah* ("migration") from Mecca was an extraordinary step. In

Arabia, where the tribe was the most sacred value, to abandon one's kins-folk and accept the permanent protection of strangers was tantamount to blasphemy. The very word *hijrah* suggests painful severance: *HJR* has been translated as "he cut himself off from friendly or loving communi-cation . . . he ceased . . . to associate with them."[14] Henceforth Meccan Muslims would be called the *Muhajirun* ("Emigrants"), this traumatic dislocation becoming central to their identity. In taking in these foreign-ers, with whom they had no blood relationship, the Arabs of Medina who had converted to Islam, the *Ansar* ("Helpers"), had also embarked on an audacious experiment. Medina was not a unified city but a series of fortified hamlets, each occupied by a different tribal group. There were two large Arab tribes—the Aws and the Khasraj—and twenty Jew-ish tribes, and they all fought one another constantly.[15] Muhammad, as a neutral outsider, became an arbitrator and crafted an agreement that united Helpers and Emigrants in a supertribe—"one community to the exclusion of all men"—that would fight all enemies as one.[16] This is how Medina became a primitive "state" and how it found, almost immedi-ately, that despite the ideology of hilm, it had no option but to engage in warfare.

· · ·

The Emigrants were a drain on the community's resources. They were merchants and bankers, but there was little opportunity for trade in Medina; they had no experience of farming, and in any case there was no available land. It was essential to find an independent source of income, and the ghazu, the accepted way of making ends meet in times of scarcity, was the obvious solution. In 624, therefore, Muhammad began to dis-patch raiding parties to attack the Meccan caravans, a step that was con-troversial only in that the Muslims attacked their own tribe. But because the Quraysh had abjured warfare long ago, the Emigrants were inexperi-enced *ghazis*, and their first raids failed. When they finally got the hang of it, the raiders broke two Arabian cardinal rules by accidentally killing a Meccan merchant and fighting during one of the Sacred Months, when violence was prohibited throughout the peninsula.[17] Muslims could now expect reprisals from Mecca. Three months later Muhammad himself led a ghazu to attack the most important Meccan caravan of the year. When they heard about it, the Quraysh immediately sent their army to defend it, but in a pitched battle at the well of Badr, the Muslims achieved a stunning victory. The Quraysh responded the following year by attacking Medina and defeating the Muslims at the Battle of Uhud, but in 627, when they attacked Medina again, the Muslims trounced the Quraysh at the Battle of the Trench, so called because Muhammad dug a defensive ditch around the settlement.

The ummah also had internal troubles. Three of Medina's Jewish tribes—the Qaynuqa, Nadir, and Qurayzah—were determined to destroy Muhammad, because he had undermined their political ascendency in the oasis. They had sizable armies and preexisting alliances with Mecca so they were a security risk. When the Qaynuqa and Nadir staged revolts and threatened to assassinate him, Muhammad expelled them from Medina. But the Nadir had joined the nearby Jewish settlement of Khaybar and drummed up support for Mecca among the local Bedouin. So after the Battle of the Trench, when the Qurayzah had put the entire settlement at risk by plotting with Mecca during the siege, Muhammad showed no mercy. In accordance with Arab custom, the seven hundred men of the tribe were slaughtered and the women and children sold as slaves. The other seventeen Jewish tribes remained in Medina, and the Quran continued to instruct Muslims to behave respectfully to "the people of the book" (*ahl al-kitab*) and stress what they all held in common.[18] Even though the Muslims sentenced the tribesmen of Qurayzah for political rather than religious reasons, this atrocity marked the lowest point in the Prophet's career. From then on, he intensified his diplomatic efforts to build relationships with the Bedouin, who had been impressed by his military success, and established a powerful confederacy. Bedouin allies did not have to convert to Islam but swore merely to fight the ummah's enemies: Muhammad must be one of the few leaders in history to build an empire largely by negotiation.[19]

In March 628, during the month of the hajj, Muhammad announced, to everybody's astonishment, that he intended to make the pilgrimage to Mecca, which, since pilgrims were forbidden to carry weapons, meant riding unarmed into enemy territory.[20] About a thousand Muslims volunteered to accompany him. The Quraysh dispatched their cavalry to attack the pilgrims, but their Bedouin allies guided them by a back route into the sanctuary of Mecca, where all violence was forbidden. Muhammad then ordered the pilgrims to sit beside the Well of Hudaybiyyah and wait for the Quraysh to negotiate. He knew that he had put them in an extremely difficult position: if the guardians of the Kabah killed pilgrims on sacred ground, they would lose all credibility in the region. Yet when the Qurayshi envoy arrived, Muhammad agreed to conditions that seemed to throw away every advantage the ummah had gained during the war. His fellow pilgrims were so horrified that they almost mutinied, yet the Quran would praise the truce of Hudaybiyyah as a "manifest victory." While the Meccans had behaved with typical jahili belligerence when they tried to slaughter the unarmed pilgrims, God had sent down the "spirit of peace" (*sakina*) upon the Muslims.[21] Muhammad's first biographer declared that this nonviolent victory was the turning point for the young movement: during the next two years "double or more than double as many entered Islam as ever before,"[22] and in 630 Mecca voluntarily opened its gates to the Muslim army.

◆ ◆ ◆

Our main source for Muhammad's life is the Quran, the collection of revelations that came to the Prophet during the twenty-three years of his mission. The official text was standardized under Uthman, the third caliph, some twenty years after Muhammad's death. But it had originally been transmitted orally, recited aloud, and learned by heart; as a result, during and after the Prophet's life, the text remained fluid, and people would have remembered and dwelled on different parts they had heard. The Quran is not a coherent revelation: it came to Muhammad piecemeal in response to particular events, so as in any scripture, there were inconsistencies—not least about warfare. *Jihad* ("struggle") is not one of the Quran's main themes: in fact, the word and its derivatives occur only forty-one times, and only ten of these refer unambiguously to warfare. The "surrender" of islam requires a constant jihad against our inherent selfishness; this sometimes involves fighting (*qital*), but bearing trials courageously and giving to the poor in times of personal hardship was also described as jihad.[23]

There is no univocal or systematic Quranic teaching about military violence.[24] Sometimes God demands patience and restraint rather than fighting;[25] sometimes he gives permission for defensive warfare and condemns aggression; but at other times he calls for offensive warfare within certain limits;[26] and occasionally these restrictions are lifted.[27] In some passages, Muslims are told to live at peace with the people of the book;[28] in others, they are required to subdue them.[29] These contradictory instructions occur throughout the Quran, and Muslims developed two exegetical strategies to rationalize them. The first linked each verse of the Quran with a historical event in Muhammad's life and used this context to establish a general principle. Yet because the extant text does not place the revelations in chronological order, the early scholars found it difficult to determine these *asbab al-nuzal* ("occasions of revelations"). The second strategy was to abrogate verses: scholars argued that while the ummah was still struggling for survival, God could only give Muslims temporary solutions to their difficulties, but once Islam was victorious, he could issue permanent commands. Thus the later revelations—some of which call for unrestrained warfare—were God's definitive words and rescinded the earlier, more lenient directives.[30]

Scholars who favored abrogation argued that when Muslims were still a vulnerable minority in Mecca, God told them to avoid fighting and confrontation.[31] However, after the hijrah, when they had achieved a degree of power, God gave them permission to fight—but only in self-defense.[32] As they grew stronger, some of these restrictions were lifted,[33] and finally, when the Prophet returned in triumph to Mecca, Muslims were told to wage war against non-Muslims wherever and whenever they could.[34] God had therefore been preparing Muslims gradually for their global conquests, tempering his instructions to their circumstances. Modern researchers have noted, though, that the early exegetes did not always agree about which revelation should be attached to which particular "occasion" or which verse abrogated which. The American scholar Reuven Firestone has suggested that the conflicting verses instead expressed the views of different groups within the ummah during the Prophet's life and after.[35]

It would not be surprising if there were disagreements and factions in the early ummah. Like the Christians, Muslims would interpret their revelation in radically divergent ways and, like any other faith, Islam developed in response to changing circumstances. The Quran seems aware that some Muslims would not be happy to hear that God had encouraged fighting: "Fighting has been ordained for you, though it is hateful to you."[36] Once the ummah had started to engage in warfare, it seems that one group, which was strong enough to warrant extensive rebuttal, consistently refused to take part:

> Believers, why, when it is said to you, "Go and fight in God's cause,"
> do you feel weighed down to the ground? Do you prefer this world

to the world to come? How small is the enjoyment of this world compared with the life to come! If you do not go out and fight, God will punish you severely and put others in your place.[37]

The Quran calls these people "laggers" and "liars," and Muhammad was reproved for allowing them to "stay at home" during campaigns.[38] They are accused of apathy and cowardice and are equated with the *kufar*, the enemies of Islam.[39] Yet this group could point to the many verses in the Quran that instruct Muslims not to retaliate but to "forgive and forbear," responding to aggression with mercy, patience, and courtesy.[40] At other times, the Quran looks forward confidently to a final reconciliation: "Let there be no argument between us and you—God will gather us together and to Him we shall return."[41] The impressive consistency of this irenic theme throughout the Quran, Firestone believes, must reflect a strong tendency that survived in the ummah for some time—perhaps until the ninth century.[42]

Ultimately, however, the more militant groups prevailed, possibly because by the ninth century, long after the Prophet's death, the more aggressive verses reflected reality, since by this time Muslims had established an empire that could be maintained only by military force. A favorite text of those involved in the wars of conquest was the "Sword Verse," which they regarded as God's last word on the subject—though even here the endorsement of total warfare segues immediately into a demand for peace and leniency:

> When the forbidden months are over wherever you encounter the idolaters, kill them, seize them, besiege them, wait for them at every look-out post; but if they repent, maintain the prayer, and pay the prescribed alms let them go on their way, for God is most merciful and forgiving.[43]

There is thus a constant juxtaposition of ruthlessness and mercy in the Quran: believers are repeatedly commanded to fight "until there is no more sedition and religion becomes God's," but they are at once told that the moment the enemy sues for peace, there must be no further hostilities.[44]

◆　◆　◆

Muhammad's confederacy broke up after his death in 632, and his "successor" (*khalifa*), Abu Bakr, fought the defecting tribes to prevent Arabia from sliding back into chronic warfare. As we have seen elsewhere, the only way to stop such infighting was to establish a strong hegemonic power that could enforce the peace. Within two years, Abu Bakr succeeded in restoring the Pax Islamica, and after his death in 634, Umar ibn al-Khattab (r. 634–44), the second caliph, believed that peace could be preserved only by an outwardly directed offensive. These campaigns were not religiously inspired: there is nothing in the Quran to suggest that Muslims must fight to conquer the world. Umar's campaigns were driven almost entirely by the precarious economy of Arabia. There could be no question of establishing a conventional agrarian empire in Arabia, because there was so little land suitable for cultivation. The Quraysh's modest market economy clearly could not sustain the entire peninsula, and the Quran forbade members of the Islamic confederacy to fight one another. How, then, could a tribe feed itself in times of scarcity? The ghazu, the acquisition raid against neighboring tribes, had been the only way to redistribute the meager resources of Arabia, but this was now off-limits. Umar's solution was to raid the rich settled lands beyond the Arabian Peninsula, which, as the Arabs knew well, were in disarray after the Persian-Byzantine wars.

Under Umar's leadership, the Arabs burst out of the peninsula, initially in small local raids but later in larger expeditions. As they expected, they met little opposition. The armies of both the great powers had been decimated, and the subject peoples were disaffected. Jews and Monophysite Christians were sick of harassment from Constantinople, and the Persians were still reeling from the political upheaval that had followed Khosrow II's assassination. Within a remarkably short period, the Arabs forced the Roman army to retreat from Syria (636) and crushed the depleted Persian army (637). In 641 they conquered Egypt, and though they had to fight some fifteen years to pacify the whole of Iran, they were eventually victorious in 652. Only Byzantium, now a rump state shorn of its southern provinces, held out. Thus, twenty years after the Battle of Badr, the Muslims found themselves masters of Mesopotamia, Syria, Palestine, and Egypt. When they finally subdued Iran, they fulfilled the dream that had eluded both the Persians and Byzantines and re-created Cyrus's empire.[45]

It is hard to explain their success. The Arabs were accomplished raiders but had little experience of protracted warfare and had no superior weapons or technology.[46] In fact, like the Prophet, in the early years of the conquest period, they gained more territory by diplomacy than by fighting: Damascus and Alexandria both surrendered because they were offered generous terms.[47] The Arabs had no experience of state building and just adopted Persian and Byzantine systems of land tenure, taxation, and government. There was no attempt to impose Islam on the subject peoples. The people of the book—Jews, Christians, and Zoroastrians— became *dhimmis* ("protected subjects"). Critics of Islam often denounce this arrangement as evidence of Islamic intolerance, but Umar had simply adapted Khosrow I's Persian system: Islam would be the religion of the Arab conquerors—just as Zoroastrianism had been the exclusive faith of the Persian aristocracy—and the dhimmis would manage their own affairs as they had in Iran and pay the *jizya*, a poll tax, in return for military protection. After centuries of forcible attempts by the Christian Roman Empire to impose religious consensus, the traditional agrarian system reasserted itself, and many of the dhimmis found this Muslim polity a relief.

When Umar conquered Jerusalem from the Byzantines in 638, he immediately signed a charter to ensure that the Christian shrines were undisturbed and cleared the site of the Jewish temple, which had been left in ruins since its destruction in 70 and was used as the city's garbage dump. Henceforth this holy site would be called the Haram al-Sharif, the "Most Noble Sanctuary," and become the third-holiest place in the Muslim world, after Mecca and Medina. Umar also invited Jews, who had been forbidden permanent residence in Judea since the Bar Kokhba revolt, to return to the City of the Prophet Daud (David).[48] In the eleventh century, a Jerusalem rabbi still recalled with gratitude the mercy God had shown his people when he allowed the "Kingdom of Ishmael" to conquer Palestine.[49] "They did not inquire about the profession of faith," wrote the twelfth-century historian Michael the Syrian, "nor did they persecute anybody because of his profession, as did the Greeks, a heretical and wicked nation."[50]

The Muslim conquerors tried at first to resist the systemic oppression and violence of empire. Umar did not allow his officers to displace the local peoples or establish estates in the rich land of Mesopotamia. Instead, Muslim soldiers lived in new "garrison towns" (*amsar,* singular: *misr*) built in strategic locations: Kufah in Iraq, Basra in Syria, Qum in

Iran, and Fustat in Egypt; Damascus was the only old city to become a misr. Umar believed that the ummah, still in its infancy, could retain its integrity only by living apart from the more sophisticated cultures. The Muslims' ability to establish and maintain a stable, centralized empire was even more surprising than their military success. Both the Persians and the Byzantines imagined that after their initial victories, the Arabs would simply ask to settle in the empires they had conquered. This, after all, was what the barbarians had done in the western provinces, and they now ruled according to Roman law and spoke Latin dialects.[51] Yet when their wars of expansion finally ceased in 750, the Muslims ruled an empire extending from the Himalayas to the Pyrenees, the largest the world had yet seen, and most of the conquered peoples would convert to Islam and speak Arabic.[52] This extraordinary achievement seemed to endorse the message of the Quran, which taught that a society founded on the Quranic principles of justice would always prosper.

Later generations would idealize the Conquest Era, but it was a difficult time. The failure to defeat Constantinople was a bitter blow. By the time Uthman, the Prophet's son-in-law, became the third caliph (r. 644–56), Muslim troops had become mutinous and discontented. The distances were now so vast that campaigning was exhausting, and they were taking less plunder. Far from home, living perpetually in strange surroundings, soldiers had no stable family life.[53] This disquiet is reflected in the *hadith* (plural: *ahadith*) literature, in which the classical doctrine of jihad began to take shape.[54] The *ahadith* ("reports") recorded sayings and stories of the Prophet not included in the Quran. Now that he was no longer with them, people wanted to know how Muhammad had behaved and what he had thought about such subjects as warfare. These traditions were collected and anthologized during the eighth and ninth centuries and became so numerous that criteria were needed to distinguish authentic reports from the obviously spurious. Few of the ahadith date back to the Prophet himself, but even the more dubious ones throw light on attitudes in the early ummah as Muslims reflected on their astounding success.

Many ahadith saw the wars as God's way of spreading the faith. "I have been sent to the human race in its entirety," the Prophet says; "I have been commanded to fight the people until they bear witness: 'There is no god but Allah.' "[55] Empire building works best when soldiers believe that they are benefiting humanity, so the conviction that they had a divine mission would cheer flagging spirits. There is also contempt for the "laggers" who "stayed at home"; these soldiers probably resented those Muslims who benefited from the conquests but did not share their hardships. Thus in some ahadith, Muhammad is made to condemn settled life: "I was sent as a mercy and a fighter, not as a merchant and a farmer; the worst people of this ummah are the merchants and the farmers, [who are] not among those who take religion [*din*] seriously."[56] Other reports emphasize the hardships of the warrior who lives daily with death and "has built a house and not lived in it, who has married a woman and not had intercourse with her."[57] These warriors were beginning to dismiss other forms of jihad, such as caring for the poor, and saw themselves as the only true jihadis. Some ahadith claim that fighting was the Sixth Pillar or "essential practice" of Islam, alongside the profession of faith (*shehadah*), almsgiving, prayer, the Ramadan fast, and the hajj. Some said that fighting was far more precious than praying all night beside the Kabah or fasting for many days.[58] The ahadith gave fighting a spiritual dimension it had never had in the Quran. There is much emphasis on the soldier's intentions: Was he fighting for God or simply for fame and glory?[59] According to the Prophet, "The monasticism of Islam is the jihad."[60] The hardship of military life segregated soldiers from civilians, and as Christian monks lived separately from the laity, the garrison towns where Muslim fighters lived apart from their wives and observed the fasts and prayers assiduously were their monasteries.

Because soldiers constantly faced the possibility of an untimely death, there was much speculation about the afterlife. There had been no detailed end-time scenario in the Quran, and paradise had been described only in vaguely poetic terms. But now some ahadith claimed that the wars of conquest heralded the Last Days[61] and imagined Muhammad speaking as a doomsday prophet: "Behold! God has sent me with a sword, just before the Hour."[62] Muslim warriors are depicted as an elite vanguard fighting the battles of the end time.[63] When the end came, all Muslims would have to abandon the ease of settled life and join the army, which would not only defeat Byzantium but complete the conquest of Central Asia, India, and Ethiopia. Some soldiers were dreaming of martyrdom, and the ahadith supplemented with Christian imagery the Quran's brief remarks about the fate of those who die in battle.[64] Like the Greek *martus,* the Arabic *shahid* meant "one who bears witness" to Islam by making the ultimate surrender. Ahadith list his heavenly rewards: he would not have to wait in the grave for the Last Judgment like everybody else, but would ascend immediately to a special place in paradise.

> In the sight of God the martyr has six [unique] qualities: He [God] forgives him at the first opportunity, and shows him his place in paradise; he is saved from the torment of the grave, he is safe from the great fright [of the Last Judgment], a crown of honor is placed upon his head—one ruby of which is better than the world and all that is in it—he is married to 72 of the houris [women of paradise], and he gains the right to intercede [with God] for 70 of his relatives.[65]

As a reward for his hard life in the army, the martyr will drink wine, wear silk clothes, and bask in the sexual delights he had forsaken for the jihad. But other Muslims, who were not so wedded to the new military ideal, would insist that any untimely death was a martyrdrom: drowning, plague, fire, or accident also "bore witness" to human finitude, showing that there was no security in the human institutions in which people put their trust but only in the illimitable God.[66]

· · ·

It was probably inevitable that, as Muslims made their astonishing transition from a life of penury to world rule, there would be disagreements about leadership, the allocation of resources, and the morality of empire.[67] In 656 Uthman was killed during a mutiny of soldiers backed by the Quran reciters, the guardians of Islamic tradition who were opposed to the growing centralization of power in the ummah. With the support of these malcontents, Ali, the Prophet's cousin and son-in-law, became the fourth caliph; a devout man, he struggled with the logic of practical politics, and his rule was not accepted in Syria, where the opposition was led by Uthman's kinsman Muawiyyah, governor of Damascus. The son of one of the Prophet's most obdurate enemies, Muawiyyah was supported by the wealthy Meccan families and by the people of Syria, who appreciated his wise and able rule. The spectacle of the Prophet's relatives and companions poised to attack one another was profoundly disturbing, and to prevent armed conflict, the two sides called for arbitration by neutral Muslims, who decided in favor of Muawiyyah. But an extremist group refused to accept this and were shocked by Ali's initial submission. They believed that the ummah should be led by the most committed Muslim (in this case, Ali) rather than a power seeker like Muawiyyah. They now regarded both rulers as apostates, so these dissidents withdrew from the ummah, setting up their own camp with an independent commander. They would be known as *kharaji*, "those who go out." After the failure of a second arbitration, Ali was murdered by a Kharajite in 661.

The trauma of this civil war marked Islamic life forever. Henceforth rival parties would draw upon these tragic events as they struggled to make sense of their Islamic vocation. From time to time, Muslims who objected to the behavior of the reigning ruler would retreat from the ummah, as the Kharajites had done, and summon all "true Muslims" to join them in a struggle (*jihad*) for higher Islamic standards.[68] The fate of Ali became for some a symbol of the structural injustice of mainstream political life, and these Muslims, who called themselves the *shiah-i Ali* ("Ali's partisans"), developed a piety of principled protest, revering Ali's male descendants as the true leaders of the ummah. But appalled by the murderous divisions that had torn the ummah apart, most Muslims decided that unity must be the first priority, even if that meant accommodating a degree of oppression and injustice. Instead of revering Ali's descendants, they would follow the *sunnah* ("customary practice") of the Prophet. As in Christianity and Judaism, radically different interpretations of the original revelation would make it impossible to speak of a pure, essentialist "Islam."

The Quran had given Muslims an historical mission: to create a just community in which all members, even the weakest and most vulnerable, would be treated with absolute respect. This would demand a constant struggle (*jihad*) with the egotism and self-interest that holds us back from the divine. Politics was therefore not a distraction from spirituality but what Christians would call a sacrament, the arena in which Muslims experienced God and that enabled the divine to function effectively in our world. Hence if state institutions did not measure up to the Quranic ideal, if their political leaders were cruel or exploitative and their community humiliated by foreign enemies, a Muslim could feel that his or her faith in life's ultimate purpose was imperiled. For Muslims, the suffering, oppression, and exploitation that arose from the systemic violence of the state were moral issues of sacred import and could not be relegated to the profane realm.

After Ali's death, Muawiyyah moved his capital from Medina to Damascus and founded a hereditary dynasty. The Umayyads would create a regular agrarian empire, with a privileged aristocracy and an unequal distribution of wealth. Herein lay the Muslim dilemma. There was now general agreement that an absolute monarchy was far more satisfactory than a military oligarchy, where commanders inevitably competed aggressively for power—as Ali and Muawiyyah had done. The Umayyads' Jewish, Christian, and Zoroastrian subjects agreed. They were weary of the chaos inflicted by the Roman-Persian wars and longed for the peace that only an autocratic empire seemed able to provide. Umayyads permitted some of the old Arab informality, but they understood the importance of the monarch's state of exception. They modeled their court ceremonial on Persian practice, shrouded the caliph from public view in the mosque, and achieved a monopoly of state violence by ruling that only the caliph could summon Muslims to war.[69]

But this adoption of the systemic violence condemned by the Quran was very disturbing to the more devout Muslims, and nearly all the institutions now regarded as critical to Islam emerged from anguished discussions that took place after the civil war. One was the Sunni/Shiah divide. Another was the discipline of jurisprudence (*fiqh*): jurists wanted to establish precise legal norms that would make the Quranic command to build a just society a real possibility rather than a pious dream. These debates also produced Islamic historiography: in order to find solutions in the present, Muslims looked back to the time of the Prophet and the first four caliphs (*rashidun*). Moreover, Muslim asceticism developed as a reaction against the growing luxury and worldliness of the aristocracy. Ascetics often wore the coarse woollen garments (*tasawwuf*) standard among the poor, as the Prophet had done, so would become known as Sufis. While the caliph and his administration struggled with the problems that beset any agrarian empire and tried to develop a powerful monarchy, these pious Muslims were adamantly opposed to any compromise with its structural inequity and oppression.

One event above all others symbolized the tragic conflict between the inherent violence of the state and Muslim ideals. After Ali's death, the Shii had pinned their hopes on Ali's descendants. Hasan, Ali's elder son, came to an agreement with Muawiyyah and retired from political life. But in 680, when Muawiyyah died, he passed the caliphate to his son Yazid. For the first time, a Muslim ruler had not been elected by his peers, and there were Shii demonstrations in Kufa in favor of Husain, Ali's younger son. This uprising was ruthlessly quashed, but Husain had already set out from Medina to Kufa, accompanied by a small band of his followers and their wives and children, convinced that the spectacle of the Prophet's family marching to end imperial injustice would remind the ummah of its Islamic priorities. But Yazid sent out the army, and they were massacred on the plain of Karbala, outside Kufa; Husain was the last to die, holding his infant son in his arms. All Muslims lament the murder of the Prophet's grandson, but for the Shiah, Karbala epitomized the Muslim dilemma. How could Islamic justice be realistically implemented in a belligerent imperial state?

Under the Umayyad caliph Abd al-Malik (r. 685–705), the wars of expansion gained new momentum, and the Middle East began to assume an Islamic face. The Dome of the Rock, built by Abd al-Malik in Jerusalem in 691, was as magnificent as any of Justinian's buildings. Yet the Umayyad economy was in trouble: it was too reliant on plunder, and its investment in public buildings was not sustainable. Umar II (r. 717–20) tried to rectify this by cutting down on state expenditure, demobilizing surplus military units, and reducing the commanders' allowances. He knew that the dhimmis resented the jizya tax, which they alone had to pay, and that many Muslims believed this arrangement violated Quranic egalitarianism. So even though it meant a drastic loss of income, Umar II became the first caliph to encourage the conversion of the dhimmis to Islam. He did not live long enough to see his reform through, however. Hisham I (724–43), his successor, launched new military offensives in Central Asia and North Africa, but when he tried to revive the economy by reimposing the jizya, there was a massive revolt of Berber converts in North Africa.

Backed by disaffected Persian converts, a new dynasty, claiming descent from Muhammad's uncle Abbas, challenged Umayyad rule, drawing heavily on Shii rhetoric. In August 749 they occupied Kufa and defeated the Umayyad caliph the following year. But as soon as they were in power, the Abbasids cast aside their Shii piety and set up an absolute monarchy on the Persian model, which was welcomed by the subject peoples but strayed wholly from Islamic principles by embracing imperial structural violence. Their first act was to massacre all the Umayyads, and a few years later Caliph Abu Jafar al-Mansur (754–75) murdered Shii leaders and moved his capital to the new city of Baghdad, just thirty-five miles south of Ctesiphon. The Abbasids were wholly oriented toward the East.[70] In the West, the victory of the Frankish king Charles Martel over a Muslim raiding party at Poitiers in 732 is often seen as the decisive event that saved Europe from Islamic domination; in fact, Christendom was saved by the Abbasids' total indifference to the West. Realizing that the empire could expand no further, they conducted foreign affairs with elaborate Persian diplomacy, and the soldier soon became an anomaly at court.

By the reign of Harun al-Rashid (786–809), the transformation of the Islamic Empire from an Arab to a Persian monarchy was complete. The caliph was hailed as the "Shadow of God" on earth, and his Muslim subjects—who had once bowed only to God—prostrated themselves before him. The executioner stood constantly beside the ruler to show that he had the power of life and death. He left the routine tasks of government to his vizier; the caliph's role was to be a judge of ultimate appeal, beyond the reach of factions and politicking. He had two significant tasks: to lead the Friday prayers and to lead the army into battle. The latter was a new departure because the Umayyads had never personally taken the field with the army, so Harun was the first autocratic ghazi-caliph.[71]

The Abbasids had given up trying to conquer Constantinople, but every year Harun conducted a raid into Byzantine territory to demonstrate his commitment to the defense of Islam: the Byzantine emperor reciprocated with a token invasion of Islamdom. Court poets praised Harun for his zeal in "exerting himself beyond the exertion [*jihad*] of one who fears God." They pointed out that Harun was a volunteer who put himself at risk in a task not required of him: "You could, if you liked, resort to some pleasant place, while others endured hardship instead of you."[72] Harun was deliberately evoking the golden age when every able-bodied man had been expected to ride into battle beside the Prophet. Despite its glorious facade, however, the empire was already in trouble, economically and militarily.[73] The Abbasids' professional army was expensive, and manpower always a problem. Yet it was imperative to defend the border against the Byzantines, so Harun reached out to committed civilians who, like himself, were ready to volunteer their services.

Increasingly, Muslims who lived near the empire's frontiers began to see "the border" as a symbol of Islamic integrity that had to be defended against a hostile world. Some of the *ulema* ("learned scholars") had objected to the Umayyads' monopoly of the jihad because it clashed with Quranic verses and hadith traditions that made jihad a duty for everybody.[74] Hence, when the Umayyads had besieged Constantinople (717–18), ulema, hadith-collectors, ascetics, and Quran-reciters had assembled on the frontier to support the army with their prayers. Their motivation was pious, but perhaps they were also attracted by the intensity and excitement of the battlefield. Now following Harun's lead, they gathered again in even greater numbers, not only on the Syrian-Byzantine border but also on the frontiers of Central Asia, North Africa, and Spain. Some of these scholars and ascetics took part in the fighting and in garrison duties, but most supplied spiritual support in the form of prayer, fasting, and study. "Volunteering" (*tatawwa*) would put down deep roots in Islam and resurface powerfully in our own day.

During the eighth century, some of these "fighting scholars" started to develop a distinctively jihadi spirituality. Abu Ishaq al-Fazari (d. c. 802) believed he was imitating the Prophet in his life of study and warfare; Ibraham ibn Adham (d. 778), who engaged in extreme fasts and heroic night vigils on the frontier, maintained that there could be no more perfect form of Islam; and Abdullah ibn Mubarak (d. 797) agreed, arguing that the dedication of the early Muslim warriors had been the glue that bonded the early ummah. Jihadis did not need the state's permission but could volunteer whether the authorities and professional soldiers liked it or not. However, these pious volunteers could not solve the empire's manpower problem, so eventually Caliph al-Mutasim (r. 833–42) would create a personal army of Turkish slaves from the steppes, who placed the formidable fighting skills of the herdsmen at the service of Islam. Each *mamluk* ("slave") was converted to Islam, but because the Quran forbade the enslaving of Muslims, their sons were born free. This policy was fraught with contradictions, but the Mamluks became a privileged caste, and in the not-too-distant future, these Turks would rule the empire.

The volunteers had created another variant of Islam and could claim that their way of life came closest to that of the Prophet who had spent years defending the ummah against its enemies. Yet their militant jihad never appealed to the wider ummah. In Mecca and Medina, where the frontier was a distant reality, almsgiving and solicitude for the poor were still seen as the most important form of jihad. Some ulema vigorously opposed the beliefs of the "fighting scholars," arguing that a man who devoted his life to scholarship and prayed every day in the mosque was just as good a Muslim as a warrior.[75] A new hadith reported that on his way home from the Battle of Badr, Muhammad had said to his companions: "We are returning from the Lesser Jihad [the battle] and returning to the Greater Jihad"—the more exacting and important effort to fight the baser passions and reform one's own society.[76]

* * *

During the Conquest Era, the ulema had begun to develop a distinctive body of Muslim law in the garrison towns. At that time the ummah had been a tiny minority; by the tenth century, 50 percent of the empire's population was Muslim, and the code of the garrisons was no longer appropriate.[77] The Abbasid aristocracy had its own Persian code known as the *adab* ("culture"), which was based on the literate artistry and courtly manners expected of the nobility and was obviously unsuitable for the masses.[78] The caliphs therefore asked the ulema to develop the standardized system of Islamic law that would become the Shariah. Four schools of law (*maddhab*) emerged, all regarded as equally valid. Each school had its distinctive outlook but was based on the practice (*sunnah*) of the Prophet and the early ummah. Like the Talmud, which was a strong influence on these developments, the new jurisprudence (*fiqh*) aimed to bring the whole of life under the canopy of the sacred. There was therefore no attempt to impose a single "rule of faith." Individuals were free to select their own maddhab and, as in Judaism, follow the rulings of the scholar of their choice.

Shariah law provided a principled alternative to the aristocratic rule of agrarian society, since it refused to accept a hereditary class system. It therefore had revolutionary potential; indeed, two of the maddhab founders—Malik ibn Anas (d. 795) and Muhammad Idris al-Shafii (d. 820)—had taken part in Shii uprisings against the early Abbasids. The Shariah insisted that every single Muslim was directly responsible to God; a Muslim needed no caliph or priest to mediate divine law, and everybody—not just the ruling class—was responsible for the ummah's well-being. Where the aristocratic adab took a pragmatic view of what was politically feasible, the Shariah was an idealistic countercultural challenge, which tacitly condemned the structural violence of the imperial state and boldly insisted that no institution—not even the caliphate— had the right to interfere with an individual's personal decisions. There was no way that an agrarian state could be run on these lines, however, and although the caliphs always acknowledged the Shariah as the law of God, they could not rule by it. Consequently, Shariah law never governed the whole of society, and the caliph's court, where justice was summary, absolute, and arbitrary, remained the supreme court of appeal; in theory, any Muslim, however lowly, could appeal to the caliph for justice against members of the lower aristocracy.[79] Nevertheless, the Shariah was a constant witness to the Islamic ideal of equality that is so deeply embedded in our humanity that despite the apparent impossibility of incorporating it in political life, we remain stubbornly convinced that it is the natural way for human beings to live together.

Al-Shafii formulated what would become the classical doctrine of jihad, which, despite Shariah aversion to autocracy, drew on standard imperial ideology: it had a dualistic worldview, claimed that the ummah had a divine mission and that Islamic rule would benefit humanity. God had decreed warfare because it was essential for the ummah's survival, Al-Shafii argued. The human race was divided into the *dar al-Islam* ("The Abode of Islam") and the non-Muslim world, the *dar al-harb* ("The Abode of War"). There could be no final peace between the two, though a temporary truce was permissible. But since all ethical faiths came from God, the ummah was only one of many divinely guided communities, and the goal of jihad was not to convert the subject population. What distinguished Islam from other revelations, however, was that it had a God-given mandate to extend its rule to the rest of humanity. Its mission was to establish the social justice and equity prescribed by God in the Quran, so that all men and women could be liberated from the tyranny of a state run on worldly principles.[80] The reality, however, was that the Abbasid caliphate was an autocracy that depended on the forcible subjugation of the majority of the population; like any agrarian state, it was constitutionally unable to implement Quranic norms fully. Yet without such idealism, which reminds us of the imperfection of our institutions, their inherent violence and injustice would go without critique. Perhaps the role of religious vision is to fill us with a divine discomfort that will not allow us wholly to accept the unacceptable.

Al-Shafii also ruled against the conviction of "fighting scholars" that militant jihad was incumbent upon every Muslim. In Shariah law, the daily prayer was binding on all Muslims without exception, so it was *fard ayn,* an obligation for each individual. But even though all Muslims were responsible for the well-being of the ummah, some tasks, such as cleaning the mosque, could be left to the appointed official and was *fard kifaya,* a duty delegated to an individual by the community. Should this job be neglected, however, others were obliged to take the initiative and step in.[81] Al-Shafii decreed that jihad against the non-Muslim world was fard kifaya and the ultimate responsibility of the caliph. Therefore, as long as there were enough soldiers to defend the frontier, civilians were exempt from military service. In the event of an enemy invasion, though, Muslims in the border regions might be obliged to help. Al-Shafii was writing at a time when the Abbasids had renounced territorial expansion, so he was legislating not for offensive jihad but only for defensive warfare. Muslims still debate the legitimacy of jihad in these terms today.

• • •

Sunni Muslims had accepted the imperfections of the agrarian system in order to keep the peace.[82] The Shii still condemned its systemic violence but found a practical way of dealing with the Abbasid regime. Jafar al-Sadiq (d. 765), the sixth in the line of Imams ("leaders") descended from Ali, formally abandoned armed struggle, because rebellions were always savagely put down and resulted only in unacceptable loss of life. Henceforth the Shiah would hold aloof from the mainstream, their disengagement a silent rebuke to Abbasid tyranny and a witness to true Islamic values. As the Prophet's descendant, Jafar enshrined his charisma and remained the rightful leader of the ummah, but henceforth he would function only as a spiritual guide. Jafar had, in effect, separated religion and politics. This sacred secularism would remain the dominant ideal of Shiism until the late twentieth century.

Yet the Imams remained an unbearable irritant to the caliphs. The Imam, a living link with the Prophet, revered by the faithful, quietly dedicated to the contemplation of scripture and charitable works, offered a striking contrast to the caliph, whose ever-present executioner was a grim reminder of the violence of empire. Which was the truly Muslim leader? The Imams embodied a sacred presence that could not exist safely or openly in a world dominated by cruelty and injustice, since they were nearly all murdered by the caliphs. When toward the end of the ninth century, the Twelfth Imam mysteriously vanished from prison, it was said that God had miraculously removed him and that he would one day return to inaugurate an era of justice. In this concealment he remained the true leader of the ummah, so all earthly government was illegitimate. Paradoxically, liberated from the confines of time and space, the Hidden Imam became a more vivid presence in the lives of Shiis. The myth reflected the tragic impossibility of implementing a truly equitable policy in a flawed and violent world. On the anniversary of Imam Husain's death on the tenth (*ashura*) of the month of Muharram, Shiis would publicly mourn his murder, processing through the streets, weeping and beating their breasts to demonstrate their undying opposition to the corruption of mainstream Muslim life. But not all Shiis subscribed to Jafar's sacred secularism. The Ismailis, who believed that Ali's line had ended with Ismail, the Seventh Imam, remained convinced that piety must be backed up by military jihad for a just society. In the tenth century, when the Abbasid regime was in serious decline, an Ismaili leader established a rival caliphate in North Africa, and this Fatimid dynasty later spread to Egypt, Syria, and Palestine.[83]

•   •   •

In the tenth century, the Muslim empire was beginning to fragment. Taking advantage of Fatimid weakness, the Byzantines conquered Antioch and important areas of Cilicia, while within the Dar al-Islam, Turkish generals established virtually independent states, although they continued to acknowledge the caliph as the supreme leader. In 945 the Turkish Buyid dynasty actually occupied Baghdad, and even though the caliph retained his court, the region became a province of the Buyid kingdom. Yet Islam was by no means a spent force. There had always been tension between the Quran and autocratic monarchy, and the new arrangement of independent rulers symbolically linked by their loyalty to the caliph was religiously more congenial if not politically effective. Muslim religious thought subsequently became less driven by current events and would become politically oriented again only in the modern period, when the ummah faced a new imperial threat.

The Seljuk Turks from Central Asia gave fullest expression to the new order. They acknowledged the sovereignty of the caliph, but under their brilliant Persian vizier Nizam al-Mulk (r. 1063–92), they created an empire extending to Yemen in the south, the Oxus River in the east, and Syria in the west. The Seljuks were not universally popular. Some of the more radical Ismailis withdrew to mountain strongholds in what is now Lebanon, where they prepared for a jihad to replace the Seljuks with a Shii regime, occasionally undertaking suicidal missions to murder prominent members of the Seljuk establishment. Their enemies called them *hashashin* because they were said to use hashish to induce mystical ecstasy, and this gave us our English word *assassin*.[84] But most Muslims accommodated easily to Seljuk rule. Theirs was not a centralized empire; the emirs who commanded the districts were virtually autonomous and worked closely with the ulema, who gave these disparate military regimes ideological unity. To raise educational standards, they created the first madrassas, and Nizam al-Mulk established these schools throughout the empire, giving the ulema a power base and drawing the scattered provinces together. Emirs came and went, but the Shariah courts became a stable authority in each region. Moreover, Sufi mystics and the more charismatic ulema traveled the length and breadth of the Seljuk Empire, giving ordinary Muslims a strong sense of belonging to an international community.

By the end of the eleventh century, however, the Seljuk Empire had also started to decline. It had succumbed to the usual problem of a military oligarchy, since the emirs began to fight one another for territory. They were so intent on these internal feuds that they neglected the frontier and were incapable of stopping the influx of pastoralists from the steppes who had begun to bring their herds into the fertile settled lands now ruled by their own people. Large groups of Turkish herdsmen moved steadily westward, taking over the choicest pasturage and driving out the local population. Eventually they arrived at the Byzantine frontier in the Armenian highlands. In 1071 the Seljuk chieftain Alp Arslan defeated the Byzantine army at Manzikert in Armenia, and as the Byzantines retreated, the nomadic Turks broke through the unguarded frontier and began to infiltrate Byzantine Anatolia. The beleaguered Byzantine emperor now appealed to the Christians of the West for help.

8

Crusade and Jihad

Pope Gregory VII (r. 1073–85) was deeply disturbed to hear that hordes of Turkish tribesmen had invaded Byzantine territory, and in 1074 he dispatched a series of letters summoning the faithful to join him in "liberating" their brothers in Anatolia. He proposed personally to lead an army to the east, which would rid Greek Christians of the Turkish menace and then liberate the holy city of Jerusalem from the infidel.[1] *Libertas* and *liberatio* were the buzzwords of eleventh-century Europe; its knights had recently "liberated" land from the Muslim occupiers of Calabria, Sardinia, Tunisia, Sicily, and Apulia and had begun the Reconquista of Spain.[2] In the future, Western imperial aggression would often be couched in the rhetoric of liberty. But *libertas* had different connotations in medieval Europe. When Roman power collapsed in the western provinces, the bishops had taken the place of the Roman senatorial aristocracy, stepping into the political vacuum left by the departing imperial officials.[3] The Roman clergy thus adopted the old aristocracy's ideal of libertas, which had little to do with freedom; rather, it referred to the maintenance of the privileged position of the ruling class, lest society lapse into barbarism.[4] As the successor of Saint Peter, Gregory believed that he had a divine mandate to rule the Christian world. His "crusade" was designed in part to reassert papal libertas in the Eastern Empire, which did not accept the supremacy of the bishop of Rome.

Throughout his pontificate, Gregory struggled but ultimately failed to assert the libertas, the supremacy and integrity, of the Church against the rising power of the lay rulers. Hence his proposed crusade came to nothing, and in his determined effort to free the clergy from lay control, he was ignominiously defeated by Henry IV, Holy Roman emperor of the West. For eight years the pontiff and the emperor had been locked in a power struggle, each trying to depose the other. In 1084, when Gregory threatened him with excommunication once again, Henry simply invaded Italy and installed an antipope in the Lateran Palace. But the popes had only themselves to blame, for the Western Empire was their creation. For centuries the Byzantines had maintained an outpost in Ravenna, Italy, to protect the Church of Rome against the barbarians. By the eighth century, however, the Lombards had become so aggressive in northern Italy that the pope needed a stronger lay protector, so in 753 Pope Stephen II made an heroic journey over the Alps in the middle of winter to the old Roman province of Gaul to seek an alliance with Pippin, son of the Frankish king Charles Martel, thus giving papal legitimacy to the Carolingian dynasty. Pippin at once began preparations for a military expedition to Italy, while his ten-year-old son, Charles—later known as Charlemagne—escorted the exhausted and bedraggled pope to his lodgings.

The Germanic tribes who established kingdoms in the old Roman provinces had embraced Christianity and revered the warrior kings of the Hebrew Bible, but their military ethos was still permeated with ancient Aryan ideals of heroism and desire for fame, glory, and loot. All these elements blended inextricably in their conduct of war. The Carolingians' wars were presented as holy wars, sanctioned by God, and they called their dynasty the New Israel.[5] Their military campaigns certainly had a religious dimension, but material profit was every bit as important. In 732 Charles Martel (d. 741) had defeated a Muslim army on its way to pillage Tours, but after his victory Charles immediately proceeded to loot the Christian communities in southern Francia as thoroughly as the Muslims would have done.[6] During his Italian wars to defend the pope, his son Pippin forced the Lombards to relinquish a third of their treasure; this massive wealth enabled his clergy to build a truly Catholic and Roman enclave north of the Alps.

Charlemagne (r. 772–814) showed what a king could do when supported by such substantial resources.[7] By 785 he had conquered northern Italy and the whole of Gaul; in 792 he moved into central Europe and attacked the Avars of western Hungary, bringing home wagonloads of plunder. These campaigns were billed as holy wars against "pagans," but the Franks remembered them for more mundane reasons. "All the Avar nobility died in the war, all their glory departed. All their wealth and their treasure assembled over so many years were dispersed," Einhard, Charlemagne's biographer, recorded complacently. "The memory of men cannot remember any war of the Franks by which they were so enriched and their material possessions so increased."[8] Far from being inspired solely by religious zeal, these wars of expansion were also informed by the economic imperative of acquiring more arable land. The episcopal sees in the occupied territories became instruments of colonial control,[9] and the mass baptisms of the conquered peoples were statements of political rather than spiritual realignment.[10]

But the religious element was prominent. On Christmas Day 800, Pope Leo III crowned Charlemagne "Holy Roman Emperor" in the Basilica of St. Peter. The congregation acclaimed him as "Augustus," and Leo prostrated himself at Charlemagne's feet. The popes and bishops of Italy had long believed that the raison d'être of the Roman Empire was to protect the libertas of the Catholic Church.[11] After the empire's fall, they knew that the Church could not survive without the king and his warriors. Between 750 and 1050, therefore, the king was a sacred figure who stood at the apex of the social pyramid. "Our Lord Jesus Christ has set you up as the ruler of the Christian people, in power more excellent than the pope or the emperor of Constantinople," wrote Alcuin, a British monk and court adviser to Charlemagne. "On you alone depends the whole safety of the churches of Christ."[12] In a letter to Leo, Charlemagne declared that as emperor it was his mission "everywhere to defend the church of Christ."[13]

The instability and chaotic flux of life in Europe after the collapse of the Roman Empire had created a hunger for tangible contact with the eternal stability of Heaven. Hence the popularity of the saints' relics, which provided a physical link with a martyr who was now with God. Even the mighty Charlemagne felt vulnerable in this violent and unstable world: his throne in Aachen had cavities stuffed with relics, and the great monasteries of Fulda, St. Gall, and Reichenau, positioned on the borders of his empire as powerhouses of prayer and sanctity, took great pride in their relic collection.[14] The monks of Europe were very different from their counterparts in Egypt and Syria. They were not peasants but members of the nobility; they lived not in desert caves but on estates farmed by serfs who were the monastery's property.[15] Most followed the Rule of St. Benedict, written in the sixth century at a time when the bonds of civil society seemed on the point of collapse. Benedict's aim had been to create communities of obedience, stability, and *religio* ("reverence" and "bonding") in a world of violence and uncertainty. The rule provided *disciplina,* similar to the military disciplina of the Roman soldier: it prescribed a series of physical rituals carefully designed to restructure emotion and desire and create an attitude of humility very different from the aggressive self-assertion of the knight.[16] Monastic disciplina set out to defeat not a physical enemy but the unruly psyche and the unseen powers of evil. The Carolingians knew that they owed their success in battle to highly disciplined troops. Hence they appreciated the Benedictine communities, and during the ninth and tenth centuries support for the rule became a central feature of government in Europe.[17]

Monks formed a social order (*ordo*), separate from the disordered world outside the monastery. Abjuring sex, money, fighting, and mutability, the most corrupting aspects of secular life, they embraced chastity, poverty, nonviolence, and stability. Unlike the restless boskoi, Benedictine monks vowed to remain in the same community for life.[18] A monastery, however, was designed not so much to cater to individual spiritual quests but to serve a social function by providing occupation for the younger sons of the nobility, who could never hope to own land and might become a disruptive influence in society. At this point, Western Christendom did not distinguish public and private, natural and supernatural. Thus by combating the demonic powers with their prayers, monks were essential to the security of the realm. There were two ways for an aristocrat to serve God: fighting or praying.[19] Monks were the spiritual counterparts of secular soldiers, their battles just as real and far more significant:

> The abbot is armed with spiritual weapons and supported by a troop of monks anointed with the dew of heavenly graces. They fight together in the strength of Christ with the sword of the spirit against the aery wiles of the devils. They defend the king and clergy of the realm from the onslaughts of their invisible enemies.[20]

The Carolingian aristocracy was convinced that the success of their earthly battles depended on their monks' disciplined warfare, even though they fought only with "vigils, hymns, prayers, psalms, alms and daily offering of masses."[21]

Originally there had been three social orders in Western Christendom: monks, clerics, and the laity. But during the Carolingian period, two distinct aristocratic orders emerged: the warrior nobility (*bellatores*) and the men of religion (*oratores*). Clerics and bishops, who worked in the world (*saeculum*) and had once formed a separate ordo, were now merged with monks and would increasingly be pressured to live like them by abjuring marriage and fighting. In Frankish and Anglo-Saxon society, still influenced by ancient Aryan values, those who shed blood on the battlefield carried a taint that disqualified them from handling sacred things or saying Mass. However, military violence was about to receive a Christian baptism.

During the ninth and tenth centuries, hordes of Norse and Magyar invaders devastated Europe and brought down the Carolingian Empire. Although they would be remembered as wicked and monstrous, in truth a Viking leader was no different from Charles Martel or Pippin: he was simply a "king on the warpath [*vik*]," fighting for tribute, plunder, and prestige.[22] In 962 the Saxon king Otto managed to repel the Magyars and re-create the Holy Roman Empire in much of Germany. Yet in Francia, the kings' power had so declined that they could no longer control the lesser aristocrats, who not only fought one another but had begun to loot church property and to terrorize the peasant villages, killing livestock and burning homes if the agricultural yield was poor.[23] A member of the lower aristocracy—called *cniht* ("soldier") or *chevaller* ("horseman")— felt no qualms about such raiding, which was essential to his way of life. For decades French knights had been engaged in almost ceaseless warfare and were now economically dependent on plunder and looting. As the French historian Marc Bloch has explained, besides bringing a knight glory and heroism, warfare was "perhaps above all, a source of profit, the nobleman's chief industry," so for the less affluent, the return of peace could be "an economic crisis as well as a disastrous loss of prestige."[24] Without war, a knight could not afford weapons and horses, tools of his trade, and would be forced into menial labor. The violent seizure of property was, as we have seen, regarded as the only honorable way for an aristocrat to acquire resources, so much so that there was "no line of demarcation" in early medieval Europe between "warlike activity" and "pillaging."[25] During the tenth century, therefore, many impoverished knights were simply doing what came naturally to them when they robbed and harassed the peasantry.

This surge of violence coincided with the development of the manors, the great landed estates, and a full-fledged agrarian system in Europe, which depended on the forcible extraction of the agricultural surplus.[26] The arrival of the structural violence that maintained it was heralded at the end of the tenth century by the appearance of a new ordo: the *imbelle vulgus,* or "unarmed commoner," whose calling was *laborare,* "to work."[27] The manorial system had abolished the ancient distinction between the free peasant, who could bear arms, and the slave, who could not. Both were now lumped together, forbidden to fight, yet unable to defend themselves from the knights' assault, and forced to live at subsistence level. A two-tier stratification had emerged in Western society: the "men of power" (*potentes*) and the "poor" (*pauperes*). The aristocracy needed the help of ordinary soldiers to subjugate the poor, so knights became retainers, exempt from servitude and taxation and members of the nobility.

The aristocratic priests naturally supported this oppressive system and indeed were largely responsible for crafting it, enraging many of the poor by their flagrant abandonment of the egalitarianism of the gospel. The Church denounced the more vocal of these malcontents as "heretics," but their dissent took the form of a religiously articulated protest against the new social and political system and was not concerned with theological issues. In the early eleventh century, for example, Robert of Arbrissel wandered barefoot through Brittany and Anjou at the head of a tattered retinue of *pauperes Christi,* his demand for a return to gospel values attracting widespread support.[28] In southern France, Henry of Lausanne also drew huge crowds when he attacked the greed and immorality of the clergy, and in Flanders, Tanchelm of Antwerp preached so effectively that people stopped attending Mass and refused to pay their tithes. Robert eventually submitted to the Church, founded a Benedictine monastery, and became a canonized saint, but Henry remained active in his "heresy" for thirty years, and Tanchelm set up his own church.

The monks of the Benedictine abbey of Cluny in Burgundy responded to the twofold crisis of internal violence and social protest by initiating a reform that attempted to limit the lawless aggression of the knights. They tried to introduce lay men and women to the values of monastic religio, in their view the only authentic form of Christianity, by promoting the practice of pilgrimage to sacred sites. Like a monk, the pilgrim made a decision to turn her back on the world (*saeculum*) and head for the centers of holiness; like a monk, she made a vow in the local church before setting out and donned a special uniform. All pilgrims had to be chaste for the duration of their pilgrimage, and knights were forbidden to carry arms, thus forced to contain their instinctive aggression for a significant period of time. During the long, difficult, and frequently dangerous journey, lay pilgrims formed a community, the rich sharing the privations and vulnerability of the poor, the poor learning that their poverty had sacred value, and both experiencing the inevitable hardship of life on the road as a form of asceticism.

At the same time, the reformers tried to give fighting spiritual value and make knightly warfare a Christian vocation. They decided that a warrior could serve God by protecting the unarmed poor from the depredations of the lower aristocracy and by pursuing the enemies of the Church. The saintly hero of the *Life of St. Gerald of Aurillac,* written circa 930 by Odo, abbot of Cluny, was neither a king, nor a monk, nor a bishop but an ordinary knight who achieved sanctity by becoming a soldier of Christ and defending the poor. To further their cult of this "holy warfare," the reformers devised rituals for the blessing of military banners and swords and encouraged devotion to such military saints as Michael, George, and Mercury (who was believed to have murdered Julian the Apostate).[29]

In a related movement, the bishops inaugurated the Peace of God to limit the knights' violence and protect Church property.[30] In central and southern France, where the monarchy was no longer functioning and society was degenerating into violent chaos, they began to convene large assemblies of churchmen, knights, and feudal lords in the fields outside the cities. During these rallies, knights were forced to swear, on pain of excommunication, that they would stop tormenting the poor:

> I will not carry off either ox or cow or any other beast of burden; I
> will seize neither peasant nor merchant; I will not take from them
> their pence, nor oblige them to ransom themselves; and I will not

beat them to obtain their subsistence. I will seize neither horse, mare nor colt from their pasture; I will not destroy or burn their houses.[31]

At these peace councils the bishops insisted that anyone who killed his fellow Christians "spills the blood of Christ."[32] They now also introduced the Truce of God, forbidding fighting from Wednesday evening to Monday morning each week in memory of Christ's days of passion, death, and resurrection. Although peace became a reality for a specific period of time, it could not be maintained without coercion. The bishops were able to enforce the Peace and the Truce only by forming "peace militias." Anyone who broke the Truce, explained the chronicler Raoul Glaber (c. 985–1047), "was to pay for it with his life or be driven from his own country and the company of his fellow-Christians."[33] These peacekeeping forces helped to make knightly violence a genuine "service" (*militia*) of God, equal to the priestly and monastic vocation.[34] The Peace movement spread throughout France, and by the end of the eleventh century, there is evidence that a significant number of knights had indeed been converted to a more "religious" lifestyle and regarded their military duties as a form of lay monasticism.[35]

But for Pope Gregory VII, one of the leading reformers of the day, knighthood could be a holy vocation only if it fought to preserve the libertas of the Church. He therefore tried to recruit kings and aristocrats into his own Militia of St. Peter to fight the Church's enemies—and it was with this militia that he intended to fight his "crusade." In his letters he linked the ideals of brotherly love for the beleaguered Eastern Christians and liberatio of the church with military aggression. But very few laymen joined his militia.[36] Why indeed would they, since it was clearly designed to enhance the power of the Church at the expense of the bellatores? The popes had blessed the predatory violence of the Carolingians because it had enabled the Church to survive. But as Gregory had learned in his struggle with Henry IV, warriors were no longer willing simply to protect the Church's privileges.

This political struggle for power between popes and emperors would inform the religiously inspired violence of the Crusading period; both sides were competing for political supremacy in Europe, and that meant gaining the monopoly of violence. In 1074 Gregory's crusade had no takers; twenty years later, the response from the laity would be very different.

• • •

On November 27, 1095, Pope Urban II, another Cluniac monk, addressed a Peace Council at Clermont in southern France and summoned the First Crusade, appealing directly to the Franks, the heirs of Charlemagne. We have no contemporary record of this speech and can only infer what Urban might have said from his letters.[37] In keeping with the recent reforms, Urban urged the knights of France to stop attacking their fellow Christians and instead fight God's enemies. Like Gregory VII, Urban urged the Franks to "liberate" their brothers, the Eastern Christians, from "the tyranny and oppression of Muslims."[38] They should then proceed to the Holy Land to liberate Jerusalem. In this way the Peace of God would be enforced in Christendom and God's war fought in the East. The Crusade, Urban was convinced, would be an act of love in which the Crusaders nobly laid down their lives for their eastern brothers, and in leaving their homes they would secure the same heavenly rewards as monks who abjured the world for the cloister.[39] Yet for all this pious talk, the Crusade was also essential to Urban's political maneuvers to secure the libertas of the Church. The previous year he had ousted Henry IV's antipope from the Lateran Palace, and at Clermont he excommunicated King Philip I of France for making an adulterous marriage. Now by dispatching a massive military expedition to the East without consulting either monarch, Urban had usurped the royal prerogative of controlling the military defense of Christendom.[40]

While a pope might say one thing, however, less educated listeners could hear something entirely different. Drawing on Cluniac ideas, Urban would always call the expedition a pilgrimage—except that these pilgrims would be heavily armed knights, and this "act of love" would result in the deaths of thousands of innocent people. Urban almost certainly quoted Jesus's words, telling his disciples to take up their cross, and he probably told the Crusaders to sew crosses on the back of their clothes and travel to the land where Jesus had lived and died. The vogue for pilgrimage had already raised the profile of Jerusalem in Europe. In 1033, the millennium of Jesus's death, Raoul Graber reported that, convinced that the end time was nigh, an "innumerable multitude" had marched to Jerusalem to fight the "miserable Antichrist."[41] Thirty years later seven thousand pilgrims had left Europe for the Holy Land to force the Antichrist to declare himself so that God could establish a better world. In

1095 many of the knights would have seen the Crusade in this populist, apocalyptic light. They would also have viewed Urban's call to help the Eastern Christians as a vendetta for their kinsmen and felt as bound to fight for Christ's patrimony in the Holy Land as they would to recover the fief of their feudal lord. One early medieval historian of the Crusades makes a priest ask his listeners: "If an outsider were to strike any of your kin down, would you not avenge your blood relative? How much more ought you to avenge your God, your father, your brother, whom you see reproached, banished from his estates, crucified, whom you hear calling for aid."[42] Pious ideas would certainly have been fused with more earthly objectives. Many would take up their cross to acquire wealth overseas, and fiefs for their descendants, as well as fame and prestige.

Events quickly spiraled out of Urban's control—a reminder of the limitations of religious authority. Urban had imagined an orderly military expedition and had urged the Crusaders to wait until after the harvest. Nevertheless, five large armies ignored this sensible advice and began their trek across Europe in the spring. Thousands either died of hunger or were repulsed by the Hungarians, who were terrified by this sudden invasion. It had never occurred to Urban that the Crusaders would attack the Jewish communities in Europe, but in 1096 an army of German Crusaders slaughtered between four to eight thousand Jews in Speyer, Worms, and Mainz. Their leader, Emicho of Leningen, had presented himself as the emperor of popular legend who would appear in the West during the Last Days and fight the Antichrist in Jerusalem. Jesus could not return, Emicho believed, until the Jews had converted to Christianity, so as his troops approached the Rhineland cities with large Jewish communities, Emicho ordered that Jews be forcibly baptized on pain of death. Some Crusaders seemed genuinely confused. Why were they going to fight Muslims thousands of miles away when the people who had actually killed Jesus—or so the Crusaders mistakenly believed—were alive and well on their very doorsteps? "Look now," a Jewish chronicler overheard the Crusaders saying to one another, "we are going to take vengeance on the Ishmaelites for our Messiah, when here are the Jews who murdered and crucified him. Let us first avenge ourselves on them."[43] Later some of the French Crusaders would also be puzzled: "Do we need to travel to distant lands in the East to attack the enemies of God, when there are Jews right before our eyes, a race that is the greatest enemy of God? We've got it all backward!"[44]

The Crusades made anti-Semitic violence a chronic disease in Europe: every time a Crusade was summoned, Christians would first attack Jews at home. This persecution was certainly inspired by religious conviction, but social, political, and economic elements were also involved. The Rhineland cities were developing the market economy that would eventually replace agrarian civilization; they were therefore in the very early stages of modernization, a transition that always strains social relations. After the demise of the Roman Empire, town life had declined, so there was virtually no commerce and no merchant class.[45] Toward the end of the eleventh century, however, increased productivity had given aristocrats a taste for luxury. To meet their demands, a class of specialists— masons, craftsmen, and merchants—had emerged from the peasantry, and the consequent exchanges of money and goods led to the rebirth of the towns.[46] The nobility's resentment of the *vilain* ("upstart") from the lower classes who was acquiring wealth that they regarded as theirs by right may also have fueled the violence of the German Crusaders, since Jews were particularly associated with this disturbing social change.[47] In the episcopally administered Rhineland cities, the townsfolk had been trying for decades to shake off feudal obligations that impeded commerce, but their bishop-rulers had particularly conservative views on trade.[48] There was also tension between rich merchants and poorer artisans, and when the bishops tried to protect the Jews, it appears these less affluent townsfolk joined the Crusaders in the killing.

Crusaders would always be motivated by social and economic factors as well as by religious zeal. Crusading was especially appealing to the *juventus,* the knightly "youth," who completed their military training by roaming freely around the countryside in search of adventure. Primed for violent action, these knights errant were free of the restraints of settled existence, and their lawlessness might account for some of the crusading atrocities.[49] Many of the first Crusaders came from regions in northeastern France and western Germany that had been devastated by years of flooding, plague, and famine and may simply have wanted to leave an intolerable life.[50] There were also inevitably adventurers, robbers, renegade monks, and brigands in the Crusading hordes, many doubtless drawn by dreams of wealth and fortune as well as a "restless heart."[51]

The leaders of the First Crusade, which left Europe in the autumn of 1096, also had mixed motives for joining the expedition. Bohemund, count of Taranto in southern Italy, had a very small fief and made no secret of his worldly ambitions: he left the Crusade at the first opportunity to become Prince of Antioch. His nephew Tancred, however, found in the Crusade the answer to a spiritual dilemma. He had "burned with anxiety" because he could not reconcile his profession of fighting with the gospel and had even considered the monastic life. But as soon as he heard Pope Urban's summons, "his eyes opened, his courage was born."[52] Godfrey of Bouillon, meanwhile, was inspired by the Cluniac ideal that saw fighting the Church's enemies as a spiritual vocation, but his brother Baldwin merely wanted fame, fortune, and an estate in the East.

The terrifying experience of Crusading soon changed their views and expectations.[53] Many of the Crusaders had never left their villages; now they were thousands of miles from home, shut off from everything they had known, and surrounded by fearsome enemies in alarming terrain. When they arrived at the Ante-Taurus range, many were paralyzed by terror, gazing at these precipitous mountains "in a great state of gloom, wringing their hands because they were so frightened and miserable."[54] The Turks operated a scorched-earth policy, so there was no food, and the poorer noncombatants and soldiers died like flies. Chroniclers report that during the siege of Antioch:

> The starving people devoured the stalks of beans still growing in the fields, many kinds of herbs unseasoned with salt, and even thistles which because of the lack of firewood were not well cooked and therefore irritated the tongues of those eating them. They also ate horses, camels, dogs, and even rats. The poorer people even ate the hides of animals and the seeds of grain found in manure.[55]

The Crusaders soon realized that they were badly led and inadequately provisioned. They also knew that they were massively outnumbered. "Where we have a count, the enemy has forty kings; where we have a regiment, the enemy has a legion," wrote the bishops who accompanied the expedition in their joint letter home; "where we have a castle, they have a kingdom."[56]

Even so, they could not have arrived at a more opportune moment. Not only was the Seljuk Empire disintegrating, but the sultan had recently died, and the emirs were fighting one another for the succession. Had the Turks preserved a united front, the Crusade could not have succeeded. The Crusaders knew nothing about local politics, and their understanding was derived almost entirely from their religious views and prejudices. Onlookers described the Crusading armies as a monastery on the march. At every crisis there were processions, prayers, and a special liturgy. Even though they were famished, they fasted before an engagement and listened as attentively to sermons as to battle instructions. Starving men had visions of Jesus, the saints, and deceased Crusaders who were now glorious martyrs in Heaven. They saw angels fighting alongside them, and at one of the lowest moments of the siege of Antioch, they discovered a holy relic—the lance that had pierced Christ's side—which so elated the despairing men that they surged out of the city and put the besieging Turks to flight. When they finally succeeded in conquering Jerusalem on July 15, 1099, they could only conclude that God had been with them. "Who could not marvel at the way we, a small people among such kingdoms of our enemies, were able not just to resist them but survive?" wrote the chaplain, Fulcher of Chartres.[57]

War has been aptly described as "a psychosis caused by an inability to see relationships."[58] The First Crusade was especially psychotic. From all accounts, the Crusaders seemed half-crazed. For three years they had had no normal dealings with the world around them, and prolonged terror and malnutrition made them susceptible to abnormal states of mind. They were fighting an enemy that was not only culturally but ethnically different—a factor that, as we have found in our own day, tends to nullify normal inhibitions—and when they fell on the inhabitants of Jerusalem, they slaughtered some thirty thousand people in three days.[59] "They killed all the Saracens and Turks they found," the author of the *Deeds of the Franks* reported approvingly. "They killed everyone, male or female."[60] The streets ran with blood. Jews were rounded up into their synagogue and put to the sword, and ten thousand Muslims who had sought sanctuary in the Haram al-Sharif were brutally massacred. "Piles of heads, hands and feet were to be seen," wrote the Provençal chronicler Raymond of Aguilers: "Men rode in blood up to their knees and bridle reins. Indeed, it was a just and splendid judgment of God that this place should be filled with the blood of unbelievers."[61] There were so many dead that the Crusaders were unable to dispose of the bodies. When Fulcher of Chartres came to celebrate Christmas in Jerusalem five months later, he was appalled by the stench from the rotting corpses that still lay unburied in the fields and ditches around the city.[62]

When they could kill no more, the Crusaders proceeded to the Church of the Resurrection, singing hymns with tears of joy rolling down their cheeks. Beside the Tomb of Christ, they sang the Easter liturgy. "This day, I say, will be famous in all future ages, for it turned our labors and sorrows into joy and exultation," Raymond exulted. "This day, I say, marks the justification of all Christianity, the humiliation of paganism, the renewal of faith."[63] Here we have evidence of another psychotic disconnect: the Crusaders were standing beside the tomb of a man who had been a victim of human cruelty, yet they were unable to question their own violent behavior. The ecstasy of battle, heightened in this case by years of terror, starvation, and isolation, merged with their religious mythology to create an illusion of utter righteousness. But victors are never blamed for their crimes, and chroniclers soon described the conquest in Jerusalem as a turning point in history. Robert the Monk made the astonishing claim that its importance had been exceeded only by the creation of the world and Jesus's crucifixion.[64] As a consequence, Muslims were now regarded in the West as a "vile and abominable race," "despicable, degenerate and enslaved by demons," "absolutely alien to God," and "fit only for extermination."[65]

This holy war and the ideology that inspired it represented a complete denial of the pacifist strain in Christianity. It was also the first imperial venture of the Christian West as, after centuries of stagnation, it fought its way back onto the international scene. Five Crusader states were established, in Jerusalem, Antioch, Galilee, Edessa, and Tripoli. These states needed a standing army, and the Church completed its canonization of warfare by giving monks a sword: the Knights Hospitaler of St. John were founded originally to care for poor and sick pilgrims, and the Knights Templar, housed in the Aqsa Mosque on the Haram, policed the roads. They took vows of poverty, chastity, and obedience to their military commander, and because they were far more disciplined than ordinary knights, they became the most professional fighting force in the West since the Roman legions.[66] Saint Bernard, abbot of the new Cistercian abbey of Clairvaux, had no time for regular knights, who with their fine clothes, jeweled bridles, and delicate hands were motivated only by "irrational anger, hunger for empty glory, or hankering after some earthly possessions."[67] The Templars, however, combined the meekness of monks with military power, and their sole motivation was to kill the enemies of Christ. A Christian, Bernard said, should exult when he saw these "pagans" "scattered," "cut away," and "dispersed."[68] The ideology of these first Western colonies was permeated through and through with religion, but although later Western imperialism was inspired by a more secular ideology, it would often share the ruthlessness and aggressive righteousness of Crusading.

. . .

The Muslims were stunned by the Crusaders' violence. By the time they reached Jerusalem, the Franj ("Franks") had already acquired a fearsome reputation; it was said that they had killed more than a hundred thousand people at Antioch, and that during the siege they had roamed the countryside, wild with hunger, openly vowing to eat the flesh of any Saracen who crossed their path.[69] But Muslims had never experienced anything like the Jerusalem massacre. For over three hundred years they had fought all the great regional powers, but these wars had always been conducted within mutually agreed limits.[70] Muslim sources reported in horror that the Franks did not spare the elderly, the women, or the sick; they even slaughtered devout ulema, "who had left their homelands to live lives of pious seclusion in the holy place."[71]

Despite this appalling beginning, not only was there no major Muslim offensive against the Franks for nearly fifty years, but the Crusaders were accepted as part of the political makeup of the region. The Crusader states fitted neatly into the Seljuk pattern of small, independent tributary states, and when emirs fought one another, they often made alliances with Frankish rulers.[72] For the Turkish commanders, the ideals of classical jihad were dead, and when the Crusaders had arrived, no "volunteers" had rushed to defend the frontiers. No longer poised to resist foreign invasion, the emirs had been lax in their defense of the borders; they were unconcerned about the "infidel" presence, since they were too intent on their campaigns against one another. Even though the Crusading ideal resonated with ahadith that saw jihad as a form of monasticism, the first Muslim chroniclers to record the Crusade completely failed to recognize the Franks' religious passion and assumed that they were driven simply by material greed. They all realized that the Franks owed their success to their own failure to form a united front, but after the Crusade there was still no serious attempt to band together. For their part, the Franks who stayed in the Holy Land realized that their survival depended on their ability to coexist with their Muslim neighbors and soon lost their rabid prejudice. They assimilated with the local culture and learned to take baths, dress in the Turkish style, and speak the local languages; they even married Muslim women.

But if the emirs had forgotten the jihad, a handful of "fighting ulema" had not. Immediately after the conquest of Jerusalem, Abu Said al-Harawi, qadi of Damascus, led a deputation of Muslim refugees from Jerusalem to the caliph's mosque in Baghdad and begged the caliph to call for a jihad against the invaders. Their terrible stories reduced the congregation to tears, but the caliph was now too weak to undertake any military action.[73] In 1105 the Syrian jurist al-Sulami wrote a treatise arguing that jihad against the Franks was *fard ayn*, an "individual obligation" incumbent on the local emirs, who must step into the vacuum created by the caliph's incapacity and drive the invaders out of the Dar al-Islam. He insisted that no military action would be successful unless it was preceded by the "Greater Jihad," a reform of hearts and minds in which Muslims battled with their fear and apathy.[74]

Yet still there was little response. Far from being maniacally programmed for holy war by their religion, the Muslims had little appetite for jihad and were preoccupied by new forms of spirituality. In particular, some of the Sufi mystics would develop an outstanding appreciation of other faith traditions. The learned and highly influential Muid ad-Din ibn al-Arabi (1165–1240) would claim that a man of God was at home equally in a synagogue, mosque, temple, or church, since all provided a valid apprehension of God:

> My heart is capable of every form.
> A cloister for the monk, a fane for idols,
> A pasture for gazelles, the votary's Kabah,
> The tables of the Torah, the Quran.
> Love is the faith I hold. Wherever turn
> His camels, still the one true faith is mine.[75]

During the twelfth and thirteenth centuries, the period of the Crusades, Sufism ceased to be a fringe movement and in many parts of the Muslim world became the dominant Islamic mood. Few were capable of achieving the higher mystical states, but Sufi disciplines of concentration, which included music and dancing, helped people to abandon simplistic and narrow notions of God and chauvinist attitudes toward other traditions.

A few ulema and ascetics found the presence of the Franks intolerable. In 1111 Ibn al-Khashab, qadi of Aleppo, led a delegation of Sufis, imams, and merchants to Baghdad, breaking into the caliph's mosque and smashing his pulpit in an unsuccessful attempt to rouse him from his inertia.[76] In 1119 the troops of Mardin and Damascus were so inspired by the qadi's preaching that they "wept with emotion and admiration" and achieved their first Muslim victory over the Franks by defeating Count Roger of Antioch.[77] But no sustained action was taken against the Crusaders until 1144, when, almost by accident, Zangi, emir of Mosul, conquered the Christian principality of Edessa during his campaign in Syria. To his surprise, Zangi, who had little interest in the Franks, became an overnight hero. The caliph hailed him as "the pillar of religion" and "the cornerstone of Islam," though it was hard to see Zangi as a devout Muslim.[78] The Turkish chroniclers condemned his "roughness, aggression, and insolence that brought death to enemies and civilians," and in 1146 he was murdered by a slave while in a drunken stupor.[79]

It was the spectacle of the huge armies arriving from Europe to recover Edessa in the Second Crusade (1148) that finally galvanized some of the emirs. Even though this Crusade was an embarrassing fiasco for the Christians, the local people were beginning to see the Franks as a real danger. The Muslim riposte was led by Nur ad-Din, Zangi's son (r. 1146–74), who took the advice of the "fighting scholars" and first dedicated himself to the Greater Jihad. He returned to the spirit of the Prophet's ummah, living a frugal life, often passing the whole night in prayer, and setting up "houses of justice" where anybody, whatever his faith or status, could find redress. He fortified the cities of the region, built madrassas and Sufi convents, and cultivated the ulema.[80] So moribund was the jihad spirit among the populace that reviving it was hard work, however. Nur ad-Din circulated anthologies of ahadith in praise of Jerusalem and commissioned a beautiful pulpit to be installed in the Aqsa Mosque when the Muslims recovered their holy city. Yet never once in his twenty-eight-year reign did he attack the Franks directly.

His greatest military achievement was the conquest of Fatimid Egypt, and it was his Kurdish governor of there, Yusuf ibn Ayyub, usually known by his title Salah ad-Din ("Honor of the Faith"), who would reconquer Jerusalem. But Saladin had to spend the first ten years of his reign fighting other emirs in order to hold Nur ad-Din's empire together, and during this struggle he made many treaties with the Franks. Saladin too first concentrated on the Greater Jihad and endeared himself to the

people by his compassion, humility, and charisma, but as his biographer
explained, his real passion was the military jihad:

> The Jihad and the suffering involved in it weighed heavily on his
> heart and his whole being in every limb; he spoke of nothing else,
> thought only about equipment for the fight, was interested only in
> those who had taken up arms. . . . For the love of Jihad in God's Path,
> he left his family and his sons, his homeland, his house and all his
> estates, and chose out of all the world to live in the shade of his tent.[81]

Like Nur ad-Din, Saladin always traveled with an entourage of ulema,
Sufis, qadis, and imams, who recited Quran and ahadith to the troops as
they marched. Jihad, which had been all but dead, was becoming a live
force in the region; it had been resurrected not by the inherently violent
nature of Islam but by a sustained assault from the West. In the future any
Western intervention in the Middle East, however secular its motivation,
would evoke the memory of the fanatical violence of the First Crusade.

Like the Crusaders, Saladin discovered that his enemy could be its
own greatest foe. He ultimately owed his military success to the chronic
infighting of the Franks and the hawkish policies of newcomers from
the West who did not understand regional politics. As a result, in July
1187 he was able to destroy the Christian army at the Horns of Hattin
in Galilee. After the battle, he released the king of Jerusalem but had
the surviving Templars and Hospitalers killed in his presence, judging
correctly that they posed the greatest danger to the Muslim reconquista.
When he took possession of Jerusalem, his first impulse was to avenge
the Crusaders' massacre of 1099 but was persuaded by a Frankish envoy
to take the city without violence.[82] Not a single Christian was killed, the
Frankish inhabitants of Jerusalem were ransomed for a very moderate
sum, and many were escorted to Tyre, where the Christians maintained a
stronghold. Christians in the West were uneasily aware that Saladin had
behaved more humanely than the Crusaders and developed legends that
made him an honorary Christian. Some Muslims, however, were more
critical: Ibn al-Athir argued that this clemency was a serious military and
political error, because the Franks managed to retain a narrow coastal
state stretching from Tyre to Beirut, which continued to threaten Muslim
Jerusalem until the late thirteenth century.[83]

Ironically, as military jihad became embedded in the spirituality of the Greater Jihad, Crusading was increasingly driven by material and political interests that sidelined the spiritual.[84] When Pope Urban summoned the First Crusade, he had usurped the kings' prerogative in his bid for papal supremacy. The Third Crusade (1189–92), led and convened by the Holy Roman emperor Frederick Barbarossa, Philip II of France, and Richard I of England, reasserted the temporal rulers' monopoly of violence. While Saladin inspired his soldiers with hadith readings, Richard offered his men money for every stone of Acre's city wall torn down. A few years later the Fourth Crusade was hijacked purely for commercial gain by the merchants of Venice, the new men of Europe, who persuaded the Crusaders to attack their fellow Christians in the port of Zara and plunder Constantinople in 1204. Western emperors governed Byzantium until 1261, when the Greeks finally managed to expel them, but their incompetence in the intervening period may have fatally weakened this sophisticated state, whose polity was far more complex than any Western kingdom at this date.[85] Pope Innocent III reclaimed papal libertas in 1213 by summoning the Fifth Crusade, which attempted to establish a Western base in Egypt, but the Crusaders' fleet was incapacitated by an epidemic and the land army cut off by the rising flood waters of the Nile during the march to Cairo.

The Sixth Crusade (1228–29) entirely subverted the original Crusading ideal because it was led by the Holy Roman emperor Frederick II, who had recently been excommunicated by Pope Gregory IX. Brought up in cosmopolitan Sicily, Frederick did not share the Islamophobia of the rest of Europe and negotiated a truce with his friend Sultan al-Kamil, who had no interest in jihad. Frederick thus recovered Jerusalem, Bethlehem, and Nazareth without fighting a single battle.[86] But both rulers had misjudged the popular mood: Muslims were now convinced that the West was their implacable enemy, and Christians seemed to think it more important to fight Muslims than to get Jerusalem back. Because no priest would perform the ceremony for an excommunicate, in March 1229 Frederick defiantly crowned himself King of Jerusalem in the Holy Sepulcher Church. The Teutonic Knights of the Holy Roman Empire proudly declared that this ceremony had made him God's vicar on earth, and that it was the emperor, not the pope, who stood "between God and mankind and was chosen to rule the entire world."[87] By now a Crusade's political impact at home seemed more important than what was happening in the Middle East.

• • •

Christians lost Jerusalem again in 1244, when the marauding Khwaraz-mian Turks in flight from the Mongol armies rampaged through the holy city, a portent of a terrifying threat to both Christendom and Islamdom. Between 1190 and 1258, Genghis Khan's Mongol hordes had overrun northern China, Korea, Tibet, Central Asia, Anatolia, Russia, and eastern Europe. Any ruler who failed to submit immediately saw his cities laid waste and his subjects massacred. In 1257 Hulugu, Genghis Khan's son, crossed the Tigris, seized Baghdad, and strangled the last Abbasid caliph; then he destroyed Aleppo and occupied Damascus, which surrendered and was spared destruction. At first King Louis IX of France and Pope Inno-cent IV hoped to convert the Mongols to Christianity and let them destroy Islam. Instead the Muslims would save the Crusaders' coastal state and, possibly, Western Christendom from the Mongols. Finally, the Mongol rulers who established states in the Middle East would convert to Islam.

In 1250 a group of disaffected Mamluks took over Saladin's Ayyubid Empire in a military coup. Ten years later the brilliant Mamluk com-mander Baibars defeated the Mongol army at the Battle of Ain Jalut in Galilee. But the Mongols had conquered vast swaths of Muslim territory in Mesopotamia, the Iranian mountains, the Syr-Oxus Basin, and the Volga region, where they established four large states. Mongol violence was not caused by religious intolerance: they acknowledged the validity of all faiths and usually built on local traditions once a region had been subjugated; so by the early fourteenth century, the Mongol rulers of all four states had converted to Islam. The Mongol aristocracy, however, still followed the Yasa, Genghis Khan's military code. Many of their Muslim subjects were dazzled by their brilliant courts and were fasci-nated by their new rulers. But so much Muslim scholarship and culture had been lost in the devastation that some jurists decreed that the "gates of *ijtihad* [independent reasoning]" had closed. This was an extreme ver-sion of the conservative tendency of agrarian civilization, which lacked the economic resources to implement innovation on a large scale, val-ued social order over originality, and felt that culture was so hard won that it was more important to conserve what had already been achieved. This narrowing of horizons was not inspired by an inherent dynamic of Islam but was a reaction to the shocking Mongol assault. Other Muslims would respond to the Mongol conquests very differently.

Muslims were always ready to learn from other cultures, and in the late fifteenth century they did so from the heirs of Genghis Khan. The Ottoman Empire in Asia Minor, the Middle East, and North Africa, the Safavid Empire in Iran, and the Moghul Empire in India would be created on the basis of the Mongol army state and become the most advanced states in the world at the time. But the Mongols also unwittingly inspired a spiritual revival. Jalal ad-Din Rumi (1207–73) had fled the Mongol armies with his family, migrating from Iran to Anatolia, where he founded a new mystical Sufi order. One of the most widely read Muslims in the West today, his philosophy is redolent of the refugee's homelessness and sense of separation, but Rumi was also enthralled by the vast extent of the Mongol Empire and encouraged Sufis to explore boundless horizons on the spiritual plane and to open their hearts and minds to other faiths.

No two people will respond to the same trauma identically, however. Another thinker of the period who has also achieved great influence in our own time was the "fighting scholar" Ahmed ibn Taymiyyah (1263–1382), also a refugee who, unlike Rumi, hated the Mongols. He saw the Mongol converts, now fellow Muslims, as *kufar* ("infidels").[88] He also disapproved of the suspension of ijtihad: in these fearful times jurists needed to think creatively and adapt Shariah to the fact that the ummah had been weakened by two ruthless enemies: the Crusaders and the Mongols. True, the Crusaders seemed a spent force, but the Mongols might still attempt the conquest of the Levant. In preparation for a military jihad to defend their lands, Ibn Taymiyyah urged Muslims to engage in the Greater Jihad and return to the pure Islam of the Prophet's time, ridding themselves of such inauthentic practices as philosophy (*falsafah*), Sufi mysticism, Shiism, and the veneration of saints and their tombs. Muslims who persisted in these false devotions were no better than infidels. When Ghazan Khan, the first of the Mongol chieftains to convert to Islam, invaded Syria in 1299, Ibn Taymiyyah issued a *fatwa* ("legal ruling") declaring that despite their conversion to Islam, the Mongols were infidels, because they observed the Yasa instead of the Shariah, and their Muslim subjects were not bound to obey them. Muslims had traditionally been wary of condemning fellow Muslims as apostates, because they believed that only God could read a person's heart. The practice of *takfir*, declaring that a fellow Muslim has apostatized, would take on new life in our own times, when Muslims have once again felt threatened by foreign powers.

• • •

During the Crusading period, Europe had adopted a narrower perspective and become what one historian has called a "persecuting society." Until the early eleventh century, Jews had been fully integrated in Europe.[89] Under Charlemagne they had enjoyed imperial protection and held important public posts. They became landowners and craftsmen in all trades; Jewish physicians were much in demand. Jews spoke the same languages as Christians—Yiddish did not develop until the thirteenth century—and gave their children Latin names. There were no "ghettos": Jews and Christians lived side by side and bought houses from one another in London until the mid-twelfth century.[90] However, during the eleventh century, there were rumors that Jews had persuaded the Fatimid caliph al-Hakim to destroy the Church of the Resurrection in Jerusalem in 1009, even though the caliph, who seemed to have been certifiably insane, had persecuted Jews and his fellow Muslims as well as Christians.[91] In consequence, Jews were attacked in Limoges, Orléans, Rouen, and Mainz. Linked with Islam in the Christian imagination, their position grew more precarious with each Crusade. After Richard I took the Cross in London in 1198, there were persecutions in East Anglia and Lincoln, and in York in 1193, Jews who refused baptism committed suicide en masse. The so-called blood libel, whereby the deaths of children were blamed on the local Jewish community, first surfaced when a child was killed in Norwich during the 1140s; there were similar cases in Gloucester (1168), Bury St. Edmunds, and Winchester (1192).[92]

This wave of persecution was certainly inspired by a distorted Christian mythology, but it was also the product of social factors. During the slow transition from a purely agrarian to a commercialized economy, towns were beginning to dominate Western Christendom, and by the end of the twelfth century were becoming important centers of prosperity, power, and creativity. There were great disparities of wealth. Low-born bankers and financiers were becoming rich at the expense of the aristocracy, while some townsfolk had not only been reduced to abject poverty but had also lost the traditional support structures of peasant life.[93] Money, in common use by the late eleventh century, came to symbolize the disturbing changes caused by this rapid economic growth that undermined the traditional social structure; it was seen as "the root of all evil," and in popular iconography the deadly sin of avarice inspired visceral loathing and dread.[94] Originally Christians had been the most successful moneylenders, but during the twelfth century Jews had their lands confiscated and many were forced to become bailiffs, financial agents of the aristocracy, or moneylenders and were thereafter tainted by their association with money.[95] The Jew in Peter Abelard's *Dialogue* (1125) explains that because Jews' land tenure is so insecure, "the principal gain that is left for us is that we sustain our miserable lives here by lending money at interest to strangers. But that just makes us more hated by those who think that they are oppressed by it."[96] Jews, of course, were not the only scapegoats of Christian anxiety. Since the Crusades, Muslims, once regarded with vague indifference in Europe, had now come to be regarded as fit only for extermination. In the mid-twelfth century Peter the Venerable, abbot of Cluny, depicted Islam as a bloodthirsty religion that had been propagated entirely by the sword—a fantasy that may have reflected hidden guilt about Christian behavior during the First Crusade.[97]

Disquiet about nascent capitalism and the growing violence of Western society, both of which were so obviously at odds with the radical teachings of Jesus, also surfaced in the "heresies" that the Church had begun to persecute actively in the late twelfth century. Again, the challenge was political rather than doctrinal. The conditions of peasants had reached their lowest level, and poverty had become a major problem.[98] Some had become rich in the towns, but population growth had fragmented inheritances and multiplied the numbers of landless villagers roaming the countryside desperately seeking employment. The structural violence of the "three estate" system was the cause of much anxious soul-searching among Christians. In orthodox as well as heretical circles, the well-to-do were coming to the conclusion that the only way to save their souls was to give away their wealth, which they now regarded as sinful. After a serious illness, Francis of Assisi (1181–1226), son of a wealthy merchant, renounced his patrimony, lived as a hermit, and founded a new order of friars dedicated to serving the poor and sharing their poverty; it increased rapidly in membership. Francis's rule was approved by Pope Innocent III, who hoped thereby to retain some control of the poverty movement that threatened the entire social order.

Other groups were not such loyal adherents of the Church. Even after they had been excommunicated in 1181, the followers of Valdes, a rich businessman of Lyons who had given all his wealth to the poor, continued to attract much support as they traveled through the towns of Europe in pairs like the apostles, barefoot, clad in simple garments and holding all things in common. Still more worrying were the Cathari, the "Pure Ones," who also roamed the countryside, begging for their bread, and were dedicated to poverty, chastity, and nonviolence. They founded churches in all the major cities of northern and central Italy, enjoyed the protection of influential laymen, and were especially powerful in Languedoc, Provence, Tuscany, and Lombardy. They embodied the gospel values far more clearly and authentically than did the worldly Catholic establishment who, perhaps because they felt at some level guilty about their reliance on a system that so clearly contradicted Jesus's teachings, responded viciously. In 1207 Pope Innocent III (r. 1198–1216) commissioned Philip II of France to lead a Crusade against the Cathars in Languedoc, who, he wrote, were worse than the Muslims. The Cathar Church "gives birth continually to a monstrous brood by which its corruption is vigorously renewed after that offspring has passed on to others the canker of its own madness and a detestable succession of criminals emerges."[99]

Philip was happy to oblige, since this would enhance his hold over southern France, but Counts Raymond VI of Toulouse and Raymond-Roger of Béziers and Carcassonne refused to join his Crusade. When one of Raymond's barons stabbed the papal legate, Innocent was convinced that the Cathars were determined "to annihilate us ourselves" and eliminate orthodox Catholicism in Languedoc.[100] In 1209 Armand-Amalric, abbot of Citeaux, led a large army there, laying siege to the city of Béziers. It is said that when his troops asked the abbot how they could distinguish orthodox Catholics from the heretics in the town, he had replied: "Kill them all; God will know his own." Indiscriminate slaughter followed. In fact, it seems that when the Catholics of Béziers were ordered to leave the town, they refused to abandon their Cathar neighbors and chose to die with them.[101] This Crusade was as much about regional solidarity against outside intrusion as it was about religious affiliation.

The extremity of both the rhetoric and the military ruthlessness of the Catharist Crusade is symptomatic of a profound denial. Popes and abbots were dedicated to the imitation of Christ, but, like Ashoka, they had come up against the dilemma of civilization, which cannot exist without the structural and military violence against which the Cathars were protesting. Innocent III was the most powerful pope in history:

he had secured the libertas of the Church and, unlike his predecessors, could command kings and emperors as their monarch. But he headed a society that had almost succumbed to barbarism after the collapse of the Roman Empire and was now in the process of creating the world's first predominantly commercial economy. All three Abrahamic faiths began with a defiant rejection of inequity and systemic violence, which reflects the persistent conviction of human beings, dating back perhaps to the hunter-gatherer period, that there should be an equitable distribution of resources. Yet this militated against the way Western society was heading. Cathars, Waldenses, and Franciscans all felt torn by this impasse, realizing perhaps that as Jesus had pointed out, all who benefit from the inherent violence of the state are implicated in its cruelty.

It seems unlikely that Innocent agonized unduly about this dilemma, though his neurotically exaggerated anti-Cathar rhetoric may express some dis-ease with his position. Far more poignant was the stance of Dominic de Guzmán (c. 1170–1221), founder of the Order of Preachers; like the Franciscans, his friars had adopted a poverty that was so extreme that they could own no property and begged for a living. The mendicant Dominicans traveled throughout Languedoc in pairs trying to bring the "heretics" back to orthodoxy peacefully, reminding them of Saint Paul's insistence that Christians obey the political authorities. But they were inevitably tainted by their association with the anti-Cathar Crusade, especially after Dominic attended the Lateran Council of 1215 to seek Innocent's approval of his order.

Those Christians who remained loyal to the Church but could see how the intrinsic violence of Christendom violated the gospel teaching were inevitably conflicted. Unable to admit that the "heretics" had a point, yet furious with them for drawing attention to their dilemma, they projected these sentiments outward, in forms monstrous and inhuman. There were paranoid fantasies of a highly organized, clandestine Catharist Church determined to destroy the human race and restore Satan's kingdom.[102] We shall see that similar conspiracy fears would later erupt in other societies that were going through a traumatic modernization process and would also result in violence. The Council of Rheims (1157) described the Cathars "hiding among the poor and under the veil of religion . . . moving from place to place and undermining the faith of simple people."[103] Soon Jews would be said to belong to a similar international conspiracy.[104] Even a fair-minded man like Peter the Venerable, abbot of Cluny, who claimed to be reaching out to the Muslim world with love rather than force, described Islam as a "heresy and diabolical sect" addicted to "bestial cruelty."[105] At the outset of the Second Crusade he wrote to King Louis VII of France that he hoped he would kill as many Muslims as Moses and Joshua had killed Amorites and Canaanites.[106] During this period Satan, often pictured as a monstrous human being with horns and a tail, became a far more menacing figure in Western Christianity than in either Judaism or Islam. As they made their stressful transition from a political backwater to a major world power, Europeans were terrified of an unseen "common enemy," representing what they could not accept in themselves and associated with absolute evil.[107]

◆ ◆ ◆

Innocent III had achieved a virtual papal monarchy in Europe, but no other pope would match his power. Secular rulers, such as Louis VII of France (1137–80), Henry II of England (r. 1154–89), and Frederick II all challenged this papal supremacy. They had built powerful kingdoms with government institutions that could intrude more than ever before into the lives of ordinary people, so they were all zealous persecutors of "heretics" who threatened the social order.[108] They were not "secularists" in our sense; they still regarded royal power as sacred and war as holy, but they had developed a Christian theology of war that was quite different from that of the official church. Again, we find it impossible to pinpoint a single, essentialist "Christian" attitude to war, fighting, and violence. The Christian template could be used to very different effect by different groups.

Bishops and popes had used both the Peace of God and the Crusades to control the warrior aristocracy, but during the thirteenth century the knights responded by developing a chivalric code that declared independence of the papal monarchy. They rejected the Cluniac reform, had no intention of converting to the monastic ideal, and were indifferent to Bernard's scathing critique of knighthood. Their Christianity was laced with the Indo-European warrior code of the Germanic tribes, with its ethos of honor, loyalty, and prowess.[109] Where the reforming popes had forbidden knights to kill their fellow Christians, urging them to slaughter Muslims instead, these rebellious knights were happy to fight any Christian who threatened their lord and his people.

In the *chansons de geste*, or "songs of deeds," composed in the early twelfth century, warfare is a natural, violent, and sacred activity. These knights clearly loved the excitement and intensity of the battlefield and experienced it with religious fervor. "Now war is upon us again, all praise to Christ!" cries one of King Arthur's knights.[110] *The Song of Roland,* composed in the late eleventh century, describes an incident that occurred at the end of Charlemagne's campaign in Muslim Spain: Archbishop Turpin kills Muslims with joyous abandon, and Roland has no doubt that the souls of his dead companions have gone straight to heaven.[111] His sword, Durendal, which has relics embedded in its hilt, is a sacred object, and his loyalty to Charlemagne inseparable from his devotion to God.[112] Far from having monastic aspirations, these knights regard monks with disdain. As Archbishop Turpin says robustly, a knight who is not "forward and fierce in battle" might as well "turn monk in monastery meek and for his sins pray daily on his knees."[113]

The Quest of the Holy Grail (c. 1225), a prose fable, takes us into the heart of knightly spirituality.[114] It shows clear influences of the Cistercian ideal, which had introduced a more introspective spirituality into monasticism, but it replaced this internal quest with heroism on the battlefield and set the knight's religious world apart from the ecclesiastical establishment. Indeed, knights alone can participate in the quest for the Grail, the cup that Jesus used at the Last Supper. Their liturgy takes place in a feudal castle rather than a church or monastery, and their clergy are not abbots or bishops but hermits, many of them former knights. Galahad, not the pope, is Christ's representative on earth. The knight's loyalty to his earthly lord is a sacred duty and no other commitment can supersede it: "For the heart of the knight must be so hard and unrelenting to his sovereign's foe that nothing in the world can soften it. And if he gives way to fear, he is not of the company of knights, a veritable companion, who would sooner meet death in battle than fail to uphold the quarrel of their lord."[115] Killing the enemies of his king, even if they are Christians, is just as holy as killing the Muslim enemies of Christ.

The ecclesiastical establishment found it impossible to control the knights' dissident Christianity. Aware that they were in an unassailable position, these knights simply refused to comply with the Church's demands.[116] "Everybody should honor [them]," wrote an early thirteenth-century cleric, ". . . for they defend Holy Church, and they uphold justice for us against those who would do us harm. . . . Our chalices would be stolen from before us at the table of God and nothing would ever stop it. . . . The good would never be able to endure if the wicked did not fear knights."[117] Why should knights obey the Church? Their victories alone proved that they had a special relationship with the Lord of Hosts.[118] Indeed, one poet argued, the physical effort, skill, tenacity, and courage that warfare required made it "a much nobler work" than any other occupation and put the knight in a superior class of his own. Chivalry, claimed another knight, was "such a difficult, tough and very costly thing to learn that no coward ventures to take it on."[119] Knights regarded fighting as an ascetic practice that was far more challenging than a monk's fasts or vigils. A knight knew what real suffering was: every day he took up his cross and followed Jesus onto the battlefield.[120]

Henry of Lancaster (1310–61), hero of the first phase of the Hundred Years' War between England and France, prayed that the wounds, pain, fatigue, and danger of the battlefield would enable him to endure for Christ "such afflictions, labors, pains, as you chose, and not merely to win a prize nor to offset my sins, but purely for love of you, as you Lord have done for love of me."[121] For Geoffroi de Charny, fighting on the other side, the physical struggle of warfare gave his life meaning. Prowess was the highest human achievement because it required such extreme "pain, travail, fear, and sorrow." Yet it also brought "great joy."[122] Monks had it easy; their so-called sufferings were "nothing in comparison" to what a soldier endured every day of his life, "beset by great terrors" and knowing that at any moment he could be "defeated, or killed, or captured, or wounded." Fighting for worldly honor alone was useless, but if knights struggled in the path of God, their "noble souls will be set in paradise for all eternity and their persons will be forever honored."[123]

◆ ◆ ◆

The kings, who also abided by this chivalric code, believed that they too had a direct link to God that was independent of the Church, and by the late thirteenth century some of them felt strong enough to challenge papal supremacy.[124] This began in 1296 with a dispute about taxation. The Fourth Lateran Council (1215) had "liberated" the clergy from the direct jurisdiction of secular princes, but now Philip IV of France and Edward I of England asserted their right to tax the clergy in their realms. Even though Pope Boniface VIII objected, they got their way—Edward by outlawing the English clergy and Philip by withholding essential resources from the papacy. In 1301 Philip again went on the offensive, when he ordered a French bishop to stand trial for treason and heresy. When Boniface issued the bull *Unam Sanctam*, insisting that all temporal power was subject to the pope, Philip simply dispatched Guillaume de Nogaret with a band of mercenaries to bring Boniface to Paris to face charges of usurpation of royal power. Nogaret arrested the pope at Anagni and held him prisoner for several days before he was able to escape. The shock proved too much for Boniface, and he died shortly afterward.

At this date no king could survive without papal support. But the outrage of Anagni convinced Clement V (r. 1305–14), Boniface's successor, to make the papacy more accommodating, and he was the first in a line of French popes to reside in Avignon. Clement meekly restored Philip's legitimacy by repealing all the bulls Boniface had issued against him and, on Philip's orders, disbanded the Templars and confiscated their vast wealth. Subject to the pope and owing no obedience to the king, the Templars were an enemy to royal ascendancy; they epitomized the Crusading ideals of the papal monarchy and had to go. The monks were tortured until they admitted to sodomy, cannibalism, and devil worship; many repudiated these confessions at the stake.[125] Philip's ruthlessness did not suggest that royal power would be more irenic than Innocent III's papal monarchy.

It is wrong to claim, as some scholars have done, that Philip created the first modern secular kingdom; these were not yet sovereign states.[126] Philip was resacralizing kingship; these ambitious kings knew that the king had once been the chief representative of the divine in Europe and argued that the pope had usurped their royal prerogative.[127] Philip was a theocratic ruler, whose subjects called him "semi-divine" (*quasi semideus*) and "king and priest" (*rex et sacerdos*). His land was "holy," and the French were the new chosen people.[128] In England too, holiness had "migrated from the crusade to the nation and its wars."[129] England, claimed the chancellor when he opened the Parliament of 1376–77, was the new Israel; her military victories proved her divine election.[130] Under this sacral kingship, defense of the realm would become sanctified.[131] Soldiers who died fighting for a territorial kingdom would, like the Crusaders, be revered as martyrs.[132] People still dreamed of going on Crusade and liberating Jerusalem, but in an important development, holy warfare was beginning to merge with the patriotism of national war.

Part Three

MODERNITY

9

The Arrival of "Religion"

On January 2, 1492, the Catholic monarchs Ferdinand of Aragon and Isabella of Castile celebrated their victory over the Muslim kingdom of Granada in southern Spain. Crowds watched the Christian banners unfurled on the city walls with deep emotion, and bells pealed triumphantly throughout Europe. Yet despite the triumph of that day, Europeans still felt threatened by Islam. In 1453 the Ottoman Turks had obliterated the Byzantine Empire, which for centuries had protected Europe from Muslim encroachment. In 1480, the year after the monarchs' accession, the Ottomans had begun a naval offensive in the Mediterranean, and Abu al-Hassan, sultan of Granada, had made a surprise attack on the port of Zahara in Castile. Spain therefore was on the front line of the war with the Muslim world, and many believed that Ferdinand was the mythical emperor who was expected to unite Christendom, defeat the Ottomans, and usher in the Age of the Holy Spirit in which Christianity would spread to the ends of the earth.[1] Western Europe was indeed about to achieve global dominance, but in 1492 it still lagged far behind Islamdom.

The Ottoman Empire was the strongest and most powerful state in the world, ruling Anatolia, the Middle East, North Africa, and Arabia. But the Safavids in Iran and the Moghuls in India had also established absolute monarchies in which almost every facet of public life was run with systematic and bureaucratic precision. Each had a strong Islamic ideology that permeated every aspect of their rule: the Ottomans were staunchly Sunni; the Safavids Shii; and the Mughals leaned toward Falsafah and Sufism. Far more efficient and powerful than any European kingdom at this time, they marked the culmination of the agrarian state, and were the last magnificent expression of the "conservative spirit" that was the hallmark of premodern society.[2] As we have seen, all agrarian societies eventually outran their intrinsically limited resources, which put a brake on innovation. Only fully industrialized societies could afford the constant replication of the infrastructure that unlimited progress required. Premodern education could not encourage originality, because it lacked the resources to implement many new ideas. If people were encouraged to think innovatively, but nothing ever came of it, the ensuing frustration could lead to social unrest. In a conservative society, stability and order were far more important than freedom of expression.

In any traditional empire, the purpose of government was not to guide or provide services for the population but to tax them. It did not usually attempt to interfere with the social customs or religious beliefs of its subjects. Rather, a government was set up to take whatever it could from its peasants and prevent other aristocrats from getting their surplus, so warfare—to conquer, expand, or maintain the tax base—was essential to these states. Indeed, between 1450 and 1700, there were only eight years when the Ottomans were not involved in warfare.[3] An Ottoman treatise expressed succinctly the agrarian state's dependence on organized violence:

> The world is before all else a verdant garden whose enclosure is the State; the State is a government whose head is the prince; the prince is a shepherd who is assisted by the army; the army is a body of guards which is maintained by money, and money is the indispensable resource which is provided by subjects.[4]

But for centuries now, Europeans had been devising a commercial economy that would result in the creation of a very different kind of state. The modern world is often said to have begun in 1492; in fact, it would take Europeans some four hundred years to create the modern state. Its economy would no longer be based on the agrarian surplus, it would interfere far more in the personal lives of its subjects, it would be run on the expectation of constant innovation, and it would separate religion from its politics.

Present at the ceremony in Granada was Christopher Columbus, the monarchs' protégé; later that year he sailed from the port of Palos in Spain to find a new trade route to the Indies, only to discover the Americas instead. In sponsoring this voyage, Ferdinand and Isabella had unwittingly taken an important step toward the creation of our globalized, Western-dominated world.[5] For some, Western modernity would be empowering, liberating, and enthralling; others would experience it as coercive, invasive, and destructive. The Spaniards and Portuguese, who pioneered the discovery of the New World, imagined that it was simply waiting to be carved up, plundered, and exploited for their benefit. So did Pope Alexander VI, who, as if he were undisputed monarch of the globe, divided it between Spain and Portugal from pole to pole and gave Ferdinand and Isabella a mandate to wage a "just war" against any native peoples who resisted the European colonialists.[6]

But Alexander was no Innocent III. Papal power had plummeted during the fourteenth century, and the balance of power had passed to the kings. Seven successive popes had resided in Avignon (1309–77), firmly under the thumb of the French kings. In 1378 a disputed papal election divided the Church between the supporters of Urban VI in Rome and Clement VII in Avignon, and the kings of Europe had taken sides according to their own rivalries. The schism ended only with the election of Martin V at the Council of Constance in 1417, but the popes, now safely back in Rome, never recovered their former prestige. There were reports of corruption and immorality, and in 1492 Rodrigo Borgia, father of Cesare and Lucrezia Borgia and two other illegitimate children, had won the papacy by flagrant bribery, taking the name of Alexander VI. His chief goal as pontiff was to break the power of the Italian princes and secure their wealth for his own family. His mandate to Ferdinand and Isabella was, therefore, of dubious spiritual value.

The early colonialists stormed violently into the New World as if they were conducting a giant acquisition raid, greed melding seamlessly with pious intent. The Portuguese set up sugar plantations in the Cape Verde Islands, and between three and five million Africans were torn from their homes and enslaved there. No American colony would be as gravely implicated in slavery. When the Portuguese finally rounded the Cape and exploded aggressively into the Indian Ocean, their bronze cannons made short work of the slender dhows and junks of their rivals. By 1524 they had seized the best ports in eastern Africa, western India, the Persian Gulf, and the Malacca Straits, and by 1560 they had an oceanwide chain of settlements based on Goa.[7] This was a purely trading empire: the Portuguese made no attempt to conquer territory inland. Meanwhile, the Spanish had invaded the Americas, slaughtering the indigenous peoples and seizing land, booty, and slaves. They may have claimed to fight in the name of Christianity, but Hernán Cortés was brutally frank about his real motivation: he simply wanted "to get rich, not to work like a peasant."[8] In Montezuma's Aztec Empire in central Mexico, in each city Cortés would invite local chieftains to the central square, and when they arrived with their retainers, his small Spanish army would gun them down, loot the city, and go on to the next.[9] When Cortés arrived in the Aztec capital in 1525, Montezuma was already dead, and his now-shattered empire passed into Spanish hands. Survivors were decimated by European diseases for which they had no immunity. Some ten years later Francisco Pizarro, using similar military tactics, brought smallpox to the Inca Empire in Peru. For Europeans, colonialism brought unimaginable wealth; for the native peoples, it brought death on an unprecedented scale. According to one estimate, between 1519 and 1595 the population of Central Mexico fell from 16.9 million to 1 million and between 1572 and 1620 the Inca population had been halved.[10]

Cortés and Pizarro were the heroes of the *conquistadores* ("conquerors"), men of low social status who went to the New World to become Spanish grandees. Their conquests were achieved with martial savagery and maintained by systematic exploitation. When they arrived in a new region, they would read out a formal statement in Spanish, informing the uncomprehending inhabitants that the pope had given their land to Spain so they must now submit to the Church and the Catholic monarchs: "We shall take you and your wives and your children, and make slaves of them and we shall take away your goods and do you all the mischief and damage that we can."[11] The Spanish did not need to import African slaves; they simply enslaved the local people to grow cash crops, work in the mines, and provide domestic labor. By the end of the sixteenth century, they were shipping on average 300 million grams of silver and 1.9 million grams of gold every year. With these unprecedented resources, Spain established the first global empire, stretching from the Americas to the Philippines and dominating large portions of Europe.[12]

The Spanish colonialists felt no compunction about their treatment of the indigenous peoples—they regarded the "savage" as scarcely human and had been horrified to discover that the Aztecs practiced human sacrifice and cannibalism.[13] But at home the Dominicans adhered more faithfully to Christian principles and spoke up for the conquered peoples. The Church had no jurisdiction over these American "kings," argued Durandus of San Poinciana in 1506; they should not be attacked unless they were actually harming Europeans. The popes should send missionaries to these new lands, Cardinal Thomas Cajetan argued, but not "for the purpose of seizing their lands or reducing them to temporal subjection."[14] Francisco de Vitoria maintained that the conquistadores had no right to "eject the enemy from their dominions and despoil them of their property."[15]

The Renaissance humanists, however, were far more sympathetic to the colonial project. In Thomas More's *Utopia* (1516), a fictional account of an ideal society, the Utopians went to war only "to drive invading armies from the territories of their friends, or to liberate oppressed people in the name of humanity from tyranny and servitude." All very admirable, but there were limits to this benevolent policy: if the population became too great for their island to support, Utopians felt entitled to send settlers to plant a colony on the mainland, "wherever the natives have plenty of unoccupied or uncultivated land." They would farm this neglected soil, which "previously had seemed too barren and paltry even to support the natives," and make it yield an abundance. Friendly natives could be absorbed into the colony, but the Utopians felt no qualms about fighting those who resisted them: "The Utopians say that it is perfectly justifiable to make war on people who leave their land idle or waste yet forbid the use and possession of it to others who, by the law of nature, ought to be supported from it."[16]

There was a strain of ruthlessness and cruelty in early modern thought.[17] The so-called humanists were pioneering a rather convenient idea of natural rights to counter the brutality and intolerance they associated with conventional religion. From the outset, however, the philosophy of human rights, still crucial to our modern political discourse, did not apply to all human beings. Because Europe was frequently afflicted by famine and seemed unable to support its growing population, humanists like Thomas More were scandalized by the idea of arable land going to waste. They looked back to Tacitus, an apologist for Roman imperialism, who had been convinced that exiles had every right to secure a place to live, since "what is possessed by none belongs to everyone." Commenting on this passage, Alberico Gentili (1552–1608), professor of civil law at Oxford, concluded that because "God did not create the world to be empty," the "the seizure of vacant places" should be "regarded as a law of nature":

> And even though such lands belong to the sovereign of that territory . . . yet because of that law of nature which abhors a vacuum, they will fall to the lot of those who take them, though the sovereign will retain jurisdiction over them.[18]

Gentili also quoted Aristotle's opinion that some men were natural slaves and that waging war against primitive peoples "who, though intended by nature to be governed, will not submit," was as necessary as hunting wild animals.[19] Gentili argued that the Mesoamericans clearly fell into this category because of their abominable lewdness and cannibalism. Where churchmen frequently condemned the violent subjugation of the New World, the Renaissance humanists who were trying to create an alternative to the cruelties committed by people of faith endorsed it.

◆ ◆ ◆

Spain had, however, embarked on a policy that would come to epitomize the fanatical violence inherent in religion. In 1480, with the Ottoman threat at its height, Ferdinand and Isabella had established the Spanish Inquisition. It is significant that, even though the Catholic monarchs remained the pope's obedient servants, they insisted that it remain separate from the papal inquisition. Ferdinand may have hoped thereby to mitigate the cruelty of his own inquisition and almost certainly never intended it to be a permanent institution.[20] The Spanish Inquisition did not target Christian heretics but focused on Jews who had converted to Christianity and were believed to have lapsed. In Muslim Spain, Jews had never been subjected to the persecution that was now habitual in the rest of Europe,[21] but as the Crusading armies of the Reconquista advanced down the peninsula in the late fourteenth century, Jews in Aragon and

Castile had been dragged to the baptismal font; others had tried to save themselves by voluntary conversion, and some of these *conversos* ("converts") became extremely successful in Christian society and inspired considerable resentment. There were riots, and converso property was seized, the violence caused by financial and social jealousy as much as by religious allegiance.[22] The monarchs were not personally anti-Semitic but simply wanted to pacify their kingdom, which had been shaken by civil war and now faced the Ottoman threat. Yet the Inquisition was a deeply flawed attempt to achieve stability. As often happens when a nation is menaced by an external power, there were paranoid fears of enemies within, in this case of a "fifth column" of lapsed conversos working secretly to undermine the kingdom's security. The Spanish Inquisition has become a byword for excessive "religious" intolerance, but its violence was caused less by theological than by political considerations.

Such interference with the religious practice of their subjects was entirely new in Spain, where confessional uniformity had never been a possibility. After centuries of Christians, Jews, and Muslims "living together" (*convivencia*), the monarchs' initiative met with strong opposition. Yet while there was no public appetite for targeting observant Jews, there was considerable anxiety about the so-called lapsed "secret Jews," known as New Christians. When the Inquisitors arrived in a district, "apostates" were promised a pardon if they confessed voluntarily, and "Old Christians" were ordered to report neighbors who refused to eat pork or work on Saturday, the emphasis always on practice and social custom rather than "belief." Many conversos who were loyal Catholics felt it wise to seize the opportunity of amnesty while the going was good, and this flood of "confessions" convinced both the Inquisitors and the public that the society of clandestine "Judaizers" really existed.[23] Seeking out dissidents in this way would not infrequently become a feature of modern states, secular as well as religious, in times of national crisis.

After the conquest of 1492, the monarchs inherited Granada's large Jewish community. The fervid patriotism unleashed by the Christian triumph led to more hysterical conspiracy fears.[24] Some remembered old tales of Jews helping the Muslim armies when they had arrived in Spain eight hundred years earlier and pressured the monarchs to deport all practicing Jews from Spain. After initial hesitation, on March 31, 1492, the monarchs signed the edict of expulsion, which gave Jews the choice of baptism or deportation. Most chose baptism and, as conversos, were now harassed by the Inquisition, but about eighty thousand crossed the border into Portugal, and fifty thousand took refuge in the Ottoman Empire.[25] Under papal pressure. Ferdinand and Isabella now turned their attention to Spain's Muslims. In 1499 Granada was split into Christian and Muslim zones, Muslims were required to convert, and by 1501 Granada was officially a kingdom of "New Christians." But the Muslim converts (*Moriscos*) were given no instruction in their new faith, and everybody knew that they continued to live, pray, and fast according to the laws of Islam. Indeed, a mufti in Oran in North Africa issued a fatwa permitting Spanish Muslims to conform outwardly to Christianity, and most Spaniards turned a blind eye to Muslim observance. A practical convivencia had been restored.

The first twenty years of the Spanish Inquisition were undoubtedly the most violent in its long history. There is no reliable documentation of the actual numbers of people killed. Historians once believed that about thirteen thousand conversos were burned during this early period.[26] More recent estimates suggest, however, that most of those who came forward were never brought to trial; that in most cases the death penalty was pronounced in absentia over conversos who had fled and were symbolically burned in effigy; and that from 1480 to 1530 only between 1,500 and 2,000 people were actually executed.[27] Nevertheless, this was a tragic and shocking development that broke with centuries of peaceful coexistence. The experience was devastating for the conversos and proved lamentably counterproductive. Many conversos who had been faithful Catholics when they were detained were so disgusted by their treatment that they reverted to Judaism and became the "secret Jews" that the Inquisition had set out to eliminate.[28]

Spain was not a modern centralized state, but in the late fifteenth century it was the most powerful kingdom in the world. Besides its colonial possessions in the Americas, Spain had holdings in the Netherlands, and the monarchs had married their children to the heirs of Portugal, England, and the Austrian Habsburg dynasty. To counter the ambitions of its archrival France, Ferdinand had campaigned in Italy against France and Venice and seized control of Upper Navarre and Naples. Spain was, therefore, feared and resented, and exaggerated tales of the Inquisition spread through the rest of Europe, which was itself in the violent throes of a major transformation.

• • •

By the sixteenth century a different kind of civilization was slowly emerging in Europe, based on new technologies and the constant reinvestment of capital. This would ultimately free the continent from many of the restrictions of agrarian society. Instead of focusing on the preservation of past achievements, Western people were acquiring the confidence to look to the future. Where older cultures had required people to remain within carefully defined limits, pioneers like Columbus were encouraging them to venture beyond the known world, where they discovered that they not only survived but prospered. Inventions were occurring simultaneously in many different fields; none of them seemed particularly momentous at the time, but their cumulative effect was decisive.[29] Specialists in one discipline found that they benefited from discoveries made in others. By 1600 innovations were occurring on such a scale and in so many areas at once that progress had become irreversible. Religion would either have to adapt to these developments or become irrelevant.

By the early seventeenth century, the Dutch had created the building blocks of Western capitalism.[30] In the joint-stock company, members pooled their capital contributions and placed them on a permanent basis under common management, which gave a colonial or trading venture abroad resources and security far greater than one person could provide. The first municipal bank in Amsterdam offered efficient, inexpensive, and safe access to deposits, money transfers, and payment services both at home and in the growing international market. Finally, the stock exchange gave merchants a center where they could trade in all kinds of commodities. These institutions, over which the church had no control, would acquire a dynamic of their own and, as the market economy developed, would increasingly undermine old agrarian structures and enable the commercial classes to develop their own power base. Successful merchants, artisans, and manufacturers would become powerful enough to participate in the politics that had formerly been the preserve of the aristocracy, even to the point of playing off one noble faction against another. They tended to ally themselves with those kings who were trying to build strong centralized monarchies, since this would facilitate trade. With the emergence of the absolute monarchy and the sovereign state in England and France, the commercial classes, or bourgeoisie, became increasingly influential as market forces gradually made the state independent of the restrictions imposed upon it by a wholly agrarian economy.[31] But would it be less structurally or militarily violent than the agrarian state?

In Germany there were no strong, centralizing monarchies, only a welter of forty-one small principalities that the Holy Roman emperor was unable to control. But in 1506 Charles V, the grandson of Ferdinand and Isabella and of the Holy Roman emperor Maximilian, inherited the Habsburg lands in Austria and on the death of Ferdinand in 1516 he also became king of Aragon and Castile; in 1519 he was elected Holy Roman emperor. By an adroit series of marriage alliances, skillful diplomacy, and warfare, the Habsburgs had brought more territories under their rule than any previous European monarchs. Charles's ambition was to create a pan-European empire similar to the Ottoman Empire, but he found that he could not control the German princes who wanted to make their principalities strong monarchies on the model of France and England. Moreover, the towns of central and southern Germany had become the most vital commercial centers in northern Europe.[32] Economic changes there led to class conflict, and as usual, discontent focused on Jewish "usurers" and venal Catholic priests who were said to leech off the poor.

In 1517 Martin Luther (1483–1546), an Augustinian friar, nailed his famous ninety-five theses on the castle church door in Wittenberg and set in motion the process known as the Reformation. His attack on the Church's sale of indulgences resonated with discontented townsfolk, who were sick of clerics extorting money from gullible people on dubious pretexts.[33] The ecclesiastical establishment treated Luther's protest with lofty disdain, but young clerics took his ideas to the people in the towns, who initiated local reforms that effectively liberated their congregations from the control of Rome. The more intellectually vigorous clergy spread Luther's ideas in their own books, which thanks to the new technology of printing, circulated with unprecedented speed, launching one of the first modern mass movements. Like other heretics in the past, Luther had created an antichurch.

Luther and the other great reformers—Ulrich Zwingli (1484–1531) and John Calvin (1509–64)—were addressing a society undergoing fundamental and far-reaching change. Modernization would always be frightening: living in medias res, people are unable to see where their society is going and find its slow but radical alteration distressing. No longer feeling at home in a changing world, they found that their faith changed too. Luther himself was prey to agonizing depressions and wrote eloquently of his inability to respond to the old rituals, which had been designed for another way of life.[34] Zwingli and Calvin both felt a sense of crippling helplessness before experiencing a profound conviction of the absolute power of God; this alone, they were convinced, could save them. In leaving the Roman Church, the reformers were making one of the earliest declarations of independence of Western modernity, and because of their aggressive stance toward the Catholic establishment, they were known as "Protestants." They demanded the freedom to read and interpret the Bible as they chose—even though each of the three could be intolerant of views opposed to his *own* teaching. The reformed Christian stood alone with his Bible before his God: Protestants thus canonized the growing individualism of the modern spirit.

Luther was also the first European Christian to advocate the separation of church and state, though his "secularist" vision was hardly irenic. God, he believed, had so retreated from the material world that it no longer had any spiritual significance. Like other rigorists before him, Luther yearned for spiritual purity and concluded that church and state should operate independently, each respecting the other's proper sphere.[35] In Luther's political writings we see the arrival of "religion" as a discrete activity, separate from the world as a whole, which it had previously permeated. True Christians, justified by a personal act of faith in God's saving power, belonged to the Kingdom of God, and because the Holy Spirit made them incapable of injustice and hatred, they were essentially free from state coercion. But Luther knew that such Christians were few in number. Most were still in thrall to sin and, together with non-Christians, belonged to the Kingdom of the World; it was essential, therefore, that these sinners be restrained by the state "in the same way as a savage wild beast is bound with chains and ropes so that it cannot bite and tear as it would normally do." Luther understood that without a strong state, "the world would be reduced to chaos," and that no government could realistically rule according to the gospel principles of love, forgiveness, and tolerance. To attempt this would be like "loosing the ropes and chains of the savage wild beasts and letting them bite and mangle everywhere."[36] The only way the Kingdom of the World, a realm of selfishness and violence ruled by the devil, could impose the peace, continuity, and order that made human society feasible was by the sword.

But the state had no jurisdiction over the conscience of the individual and no right, therefore, to fight heresy or lead a holy war. While it could have nothing to do with the spiritual realm, the state *must* have unqualified and absolute authority in temporal affairs. Even if the state were cruel, tyrannical, and forbade the teaching of God's word, Christians must not resist its power.[37] For its part, the true church, the Kingdom of God, must hold aloof from the inherently corrupt and depraved policies of the Kingdom of the World, dealing only with spiritual affairs. Protestants believed that the Roman Church had failed in its true mission because it had dallied with the sinful Kingdom of the World.

Where premodern faith had emphasized the sacredness of community—the Sangha, the ummah, and the Body of Christ—for Luther "religion" was a wholly personal and private matter. Where previous sages, prophets, and reformers had felt impelled to take a stand against the systemic violence of the state, Luther's Christian was supposed to retreat into his own interior world of righteousness and let society, quite literally, go to hell. And in his emphasis on the limited and inferior nature of earthly politics, Luther had given a potentially dangerous endorsement of unqualified state power.[38] Luther's response to the Peasants' War in Germany showed that a secularized political theory would not necessarily lead to a reduction of state violence. Between March and May 1525, peasant communities in southern and central Germany had resisted the centralizing policies of the princes that deprived them of traditional rights, and by hardheaded bargaining, many villages had managed to wrest concessions from them without resorting to violence. But in Thuringia, in central Germany, lawless peasant bands roamed the countryside, looting and burning convents, churches, and monasteries.[39]

In his first pamphlet on the Peasants' War, Luther had tried to be even-handed and had castigated the "cheating" and "robbing" of the aristocracy. But in his view the peasants had committed the unpardonable sin of mixing religion and politics. Suffering, he maintained, was their lot; they must obey the gospel, turn the other cheek, and accept the loss of their lives and property. They had had the temerity to argue that Christ had made all men free—an opinion that clearly chimed with New Testament teachings but cut no ice with Luther. He insisted that "a worldly kingdom cannot exist without an inequality of persons, some being free, some imprisoned, some lords, some subjects."[40] Luther encouraged the princes to use every possible means to suppress the peasant agitators:

Let everyone who can, smite, slay and stab, secretly or openly, remembering that nothing can be more poisoned, hurtful or devilish than a rebel. It is just as when one must kill a mad dog: if you do not strike him, he will strike you and a whole land with you.[41]

The rebels, he concluded, were in thrall to the devil, and killing them was an act of mercy, because it would rescue them from this satanic bondage.

Because this rebellion threatened the entire social structure, the state suppressed it savagely: as many as a hundred thousand peasants may have died. The crisis was an ominous sign of the instability of early modern states at a time when traditional ideas were being widely questioned. The reformers had called for reliance on scripture alone but would find that the Bible could be a dangerous weapon if it got into the wrong hands. Once people began reading their Bibles for themselves, they soon saw glaring discrepancies between Jesus's teachings and current ecclesiastical and political practice. The Anabaptists ("Re-baptizers") were especially disruptive because their literal reading of the gospel led them to condemn such institutions as the Holy Roman Empire, the city council, and the trade guild.[42] When some Dutch Anabaptists managed to seize control of Münster in northwestern Germany in 1534, instituting polygamy and banning private property, Catholics and Protestants—for once in firm agreement—saw this as a political threat that could easily be emulated by other towns.[43] The following year, the Anabaptists of Münster were massacred by joint Catholic and Protestant forces.[44]

· · ·

The Münster catastrophe and the Peasants' War both affected the way other rulers dealt with religious dissidents. In western Europe, "heresy" had always been a political rather than a purely theological matter and had been suppressed violently because it threatened public order. Very few of the elite, therefore, considered it wrong to prosecute and execute "heretics," who were killed not so much for what they believed as for what they did or failed to do. The Reformation, however, had introduced an entirely new emphasis on "belief." Hitherto the Middle English *beleven* (like the Greek *pistis* and the Latin *credo*) had been a practically expressed "commitment" or "loyalty"; now it would increasingly come to mean an intellectual acceptance of a set of doctrinal opinions.[45] As the

Reformation progressed, it became important to explain the differences between the new and the old religion, as well as between the different Protestant sects—hence the lists of obligatory "beliefs" in the Thirty-Nine Articles, the Lambeth Articles, and the Westminster Confession.[46] Catholics would do likewise in their own reformation, formulated by the Council of Trent (1545–63), which created a catechism of propositional, standardized opinions.

The doctrinal divisions created by the Reformation became especially important in states aspiring to strong, centralized rule. Hitherto the traditional agrarian state had neither the means nor, usually, the inclination to supervise the religious lives of the lower classes. Yet those monarchs striving for absolute rule had developed a state machinery that enabled them to supervise their subjects' lives more closely, and increasingly confessional allegiance would become the criterion of political loyalty. Henry VIII (r. 1509–47) and Elizabeth I (r. 1558–1603) of England both persecuted Catholics not as religious apostates but as traitors to the state. When he was Henry VIII's chancellor, Thomas More had passed harsh sentences on politically dangerous heretics, only to be himself executed for refusing to take the Oath of Supremacy that made Henry head of the church in England.[47] In France the Edict of Paris (1543) described Protestant "heretics" as "the seditious disturbers of the peace and tranquillity of our subjects and secret conspirators against the prosperity of our state, which depends chiefly on the preservation of the Catholic faith in our kingdom."[48]

Although the Reformation produced fruitful forms of Christianity, it was in many ways a tragedy. It has been estimated that as many as eight thousand men and women were judicially executed as heretics in Europe during the sixteenth and seventeenth centuries.[49] Policies differed from region to region. In France judicial proceedings had given way to open warfare, massacre, and popular violence by the 1550s. The German Catholic inquisitors were never overly zealous in pursuing Protestants, but Holy Roman Emperor Charles V and his son Philip II of Spain (r. 1555–98) regarded Protestantism in the Netherlands as a political as well as a religious threat, so they were unwavering in their attempts to suppress it. In England policy changed with the faith allegiance of the monarch. Henry VIII, who upheld his Catholicism, was unswervingly hostile to Lutherans, but regarded fidelity to the pope as a capital offense because it threatened his political supremacy. Under his son Edward VI

(r. 1547–53), the pendulum swung in favor of Calvinism, then veered back under the Catholic Mary Tudor (r. 1553–58), who burned some three hundred Protestants. Under Elizabeth I, England became officially Protestant again, and the main victims were Catholic missionary-priests, trained in seminaries abroad and living in England clandestinely, saying Mass and administering the sacraments to recusant Catholics.

We cannot expect these early modern states to have shared the outlook of the Enlightenment. Civilization had always depended upon coercion, so state violence was regarded as essential to public order. Petty theft, murder, forgery, arson, and the abduction of women were all capital offenses, so the death penalty for heresy was neither unusual nor extreme.[50] Executions were usually carried out in public as a ritualized deterrent that expressed and enforced state and local authority.[51] Without a professional police force and modern methods of surveillance, public order was dependent on such spectacles. Utterly repugnant as it is to us today, killing dissenters was seen as essential to the exercise of power, especially when the state was still fragile.[52]

But the suppression of heterodoxy was not wholly pragmatic; an ideology that was central to an individual's integrity also played a role. Thomas More, once a ruthless persecutor, would have taken the oath had he been motivated solely by political concerns; and Mary Tudor could have strengthened her regime had she been less zealous against Protestants. Yet heresy was different from other capital crimes, because if the accused recanted, she was pardoned and her life spared. Modern scholars have shown that officials often genuinely wanted to bring the wayward back into the fold and that the death of an unrepentant heretic was seen as a defeat.[53] During the 1550s, the zealous inquisitor Pieter Titlemaus presided over at least 1,120 heresy trials in Flanders, but only 127 ended in execution. Twelve attempts were made by inquisitors, civic authorities, and priests to save the Anabaptist Soetken van den Houte and her three women companions in 1560. Under Mary Tudor, Edmund Bonner, Catholic bishop of London, tried fifteen times to rescue the Protestant John Philpot, six times to save Richard Woodman, and nine times to redeem Elizabeth Young.[54]

Catholics, Lutherans, and Calvinists could all find biblical texts to justify the execution of heretics.[55] Some quoted scriptural teachings that preached mercy and tolerance, but these kinder counsels were rejected by the majority. Yet even though thousands were indeed beheaded, burned, or hanged, drawn and quartered, there was no headlong rush to martyr-dom. The vast majority were content to keep their convictions to themselves and conform outwardly to state decrees. Calvin inveighed against such cowardice, comparing closet Calvinists to Nicodemus, the Pharisee who kept his faith in Jesus secret. But "Nicodemites" in France and Italy retorted that it was easy for Calvin to take this heroic line while living safely in Geneva.[56] Under Elizabeth I, there was a strong cult of martyr-dom only among the Jesuits and seminarians training for the English mission who believed that their sacrifice would save their country.[57] But recruits were also warned against excessive enthusiasm. A manual of the English College in Rome during the 1580s pointed out that not every-body was called to martyrdom and that no one should put himself at risk unnecessarily.[58]

The one thing on which Catholics and Protestants could agree was their hatred of the Spanish Inquisition. But despite its gruesome reputa-tion, the crimes of the Inquisition were exaggerated. Even the *auto-da-fé* ("declaration of faith"), with its solemn processions, sinister costumes, and burning of heretics, which to foreigners seemed the epitome of Span-ish fanaticism, was not all it was cracked up to be. The auto-da-fé had no deep roots in Spanish culture. Originally a simple service of recon-ciliation, it took on this spectacular form only in the mid-sixteenth cen-tury and after its brief heyday (1559–70) was held very rarely. Moreover, the burning of the recalcitrant was not the centerpiece of the ritual: the accused were usually put to death unceremoniously outside the city, and scores of autos were held without a single execution. After the Inquisi-tion's first twenty years, less than 2 percent of those who were accused were convicted, and of these most were burned in effigy in absentia. Between 1559 and 1566, when the auto was at the peak of its popularity, about a hundred people died, whereas three hundred Protestants were put to death under Mary Tudor; twice that number were executed under Henry II of France (r. 1547–59), and ten times as many were killed in the Netherlands.[59]

Very few Protestants were killed by the Spanish Inquisition; most of its victims were the "New Christians." By the 1580s, when Spain was at war with other European states, the crown once again turned on the "enemy within," this time the Moriscos, who, like the Jews before them, were resented less for their beliefs than for their cultural difference and financial success. "They marry among themselves and do not mix with Old Christians," a Toledo tribunal complained to Philip II in 1589; "none of them enters religion, nor joins the army, none enters domestic service . . . they take part in trade and are rich."[60] Yet again, persecution proved counterproductive because it transformed the beleaguered Moriscos from imaginary to real enemies, courted by the Huguenots and Henry IV of France or turning to the sultan of Morocco for help. As a result, in 1609, the Moriscos were expelled from Spain, eliminating the last substantial Muslim community from Europe.

⋆ ⋆ ⋆

Spain was heavily involved in the Wars of Religion that culminated in the horror of the Thirty Years' War (1618–48). These conflicts gave rise to what has been called the "creation myth" of the modern West, because it explains how our distinctively secular mode of governance came into being.[61] The theological quarrels of the Reformation, it is said, so inflamed Catholics and Protestants that they slaughtered one another in senseless wars, until the violence was finally contained by the creation of the liberal state that separated religion from politics. Europe had learned the hard way that once a conflict becomes "holy," violence will know no bounds and compromise becomes impossible because all combatants are convinced that God is on their side. Consequently, religion should never again be allowed to influence political life.

But nothing is ever quite that simple. After the Reformation, northeastern Germany and Scandinavia were, roughly speaking, Lutheran; England, Scotland, the northern Netherlands, the Rhineland, and southern France were predominantly Calvinist; and the rest of the continent remained mostly Catholic. This naturally affected international relations, but European rulers had other concerns. Many, especially those trying to create absolutist states, were alarmed by the extraordinary success of the Habsburgs, who now ruled the German territories, Spain, and the southern Netherlands. Charles V's aspiration to achieve trans-European hegemony on the Ottoman model was opposed by the more pluralistic dynamics in Europe that inclined toward the sovereign nation-state.[62] The German princes naturally struggled to resist Charles's ambitions and retain their local power and traditional privileges.

In the minds of the participants, however, these wars were certainly experienced as a life-and-death struggle between Protestants and Catholics. Religious sentiments helped soldiers and generals to distance themselves from the enemy, blot out all sense of a shared humanity, and infuse the cruel struggle with a moral fervor that made it not only palatable but noble: they gave participants an uplifting sense of righteousness. But secular ideologies can do all this too. These wars were not simply and quintessentially "religious" in the modern sense. If they had been, we would not expect to find Protestants and Catholics fighting on the same side, for example. In fact, they often did so and consequently fought their co-religionists.[63] Just two years after Charles became Holy Roman emperor, the Catholic Church had condemned Luther at the Diet of Worms (1521). For the first ten years of his reign, Charles, a Catholic, paid little attention to the Lutherans in Germany and instead concentrated on fighting the pope and the Catholic kings of France in Italy. Catholic rulers were particularly hostile to decrees of the Council of Trent that sought to limit their powers; this was yet another episode in the long struggle of European monarchs to control the church in their own realms.[64] As late as 1556, Pope Paul IV went to war against Charles's son Philip II, the devout Catholic ruler of Spain.[65] The Catholic kings of France were so alarmed by the Habsburgs that they were even prepared to make alliances with the Ottoman Turks against them.[66] For over thirty years (1521–52) they engaged in five military campaigns against the Catholic emperor, who was supported in these conflicts by many of the Protestant German princes; Charles rewarded them by granting them extensive powers over the churches in their domains.[67]

The German princes, Catholic and Lutheran alike, were also alarmed by Charles's centralizing ambitions. In 1531 some Protestant princes and townsfolk united to form the Schmalkaldic League against him. But during the First Schmalkaldic War, other prominent Lutheran princes fought on Charles's side, while the Catholic king Henry II of France joined the Lutheran League in an attack on the emperor's forces, and the Catholic German princes remained neutral.[68] Moreover, many of Charles's soldiers in the imperial army were mercenaries fighting for money rather than faith, and some were Protestants.[69] Clearly these wars were not simply driven by sectarian fervor. Eventually, Charles had to admit defeat and signed the Peace of Augsburg in 1555. The Protestant princes were allowed to keep the Catholic ecclesiastical properties they had seized, and henceforth in Europe the religious allegiance of the local ruler determined the faith of his subjects—a principle later enshrined in the maxim *cuius regio, eius religio*.[70] Charles abdicated and retired to a monastery, and the empire was divided between his brother Ferdinand, who ruled the German territories, and his son Philip II, who governed Spain and the Netherlands.

This was a political victory of one set of state builders over another.[71] The Catholic and Lutheran princes of Germany had ganged up on Charles, realizing quite correctly that his aim had not been simply to crush heresy but also to increase his own power at their expense. The peasantry and the lower classes showed little theological conviction but switched from Catholicism to Lutheranism and back again as their lords and masters required.[72] At the end of the struggle, the Peace of Augsburg greatly enhanced the political power of the princes, Catholic and Protestant alike. They could now use the Reformation to their own advantage, taxing their clergy, appropriating church estates, controlling education, and potentially extending their authority, through the parishes, to every one of their subjects.[73]

A similar complexity can be observed in the French Wars of Religion (1562–98). These too were not simply a fight between the Calvinist Huguenots and the Catholic majority but were also a political contest among competing aristocratic factions.[74] The Guises were Catholic and the southern Bourbons Huguenot; the Montmorencies were split, the older generation inclining to Catholicism, the younger to the Huguenots. These aristocrats were defending their traditional rights against the kings' ambition to create a centralized state with *un roi, une foi, une loi* ("one king, one faith, one law"). The social and political elements of these struggles were so evident that until the 1970s, most scholars believed that faith was merely a front for the purely secular ambitions of kings and nobles.[75] But in a landmark 1973 article, Natalie Zemon Davis examined the popular rituals in which both Catholics and Protestants drew on the Bible, the liturgy, and folk traditions to dehumanize their enemies and concluded that the French civil wars were "essentially religious."[76] Since then, scholars have reemphasized the role of religion, pointing out, however, that it is still anachronistic to separate the "political" from the "religious" at this date.[77]

On October 25, 1534, Calvinists had pasted vitriolic and satirical posters attacking the Catholic Mass on public landmarks all over Paris, Blois, Orléans, and Tours. One even appeared on the door of Francis I's bedchamber. As Catholics made their way to morning Mass, they were confronted by a headline printed in capital letters: "TRUE ARTICLES ON THE

HORRIBLE, GROSS AND INSUFFERABLE ABUSE OF THE PAPAL MASS." The French pamphleteer Antoine Marcourt listed four arguments against the Eucharist, "by which the whole world . . . will be completely ruined, cast down, lost and desolated": it was blasphemous for the Mass to claim that it repeated Christ's perfect sacrifice on Calvary; Jesus's body was with God in Heaven so could not be present in the bread and wine; transubstantiation had no scriptural warrant; and communion was simply an act of remembrance. The diatribe concluded with a vicious attack on the clergy:

> By this [Mass] they have seized, destroyed and swallowed up everything imaginable, dead or alive. Because of it they live without any duties or responsibility to anyone or anything even to the need to study. . . . They kill, burn, destroy and murder as brigands all those who contradict them, for now all they have left is force.[78]

The polemic was so extreme that even Theodore Beza, Calvin's future deputy in Geneva, condemned it in his history of the French Protestant Church. Yet it was this disreputable attack that sparked the French Wars of Religion.

As soon as the king saw the placards, he initiated a nationwide persecution of the Huguenots that forced many, including Calvin himself, to flee the country. King Francis was not a theological bigot; he was open to new ideas and had entertained Erasmus and other humanists at his court. But he rightly saw the placards not simply as a theological denunciation but also as an assault on the entire political system. The Eucharist was the supreme expression of social bonding, experienced not principally as a private communion with Christ but as a rite that bound the community together,[79] a ritual of "greeting, sharing, giving, receiving, and making peace."[80] Before receiving the sacrament, Catholics had to beg their neighbors' pardon for outstanding grievances; king, priests, aristocrats, and the common folk all ate the same consecrated bread and in so doing were integrated as one in the Body of Christ. The placards were also understood by both Catholics and Protestants as an implicit critique of the monarchy. The kings of France had always been revered as semidivine; the Calvinists' denial of the real presence of Christ now tacitly denied the fusion of the physical and the sacred that had been crucial to medieval Christianity and that the king embodied in his person.[81] Past-ing the scurrilous placard on Francis's door was both a religious and a political act; and for Francis, the two were inseparable.

Yet during the ensuing wars, it was impossible to divide the French population into neat communities of Protestants and Catholics.[82] Here too people crossed the confessional lines and even changed their religious allegiance.[83] In 1574 Henry of Montmorency, Catholic governor of Languedoc, joined his Huguenot neighbors in supporting a constitution attacking the monarchy.[84] In 1579 a significant number of Huguenots were prepared to fight the king under the banner of the ultra-Catholic Duke of Guise, a pretender to the throne.[85] Even the Catholic kings made alliances with Protestants in their struggle against the Habsburgs, whom the Peace of Augsburg had set back but hardly neutralized. Charles IX (r. 1560–74) fought with the Huguenots against the Spanish Habsburgs in the Netherlands, and in 1580 Henry III (r. 1575–89) was prepared to support Dutch Calvinists against Catholic Spain.

In their struggle against the aristocracy, the lower classes also transcended sectarian allegiance. In 1562 hundreds of Catholic peasants joined a revolt against a Catholic nobleman who had forbidden his Huguenot peasants to hold Protestant services.[86] Catholic and Protestant peasants joined forces again to oppose Henry III's excessive tax levy in 1578, rampaging through the countryside for almost a year until they were slaughtered by the royal troops. In another tax protest during the 1590s, twenty-four Protestant and Catholic villages in the Haut-Biterrois set up an alternative system of self-government,[87] and in the southwest Protestants and Catholics engaged in dozens of joint uprisings against the nobility, some of which involved as many as forty thousand people. In Croquants, the most famous of these associations, ignoring religious difference was a condition of membership.[88]

After the murder of Henry III in 1589, the Huguenot leader Henry of Navarre succeeded to the throne as Henry IV and brought the French Wars of Religion to an end by converting to Catholicism and adopting a policy of strict neutrality. In the Edict of Nantes (1598), he granted religious and civil liberties to the Huguenots, and when the *parlement* expelled the Jesuits from France, he had them reinstated. This did not mark the birth of the tolerant secular state, however, since Henry had not abandoned the ideal of *une foi;* the Edict of Nantes was simply a temporary settlement, an attempt to buy time by winning the Huguenots over.

The French crown was still too weak to achieve the religious uniformity that, the kings believed, would help to centralize the state and bind the nation together.[89]

Despite Henry's policy of toleration, though, Europe drifted inexorably toward the horror of the Thirty Years' War, which would kill about 35 percent of the population of central Europe. Here again, though religious solidarities were certainly a factor in this series of conflicts, it was never their sole motivation.[90] This was already clear in 1609, nine years before the war began, when the Calvinist Frederick V, elector palatine, tried to create a pan-European Union of Protestant principalities against the Habsburgs. Very few of the Protestant princes joined, but the union did gain Catholic support from Henry IV and Carlo Emmanuele of Savoy. The war started in earnest with an uprising in Catholic Bohemia against the Catholic Habsburg emperor Ferdinand II: in 1618 the rebels defiantly offered the crown of Bohemia to the Calvinist Frederick V, but the other members of the Protestant Union refused to support him, and two years later the union disbanded.[91] It took two years for the Habsburgs to quash the revolt and re-Catholicize Bohemia, and meanwhile the Dutch had opened a new round of hostilities against Habsburg rule.

The princes of Europe resisted Habsburg imperialism, but there was rarely a wholly solid "Catholic" or "Protestant" response. Catholic France nearly always supported the Protestant princes of Germany against the empire. The war was fought by mercenaries available to the highest bidder, so Protestants from Scotland and England, for example, served in the armies of Catholic France.[92] The Catholic general Ernst von Mansfeld led the imperial army against the Catholic Bohemian rebels at the start of the war but in 1621 switched sides and commanded the troops of the Calvinist Frederick V in Bohemia.[93] Albrecht von Wallenstein, the Bohemian mercenary leader who became the supreme commander of the Catholic imperial army, was a Lutheran, and many of his foot soldiers were Protestants who had fled Catholic persecution in their own countries. Wallenstein seemed more interested in military entrepreneurism than religion.[94] He transformed his huge estates into a vast arsenal for his private army of half a million men. Indifferent to the social standing or religious convictions of his associates, he demanded only obedience and efficiency from his troops, who were allowed to live off the countryside and terrorize the rural population.

By 1629 Emperor Ferdinand seemed to have regained control of the empire. However, a year later the tide turned, when Cardinal Richelieu, chief minister of France, persuaded the Protestant warrior-king Gustavus Adolphus of Sweden to invade the Habsburg Empire. Adolphus is often presented as the hero of the Protestant cause, but he did not mention religion in his declaration of intent in June 1630 and found it difficult at first to attract allies.[95] The most powerful German Protestant princes saw the Swedish invasion as a threat and formed a third party, holding aloof from both the Swedes and the Habsburgs. When Lutheran German peasants tried to drive the Lutheran Swedes out of their country in November 1632, they were simply massacred.[96] Eventually, however, after Adolphus's first victory over the Catholic League of German princes at Magdeburg in 1631, many territories that had tried to remain neutral joined the Swedish offensive. Inadequate methods of financing, supplying, and controlling the troops meant that Swedish soldiers resorted to looting the countryside, killing huge numbers of civilians.[97] The mass casualties of the Thirty Years' War can partly be attributed to the use of mercenary armies who had to provision themselves and could only do so by brutally sacking civilian populations, abusing women and children, and slaughtering their prisoners.

Catholic France had come to the rescue of the Protestant Swedes in January 1631, promising to supply their campaign, and later dispatched troops to fight the imperial forces in the winter of 1634–35. They received the backing of Pope Urban VIII, who wanted to weaken Habsburg control of the Papal States in Italy. To counter the combined Swedish, French, and papal alliance, the Protestant principalities of Brandenburg and Saxony were reconciled with the Catholic emperor at the Peace of Prague (1635), and within a few months most of the Lutheran states also made peace with Ferdinand. The Protestant armies were absorbed into the imperial forces, and German Catholics and Protestants fought together against the Swedes. The rest of the Thirty Years' War now became largely a struggle between Catholic France and the Catholic Habsburgs. Neither could achieve a decisive victory, and after a long, enervating struggle, treaties were signed, known collectively as the Peace of Westphalia (1648), which left the Austrian Habsburgs in control of their hereditary lands and the Swedes in possession of Pomerania, Bremen, and the Baltic region. Prussia emerged as the leading German Protestant state, and France gained much of the Alsace. Finally Calvinism became a licit religion in the Holy Roman Empire.[98] By the end of the

Thirty Years' War, Europeans had fought off the danger of imperial rule. There would never be a large unified empire on the Persian, Roman, or Ottoman model; instead, Europe would be divided into smaller states, each claiming sovereign power in its own territory, each supported by a standing, professional army and governed by a prince who aspired to absolute rule—a recipe, perhaps, for chronic interstate warfare.

"Religious" sentiments were certainly present in the minds of those who fought these wars, but to imagine that "religion" was yet distinguishable from the social, economic, and political issues is essentially anachronistic. As the historian John Bossy has reminded us, before 1700 there was no concept of "religion" as separate from society or politics. As we shall see later in this chapter, that distinction would not be made until the formal separation of church and state by early modern philosophers and statesmen, and even then the liberal state was slow to arrive. Before that time, "there simply was no coherent way yet to divide religious causes from social causes; the divide is a modern invention."[99] People were fighting for different visions of society, but they had as yet no way to separate religious from temporal factors.

This was also true of the English Civil War (1642–48), which resulted in the execution of Charles I and the creation in England of a short-lived Puritan republic under Oliver Cromwell (1599–1658). It is more difficult to list examples of participants in this war crossing denominational lines, since Cromwell's Puritan army and the royalist troops were all members of the Church of England. They held different views of their faith, however. The "Puritans" were dissatisfied with the slow and limited progress of the Reformation in their country and wanted to "purge" the Anglican establishment of "popish" practices. Instead of worshipping in elaborate church buildings with authoritarian bishops, they formed small, exclusive congregations of those who had experienced a "born-again" conversion. Certainly the heavy-handed attempts of William Laud, Archbishop of Canterbury (1573–1645), to root out Calvinism in the English and Scottish churches, his suspension of Puritan ministers, and his support of royal absolutism were crucial irritants. Cromwell was convinced that God controlled events on earth and had singled out the English to be his new chosen people.[100] The success of his New Model Army in defeating the royalists at the Battle of Naseby in 1645 seemed to prove the "remarkable providences and appearances of the Lord," and he justified his brutal subjugation of Ireland as a "righteous judgment of God."[101]

But the civil war is no longer regarded as a last eruption of religious bigotry laid to rest by Charles II's constitutional monarchy in 1660.[102] It too was part of the larger European struggle against state centralization. Charles I had been trying to achieve an absolute monarchy similar to those established on the continent after the Thirty Years' War, and the civil war was an attempt to resist this centralization and protect local interests, freedoms, and privileges. Again, transcending sectarian divisions, Scottish Presbyterians and Irish Catholics had for a time fought alongside the Puritans to weaken the monarchy. Even though Charles had tried to impose episcopal rule on the Scots, they made it clear in their Proclamation of 1639 that they were fighting not only for religion but also "to shake off all monarchical government." In the Grand Remonstrance, presented to Charles in 1641, the Puritans took it for granted that religion and politics were inseparable: "The root of all this mischief we find to be a malignant and pernicious design of subverting the fundamental laws and principles of government upon which the religion and justice of this kingdom are firmly established."[103]

As William Cavanaugh explains in *The Myth of Religious Violence*, these wars were neither "all about religion" nor "all about politics." Yet it is true that these wars helped create the idea of "religion" as a private and personal activity, separate from mundane affairs.[104] Chancellor Axel Oxenstierna, who masterminded Sweden's participation in the Thirty Years' War, told the Swedish Council that the conflict was "not so much a matter of religion, but rather of serving the status publicus, wherein religion is also comprehended."[105] He could speak in this way because the Lutheran church had already been absorbed or "comprehended" by the Swedish state. New configurations of political power were beginning to force the Church into a subordinate realm, a process that involved a fundamental reallocation of authority and resources. When the new word *secularization* was coined in France during the late sixteenth century, it originally referred to "the transfer of goods from the possession of the Church into that of the 'world' [*saeculum*]."[106] Legislative and judicial powers that had been in the Church's remit were gradually transferred to the new sovereign state.

Like most states, these early modern kingdoms were achieved by force: all struggled to annex as much land as possible and had internal battles with the cities, clergy, local associations, and aristocracies who jealously guarded traditional privileges and immunities that sovereign states could not permit.[107] The modern state had come into being by militarily defeating rival political institutions: the empire, the city-state, and the feudal lordship.[108] The church, which had been so integral to medieval government, also had to be subdued. Thus the sixteenth- and seventeenth-century wars were "the crucible in which some of the competing forces from an earlier age were consumed in the fire and others blended and transmuted into new compounds . . . the matrix of all that came after."[109]

• • •

These political and social developments required a new understanding of the word *religion*.[110] One of the characteristics of early modern thought was a tendency to assume binary contrasts. In an attempt to define phenomena more exactly, categories of experience that had once co-inhered were now set off against each other: faith and reason, intellect and emotion, and church and state. Hitherto, the "internal" and "external" worlds had been complementary, but now "religion" was becoming a private, internalized commitment separate from such "external" activities as politics. Protestants, whose reinterpretation of Christianity was itself a product of early modernity, would define *religion* and set an agenda to which other faith traditions would be expected to conform. This new definition mirrored the programs of the new sovereign states, which were relegating "religion" to the private sphere.

A crucial figure in this development was Edward, Lord Herbert of Cherbury (1583–1648), who was not only a philosopher but also a statesman committed to the state control of ecclesiastical affairs. His most important work, *De Veritate,* which influenced such important philosophers as Hugo Grotius (1583–1645), René Descartes (1596–1650), and John Locke (1632–1704), argued that Christianity was neither an institution nor a way of life but a set of five truths that were innate in the human mind: (1) a supreme deity existed, (2) which should be worshipped (3) and served by ethical living and natural piety; (4) human beings were thus required to reject sin and (5) would be rewarded or punished by God after death. Because these notions were instinctive, self-evident, and accessible to the meanest intelligence, the rituals and guidance of a church were entirely unnecessary.[111] These "truths" would, however, seem strange indeed to Buddhists, Hindus, Confucians, or Daoists, and many Jews, Christians, and Muslims would also find them bleakly unrepresentative of their faith. Herbert was convinced that "all men will be unanimously eager for this austere worship of God," and since everybody would agree on "these natural tokens of faith," it was the key to peace; "insolent spirits" who refused to accept them must be punished by the secular magistracy.[112] Emphasis on the "natural," "normal," and "innate" character of these core ideas implied that those who did not discover them in their minds were in some way unnatural and abnormal: a dark current was emerging in early modern thought. This extreme privatization of faith, therefore, had the potential to become as divisive, coercive, and intolerant as the so-called *religious* passions it was trying to abolish.

Thomas Hobbes (1588–1679) also saw state control of the church as essential to peace and wanted a strong monarch to take over the church and enforce religious unity. A committed royalist, he wrote his classic *Leviathan* (1651) in exile in Paris after the English Civil War. The disruptive forces of religion, Hobbes argued, must be curbed as effectively as God had subdued Leviathan, the biblical chaos-monster, to create an ordered universe. Hobbes was adamant that pointless squabbling about irrational dogmas had been entirely responsible for the Wars of Religion. Not everybody shared this view, however. In *Commonwealth of Oceana* (1656), the English political theorist James Harrington discussed the economic and legal issues that had contributed to these conflicts, but Hobbes would have none of it. The preachers alone, he insisted, had been "the cause of all our late mischief" by leading the people astray with "disreputable doctrines." The Presbyterian divines, he believed, had been particularly culpable in stirring up unruly passions before the English Civil War and were "therefore guilty of all that fell."[113] Hobbes's solution was to create an absolute state that would crush the tendency of human beings to cling obstinately to their own beliefs, which doomed them to perpetual warfare. Instead, they must learn to recognize the frailty of our grasp on truth, enter into a contractual relationship with one another, elect an absolute monarch, and accept his ideas as their own.[114] This ruler would control the clergy in such a way as to prevent even the possibility of sectarian conflict.[115] Alas, history would show that Hobbes's solution was too simplistic; the states of Europe would continue to fight one another savagely, with or without sectarian strife.

John Locke's solution was religious freedom, since, in his view, the Wars of Religion had been caused by a fatal inability to entertain other points of view. "Religion," he argued, was a "private search" and as such could not be policed by the government; in this personal quest, everyone must rely on "his own endeavours" rather than an external authority. To mingle "religion" and politics was a grievous, dangerous, and existential error:

> The church itself is a thing absolutely separate and distinct from the commonwealth. The boundaries on both sides are fixed and immoveable. He jumbles heaven and earth together, the things most remote and opposite, who mixes these two societies, which are in their original end, business, and in everything perfectly and infinitely different from each other.[116]

Locke assumed that the separation of politics and religion was written into the very nature of things. But this, of course, was a radical innovation that most of his contemporaries would find extraordinary and unacceptable. It would make modern "religion" entirely different from anything that had gone before. Yet because of the violent passions it supposedly unleashed, Locke insisted that the segregation of "religion" from government was "above all things necessary" for the creation of a peaceful society.[117] In Locke we see the birth of the "myth of religious violence" that would become ingrained in the Western ethos.

It is true that Western Christianity had become more internalized during the early modern period. This is evident in Luther's conception of faith as an interior appropriation of Christ's saving power, in the mysticism of Teresa of Ávila (1515–82), and in the *Spiritual Exercises* of Ignatius of Loyola (1491–1556). In the past the exploration of the inner world had compelled Buddhist monks to work "for the welfare and happiness of the people" and Confucians to engage in a political effort to reform society. After his solitary struggle with Satan in the wilderness, Jesus had embarked on a ministry of healing in the troubled villages of Galilee that led to his execution by the Roman authorities. Muhammad had left his cave on Mount Hira for a political struggle against the structural violence of Mecca. In the early modern period too, the *Spiritual Exercises* had propelled Ignatius's Jesuits all over the world—to Japan, India, China, and the Americas. But modern "religion" would try to subvert this natural dynamic by turning the seeker in upon himself, and inevitably, many would rebel against this unnatural privatization of their faith.

Unable to extend the natural human rights they were establishing to the indigenous peoples of the New World, the Renaissance humanists had already revealed the insidious underside of early modern ideas that still inform our political life. Locke, who was among the first to formulate the liberal ethos of modern politics, also revealed the darker aspect of the secularism he proposed. A pioneer of tolerance, he was adamant that the sovereign state could not accommodate either Catholicism or Islam;[118] he endorsed a master's "Absolute, Arbitrary, Despotical Power" over a slave that included "the power to kill him at any time." Himself directly involved in the colonization of the Carolinas, Locke argued that the native "kings" of America had no legal jurisdiction or right of ownership of their land. Like the urbane Thomas More, he found it intolerable that the "wild woods and uncultivated waste of America be left to nature, without any improvement, tillage and husbandry," when it could be used to support the "needy and wretched" of Europe.[119] A new system of violent oppression was emerging that would privilege the liberal, secular West at the expense of the indigenous peoples of its colonies.

On the issue of colonization, most early modern thinkers agreed with Locke. Grotius contended that any military action against the natives was just because they had no legal claim to their territory.[120] Hobbes believed that because they had not developed an agrarian economy, the Native Americans—"few, savage, short-lived, poor and mean"—must relinquish their land.[121] And in a sermon delivered in London in 1622 to the Virginia Company, which had received a royal charter to settle all the terrain between what is now New York and South Carolina, John Donne, dean of St. Paul's Cathedral, argued that: "In the Law of Nature and Nations, a Land never inhabited by any or utterly derelicted and immemorially abandoned by the former Inhabitants, becomes theirs that will possess it."[122] The colonists would take this belief with them to North America—but unlike these early modern thinkers, they had absolutely no intention of separating church and state.

—◆◆◆—

10

The Triumph of the Secular

When the Pilgrim Fathers arrived in Massachusetts Bay in 1630, they would have been horrified to hear that they were about to lay the foundations of the world's first secular republic. They had left England because Archbishop Laud, they believed, had corrupted their church with popish practices; they regarded their migration as a new Exodus and America, the "English Canaan," as their "land of Promise."[1] Before landing, John Winthrop, first governor of the Bay Colony, reminded them that they had come to the American wilderness to build a truly Protestant community that would be a light to other nations and inspire Old England to revive the Reformation:[2] "We must consider that we shall be as a city upon a hill. The eyes of all people are upon us, so that if we shall deal falsely with our God in this work we have undertaken, and so cause him to withdraw his present help from us, we shall be made a story and a by-word throughout the world."[3] One of their most important missions was to save the Native Americans from the wiles of the French Catholic settlers in North America, making New England a "bulwark against the kingdom of Antichrist, which the Jesuits labour to rear up in these parts."[4] Winthrop would have found the notion of a secular state inconceivable, and like most of the colonists, he had no time for democracy. Before they set foot on American soil, he reminded the migrants firmly that God had "so disposed the condition of mankind, as in all times some must be rich, some poor, some high and eminent in power and dignity, others mean and in subjection."[5]

The Puritans were convinced that God had given the land to them by a special dispensation, but this covenantal faith blended seamlessly with the humanists' more secular doctrine of natural human rights. On the eve of their departure from Southampton in 1630, their minister, John Cotton, had listed all the biblical precedents for their migration. After showing that God had given the children of Adam and Noah, who had both colonized an "empty" world, the "liberty" to inhabit a "vacant place" without either buying it from the original inhabitants or asking their leave, he segued quite naturally into the argument: "It is a principle in nature, that in a vacant soil he that taketh possession of it, and bestoweth culture and husbandry upon it, his right it is."[6] England was overcrowded, contended Robert Cushman, business manager of the Bay Company, and America was "a vast and empty chaos" because the Indians were "not industrious, neither having art, science, skill or faculty to use either the land or the commodities but all spoils, rots and is marred for want of manuring, gathering, ordering etc." It was therefore "lawful" for the settlers "to take a land which none useth."[7] This liberal doctrine would inform their dealings with the Native Americans quite as much as the biblical teachings.

The centrality of Original Sin in their theology predisposed these staunchly Protestant colonists toward an absolutist remedy for man's fallen nature in their polity. If Adam had not sinned, government would have been unnecessary; but unredeemed men and women were naturally prone to lie, steal, and murder, and these evil impulses could be forcibly held in check only by a strong, authoritative government. Those who had been "born again" enjoyed the freedom of the sons of God but were at liberty only to do what God commanded. At their conversion, they had surrendered the right to follow their own inclinations and must submit to the authorities God had placed over them.[8]

The Massachusetts Bay Colony was, of course, not the first English settlement in North America. The founders of Jamestown in Virginia had arrived in 1607. They were not ardent Puritan dissenters but mercantilists, intent on making their colony a profitable commercial enterprise. Yet on disembarking, the first thing they did was build a makeshift church, with a sail for a roof and logs for pews. Their colony was almost as strict as Massachusetts.[9] Church services were obligatory, and there

were fines for drunkenness, gambling, adultery, idleness, and ostenta-
tious dress. If an offender failed to change his ways, he was excommunicated and his property confiscated.[10] This was a Christian as well as a
commercial enterprise, hailed in London as a pivotal moment in salvation history. According to its royal charter, the Virginia Company's chief
objective was the conversion of the native peoples rather than financial
success.[11] As good early-modern Protestants, Virginians adhered to the
principles of the Treaty of Augsburg: *cuius regio, eius religio* ("whoever
controls the region controls religion"). Where most agrarian rulers had
rarely attempted to control the spiritual lives of their subjects, the com-
mercially minded Virginians took it for granted that in a properly regulated society all citizens should have the same faith and that it was the
duty of any government to enforce religious observance.

John Locke was not yet born, so in the American colonies, religion,
politics, and economics were still inseparable. Indeed, the Virginians
were incapable of thinking of commerce as a purely secular activity.[12]
Samuel Purchas, the company's propagandist, gave fullest expression to
their ideology.[13] If Adam had not fallen, the whole world would have
retained its original perfection and exploration would have been easy.
With the arrival of sin, though, men became so depraved that they would
have slaughtered one another had not God scattered them over the earth
after the destruction of the Tower of Babel and kept them in ignorance of
one another. Yet he had also decreed that commerce would bring them
together again. In Eden, Adam had enjoyed all essential commodities,
but these too had been dispersed after the Fall. Now, thanks to modern maritime technology, a country in one region could supply what was
lacking in other places, and God could use the global market to redeem
the non-Christian world. In America the Virginians would supply staples
for famine-prone England and at the same time bring the gospel to the
Indians. A company broadsheet explained that God no longer worked
through prophets and miracles; the only way to evangelize the world
these days was "mixtly, by discoverie, and trade of marchants." Living
on the Indians' land and trading with them, the colonists would "sell to
them the pearles of heaven" by "dailie conversation."[14] So the quest for
commodities, Purchas insisted, was not an end in itself, and the company
would fail if it sought only profit.

Purchas initially believed that the land must not be forcibly taken
from the Indians because it had been assigned to them by God.[15] His

Protestant ideology may have been paternalistic, but it also had a measure of respect for the indigenous peoples. Yet during the first two terrible winters, when the colonists were starving to death, some of their conscripted laborers had fled to the local Powhattans, and when the English governor asked their chief to return the fugitives, he disdainfully refused. Whereupon the English militia descended on the settlement, killed fifteen Native Americans, burned their houses, cut down their corn, and abducted the queen, killing her children. So much for peaceful "dailie conversation." The Indians were bewildered: "Why will you destroy us who supply you with food?" asked Chief Powhattan: "Why are you jealous of us? We are unarmed and willing to give you what you ask, if you come in a friendly manner."[16]

By 1622 the Indians had become seriously alarmed by the rapid growth of the colony; the English had taken over a significant acreage of their hunting grounds, depriving them of essential resources.[17] In a sudden attack on Jamestown, the Powhattans killed about a third of the English population. The Virginians retaliated in a ruthless war of attrition: they would allow local tribes to settle and plant their corn and then, just before the harvest, attack them, killing as many natives as possible. Within three years they had avenged the Jamestown massacre many times over. Instead of founding their colony on the compassionate principles of the gospel, they had inaugurated a policy of elimination imposed by ruthless military force. Even Purchas was forced to abandon the Bible and rely on the humanists' aggressive doctrine of human rights when he finally agreed that the Indians deserved their fate because, by resisting English settlement, they had broken the law of nature.[18] More pragmatic considerations were beginning to replace the old piety. The company had not been able to produce the staples England needed, and investors had not seen an adequate return. The only way their colony could function was to cultivate tobacco and sell it at five shillings a pound. Begun as a holy enterprise, Virginia would gradually be secularized not by Locke's liberal ideology but by pressure of events.

The Puritans of Massachusetts had no qualms about killing Indians. They had left England during the Thirty Years' War, had absorbed the militancy of that fearsome time, and justified their violence by a highly selective reading of the Bible. Ignoring Jesus's pacifist teachings, they drew on the bellicosity of some of the Hebrew scriptures. "God is an excellent Man of War," preached Alexander Leighton, and the Bible "the best handbook on war." Their revered minister John Cotton had instructed them that they could attack the natives "without provocation"—a procedure normally unlawful—because they had not only a natural right to their territory, but "a special Commission from God" to take their land.[19] Already there were signs of the exceptionalist thinking that would in the future often characterize American politics. In 1636 William Bradford described a raid on the Pequot village of Fort Mystic on the Connecticut shore to avenge the murder of an English trader, contemplating the fearsome carnage with lofty complacency:

> Those that escaped the fire were slain with the sword; some hewed to pieces, others run through with rapiers, so as they were quickly dispatched, and very few escaped. It was conceived they thus destroyed about 400 at this time. It was a fearful sight to see them thus frying in the fire, and the streams of blood quenching the same, and horrible was the stink and scent thereof, but the victory seemed a sweet sacrifice, and they gave the prayers thereof to God, who had wrought so wonderfully for them.[20]

When the Puritans negotiated the Treaty of Hertford (1638) with the few Pequot survivors, they insisted on the destruction of all Pequot villages and sold the women and children into slavery. Should Christians have behaved more compassionately? asked Captain John Underhill, a veteran of the Thirty Years' War. He answered his rhetorical question with a decided negative: God supported the English, "so we had sufficient light for our proceedings."[21]

Thirty years later, when Europeans were recoiling from the violence in the Thirty Years' War, some Puritans had begun to question the validity of these Indian campaigns.[22] After the murder of an Indian convert to Christianity in 1675, the Plymouth authorities, on very shaky evidence, pinned the blame on Metacom, chief of the Wampanoag, whom the English called "King Philip." When they executed three of his aides, Metacom with his Indian allies promptly devastated fifty out of the ninety English towns in Plymouth and Rhode Island; by the spring of 1676 the Indian armies were within ten miles of Boston. In the autumn the war turned in the colonists' favor. Yet they were facing a hard winter and the Narragansetts on Rhode Island had food and supplies. Accusing them—again on dubious grounds—of aiding Metacom, the English militia attacked and looted the village, massacred its inhabitants—most of them noncombatant refugees—and burned the settlement to the ground. The war continued with atrocities on both sides—Indian warriors scalped their prisoners alive; the English disemboweled and quartered theirs—but in the summer of 1676, both sides abandoned the struggle. Almost half the prewar Indian population had been eliminated: 1,250 were killed in battle, 625 died of wounds, and 3,000 died of disease in captivity. The colonies, however, suffered only about 800 casualties, a mere 1.6 percent of the total English population of 50,000.

The Puritan establishment believed that God had used the Indians to punish the colonists for their backsliding from godly ways and for the decline in church attendance and were therefore unconcerned about the Indian casualties. But many of the colonists were now less convinced of the morality of all-out warfare. This time a vocal minority spoke out against the war. The Quakers, who had first arrived in Boston in 1656 and had themselves been the victims of Puritan intolerance, vigorously condemned the atrocities. John Easton, governor of Rhode Island, accused the Puritans of Plymouth of arrogance and overconfidence in provocatively expanding their settlements and mischievously playing the tribes off against one another. John Eliot, a missionary to the Indians, argued that this had not been a war of self-defense; the real aggressors were the Plymouth authorities who had fudged evidence and treated the Indians with rough justice. As in Virginia, flagging piety meant that gradually more rational and naturalistic arguments would replace theological ones in their politics.[23]

As is often the case, a general decline in religious fervor tends to inspire a revival from some dissatisfied element of society. By the early eighteenth century, worship had become more formal in the colonies and elegant churches transformed the skylines of New York and Boston. But to the horror of these polite congregations, a frenzied piety had erupted in the rural areas. The Great Awakening broke out first in Northampton, Connecticut, in 1734, when the death of two young people and the powerful preaching of its minister Jonathan Edwards (1703–58) whipped the town into a devotional fever that spread to Massachusetts and Long Island. During Edwards's sermons, the congregation screamed, yelled, writhed in the aisles, and crowded around the pulpit, begging him to stop. But Edwards continued inexorably, never looking at the hysterical masses, offering them no comfort, but staring rigidly at the bell rope.

Three hundred people experienced a wrenching conversion, could not tear themselves away from their Bibles, and forgot to eat. Yet they also experienced, Edwards recalled, a joyous perception of beauty that was quite different from any natural sensation "so that they could not forbear crying out with a loud voice, expressing their great admiration."[24] Others, broken by the fear of God, would sink into an abyss of despair only to soar to an equally extreme elation in the sudden conviction that they were free of sin.

The Great Awakening showed that religion, instead of being an obstacle to progress and democracy, could be a positive force for modernization. Strangely enough, this seemingly primitive hysteria helped these Puritans to embrace an egalitarianism that would have shocked Winthrop but was far closer to our present norms. The Awakening appalled the Harvard faculty, and Yale, Edwards's own university, disowned him, but Edwards believed that a different order—nothing less than the Kingdom of God—was coming painfully to birth in the New World. Edwards was, in fact, presiding over a revolution. The Awakening flourished in the poorer colonies, where people had little hope of earthly fulfillment. While the educated classes were turning to the rational consolations of the European Enlightenment, Edwards brought the Enlightenment ideal of the pursuit of happiness to his unlettered congregation in a form that they could understand and prepared them for the revolutionary upheavals of 1775.[25]

At this date, most colonists still believed that democracy was the worst form of government and that some form of social stratification was God's will. Their Christian horizons were bound by the systemic violence that had been essential to the agrarian state. In the congregations of New England, only the "saints" who had experienced a born-again conversion were allowed to participate in the Lord's Supper. Even though they comprised only a fifth of the English population, they alone had a share in God's Covenant with the New Israel. Yet not even the saints were allowed to speak in church but had to wait in silent attendance on the minister, and the unregenerate majority had equality before the law but no voice in government.[26] Edwards's grandfather, Solomon Stoddard of Northampton, had brusquely dismissed the masses as incapable of serious thought: "Let the government be put into their hands and things will be carried by a tumultuous cry . . . things would quickly be turned upside down."[27] Yet Stoddard had urged his entire congregation, including the unconverted, to partake of the Lord's Supper and ordered them, in highly emotional gatherings, to stand up and publicly claim the covenant for themselves.

Jonathan Edwards understood that, despite his autocratic views, his grandfather had in fact given the masses a voice. He now demanded that his congregants speak out in church or be forever lost. Edwards belonged to the New England aristocracy; he had no interest in political revolution, but he had realized that a preacher could no longer expect his audience to listen submissively to eternal verities that did not speak convincingly to their condition. That might have worked in seventeenth-century England, but a different kind of society was coming into being in America, one that was not in thrall to an established aristocracy. In 1748, at the funeral of his uncle, Colonel John Stoddard, Edwards delivered a remarkable eulogy that listed the qualities of a great leader. In this New World, a leader must come down to the people's level.[28] He must have a "great knowledge of human nature" and acquaint himself with "the state and circumstances" of the nation, adapting his ideas to the realities of human and social experience. A leader must get to know his people, be attentive to current events and foresee crises.

Only at the very end did Edwards say that a leader should belong to a "good family," but that was simply because education was "useful" and would make him more effective. A great man could have nothing to do with self-interested people of a "narrow, private spirit." Standing before the merchants, businessmen, and land speculators of Northampton, Edwards uttered a blistering condemnation of men who "shamefully defile their hands to gain a few pounds, and . . . grind the faces of the poor and screw upon their neighbors, and will take advantage of their authority to line their own pockets."[29] This revolutionary assault on the structural violence of colonial society spread to other towns, and two years later, Edwards was driven from his pulpit and forced to take refuge for a time on the frontier with other misfits, acting as chaplain to the Indians of Stockbridge. Edwards was well versed in modern thought and had read Locke and Newton, but it was his Christianity that enabled him to bring the modern egalitarian ideal to the common people.

The Great Awakening was America's first mass movement; it gave many ordinary folk their first experience of participating in a nationwide event that could change the course of history.[30] Their ecstatic illumination left many Americans, who could not easily relate to the secular lean-ings of the revolutionary leaders, with the memory of a blissful state that they called "liberty." The revival had also encouraged them to see their emotional faith as superior to the cerebral piety of the respectable classes. Those who remembered the aristocratic clerics' disdain of their enthusiasm retained a distrust of institutional authority that prepared them later to take the drastic step of rejecting the king of England.

In 1775, when the British government tried to tax the colonists to pay for its colonial wars against France, anger flared into outright rebellion. The leaders experienced the American Revolution as a secular event, a sober, pragmatic struggle against an imperial power. They were men of the Enlightenment, inspired by Locke and Newton, and were also deists, who differed from orthodox Christians by rejecting the doctrines of revelation and the divinity of Christ. The Declaration of Independence, drafted by Thomas Jefferson, John Adams, and Benjamin Franklin, and ratified by the Colonial Congress on July 4, 1776, was an Enlightenment document, based on Locke's theory of self-evident human rights—life, liberty, and property[31]—and the Enlightenment ideals of freedom and equality. These men had no utopian ideas about redistributing wealth or abolishing the class system. For them, this was simply a practical, far-reaching, but sustainable war of independence.

The Founding Fathers, however, belonged to the gentry, and their ideas were far from typical; most Americans were Calvinists who could not relate to this rationalist ethos. Reluctant initially to break with Britain, not all the colonists joined the struggle, but those that did were motivated as much by the millennial myths of Christianity as by the Founders' ideals. During the revolution, secularist ideology blended creatively with the religious aspirations of the majority in a way that enabled Americans with very divergent beliefs to join forces against the might of England. When ministers spoke of the importance of virtue and responsibility in government, they helped people make sense of Sam Adams's fiery denunciations of British tyranny.[32] When the Founders spoke of "liberty," they used a word charged with religious meaning.[33] Timothy Dwight, Jonathan Edwards's grandson and president of Yale University, predicted that the revolution would usher in "Immanuel's land";[34] the Connecticut preacher Ebenezer Baldwin argued that liberty, religion, and learning had been driven out of Europe and moved to America, where Jesus would establish his kingdom; and Provost William Smith of Philadelphia maintained that the colonies were God's "chosen seat of Freedom,

Arts and Heavenly Knowledge." John Adams saw the English settlement of America as part of God's plan for the world's enlightenment,[35] and Thomas Paine was convinced that "we have it in our power to begin the world over again. A situation such as the present hath not happened since the days of Noah."[36]

This exaltation, though, was laced with hatred for the enemies of God's kingdom. After the passing of the Stamp Act (1765), patriotic songs portrayed its perpetrators—Lords Bute, Grenville, and North—as the minions of Satan, and during political demonstrations their pictures were carried alongside effigies of the devil. When George III granted religious freedom to the French Catholics in the Canadian territory, he was denounced by the American colonists as the ally of Antichrist; and even the presidents of Harvard and Yale saw the War of Independence as part of God's design for the overthrow of Catholicism.[37] This virulent sectarian hostility enabled the colonists to separate themselves definitively from the Old World, for which many still felt a strong residual affection; hatred of Catholic "tyranny" would long remain a crucial element in American national identity. The Founders may have been followers of Locke, but "religion" had not yet been banished from the colonies; had it been so, the revolution might not have succeeded.

As soon as independence was declared in July 1776, the colonies began to compose their new constitutions. In Virginia, Thomas Jefferson (1743–1826) proposed a formula that would not survive the ratification process: "All persons shall have full and free liberty of religious opinion; nor shall any be compelled to frequent or maintain any religious institution."[38] This guaranteed freedom *for* religion and freedom *from* it. But we must bear in mind that Jefferson's conception of "religion" was based on two early modern innovations to which most of his countrymen did not subscribe. First was the reduction of religion to "belief" and "opinion." As an apostle of Enlightenment empiricism, Jefferson rejected the idea that religious knowledge was acquired by revelation, ritual, or communal experience; it was merely a set of beliefs shared by some. Like all Enlightenment philosophes, Jefferson and James Madison (1751–1836), the pioneers of religious liberty in America, believed that no idea should be immune from investigation or even outright rejection. Nevertheless, they also insisted on the right of conscience: a man's personal convictions were his own, not subject to the coercion of government. Obligatory belief, therefore, violated a fundamental human right. "Religious bondage shackles and debilitates the mind and unfits it for every noble enterprise, every expected prospect," Madison objected.[39] The last fifteen hundred years, he claimed sweepingly, had resulted in "more or less all places" in "pride and indolence in the clergy, ignorance and servility in the laity; in both, superstition, bigotry and persecution."[40] The "myth of religious violence" had clearly taken root in the minds of the Founders. In the new enlightened age, Jefferson declared in his *Statute for Establishing Religious Freedom in Virginia,* "our civil rights have no dependence upon our religious opinions, any more than our opinions in physics or geometry."[41]

The critique of Jefferson and Madison was a healthy corrective to the idolatrous tendency to give man-made ideas divine status. Freedom of thought would become a sacred value in the modern secular West, an inviolable and nonnegotiable human right. It would advance scientific and technological progress and enable the arts to flourish. But the intellectual freedom proclaimed by the Enlightenment philosophes was a luxury of modernization. In the premodern agrarian state, it had never been possible to permit an entire population to cast tradition aside and freely criticize the established order. Most of the aristocratic Founders, moreover, had no intention of extending this privilege to the common people. They still took it for granted that it was their task, as enlightened statesmen, to lead from above.[42] Like most of the elite, John Adams, second president of the United States (r. 1796–1800), was suspicious of any policy that might lead to "mob-rule" or the impoverishment of the gentry, though Jefferson's more radical followers protested this "tyranny" and, like Edwards, demanded that the people's voices be heard.[43] Still, it was not until the Industrial Revolution shook up the social order that the ideals enshrined by the Founding Fathers could apply broadly to social reality.

The second assumption of Jefferson and Madison was that "religion" was an autonomous, private human activity essentially separate from politics and that mixing the two had been a great aberration. This may have been a self-evident idea to Locke, but it would have still been a very strange notion to most Americans. The Founders knew their countrymen: a federal constitution would never gain the support of all the states unless it refrained from making any single Protestant denomination official, as many of the state constitutions had done. Precisely because most Americans still approved of religion in their governments, therefore, uniting the several states would require religious neutrality at the federal level.[44] Hence the first lapidary clause of the First Amendment to the Constitution in the Bill of Rights (1791) decreed that "Congress shall make no law respecting the establishment of religion, or prohibiting the free exercise thereof." The state would neither promote nor obstruct religion but simply leave it alone.[45] Yet there were political consequences even for that. During the bitterly contested presidential election of 1800, Jefferson the deist was accused of being an atheist and even a Muslim. He replied that while he was not hostile to faith, he was adamantly opposed to government meddling in religious affairs. When a group of his Baptist supporters in Danbury, Connecticut, asked him to appoint a day of fasting to bring the nation together, Jefferson replied that this lay beyond the president's competence:

> Believing with you that religion is a matter which lies solely between man and his God, that he owes to none other for his faith and worship, that the legislative powers of government reach actions only, and not opinions, I contemplate with solemn reverence that act of the whole American people which declared that their legislature should "make no law respecting an establishment of religion or prohibiting the free exercise thereof," thus building a wall of separation of Church and State.

While such separation could be beneficial to both church and state, it was not, as Jefferson assumed, written into the very nature of things but was a modern innovation. The United States was attempting something entirely new.

Jefferson had borrowed the image of the "wall of separation" from Roger Williams (1604–83), founder of Providence, Rhode Island, who had been expelled from New England because of his opposition to the intolerant policies of the Puritan government.[46] But Williams was less concerned about the welfare of the state than that of his faith, which he believed would be contaminated by any involvement with government.[47] He intended Rhode Island to be an alternative Christian community that came closer to the spirit of the gospels. Jefferson, by contrast, was more concerned to protect the state from the "loathsome combination of church and state" that had reduced human beings to "dupes and drudges."[48] He seemed to assume—quite wrongly—that there had been states in the past that had *not* been guilty of this "loathsome combination." It remained to be seen whether the secularized United States would be less violent and coercive than its more religious predecessors.

Whatever the Founders wanted, most Americans still took it for granted that the United States would be based on Christian principles. By 1790, some 40 percent of the new nation lived on the frontiers and were becoming increasingly resentful of the republican government that did not share their hardships but taxed them as harshly as the British had done. A new wave of revivals, known as the Second Great Awakening, represented a grassroots campaign for a more democratic and Bible-based America.[49] The new revivalists were not intellectuals like Edwards but men of the people who used wild gestures, earthy humor, and slang and relied on dreams, visions, and celestial signs. During their mass rallies, they pitched huge tents outside the towns, and their gospel songs transported the crowds to ecstasy. However, these prophets were not pre-Enlightenment throwbacks. Lorenzo Dow may have looked like John the Baptist, but he quoted Jefferson and Paine and, like any Enlightenment philosophe, urged the people to think for themselves. In the Christian commonwealth the first should be last and the last first. God had sent his insights to the poor and unlettered, and Jesus and his disciples had not had college degrees.

James Kelly and Barton Stone railed against the aristocratic clergy who tried to force the erudite faith of Harvard on the people. Enlightenment philosophers had insisted that people must have the courage to throw off their dependence on authority, use their natural reason to discover the truth, and think for themselves. Now the revivalists insisted that American Christians could read the Bible without direction from upper-class scholars. When Stone founded his own denomination, he called it a "declaration of independence": the revivalists were bringing the modern ideals of democracy, equality, freedom of speech, and independence to the folk in an idiom that uneducated people could make their own. This Second Awakening may have seemed retrograde to the elite, but it was actually a Protestant version of the Enlightenment. Demanding a degree of equality that the American ruling class was not yet ready to give them, the revivalists represented a populist discontent that it could not safely ignore.

At first, this rough, democratic Christianity was confined to the poorer Americans, but during the 1840s Charles Finney (1792–1875) brought it to the middle classes, creating an "evangelical" Christianity based on a literal reading of the gospels. Evangelicals were determined to convert the secular republic to Christ, and by the mid-nineteenth century, evangelicalism had become the dominant faith of the United States.[50] Without waiting for guidance from the government, from about 1810 these Protestants began to work in churches and schools and established reform associations that mushroomed in the northern states. Some campaigned against slavery, others against liquor; some worked to end the oppression of women and other disadvantaged groups, others for penal and educational reform. Like the Second Great Awakening, these modernizing movements helped ordinary Americans to embrace the ideal of inalienable human rights in a Protestant package. Their members learned to plan, organize, and pursue a clearly defined objective in a rational way that empowered them against the establishment. We in the West tend to evaluate other cultural traditions by measuring them against the Enlightenment: the Great Awakenings in America show that people can reach these ideals by another, specifically religious route.

In fact, American evangelicals had appropriated some Enlightenment ideals so thoroughly that they created a curious hybrid that some historians have called "Enlightenment Protestantism."[51] This paradox had been noted by Alexis de Tocqueville when he visited the United States during the 1830s, remarking that the character of the country combined "two perfectly distinct elements that elsewhere have often made war with each other, but which, in America, . . . they have succeeded in incorporating somehow one into another and combining marvellously: I mean to speak of the *spirit of religion* and the *spirit of freedom*."[52] The Founding Fathers had been inspired by the so-called moderate Enlightenment of Isaac Newton and John Locke. The evangelicals, however, repudiated the "skeptical" Enlightenment of Voltaire and David Hume as well as the "revolutionary" Enlightenment of Rousseau but embraced the "common sense" philosophy of the Scottish thinkers Francis Hutcheson (1694–1746), Thomas Reid (1710–96), Adam Smith (1723–90), and Dugald Stewart (1753–1828).[53] This taught them that human beings had an innate and infallible ability to see clear connections between moral causes and their effects in public life. Understanding things was simple, a matter of common sense. Even a child could grasp the essence of the gospel and figure out for herself what was right. Enlightenment philosophers had told people to cast aside the habit of tutelage and work out the truth for themselves, without relying on authoritarian institutions and learned experts. American evangelicals, therefore, were confident that if they put their minds to it, they could create a society in the New World that fully implemented Christian values.[54] The Constitution had established a secular state but had done nothing to encourage the development of a national culture; the Founders had assumed that this would evolve naturally in response to government action.[55] Yet thanks to the evangelical welfare and reform associations, "Enlightenment Protestantism," somewhat ironically, became the national ethos of the secular state.[56] You can take religion out of the state, but you can't take religion out of the nation. By dint of their energetic missionary work, reform organizations, and publications, the evangelicals created a Bible-based culture that pulled the new nation together.

◆ ◆ ◆

The Americans had shown that it was possible to organize society on a more just and rational basis. In France the leaders of the bourgeoisie, the rising middle classes, watched these events very carefully because they too had developed ideologies that emphasized the freedom of the individual.[57] They had a more difficult task, however, because they had to depose a long-established ruling class with a professional army, a centralized bureaucracy, and an absolute monarchy.[58] But by the end of the eighteenth century, traditional agrarian society was coming under increasing strain in Europe: more people were moving to the towns and working in nonagricultural trades and professions, literacy was more widespread, and there was unprecedented social mobility.

In the spring of 1789, Louis XVI's absolutist monarchy was in trouble. Profligate stewardship had plunged the French economy into crisis, and now the clergy and nobility (the First and Second Estates) were refusing a new regime of taxation by the crown. To break the deadlock, the king called the Estates General to meet at Versailles on May 2.[59] The king wanted the three estates—clergy, nobility, and commoners—to deliberate and vote separately, but the Third Estate refused to allow the aristocracy to dominate the proceedings and invited the clergy and nobility to join them in a new National Assembly. The first to defect to the Third Estate were 150 of the lower clergy, who came from the same background as the commoners, were weary of the bishops' hauteur, and wanted a more collegial church.[60] There were also defections from the

Second Estate: the rural gentry disdained by the Parisian aristocracy and the wealthy bourgeois who were impatient with the nobility's conservatism. On June 17 members of the new National Assembly swore that they would not disperse until they had a new constitution.

The Assembly had intended to conduct a reasoned, enlightened debate on the American model, but it had reckoned without the people. After a bad harvest, food supplies were dangerously low, the price of bread rocketed in the towns, and there was widespread unemployment. In April five thousand artisans had rioted in Paris, and revolutionary committees and citizen militias had formed across the country to contain the unrest. During the Assembly's discussions, delegates were booed and heckled from the public galleries, and the distraught crowds took to the street, attacking any representative of the Old Regime who crossed their path. In a crucial development, some of the troops dispatched to quell these riots joined the rebels instead. On June 14 the mob stormed the Bastille in eastern Paris, released the prisoners, and hacked the jail's governor to pieces. Other senior officials met the same fate. In the countryside, the famished peasantry were gripped by the "Great Fear," convinced that the grain shortages had been engineered by the regime to starve them into submission. This suspicion was compounded by the arrival of impoverished laborers seeking work, who were thought to be the nobility's advance troops.[61] Villagers raided the châteaux, attacked Jewish moneylenders, and refused to pay their tithes and taxes.

As the country spun out of control, the Assembly became more radical. It produced the Declaration of the Rights of Man and the Citizen that vested sovereignty in the people rather than in the monarch and proclaimed that all men had natural rights of liberty of conscience, property, and free speech and must enjoy equality before the law, personal security, and equal opportunity. Then the Assembly set about dismantling the Catholic Church in France. As we have seen, the "myth of religious violence" was founded on the belief that the separation of church and state would liberate society from the inherent belligerence of "religion." But almost every secularizing reform in Europe and in other parts of the world would begin with an aggressive assault on religious institutions, which would inspire resentment, anomie, distress, and in some cases, a violent riposte. On November 2, 1789, the Assembly voted by 568 to 346 to pay off the national debt by confiscating the wealth of the Church. The bishop of Autun, Charles Maurice de Talleyrand, pointed out that the

Church did not own property in the ordinary way; its lands and estates had been given to it so that it could do good works.[62] The state could now pay the clergy a salary and finance these charitable activities itself. This decision was followed on February 3, 1790, by the abolition of all religious orders except those engaged in teaching or hospital work. Many clerics protested vigorously against these measures, and they gravely disturbed many of the common people, but some priests saw them as an opportunity for reform that could return the Church to its pristine purity and even inaugurate a new "national religion."

The secular regime thus began with a policy of coercion, disempowerment, and dispossession. On May 29, 1790, the Assembly issued the Civil Constitution of the Clergy that relegated the Church to a state department. Fifty sees were abolished, and in Brittany many parishioners found themselves without a bishop. Four thousand parishes were eliminated, bishops' salaries were reduced, and in the future bishops were to be elected by the people. On November 26, the clergy were given eight days to take an oath of loyalty to the nation, the law, and the king. Forty-four clerics in the Assembly refused to take the oath, and there were riots in protest against this humiliating order in Alsace, Anjou, Artois, Brittany, Flanders, Languedoc, and Normandy.[63] Catholicism was so deeply entwined with almost every detail of daily life that, aghast, many of the Third Estate turned against the regime. In western France, parishioners pressured their priests to refuse the oath and would have nothing to do with the Constitutional clerics sent in to replace them.

The aggression of the secular state soon segued into outright violence. Neighboring monarchies began to mobilize against the revolution. As so often happens, an external threat led to widespread fears of the "enemy within." When French troops were routed by the Austrians in the summer of 1792, wild rumors circulated of a "fifth column" of counterrevolutionary priests aiding the enemy. When the Prussian army broke through the frontier and threatened Verdun, the last line of defense before Paris, recalcitrant clergy were imprisoned. In September, amid fears of royalist clerics planning simultaneous uprisings, violent mobs descended on the prisons and murdered between two to three thousand prisoners, many of them priests. Two weeks later France was declared a republic.

The French and the Americans had adopted diametrically opposed policies toward religion: all the American states eventually disestablished their churches, but because their clergy were not implicated in a long-established aristocratic regime, there was no virulent hostility toward the traditional denominations. In France, however, the Church, which had been so deeply involved in aristocratic rule, could be dismantled only by an outright assault.[64] By now it was clear that a nonreligious regime had just as much potential for violence as a religiously constituted one. After the September Massacres, there were more atrocities. On March 12, 1793, an uprising began in the Vendée in western France in protest against conscription to the army, unfair taxation, and above all, the anti-Catholic policies of the revolution.[65] The rebels were especially incensed by the arrival in the Vendée of Constitutional clergy, who had no roots in the region, to replace priests who were known and loved. They formed the Catholic and Royal Army, carried banners of the Virgin, and sang hymns as they marched. This was not an aristocratic uprising but an army of the people, who were determined to retain their Catholicism: over 60 percent were farmers, and the others, artisans and shopkeepers. Three armies dispatched from Paris to quell the uprising were diverted to deal with the Federalist Revolt, in which moderate provincial bourgeois and republicans joined forces with royalists in Bordeaux, Lyons, Marseilles, Toulouse, and Toulon to protest measures taken in Paris.

Once the Federalists were put down with horrible reprisals, four revolutionary armies arrived in the Vendée early in 1794 with instructions from the Committee of Public Safety that recalled the rhetoric of the Catharist Crusade: "Spear with your bayonets all the inhabitants you encounter along the way. I know there may be a few patriots in this region—it matters not, we must sacrifice all."[66] "All brigands found with weapons or suspected of having carried them will be speared by the bayonet," General Turreau instructed his soldiers. "We will act equally with women, girls and children. . . . Even people only suspected will not be spared."[67] "The Vendée no longer exists," François-Joseph Westermann reported to his superiors at the end of the campaign. "Following the orders I have received, I have crushed children beneath the hooves of our horses, and massacred women. . . . The roads are littered with corpses."[68] The revolution that had promised liberty and fraternity may have slaughtered a quarter of a million people in one of the worst atrocities of the early modern period.

Human beings have always sought intensity and moments of ecstasy that give their lives meaning and purpose. If a symbol, icon, myth, ritual, or doctrine no longer yields a sense of transcendent value, they tend to replace it with something else. Historians of religion tell us that absolutely anything can become a symbol of the divine, and that such epiphanies occur "in every area of psychological, economic, spiritual and social life."[69] This was soon evident in France. No sooner had the revolutionaries rid themselves of one religion than they invented another, making the nation an embodiment of the sacred. It was the audacious genius of the revolutionary leadership to recognize that the potent emotions traditionally connected with the Church could be just as powerfully felt if directed toward a new symbol. On August 10, 1793, while the nation was tearing itself apart in war and bloodshed, a festival choreographed by the artist Jacques-Louis David celebrated the Unity and Indivisibility of the Republic in Paris. It began at sunrise on the site of the Bastille, where an imposing statue of Nature decanted water from her breasts into a cup held by the president of the National Convention; he then passed it to eighty-six elderly men representing the French *départements* in a holy communion. In the Place de la Révolution the president torched a great bonfire of heraldic symbols, scepters, and thrones before a statue of Liberty, and at the Invalides the public gazed at a giant effigy of the French people as Hercules. These festivals became so frequent that people wrote of "festomania."[70] As the nineteenth-century historian Jules Michelet explained, the state festivals celebrated the arrival of "a strange *vita nuova,* one eminently spiritual."[71]

The Catholic Mass had been a central feature of the early festivals, but by 1793 the priests had been eliminated from these national rites. This was the year that Jacques Hébert enthroned the Goddess of Reason on the high altar of Notre Dame Cathedral, transforming it into a temple of philosophy. Revolutionary politics was itself becoming an object of worship. Leaders made great use of such terms as *credo, zealot, sacrament,* and *sermon* when describing political events.[72] Honoré Mirabeau wrote that "the Declaration of the Rights of Man has become a political Gospel and the French Constitution a religion for which the people is prepared to die." The poet Marie-Joseph Chénier told the National Convention: "You will know how to found on the ruins of dethroned superstition, the single universal religion of which our lawmakers are the preachers, the magistrates the pontiffs, and in which the human family burns its incense only at the altar of the Patrie, common mother and divinity."[73] Because the revolution "seemed to be striving for the regeneration of the human race even more than for the reform of France," Tocqueville would observe, "a new kind of religion, an incomplete religion, it is true, without God, without ritual, and without life after death, but one which nevertheless, like Islam, flooded the earth with its soldiers, apostles and martyrs."[74] It is interesting that he equated this defiantly secular religiosity with the fanatical violence that Europeans had long attributed to Islam.

The "civil religion" described first by Jean-Jacques Rousseau (1712–78) was based on belief in God and the afterlife, the social contract, and the prohibition of intolerance. Its festivals, Rousseau wrote, would create a sacred bond between participants: "Let the spectators become an entertainment to themselves; make them actors themselves; do it so that each sees and loves himself in the others so that all will be better united."[75] But Rousseau's loving tolerance did not extend to anyone who refused to obey the precepts of civil religion, and a similar rigor entered the revolution.[76] A month after the festival celebrating the Unity and Indivisibility of the Republic, the reign of terror began, when Maximilien de Robespierre appointed a tribunal to seek out traitors and pursued dissidents with all the zeal of a militant pope. Not only were the king and queen, members of the royal family, and the aristocracy executed, but one group of apparently loyal patriots after another went to the guillotine. The distinguished chemist Antoine Lavoisier, who had worked all his professional life to improve conditions in French prisons and hospitals, and Gilbert Romme, who had designed the revolutionary calendar, were both beheaded. When the purge ended in July 1794, some seventeen thousand men, women, and children had been guillotined, and twice as many more had either died in the disease-ridden prisons or were slaughtered by local vigilantes.[77]

Meanwhile, the revolutionary leaders were waging a holy war against the nonrevolutionary regimes of Europe.[78] After the Peace of Westphalia, the continent had known nearly two hundred years of relative peace. A balance of power kept the sovereign states in harmony. Brutality on the battlefield was no longer acceptable; moderation and restraint were the new watchwords.[79] Armies were now adequately provisioned so soldiers no longer had to terrorize the peasant population by foraging for themselves.[80] There was greater emphasis on drill, discipline, and correct methods of procedure, and between 1700 and 1850 there were no significant developments in military technology.[81] But this peace was shattered when first the revolutionary armies and then Napoleon threw these restraints to the wind.

The French state had certainly not become more irenic after eliminating the Church from government. On August 16, 1793, the National Convention issued the *levée en masse:* for the first time in history, an entire society was mobilized for war.

> All Frenchmen are permanently requisitioned for service into the armies. Young men will go forth into battle; married men will forge weapons and transport munitions; women will make tents and clothing and serve in the hospitals; children will make lint from old linen; and old men will be brought into the public squares to arouse the courage of the soldiers, while preaching the unity of the Republic and hatred against Kings.[82]

Some 300,000 volunteers, aged between eighteen and twenty-five, brought the French army up to a record-breaking million strong. Hitherto peasants and artisans had been tricked or press-ganged into the military, but in this "Free Army" soldiers were well paid and for the first year officers were elected from the ranks on merit. In 1789 over 90 percent of French officers had been aristocrats; by 1794 a mere 3 percent were of noble birth. Even though over a million young men died in the Revolutionary and Napoleonic Wars, more were willing to volunteer. These soldiers fought not with professional decorum but with the raw violence they had learned in the revolution's street battles, and they probably relished the ecstasy of warfare.[83] Because they had to feed themselves, they committed the same kind of atrocities as the mercenaries in the Thirty Years' War.[84] For nearly twenty years, the French armies seemed unstoppable, overrunning Belgium, the Netherlands, and Germany and effortlessly brushing aside the Austrian and Prussian armies that tried to halt this triumphant progress.

Revolutionary France did not bring liberty to the peoples of Europe, however; instead, Napoleon, the revolution's heir, created a traditional tributary empire that threatened the imperial ambitions of Britain. In 1798, to establish a base in Suez that would cut off the British sea routes to India, Napoleon invaded Egypt and at the Battle of the Pyramids inflicted a devastating defeat on the Mamluk army: only ten French soldiers were killed, but the Mamluks lost more than two thousand men.[85] With consummate cynicism, Napoleon then presented himself as the liberator of the Egyptian people. Carefully briefed by the French Institut d'Égypte, he addressed the sheikhs of the Azhar madrassa in Arabic, expressing his deep respect for the Prophet and promising to free Egypt from the oppression of the Ottomans and their Mamluk agents. Accompanying the French army was a corps of scholars, a library of modern European literature, a laboratory, and a printing press with Arabic type. The ulema were not impressed: "All this is nothing but deceit and trickery," they said, "to entice us."[86] They were right. Napoleon's invasion, exploiting Enlightenment scholarship and science to subjugate the region, marked the beginning of Western domination of the Middle East.

To many it seemed that the French Revolution had failed. The systemic violence of Napoleon's empire betrayed revolutionary principles, and Napoleon also reinstated the Catholic Church. For decades the hopes of 1789 were dashed by one disillusioning event after another. The glory days of the fall of the Bastille were followed by the September Massacres, the Reign of Terror, the Vendée genocide, and a military dictatorship. After Napoleon's fall from power in 1814, Louis XVIII (the brother of Louis XVI) was returned to the throne. But the republican dream refused to die. The republic was revived for two brief periods, during the Hundred Days before Napoleon's final defeat at Waterloo in 1815 and for a brief period between 1848 and 1852. In 1870 it was restored yet again, this time lasting until it was destroyed by the Nazis in 1940. Instead of seeing the French Revolution as a failure, therefore, we should perhaps see it as the explosive start of a lengthy process. Such massive social and political change overturning millennia of autocracy cannot be achieved overnight. Revolutions take a long time. But unlike several other European countries, where aristocratic regimes were so deeply entrenched that they managed to hang on, albeit in limited form, France eventually achieved its secular republic. We should bear this long-drawn-out and painful process in mind before dismissing as failures revolutions that have taken place in our own time in Iran, Egypt, and Tunisia, for example.

• • •

The French Revolution may have changed the politics of Europe, but it did not affect the agrarian economy. Modernity came of age in Britain's Industrial Revolution, which began in the later eighteenth century, though its social effects would not be truly felt until the early nineteenth.[87] It started with the invention of the steam engine, which provided more energy than the country's entire workforce put together, so the economy grew at an unprecedented rate. It was not long before Germany, France, Japan, and the United States followed Britain's lead, and all these industrialized countries were forever transformed. To man the new machines, the population had to be mobilized for industry instead of agriculture; economic self-sufficiency now became a thing of the past. The government also began to control the lives of ordinary folk in ways that had been impossible in agrarian society.[88] In *Hard Times* (1864) Charles Dickens portrayed the industrial city as an inferno: workers—referred to contemptuously as "the Hands"—live in abject poverty and have only instrumental value. The oppression of the agrarian state had been replaced by the structural violence of industrialization. More benign state ideologies would develop, and more people than ever before would enjoy comforts previously available only to the nobility, but despite the best efforts of some politicians, a seemingly unbridgeable gap would always separate rich and poor.

The Enlightenment ideals of toleration, independence, democracy, and intellectual freedom were no longer simply noble aspirations but had become practical necessities. Mass production required a mass market, so the common people could no longer be kept at subsistence level but had to be able to afford manufactured goods. More and more people were drawn into the productive process—as factory workers, printers, or office clerks—and needed at least a modicum of education. Inevitably they would begin to demand representation in government, and modern communications would make it easier for workers to organize politically. Because no single group could either dominate or even effectively oppose the government, different parties had to compete for power.[89] Intellectual liberty was now essential to the economy, as people could achieve the innovation that was crucial to progress only by thinking freely, unconstrained by their class, guild, or church. Governments had to exploit all their human resources, so outsiders, such as the Jews in Europe and Catholics in England and America, were brought into the mainstream.

Industrialized countries were soon compelled to seek new markets and resources abroad and would therefore, as the German philosopher

Georg Wilhelm Hegel (1770–1831) had predicted, be pushed toward colonialism.[90] In these new empires, the economic relationship between the imperial power and the subject peoples became just as one-sided as it had been in the agrarian empires. The new colonial power did not help its colonies to industrialize but simply appropriated an "undeveloped" country to extract raw materials that could feed the European industrial process.[91] In return the colony received cheap manufactured goods from the West that ruined local businesses. Not surprisingly, colonialism was experienced as intrusive and coercive. The colonialists built modern transport and communications but chiefly for their own convenience.[92] In India, British traders ransacked the assets of Bengal so ruthlessly during the late eighteenth century that this period is regularly described as "the plundering of Bengal." The region was pushed into a chronically dependent role, and instead of growing their own food, villagers were forced to cultivate jute and indigo for the world market. The British did help keep disease and famine at bay, but the consequent population growth led to poverty and overcrowding.[93]

This combination of industrialized technology and empire was creating a global form of systemic violence, driven not by religion but by the wholly secular values of the market. The West was so far ahead that it was virtually impossible for the subject peoples to catch up. Increasingly the world would be divided between the West and the Rest, and this systemic political and economic inequality was sustained by military force. By the mid-nineteenth century, Britain controlled most of the Indian subcontinent, and after the Indian Mutiny (1857), in which atrocities were committed on both sides and some seventy thousand Indians were killed in a final desperate protest against foreign rule, the British formally deposed the last Moghul emperor.[94] Because the colony had to fit into the global market, a degree of modernization was essential: policing, the army, and the local economy had to be completely reorganized, and some of the "natives" introduced to modern ideas. Only very rarely had agrarian empires attempted to change the religious traditions of the common people, but in India British innovations had a drastic effect on the religious and political life of the subcontinent.

The ease with which they had been so thoroughly subjugated was profoundly disturbing to the people of India since it implied that something was radically amiss with their social systems.[95] Traditional Indian aristocracies now had to cope not only with a foreign ruling class but with a wholly different socioeconomic order and with the new native cadres of clerks and bureaucrats, created by the British, who often earned more than the old elites. These Westernized Indians had become in effect a new caste, separated by a gulf of incomprehension from the unmodernized majority. The increasing democratization of their British rulers was alien to the social arrangements of India, which had always been strongly hierarchical and had encouraged synergy among disparate groups rather than organized unity. Moreover, confronted with the bewildering social variety of the subcontinent, the British latched on to the groups they mistakenly thought they understood and divided the population into "Hindu," "Muslim," "Sikh," and "Christian" communities.

The "Hindu" majority, however, consisted of multifarious castes, cults, and groups that did not see themselves as forming an organized religion, as Western people now understood this term. They had no unifying hierarchy and no standard set of rituals, practices, and beliefs. They worshipped numerous unrelated gods and engaged in devotions that had no logical connection with one another. Yet now they all found themselves lumped together into something the British called "Hinduism."[96] The term *hindu* had been used first by the Muslim conquerors to describe the indigenous people; it had no specifically religious connotation but simply meant "native" or "local," and the indigenous peoples, including Buddhists, Jains, and Sikhs, came to use it of themselves. Under the British, however, "Hindus" had to become a close-knit group and cultivate a broad, casteless communal identity that was alien to their age-old traditions.

It was ironic that the British, who had banished "religion" from the public sphere at home, should classify the subcontinent in such tightly religious terms. They based the Indian electoral system on religious affiliation and in 1871 conducted a census that made these religious communities acutely aware of their numbers and areas of strength in relation to one another. By bringing religion to the fore in this way, the British inadvertently bequeathed a history of communal conflict to South Asia. In the Moghul Empire, there had certainly been tension between the Muslim ruling class and its *hindu* subjects, but this had not always had a religious coloration. While Western Christians had become more sectarian during their Reformation, India had been going in the opposite direction. During the thirteenth century, Vedic orthodoxy had begun to be transformed by *bhakti*, a "devotion" to a personal deity that refused to acknowledge differences of caste or creed. Bhakti drew much inspiration from Sufism, which had become the dominant mode of Islam in the subcontinent and had long insisted that because the omniscient and omnipresent God could not be confined to a single creed, belligerent assertion of orthodoxy was a form of idolatry (*shirk*).

Sikhism had been born in this climate of open-hearted tolerance. The word *sikh* derived from the Sanskrit *shishya* ("disciple"), for Sikhs followed the teachings of Guru Nanak (1469–1539), founder of their tradition, and his nine inspired successors. Born in a village near Lahore in the Punjab, Nanak had insisted that interior apprehension of God was far more important than a strict adherence to doctrines and customs that could divide people from one another—though he scrupulously avoided deriding anybody's faith. Like the Sufis, he believed that human beings must be weaned from the fanaticism that made them attack the beliefs of others. "Religion lives not in empty words," he once said. "He who regards all men as equals is religious."[97] One of his earliest maxims stated categorically: "There is no *hindu*; there is no Muslim; who shall I follow? I shall follow the way of God."[98]

Another leading proponent of this openness to other faiths was Akbar, the third Moghul emperor (r. 1556–1605). Out of respect for *hindu* sensitivity, he gave up hunting, forbade the sacrifice of animals on his birthday, and became a vegetarian. In 1575 he founded a House of Worship, where scholars from all religious traditions met freely to discuss spiritual matters, and a Sufi order, dedicated to "divine monotheism" (*tawhid-e-ilahi*) based on the conviction that the one God could reveal himself in any rightly guided religion. But not all Muslims shared this vision, and this policy could be sustained only while the Moghuls were in a position of strength. When their power began to decline and various groups began to revolt against imperial rule, religious conflict escalated. Akbar's son Jahangir (r. 1605–27) had to put down one rebellion after another, and Aurangzeb (r. 1658–1707) seems to have believed that political unity could be restored only by greater discipline within the Muslim ruling class. He therefore outlawed laxities such as wine drinking, made Muslim cooperation with their *hindu* subjects impossible, and engaged in the widespread destruction of their temples. These violent policies, the result of political insecurity as much as religious zeal, were reversed immediately after Aurangzeb's death but were never forgotten.

Sikhs had suffered from this imperial violence. By this time Sikhs, who had once eschewed all external symbols, had developed some of their own. The fifth guru, Arjan Dev, had made the Golden Temple at Amritsar in the Punjab a place of pilgrimage and had enshrined the Sikh scriptures there in 1604. Sikhism had always abstained from violence. Guru Nanak had said: "Take up arms that hurt no one; let your coat of mail be understanding; convert your enemies to friends."[99] The first four gurus had had no need to bear arms. But Jahangir had tortured the fifth guru to death in 1606, and in 1675 Aurangzeb beheaded Tegh Bahadur, the ninth guru. His successor, Gobind Singh, therefore faced an entirely different world. Henceforth, the tenth guru declared, there would be no more human leaders: in the future the Sikhs' only guru would be their scripture. In 1699 he instituted the Sikh Order of Khalsa (the "purified" or "chosen"). Like Kshatriya warriors, its members would call themselves Singh ("Lion"), carry swords, and distinguish themselves from the rest of the population by wearing soldiers' garb and keeping their hair unshorn. Yet again, imperial violence had radicalized an originally irenic tradition and had also introduced a particularism that was entirely alien to the original Sikh vision. Gobind is believed to have written to Aurangzeb that when all else failed, it was only right to lift the sword and fight. Militancy might be necessary to defend the community—but only as a last resort.[100]

•   •   •

The Hindu, Sikh, and Muslim communities were now in competition for British favor, resources, and political influence. Their leaders discovered that the British were more receptive to their ideas if they believed that they represented a larger group and realized that in order to prosper under colonial rule, they would have to adapt to the Western understanding of religion. So new reform movements tended to adopt contemporaneous Protestant norms in a way that distorted these traditions. Luther had tried to return to the practice of the early church, so the Arya Samaj ("Society of Aryans"), which was founded in the Punjab in 1875 by Swami Dayananda, attempted a return to Vedic orthodoxy. He also tried to create an authoritative scriptural canon, which had no precedent in India. The Arya was, therefore, an extremely reductive form of "Hinduism," since the Vedic tradition had long been the faith of only a small elite, and very few people were able to understand ancient Sanskrit. It thus tended to appeal only to the educated classes. But by 1947, when British rule ended, the Arya had 1.5 million members. In other parts of the world too, wherever secular modernity was imposed, there would be similar attempts to return to "fundamentals." The Arya illustrated the aggression inherent in such fundamentalism. In his book *Satyarth Prakash* ("The Light of Truth"), Dayananda dismissed Buddhists and Jains as mere offshoots of "Hinduism," derided Christian theology, claimed that Sikhism was merely a Hindu sect, dismissing Guru Nanak as a well-meaning ignoramus who had no understanding of the Vedic traditions, and was vitriolic in his abuse of the Prophet Muhammad. In 1943 the book inspired violent protests among Muslims in Sind and became a rallying point for those Hindus who were campaigning for an India free of both the British and Islam.[101]

After Devananda's death, the Arya became even more insulting and disrespectful in their denunciation of the Sikh gurus and, perhaps inevitably, inspired an aggressive assertion of Sikh identity. When Arya pamphlets argued that *Sikh Hindu hain* ("The Sikhs are Hindus"), the prominent Sikh scholar Kahim Singh retaliated with his highly influential tract *Ham Hindu nahin* ("We are not Hindus").[102] The irony was, of course, that until the British had arrived, nobody had thought of themselves as "Hindu" in this sectarian way. The British tendency to see the different faith communities in stereotypical ways also helped to radicalize the Sikh tradition; they promoted the idea that Sikhs were an essentially warlike and heroic people.[103] In recognition of Sikh support during the 1857 mutiny, the British had overcome their initial reluctance to admit members of the Khalsa into the army; moreover, once they were recruited, they were allowed to wear their traditional uniforms. This special treatment meant that gradually the idea that Sikhs were a separate and distinctive race gained ground.

Hitherto Sikhs and Hindus had lived together peacefully in the Punjab, sharing the same cultural traditions. There had been no central Sikh authority, so variant forms of Sikhism flourished. This had always been the norm in India, where religious identities had been multiple and defined regionally.[104] But during the 1870s Sikhs began to develop their own reform movement in an attempt to adapt to these new realities. By the end of the nineteenth century, there were about a hundred Sikh Sabha groups all over the Punjab, dedicated to an assertion of Sikh distinctiveness, building Sikh schools and colleges, and producing a flood of polemical literature.[105] On the surface these groups seemed in tune with Sikh tradition, but this separation entirely subverted Nanak's original vision. Sikhs were now expected to adopt a single identity. Over the years a Sikh fundamentalism would emerge that interpreted the tradition selectively, claiming to return to the martial teachings of the tenth guru but ignoring the peaceful ethos of the early gurus. This new Sikhism was passionately opposed to secularism: Sikhs must have political power in order to enforce this conformity. A tradition that once had been open to all had been invaded by fear of the "other," represented by a host of enemies—Hindus, heretics, modernizers, secularists, and any form of political dominance.[106]

There was a similar distortion of the Muslim tradition. The British abolition of the Moghul Empire had been a traumatic watershed, summarily demoting a people who hitherto had seemed virtual masters of the globe. For the first time, they were being ruled by hostile infidels in one of the core cultures of the civilized world. Given the symbolic importance of the ummah's well-being, this was not simply a political anxiety but one that touched the spiritual recesses of their being. Some Muslims would therefore cultivate a history of grievance. We have previously seen that the experience of humiliation can damage a tradition and become a catalyst for violence. Segments of the Hindu population, who had been subjected to Muslim rule for seven hundred years, had their own smoldering resentment of Moghul imperialism, so Muslims suddenly felt extremely vulnerable, especially since the British blamed them for the Mutiny of 1857.[107]

Many were afraid that Islam would disappear from the subcontinent and that Muslims would entirely lose their identity. Their first impulse was to withdraw from the mainstream and cling to the glories of the distant past. In 1867 in Deoband, near Delhi, a cadre of ulema began to issue detailed fatwas that governed every single aspect of life to help Muslims live authentically under foreign rule. Over time the Deobandis established a network of madrassas throughout the subcontinent that promoted a form of Islam that was as reductive in its own way as the Arya Samaj. They too attempted a return to "fundamentals"—the pristine Islam of the Prophet and the rashidun—and vehemently decried such later developments as the Shiah. Islam had for centuries displayed a remarkable ability to assimilate other cultural traditions, but their colonial humiliation caused the Deobandis to retreat from the West in rather the same way as Ibn Taymiyyah had recoiled from Mongol civilization.

Deobandi Islam refused to countenance *itjihad* ("independent reasoning") and argued for an overly strict and literal interpretation of the Shariah. The Deobandis were socially progressive in their rejection of the caste system and their determination to educate the poorest Muslims, but they were virulently opposed to any innovation—adamant, for instance, in their condemnation of the compulsory education of women. In the early days, Deobandis were not violent, but they would later become more militant. They would have a drastic effect on subcontinental Islam, which had traditionally leaned toward the more inclusive spiritualities of Sufism and Falsafah, both of which the Deobandis now utterly condemned. During the twentieth century they would gain considerable influence in the Muslim world and would rank in importance with the prestigious al-Azha Madrassa in Cairo. The British subjugation of India had driven some Hindus, Sikhs, and Muslims into a defensive posture that could easily segue into violence.

• • •

With the transformation of manufacturing came one particularly portentous technological development: the creation of modern weaponry. The new guns and shells developed by William Armstrong, Claude Minié, and Henry Shrapnel made it easy for Europeans to keep their colonial subjects in line. They were initially unwilling to use these new machine guns against their fellow Europeans, but by 1851 Minié ball–firing rifles had been issued to British troops overseas. When they were used the following year against Bantu tribesmen, marksmen found that they could pick off the Bantu at a distance of thirteen hundred yards without having to see the devastating consequences of their action. This distance led to a dulling of the innate reluctance to kill at close quarters. In the early 1890s, during an encounter between the German East Africa Company and the Hehe tribesmen, an officer and a soldier killed around a thousand natives with two machine guns.[108] In 1898 at the Battle of Omdurman in the Sudan, a mere six Maxim guns firing at six hundred shots a minute mowed down thousands of the Mahdi's followers. "It was not a battle, but an execution," an onlooker reported. "The bodies were not in heaps . . . but . . . spread evenly over acres and acres."[109]

The new secular ethos was quickly able to adapt to this horrific violence. It certainly did not share the universalist outlook promoted by some religious traditions that had helped people cultivate a reverence for the sanctity of all human beings. At a conference in The Hague that debated the legality of these weapons the following year, Sir John Armagh explained that "civilized man is much more susceptible to injury than savages. . . . The savage, like the tiger, is not so impressionable, and will go on fighting even when desperately wounded."[110] As late as 1927, U.S. Army Captain Elbridge Colby could argue that "the real essence of the matter is that devastation and annihilation is the principal method of warfare that savage tribes know." It was a mistake to allow "excessive humanitarian ideas" to inhibit the use of superior firepower. A commander who gives in to this misplaced compassion "is simply being unkind to his own people." If a few "non-combatants" were killed, "the loss of life is probably far less than might have been sustained in prolonged operations of a more polite character. The *inhuman* act thus becomes *actually humane*."[111] The pervasive view that ethnic difference rendered other groups not quite human had resulted in a casual acceptance of the mass slaughter that mechanized arms had made possible. An age of unimagined violence was dawning.

◆ ◆ ◆

Industrialization also gave birth to the nation-state.[112] Agrarian empires had lacked the technology to impose a uniform culture; the borders and territorial reach of premodern kingdoms could be only loosely defined and the monarch's authority enforced in a series of overlapping loyalties.[113] But during the nineteenth century, Europe was reconfigured into clearly defined states ruled by a central government.[114] Industrialized society required standardized literacy, a shared language, and a unified control of human resources. Even if they spoke a different language from the ruler, subjects now belonged to an integrated "nation," an "imaginary community" of people who were encouraged to feel a deep connection with persons they knew nothing about.[115]

Religiously organized agrarian societies had often persecuted "heretics"; in the secularized nation-state, it was "minorities" who had either to assimilate or disappear. In 1807 Jefferson had instructed his secretary of war that the Native Americans were "backward peoples" who must either be "exterminated" or driven "beyond our reach" to the other side of the Mississippi "with the beasts of the forest."[116] In 1806 Napoleon made Jews full citizens of France, but two years later he issued the "Infamous Decrees" ordering them to take French names, privatize their faith, and ensure that at least one in every three marriages per family was with a gentile.[117] This forcible integration was regarded as progress. Surely, argued the British philosopher John Stuart Mill (1806–73), it was better for a Breton to accept French citizenship "than to sulk on his own rocks, the half-savage remnant of past times, revolving in his own little mental orbit, without participation or interest in the general movement of the world."[118] But the English historian Lord Acton (1834–1902) deplored the notion of nationality, fearing that the "fictitious" general will of the people that it promoted would crush "all natural rights and all established liberties for the purpose of vindicating itself."[119] He could see that the desire to preserve the nation could become an absolute used to justify the most inhumane policies. Even worse,

> By making the State and the nation commensurate with each other in theory, [nationality] reduces practically to a subject condition all other nationalities that may be within the boundary. . . . According, therefore, to the degree of humanity and civilization in that dominant body which claims all the rights of the community, the inferior races are exterminated or reduced to servitude, or put in a condition of dependence.[120]

His reservations about nationalism would prove to be all too well grounded.

The new nation-state would labor under a fundamental contradiction: the *state* (the governmental apparatus) was supposed to be secular, but the *nation* ("the people") aroused quasi-religious emotions.[121] In 1807–08, while Napoleon was conquering Prussia, the German philosopher Johann Gottlieb Fichte had delivered a series of lectures in Berlin, looking forward to the time when the forty-one separate German principalities would become a unified nation-state. The Fatherland, he claimed, was a manifestation of the divine, the repository of the spiritual essence of the *Volk* and therefore eternal. Germans must be ready to die for the nation, which alone gave human beings the immortality they craved because it had existed since the dawn of time and would continue after their deaths.[122] Early modern philosophers, such as Hobbes, had called for a strong state to restrain the violence of Europe, which, they believed, had been solely inspired by "religion." Yet in France, the nation had been evoked to mobilize all citizens for war, and Fichte now encouraged Germans to fight French imperialism for the sake of the Fatherland. The *state* had been devised to contain violence, but the *nation* was now being used to release it.

If we can define the sacred as something for which one is prepared to die, the nation had certainly become an embodiment of the divine, a supreme value. Hence national mythology would encourage cohesion, solidarity, and loyalty within the confines of the nation. But it had yet to develop the "concern for everybody" that had been such an important ideal in many of the spiritual traditions associated with religion. The national mythos would not encourage citizens to extend their sympathy to the ends of the earth, to love the stranger in their midst, be loyal even to their enemies, to wish happiness for all beings, and to become aware of the world's pain. True, this universal empathy had rarely affected the violence of the warrior aristocracy, but it had at least offered an alternative and a continuing challenge. Now that religion was being privatized, there was no "international" ethos to counter the growing structural and military violence to which weaker nations were increasingly subjected. Secular nationalism seemed to regard the foreigner as fair game for exploitation and mass slaughter, especially if he belonged to a different ethnic group.

◆ ◆ ◆

In America, the colonies and later the states had lacked the manpower to maintain productivity, so by 1800 between ten and fifteen million African slaves had been forcibly transported to North America.[123] They were subdued brutally: slaves were repeatedly reminded of their racial inferiority, their families were broken up, and they were subjected to hard labor, flogging, and mutilation. None of this seemed to bother the Founders, who had so proudly asserted that "all men are created equal" and "endowed by their Creator with certain inalienable rights." Those who would object did so by invoking not Enlightenment principles but Christian morals. In the northern states, Christian abolitionists condemned slavery as a blot on the nation, and in 1860 president-elect Abraham Lincoln (1809–65) announced that he would prohibit it in any newly conquered territory. Almost at once South Carolina seceded from the Union, and it was clear that other Southern states would follow.

The political issue—the preservation or dissolution of the Union— was not in doubt, but to their dismay, both Northerners and Southerners found that the clergy on whom they relied for ideological guidance could find no common ground. Supporters of slavery had a host of biblical texts at their command,[124] but in the absence of any explicit biblical condemnation of slave ownership, abolitionists could only appeal to the spirit of scripture. The Southern preacher James Henry Thornhill argued that slavery was a "good and merciful" way of organizing labor,[125] while in New York Henry Ward Beecher maintained that it was "the most alarming and most fertile cause of national sin."[126] But the theological split did not coincide neatly with the North-South divide. In Brooklyn, Henry Van Dyke argued that abolition was evil because it amounted to an "utter rejection of the Scriptures,"[127] but Taylor Lewis, a professor of Greek and Oriental studies at New York University, retorted that Van Dyke was not taking "the vastly changed condition of the world" sufficiently into account: it was a "malignant falsehood" to suggest that ancient institutions could be transplanted wholesale to the modern world.[128]

Lewis's nuanced approach to scripture was based on a scholarly understanding of ancient slavery that was anathema to evangelicals in the North, who had led the Abolitionist movement since its founding in the 1830s.[129] They still approached scripture with the Enlightenment conviction that human beings could discover the truth for themselves without authoritative or expert guidance, but now, to their dismay, they found that the Bible that had united the nation after the War of Independence was tearing it apart.[130] The evangelicals had failed to guide the nation at this moment of grave crisis. When, however, the political unity of the states foundered with the election of Abraham Lincoln and the secession of the Confederacy, the problem of slavery was settled by the battles of the Civil War (1861–65), not by the Bible.

This is not to say that wartime saw an eclipse of religious sentiment. On the contrary: though the American state would regard its effort as a principled defense of the Constitution, for the American nation it was a conflict charged with religious conviction. The Civil War armies have been described as the most religiously motivated in American history.[131] Northerners and Southerners both believed that God was on their side and that they knew exactly what he was doing.[132] And when it was all over, Southerners would see their defeat as divine retribution, while Northern preachers would celebrate their victory as God's endorsement of their political arrangements. "Republican institutions have been vindicated in this experience as they never were before," Beecher exulted;

"God, I think, has said, by the voice of this event to all the nations of the earth: 'Republican liberty, based upon true Christianity, is firm as the foundation of the globe.'"[133] "The Union will no more be thought of as a mere human compact," exclaimed Howard Bushnell at the Yale Commencement of 1865. "The sense of nationality becomes even a kind of religion."[134]

In fact, however, the outcome had been decided not by God but by modern weaponry. Both sides were armed with Minié rifles, which made it impossible for either to charge—the traditional mode of engagement—without being vulnerable to the gun's substantial range and suffering horrific casualties.[135] Despite the appalling loss of life—two thousand men could be lost in a single charge—generals continued to order their men to take the offensive.[136] As a result, in eight of the first twelve battles of the war, the Southern Confederacy lost 97,000 men, and in 1864 the Northern general Ulysses Grant lost 64,000 men in the first six months of his campaign against Robert E. Lee in the Wilderness.[137] The infantrymen caught on to this problem before the political or military leaders. Because one had to fire the Minié standing up, foot soldiers on both sides started to dig the trenches that would become the hallmark of early industrialized warfare with its protracted stalemates.[138] With both sides "dug in," unable to advance decisively, modern wars would drag on battle after battle.

After the war, the more reflective leaders—such as Oliver Wendell Holmes Jr., Andrew Dixon White, and John Dewey—retreated from the certainties of Enlightenment Protestantism.[139] In Europe too, Enlightenment confidence had been undermined. In Germany during the late eighteenth and early nineteenth centuries, scholars had applied to scripture the modern historical-critical methodology used to study classical texts. This "Higher Criticism" revealed that there was no univocal message in scripture; that Moses had not written the Pentateuch, which was composed of at least four different sources; that the miracle stories were little more than a literary trope; and that King David was not the author of the psalms. A little later Charles Lyell (1797–1875) argued that the earth's crust had not been shaped by God but by the incremental effects of wind and water; Charles Darwin (1809–82) put forward the hypothesis that Homo sapiens had evolved from the same protoape as the chimpanzee; and studies revealed that the revered philosopher Immanuel Kant had actually undercut the entire Enlightenment project by maintaining that our ways of thinking bear no relation to objective reality.

In Europe the rising tide of unbelief was born not merely from skepticism but from a hunger for radical social and political change. The Germans had been enthralled by the French Revolution, but the social and political situation in their country ruled out anything similar; it seemed better to try to change the way people thought than to resort to violence. By the 1830s, a radical cadre of intellectuals had emerged who were theologically literate, were particularly incensed by the social privileges of the clergy, and saw the Lutheran Church as a bastion of conservatism. As part of this corrupt Old Regime, they argued, the churches had to go, together with the God who had supported the system. Ludwig Feuerbach's atheistic statement *The Essence of Christianity* (1841) was avidly read as a revolutionary as well as a theological tract.[140]

In the United States, however, the urban elite had been appalled by the violence of the French Revolution and used Christianity to promote the social reform that would hold such turbulence at bay. Lyell's revelations had caused a brief panic, but most Americans remained convinced by Newton's vision of a design in the universe that proved the existence of an intelligent, benign Creator. These more liberal Christians were open to the Higher Criticism and willing to "christen" Darwinism, largely because they had not yet fully absorbed its implications. Evolution was not yet the bogey in America that it would become during the 1920s. At this point the liberal elite believed that God had been at work in the process of natural selection and that humanity was gradually evolving to a greater spiritual perfection.[141]

After the Civil War, demoralized by their failure to resolve the slavery question, many of the Evangelicals withdrew from public life, realizing that they had marginalized themselves politically.[142] Their religion thus became separate from their politics, a private affair—just as the Founders had hoped. Instead of bringing a Christian voice to the great questions of the day, they turned inward, and perhaps because the Bible had seemed to fail them in the nation's darkest hour, they became preoccupied with the minutiae of biblical orthodoxy. That retreat was in some ways a positive development. Evangelicals were still staunchly anti-Catholic, and their withdrawal made it easier for Catholic immigrants to be accepted into the American nation, but it also deprived that nation of salutary criticism. Before the war, preachers had concentrated on the legitimacy of slavery as an institution but had neglected the issue of race. Tragically, they would remain unable to bring the gospel to bear on this major American problem. For a hundred years after the abolition of slavery, African Americans in the South would continue to suffer segregation, discrimination, and routine terrorism at the hands of white supremacist mobs, which the local authorities did little to suppress.[143]

• • •

Shaken by the catastrophe of the Civil War, Americans dismantled their military. Europeans meanwhile came to believe that they had discovered a more civilized and sustainable mode of warfare.[144] Their model for this supposedly efficient warfare was the Prussian chancellor Otto von Bismarck (1815–98), who had invested heavily in railways and telegraph systems and issued his army with new needle guns and steel cannons. In three relatively short, bloodless, but spectacularly successful wars against states that did not have this advanced technology—the Danish War (1864), the Austro-Prussian War (1866), and the Franco-Prussian War (1870)—Bismarck created a united Germany. Fired by their national myths, the nation-states of Europe now embarked on an arms race, each convinced that it too could fight its way to a unique and glorious destiny. The British writer I. F. Clarke has shown that between 1871 and 1914, not a single year passed in which a novel or short story about a future catastrophic conflict did not appear in a European country.[145] The "Next Great War" was invariably imagined as a terrible but inevitable ordeal, after which the nation would rise to enhanced life. This would not be as easy as they imagined, however. What each power failed to reckon was that when all nations had the same new weapons, none would have an advantage and that Bismarck's victories were, therefore, not replicable.

As Lord Acton had predicted, this aggressive nationalism made life even more problematic for minorities. In the nation-state, Jews increasingly appeared chronically rootless and cosmopolitan. There were pogroms in Russia, condoned and even orchestrated by the government;[146] in Germany anti-Semitic parties began to emerge in the 1880s; and in 1893 Captain Alfred Dreyfus, the only Jewish officer on the French General Staff, was convicted on false evidence of transmitting secrets to Germany. Many were convinced that Dreyfus was part of an international Jewish conspiracy that was plotting to weaken France. The new anti-

Semitism drew on centuries of Christian prejudice but gave it a scientific rationale.[147] Anti-Semites claimed that Jews did not fit the biological and genetic profile of the Volk, and some argued that they should be eliminated, in the same way as modern medicine cut out a cancer.

It was perhaps inevitable that, correctly anticipating an anti-Semitic disaster, some Jews would develop their own national mythology. Loosely based on the Bible, Zionism campaigned for a safe haven for Jews in their ancestral land, but Zionists also drew on varied currents of modern thought—Marxism, secularism, capitalism, and colonialism. Some wanted to build a socialist utopia in the Land of Israel. The earliest and most vociferous Zionists were atheists who were convinced that religious Judaism had made Jews passive in the face of persecution: they horrified Orthodox Jews, who insisted that only the Messiah could lead Jews back to the Promised Land. Like most forms of nationalism, though, Zionism had a religiosity of its own. Zionists who settled in agricultural colonies in Palestine were called *chalutzim,* a term with biblical connotations of salvation, liberation, and rescue; they described their agricultural work as *avodah,* which in the Bible had referred to temple worship; and their migration to Palestine was *aliyah,* a spiritual "ascent." Their slogan, however, was "A land without a people for a people without a land."[148] Like other European colonists, they believed that an endangered people had a natural right to settle in "empty" land. But the land was not empty. Palestinians had their own dreams of national independence, and when the Zionists finally persuaded the international community to create the State of Israel in 1948, the Palestinians became a rootless, endangered people without a land of their own in a world that now defined itself by nationality.

◆　◆　◆

The First World War (1914–18) destroyed a generation of young men, yet many Europeans initially embraced it with an enthusiasm that shows how difficult it is to resist those emotions long activated by religion and now by nationalism, the new faith of the secular age. In August 1914 the cities of Europe were swept up in a festival atmosphere that, like the rituals of the French Revolution, made the "imaginary community" of the nation an incarnate reality. Total strangers gazed enraptured into each other's eyes; estranged friends embraced, feeling a luminous cohesion that defied rational explanation. The euphoria has been dismissed as an outbreak of communal madness, but those who experienced it said that it was the "most deeply lived" event of their lives. It has also been called an "escape from modernity" since it sprang from a profound discontent with industrialized society, in which people were defined and classified by their function and everything was subordinated to a purely material end.[149] The declaration of war seemed a summons to the nobility of altruism and self-sacrifice that gave life meaning.

"All differences of class, rank and language were flooded over at that moment by the rushing feeling of fraternity," the Austrian writer Stefan Zweig recalled. Everyone "had been incorporated into the mass, he was a part of the people, and his person, his hitherto unnoticed person, had been given meaning. . . . Each one was called upon to cast his infinitesimal self into the glowing mass and there to be purified of all selfishness."[150] There was a yearning to cast aside an identity that felt too lonely, narrow, and confining and to escape from the privacy imposed by modernity.[151] An individual "was no longer the isolated person of former times," said Zweig.[152] "No more are we what we had been so long: alone," declared Marianne Weber.[153] A new era seemed to have begun. "People realized that they *were* equal," remembered Rudolf Binding. "No one wished to count for more than anyone else. . . . It was like a rebirth."[154] It "transported the body as well as the soul into a trance-like, enormously enhanced love of life and existence," recalled Carl Zuckmayer, "a joy of participation, of living-along-with, a feeling, even, of grace."[155] The triviality of the "petty, aimless lounging life of peacetime is done with," Franz Schauwecker exulted.[156] For the first time, said Konrad Haenisch, a lifelong critic of German capitalism, he could join "with a full heart, a clean conscience, and without a sense of treason in the sweeping, stormy song: Deutschland, Deutschland über alles."[157]

In the trenches, however, volunteers discovered that far from escaping industrialization, they were entirely dominated by it. Like a sinister religious revelation, the war laid bare the material, technological, and mechanical reality that twentieth-century civilization concealed.[158] "Everything becomes machine-like," one soldier wrote; "one might almost term the war an industry of professionalized human slaughter."[159] It is a telling indictment of the loneliness and segmentation of modern society that many of these soldiers never forgot the profound sense of community they experienced in the trenches. "There enwrapped us, never to be lost, the sudden comradeship of the ranks," T. E. Lawrence recalled.[160] One of Simone de Beauvoir's professors "discovered the joys of comradeship which overcome all social barriers" and determined never again to submit to "the segregation which in civil life separates young middle-class men from working chaps . . . something he felt like a personal mutilation."[161] Many found that they could not even hate the invisible enemy and were shocked when they finally saw the people they had been shelling for months. "They were showing themselves to us as they really were, men and soldiers like us, in uniform like us," an Italian soldier explained.[162]

This secular war for the nation had given some of the participants experiences associated with the religious traditions: an *ekstasis,* a sense of liberation, freedom, equanimity, community, and a profound relationship with other human beings, even the enemy. Yet the First World War heralded a century of unprecedented slaughter and genocide that was inspired not by religion as people had come to know it but by an equally commanding notion of the sacred: men fought for power, glory, scarce resources, and above all, their nation.

11

Religion Fights Back

During the twentieth century, there would be many attempts to resist the modern state's banishment of religion to the private sphere. To committed secularists, these religious efforts seemed like so many efforts to turn the clock back, but in fact all were modern movements that could have flourished only in our own time. Indeed, some commentators have seen them as postmodern, since they represented a widespread dissatisfaction with many of the canons of modernity. Whatever the philosophers, pundits, or politicians claimed, people all over the world expressed a wish to see religion playing a more central role in public life. This type of religiosity is often called *fundamentalism*—an unsatisfactory term because it does not translate easily into other languages and suggests a monolithic phenomenon. In fact, though these movements share certain family resemblances, each has its own focus and trigger. In almost every region where a secular government has been established, a religious countercultural protest has developed as well, similar to the Muslim and Hindu reform movements that had emerged in British-controlled India. The attempt to confine religion to the individual conscience had originated in the West as part of Western modernization, but to others it made no sense. Indeed, many would find the expectation unnatural, reductive, and even damaging.

As I have written elsewhere in detail, fundamentalism, be it Jewish, Christian, or Muslim, is not in itself a violent phenomenon.[1] Only a tiny proportion of fundamentalists commit acts of terror; most are simply trying to live a devout life in a world that seems increasingly hostile to faith, and nearly all begin with what is perceived as an assault on them by the secular, liberal establishment. These movements tend to follow a basic pattern: first they retreat from mainstream society to create an enclave of authentic faith, rather as the Deobandis did in the subcontinent; at a later stage, some—but by no means all—engage in a counteroffensive to "convert" the broader society. Every one of the movements I have studied is rooted in fear—in the conviction that modern society is out to destroy not only their faith but also themselves and their entire way of life. This is not simply, or even mainly, paranoid. Fundamentalism first became a force in Jewish life, for example, after the Holocaust, Hitler's attempt to exterminate European Jewry. Moreover, we have seen that in the past when people fear annihilation, their horizons tend to shrink, and they can lash out violently—though most "fundamentalists" have confined their antagonism to rhetoric or nonviolent political activity. It will be our concern to consider the reasons why those exceptional cases turn out as they do.

We can learn a great deal about fundamentalism generally from a crisis in one of the first of these movements, which developed in the United States during and immediately after the First World War. The term itself was coined in the 1920s by American Protestants who resolved to return to the "fundamentals" of Christianity. Their retreat from public life after the Civil War had narrowed and, perhaps, distorted their vision. Instead of engaging as before with such issues as racial or economic inequality, they focused on biblical literalism, convinced that every single assertion of scripture was literally true. And so their enemy was no longer social injustice but the German Higher Criticism of the Bible, which had been embraced by the more liberal American Christians who were still attempting to bring the gospel to bear on social problems. For all the claims that fundamentalisms make of a return to basics, however, these movements are highly innovative. Before the sixteenth century, for instance, Christians had always been encouraged to read scripture allegorically; even Calvin did not believe that the first chapter of Genesis was a factual account of the origins of life, and he took severely to task those "frantic persons" who believed that it was.[2] The new fundamentalist outlook now required a wholesale denial of glaring discrepancies in scripture itself. Closed to any alternative and coherent only in its own terms, biblical inerrancy created a shuttered mind-set born of great fear. "Religion has to fight for its life against a large class of scientific men," warned Charles Hodge, who formulated this dogma in 1874.[3] This embattled preoccupation with the status of the biblical text reflected a wider Christian concern about the nature of religious authority. Just four years earlier the First Vatican Council (1870) had promulgated the new—and highly controversial—doctrine of papal infallibility. At a time when modernity was demolishing old truths and leaving crucial questions unanswered, there was a yearning for absolute certainty.

Fundamentalisms are also often preoccupied by the horror of modern warfare and violence. The shocking slaughter in Europe during the First World War could only be the beginning of the end, the evangelicals concluded; these times of unprecedented carnage must be the battles foretold in the book of Revelation. There was a deep anxiety about the centralization of modern society and anything approaching world rule. In the new League of Nations, they saw the revival of the Roman Empire predicted in Revelation, the abode of Antichrist.[4] Fundamentalists now saw themselves grappling with satanic forces that would shortly destroy the world. Their spirituality was defensive and filled with a paranoid terror of the sinister influence of the Catholic minority; they even described American democracy as the "most devilish rule this world has ever seen."[5] The American fundamentalists' chilling scenario of the end time, with its wars, bloodshed, and slaughter, is symptomatic of a deep-rooted distress that cannot be assuaged by cool rational analysis. In less stable countries, it would be all too easy for a similar malaise, despair, and fear to erupt in physical violence.

Their horrified recoil from the violence of the First World War also led American fundamentalists to veto modern science. They became obsessed with evolutionary theory. There was a widespread belief that German wartime atrocities were the result of the nation's devotion to Darwinian social theory, according to which existence was a brutal, godless struggle in which only the strongest should survive. This was, of course, a vulgar distortion of Darwin's hypothesis, but at a time when people were trying to make sense of the bloodiest war in human history, evolution seemed to symbolize everything that was most ruthless in modern life. These ideas were particularly disturbing to small-town Americans who felt that their culture was being taken over by the secularist elite— almost as though they were being colonized by a foreign power. This distress came to a head in the famous Scopes Trial in Dayton, Tennessee, when the fundamentalists, represented by the Democratic politician William Jennings Bryan, tried to defend the state legislature's prohibition of the teaching of evolution in the public schools. They were opposed by the rationalist campaigner Clarence Darrow, supported by the newly founded American Civil Liberties Union.[6] Even though the state law was upheld, Bryan's bumbling performance under Darrow's sharp interrogation thoroughly discredited the fundamentalists' cause.

Their response to this humiliation is instructive. The press mounted a virulent campaign exposing Bryan and his fundamentalist supporters as hopeless anachronisms. Fundamentalists had no place in modern society, argued the journalist H. L. Mencken: "They are everywhere where learning is too heavy a burden for human minds to carry, even the vague, pathetic learning on tap in the little red schoolhouses." He mocked Dayton as a "one-horse Tennessee village" and its citizens the "gaping primates of the upland valleys."[7] Yet whenever a fundamentalist movement is attacked, either with violence or in a media campaign, it almost invariably becomes more extreme. It shows malcontents that their fear is well grounded: the secular world really *is* out to destroy them. Before the Scopes Trial, not even Hodge had believed that Genesis was scientifically sound in every detail, but afterward "creation science" became the rallying cry of the fundamentalist movement. Before Dayton, some leading fundamentalists still engaged in social work with people on the left; afterward, they swung to the far right, retreating altogether from the mainstream and creating their own churches, colleges, broadcasting stations, and publishing houses. They grew and grew below the mainstream cultural radar. Once they became aware of their considerable public support, in the late 1970s they would reemerge from the margins with Jerry Falwell's Moral Majority.

American fundamentalism would ever after vie to be heard as a decisive voice in American politics—with notable success. It would not resort to violence, largely because American Protestants did not suffer as greatly as did, for example, the Muslims of the Middle East. Unlike the secular rulers of Egypt or Iran, the U.S. government did not confiscate their property, torture and assassinate their clergy, or cruelly dismantle their institutions. In America secular modernity was a homegrown product, which was not imposed militarily from outside but had evolved organically over time, and when they arrived on the public scene in the late

1970s, American fundamentalists could use well-established democratic channels to make their point. Although American Protestant fundamentalism was not usually an agent of violence, it was, to a degree, a response to violence: the trauma of modern warfare and the psychological assault of the aggressive disdain of the secularist establishment. Both can distort a religious tradition in ways that reverberate far beyond the community of the faithful. Nevertheless, fundamentalism in America shares with other disaffected groups the sensibility of the colonized, in its defiant self-assertion and in a determination to recover one's own identity and culture against a powerful Other.

◆　◆　◆

Muslim fundamentalism, by contrast, has often—though again, not always—segued into physical aggression. This is not because Islam is constitutionally more prone to violence than Protestant Christianity but rather because Muslims had a much harsher introduction to modernity. Before the birth of the modern state in the crucible of colonialism, Islam had continued in many Muslim lands to operate as the organizing principle of society. In 1920, after the First World War and the defeat of the Ottoman Empire, Britain and France divided Ottoman territories into Western-style nation-states and established mandates and protectorates there before granting these new countries independence. But the inherent contradictions of the nation-state would be especially wrenching in the Muslim world, where there was no tradition of nationalism. The frontiers drawn up by the Europeans were so arbitrary that it was extremely difficult to create a national "imaginary community." In Iraq, for example, where Sunnis were a minority, the British appointed a Sunni ruler to govern both the Shii majority and the Kurds in the north. In Lebanon, 50 percent of the population was Muslim and naturally wanted close economic and political relations with their Arab neighbors, but the Christian government selected by the French preferred stronger ties with Europe. The partition of Palestine and the creation of the Jewish State of Israel by the United Nations in 1948 proved no less mischievous. It resulted in the forcible displacement of 750,000 Arab Palestinians, and those who remained found themselves living in a state that was hostile to their nation. There was the added complication that Israel was a secular state founded for adherents of one of the world's ancient religions. Yet for the first twenty years of its existence, the Israeli leadership was aggressively secular, and the violence inflicted on the Palestinians, Israel's wars with its neighbors, and the Palestinian riposte were fought not for religion but for secular nationalism.

The British partition of the subcontinent into Hindu India and Muslim Pakistan in 1947 was similarly problematic, since both were established as secular states in the name of religion. The brutal process of partition caused the displacement of over seven million people and the deaths of a million others who were attempting to flee from one state to join their coreligionists in the other. In both India and Pakistan, vast numbers found themselves unable to speak the so-called national language. A particularly volatile situation was created in Kashmir, which despite a Muslim majority was given to India, because it was ruled by a Hindu maharaja. That British decision is still contested, and a similar arbitrariness was felt in the separation of eastern and western Pakistan by a thousand miles of Indian territory.

As they struggled for independence before partition, Hindus had engaged in an intense discussion about the legitimacy of fighting the British, shaped in large part by the *Bhagavad-Gita,* a text that has deeply shaped the collective memory of India. Ahimsa was an important spiritual value in India, yet the *Gita* seemed to sanction violence. Mohandas Gandhi (1869–1948), however, disagreed with this interpretation. He had been born into a vaishya family and had many Jain friends who influenced his later attitudes. In 1914, after working for years as a lawyer in South Africa to oppose discriminatory legislation against Indians, he had returned to India and become interested in the issue of home rule, founding the Natal Indian Congress Party and developing his unique method of resisting colonial oppression by nonresistance. Besides the Hindu religious tradition, he had been influenced by Jesus's Sermon on the Mount, Leo Tolstoy's *The Kingdom of God Is Within You,* John Ruskin's *Unto This Last,* and Henry David Thoreau's *Civil Disobedience.*

Central to Gandhi's worldview was the insight, first developed in the Upanishads, that all beings were manifestations of the Brahman. Since everybody shared the same sacred core, violence went against the metaphysical bias of the entire universe. This deeply spiritual vision of the oneness of existence directly countered the aggressive separatism and chauvinism of the nation-state. Gandhi's peaceable refusal to obey the self-serving obduracy of the British regime was based on three principles: ahimsa, *satyagraha* (the "soul force" that comes with the realization of the profound unity of humanity), and *swaraj* ("self-rule"). In the *Gita*, Gandhi maintained, Arjuna's initial refusal to fight had not been true ahimsa, because he still regarded himself as different from his enemies and had not realized that they were all, friend and foe alike, embodiments of the Brahman. Had Arjuna truly understood that he and Duryodana, the adversary he was about to fight, were ultimately one, he would have acquired the "soul force" that had the power to transform an enemy's hatred into love.

But as we have seen, the same texts and spiritual practices can lead to entirely different courses of actions. Others opposed this interpretation of the *Gita*. The Hindu scholar Aurobindo Ghose (1872–1950) argued that Krishna's validation of violence in the *Gita* was simply an acknowledgment of life's grim reality. Yes, it would be nice to remain peacefully above the fray, but until Gandhi's "soul force" actually became an effective reality in the world, the natural aggression inherent in both men and nations "tramples down, breaks, slaughters, burns, pollutes as we see it doing today." Gandhi might discover that he had caused as much destruction of life by abjuring violence as those who had resorted to fighting.[8] Aurobindo was voicing the view of Gandhi's critics, who thought that he closed his eyes to the fact that the British response to his nonviolent campaigns actually resulted in hideous bloodshed. But Aurobindo was also articulating the eternal dilemma of Ashoka: Is nonviolence feasible in the inescapably violent world of politics?

Nevertheless, Gandhi saw his theory through to its ultimate conclusion. Nonviolence meant not only loving your enemies, he maintained, but realizing that they were not your enemies at all. He might hate the systemic and military ruthlessness of colonial rule, but he could not allow himself to hate the people who implemented it:

> Mine is not an exclusive love. I cannot love Moslems or Hindus and hate Englishmen. For if I love merely Hindus and Moslems because their ways are on the whole pleasing to me, I shall soon begin to hate them when their ways displease me, which they may well do any moment. A love that is based on the goodness of those whom you love is a mercenary affair.[9]

Without reverence for the sanctity of every single human being and the "equanimity" long seen in India as the pinnacle of the spiritual quest, "politics bereft of religion," Gandhi believed, were a "death-trap because they kill the soul."[10] Secular nationalism seems unable to cultivate a similarly universal ideology, even though our globalized world is so deeply interconnected. Gandhi could not countenance Western secularism: "To see the universal and all-pervading Spirit of Truth face to face one must be able to love the meanest creature as oneself," he concluded in his autobiography. Devotion to this truth required one to be involved in every field of life; it had brought him into politics, for "those who say that religion has nothing to do with politics do not know what religion means."[11] Gandhi's last years were darkened by the communal violence that had erupted during and after partition. He was assassinated in 1948 by a radical nationalist who believed that Gandhi had given too many concessions to the Muslims and had made a large monetary donation to Pakistan.

As they forged their national identities in the peculiarly tense conditions of India, Muslims and Hindus would both fall prey to the besetting sin of secular nationalism: its inability to tolerate minorities. And because their outlook was still permeated by spirituality, this nationalist bias distorted their traditional religious vision. As violence between Muslims and Hindus escalated during the 1920s, the Arya Samaj became more militant.[12] At a conference in 1927, it formed a military cadre, the Arya Vir Dal ("Troop of Aryan Horses"). It declared that the new Aryan hero must develop the virtues of the Kshatriya—courage, physical strength, and, especially, proficiency in the use of weapons. His principal duty was to defend the rights of the Aryan nation against the Muslims and the British.[13] The Arya was anxious not to be outdone by the Rashtriya Svayamsevak Sangh ("National Volunteer Association"), usually referred to as RSS, founded in central India three years earlier by Keshav B. Hedgewar. Where the Arya had adapted the British idea of "religion" to "Hinduism," RSS had fused traditional religious ideals with Western nationalism. It was primarily a character-building organization designed to develop an ethos of service, based on loyalty, discipline, and a respect for the Hindu heritage, and it appealed particularly to the urban middle classes. Its hero was the seventeenth-century warrior Shivaji who, empowered by his fidelity to traditional Hindu ritual as well as his organizational skills, had led a successful revolt against the Moghuls. He had managed to weld recruits from disparate peasant castes into a unified army, and RSS vowed to do the same in British India.[14]

Thus a new religiosity was coming to birth in India, one that cultivated Hindu strength not by evoking ahimsa but by developing the traditional warrior ethos. Yet this combination of the Kshatriya ideal with
secular nationalism was dangerous. For RSS, Mother India was not simply a territorial entity but a living goddess. She had always been revered
as a holy land, and her seas, rivers, and mountains were sacred, but for
centuries she had been desecrated by foreigners and would shortly be
raped by partition. Traditionally, the Mother Goddess had embraced
everyone, but with its new nationalist intolerance of minorities, RSS
insisted that she could no longer admit Muslims or East Asian Buddhists.

Hedgewar was an activist rather than an intellectual, his thinking
deeply influenced by V. D. Savarkar, a brilliant radical imprisoned by the
British whose classic *Hindutva* ("Hinduness") had been smuggled out
of prison and published in 1923. It defined the Hindu as a person who
acknowledged the integrity of Greater India (which stretched from the
Himalayas to Iran and Singapore) and revered her not only as Mother-
land, as other nationalists did, but also as Holy Land.[15] This fusion of
religion and secular nationalism was potentially toxic. In Savarkar's
books, the emerging Hindu national identity depended upon the exclusion of Islam: the whole complex history of India was presented as a
struggle to the death with Muslim imperialism. Even though Hindus had
always been the majority population, they had been conditioned by centuries of imperial domination to see themselves as an embattled, endangered minority.[16] Like so many subject peoples, they had developed a
history of injury and humiliation, which can corrode a religious tradition
and incline it toward violence. Some experienced their long oppression as
a national disgrace. During the 1930s M. S. Golwalkar, the second leader
of the RSS, felt an affinity with the ideals of National Socialism, in part
the product of Germany's humiliation by the Allies after the First World
War. Foreigners in India had only two options, Golwalkar argued: "The
foreign races must lose their separate existence . . . or [they] may stay in
the country, wholly subordinated to the Hindu Nation, claiming nothing, deserving no privileges, far less any preferential treatment—not even
citizen's rights." Golwalkar praised the Germans for "purging the country of the Semitic Races"; India, he believed, had much to learn from this
Aryan "Race pride."[17]

The horror of partition could only inflame the history of grievance
that was so dangerously poisoning relations between Muslims and

Hindus. As the psychologist Sudhir Kakar has explained, for decades hundreds of thousands of Hindu and Muslim children have listened to tales of the violence of that time, which "dwell on the fierceness of the implacable enemy. This is a primary channel through which historical enmity is transmitted from one generation or the next." It also created a rift between secularist and religious Hindus.[18] Secularists convinced themselves that this violence could never happen again. Many blamed the British for the tragedy; others regarded it merely as a terrifying aberration. Jawaharlal Nehru, India's first prime minister, believed that the industrialization of the country and the spread of scientific rationalism and democracy would counter these communal passions.

But there was a disturbing portent of future trouble. In 1949 an image of Ram, incarnation of Vishnu and chief exemplar of Hindu virtue, was discovered in a building at the site of his mythological birthplace in Ayodhya on the eastern Gangetic plain. This was also the site of a mosque said to have been established by Babur, the first Moghul emperor, in 1528.[19] Devout Hindus claimed that Ram's image had been placed there by God; Muslims, naturally, denied this. There were violent clashes, and the district magistrate, a member of RSS, refused to remove the image. Because their images require regular worship, Hindus were henceforth permitted to enter the building for devotional chanting on the anniversary of the miraculous arrival of Ram's statue. Forty years later this sacred geography would trump the scientific rationalism so confidently predicted by the secularists.

◆　◆　◆

The founder of Pakistan, Muhammad Ali Jinnah (1876–1948), was an unabashed secularist who simply wanted to create a state in which Muslims would not be defined or limited by their religious affiliation. In fact, the nation was defined by Islam before it had even begun. This inevitably raised certain expectations, and from the beginning, while the government was still resolutely secularist, there was pressure to resacralize political life. The Deobandis became particularly powerful in Pakistan. They endorsed the modern system of territorial nationalism and secular democracy and offered free education to the poor in their madrassas at a time when the state school system was collapsing due to lack of funding. Their students would be isolated from mainstream secular life and schooled in the Deobandis' peculiarly rigid and intolerant form of Islam.

To protect their Islamic lifestyle, the Deobandis also founded a political party, the JUI (Association of Ulema of Islam). By the late 1960s, having accumulated tens of thousands of students and alumni, they were in an excellent position to pressure the government to Islamize civil law and the banking system, thereby creating jobs for their ultrareligious graduates.

Quite different was the Jamaat-i-Islami, which had been founded in India in 1941 to oppose the creation of a separate secular state. Jamaat had no madrassa base and did not cling to the past, as the Deobandis did, but developed an Islamic ideology influenced by the modern ideals of liberty and independence. Abul Ala Maududi (1903–79), its founder, argued that because God alone ruled human affairs, nothing else—"be it a human being, a family, a class, or a group of people, or even the human race as a whole"—could claim sovereignty.[20] Therefore nobody was obliged to obey any mortal authority. Each generation had to fight the jahiliyyah of its day, as the Prophet had done, since jahili violence, greed, and Godlessness were an ever-present danger. Western secularism epitomized the modern jahiliyyah because it amounted to a rebellion against God's rule.[21] Islam, Maududi insisted, was not a Western-style "religion," separate from politics; here he was in full agreement with Gandhi. Rather, Islam was a *din,* a whole way of life that had to include economic, social, and political as well as ritualized activities:[22]

> The use of the word [*din*] categorically refutes the views of those who believe a prophet's message is principally aimed at ensuring worship of the one God, adherence to a set of beliefs, and observance of a few rituals. This also refutes the views of those who think that din has nothing to do with cultural, political, economic, legal, judicial, and other matters pertaining to this world.[23]

Muslims had been charged to reject the structural violence of the jahili state and to implement economic justice, social harmony, and political equality in public as well as private life, all based on a profound awareness of God (*taqwah*).

Before partition, Jamaat had concentrated on training its members to reform their own lives in the Greater Jihad; only by living an authentically Quranic life could they hope to inspire the people with a longing for Islamic government. But after partition, the movement split. Of its 625 members, 240 remained in India. Since only 11 percent of the population of India was Muslim, Indian Jamaat could not hope to create an Islamic state; instead, its members acquired a qualified appreciation of the moderate (as opposed to atheistic) secularism of the new state of India that forbade discrimination on the basis of religious belief. This, they declared, was a "blessing" and a "guarantee for a safe future for Islam in India."[24] But in Pakistan, where there was a possibility of an Islamic state, Maududi and his 385 Jamaat disciples felt no such constraints. They became the most organized Pakistani political party, gained the support of the educated urban classes, and campaigned vigorously against the dictatorship of Ayub Khan (r. 1958–69), who confiscated all clerical property, and the socialist regime of Zulfiqar Ali Bhutto (r. 1970–77), who used Islamic symbols and slogans to win popular support but in reality had nothing but contempt for religion.

Maududi, therefore, was still committed to the struggle (*jihad*) against jahili secularism, but he always interpreted jihad broadly in the traditional manner so that it did not simply mean "holy war"; one could "strive" to achieve God's sovereignty by peaceful political activities, such as writing books or working in education.[25] It is a mistake, therefore, to brand Pakistani Jamaat as fanatically intent on violence; the fact that the party went in two such different directions after partition shows that it had the flexibility to adapt to circumstances. Maududi would have nothing to do with revolutionary coups, assassinations, or policies that stirred up hatred and conflict, insisting that an Islamic state could put down firm roots only if ends and means were "clean and commendable."[26] The transition from a secular nation-state to a truly Islamic society must, he would always maintain, be "natural, evolutionary and peaceful."[27]

But in Pakistan physical force had become one of the chief ways of doing politics.[28] Leaders regularly came to power in military coups, and in their ruthless suppression of political opposition, neither Khan nor Bhutto could be seen as examples of benign, peaceable secularism. So prevalent was armed conflict in Pakistani society that a group that abjured it had little hope of success. In an effort to gain popular support for Jamaat, Maududi agreed to lead a campaign against the so-called heretical Ahmadi sect in 1953 and wrote an inflammatory pamphlet, which sparked riots and put him in prison.[29] This, however, was an aberration. Maududi continued to denounce the violence of Pakistani politics and condemned the aggressive activities of Jamaat's affiliate IJT (Islami Jamiat-i-Taliban), the Society of Islamic Students, which organized strikes and demonstrations against Bhutto, paralyzed the communication systems, disrupted urban commerce and educational establishments, and led militant confrontations with the police. While other members of Jamaat succumbed to Pakistan's endemic violence, Maududi remained committed to achieving an Islamic state democratically. He repeatedly insisted that an Islamic state could not be a theocracy, because no group or individual had the right to rule in God's name. An Islamic government must be elected by the people for a fixed term; there must be universal adult franchise, regular elections, a multiparty system, an independent judiciary, and guaranteed human rights and civil liberties—a system not very different from the parliamentary democracy of Westminster.[30]

When Zia al-Haqq seized power in a coup in 1977, established a dictatorship, and announced that Pakistan would follow Shariah law, he drew heavily on Maududi's writings in his speeches. He also brought several senior Jamaat officials into his cabinet and employed thousands of Jamaat activists in the civil service, education, and the army. Shariah courts were established, and traditional Islamic penalties for alcohol, theft, prostitution, and adultery were introduced. By this time, Maududi was in failing health, and the current Jamaat leaders supported Zia's military regime, regarding it as a promising beginning. But Maududi had profound misgivings. How could a dictatorship, which usurped God's sovereignty and ruled with martial and structural violence, be truly Islamic? Shortly before his death, he penned a brief note to this effect:

> The implementation of Islamic laws alone cannot yield the positive result Islam really aims at. . . . For, merely by dint of this announcement [of Islamic laws] you cannot kindle the hearts of the people with the light of faith, enlighten their minds with the teachings of Islam, and mold their habits and manners corresponding to the virtues of Islam.[31]

Future generations of Muslim activists would have done well to heed this lesson.

◆   ◆   ◆

Western modernity had conferred two blessings in the places it was first conceived: political independence and technical innovation. But in the

Middle East, modernity arrived as colonial subjugation, and there was little potential for innovation, with the West so far ahead that Muslims could only imitate.[32] The unwelcome changes, imposed as foreign imports from without, were uncongenially abrupt. A process that had taken centuries in Europe had to be effected in a matter of decades, superficially and often violently. The almost insuperable problems faced by modernizers had already become clear in the career of Muhammad Ali (1769–1849). He had become governor of Egypt after Napoleon's invasion and managed the monumental feat of dragging this backward Ottoman province into the modern world within a mere forty years. Yet he could do so only by ruthless coercion. Twenty-three thousand peasants died in the forced labor bands that improved Egypt's irrigation and communications. Thousands more were conscripted into the army; some cut off their fingers and even blinded themselves to avoid military service. There could never be technological self-sufficiency, because Muhammad Ali had to buy all his machinery, weapons, and manufactured goods from Europe.[33] And there could be no independence: despite his achieving a degree of autonomy from the Ottomans, modernization eventually led to Egypt's becoming a virtual British colony. Ismail Pasha (1830–95), Muhammad Ali's grandson, made the country too desirable to the Europeans: he had commissioned French engineers to construct the Suez Canal, built nine hundred miles of railways, irrigated over a million acres of hitherto uncultivable land, set up modern schools for both boys and girls, and transformed Cairo into an elegant modern city. In the process, he bankrupted the country, ultimately giving the British the pretext they needed in 1882 to establish a military occupation to protect the interests of shareholders.

Even when a degree of modernization was achieved, the European colonial powers managed to snuff it out. Perhaps Muhammad Ali's greatest achievement had been the creation of the cotton industry, which promised to give Egypt a reliable economic base until Lord Cromer, the first consul-general of Egypt, put a brake on production, since Egyptian cotton damaged British interests. No friend to the emancipation of women—he was a founding member of the Anti-Women's Suffrage League in London—Cromer also scaled back Ismail's programs to educate women and blocked them from entering the professions. Every benefaction was less than it seemed. In 1922 the British allowed Egypt a modicum of independence, with a new king, a parliamentary body, and a liberal Western-style constitution, but they retained control of military and foreign policy. Between 1923 and 1930 there were three general elections, each won by the Wafd party, which campaigned for a reduced British presence in Egypt; but each time the British forced the elected government to resign.[34] In the same way, Europeans obstructed the development of democracy in Iran, where modernizing clergy and intellectuals had led a successful revolution against the Qajar shah in 1906, demanding constitutional rule and representative government. But almost immediately the Russians helped the shah to close the new parliament (*majlis*), and during the 1920s, the British routinely rigged elections to prevent the majlis from nationalizing the Iranian oil that fueled their navy.[35]

The Muslims of the Middle East had therefore experienced the secular rule of the colonial powers as militarily and systemically violent. Things did not improve after they achieved independence in the twentieth century. As the Europeans dismantled their empires and left the region, they ceded power to the precolonial ruling classes, which were so embedded in the old aristocratic ethos that they were incapable of modernization. They were usually deposed in coups organized by reform-minded army officers, who were virtually the only commoners to receive a Western-style education: Reza Khan in Iran (1921), Colonel Adib Shissak in Syria (1949), and Gemal Abd al-Nasser in Egypt (1952). Like Muhammad Ali, these reformers modernized rapidly, superficially, and even more violently than the Europeans. Used to barracks life and the following of orders without question, they cut down opposition ruthlessly and underestimated the complexities of modernization.[36] Secularism did not come to their subjects as liberating and irenic. Instead, these secularizing rulers effectually terrorized their subjects by tearing down familiar institutions, so that their world became unrecognizable.

Again, you could take religion out of the state but not out of the nation. The army officers wanted to secularize but found themselves ruling devout nations for whom a secularized Islam was a contradiction in terms.[37] Undeterred, these rulers declared war on the religious establishment. Following the aggressive methods of the French revolutionaries, Muhammad Ali had starved the clergy financially, taking away their tax exemption, confiscating the religiously endowed properties (*awqaf*) that were their principal source of income, and systematically robbing them of any shred of power.[38] For the Egyptian ulema, modernity was forever tainted by this ruthless assault, and they became cowed and reactionary. Nasser changed tack and turned them into state officials. For centuries the ulema's learned expertise had guided the people through the intricacies of Islamic law, but they had also stood as a protective bulwark between the people and the systemic violence of the state. Now the people came to despise them as government lackeys. This deprived them of responsible and expert religious authority that was aware of the complexity of the Islamic tradition. Self-appointed religious leaders and more simple-minded radicals would step into the breach, often to disastrous effect.[39]

Throughout the Muslim world, Mustafa Kemal Atatürk (1881–1938), founder of the modern republic of Turkey, seemed to personify the violence of secularism. After the First World War, he had managed to keep the British and French out of Anatolia, the Ottoman heartland, so Turkey had the great advantage of avoiding colonization. Determined to deprive Islam of all legal, political, and economic influence, Atatürk is often admired in the West as an enlightened Muslim leader.[40] In fact, he was a dictator who hated Islam, which he described as a "putrefied corpse."[41] He proceeded in the usual belligerent manner to outlaw the Sufi orders, seize their properties, shut down the madrassas, and appropriate the awqaf. Most important, he abolished Shariah law, replacing it with a legal code essentially adopted from Switzerland that was meaningless to most of the population.[42] Finally, in 1925, Atatürk declared the caliphate null and void. It had long been a dead letter politically but had symbolized the unity of the ummah and its link with the Prophet; at this bleak moment in their history, Sunni Muslims everywhere experienced its loss as a spiritual and cultural trauma. Western approval of Atatürk led many to believe that the West sought to destroy Islam itself.

In order to control the rising merchant class, the last Ottoman sultans had systematically deported or killed their Greek and Armenian subjects, who constituted about 90 percent of the bourgeoisie. In 1908 the Young Turks, a party of modernizers, deposed Sultan Abdul-Hamid II in a coup. They had absorbed the antireligious positivism of such Western thinkers as Auguste Comte (1798–1857) as well as the new "scientific" racism, an outgrowth of the Age of Reason that came into good use in the Age of Empire. During the First World War, in order to create a purely Turkic state, the Young Turks ordered the deportation and "resettlement" of Armenian Christians from the empire on the pretext that they were conniving with the enemy. This led to the first genocide of the twentieth century, committed not by religious fanatics but by avowed secularists. Over a million Armenians were slaughtered: men and youths were killed where they stood, while women, children, and the elderly were driven into the desert where they were raped, shot, starved, poisoned, suffocated, or burned to death.[43] "I came into this world a Turk," declared the physician Mehmet Resid, the "Executioner Governor." "Armenian traitors had found a niche for themselves in the bosom of the fatherland; they were dangerous microbes. Isn't it a duty of a doctor to destroy these microbes?"[44]

When Atatürk came to power, he completed this racial purge. For centuries Greeks and Turks had dwelled together on both sides of the Aegean. Atatürk now partitioned the region and organized a massive exchange of populations. Greek-speaking Christians living in what is now Turkey were deported to what would become Greece, while Turkish-speaking Muslims living in Greece were sent the other way. For many in the Muslim world, therefore, Western secularism and nationalism would be forever associated with ethnic cleansing, virulent religious intolerance, and a violent destruction of precious Islamic institutions.

In Iran, Reza Khan courted the Westernized upper and middle classes but took no interest in the peasant masses, who therefore relied more than ever on the ulema. Two nations were developing in the country, one modernized, the other excluded from the benefits of modernity and cruelly deprived of the religious traditions that gave their life meaning. Determined to base the state's identity on ancient Persian culture rather than on Islam, Reza summarily outlawed the ashura mourning rituals for Husain, forbade Iranians to make the hajj, and drastically curtailed the scope of the Shariah courts. When Ayatollah Modarris objected, he was imprisoned and executed.[45] In 1928 Reza issued the Laws on the Uniformity of Dress, and with their bayonets his soldiers tore off the women's veils and ripped them to pieces in the street.[46] On Ashura 1929, the police surrounded the prestigious Fayziyah Madrassa in Qum, and when the students spilled out after their classes, they were stripped of their traditional clothes and forced into Western garb. In 1935 the police were ordered to open fire on a crowd who had staged a peaceful demonstration against the dress laws in the holy shrine of the Eighth Imam in Mashhad and killed hundreds of unarmed Iranians.[47] In the West, the secular nation-state had been set up to curb the violence of religion; for many thousands of people in the Middle East, secular nationalism seemed a bloodthirsty, destructive force that deprived them of the spiritual support that had been their mainstay.

◆ ◆ ◆

The Middle East had thus been brutally initiated into the new system of oppression and violence that had come into being during the colonial period. These former provinces of the mighty Ottoman Empire had been aggressively reduced by the colonialists almost overnight to a dependent bloc, their laws replaced by foreign codes, their age-old rituals abolished, and their clergy executed, impoverished, and publicly humiliated. Surrounded by modern buildings, institutions, and Western-style street layouts, people no longer felt at home in their own countries. The effect of their transformation has been compared to watching a beloved friend become slowly disfigured before one's eyes by mortal sickness. Egypt, always a leader in the Arab world, had had a particularly difficult transition to modernity, with a much longer period of direct Western rule than many other Middle Eastern countries. This persistent foreign presence and the lack of spiritual and moral leadership had created a dangerous malaise in the country and a corrosive sense of humiliation, which neither the British nor the new Egyptian government seemed willing to address. Some reformers belonging to the traditional Egyptian elite tried to counter this growing alienation. Muhammad Abdu (1849–1905), sheikh of Al-Azhar, suggested that modern legal and constitutional arrangements should be linked to traditional Islamic norms that would make them comprehensible. As it was, the people were so bewildered by the secular legal system that Egypt was effectively becoming a country without law.[48] Lord Cromer, however, who regarded the social system of Islam as "politically and socially moribund," would have none of it.[49] In the same vein, Rashid Rida (1865–1935), Abdu's biographer, wanted to establish a college where students would be introduced to modern jurisprudence, sociology, and science at the same time as they studied Islamic law, so that it might be possible one day to modernize the Shariah without diluting it and to formulate laws based on authentic Muslim tradition instead of a foreign ideology.[50]

But these reformers failed to inspire disciples who could carry their ideas forward. Far more successful was Hassan al-Banna (1906–49), founder of the Muslim Brotherhood and one of the more positive "free lances" who would step into the spiritual leadership vacuum created by the modernizers.[51] A schoolteacher who had studied modern science, Banna knew that modernization was essential but believed that because Egyptians were deeply religious, it could succeed only if accompanied by a spiritual reformation. Their own cultural traditions would serve them better than alien ideologies that they could never make fully their own. Banna and his friends had been shocked and saddened by the political and social confusion in Egypt and by the stark contrast between the luxurious homes of the British and the hovels of the Egyptian workers in the Canal Zone. One night in March 1928, six of his students begged Banna to take action, eloquently articulating the inchoate distress experienced by so many:

> We know not the practical way to reach the glory of Islam and to serve the welfare of the Muslims. We are weary of this life of humiliation and restriction. So we see that the Arabs and the Muslims have no status and no dignity. They are no more than mere hirelings belonging to foreigners. . . . We are unable to perceive the road to action as you perceive it, or to know the path to the service of the fatherland, the religion and the ummah.[52]

That very night Banna created the Society of Muslim Brothers, which inaugurated a grassroots reformation of Egyptian society.

The Society clearly answered an urgent need because it would become one of the most powerful players in Egyptian politics. By the time of Banna's assassination in 1949, it had two thousand branches throughout Egypt, and the Brotherhood was the only Egyptian organization that represented every social group—civil servants, students, urban workers, and peasants.[53] The Society was not a militant organization but sought simply to bring modern institutions to the Egyptian public in a familiar Islamic setting. The Brothers built schools for girls and boys beside the mosque and founded the Rovers, a scout movement that became the most popular youth group in the country; they set up night schools for workers and tutorial colleges to prepare students for the civil service examinations; they built clinics and hospitals in the rural areas; and they involved the Rovers in improving sanitation and health education in the poorer districts. The Society also set up trade unions that acquainted workers with their rights; in the factories where the Brotherhood was a presence, they earned a just wage, had health insurance and paid holidays, and could pray in the company's mosque. Banna's counterculture thus proved that, far from being some obsolete vestige of another era, Islam could become an effective modernizing force as well as promote spiritual vitality. But the Brotherhood's success would prove double-edged, for it called attention to the government's neglect of education and labor conditions. Banna's Society of Muslim Brothers thus came to be perceived not as a help but as a grave threat to the regime.

The Society was not perfect: it tended to be anti-intellectual, its pronouncements often defensive and self-righteous, its view of the West distorted by the colonial experience, and its leaders intolerant of dissent. Most seriously, it had developed a terrorist wing. After the creation of the State of Israel, the plight of the Palestinian refugees became a disturbing symbol of Muslims' impotence in the modern world. For some, violence seemed the only way forward. Anwar Sadat, future president of Egypt, founded a "murder society" to attack the British in the Canal Zone.[54] Other paramilitary groups were attached to the palace and the Wafd, and so it was perhaps inevitable that some Brothers should form the "Secret Apparatus" (*al-jihaz al-sirri*). Numbering only about a thousand, the Apparatus was so clandestine that even most of the Brothers had never heard of it. Banna denounced the Apparatus but could not control it and eventually it would both taint and endanger the Society.[55] When the Apparatus assassinated Prime Minister Muhammad al-Nuqrashi on December 28, 1948, the Society condemned the atrocity in the strongest terms. But the government seized this opportunity to suppress it. On February 12, 1949, almost certainly at the behest of the new prime minister, Banna was gunned down in the street.

When Nasser seized power in 1952, the Society had regrouped but was deeply divided. In the early days while he was still unpopular, Nasser courted the Brotherhood, even though he was a committed secularist and an ally of the Soviet Union. When it became clear that he had no intention of creating an Islamic state, however, a member of the Apparatus shot him during a rally. Nasser survived, and his courage under attack did wonders for his popularity. He now felt able to move against the Society, and by the end of 1954 more than a thousand Brothers had been brought to trial, and uncounted others, many of whom had committed no greater offense than distributing leaflets, never had even a day in court but languished in prison uncharged for fifteen years. After

Nasser became a hero in the larger Arab world by defying the West during the Suez Crisis of 1956, he intensified his efforts to secularize the country. But this state violence simply spawned a more extreme form of Islam that called for armed opposition to the regime.

Religious extremism often develops in a symbiotic relationship with a virulently aggressive secularism. One of the Brothers detained in 1954 was Sayyid Qutb (1906–66), the Society's chief propagandist.[56] As a young man, Qutb had felt no conflict between his faith and secular politics, but he had been alienated by the ruthless policies of the British and shocked by the racial prejudice he experienced during a visit to the United States. Still, his views had remained moderate and tentative; what radicalized him was the violence of Nasser's prison. Qutb was himself tortured and was horrified to see twenty prisoners slaughtered in a single incident. Dozens more were tortured and executed—and not by foreigners but by their own people. Secularism no longer seemed benign but cruel, aggressive, and immoral. In prison, Qutb took Maududi's ideas a step further. When he heard Nasser vowing to privatize Islam on the Western model and observed the unfolding horror of his prison life, Qutb came to believe that even a so-called Muslim ruler could be as violently jahili as any Western power. Like so many others terrorized by violence and injustice, Qutb had developed a dualistic ideology that divided the world starkly into two camps: one accepted God's sovereignty, and the other did not. In the career of Muhammad, God had revealed a practical program for the creation of a properly ordered society. First, acting under God's orders, he had created a *jamaat,* a "party" committed to justice and equity that held aloof from the pagan establishment. Second, at the hijrah, he had effected a complete severance between the Godly and the Godless. Third, Muhammad had established an Islamic state in Medina; and fourth, he began his jihad against jahili Mecca, which eventually bowed to God's sovereignty.

Qutb formulated these ideas in his book *Milestones,* which was smuggled out of prison and read avidly. He was a learned man, but *Milestones* is not the work of an official Islamic authority; rather, it is the outcry of a man who has been pushed too far. Qutb's program distorted Islamic history, since it made no mention of Muhammad's nonviolent policy at Hudaybiyya, the turning point of the conflict with Mecca. Humiliation, foreign occupation, and secularizing aggression had created an Islamic history of grievance. Qutb now had a paranoid vision of the past, seeing only a relentless succession of jahili enemies—pagans, Jews, Christians, Crusaders, Mongols, Communists, capitalists, colonialists, and Zionists—intent on the destruction of Islam.[57] Executed in 1966, he did not live long enough to work out the practical implications of his program. Yet unlike some of his later followers, he seems to have realized that Muslims would have to undergo a long spiritual, social, and political preparation before they were ready for armed struggle. After his death, however, the political situation in the Middle East deteriorated, and the increasing violence and consequent alienation meant that Qutb's work would resonate with the disaffected youth, especially those Brothers who had been likewise hardened in Egyptian jails and felt that there was no time for such a ripening process. When they were released in the early 1970s, they would bring Qutb's ideas into mainstream society and try to implement them practically.

• • •

After the Six-Day War between Israel and its Arab neighbors in June 1967, the region experienced a religious revival not only in the Muslim countries but also in Israel. Zionism, we have seen, had begun as a defiantly secular movement, and the military campaigns of the Jewish state had had no religious content; their violent suppression of the Palestinian people had been the result of their secular nationalism rather than a religious imperative. Before the war, as they listened to Nasser vowing to throw them all into the sea, many Israelis had been convinced that yet another attempt would be made to exterminate them. They responded with lightning speed, achieving a spectacular victory in which they took the Golan Heights from Syria, the Sinai Peninsula from Egypt, and the West Bank and the Old City of Jerusalem from Jordan.

Although religion had not figured in the action, many Israelis would experience this dramatic reversal of fortune as a miracle similar to the crossing of the Red Sea.[58] Above all, the conquest of the Old City of Jerusalem, closed to Israelis since 1948, was a numinous experience. When in 1898 the Zionist ideologue Theodor Herzl had visited the Western Wall, the last relic of Herod's temple, he had been repelled by the sight of the Jewish worshippers clinging cravenly to its stones.[59] But in June 1967 tough paratroopers with blackened faces and their atheistic officers leaned against the Wall and wept, their secular ethos momentarily transformed by sacred geography. Nationalism, as we have seen, easily segues into a quasi-religious fervor, especially in moments of heightened tension and emotion. Devotion to Jerusalem had been central to Jewish identity for millennia. Long before people began to map their landscape scientifically, they had defined their place in the world emotionally and spiritually, drawn irresistibly to localities that they experienced as radically different from all others. The Israeli experience in 1967 shows that we have still not entirely desacralized the world.[60] The soldiers' "beliefs" had not changed, but the Wall evoked in them something akin to the way others experienced the sacred—"something big and terrible and from another world," yet also "an old friend, impossible to mistake." Just as they had narrowly escaped destruction, they recognized the Wall as a survivor like themselves. "There will be no more destruction," one soldier said as he kissed the stones, "and the Wall will never again be deserted."[61]

"Never again" had been a Jewish watchword since the Holocaust, and now generals and soldiers were using it once more. For the first time too, the term *holy city* entered Zionist rhetoric. According to the ancient sacred geography of the Middle East, the whole point of a "holy city" was that nobody could own it because it belonged to the god—to Marduk, Baal, or Yahweh. The "City of David" had been ruled by Yahweh from his throne in the temple, the king merely acting as his anointed representative. Instead of becoming the personal property of the ruler, Jerusalem was "holy" (*qaddosh*) precisely because it was "set apart" for Yahweh. But once the emotions of sacred geography were fused with the Israelis' secular nationalism, in which territorial integrity was all important, politicians had no doubt that Jerusalem belonged absolutely to the Israeli state. "We have returned to our most holy places," said the avowed secularist commander Moshe Dayan; "we have returned and we shall never leave them."[62] Jerusalem had become a nonnegotiable absolute that transcended all other claims. Even though international law forbade the permanent occupation of territory conquered during a conflict, Abba Eban, Israel's delegate to the United Nations, argued that Jerusalem "lies beyond and above, before and after, all political and secular considerations."[63]

The sacred geography of Israel also had a strong moral and political dimension. While Israelis lauded Jerusalem as the city of *shalom* ("peace," "wholeness"), the Psalms had insisted that there would be no shalom in Jerusalem without justice (*tzeddek*). The king was charged by

Yahweh to "defend the poorest, save the children of those in need and crush their oppressors."[64] In Yahweh's Zion there could be no oppression and violence; rather, it must be a haven for the poor (*evionim*). But once the "holiness" of Jerusalem had been fused with the secular nation-state, its Palestinian inhabitants became a vulnerable minority and their presence a contamination. On the night of June 10, 1967, after the signing of the armistice, the 619 Palestinian inhabitants of the Maghribi Quarter beside the Wall were given three hours to evacuate their homes. Then, in contravention of international law, the bulldozers came in and reduced this historic district—one of the earliest Jerusalem awqaf—to rubble. On June 28 the Israeli Knesset formally annexed the Old City and East Jerusalem, declaring them part of the State of Israel.

Secular nationalism had exploited and distorted a religious ideal; but a religious embrace of the modern nation-state could be equally dangerous. Well before 1967, Orthodox Jews had sacralized the secular state of Israel and made it a supreme value. A somewhat despised religious version of Zionism had always existed alongside the secular nationalism of most Israelis.[65] It became slightly more prominent during the 1950s, when a group of young Orthodox, including Moshe Levinger, Shlomo Aviner, Yaakov Ariel, and Eliezer Waldman, had fallen under the spell of the aging Rabbi Zvi Yehuda Kook, who regarded the secular State of Israel as a "divine entity" and the Kingdom of God on earth. In exile it had been impossible to observe the commandments tied to the Land; now there was a yearning for wholeness. Instead of excluding the sacred from political life, Kookists, as the rabbi's followers became known, intended it to pervade the whole of existence once again—"all the time and in every area." Political engagement, therefore, had become an "ascent to the pinnacles of holiness." The Kookists transformed the Land into an idol, an earthly object that had absolute status and required the unquestioning veneration and commitment that traditionally applied only to the transcendence we call God. "Zionism is a heavenly matter," Kook insisted. "The State of Israel is a divine entity, our holy and exalted state."[66] For Kook, every clod of Israel's soil was holy; its institutions were divine; and the weapons of Israeli soldiers were as sacred as prayer shawls. But Israel, like any state, was far from ideal and guilty of both structural and martial violence. In the past, prophets had challenged the systemic injustice of the state, and priests had been critical even of its holy wars. For the Kookists, however, secular Israel was beyond criticism and essential to the world's salvation. With the establishment of Israel, Messianic redemption had already begun: "Every Jew who comes to Eretz Yisrael, every tree that is planted in the soil of Israel, every soldier added to the army of Israel constitutes another spiritual stage; literally, another stage in the process of redemption."[67]

As we have seen, ancient Israel from the very first had looked askance at state violence; now the Kookists gave it supreme sanction. Once the nation-state becomes the highest value, however, as Lord Acton had predicted, there is no limit to what it can do—literally, anything goes. By elevating the state to the divine level, Kookists had also given sacred endorsement to nationalism's shadow side: its intolerance of minorities. Unless Jews occupied the entire Land, Israel would remain tragically incomplete, so annexing Arab territory was a supreme religious duty.[68] A few days after the Six-Day War, the Labor government proposed to return some of the occupied territories—including some of the most important biblical sites on the West Bank—to the Arabs in exchange for peace and recognition. The Kookists vehemently opposed the plan and, to their surprise, found that for the first time they had secular allies. A group of Israeli poets, philosophers, and army officers, fired by the victory, had come together to prevent any such handover and offered the Kookists moral and financial support. Secular nationalists made common cause with the hitherto despised religious Zionists, realizing that they had exactly the same objectives.

Enthused by this backing, in April 1968, Moshe Levinger led a small group of families to celebrate Passover in Hebron on the West Bank. They checked into the Park Hotel and, to the embarrassment of the Labor government, refused to leave. But their chutzpah tugged at Laborite heartstrings because it recalled the audacity of the chalutzim, who in the days before the state had defied the British by squatting aggressively in Arab land.[69] Yet again, secular and religious enthusiasms merged dangerously. For the Kookists, Hebron—the burial place of Abraham, Isaac, and Jacob—was contaminated by the presence of the Palestinians, who also revered these prophets. They now refused to leave the Cave of the Patriarchs in time for Muslim communal prayer, noisily blocking the entrances and flying the Israeli flag at the shrine on Independence Day.[70] When a Palestinian finally threw a hand grenade, the Israeli government reluctantly established an enclave guarded by the IDF for the settlers outside Hebron; by 1972 Kiryat Arba had five thousand inhabitants. For

Kookists it was an outpost pushing against the frontiers of the demonic world of the "Other Side."

Yet still Labor refused to annex the territories. After the October War of 1973, when Egypt and Syria invaded Sinai and the Golan Heights and were repelled only with great difficulty, a group of Kookists, rabbis, and hawkish secularists formed Gush Emunim, the "Bloc of the Faithful." A pressure group rather than a political party, its objective was nothing less than "the full redemption of Israel and the entire world."[71] As a "holy people," Israel was not bound by UN resolutions or international law. Gush's ultimate plan was to colonize the entire West Bank and transplant hundreds of thousands of Jews into the occupied territories. To make their point, they organized hikes and rallies in the West Bank, and on Independence Day 1975 nearly twenty thousand armed Jews attended a West Bank "picnic," marching militantly from one location to another.[72]

The Gush experienced their marches, battles with the army, and illegal squats as rituals that brought them a sense of ecstasy and release.[73] The fact that they attracted so much secularist support showed that they were tapping into nationalistic passions that were felt just as strongly by Israelis who had no time at all for religion. They could also draw on the Western tradition of natural human rights that had long declared that an endangered people—and after the October War, who, they asked, could deny that Israelis *were* endangered?—were entitled to settle in "vacant" land. Their sacred task was to ensure that it was truly "empty." When the Likud party led by Menachem Begin defeated Labor in the 1977 elections and declared its commitment to Israeli settlement on both sides of the Jordan, Kookists believed that God was at work. But the honeymoon was short-lived. On November 20, 1977, President Anwar Sadat of Egypt made his historic journey to Jerusalem to initiate a peace process, and the following year Begin and Sadat, two former terrorists, signed the Camp David Accords: Israel would return the Sinai Peninsula to Egypt in exchange for Egypt's formal recognition of the State of Israel. Observing this unexpected development, many Western people concluded that secular pragmatism would prevail after all.

· · ·

The Iranian Revolution shattered that hope. Western politicians had regarded Shah Muhammad Reza Pahlavi as a progressive leader and had put their muscle behind his regime, regardless of the fact that he had no legitimacy among his own people. Iranians were in fact experiencing the structural violence of "the West and the Rest" in an acute form. Independence, democracy, human rights, and national self-determination were for "the West"; but for Iranians, violence, domination, exploitation, and tyranny were to be the order of the day. In 1953 a coup organized by the CIA and British Intelligence had unseated the secular nationalist premier Muhammad Musaddiq (who had tried to nationalize the Iranian oil industry) and reinstated the shah. This event showed Iranians how little they could command their own destiny. After 1953, like the British before them, the United States controlled the monarch and Iran's oil reserves, demanding diplomatic privileges and trade concessions. American businessmen and consultants poured into the country, and though a few Iranians benefited from the boom, most did not. In 1962 the shah began his White Revolution by closing the Majlis legislature and pushed his unpopular reforms through with the support of SAVAK, the dreaded secret police trained by the CIA and Israeli Mossad. These reforms were applauded in the West, since they established capitalism, undermined feudal landownership, and promoted literacy and women's rights, but in fact they favored the rich, concentrated on city dwellers, and ignored the peasantry.[74] There were the usual symptoms of an economy modernizing too rapidly: agriculture declined, and rural migrants poured into the cities, living in desolate shantytowns and eking out a precarious existence as porters and street vendors.[75] SAVAK made Iranians feel like prisoners in their own country, and clandestine Marxist and Islamist guerrilla groups formed in opposition to a secular government that violently suppressed all opposition.

One little-known cleric had the courage to speak out publicly against this oppressive regime. In 1963 Ayatollah Ruhollah Khomeini (1902–89), professor of ethics at the Fayziyah Madrassa in Qum, began a sustained attack on the shah, condemning his use of torture, his closing the Majlis, his spineless subservience to the United States, and his support for Israel, which denied Palestinians fundamental human rights. On one occasion he stood with the Quran in one hand and the 1906 constitution in the other, and accused the shah of betraying both.[76] On March 22, 1963, the anniversary of the martyrdom of the Sixth Imam, SAVAK attacked the madrassa, arrested Khomeini, and killed some of the students. After his release, Khomeini resumed the offensive. During the Ashura rituals, in his eulogy for Husain, he compared the shah to Caliph Yazid, the villain of the Karbala tragedy.[77] When Khomeini was arrested for a second time, thousands of Iranians poured onto the streets, laymen and mullahs protesting side by side. SAVAK was given shoot-to-kill orders, and clerics braved the guns wearing the white shroud of the martyr, demonstrating their willingness to die like Husain in the struggle against tyranny. By the time peace was finally restored, hundreds of civilians had been killed.[78]

The regime, Khomeini protested, was assaulting its own people. Always he championed the poor, the chief victims of its systemic injustice, ordering the shah to leave his palace and look at the deplorable conditions in the shantytowns. Iran, he claimed on October 27, 1964, was virtually an American colony. It was a rich country, and it was a disgrace that people were sleeping in the streets. For decades foreigners had been plundering their oil, so that it was of no benefit to the Iranian people. "I am deeply concerned about the conditions of the poor next winter, as I expect many to die, God forbid, from cold and starvation," he concluded. "The ulema should think of the poor and take action now to prevent the atrocities of last winter."[79] After this speech Khomeini was deported and went into exile in Iraq. Overnight, he had become a hero in Iran, a symbol of resolute Shii opposition to oppression. Marxist or liberal ideology could have appealed to only a few Iranians, but everybody, especially the urban poor, understood the imagery of Karbala. In the West we are accustomed to extrovert and crowd-pleasing politicians, so it was hard for us to understand Khomeini's appeal, but Iranians recognized his withdrawn demeanor, inward-seeming gaze, and monotonous delivery as the sign of a "sober" mystic who had achieved full control of the senses.[80] In exile in Najaf too, near the tomb of Imam Ali, Khomeini became closely associated with the Twelve Imams in the minds of the people, and thanks to modern communications, he would continue to direct events from afar—not unlike the Hidden Imam.

In the West, Khomeini would be widely regarded as a fanatic and his success seen as a triumph of superstition over rationality. Yet his principled opposition to systemic violence and demand for global justice was deeply in tune with contemporaneous religious developments in the West. His message was not dissimilar to that of Pope John XXIII (r. 1958–63), whose encyclical letter *Mater et Magistra* (1961) insisted that unfettered capitalism was immoral and unsustainable; instead, "all forms of economic enterprise must be governed by the principles of social justice and charity." The pope also called for global equity. National prosperity was not enough: "Man's aim must be to achieve in social justice a national and international juridical order . . . in which all economic activity can be conducted not merely for private gain but also in the interests of the common good."[81] In *Pacem in Terris* (1963), the pope insisted that human rights rather than economic profit must be the basis of international relations—a plea clearly critical of the exploitative Western policies in undeveloped countries.

At about the same time as Khomeini was inveighing against the injustice of the shah, the Catholic Church in Latin America was evolving its Liberation Theology. Priests and nuns encouraged small communities of the poor to study the Bible in order to redress the systemic violence of Brazilian society. In 1968 Latin American bishops met in Medellín, Colombia, to support the emerging themes of this new movement, which argued that Jesus was on the side of the poor and oppressed and that Christians must struggle for justice and equality. In Latin America, as in Iran, this kind of theology was deeply threatening to the political and economic elites. Liberation priests were dubbed "communists" and, like Iranian clerics, were imprisoned, tortured, and executed because they made it clear that the economic order imposed on the "Third World" by the colonial West was inherently violent:

> For centuries, Latin America has been a region of violence. We are talking of the violence that a privileged minority has been using, since the colonial period, to exploit the vast majority of the people. We are talking of the violence of hunger, of helplessness, of underdevelopment . . . of illegal but existing slavery, of social, intellectual, and economic discrimination.[82]

They insisted that because the world was now so economically interdependent, a North American individual was able to live a comfortable life only because other people, living perhaps in a Brazilian slum, were impoverished; they could purchase goods cheaply because others had been exploited in their production.[83]

In the United States too, religion acquired a revolutionary edge and for the first time in the twentieth century opposed the policies of the American government. While presidents John F. Kennedy and Lyndon B. Johnson were careful to keep religion out of politics, liberal Catholics, Protestants, and Jews campaigned in the name of their faith against the structural and military violence of the United States. Like Iranian Shii Muslims, they took to the streets to protest the Vietnam War and joined Martin Luther King's civil rights movement against racial discrimination at home. In 1962 the National Council of Churches asked Kennedy to commit the nation to "an all-out effort to abolish [poverty], both at home and abroad."[84]

Khomeini, often thought in the West to be a rabble-rouser, was not advocating violence. The crowds who protested on the streets were unarmed, and their deaths laid bare the ruthless ferocity of the shah's secular regime. The assassination of Martin Luther King, who had insisted that a nonviolent response to injury was "an absolute necessity for our survival . . . the key to the solution of the problems of our world,"[85] also revealed the latent violence of American society. King would have agreed with Khomeini's demand for global justice. He had lamented Kennedy's disastrous colonial misadventure in the Bay of Pigs (1961), and even though Johnson had given African Americans more than any previous president, he refused to support his war in Vietnam. But in the late 1970s, when the Iranian revolution broke out, the mood in the West had changed. In 1978 the conservative bishop of Cracow Karol Wojtyla, a fierce opponent of Liberation Theology, was elected to the papacy, taking the name of John Paul II. The fundamentalist Moral Majority had surged to the forefront of American religious life, and the Democratic president Jimmy Carter, a "born-again" Christian who campaigned vigorously for human rights, was a loyal supporter of the shah's dictatorship.

* * *

Viewed from the West, Iran seemed to be booming during the 1970s, but the state had become rich at the expense of the nation; a million people were unemployed, local merchants had been ruined by the influx of foreign goods, and there was widespread resentment of the flourishing American expatriates.[86] After Khomeini's departure, the shah had become even more autocratic and started to secularize more aggressively, confiscating the awqaf and bringing the madrassas under strict bureaucratic control.[87] When Ayatollah Riza Saidi denounced the regime, he was tortured to death, and thousands of demonstrators poured onto the streets of Qum.[88] The charismatic lay philosopher Ali Shariati (1933–77), who had studied at the Sorbonne, kept the revolutionary flame alive among the young Westernized Iranians.[89] He told them that if they tried to conform too closely to the Western ideal and abandoned the Shiah, they would lose themselves; the example of Ali and Husain compelled Muslims to stand up and say no to injustice, coercion, and tyranny. Shariati too was tortured, imprisoned, and died in exile, almost certainly the victim of SAVAK agents. In Najaf in 1971, Khomeini published *Islamic Government*, arguing that the ulema should rule the state. His doctrine of *velayat-e faqih* ("the government of a [Muslim] jurist") seemed to fly in the face of Western modernity and was shocking to most Shiis, since for centuries the clergy had refused official posts—in the absence of the Hidden Imam, they regarded any government as corrupt. But Khomeini's thought was clearly in line with those Third World intellectuals who defied global structural violence. Islam, he would always claim, was "the religion of militant individuals who are committed to faith and justice. It is the religion of those who desire freedom and independence. It is the school of those who struggle against imperialism."[90]

Even though nobody at this date, Khomeini included, believed that it was possible to topple the shah, events were moving faster than he had anticipated. In November 1977, his son Mustafa was assassinated in Iraq, again almost certainly by SAVAK agents,[91] and the shah forbade mourning ceremonies to be held. This only identified Khomeini even more closely with the Shii Imams, since like Husain, his son had been murdered by an unjust ruler, casting the shah yet again as Yazid. And at this critical juncture, U.S. president Jimmy Carter cast himself as the "Great Satan." In November 1977, while Iran was mourning Mustafa Khomeini, the shah visited Washington, and Carter spoke with great emotion of the United States' "special relationship" with Iran, "an island of stability in a turbulent corner of the world."[92] He thus entered the unfolding Karbala drama as the *shaytan*, the "tempter," who lured the shah to follow the United States to the detriment of his own people.

The revolution began on January 8, 1978, when the semiofficial newspaper *Ettelaat* published a preposterous attack on Khomeini.[93] The next day four thousand unarmed students in Qum demanded a revival of the 1906 constitution, freedom of speech, the release of political prisoners, and the return of Khomeini. Throughout, Iranians showed that they had fully absorbed the modern ethos, demanding the independence, liberty, and constitutional rule that they had been consistently denied by the shah's secular government and the international community. Seventy of these students were killed. With this massacre, the regime crossed a line. A pattern now emerged. Forty days after the Qum massacre, crowds gathered for the traditional mourning ceremonies for the dead, and more people were shot down. Forty days later there were more ritualized rallies in honor of the new martyrs. Marxists, secularists, and liberals who opposed the shah but knew that they had no grassroots appeal joined forces with the religiously minded revolutionaries. This was not a violent uprising, however. Cinemas, banks, and liquor stores—symbols of the "great shaytan"—were attacked, but not people.[94] By now the jails were full of political prisoners, and the mounting death toll showed the world that the shah's secular regime, lauded in the West as progressive and peaceful, was slaughtering its own people.

The revolution was experienced as a religious as well as a political event. Demonstrators carried placards reading "Everywhere is Karbala, and every day is Ashura," convinced that they were following Husain in their struggle against oppression.[95] They spoke of the revolution as a transforming and purifying experience, as if they were purging themselves of a debilitating poison and regaining authenticity.[96] Many felt as though Husain himself were leading them and that Khomeini, like the Hidden Imam, was directing them from afar.[97] On the last night of Ramadan, September 4, vast crowds prostrated themselves in prayer in the streets, but—an important turning point—this time the army did not open fire. Even more significant, the middle classes began to join in the protests, marching with placards reading: "Independence, Freedom and Islamic Government!"[98] At six a.m. on September 8, martial law was declared, but the twenty thousand demonstrators who were already gathering in Jaleh Square did not know it; when they refused to disperse, the soldiers opened fire. As many as nine hundred people may have died that day.[99]

That evening Carter called the shah from Camp David to assure him of his support, and the White House, while regretting the loss of life, reaffirmed its special relationship with Iran. The liberty and independence for which the American revolutionaries had fought were clearly not for everybody. On the first three nights of Muharram, men donned the white shroud of the martyr and ran through the streets defying the curfew, while others shouted anti-shah slogans from the rooftops. The BBC estimated that seven hundred people had been killed by the Iranian army and police in these few days alone.[100] Yet still there was no mob violence. On December 9, for six hours a vast procession—at different times numbering between 300,000 and 1.5 million people—wound through the streets of Tehran, walking quietly four abreast. Two million more marched on the day of Ashura itself, carrying green, red, and black flags, representing Islam, martyrdom, and the Shiah.[101]

A month later it was all over. The shah and the royal family flew to Egypt, and on February 1, 1979, Khomeini returned to Tehran. His arrival was one of those events, like the storming of the Bastille, that seemed to change the world forever. For committed liberal secularists, it was a dark moment, the triumph of the forces of unreason over rationality. But for many Muslims, Sunni as well as Shii, it seemed a luminous reversal. As he drove through the streets of Tehran, the crowds greeted him as if he were the returned Hidden Imam, confident that a new age had dawned. Taha Hejazi published a poem of celebration, a tremulous hope for the justice that the shah and the international community had denied them:

> When the Imam returns,
> Iran—this broken, wounded mother—
> Will be forever liberated
> From the shackles of tyranny and ignorance
> And the chains of plunder, torture and prison.[102]

Khomeini liked to quote the hadith in which the Prophet announced after a battle that he was returning from the lesser to the "greater jihad," the implementation of truly Islamic values in society, a struggle far more exacting than the "lesser" military one. As he looked at the ecstatic crowds that day, he must surely have felt apprehension at the more onerous jihad about to begin.

◆ ◆ ◆

It was indeed a struggle: almost at once, perhaps predictably, the fragile coalition of Marxists, liberals, and the devout seemed to unravel. There was opposition to the new constitution, in 1980 four separate plots against the regime were uncovered, and there were constant street battles between secularist guerrillas and Khomeini's Revolutionary Guards. A reign of terror ensued, not unlike those that followed the French and Russian Revolutions, when so-called revolutionary councils, which the government could not control, executed hundreds of people for "un-Islamic behavior." As a crowning blow, on September 20, 1980, the southwest of the country was invaded by Saddam Hussein's Iraqi forces. During this turbulent period, the American hostage crisis proved a godsend to Khomeini. On November 4, 1979, three thousand Iranian students had stormed the U.S. embassy in Tehran and taken ninety prisoners. It is not clear whether Khomeini knew of their plan beforehand, and everyone expected him to release the hostages immediately. But although the women hostages and the embassy's Marine guards were allowed to return to America, the remaining fifty-two diplomats were held for 444 days. In the West, this disreputable affair seemed to epitomize Islamic radicalism.

Yet Khomeini's decision to retain the hostages was inspired not by an Islamic imperative but simply by politics. He could see that this focus on the Great Satan would unite Iranians behind him at his difficult juncture. As he explained to his prime minister Bani Sadr:

> This action has many benefits. The Americans do not want to see the Islamic Republic taking root. We keep the hostages, finish our internal work, and then release them. This has united our people. Our opponents do not dare act against us. We can put the constitution to the people's vote without difficulty, and carry out presidential and parliamentary elections. When we have finished all these jobs, we can let the hostages go.[103]

As soon as they were no longer useful, the hostages were released on January 20, 1981, the inauguration day of the new U.S. president Ronald Reagan and the departure of his "satanic" predecessor Jimmy Carter. Inevitably the hostage crisis tainted the image and idealism of the Islamic Revolution. Many Iranians were unhappy about it, even while appreciating its symbolism. A nation's embassy is regarded as its sovereign territory on foreign soil, and some thought it apt that American citizens should be held there, just as for decades Iranians had felt imprisoned in their own country with the connivance of the United States. But this was simply revenge politics, and the cruel treatment meted out to the hostages violated cardinal principles of all faith traditions, not least those of Islam. Whatever the regime gained by stopping the clock while it achieved a degree of stability, it would pay for over many years in the ledger of the privileged free world.

The great genius of the Shiah was its tragic perception that it is impossible fully to implement the ideals of religion in the inescapably violent realm of politics. Ashoka had discovered this even earlier than the Shii Imams when he promoted his compassionate dharma but could not disband his army. At best, people of faith can either bear witness to these values, as Khomeini did when he castigated the injustice of the Pahlavi regime in the 1960s, or provide an alternative that either challenges or seeks to mitigate state violence. But as we have seen throughout this story, even the most humanitarian traditions are unable to implement their ideals if they identify with a state ideology that inevitably depends upon force. Khomeini believed that the revolution had been a rebellion against the rational pragmatism of the modern world. The goal of his theory of velayat-e faqih was to institutionalize Shii values: the supreme jurist (*faqih*) and the ulema on the Council of Guardians would have the power to veto any legislation that violated the principles of Islamic justice.[104] But in practice, Khomeini would often have to reprove the guardians for playing selfish power games, just as he himself had felt compelled to pursue a cynical realpolitik during the hostage crisis.

We have seen that revolutions can take a long time, and like the French Revolution, the Iranian Revolution has passed through many stages and is still in progress. As in France, Iranians feared that powerful external enemies would destroy the Islamic regime. In the summer of 1983 the Iraqis attacked Iranian troops with mustard gas and then with nerve gas the following year.[105] Khomeini was convinced that America would organize a coup similar to the one that had deposed Musaddiq in 1953. Because Iran had antagonized the West, she had forfeited essential equipment, spare parts, and technical advice; inflation was high, and by 1982 unemployment had risen to 30 percent of the general population and 50 percent in the cities.[106] The poor, whose plight Khomeini had championed, were not doing much better under the revolution. Yet Western observers had to acknowledge that, despite the growing opposition of Westernized Iranians, Khomeini never lost the love of the masses, especially the *bazaaris,* the madrassa students, the less-eminent ulema, and the poor.[107] These people, whom the shah's modernization program had overlooked, still thought and spoke in a traditionally religious, premodern way that many Westerners could not even comprehend.

After the Iranian Revolution, one exasperated U.S. official was heard to exclaim: "Whoever took religion seriously?"[108] Since the Enlightenment, revolutions were understood to occur at a time when the *saeculum* had reached maturity and was strong enough to declare its independence of faith.[109] The idea of a popular uprising ushering in a religiously oriented state was almost embarrassing in its upending of accepted wisdom; many Westerners deplored it as atavistic and perverse. But they seemed unable to see that by pursuing their own political and economic agendas that did violence to the Iranian people, Western governments had bred a new species of religion. They had been blind to the particular problems of the postcolonial state and the pitfalls of a modernization imposed from without rather than effected organically from within.[110] And in deploring the new theocracy, they failed to appreciate a central irony. The Western ideals of liberty had fired the Iranian imagination and inspired Iranians to demand basic freedoms, but the Western secular ideal had been irredeemably tainted for Iranians by the self-interest and cruelty with which it had been pursued. The United States declared that it had a God-given mission to spread liberty throughout the world, but this had evidently not included the people of Iran. "We did not expect Carter to defend the shah, for he is a religious man who has raised the slogan of defending human rights," an ayatollah explained to an interviewer after the revolution. "How can Carter, the devout Christian, defend the shah?"[111] Such perplexity reveals how strange a premodern sensibility must find the idea of religion as a private matter.

The Iranian Revolution had dramatically changed the status quo in the Persian Gulf. The shah had been one of the key pillars of U.S. policy in the region, permitting the West to access its vast oil reserves at a viable price. In December 1979, the Soviet Union sought to capitalize on America's loss of influence in the region by invading Iran's neighbor Afghanistan. This Cold War struggle between the superpowers helped to inspire a global jihad that would eventually target the United States and its allies. But it would be some time before the West recognized this danger, because during the 1980s and 1990s, it was more concerned with terrorist atrocities and violence in the Middle East and the Indian subcontinent that seemed wholly inspired by "religion."

12

Holy Terror

On November 18, 1978, nine hundred and thirteen American citizens died of self-administered cyanide poisoning in the agricultural colony of Jonestown, Guyana.[1] It was to date the largest loss of civilian life in a single incident in U.S. history. The deceased men, women, and children were members of the People's Temple founded during the 1950s in Indianapolis, Indiana, by the charismatic preacher James Warren Jones (1938–78). Its commitment to racial and social equality had attracted chiefly poor, working-class white Americans and African Americans. Members lived a strictly communal life based on what Jones called the "apostolic socialism" of the Acts of the Apostles. In 1965, after having a vision of a nuclear bomb destroying Chicago, Jones had persuaded his followers to move with him and his family to safety in California. The Temple opened facilities in San Francisco and Los Angeles and gained a reputation for being politically progressive, offering legal services, child care, housing, and drug and alcohol rehabilitation. Membership increased to about one thousand, and in 1976, to escape the systemic violence and injustice that it believed to be inherent in the United States, the Temple moved to Guyana.

Jonestown is often cited by those who claim that religion has been responsible for more death and suffering than any other human activity. Yet even though Jones was an ordained Methodist pastor who often quoted the gospels and used religion in recruitment, he was a self-confessed atheist and communist who often ridiculed conventional Christianity. Stories about the Temple's violence had begun to circulate in 1972: defectors spoke of beatings, verbal abuse, and emotional cruelty. Members were viciously castigated for making racist or sexist remarks, complaining about the communal living arrangements, or wasting food. Culprits were subjected to brutal physical punishment and other humiliations in public, and the community was kept in a state of constant terror. Jones filled their minds with graphic descriptions of CIA torture methods, Nazi concentration camps, and Ku Klux Klan lynchings. In 1972, while still in California, he announced that the U.S. government was

> gonna put people in this country in concentration camps. They're gonna put them in gas ovens, just like they did the Jews. . . . They're gonna put you in the concentration camps that're already in Tule Lake, California, Allentown, Pennsylvania, near Birmingham, outside El Reno, Oklahoma. They've got them all ready. . . . They still have the concentration camps, they did it to the Japanese, and they'll do it to us.[2]

"I tell you, we're in danger from a corporate dictatorship," Jones insisted, "a great fascist state, a great communist state."[3]

The ultimate terror began in 1978, when members started to rehearse their mass suicide. On "white nights" they would be roused suddenly from sleep and informed that they were about to be killed by U.S. agents; suicide was said to be the only viable option. They were then given a drink that they believed to be poisoned and waited to die. On November 18, 1978, the community had been visited by U.S. congressman Leo Ryan, who had come to investigate reports of human rights abuses. After Ryan left, Jones dispatched Temple members to shoot him at the airstrip and then summoned the entire community to the Jonestown pavilion. There medical staff administered potassium cyanide in a batch of the soft drink Flavor-Aid, which parents fed to their children before taking it themselves. Most seem to have died willingly, though the two hundred children were certainly murdered and about a hundred of the elderly may have been injected involuntarily.

They recorded their last messages on audiotape. Jones had taken the concept of "revolutionary suicide" from Black Panther leader Huey Newton.[4] "I made the decision to commit revolutionary suicide. My decision has been well thought out," said one Jonestown resident. "And in my death, I hope that it would be used as an instrument to further liberation." "It's been my pleasure walking with all of you in this revolutionary struggle," one woman stated. "No other way I would rather go [than] to give my life for socialism, communism." People who were convinced that they had no voice in their own society had come to believe that they could be heard only in the shocking spectacle of their dying. Jones was the last to take the poison: "We said—one thousand people who said, we don't like the way the world is. We didn't commit suicide. We committed an act of revolutionary suicide, protesting the conditions of an inhumane world."[5]

The community dynamics of Jonestown were, of course, complex and imponderable. Although religion was clearly not the cause of this tragedy, it has much in common with instances of "revolutionary suicide" that have been articulated in religious terms. The Temple was a protest against the structural violence of American society; it had developed a highly developed history of grievance and suffering that, its members claimed, mainstream society chose to ignore. Jonestown was an assault as well as a protest: Temple members were laying their deaths at the door of the United States, a demonstration that its systemic injustice had made their lives so intolerable that death was preferable. Jones clearly believed, however psychotically, that he was engaged in an asymmetrical struggle with a superpower that held all the cards. All these elements would also surface in the wave of religiously inspired terrorism that broke out in the 1980s.

One of the many reasons the drama of Jonestown is so disturbing is the germ of nihilism it reveals in modern culture. The Temple was clearly haunted by two of the dark icons of modernity: the concentration camp and the mushroom cloud. Sigmund Freud (1856–1939) had found that human beings were as strongly motivated by a death wish as by a desire for procreation. The French existentialist Jean-Paul Sartre (1905–80) spoke of a God-shaped hole in human consciousness, a void at the heart of modern culture. By the mid-twentieth century, that psychic void had been filled with a terrible reality. Between 1914 and 1945, seventy million people in Europe and the Soviet Union had died violent deaths.[6] Some of the worst atrocities had been perpetrated by Germans who lived in one of the most cultivated societies in Europe. The Holocaust shook the

Enlightenment optimism that education would eliminate barbarism, since it showed that a concentration camp could exist in the same vicinity as a great university. The sheer scale of the Nazi genocide reveals its debt to modernity; no previous society could have implemented such a grandiose scheme of extermination. The Nazis used many of the tools and achievements of the industrial age—the factory, the railways, and the advanced chemical industry—to deadly effect, relying on modern scientific and rational planning in which everything is subordinated to a single, limited, and defined objective.[7] Born of modern scientific racism, the Holocaust was the ultimate step in social engineering and the most extreme demonstration of the inability of the nation to tolerate minorities. It showed what can happen once the sense of the sacredness of every single human being—a conviction at the heart of traditional religions that quasi-religious systems seem unable or disinclined to re-create—is lost.

On August 6, 1945, a 3,600-kilogram atomic bomb was dropped on Hiroshima, killing approximately 140,000 people instantaneously. Three days later a plutonium-type bomb was dropped on Nagasaki, killing some 24,000 people.[8] For centuries people had dreamed of a final apocalypse wrought by God; now, with weapons of mass destruction, it appeared that human beings no longer needed God to achieve apocalyptic effects. The nation had become a supreme value, and the international community acknowledged the legitimacy of a nuclear strike to protect it, despite the prospect of total annihilation that such means suggested. There could be no more potent evidence of the death wish Freud had described. But it also, perhaps, suggests a flaw in the purely secular ideal that eliminates "holiness" from its politics—the conviction that some things or people must be "set apart" from our personal interests. The cultivation of that transcendence—be it God, Dao, Brahman, or Nirvana—had, at its best, helped people to appreciate human finitude. But if the nation becomes the absolute value (in religious terms, an "idol"), there is no reason why we should not liquidate those who appear to threaten it.

This death wish was, however, not only present in the godless violence of secular nationalism but is also evident in the religiously articulated violence of the late twentieth century. Westerners were quite rightly horrified by the Iranian child-martyrs who died on the battlefields of the Iraq-Iran War. As soon as war was declared, adolescents from the slums and shantytowns had crowded into the mosques, begging to be sent to the front. Radicalized by the excitement of the revolution, they hoped to escape the tedium of their grim lives. And so, as in traditional societies of times past, the potential for ecstasy and intensity through warfare beckoned. The government issued an edict allowing male children as young as twelve to enlist at the front without their parents' permission. They became wards of the imam and were promised a place in paradise. Tens of thousands of adolescents poured into the war zone, wearing the martyrs' insignia of crimson headbands. Some, trying to clear minefields, ran ahead of the troops and were blown to pieces. Others attacked as suicide bombers, deploying a tactic that has been used in various contexts of asymmetrical warfare since the eleventh century. Scribes were sent to the front to write the martyrs' wills, many of which took the form of letters to the Imam and spoke of their joy in fighting "alongside friends on the road to Paradise."[9] The child-martyrs restored Khomeini's faith in the revolution; like Imam Husain, he claimed, they were dying to witness to the primacy of the Unseen. But they had also been exploited to serve the interests of the nation.

Religiously articulated militarism has not been restricted to cultures with a premodern religious outlook, though. In the secularized West it has surfaced in response to the terrors of modernity, particularly those of modern industrialized warfare. During the early 1980s, disaffected American Protestant groups fearing a Soviet nuclear attack during a particularly tense period of the Cold War established fortified strongholds in remote areas of the Northwest. These survivalists, who trained militarily and stockpiled ammunition and other supplies, felt threatened not only by the godless Soviet bloc but by the U.S. government as well. Loosely affiliated as Christian Identity, these groups had very little in common with orthodox Christian churches.[10] Claiming direct descent from the Twelve Tribes of Israel (through a preposterous ethnography known as "British Israelism"), they espoused a brand of white supremacy that saw the federal government and its toxic pluralism as a mortal threat. It is difficult to estimate its numbers, because Identity was and remains merely a network of organizations, but it probably had no more than 100,000 members.[11] And not all shared the same concerns: some were strictly secular survivalists who were simply fleeing the threat of nuclear catastrophe.[12] Yet there is a religious patina to some of these extremist groups, who use the language of faith to express fears, anxieties, and enthusiasms that are widespread, though not openly expressed, in the mainstream.

The reach of the message can be dramatic. Christian Identity's brand of ideology would inspire Timothy McVeigh's bombing of the Alfred P. Murrah Federal Building in Oklahoma City on April 19, 1995. McVeigh was a self-professed agnostic, however. Like several Identity leaders, he had served in the U.S. Army and had a pathological attraction to violence. During the 1991 Gulf War he had helped massacre a group of trapped Iraqi soldiers and taken photographs of their corpses for his personal collection. He was not officially a member of Christian Identity but read its newsletter, had telephone conversations with its officers, and had visited its compound on the Oklahoma-Arkansas border.[13]

How, then, can we try to understand terrorism as a particular species of violence?

Like religion, "terrorism" is notoriously difficult to define. There are so many competing and contradictory formulations that, according to one scholar, the word is now "shrouded in terminological confusion."[14] Part of the problem is that it is such an emotive word, one of the most powerful terms of abuse in the English language, and the most censorious way of characterizing any violent act.[15] As such, it is never used of anything we do ourselves, except perhaps in some abjectly penitential confession. Connoting more than it denotes, the word stubbornly refuses to reveal much, especially when both sides in a conflict hurl the same charge at each other with equal passion. Its effect is to accuse an opponent much more than to clarify the nature of the underlying conflict.[16]

One attempt at definition describes the phenomenon as "the deliberate use of violence, or threat of its use, against innocent people, with the aim of intimidating them specifically or others into a course of action they would not otherwise take." Yet this could also be said of some forms of conventional warfare.[17] Indeed, there is a general scholarly agreement that some of the largest-scale acts of terrorizing violence against civilians have been carried out by states rather than by independent groups or individuals.[18] In the national wars of the twentieth century, hundreds of thousands of civilians were firebombed, napalmed, or vaporized. During the Second World War, Allied scientists carefully calculated the mix of explosives and wind patterns to create devastating firestorms in densely populated residential areas in German and Japanese cities precisely to create terror in the population.[19]

There is, however, at least one point on which everybody is in agreement: terrorism is fundamentally and inherently political, even when other motives—religious, economic, or social—are involved.[20] Terrorism is *always* about "power—acquiring it or keeping it."[21] And so, according to one of the pioneering experts in the field, "all terrorist organizations, whether their long-term political aim is revolution, national self-determination, preservation or restoration of the status quo, or reform, are engaged in a struggle for political power with a government they wish to influence and replace."[22] The claim that the primary motivation of a terrorist action is political may seem obvious—but not to those who seem determined to regard such atrocious acts of violence as merely "senseless." Many of that view, not surprisingly, find religion, which they regard as a byword for irrationality, to be the ultimate cause. One of the most prominent is Richard Dawkins, who has argued that "only religious faith is a strong enough force to motivate such utter madness in otherwise sane and decent people."[23] This dangerous oversimplification springs from a misunderstanding of both religion and terrorism. It is, of course, a familiar enough expression of the secularist bias of modernity, which has cast "religion" as a violent, unreasonable force that must be excluded from the politics of civilized nations.[24] Somehow it fails to consider that all the world's great religious traditions share as one of their most essential tenets the imperative of treating others as one would wish to be treated oneself. This, of course, is not to deny that religion has often been implicated in terrorist atrocities, but it is far too easy to make it a scapegoat rather than trying to see what is really going on in the world.

◆ ◆ ◆

The first act of Islamic terrorism to grab the world's attention was the murder of President Anwar Sadat, winner of the Nobel Peace Prize, hero of the Camp David Accords, and widely regarded in the West as a progressive Muslim leader. Western peoples were aghast at the ferocity of the attack. On October 6, 1981, during a parade celebrating Egypt's victories in the October War of 1973, First Lieutenant Khaled Islambouli jumped out of his truck, ran toward the presidential stand, and opened fire with a machine gun, shooting round after round into Sadat and killing seven people besides the president and injuring twenty-eight others. His political motivation was clearly regime change, but revolutionary fervor was fused with Islamic sentiment. At his trial Islambouli gave three reasons for murdering Sadat: the suffering of Egyptian Muslims under his tyrannical rule; the Camp David Accords; and Sadat's imprisonment of Islamists a month earlier.

A bevy of Western princes, politicians, and celebrities attended Sadat's funeral, but no Arab leaders were present, and the streets of Cairo were eerily silent—a very different scene from the tumultuous lamentations at Nasser's funeral. Western politicians had admired Sadat's peace initiative, but many people in Egypt regarded it as opportunistic and self-serving, especially since, three years after Camp David, the plight of the Palestinians had not improved. Sadat had also won Western approval by switching to the "right" side of the Cold War, dismissing the fifteen hundred Soviet advisers installed by Nasser in 1972 and announcing an "Open Door" policy designed to bring Egypt into the capitalist free market.[25] But, as in Iran, while a few entrepreneurs flourished, local businessmen were ruined when foreign imports flooded the markets. Only 4 percent of the young could find a decent job, and housing was so expensive that couples often had to wait years before they could marry. No longer able to afford living in their own country, thousands of Egyptians went to work in Saudi Arabia or the Gulf states, sending money home to their families.[26] The social dislocation of the abrupt Westernization of Sadat's Egypt was also disturbing. As one observer tried to explain, it was impossible for an Egyptian peasant to maintain his dignity as "a culture bearer in his own culture" when, after a day's toiling in the hot sun, he had to stand in line for a frozen American chicken and spend the evening in front of the television set purchased with money sent by his son from Saudi Arabia, watching the antics of J. R. Ewing and Sue Ellen on *Dallas*.[27]

The devout element of Egyptian society felt especially betrayed by Sadat. At first, anxious to create an identity for his regime that was distinct from Nasser's, he had courted them, releasing the Muslim Brothers from prison, encouraging Muslim student associations to wrest the campuses away from the socialists and Nasserites, and styling himself the Pious President. There was much mosque building and plenty of airtime devoted to religion. But there was nothing Islamic about Open Door. This was blatant structural violence, which revealed the hollowness of Sadat's devout stance, since he had created conditions of inequity explicitly condemned by the Quran. The president discovered that his economic and political assault on the Egyptian people had inadvertently spawned political Islamist movements that were dangerously hostile to his regime.

One of these was the Society of Muslims, founded in 1971 by Shukri Mustafa, a member of the Muslim Brotherhood, after his release from prison.[28] He would be one of the most misguided "free lances" that stepped into the vacuum created by the ulema's marginalization. By 1976 the Society had about two thousand members, men and women convinced that they were divinely commissioned to build a pure ummah on the ruins of Sadat's jahiliyyah. Taking Qutb's program in *Milestones* to the limit, Shukri declared not only the government but the entire Egyptian population to be apostate, and he and his followers withdrew from the mainstream, living in caves in the desert outside Cairo or in the city's most deprived neighborhoods. Their experiment ended in violence and lethal immorality when members killed defectors from the group and Shukri murdered a respected judge who had condemned the Society. Yet deeply misguided as it was, Shukri's society held up a mirror image that revealed the darker side Sadat's regime. Shukri's excommunication of Egypt was extreme, but in Quranic terms, Sadat's systemic violence was indeed jahili. The hijrah to the most desperate quarters of Cairo reflected the plight of many young Egyptians who felt there was no place for them in their country; the society's communes were supported by young men who, like so many others, were sent to work in the Gulf States. The Society condemned all secular learning as a waste of time, and there was a grain of truth in this since a lady's maid in a foreign household could earn more than a junior lecturer.

Far more constructive than the Society of Muslims, however, were the *jamaat al-islamiyyah,* the student organizations that dominated the university campuses during Sadat's presidency, which tried to help themselves in a society that ignored the needs of the young. By 1973 they had organized summer camps at nearly all the major universities, where students could immerse themselves in an Islamic milieu, studying the Quran, keeping night vigils, listening to sermons about the Prophet, and attending classes in sport and self-defense—creating an Islamic alternative to the inadequacies of the secular state.[29] On the lamentably ill-equipped campuses, they segregated the sexes during lectures, where several students often had to share a single seat, in order to protect women from harassment and arranged study hours in the mosque, which was quieter than the overcrowded halls of residence. Those who came from rural backgrounds and were experiencing life in a modern city for the first time were now able to make their way to modernity in a familiar Islamic setting.

Student protests became more aggressive as Sadat drew closer to the West and became more autocratic. In 1978 he issued the Law of Shame: any deviation in thought, word, or deed from the establishment was to be punished with loss of civil rights and confiscation of passports and property. Citizens were forbidden to join any group, take part in any broadcast, or publish anything that would threaten "national unity or social peace." Even a casual remark, made in the privacy of one's own home, would not go unpunished.[30] In response to government oppression, at the University of Mina students started vandalizing Christian churches—associated with Western imperialism—and attacking those who wore Western dress. Sadat closed down the jamaat, but suppression nearly always makes such movements more extreme, and some students joined a clandestine movement dedicated to armed jihad. Khaled Islambouli had studied at the University of Mina and joined one of these cells. Shortly before his assassination, Sadat had rounded up over fifteen hundred opposition figures in September 1981, including cabinet ministers, politicians, intellectuals, journalists, and ulema as well as Islamists; one of the latter was Khaled's brother Muhammad.[31]

The ideology of Sadat's murderers had been shaped by Abd al-Salam Faraj, spiritual guide of the Jihad Network, who was executed with Khaled in 1982. His treatise, *The Neglected Duty,* had been circulated privately among members of the organization and was published after the assassination. This plodding, graceless, and ill-informed document also shows how misguided the secularizing reformers had been to deprive the people of adequate religious guidance. Faraj was another freelancer: he had graduated in electrical engineering and had no expertise in Islamic law. But it seems that by the 1980s, the maverick ideas that he was expressing had spread, unchecked by the sidelined ulema, until they were widely accepted in society. The "neglected duty" of the title was aggressive jihad. Muslims, Faraj argued, had been convinced by feeble-minded apologists that fighting was permissible only in self-defense. Hence Muslims were living in subjection and humiliation and could recover their dignity only by resorting to arms. Sadat was no better than an infidel because he ruled by the "laws of unbelief" imposed on the ummah by the colonialists.[32] Despite their apparent orthodoxy, Sadat and his government were a pack of apostates who deserved to die. Faraj cited Ibn Taymiyyah's fatwa against the Mongol rulers, who, just like Sadat, had been Muslims only in name. In the time of al-Shafii, Muslims had feared only an external attack; now infidels were actually ruling the ummah. In order to create a truly Islamic state, therefore, jihad was *fard ayn,* the duty of every able-bodied Muslim.

Faraj reveals the "idolatry" that is every bit as present in some forms of political Islamism as in secularist discourse, for he made the ummah a supreme value. "It is obligatory for every Muslim to seriously strive for the return of the Caliphate," Faraj argued; anyone who fails to do so "does not die as a Muslim."[33] In the past Islam had been a religion validated by its success. Until the modern period, the powerful position of the ummah had seemed to confirm the Quran's teaching: that a rightly guided community would prosper because it was in tune with the way things ought to be. The ummah's sudden demotion has been as theologically shattering for some Muslims as Darwin's evolutionary theory has been for some Christians. The sense of shame and humiliation has been acute and is exacerbated by a sense of past greatness. Much of modern Islamism represents a desperate struggle to put history back on track. But this dream of a gloriously restored ummah has become an absolute, an end in itself, and as such justifies the means of an aggressive jihad—in this case, a criminal assassination. In Islamic terms, this constitutes the prime sin of *shirk,* an idolatry that places a political ideal on the same level as Allah. As one commentator observed, far from condoning lawless violence, the ideal of jihad originally expressed the important insight that "the final truth for man lies not in some remote and untarnished utopia but in the tension and struggle of applying its ideals to the recalcitrant and obstructive stuff of worldly sorrow."[34]

Faraj's primitive theology is apparent when he explains why it was more important to fight Sadat than the Israelis: if a truly Islamic state were established in Egypt, he believed, Jerusalem would automatically revert to Muslim rule. In the Quran, God promised Muslims that he would bring disgrace on their enemies and come to the Muslims' aid. In a nihilistic abandonment not only of his modern scientific training but also of the Quranic insistence that Muslims use their natural intelligence, Faraj reverted to a particularly naive form of the perennial philosophy that amounted to little more than magical thinking: if Muslims took the initiative, God would "intervene [and change] the laws of nature." Could the militants expect a miracle? Faraj answered yes. Observers were puzzled that there was no planned uprising after the assassination. Faraj believed that God would step in and do the rest.[35] He did not. Hosni Mubarak became president with a minimum of fuss, and his secular dictatorship remained in power for thirty years.

◆　◆　◆

Terrorism has often cropped up in the Muslim world when the nation's boundaries do not accord with those set up by the colonial powers for the state.[36] Lebanon had been put together particularly ineptly by the colonialists. It had also inherited a pattern of economic disparity and had its own unique and tragic problems. Its Shii population inhabited the infertile country between Tyre and Sidon, which until 1920 had been part of Greater Syria and so had no historic ties with the Sunni Muslims and Maronite Christians of the north; and they had not participated in the modernization process, whereby a prosperous bourgeoisie had made Beirut the intellectual capital of the Middle East. Southern Lebanon remained undeveloped, because the constitution made each confessional community responsible for its own welfare and social institutions. Shii poverty meant that most of their three hundred villages had neither hospitals nor irrigation, and because Shii tended to be uneducated, they were inadequately represented in the national government. During the 1950s, unable to make a living on the land, thousands migrated to Beirut, where they lived in the shantytowns of Maslakh and Karantina, known locally as the "misery belt." They never assimilated and were regarded with disdain by the more sophisticated population.

In 1959, however, Musa al-Sadr, a brilliant, cosmopolitan Iranian cleric, arrived from Najaf, where a circle of ulema had created a revisionist form of Shiism. Using Shii ideas to help the people reflect on their political and social position, Sadr began to transform this backward community into one of the leading factions in Lebanon. Part of the problem, Sadr believed, was that the traditional quietism of the Shiah had contributed to Shii marginalization. The Sixth Imam had adopted this policy of sacred secularism in order to protect Shiis from Abbasid violence. But the conditions of the modern world required Shiis to go back to the spirit of Imam Husain and take their destiny into their own hands. In Husain they should find a model of courage and political choice.[37] Sadr criticized the ulema and feudal landlords for failing to provide their community with adequate guidance. Together with Ayatollah Muhammad Fadl Allah, another member of the Najaf circle, he provided the community with badly needed social services and began to build a culture of Shii self-reliance and resistance to the systemic injustice of Lebanon.[38]

All the elements of the structural violence that typically contributes to the development of an Islamist movement were therefore present in Lebanon. A gulf separated a Westernized, privileged elite from the unmodernized masses; urbanization had been too rapid; there was an inequitable social system, and also physical and social dislocation. The situation of Lebanon was further complicated by the intractable Arab-Israeli conflict. After the Cairo Agreement of 1969, the Palestinian Liberation Organization (PLO) was allowed to establish bases in southern Lebanon from which to attack Israel, and once the PLO had been expelled from Jordan in 1970, Lebanon became its main base. In southern Lebanon, therefore, the Shii suffered heavy casualties in Israel's retaliatory bombardment. The demography of the country had also changed. The Shii birthrate had increased dramatically, with the population rising from 100,000 in 1921 to 750,000 in 1975. Because the Sunni and Maronite birthrates had declined, by the mid-1970s the Shii formed 30 percent of the population and had become the largest confessional community in Lebanon.[39] When both Sunni and Shii Muslims requested a restructuring of political institutions to reflect this change, a catastrophic civil war broke out (1975–78). Lebanon became a dangerously violent place, where fighting was no longer a choice but essential to personal survival.

Shii Islam became militant as a result of ubiquitous warfare and the systemic oppression of Lebanese society. Sadr had already established training camps to teach Shii youth self-defense and after the outbreak of the civil war founded AMAL ("Battalions for Lebanese Resistance"), which brought the poorer classes together with the "new men"—Shii businessmen and professionals who had managed to climb the economic ladder. They fought Maronite supremacy alongside the Druze, a small, esoteric Shii sect. The Shii probably suffered more than any other group during the civil war. Their shantytowns were destroyed by the Christian militias, thousands were left homeless, and thousands more had to flee the south of the country during the ongoing struggle between Israel and the PLO. When Israel invaded Lebanon in 1978 to oust the PLO, Shii homes were destroyed, and hundreds of thousands were forced to seek refuge in Beirut.

At this crucial moment, Musa al-Sadr made a visit to Libya and disappeared, perhaps murdered by Qaddafi, thus becoming the Lebanese "Hidden Imam." This loss split AMAL: some followed the secularist, American-educated Nabih Berri, who advocated peaceful action, but the more literate "new men" followed Fadl Allah, a scholar whose views would come to be very controversial in the community of learned authorities. His *Islam and the Use of Force* (1976), written in a society torn apart by violent conflict, had argued that Muslims must be ready to fight and, if necessary, die like Husain in the struggle for justice and equity. Martyrdom was not just a pious deed but a revolutionary political act, a refusal to submit to oppression and cruelty. Rightly used, force enabled a person to take charge of his life and was the only way to survive with dignity in a violent world:

> Force means that the world gives you resources and wealth; conversely in conditions of weakness, a man's life degenerates, his energies are wasted, he becomes subject to something that resembles suffocation and paralysis. History, the history of war and peace, of science and wealth, is the history of the strong.[40]

Muslims should not shy away from economic success and modern technology but use them to resist injustice and marginalization. They would not be aping the West, because instead of making the nation-state an instrument of the market economy, Shii would build a humane state based on the values of community and self-respect. The ends were Islamic, but the means were new.

In 1979, inspired by the Iranian Revolution and with funding and training from Tehran, Fadl Allah founded Hizbollah, the "Party of God." Western people were puzzled that the revolution had failed to spread to Shii communities closer to Iran in the Gulf and Saudi Arabia but had taken root immediately in faraway Lebanon.[41] In fact, Iran and Lebanon had a long relationship. In the sixteenth century, when the Safavids had founded their Shii Empire in Iran, then a largely Sunni country, they had asked the Shii scholars of Lebanon to instruct and guide them; so it was natural for Lebanese Shii to join the Iranian revolutionary network. Hizbollah first came to the world's attention during the Israeli invasion (1982) and the subsequent U.S. military intervention (1983–84), when on October 25, 1983, Hizbollah suicide bombers killed 241 American and

58 French peacekeeping troops in their military compound near Beirut airport; this martyrdom operation was followed by further attacks on the U.S. embassy and the U.S. barracks.

To explain its violent actions, Hizbollah communiqúes cited the United States' opposition to Khomeini and its support for Saddam Hussein, Israel, and the Christian Maronites. Fadl Allah spoke of the "arrogant silence" of Western powers in the face of Third World suffering.[42] These operations were not simply inspired by religious zeal but had a clear political objective: to compel foreign occupiers to leave Lebanon. This was "revolutionary suicide." As to methods, Fadl Allah pointed out that the Shii were engaged in an asymmetrical struggle:

> The oppressed nations do not have the technology and destructive weapons that America and Europe have. They must fight with special means of their own. . . . We . . . do not regard what oppressed Muslims of the world do with primitive and unconventional means to confront aggressive powers as terrorism. We view this as lawful warfare against the world's imperial powers.[43]

These were not random, bigoted, and irrational acts but "legal obligations governed by rules" that Muslims must not transgress.[44] One of these rules forbade the deliberate targeting of civilians, which is prohibited under Islamic law—though Hizbollah did take American, British, French, and German civilians as hostages to secure the release of Shii prisoners held elsewhere. In the West the suicide attack immediately recalled the Assassins, who symbolized the fanaticism that Westerners had long attributed to Islam. But while Hizbollah had indeed pioneered this controversial method in the Middle East, most suicide bombing in Lebanon during the 1980s would be carried out by secularists. According to one survey, Hizbollah was responsible for seven suicide operations; the secular Syrian Nationalist Party for twenty-two, and the socialist Baath party for ten.[45]

By 1986, however, the resistance leaders had decided that Hizbollah must change direction, since its operations were too often irresponsible and counterproductive; it was suffering heavy casualties and dividing the Shii community. There was tension between Hizbollah and AMAL, and the villages resisted Hizbollah's attempts to impose Islamic rules.[46] By this time Fadl Allah had concluded that violence, after all, did not bring results: What had the PLO achieved with the terrorism that had shocked the world? Lebanese Shii must take a new path, he argued, working "from within the objective and actual circumstances" in which they found themselves.[47] Fadl Allah knew that it was impossible to establish an Islamic state in Lebanon and in 1989 even suggested that it was time for the Iranians to begin "the normalization of relations with the rest of the world," since like any political movement, revolutions go through many stages and change with a changing world:

> Like all revolutions, including the French Revolution, the Islamic Revolution didn't have a realistic line at first. At that time it served to create a state, it proclaimed a mobilization, a new religious way of thinking and living, with the aim of winning Muslim autonomy and independence from the superpowers.[48]

Hizbollah, therefore, renounced terrorism and became a political party answerable to the electorate, focusing on social activism and a grassroots transformation.

It had already begun to disentangle itself from the melee of Shii militias by developing an underground cell structure and devised a spiritual process designed to replace what Khomeini had called the "colonized brain" with one that could think outside the parameters imposed by the West. All Hizbollah leaders still attend philosophy classes to develop their capacity to think critically and independently. As the American civil rights activists did, they work with small groups in the villages to discover how each individual can best contribute to the community: they may set someone up in business or train him for an elite militia. Their goal, reminiscent of the Confucian ideal, is to develop a Shii community in which everybody receives and gives a measure of respect and feels valued and needed. Since the 2006 war with Israel, Hizbollah has concentrated especially on anger management: "We want to turn this anger from a destructive course into something politically useful—building resistance, perhaps—or into some socially constructive activity."[49]

During that war, Hizbollah modeled an alternative solution to the problem of asymmetrical warfare.[50] In preparation for such a contingency, it had constructed deep underground tunnels and bunkers, some forty feet below the surface, where its militias could sit out Israeli air strikes, before emerging to mount a prolonged rocket and missile attack.

Hizbollah knew that these could not seriously damage the powerful Israeli war machine, but the long duration and unremitting nature of these missile barrages did affect Israeli morale. Hizbollah's goal was to force Israel to launch a ground invasion, whereupon the well-trained Hizbollah guerrilla forces, with intimate knowledge of the terrain, could effectively assault Israel's armored tanks with their shoulder-launched missiles. They had also achieved such a mastery of intelligence and public relations that many Israeli journalists frankly admitted that they preferred Hizbollah's dispatches to the IDF's. Their victory in compelling the Israelis to withdraw demonstrated that terrorism need not be the only way to repel a militarily superior enemy.

• • •

As an inspiration for terrorism, however, nationalism has been far more productive than religion. Terrorism experts agree that the denial of a people's right to national self-determination and the occupation of its homeland by foreign forces has historically been the most powerful recruiting agent of terrorist organizations, whether their ideology is religious (the Lebanese Shii) or secular (the PLO).[51] In Israel, however, we have seen a different dynamic of secular nationalism pushing a religious tradition into a more militant direction: its tendency to make the nation-state a supreme value so that its preservation and integrity permit any form of action, however extreme. In May 1980, after the murder of six yeshiva students in Hebron, Gush settlers Menachem Livni and Yehuda Etzion planted bombs in the cars of five Arab mayors, intending not to kill but to mutilate them so that they became living reminders of the consequences of any opposition to Israel.[52] But this operation was only a sideline. In April 1984 the Israeli government revealed the existence of a Jewish underground movement that had plotted to blow up the Dome of the Rock in order to bring the Camp David talks to an end.

In order to curb Jewish aggression that could endanger the nation's survival, the Talmudic rabbis had insisted that the Temple could be rebuilt only by the Messiah, and over the centuries this had acquired the force of a taboo. But Jewish extremists were intensely disturbed by the Dome of the Rock, the third-holiest place in the Muslim world, which was said to stand on the site of Solomon's temple. This magnificent shrine, which dominates the skyline of East Jerusalem and is so perfectly attuned to the natural environment, was a permanent reminder of the centuries of Islamic domination of the Holy Land. For the Gush, this symbol of the Muslim minority had become demonic. Livni and Etzion described it as an "abomination" and the "root cause of all the spiritual errors of our generation." For Yeshua ben Shoshan, the underground's spiritual adviser, the Dome was the haunt of the evil forces that inspired the Camp David negotiations.[53] All three were convinced that, according to Kabbalistic perennial philosophy, their actions here on earth would activate events in heaven, forcing God, as it were, to effect the Messianic redemption.[54] As an explosives expert in the IDF, Livni manufactured twenty-eight precision bombs that would have destroyed the Dome but not its surroundings.[55] Their only reason for not going ahead was that they could not find a rabbi to bless their operation. The plot was another demonstration of the modern death wish. The destruction of the iconic Dome would almost certainly have caused a war in which, for the first time, the entire Muslim world would have united to fight Israel. Strategists in Washington believed that during the Cold War, when the Soviets supported the Arabs and the United States Israel, this might even have sparked a Third World War.[56] So crucial was the survival and territorial integrity of the State of Israel to the militants that it justified risking the destruction of the human race.

Yet far from being inspired by their religious tradition, the militants' conviction violated core teachings of Rabbinic Judaism. The rabbis had repeatedly insisted that violence toward other human beings was tantamount to a denial of God, who had made men and women in his image; murder, therefore, was a sacrilege. God had created *adam,* a single man, to teach us that whoever destroyed a single human life would be punished as though he had destroyed the whole world.[57]

The Dome as a perceived symbol of Jewish humiliation, subjugation, and obliteration fed dangerously into the Jewish history of grievance and suffering, a phenomenon that, as we have seen, can fester dangerously and inspire a violent riposte. Jews had fought back and achieved a superpower status in the Middle East that would once have seemed inconceivable. For the Gush, the peace process seemed to threaten this hard-won status, and like the monks who obliterated the iconic pagan temples after Julian's attempt to suppress Christianity, they instinctively responded, "Never again." Hence Jewish radicals, with or without rabbinic approval, continue to flirt with Livni's dangerous idea, convinced that their political designs have some basis in eternal truth. The Temple

Mount Faithful have drawn up plans for the Jewish temple that will one day replace the Dome, which they display in a museum provocatively close to the Haram al-Sharif with the ritual utensils and ceremonial robes that they have prepared for the cult. For many, Jewish Jerusalem rising phoenixlike from the ashes of Auschwitz has acquired a symbolic value that is nonnegotiable.

The history of Jerusalem shows that a holy place always becomes more precious to a people after they have lost it or feel that their tenure is endangered. Livni's plot therefore helped to make the Haram al-Sharif even more sacred to the Palestinians. When Islam was a great world power, Muslims had the confidence to be inclusive in their devotion to this sacred space. Calling Jerusalem al-Quds ("the Holy"), they understood that a holy place belongs to God and can never be the exclusive preserve of a state. When Umar conquered the city, he left the Christian shrines intact and invited Jews to return to the city from which they had been excluded for centuries. But now, as they feel that they are losing their city, Palestinian Muslims have become more possessive. Hence the tension between Muslims and Jews frequently erupts into violence at this holy place: in 2000 the provocative visit of the hawkish Israeli politician Ariel Sharon with his right-wing entourage sparked the Palestinian uprising known as the Second Intifada.

Rabbi Meir Kahane also plotted to destroy what he called "the gentiles' abomination on the Temple Mount." Most Israelis were horrified when he was elected to a seat in the 1984 Knesset with 1.2 percent of the vote.[58] For Kahane, to attack any gentile who posed the slightest threat to the Jewish nation was a sacred duty. In New York he had founded the Jewish Defense League to avenge attacks on Jews by black youths, but when he arrived in Israel and settled in Kiryat Arba, he changed its name to Kach ("Thus it is!"), its goal to force the Palestinians to leave the Land. Kahane's ideology symbolizes the "miniaturization" of identity that is one of the catalysts of violence.[59] His "fundamentalism" was so extreme that it reduced Judaism to a single precept. "There are not several messages in Judaism," he insisted. "There is only one": God simply wanted Jews to "come to this country to create a Jewish state." Israel was commanded to be a "holy" nation, set apart from all others, so "God wants us to live in a country on our own, isolated, so that we have the least possible contact with what is foreign."[60] In the Bible the cult of holiness had prompted the priestly writers to honor the essential "otherness" of every single human being; it had urged Jews to love the foreigner who lived in their land, using their memories of past suffering not to justify persecution but to sympathize with the distress that these uprooted people were enduring. Kahane, however, embodied an extreme version of the secular nationalism whose inability to tolerate minorities had caused such suffering to his own people. In his view, "holiness" meant the isolation of Jews, who must be "set apart" in their own Land and the Palestinians expelled.

Some Jews argue that the Holocaust "summons us all to preserve democracy, to fight racism, and to defend human rights," but many Israelis have concluded that the world's failure to save the Jewish people requires the existence of a militarily strong Israel, and they are, therefore, reluctant to engage in peace negotiations.[61] Kahane, however, went much further. Messianic redemption, he argued, had begun after the Six-Day War. Had Israel annexed the territories, expelled the Arabs, and torn down the Dome, redemption would have come painlessly. But because the Israeli government wanted to appease the international community and refrained from this violence, redemption would come in a terrible anti-Semitic calamity, far worse than the Holocaust, that would force all Jews to leave the diaspora.[62] The Holocaust overshadowed Kahane's ideology. The State of Israel, he believed, was not a blessing for Jews but God's revenge on the gentiles: "He could no longer take the desecration of his Name and the laughter, the disgrace, and the persecution of the people that were named after Him." Every attack on a Jew, therefore, amounted to blasphemy, and every act of Jewish retaliation was *Kiddush ha-Shem*, a sanctification of God's name: "a Jewish fist in the face of the astonished gentile world that has not seen it for two millenniums [*sic*]."[63] This was the ideology that inspired Kiryat Arba settler Baruch Goldstein to shoot twenty-nine Palestinian worshippers in the Cave of the Patriarchs in Hebron on the festival of Purim, February 25, 1994. The massacre was revenge for the murder of fifty-nine Jews in Hebron on August 24, 1929. Goldstein died in the attack and is revered by the Israeli far right as a martyr. His action would inspire the first wave of Muslim suicide bombing in Israel and Palestine.

◆   ◆   ◆

A collective memory of humiliation and imperial domination has also inspired a desire for a national character of strength in India.[64] When they look back in history, Hindus are divided. Some see a paradise of coexistence and a culture in which Hindu and Muslim traditions combine. But Hindu nationalists see the period of Muslim rule as a clash of civilizations, in which a militant Islam forced its culture on the oppressed Hindu majority.[65] The structural violence of empire is always resented by subject peoples and can persist long after the imperialists have left. Founded in the early 1980s, the Bharatiya Janata Party (BJP), the "Indian National Party," an affiliate of RSS (Hedgewar's nationalist religious party), feeds on this bitterness and enhances it. It campaigned for a militarily strong India, a nuclear arsenal (whose warheads are named after Hindu gods), and national distinctiveness. At first, however, it made no headway in the polls, but its fortunes changed dramatically in 1989, when the issue of the Babri mosque once again hit the headlines.[66] In India as in Israel, sacred geography has become emblematic of the nation's disgrace. Here too, the spectacle of a Muslim shrine atop a ruined temple aroused huge passions, because it so graphically symbolized the Hindu collective memory of Islamic imperial dominance. In February 1989 activists resolved to build a new temple to Ram on the site of the mosque and collected donations from the poorer castes throughout India; in the smallest villages bricks for the new shrine were cast and consecrated. Not surprisingly, tensions flared between Muslims and Hindus in the north, and Rajiv Gandhi, who had tried to mediate, lost the election.

The BJP, however, had made large gains at the polls, and the following year its president, L. K. Advani, began a *rath yatra* ("chariot pilgrimage"), a thirty-day journey from the west coast to Ayodhya, that was to culminate in the rebuilding of the Rama temple. His Toyota van was decorated to resemble Arjuna's chariot in the last battle of the *Mahabharata* and was cheered by fervent crowds lining the route.[67] The pilgrimage began, significantly, at Somnath, where, legend has it, Sultan Mahmud of the Central Asian kingdom of Ghazni had slaughtered thousands of Hindus way back in the eleventh century, razing Shiva's ancient temple to the ground and plundering its treasure. Advani never made it to Ayodhya, because he was arrested on October 23, 1990, but thousands of Hindu nationalists from every region of India had already assembled at the site to begin the mosque's demolition. Scores of them were shot down by the police and hailed as martyrs, and Hindu-Muslim riots exploded throughout the country. The Babri mosque was finally dismantled in December 1992, while the press and army stood by and watched. For Muslims, its brutal destruction evoked the horrifying specter of Islam's annihilation in the subcontinent. There were more riots, the most notorious being a Muslim attack on a train conveying Hindu pilgrims to Ayodhya, which was avenged by a massacre of Muslims in Gujarat.

Like the Islamists, Hindu nationalists are lured by the prospect of rebuilding a glorious civilization, one that will revive the splendors of India before the Muslims' arrival. They have convinced themselves that their path to this utopian future is blocked by the relics of Moghul civilization, which have wounded the body of Mother India. Countless Hindus experienced the demolition of the Babri mosque as a liberation from "slavery"; but others argue that the process is far from complete and dream of erasing the great mosques at Mathura and Varanasi.[68] Many other Hindus, however, were religiously appalled by the Ayodhya tragedy, so this iconoclasm cannot be traced to a violence inherent in "Hinduism," which has, of course, no single essence, either for or against violence. Rather, Hindu mythology and devotion had blended with the passions of secular nationalism—especially its inability to countenance minorities.

All this meant that the new Ram temple had become a symbol of a liberated India. The emotions involved were memorably expressed in a speech by the revered renouncer Rithambra at Hyderabad in April 1991, which she delivered in the mesmerizing rhymed couplets of Indian epic poetry. The temple would not be a mere building; nor was Ayodhya important simply because it was Ram's birthplace: "The Ram temple is our honor. It is our self-esteem. It is the image of Hindu unity . . . We shall build the temple!" Ram was "the representation of mass-consciousness"; he was the god of the lowest castes—the fishermen, cobblers, and washermen.[69] Hindus were in mourning for the dignity, self-esteem, and Hindutva, the Hindu identity, that they had lost. But this new Hindu identity could be reconstructed only by the destruction of the antithetical "other." The Muslim was the obverse of the tolerant, benign Hindu: fanatically intolerant, a destroyer of shrines, and an arch-tyrant. Throughout, Rithambra laced her speech with vivid images of mutilated corpses, amputated arms, chests cut open like those of dissected frogs, and bodies slashed, burned, raped, and violated, all evoking Mother India, desecrated and ravaged by Islam. The 800 million Hindus of India can hardly claim to be economically or socially oppressed, so Hindu nationalists feed on such images of persecution and insist that a strong Hindu identity can be restored only by decisive, violent action.

◆ ◆ ◆

Until the 1980s, the Palestinians had held aloof from the religious revival in the rest of the Middle East. Yasser Arafat's PLO was a secular national-ist organization. Most Palestinians admired him, but the PLO's secular-ism appealed mainly to the Westernized Palestinian elite, and observant Muslims played virtually no part in its terrorist actions.[70] When the PLO was supressed in the Gaza Strip in 1971, Sheikh Ahmed Yassin founded Mujama ("Congress"), an offshoot of the Muslim Brotherhood, which focused on social welfare work. By 1987 Mujama had established clinics, drug rehabilitation centers, youth clubs, sporting facilities, and Quran classes throughout Gaza, supported not only by Muslim alms (*zakat*) but also by the Israeli government in an attempt to undermine the PLO. At this point Yassin had no interest in armed struggle. When the PLO accused him of being Israel's puppet, he replied that, on the contrary, it was their secular ethos that was destroying Palestinian identity. Mujama was far more popular than Islamic Jihad (IJ), formed during the 1980s, which attempted to apply Qutb's ideas to the Palestinian tragedy and regarded itself as the vanguard of a larger global struggle "against the forces of arrogance [*jahiliyyah*], the colonial enemy, all over the world."[71] IJ engaged in terrorist attacks against the Israeli military but rarely quoted the Quran; its rhetoric was frankly secular. Ironically, the only thing that was religious about this organization was its name—and this may explain its lack of mass support.[72]

The outbreak of the First Intifada (1987–93), led by young secular-ist Palestinians, changed everything. Impatient with the corruption and ineffectiveness of Fatah, the leading PLO party, they urged the entire population to rise up and refuse to submit to the Israeli occupation. Women and children threw stones at Israeli soldiers, and those shot by the IDF were hailed as martyrs. The intifada made a strong impres-sion on the international community: Israel had long presented itself as plucky David fighting the Arab Goliath, but now the world watched heavily armored Israeli soldiers pursuing unarmed children. As a mili-tary man, Yitzhak Rabin realized that harassing women and children would ruin IDF morale, and when he became prime minister in 1992, he was prepared to negotiate with Arafat. The following year Israel and the PLO signed the Oslo Accords. The PLO recognized Israel's existence within its 1948 borders and promised to end the insurrection; in return,

Palestinians were offered limited autonomy in the West Bank and Gaza for a five-year period, after which final status negotiations would begin on the issue of Israeli settlements, compensation for Palestinian refugees, and the future of Jerusalem.

The Kookists, of course, regarded this as a criminal act. In July 1995 fifteen Gush rabbis ordered soldiers to defy their commanding officers when the IDF began to evacuate the territories—an act that was tantamount to civil war. Other Gush rabbis ruled that Rabin was a *rodef* ("pursuer"), worthy of death under Jewish law for endangering Jewish life. On November 4, 1995, Yigal Amir, an army veteran and student at Bar Ilan University, took this ruling to heart, shooting the prime minister during a peace rally in Tel Aviv.[73]

The success of the Intifada made younger Mujama members aware that its welfare program was not truly addressing the Palestinian problem, so they broke away to form Hamas, an acronym of Haqamat al-Muqamah al-Islamiyya ("Islamic Resistance Movement"), meaning "Fervor." They would fight both the PLO and the Israeli occupation. Young men flocked to join up, finding the egalitarian ethos of the Quran more congenial than the secularism of the Palestinian elite. Many recruits came from the lower-middle-class intelligentsia, educated now in Palestinian universities, which was no longer prepared to kowtow to the traditional authorities.[74] Sheikh Yassin lent his support, and some of his closest associates staffed Hamas's political wing. Instead of drawing on Western ideology, Hamas found inspiration in the history of secular Palestinian resistance as well as Islamic history; religion and politics were inseparable and intertwined.[75] In its communiqúes Hamas celebrated the Prophet's victory over the Jewish tribes at the Battle of Khaybar,[76] Saladin's victory over the Crusaders, and the spiritual status of Jerusalem in Islam.[77] The Charter of Hamas evoked the venerable tradition of "volunteering" when it urged Palestinians to become *murabitun* ("guardians of the frontiers"),[78] defending the Palestinian struggle as a classical defensive jihad: "When our enemies usurp some lands, jihad becomes a duty on all Muslims [*fard ayn*]."[79]

In the early days, though, fighting was a secondary concern; the charter quoted none of the Quranic jihad verses.[80] The first priority was the Greater Jihad, the struggle to become a better Muslim. Palestinians, Hamas believed, had been weakened by the inauthentic adoption of Western secularism under the PLO, when, the Charter explained, "Islam disappeared from life. Thus, rules were broken, concepts were vilified, values changed . . . homelands were invaded, people were subdued."[81] Hamas did not resort to violence until 1993, the year of the Oslo Accords, when seventeen Palestinians were killed on the Haram al-Sharif, and Hamas activists retaliated in a series of operations against Israeli military targets and Palestinian collaborators. After Oslo, support for the militant Islamist groups dropped to 13 percent of the Palestinian population, but it rose to a third when Palestinians found that they were subjected to harsh and exceptional regulations and that Israel would retain indefinite sovereignty over Gaza and the West Bank.[82]

The Hebron massacre was a watershed. After the forty-day mourning period, a Hamas suicide bomber killed seven Israeli citizens in Afula in Israel proper, and this was followed by four operations in Jerusalem and Tel Aviv, the most deadly of which was a bus bombing in Tel Aviv on October 19, 1994, which killed twenty-three people and injured nearly fifty. The murder of innocent civilians and the exploitation of adolescents for these actions was morally repugnant, damaged the Palestinian cause abroad, and split the movement. Some Hamas leaders argued that by losing the moral high ground, Hamas had strengthened the Israeli position.[83] Others retorted that Hamas was merely responding in kind to Israel's aggression against Palestinian civilians, which indeed had increased after the outbreak of the Second Intifada, when there were more bombings, missile attacks, and assassinations of Palestinian leaders. Ulema abroad were equally divided. Sheikh Tantawi, grand mufti of Egypt, defended suicide bombing as the only way for Palestinians to counter the military might of Israel, and Sheikh al-Qaradawi in Yemen argued that it was legitimate self-defense.[84] But Sheikh al-Sheikh, grand mufti of Saudi Arabia, protested that the Quran strictly forbade suicide and that Islamic law prohibited the killing of civilians. In 2005 Hamas abandoned the suicide attack and focused instead on creating a conventional military apparatus in Gaza.

Some Western analysts have argued that suicide killing is deeply embedded in the Islamic tradition.[85] But if that were so, why was "revolutionary suicide" unknown in Sunni Islam before the late twentieth century? Why have not more militant Islamist movements adopted this tactic? And why have both Hamas and Hizbollah abandoned it?[86] It is certainly true that Hamas drew upon the Quran and ahadith to motivate the bombers with fantasies of paradise. But the suicide attack was in fact invented by the Tamil Tigers of Sri Lanka, a nationalist separatist group with no time for religion, who have claimed responsibility for over 260 suicide operations in two decades.[87] Robert Pape of the University of Chicago has investigated every suicide attack worldwide between 1980 and 2004 and concluded that "there is little connection between suicide terrorism and Islamic fundamentalism, or any religion for that matter." For instance, of 38 suicide attacks in Lebanon during the 1980s, 8 were committed by Muslims, 3 by Christians, and 27 by secularists and socialists.[88] What all suicide operations do have in common, however, is a strategic goal: "to compel liberal democracies to withdraw military forces from territory that the terrorists consider to be their homeland." Suicide bombing is therefore essentially a political response to military occupation.[89] IDF statistics show that of all Hamas's suicide attacks, only 4 percent targeted civilians in Israel proper, the rest being directed against West Bank settlers and the Israeli army.[90]

This is not to deny that Hamas is as much a religious as a national movement, only that the fusion of the two is a modern innovation. The exalted love of the fatherland, which has no roots in Islamic culture, is now suffused with Muslim fervor.[91] Islamic and nationalist themes alternate seamlessly in the final videotaped messages of Hamas martyrs. Twenty-year-old Abu Surah, for example, began with a traditional Muslim invocation: "It is the day of meeting the Lord of the Worlds and bearing witness to the Messenger." He then called upon "all the saints and all the mujahidin of Palestine and of every part of the world," moving unselfconsciously from holy men to Palestinian nationalists before finally shifting to a global perspective. Martyrs shed their blood "for the sake of Allah and out of love for this homeland and for the sake and honor of this people in order that Palestine remain Islamic, and Hamas remain a torch lighting the road of all the perplexed and all the tormented and oppressed and that Palestine be liberated."[92]

Like the Iranians, Palestinians regard their jihad against Israeli occupation as part of a Third World struggle against imperialism. Moreover, they may have fought the secular Palestinian Authority, but both share the same nationalist passions: both regard death for Palestine as a great privilege and hate the enemy with the virulence of any ultranationalist when his country is at war.[93]

Highly stylized videos notwithstanding, one can never know what goes through the mind of suicide bombers at the moment when they drive trucks into a building or detonate bombs in a crowded marketplace. To imagine they do this entirely for God or that they are impelled solely by Islamic teaching is to ignore the natural complexity of all human motivation. Forensic psychiatrists who have interviewed survivors found that the desire to become a hero and achieve posthumous immortality was also a strong factor. Other would-be martyrs cited the ekstasis of battle that gives life meaning and purpose, a feeling that is close to religious exaltation, as we have seen. In fact, it is said, the Hamas rank-and-file lived not for "politics, nor ideology, nor religion . . . but rather an ecstatic camaraderie in the face of death 'on the path of Allah.' "[94] Life under occupation held little attraction for many of the volunteers; their bleak life in Gaza's refugee camps made the possibility of a blissful hereafter and a glorious reputation here on earth powerfully alluring. But then all communities throughout history have praised the warrior who gives his life for his people. Palestinians also honor those who are killed involuntarily in the conflict with Israel; they too are *shahid,* because as the ahadith made clear, any untimely death was a "witness" to both human finitude and the nation's plight.[95]

It further complicates the question of faith and terrorism that the suicide killer has been revered as a hero in other religious traditions as well. In the story of Samson, the judge who died pulling the Temple of Dagon down upon the Philistine chieftains, the biblical author does not agonize over his motives but simply celebrates his courage.[96] Samson "heroically hath finished a life heroic," the devout Puritan John Milton likewise concluded in *Samson Agonistes:*[97]

> Nothing is here for tears, nothing to wail
> Or knock the breast; no weakness, no contempt,
> Dispraise or blame; nothing but well and fair,
> And what may quiet us in a death so noble.[98]

Far from inspiring horror, Samson's end left those who witnessed it with a sense of "peace and consolation . . . and calm of mind, all passion spent."[99] Not coincidentally, Israel calls its nuclear capacity "the Samson Option," regarding a strike that would inevitably result in the destruction of the nation to be an honorable duty and a possibility that the Jewish state has freely chosen.[100] The anthropologist Talal Asad has suggested that the suicide bomber is simply acting out this same appalling scenario on a smaller scale and can therefore "be seen to belong to the modern Western tradition of armed conflict for the defense of the free political community. To save the tradition (or to found its state) in confronting a dangerous enemy, it may be necessary to act without being bound by ordinary moral constraints."[101]

We are absolutely right to condemn the suicide bomber's targeting of innocent civilians and mourn his victims. But as we have seen, in war the state also targets such victims; during the twentieth century, the rate of civilian deaths rose sharply and now stands at 90 percent.[102] In the West we solemnize the deaths of our regular troops carefully and recurrently honor the memory of the soldier who dies for his country. Yet the civilian deaths we cause are rarely mentioned, and there has been no sustained outcry in the West against them. Suicide bombing shocks us to the core; but should it be more shocking than the deaths of thousands of children in their homelands every year because of land mines? Or collateral damage in a drone strike? "Dropping cluster bombs from the air is not only less repugnant: it is somehow deemed, by Western people at least, to be morally superior," says British psychologist Jacqueline Rose. "Why dying with your victim should be seen as a greater sin than saving yourself is unclear."[103] The colonial West had created a two-tier hierarchy that privileged itself at the expense of "the Rest." The Enlightenment had preached the equality of all human beings, yet Western policy in the developing world had often adopted a double standard so that we failed to treat others as we would wish to be treated. Our focus on the nation seems to have made it hard for us to cultivate the global outlook that we need in our increasingly interrelated world. We must deplore any action that spills innocent blood or sows terror for its own sake. But we must also acknowledge and sincerely mourn the blood that we have shed in the pursuit of our national interests. Otherwise we can hardly defend ourselves against the accusation of maintaining an "arrogant silence" in the face of others' pain and of creating a world order in which some people's lives are deemed more valuable than others.

13

Global Jihad

I n the early 1980s a steady stream of young men from the Arab world
made their way to northwestern Pakistan, near the Afghan border,
to join the jihad against the Soviet Union. The charismatic Jordanian-
Palestinian scholar Abdullah Azzam had summoned Muslims to fight
alongside their Afghan brothers.[1] Like the "fighting scholars" who flocked
to the frontiers during the classical period, Azzam was convinced that
repelling the Soviet occupation was a duty for every able-bodied Muslim.
"I believe that the Muslim ummah is responsible for the honor of every
Muslim woman that is being violated in Afghanistan and is responsible
for every drop of Muslim blood that is being shed unjustly," he declared.[2]
Azzam's sermons and lectures electrified a generation distressed by the
suffering of their fellow Muslims, frustrated by an inability to help, and
youthfully eager to do something about it. By 1984 recruits were arriving in ever-larger numbers from Saudi Arabia, the Gulf States, Yemen,
Egypt, Algeria, Sudan, Indonesia, the Philippines, Malaysia, and Iraq.[3]
One of these volunteers was the scion of a great family fortune, Osama
bin Laden, who became the main sponsor for the Services Bureau established in Peshawar to support his comrades, organize recruitment and
funding, and provide health care, food, and shelter for Afghan orphans
and refugees.

President Ronald Reagan also spoke of the Afghan campaign as a
holy war. In 1983, addressing the National Association of Evangelicals,

he branded the Soviet Union an "evil empire." "There is sin and evil in the world," he told his highly receptive audience, "and we're enjoined by Scripture and the Lord Jesus to oppose it with all our might."[4] It seemed entirely proper to Reagan and CIA director William Casey, a devout Catholic, to support Muslim mujahidin against atheistic Communists. The massive aid package of $600 million (annually renewed and matched each year by Saudi Arabia and the Gulf States) transformed the Afghan guerrilla forces into a military juggernaut that battled with the Russians as fiercely as their ancestors had fought the British in the nineteenth century. Some of the Afghan fighters had studied in Egypt and been influenced by Qutb and Maududi, but most were from rural societies, and their Sufi devotion to saints and shrines was wholly untouched by any hint of modern Islamic thought.

The Americans also gave the "Arab-Afghans" (as the foreign volunteers were called) every possible encouragement. Supported by funds from Arab entrepreneurs like Bin Laden, they were armed by the Americans and trained by Pakistani troops.[5] In training camps around Peshawar, they fought alongside the Afghan guerrillas, but their contribution should not be exaggerated. Few actually took part in the fighting; many would engage solely in humanitarian work, never to leave Peshawar, and some would stay only a few weeks. There were rarely more than three thousand Arab fighters in the region at any one time. Some merely spent part of their summer vacation on "jihad tours," which included a trip over the Khyber Pass, where they could be photographed on location. Known as "The Brigade of the Strangers," the Arab-Afghans tended to keep to themselves; the Pakistanis and Afghans regarded them as somewhat bizarre.

Leading Muslim ulema looked somewhat askance at Azzam, but his integrity was very appealing to the young Arab-Afghans, who were disillusioned by the corruption and hypocrisy of their leaders at home. They knew that Azzam had always practiced what he preached, thoughout his life combining scholarship with political activism. He had joined the Muslim Brotherhood at the age of eighteen while studying Shariah in Syria, had fought in the Six-Day War, and as a student at the Azhar had supervised Brotherhood Youth. While he was a lecturer at Abd al-Aziz University in Jeddah, Saudi Arabia, one of his pupils was the young Bin Laden. "The life of the Muslim ummah," Azzam declared, "is solely dependent on the ink of its scholars and the blood of its martyrs."[6] Scholarship was essential to deepen the ummah's spirituality, but so was the self-sacrifice of its warriors, since no nation had ever achieved distinction without a strong military. "History does not write its lines, except in blood," Azzam insisted. "Honor and respect cannot be established except on a foundation of cripples and corpses."

> Empires, distinguished peoples, states, and societies cannot be established except with examples. Indeed, those who think that they can change reality or change societies without blood, sacrifices and invalids—without pure innocent souls—do not understand the essence of this *din* [Islam] and they do not know the method of the best of Messengers.[7]

Other Muslim leaders had praised the glory of martyrdom, but none had dwelled so graphically on its violent reality. A community that cannot defend itself, Azzam insisted, will inevitably be dominated by military power. His goal was to create a cadre of scholar-warriors, whose sacrifice would inspire the rest of the ummah.[8] Jihad, he believed, was the Sixth Pillar, on a par with the shehadah, prayer, almsgiving, the Ramadan fast, and hajj. A Muslim who neglected jihad would have to answer to God on the Day of Judgment.[9]

Azzam did not make up this theory out of whole cloth. He followed al-Shafii, the eighth-century scholar who had ruled that when the Dar al-Islam was invaded by a foreign power, jihad could become fard ayn, the responsibility of every fit Muslim who lived near the frontier. Modern transport now made it possible for *all* Muslims to reach the border of Afghanistan, so jihad, Azzam reasoned, was "compulsory upon each and every Muslim on earth." Once they had liberated Afghanistan, the Arab-Afghans should go on to recover all the other lands wrested from the ummah by non-Muslims—Palestine, Lebanon, Bokhara, Chad, Eritrea, Somalia, the Philippines, Burma, South Yemen, Tashkent, and Spain.[10]

In his lectures and writings, Azzam depicted the Afghans somewhat idealistically as untouched by the brutal mechanization of modern jahiliyyah; they represented pristine humanity. Fighting the Soviet Goliath, they reminded him of David when he was but a shepherd boy. His tales of the Afghans and Arabs who died as martyrs in this war inspired Muslim audiences worldwide. But Azzam's martyrs were not suicide bombers or terrorists of any kind. They did not cause their own deaths or kill civilians: they were regular soldiers killed in battle by Soviet troops. Azzam was in fact adamantly opposed to terrorism, and on this point he would eventually part company with Bin Laden and the Egyptian radical Ayman al-Zawahiri. Azzam insistently maintained the orthodox view that killing noncombatants or fellow Muslims like Sadat violated fundamental Islamic teaching. In fact, he believed that a martyr could be a "witness" to divine truth even if he died peacefully in bed.[11] Azzam's classical jihadism was condemned by some scholars, but it had strong appeal for young Sunnis who were embarrassed by the success of the Shii revolution in Iran. Yet not all the volunteers were devout; some were not even observant, although in Peshawar many would be influenced by such hard-line Islamists as Zawahiri, who had suffered arrest, torture, and imprisonment in Egypt for alleged involvement in the Sadat assassination. And so Afghanistan became a new Islamist hub. Young militants from East Asia and North Africa were sent to the front to increase their commitment, and the government of Saudi Arabia actually encouraged its own young to volunteer.[12]

· · ·

To understand the Saudi influence, one must reckon with what may seem a contradiction. On the one hand, after the Iranian Revolution, the kingdom had become one of America's chief regional allies. On the other hand, it subscribed to an extremely reductive form of Islam, which had been developed in the eighteenth century by the Arabian reformer Muhammad ibn Abd al-Wahhab (1703–92). Ibn Abd al-Wahhab had preached a return to the pristine Islam of the Prophet and repudiated such later developments as the Shiah, Sufism, Falsafah, and the jurisprudence (*fiqh*) on which all other Muslim ulema depended. He was particularly distressed by the popular veneration of holy men and their tombs, which he condemned as idolatry. Even so, Wahhabism was not inherently violent; indeed, Ibn Abd al-Wahhab had refused to sanction the wars of his patron, Ibn Saud of Najd, because he was fighting simply for wealth and glory.[13] It was only after his retirement that Wahhabis became more aggressive, even to the point of destroying Imam Husain's shrine in Karbala in 1802 as well as monuments in Arabia connected with Muhammad and his companions. At this time too, the sect insisted that Muslims who did not accept their doctrines were infidels (*kufar*).[14] During the early nineteenth century, Wahhabis incorporated the writings of Ibn Taymiyyah into their canon, and *takfir,* the practice of declaring another Muslim an unbeliever, which Ibn Abd al-Wahhab himself had rejected, became central to their practice.[15]

The oil embargo imposed by the Gulf States during the 1973 October War had sent the price soaring, and the kingdom now had all the petrodollars it needed to find practical ways of imposing Wahhabism on the entire ummah.[16] Deeply disconcerted by the success of the Shii revolution in Iran, which threatened their leadership of the Muslim world, the Saudis intensified their efforts to counter Iranian influence and replaced Iran as the chief ally of the United States in the region. The Saudi-based Muslim World League opened offices in every region inhabited by Muslims, and the Saudi ministry of religion printed and distributed translations of the Quran, Wahhabi doctrinal tracts, and the works of Ibn Taymiyyah, Qutb, and Maududi to Muslim communities in the Middle East, Africa, Indonesia, the United States, and Europe. In all these places, they funded the building of Saudi-style mosques, creating an international aesthetic that broke with local architectural traditions, and established madrassas that provided free education for the poor, with, of course, a Wahhabi curriculum. At the same time, the young men from the more disadvantaged Muslim countries, such as Egypt and Pakistan, who came to work in the Gulf, associated their new affluence with Wahhabism. When they returned home, they chose to live in new neighborhoods with Saudi mosques and shopping malls that segregated the sexes. In return for their munificence, Saudis demanded religious conformity. The Wahhabi rejection of all other forms of Islam as well as other faith traditions would reach as deeply into Bradford, England, and Buffalo, New York, as into Pakistan, Jordan, or Syria, everywhere gravely undermining Islam's traditional pluralism. The West played an unwitting role in this surge of intolerance, since the United States welcomed the Saudis' opposition to Iran, and the kingdom depended on the U.S. military for its very survival.[17]

The Saudis' experience of modernity had been very different from that of the Egyptians, Pakistanis, or Palestinians. The Arabian Peninsula had not been colonized; it was rich and had never been forced to secularize. Instead of fighting tyranny and corruption at home, therefore, Saudi Islamists focused on the suffering of Muslims worldwide, their pan-Islamism close in spirit to Azzam's global jihad. The Quran told Muslims that they must take responsibility for one another; King Feisal had always framed his support for the Palestinians in these terms, and the Saudi-based Muslim World League and the Organization of Islamic Conferences had regularly expressed solidarity with member states in conflict with non-Muslim regimes. Now television brought images of Muslim suffering in Palestine and Lebanon into comfortable Saudi homes. They saw pictures of Israelis bulldozing Palestinian houses and in September 1982 witnessed the Christian Maronites' massacre, with the tacit approval of the IDF, of two thousand Palestinians in the refugee camps of Sabra and Chatila. With so much suffering of this kind in the Muslim world, pan-Islamist sentiment increased during the 1980s, and the government exploited it as a way of distracting their subjects from the kingdom's internal problems.[18] It was for this reason too that the Saudis encouraged the young to go to the Afghan jihad, offering airfare discounts, while the state press celebrated their feats on the frontier. The Wahhabi clerical establishment, however, disapproved of the Afghans' Sufi practices and insisted that jihad was not an individual duty for civilians but was still the ruler's responsibility. Yet the Saudi king's civil government supported Azzam's teaching for its own temporal reasons.

A study of Saudis who volunteered for Afghanistan and later fought in Bosnia and Chechnya shows that most were chiefly motivated by the desire to help their Muslim brothers and sisters.[19] Nasir al-Bahri, who would become Bin Laden's bodyguard, gave the fullest and most perceptive explanation of this concern:

> We were greatly affected by the tragedies we were witnessing and the events we were seeing: children crying, women widowed, and the high number of incidents of rape. When we went forward for jihad, we experienced a bitter reality. We saw things that were more awful than anything we had expected or had heard or seen in the media. It was as though we were like "a cat with closed eyes" that opened its eyes at these woes.[20]

This was, he said, a political awakening, and the volunteers began to acquire a global sense of the ummah that transcended national boundaries: "The idea of the umma began to evolve in our minds. We realised we were a nation [*ummah*] that had a distinguished place among nations. . . . The issue of nationalism was put out of our minds, and we acquired a wider view than that, namely the issue of the umma." The welfare of the ummah had always been a deeply spiritual as well as a political concern in Islam, so the plight of their fellow Muslims cut to the core of their Islamic identity. Many were ashamed that Muslim leaders had responded so inadequately to these disasters. "After all those years of humiliation, they could finally do something to help their Muslim brothers," one respondent explained. Another said that "he would follow the news of his brothers with the deepest empathy, and he wanted to do something, anything, to help them." One volunteer's friend remembered that "we would often sit and talk about the slaughtering to which Muslims are subjected, and his eyes would fill with tears."[21]

The survey also found that in nearly every case, there was more sympathy for the victims than hatred for their oppressors. And despite the United States' support for Israel, there was as yet not much anti-Americanism. "We did not go because of the Americans," insisted Nasir al-Bahri. Some recruits longed for the glamour of a glorious martyrdom, but many were also lured by the sheer excitement of warfare, the possibility of heroism, and the comradeship of brothers-at-arms. As ever, the warrior's transcendence of mundane circumstance seemed very much akin to the believer's spiritual transcendence. Nasir al-Bahri remembered how they idolized the volunteers: "When we used to look at the Afghan suits that the mujahidin who returned from Afghanistan wore as they walked the streets of Jidda, Mecca or Medina, we used to feel that we were living with the generation of the triumphant companions of the Prophet, and hence looked up to them as an example."[22]

When finally the Soviets were forced to withdraw from Afghanistan in February 1989 and the Soviet Union itself collapsed in 1991, the Arab-Afghans relished a heady, if inaccurate, sense of having defeated a great world power. They now planned to fulfill Azzam's dream of reconquering all the lost Muslim lands. Throughout the world at this time, political Islam seemed in the ascendant. Hamas had become a serious challenge to Fatah. In Algeria, the Islamic Salvation Front (FIS) had won a decisive victory over the secular National Liberation Front (FLN) in the municipal polls of 1990, and the Islamist ideologue Hassan Al-Turabi had come to power in the Sudan. After the Soviet withdrawal, Bin Laden founded al-Qaeda, which began humbly as an alumni organization for those Arab-Afghans who wanted to take the jihad forward. At this point the entity, whose name simply means "the Base," had no coherent ideology or clear goal. And so some of its affiliates returned home as freelances with the aim of deposing corrupt secularist regimes and replacing them with an Islamic government. Others, still committed to Azzam's classical jihadism, joined local Muslims in their struggle against the Russians in Chechnya and Tajikistan and the Serbs in Bosnia. Yet to their dismay, they found that they were unable to transform these national conflicts into what they considered a true jihad. Indeed, in Bosnia they were not only *de trop* but a positive liability.

• • •

The Bosnian War (1992–95) saw one of the last genocides of the twentieth century. Unlike the two preceding it, the Armenian genocide and the Holocaust, this mass killing was conducted on the basis of religious rather than ethnic identity. Despite the widespread assumption in the West that the divisions in the Balkans were ancient and ingrained and that the violence was ineradicable because of its strong "religious" element, this communal intolerance was relatively new. Jews, Christians, and Muslims had lived together peacefully under Ottoman rule for five hundred years and continued doing so after the fall of the Ottoman Empire in 1918, when Serbs, Slovenians, Slavic Muslims, and Croats had formed the multireligious federation of Yugoslavia ("Land of the South Slavs"). Yugoslavia was dismantled by Nazi Germany in 1941 but was revived after the Second World War by the communist leader Josip Broz Tito (r. 1945–80) under the slogan "Brotherhood and Unity." After his death, however, the radical Serbian nationalism of Slobodan Milosevic and the equally assertive Croatian nationalism of Franjo Tudjman pulled the country apart, with Bosnia caught in the middle. Slavic nationalism had a strongly Christian flavor—Serbs were Orthodox and Croatians Roman Catholic—but Bosnia, with a Muslim majority and Serbian, Croatian, Jewish, and Gypsy communities, opted for a secular state that respected all religions. Lacking the military capacity to defend themselves, Bosnian Muslims knew they would be persecuted if they remained part of Serbia, and so in April 1992 they declared independence. The United States and the European Union recognized Bosnia-Herzegovina as a sovereign state.

Milosevic depicted Serbia as "a fortress, defending European culture and religion" from the Islamic world, and Serbian clerics and academics similarly described their nation as a bulwark against the Asiatic hordes. Another radical Serbian nationalist, Radovan Karadzic, had warned the Bosnian Assembly that if it declared independence, it would lead their nation "into hell" and "make the Muslim people disappear." But this latent hatred of Islam dated only to the nineteenth century, when Serbian nationalists had created a myth that blended Christianity with a national sentiment based on ethnicity: it cast Prince Lazlo, defeated by the Ottomans in 1389, as a Christ figure; the Turkish sultan as a Christ slayer; and the Slavs who converted to Islam as "Turkified" (isturciti). By adopting a non-Christian religion, they had renounced their Slavic ethnicity and become Orientals; the Serbian nation would not rise again until these aliens were exterminated. Yet so deep-rooted were the habits of coexistence that it took Milosevic three years of relentless propaganda to persuade the Serbs to revive this lethal blend of secular nationalism, religion, and racism. Significantly, the war began with a frantic attempt to expunge the documentary evidence that for centuries Jews, Christians, and Muslims had enjoyed a rich coexistence. A month after the Bosnian declaration of independence, Serbian militias destroyed the Oriental Institute in Sarajevo, which housed the largest collection of Islamic and Jewish manuscripts in the Balkans, burned down the National Library and National Museum, and targeted all such manuscript collections for destruction. Between them, Serbian and Croat nationalists also destroyed some fourteen hundred mosques, turning the sites into parks and parking lots to erase all memory of the inconvenient past.[23]

While they were burning the museums, Serbian militias and the heavily armed Yugoslav National Army overran Bosnia, and in the autumn of 1992 the process that Karadzic called "ethnic cleansing" began.[24] Milosevic had opened the prisons and recruited petty gangsters into the militias, letting them pillage, rape, burn, and kill with impunity.[25] No Muslim was to be spared, and any Bosnian Serb who refused to cooperate must also die. Muslims were herded into concentration camps, and without toilets or other sanitation, filthy, emaciated, and traumatized, they seemed scarcely human either to themselves or to their tormentors. Militia leaders dulled the inhibitions of their troops with alcohol, forcing them to gang-rape, murder, and torture. When Srebrenica, a UN "safe area," was turned over to the Serb army in the summer of 1995, at least eight thousand men and boys were massacred, and by the autumn the last Muslims were either killed or expelled from the Banja Luka region.[26]

The international community was horrified but made no urgent demand for the killing to be stopped; rather, the prevailing feeling was that all parties were equally guilty.[27] "I don't care two cents about Bosnia. Not two cents," said *New York Times* columnist Thomas Friedman. "The people there have brought on their own troubles. Let them keep on killing one another and the problem will be solved."[28] To their credit, the Arab-Afghans were the only people to provide military help, but the Bosnian Muslims found them intolerant, were baffled by their global jihadism, and adamantly rejected all their plans for an Islamic state. Unfortunately, the Arab-Afghans' presence gave the impression abroad that the Bosnian Muslims were also fundamentalists, though in fact many wore their Islam very lightly. Stereotypical views about Islam and fears of an Islamic state on the threshold of Europe may well have contributed to the Western reluctance to intervene; Serbian rhetoric of defensive walls may not have seemed such a bad idea to some Europeans and Americans. Nevertheless, in August 1995, NATO did intervene with a series of air strikes against Bosnian Serb positions, which finally brought this tragic conflict to an end. A peace agreement was signed in Dayton, Ohio, on November 21, 1995. But the world was left with a troubling memory. Once again there had been concentration camps in Europe, this time with Muslims in them. After the Holocaust, the cry had been "Never again," but this did not seem to apply to Europe's Muslim population.

◆ ◆ ◆

Other Arab-Afghan veterans found that when they returned home, they were too radical for the local Muslims who had not shared their experience in Afghanistan. The vast majority vehemently rejected their ruthless militancy. In Algeria, Afghan veterans had high hopes of creating an Islamic state, because the Islamic Salvation Front (FIS) seemed certain to gain a majority in the national elections in 1992. But at the last moment, the military staged a coup, and the liberal secularist FLN president Benjedid, who had promised democratic reforms, suppressed the FIS and imprisoned its leaders. Had a democratic process been thwarted in such an unconstitutional manner in Iran or Pakistan, there would have been worldwide outrage. Yet because it was an Islamic government that had been blocked by the coup, there was jubilation in some sectors of the Western press, which seemed to suggest that in some mysterious way this undemocratic action had made Algeria safe for democracy. The French government threw its support behind the new hard-line FLN president Liamine Zeroual and strengthened his resolve to hold no further dialogue with the FIS.

As we have seen elsewhere, when suppressed, these movements tend almost invariably to become more extreme. The more radical members of the FIS broke away to form a guerrilla organization, the Armed Islamic Group (GIA), and were joined by the returning Arab-Afghans. At first the veterans' military training was welcome, but their unsparing methods soon shocked the Algerians. They began a terror campaign in the mountains south of Algiers, assassinating monks, journalists, and secular and religious intellectuals as well as the inhabitants of entire villages. There are indications, however, that the military not only acquiesced but may even have participated in this violence to eliminate populations sympathetic to the FIS and to discredit the GIA. There was also a chilling preview of future events, when the GIA hijacked a plane flying to France intending to crash it over Paris to prevent the French government from supporting the Algerian regime. Fortunately, the plane was captured by commandos at Marseilles.[29]

The returning Egyptian Arab-Afghans also found that they had become too extreme for their fellow countrymen. Zawahiri founded Islamic Jihad (IJ) with the intention of assassinating the entire Mubarak government and establishing an Islamic state. In June 1995 IJ attempted but failed to murder the president. In April 1996 it killed a busload of thirty Greek tourists—the intended targets had been Israelis who had switched buses at the last moment—and finally, to weaken the economy by damaging the all-essential tourist industry, it massacred sixty people, most of them foreign visitors, at Luxor in November 1997. IJ discovered, however, that it had wholly misjudged the mood of the country. Egyptians saw this violent obsession with an Islamic state as blatant idolatry that violated core Muslim values; they were so appalled by the Luxor atrocity that Zawahiri had no option but to rejoin Bin Laden in Afghanistan and merge his Islamic Jihad with al-Qaeda.

Bin Laden fared no better than the other veterans when he returned to Saudi Arabia.[30] When Saddam Hussein invaded Kuwait in 1990, he offered the royal family the services of his Arab-Afghan fighters to protect the kingdom's oil fields, but to his fury they turned him down in favor of the U.S. Army. This began his estrangement from the Saudi regime. When in 1994 the Saudi government suppressed Sahwa ("Awakening"), a nonviolent reformist party that shared Bin Laden's disapproval of American troop deployment in Arabia, his alienation was complete. Convinced now that peaceful resistance was futile, Bin Laden spent four years in Sudan, organizing financial backing for Arab-Afghan projects. In 1996, when the United States and the Saudis pressured the Turabi government to expel him, he returned to Afghanistan, where the Taliban had just seized power.

• • •

After the Soviet withdrawal, the West lost interest in the region, but both Afghanistan and Pakistan had been gravely derailed by the long conflict. A flood of money and weapons had flowed into Pakistan from the United States as well as from the Persian Gulf, giving extremist groups access to advanced armaments, which were simply stolen as they were being unloaded. These heavily armed extremists had therefore broken the state's monopoly on violence and henceforth could operate outside the law. To defend themselves, nearly all groups in the country, religious and secular, developed paramilitary wings. Moreover, after the Iranian Revolution, Saudi Arabia, aware of the significant Shii community in Pakistan, had stepped up its funding of Deobandi madrassas to counter Shii influence. This enabled the Deobandis to educate even more students from poorer backgrounds, and they sheltered the children of impoverished peasants, who were tenants of Shii landlords. These entered the madrassas, therefore, with an anti-Shii bias that was greatly enhanced by their education there.

Isolated from the rest of Pakistani society, these "students" (*taliban*) bonded tightly with the three million Afghan children who had been orphaned during the war and were brought to Pakistan as refugees. They had all arrived traumatized by war and poverty and were introduced to a rule-bound, restricted, and highly intolerant form of Islam. They had no training in critical thought, were shielded from outside influence, and became rabidly anti-Shii.[31] In 1985 the Deobandis founded the Soldiers of the Companions of the Prophet in Pakistan (SCPP) specifically to harass the Shii, and in the mid-1990s two even more violent Deobandi movements emerged: the Army of Jhangvi, which specialized in assassinating Shiis, and the Partisan Movement, which fought for the liberation of Kashmir. As a result of this onslaught, the Shii formed the Soldiers of the Prophet in Pakistan (SPP), which killed a number of Sunnis. For centuries Shiis and Sunnis had coexisted amicably in the region. Thanks to the United States' Cold War struggle in Afghanistan and to Saudi-Iranian rivalry, they were now tearing the country apart in what amounted to a civil war.

The Afghan Taliban combined their Pashtun tribal chauvinism with Deobandi rigorism, an unholy hybrid and maverick form of Islam that expressed itself in violent opposition to any rival ideology. After the Soviet withdrawal, Afghanistan had descended into chaos, and when the Taliban managed to take control, they seemed to both the Pakistanis and the Americans to be an acceptable alternative to anarchy. Their leader, Mullah Omar, believed that human beings were naturally virtuous and, if placed on the right path, needed no government coercion, social services, or public health care. There was therefore no centralized government, and the population was ruled by local Taliban *komitehs*, whose punishments for the smallest infringement of Islamic law were so draconian that a degree of order was indeed restored. Fiercely opposed to modernity, which had, after all, come to them in the form of Soviet guns and air strikes, the Taliban ruled by their traditional tribal norms, which they identified with the rule of God. Their focus was purely local, and they had no sympathy with Bin Laden's global vision. But Mullah Omar was grateful to the Arab-Afghans for their support during the war, and when Bin Laden was expelled from Sudan, he admitted him to Afghanistan, in return for which Bin Laden improved the country's infrastructure.[32]

Other uprooted radicals gathered around Bin Laden in Afghanistan—Zawahiri and his Egyptian radicals most especially.[33] Yet al-Qaeda was still a minor player in Islamist politics. A former militant told ABC television that even though he had spent ten months in training camps run by Bin Laden's aides, he had never heard of the organization.[34] It seems that, even though he expressed his approval of both operations, Bin Laden played no part in the 1993 bombing of the World Trade Center in New York by Arab-Afghan veteran Ramzi Youssef or in the 1995 truck bombing in Riyadh that killed five Americans. However, al-Qaeda may have provided an ideological focus for militants in Afghanistan, who were feeling increasingly dispirited.[35] Not only had they failed to advance on their three main fronts of Bosnia, Algeria, and Egypt, but by the end of the 1990s, political Islam itself seemed in terminal decline.[36] In a dramatic turnabout, Hojjat ol-Islam Seyyed Muhammad Khatami, running on a democratic ticket, won a landslide victory in the 1997 elections in Iran. He immediately signaled that he wanted a more positive relationship with the West and dissociated his government from Khomeini's fatwa against Salman Rushdie. In Algeria the government of President Abdul-Aziz Bouteflika included militant secularists as well as moderate Islamists, and in Pakistan the secularist colonel Pervez Musharraf toppled Nawaz Sharif, patron of the Islamist parties. In Turkey the Islamist prime minister Necmettin Erkbakan had to resign after a single year in office, and Turabi was deposed in a military coup in Sudan. It seemed increasingly urgent to Bin Laden to reignite the jihad in a spectacular operation that would catch the attention of the whole world.

In August 1996 he issued his *Declaration of War* on the United States and Israel, the "Crusader-Zionist Alliance," which he accused of "aggression, iniquity, and injustice" against Muslims.[37] He condemned the American military presence in the Arabian Peninsula, equating it with the Israeli occupation of Palestine, and denounced American support for corrupt governments in the Muslim world and the sanctions led by Israel and the United States against Iraq, which, he claimed, had caused a million Iraqi deaths. In February 1998 he announced the World Islamic Front Against Zionists and Crusaders, stating that all Muslims had a religious obligation to attack the United States and its allies "in any country in which it is possible to do it" and to drive American troops from Arabia.[38] Three entirely new themes were emerging in Bin Laden's ideology.[39] The first was his identification of the United States as the prime enemy rather than Russians, Serbs, or "apostate" Muslim rulers. Second was his call to attack the United States and its allies anywhere in the world, even in America itself—an unusual step, because terrorists usually avoided operations outside their own country, which cost them international support. Third, even though Bin Laden never wholly abandoned Qutb's terminology, he drew chiefly on pan-Islamic themes, focusing particularly on the suffering that Muslims were enduring worldwide.

This last was the core of Bin Laden's message and enabled him to claim that his jihad was defensive.[40] In his *Declaration of War* he exploited the culture of grievance that had been developing in the Muslim world, insisting that for centuries "the people of Islam have suffered from aggression, iniquity, and injustice imposed upon them by the Crusader-Zionist alliance."[41] In al-Qaeda's propaganda videos, this verbal message is relayed against a collage of pain. They show Palestinian children harassed by

Israeli soldiers; piles of corpses in Lebanon, Bosnia, and Chechnya; the shooting of a Palestinian child in Gaza; houses bombed and bulldozed; and blind, limbless patients lying inertly in hospital beds. A survey of men recruited by al-Qaeda after 1999 revealed that most of them were still primarily motivated by the desire to assuage such suffering. "I did not know exactly in what way I would help," said a Saudi prisoner in Guantánamo, "but I went to help the people, not to fight." Feisal al-Dukhayyil, who was not an observant Muslim, was so distressed by a television program on the plight of Chechen women and children that he enlisted immediately.[42] Despite Bin Laden's anti-American rhetoric, hatred of the United States was not a major preoccupation among his recruits; this seems to have developed only during their indoctrination in the al-Qaeda camps in Pakistan, where all, even those intending to fight in Chechnya, were diverted. Muslims from Buffalo, New York, known as the "Lackawanna Six," later explained that they left their training camp in 2001 because they were shocked by its anti-Americanism.[43]

Bin Laden's "Crusader-Zionist Alliance" model exploited the conspiracy fears that are widespread in Muslim countries where lack of government transparency makes accurate information hard to come by.[44] It provides an explanation for an otherwise inexplicable concatenation of disasters. Islamists often quote a hadith that was rarely cited in the classical period but became very popular during the Crusades and the Mongol invasions:[45] "The nations are about to flock against you from every horizon," the Prophet had told his companions, and Muslims would be helpless because "weakness [*wahn*] will be placed in your hearts." What did *wahn* mean? "Love of this world and fear of death," Muhammad replied.[46] Muslims had become soft and had abandoned jihad because they were afraid of dying. Their only hope was to summon again the courage at the heart of Islam. Hence the importance of the huge martyrdom operation that would show the world that Muslims were no longer fearful. Their plight was so desperate that they must either fight or be killed. Radicals also love the Quranic story of David and Goliath that concludes: "How often a small force has defeated a large army!"[47] The more powerful the enemy, therefore, the more heroic the struggle. Killing civilians is regrettable but, fighters argue, the Crusader-Zionists have also shed innocent blood, and the Quran commands retaliation.[48] So the martyr must soldier on bravely, stoically repressing pity or moral revulsion for the terrible acts that he is tragically obliged to commit.[49]

The al-Qaeda leadership had been planning the "spectacular" attack of September 11, 2001, for some time but could not proceed until they found the right recruits. They needed men who were technologically competent, were at home in Western society, and had the ability to work independently.[50] In November 1999 Muhammad Ata, Ramzi bin al-Shibh, Marwan al-Shehhi, and Ziad Jarrah, on their way (or so they thought) to Chechnya, were diverted to an al-Qaeda safe house in Kandahar. They came from privileged backgrounds, had studied engineering and technology in Europe—Jarrah and al-Shehhi were engineers, and Ata was an architect—and would blend easily into American society while they trained as pilots. They were members of a group now known as the Hamburg Cell. Of the four, only Bin al-Shibh had a deep knowledge of the Quran. None had the madrassa training that is often blamed for Muslim terrorism but had attended secular schools; until he met the group, Jarrah was not even observant.[51] Unused to allegoric and symbolic thought, their scientific education inclined them not to skepticism but toward a literalist reading of the Quran that diverged radically from traditional Muslim exegesis. They also had no training in the traditional fiqh, so their knowledge of mainstream Muslim law was at best superficial.

In his study of the 9/11 terrorists and those who worked closely with them—five hundred people in all—the forensic psychiatrist Marc Sageman found that only 25 percent had a traditional Islamic upbringing; that two-thirds were secularly minded until they encountered al-Qaeda; and the rest were recent converts. Their knowledge of Islam was therefore limited. Many were self-taught, and some would not study the Quran thoroughly until they were in prison. Perhaps, Sageman concludes, the problem was not Islam but ignorance of Islam.[52] The Saudis who took part in the 9/11 operation had had a Wahhabi education, but they were not influenced chiefly by Wahhabism but by pan-Islamist ideals, which the Wahhabi ulema had often opposed. The martyr videos of Ahmed al-Haznawi, who died in the plane that crashed in Pennsylvania, and Abdul-Aziz al-Omari, who was in the first plane to hit the World Trade Center, dwell intensely on Muslim suffering worldwide. Yet while the Quran certainly orders Muslims to come to the aid of their brothers, Shariah law forbids violence against civilians and the use of fire in warfare, and it prohibits any attack on a country where Muslims are allowed to practice their religion freely.

Muhammad Ata, leader of the Hamburg Cell, was motivated by Azzam's global vision, convinced that every able-bodied Muslim was obliged to defend his brothers and sisters in Chechnya or Tajikistan.[53] But Azzam would have deplored the terrorist activity that this group would embrace. As moderate members fell away from the cell, they were replaced by others who shared Ata's views. In such closed groups, isolated from any divergent opinion, Sageman believes, "the cause" becomes the milieu in which they live and breathe.[54] Members became deeply attached to one another, shared apartments, ate and prayed together, and watched endless battlefield videos from Chechnya.[55] Most important, they identified closely with these distant struggles. Modern media enables people in one part of the world to be influenced by events that happen far away—something that would have been impossible in premodern times—and to apply these foreign narratives to their own problems.[56] It is a highly artificial state of consciousness.

The story of the 9/11 terrorists is now well known. Years after this tragedy, the events of that day are still horrifying. Our task in this book is to assess the role of religion in this atrocity. In the West there was a widespread conviction that Islam, an inherently violent religion, was the chief culprit. A few weeks after September 11, in an article entitled "This Is a Religious War," the American journalist Andrew Sullivan quoted from Bin Laden's *Declaration of War*:

> The call to wage war against America was made because America spearheaded the Crusade against the Islamic nation, sending thousands of troops to the Land of the Two Holy Mosques, over and above its meddling in Saudi affairs and its politics, and its support of the oppressive, corrupt, and tyrannical regime that is in control.[57]

Sullivan alerted his readers to the use of the word *Crusade,* "an explicitly religious term," and pointed out that "bin Laden's beef is with American troops defiling the land of Saudi Arabia, 'the land of the Two Holy Mosques' in Mecca and Medina."[58] The words *Crusade* and *holy mosques* were enough to persuade Sullivan that this really *was* a religious war, whereupon he felt free to embark on a paean to the Western liberal tradition. Way back in the seventeenth century, the West had understood how dangerous it was to mix religion and politics, Sullivan reasoned, but the Muslim world, alas, had yet to learn this important lesson. Yet Sullivan failed to discuss or even dwell upon the two highly specific and clearly political aspects of American foreign policy mentioned by Bin Laden in the quoted extract: its interference in the internal affairs of Saudi Arabia and its support for the despotic Saudi regime.[59]

Even the "explicitly religious" terms—*Crusade* and *holy mosques*—in fact had political and economic connotations. Since the early twentieth century, the Arabic *al-salibiyyah* ("crusade") has become an explicitly *political* term, applied routinely to colonialism and Western imperialism.[60] The deployment of American troops in Saudi Arabia was not only a violation of sacred space but also a humiliating demonstration of the kingdom's dependence on the United States and of America's domination of the region. The American troops involved the kingdom in expensive arms deals; its Saudi base gave the United States easy access to Saudi oil and had enabled the U.S. military to launch air strikes against Sunni Muslims during the Gulf War.[61]

The hijackers themselves certainly regarded the 9/11 atrocities as a religious act but one that bore very little resemblance to normative Islam. A document found in Ata's suitcase outlined a program of prayer and reflection to help them through the ordeal.[62] If psychosis is "an inability to see relationships," this is a deeply psychotic document. The principal imperative of Islamic spirituality is *tawhid* ("making one"): Muslims truly understand the unity of God only if they integrate all their activities and thoughts. But this document atomizes the mission, dividing it into segments—the "last night," the journey to the airport, boarding the planes, etc.—so that the unbearable whole is never considered. The terrorists were told to look forward to paradise and back to the time of the Prophet—in fact, to contemplate anything but the atrocity they were committing in the present.[63] Living from one moment to another, their minds were to be diverted from the appalling finale. The prayers themselves are jarring. Like all Muslim discourse, the document begins with the *bismallah*—"In the Name of God, the most Merciful and most Compassionate"—but it initiates an action devoid of either mercy or compassion. It then segues to a remark that most Muslims, I suspect, would find idolatrous: "In the name of God, of myself, and my family."[64] The hijacker is told to cut off any feelings of pity for his fellow passengers or fear for his own life and exert an immense effort to put himself into this abnormal mind-set. He must "resist" these impulses, "tame," "purify," and "convince" his soul, "incite" it, and "make it understand."[65]

The imitation of Muhammad is central to Islamic piety; by imitating his external behavior, Muslims hope to acquire his interior attitude of total surrender to God. But Ata's document determinedly steers the terrorists away from their inner world by an almost perverse emphasis on the external. As a result, the devotions seem primitive and superstitious. While packing, they were to whisper Quranic verses into their hands and rub this holiness onto their luggage, box cutters, knives, ID, and passports. Their clothes must fit snugly, like the garments of the Prophet and his companions. When they begin to fight the passengers and crew, as a sign of resolution, each one must "clench his teeth just as the pious forefathers did prior to entering into battle" and "strike in the manner of champions who are not desirous of returning to this world, and shout *Allahu akbar!* For this shout causes fear in the hearts of the unbelievers." They must not "become gloomy" but recite Quranic verses while they are fighting, "just as the pious ancestors would compose poetry in the midst of battles to calm their brothers and to cause tranquillity and joy to enter their souls."[66] To imagine that a possibility of serenity and joy would be possible in such circumstances indicates a truly psychotic inability to relate their faith with the reality of what they were about to do.

We find here the kind of magical thinking that we noted in Faraj's *The Neglected Duty*. As they went through the security gates of the airport, the hijackers were instructed to recite a verse that was almost "a creedal statement" for radicals.[67] It is found in a Quranic passage about the Battle of Uhud, when the "laggers" urged the more intrepid Muslims to "stay at home." But they had simply replied: "God is enough for us: He is the best protector," and because of their faith, they had "returned with grace and bounty from God; no harm befell them."[68] If they repeated these words, the document assured the hijackers, "You will find matters straightened; and [God's] protection will surround you; no power can penetrate that." The recitation of this verse would not only keep their fear at bay but overcome all physical obstacles: "All of their devices, their [security] gates and their technology will not save [the Americans]."[69] The mere repetition of the first part of the shehadah, "There is no god but God," would itself be enough to secure their entry into paradise. The hijackers are told to "consider the awesomeness of this statement while they were fighting the Americans," remembering that in the Arabic script this verse had "no pointed letters—this is a sign of perfection and completeness, as the pointed words or letters lessen its power."[70]

Just over a year after 9/11, Louis Atiyat Allah would write an essay for a jihad website after watching al-Omari's martyr video. There is absurdity in Allah's extravagant eulogy, which imagines the hijackers— "mountains of courage, stars of masculinity, and galaxies of merit"— weeping for joy as the planes hit the target. However, it was obviously written to rebut widespread criticism of the 9/11 perpetrators. It was not only "moderates" who deplored the atrocity; even in radical circles, Muslims were apparently objecting that the Quran forbids suicide; they believed that the hijackers had acted irresponsibly. Their action had been counterproductive too: not only had the atrocity inspired worldwide sympathy for America, but it had weakened the Palestinian cause by strengthening Israel's bond with the United States. In his article rebutting these complaints, Allah retorted that the hijackers had not "committed suicide"; nor were they simply "crazy people who found planes to hijack." No, they had had a clearly defined political objective: "to smash the foundations of the tyrant and to demolish the idol of the age, America." They had also struck a blow against the structural violence of the American-dominated Middle East, rejecting the "silly [rulers] of Ibn Saud, and Husni [Mubarak], and all the other retards who falsely call themselves 'those in authority'" (Quran 4:59) but who were actually "nothing but tentacles of the octopus upon you, with the head of the [octopus] being in New York and Washington DC." The purpose of this operation was to take a "terrifying historical leap which will . . . extricate the Muslims in one fell swoop from humiliation, dependency and servility."[71]

These political objectives were certainly uppermost in Bin Laden's mind too in the immediate aftermath of 9/11, although he would also invoke the divine will. In the videotape released on October 7, 2001, he crowed: "Here is America struck by God in one of its vital organs, so that its greatest buildings are destroyed,"[72] buildings that had been carefully selected as "America's icons of military and economic power."[73] Five times Bin Laden applied the word *kafir* ("infidel") to the United States, though each time it referred not to the religious beliefs of America but to its violation of Muslim sovereignty in Arabia and Palestine:[74] on the same day, President George W. Bush announced Operation Enduring Freedom, a

U.S.-led war against the Taliban in Afghanistan. Like the First Crusade against Islam, this military offensive was couched in the language of liberty: "We defend not only our precious freedoms, but also the freedom of people everywhere."[75] He assured the people of Afghanistan that the United States had no quarrel with them, would strike only at military targets, and promised airdrops of food, medicine, and supplies. Also, just a week following the attacks, Bush had made clear that America's quarrel was not with Islam: "The face of terror is not the true faith of Islam. That's not what Islam is all about. Islam is peace. These terrorists don't represent peace. They represent evil and war."[76] Like Bin Laden, Bush, in this carefully secular presentation, also saw the world starkly divided into two camps, one good, the other evil: "In this conflict there is no neutral ground. If any government sponsors the outlaws and killers of innocents, they have become outlaws and murderers themselves."[77]

Bush's Manichean worldview reflected the thinking of the neoconservatives prominent in his administration, who had a semimystical belief that nothing must impede America's unique historical mission in the twenty-first century. The "War on Terror" would be waged against any forces that threatened America's global leadership. Indeed, neoconservatism has been described as "a faith-based system" because it required absolute fidelity to its doctrine, permitting no deviation from its beliefs.[78] And so the politics of the secular nation was imbued with a quasi-religious fervor and conviction. The United States had a mission to promote the global free market, the One True Economy, everywhere. It was not a religious message but one that nevertheless resonated strongly as such with Bush's base of 100 million American evangelical Christians, who still subscribed to the vision of America as a "city on a hill."

The first three months of the war against Afghanistan, where Taliban gave sanctuary to al-Qaeda, seemed remarkably successful. The Taliban were defeated, al-Qaeda personnel scattered, and the United States established two large military bases, at Bagram and Kandahar. But there were two ominous developments. Even though Bush had given instructions that prisoners be treated humanely in accordance with the Geneva Conventions, it seems that in practice troops were told that they could "deviate slightly from the rules" since terrorists were not covered by the laws relating to prisoners of war. Bush had been careful to insist that this was not a war against Islam, but that was not how it appeared on the ground, where there was little punctiliousness about religious sensibilities. On September 26, 2002, a convoy of mujahidin were captured in Takhar. According to one Muslim account, U.S. troops "hung one mujahid by his arms for six days, questioning him about Usama bin Laden." Eventually they gave up and asked him about his faith: he replied that

> he trusted in Allah, the Prophet Muhammad and the holy Qur'an. Upon receiving this answer, the U.S. troops replied that "Your Allah and Muhammad are not here, but the Qur'an is, so let's see what it will do to us." After this, one U.S. soldier brought a Holy Qur'an and began urinating over it, only to be joined by other U.S. and Northern Alliance troops who did the same.[79]

Despite their manifest contempt for Islam, this does not mean that U.S. troops saw themselves as fighting a war that was specifically directed against Islam. Rather, the unconventional nature of the campaign, defined as a "War on Terror," a "different kind of war," had changed the rules of engagement. With this terminology the United States had liberated itself from the rules of conventional conflict.[80] Ground troops seem to have absorbed the view that terrorists were not entitled to the same protection as regular combatants.

Since 9/11, the United States, which still regards itself as a uniquely benign hegemon, has, with the support of its allies, indefinitely retained people who deny any involvement in any conflict, conducted violent and humiliating interrogations, or else sent prisoners to countries known to practice torture. As early as December 2001, hundreds of prisoners—by means of "extraordinary rendition"—were being detained in Guantánamo Bay and Diego Garcia without due process and were subjected to "stress and duress" (i.e., torture).[81] The frequent—almost routine— reports of abuse in these U.S. prisons suggest that military and political authorities may have condoned a policy of systematic brutality.[82] The second disturbing development in the War on Terror was the large number of civilian casualties. About three thousand civilians were killed in the first three months—roughly the same number as had died in New York, Pennsylvania, and Washington on September 11. Thousands more displaced Afghans would die later in refugee camps.[83] As the war dragged on, the casualties became catastrophic: it has been estimated that 16,179 Afghan civilians perished between 2006 and 2012.[84]

There was a second wave of terrorist incidents, directed by the "second generation" of al-Qaeda, which included the failed plot of British "shoe bomber" Richard Reid (December 2001), the Djerba bombing in Tunisia (April 2002), and the Bali nightclub attack (October 2002), which killed over two hundred people. After Iyman Faris's foiled plot to destroy the Brooklyn Bridge, however, most of the al-Qaeda central command had either been killed or captured, and there were no more major incidents.[85] But just as the situation seemed to be improving, in March 2003, the United States, Britain, and their allies invaded Iraq, despite considerable opposition from the international community and strong protests throughout the Muslim world. The reasons for this invasion were allegations that Saddam Hussein possessed weapons of mass destruction and had furnished support for al-Qaeda, both of which eventually proved to be groundless.

Again, the United States presented itself as the bearer of freedom. "If we must use force," Bush had promised the American people, "the United States and our coalition stand ready to help the citizens of a liberated Iraq."[86] "We don't seek an empire," he insisted on another occasion. "Our nation is committed to freedom for ourselves and for others."[87] Cheered on by such neoimperialist intellectuals as Niall Ferguson, the Bush regime believed that it could use the colonial methods of invasion and occupation for purposes of liberation.[88] America would force Iraq into the free global economy and change the politics of the Middle East by creating a liberal, democratic, and pro-Western Arab state, one that would also support Israel, embrace market capitalism, and at the same time provide the United States with a military base and access to vast oil reserves.

On May 1, 2003, Bush's Viking jet swooped onto the deck of USS *Abraham Lincoln,* where the president announced a victorious end to the Iraq War.[89] "We have fought for the cause of liberty and for the peace of the world," he told the assembled troops. "Because of you, the tyrant is fallen and Iraq is free." In this political message too were the overtones of a holy war. This war of the American nation was directed by God himself. "All of you—all in this generation of our military—have taken up the highest calling of history," he proclaimed, quoting the Prophet Isaiah: "And wherever you go, you carry a message of hope—a message that is ancient and ever new. To the captives, 'come out'—and to those in darkness 'be free.' "[90] Use of this biblical verse, which Jesus had quoted to describe his own mission,[91] revealed the messianic streak of the Bush administration.

It was ironic that Bush announced the liberation of captives. In October 2003, the media published photographs of U.S. military police abusing Iraqi prisoners in Abu Ghraib, Saddam's notorious prison; later, almost identical cruelty was shown to have taken place in British-run prisons. These photographs were a cruder vision of the official U.S. media presentation of the Iraq War. Hooded, naked, writhing on the ground, the Iraqis were depicted as dehumanized, craven, bestial, and utterly dominated by America's superior power. The cocky stance of the low-ranking GIs implied: "We are high, they are low; we are clean, they are dirty; we are strong and brave, they are weak and cowardly; we are lordly, they are virtually animals; we are God's chosen, they are estranged from everything divine."[92] "The photos are us," the late Susan Sontag declared. Nazis were not the only people to commit atrocities; Americans do so too, "when they are led to believe that the people they are torturing belong to an inferior, despicable race or religion."[93] Clearly the GIs saw nothing untoward in their behavior and had no fear of punishment. "It was just for fun," said Private Lynndie England, who had appeared in the photographs walking a prisoner on a leash like a dog. They behaved in this way, the official investigation concluded, "simply because they could."[94]

Within a month of Bush's carrier speech, Iraq had descended into chaos. Most Iraqis gave no credence to Bush's exalted rhetoric; instead they were convinced that the United States simply wanted their oil and intended to use their country as a military base from which to defend Israel. They may have been glad to get rid of Saddam, but they did not regard the American and British troops as liberators. "They're walking over my heart," said one Baghdad resident. "Liberate us from what?" demanded another. "We have [our own] traditions, morals, customs."[95] The Iraqi cleric Sheikh Muhammad Bashir complained that if the Americans had brought freedom to the country, it was not for the Iraqis:

> It is the freedom of occupying soldiers in doing what they like. . . . No one can ask them what they are doing, because they are protected by their freedom. . . . No one can punish them, whether in our country or in their country. They expressed the freedom of rape, the freedom of nudity, and the freedom of humiliation.[96]

The overwhelming 2004 U.S. assault on Fallujah, the iconic "city of mosques," has been called the Arab 9/11: hundreds of civilians were killed and 200,000 made homeless. By the following year 24,000 civilians had been killed in Iraq and 70,000 injured.[97] Instead of bringing peace to the region, the occupation inspired an insurgency of Iraqis and mujahidin from Saudi Arabia, Syria, and Jordan, who responded to this foreign invasion with the heretofore unusual technique of suicide bombing, eventually breaking the long-standing record of the Tamil Tigers.[98]

As to global terrorism, the situation has become only more dangerous than it was before the Iraq War.[99] Following the assassination of Bin Laden in 2011, al-Qaeda still thrives. Its strength was always more conceptual than organizational—global revolutionary fervor combining an intense political militancy with dubious claims to divine sanction. Its branch affiliates, including the one founded in Iraq (as of this writing increasingly active there and also in the Syrian civil war) as well as those in Somalia and Yemen, continue to promote a restoration of the caliphate as the ultimate objective of their interventions in local politics. Elsewhere, in the absence of any tightly organized cadre, there are thousands of freelance aspirants to terrorism worldwide—radicalized in Internet chat rooms, self-trained, poorly educated, and lacking any clear practical objective. Such was the case with Michael Adebolajo and Michael Adebolawe, two British-born converts to Islam, who murdered the British soldier Lee Rigby in 2013 in southeastern London, claiming to avenge the deaths of Muslim innocents by British troops. Like Muhammad Bouyeri, who assassinated the Dutch filmmaker Theo Van Gogh in 2004, and the Madrid train bombers, who killed 191 people in the same year, they were not directly linked to al-Qaeda.[100] Some self-starters do seek out the al-Qaeda leadership for credentialing and in hope of being sent to some important operational theater, but it seems that trainers in Pakistan prefer to send them home to destabilize Western countries instead—as happened with the 7/7 London bombings (July 2005), the Australian bombing plan (November 2005), the Toronto plot (June 2006), and the foiled British project of blowing up several planes over the Atlantic (August 2006).

These freelance terrorists have very little knowledge of the Quran, and so it is pointless to attempt a debate about their interpretation of scripture or to blame "Islam" for their crimes.[101] Indeed, Marc Sageman, who has talked with several of them, believes that a regular religious education might have deterred them from lawless violence. They are, he has found, chiefly motivated by the desire to escape a stifling sense of insignificance and pointlessness in secular nation-states that struggle to absorb foreign minorities. They seek to fulfill the age-old dream of military glory and believe that by dying a heroic death, they will give their lives meaning as local heroes.[102] In these cases, suffice it to say, what we call "Islamic terrorism" has been transformed from a political cause— inflamed with pious exhortations contrary to Islamic teachings—into a violent expression out of youthful rage. They may claim to be acting in the name of Islam, but when an untalented beginner claims to be playing a Beethoven sonata, we hear only cacophony.

One of Bin Laden's objectives had been to draw Muslims all over the world to his vision of jihad. Though he did become a charismatic folk hero to some—a kind of Saudi Che—in this central mission he ultimately failed. Between 2001 and 2007, a Gallup poll conducted in thirty-five predominantly Muslim countries found that only 7 percent of respondents thought the 9/11 attacks were "completely justified"; for these people, the reasons were entirely political. As for the 93 percent who condemned the attacks, they quoted Quranic verses to show that the killing of innocent people could have no place in Islam.[103] One might well wonder how much more unanimously opposed to terror the Muslim world might have become, but for the course the United States and its allies took in the wake of 9/11. At a time when even in Tehran there were demonstrations of solidarity with America, the Bush and Blair coalition lashed out with its own violent rejoinder, a drive that would culminate in the tragically misbegotten Iraq invasion of 2003. Its most decisive result was to present the world with a new set of images of Muslim suffering in which the West was not only implicated but for which it was, this time, directly responsible. When considering the tenacity of al-Qaeda, it is well to remember that such images of Muslim suffering, more than any expansive theory of jihad, were what had drawn so many young Muslims to the camps of Peshawar in the first instance.

We routinely and rightly condemn the terrorism that kills civilians in the name of God, but we cannot claim the high moral ground if we dismiss the suffering and death of the many thousands of civilians who die in our wars as "collateral damage." Ancient religious mythologies helped people to face up to the dilemma of state violence, but our current nationalist ideologies seem by contrast to promote a retreat into denial or hardening of our hearts. Nothing shows this more clearly than a remark of Madeleine Albright's when she was still Bill Clinton's ambassador to the United Nations. She later retracted it, but among people all around the world, it has never been forgotten. In 1996, on CBS's *60 Minutes,* Lesley Stahl asked her whether the cost of international sanctions against Iraq was justified: "We have heard that half a million children have died. I mean, that is more than died in Hiroshima. . . . Is the price worth it?" "I think this is a very hard choice," Albright replied, "but the price, we think the price is worth it."[104]

On October 24, 2012, Mamana Bibi, a sixty-five-year-old woman picking vegetables in her family's large open land in northern Waziristan, Pakistan, was killed by a U.S. drone aircraft. She was not a terrorist but a midwife married to a retired schoolteacher, yet she was blown to pieces in front of her nine young grandchildren. Some of the children have had multiple surgeries that the family could ill afford because they lost all their livestock; the smaller children still scream in terror all night long. We do not know who the real targets were. Yet even though the U.S. government claims to carry out thorough poststrike assessments, it has never apologized, never offered compensation to the family, nor even admitted what happened to the American people. CIA director John O. Brennan had previously claimed that drone strikes caused absolutely no civilian casualties; more recently he has admitted otherwise while maintaining that such deaths are extremely rare. Since then, Amnesty International reviewed some forty-five strikes in the region, finding evidence of unlawful civilian deaths, and has reported several strikes that appear to have killed civilians outside the bounds of law.[105] "Bombs create only hatred in the hearts of people. And that hatred and anger breed more terrorism," said Bibi's son. "No one ever asked *us* who was killed or injured that day. Not the United States or my own government. Nobody has come to investigate nor has anyone been held accountable. Quite simply, nobody seems to care."[106]

"Am I my brother's guardian?" Cain asked after he had killed his brother, Abel. We are now living in such an interconnected world that we are all implicated in one another's history and one another's tragedies. As we—quite rightly—condemn those terrorists who kill innocent people, we also have to find a way to acknowledge our relationship with and responsibility for Mamana Bibi, her family, and the hundreds of thousands of civilians who have died or been mutilated in our modern wars simply because they were in the wrong place at the wrong time.

Afterword

We have seen that, like the weather, religion "does lots of different things." To claim that it has a single, unchanging, and inherently violent essence is not accurate. Identical religious beliefs and practices have inspired diametrically opposed courses of action. In the Hebrew Bible, the Deuteronomists and the Priestly authors all meditated on the same stories, but the Deuteronomists turned virulently against foreign peoples, while the Priestly authors sought reconciliation. Chinese Daoists, Legalists, and military strategists shared the same set of ideas and meditative disciplines but put them to entirely different uses. Saint Luke and the Johannine authors all reflected on Jesus's message of love, but Luke reached out to marginalized members of society, while the Johannines confined their love to their own group. Antony and the Syrian boskoi both set out to practice "freedom from care," but Antony spent his life trying to empty his mind of anger and hatred, while the Syrian monks surrendered to the aggressive drives of the reptilian brain. Ibn Taymiyyah and Rumi were both victims of the Mongol invasions, but they used the teachings of Islam to come to entirely different conclusions. For centuries the story of Imam Husain's tragic death inspired Shiis to withdraw from political life in principled protest against systemic injustice; more recently it has inspired them to take political action and say no to tyranny.

Until the modern period, religion permeated all aspects of life, including politics and warfare, not because ambitious churchmen had "mixed up" two essentially distinct activities but because people wanted to endow everything they did with significance. Every state ideology was religious. The kings of Europe who struggled to liberate themselves from papal control were not "secularists" but were revered as semidivine. Every successful empire has claimed that it had a divine mission; that its enemies were evil, misguided, or tyrannical; and that it would benefit humanity. And because these states and empires were all created and maintained by force, religion has been implicated in their violence. It was not until the seventeenth and eighteenth centuries that religion was ejected from political life in the West. When, therefore, people claim that religion has been responsible for *more* war, oppression, and suffering than any other human institution, one has to ask, "More than *what*?" Until the American and French Revolutions, there were no "secular" societies. So ingrained is our impulse to "sanctify" our political activities that no sooner had the French revolutionaries successfully marginalized the Catholic Church than they created a new national religion. In the United States, the first secular republic, the state has always had a religious aura, a manifest destiny, and a divinely sanctioned mission.

John Locke believed that the separation of church and state was the key to peace, but the nation-state has been far from war-averse. The problem lies not in the multifaceted activity that we call "religion" but in the violence embedded in our human nature and the nature of the state, which from the start required the forcible subjugation of at least 90 percent of the population. As Ashoka discovered, even if a ruler shrank from state aggression, it was impossible to disband the army. The *Mahabharata* lamented the dilemma of the warrior-king doomed to a life of warfare. The Chinese realized very early that a degree of force was essential to civilized life. Ancient Israel tried initially to escape the agrarian state, yet Israelites soon discovered that much as they hated the exploitation and cruelty of urban civilization, they could not live without it; they too had to become "like all the nations." Jesus preached an inclusive and compassionate kingdom that defied the imperial ethos, and he was crucified for his pains. The Muslim ummah began as an alternative to the jahili injustice of commercial Mecca, but eventually it had to become an empire, because an absolute monarchy was the best and perhaps the only way to keep the peace. Modern military historians agree that without professional and responsible armies, human society would either have remained in a primitive state or would have degenerated into ceaselessly warring hordes.

Before the creation of the nation-state, people thought about politics in a religious way. Constantine's empire showed what could happen when an originally peaceful tradition became too closely associated with the government; the Christian emperors enforced the Pax Christiana as belligerently as their pagan predecessors had imposed the Pax Romana. The Crusades were inspired by religious passion but were also deeply political: Pope Urban II let the knights of Christendom loose on the Muslim world to extend the power of the Church eastward, and create a papal monarchy that would control Christian Europe. The Inquisition was a deeply flawed attempt to secure the internal order of Spain after a divisive civil war. The Wars of Religion and the Thirty Years' War may have been pervaded by the sectarian quarrels of the Reformation, but they were also the birth pangs of the modern nation-state.

When we fight, we need to distance ourselves from the adversary, and because religion was so central to the state, its rites and myths depicted its enemies as monsters of evil that threatened cosmic and political order. During the Middle Ages, Christians denounced Jews as child-killers, Muslims as "an evil and despicable race," and Cathars as a cancerous growth in the body of Christendom. Again, this hatred was certainly religiously motivated, but it was also a response to the social distress that accompanied early modernization. Christians made Jews the scapegoat for their excessive anxiety about the money economy, and popes blamed Cathars for their own inability to live up to the gospel. In the process they created imaginary enemies who were distorted mirror images of themselves. Yet casting off the mantle of religion did not bring an end to prejudice. A "scientific racism" developed in the modern period that drew on the old religious patterns of hatred and inspired the Armenian genocide and Hitler's death camps. Secular nationalism, imposed so unceremoniously by the colonialists, would regularly merge with local religious traditions, where people had not yet abstracted "religion" from politics; as a result, these religious traditions were often distorted and developed an aggressive strain.

The sectarian hatreds that develop within a faith tradition are often cited to prove that "religion" is chronically intolerant. These internal feuds have indeed been bitter and virulent, but they too have nearly always had a political dimension. Christian "heretics" were persecuted for using the gospel to articulate their rejection of the systemic injustice and violence of the agrarian state. Even the abstruse debates about the nature of Christ in the Eastern Church were fueled by the political ambitions of the "tyrant-bishops." Heretics were often persecuted when the nation feared external attack. The xenophobic theology of the Deuteronomists developed when the Kingdom of Judah faced political annihilation. Ibn Taymiyyah introduced the practice of takfir when Muslims in the Near East were menaced by the Crusaders from the West and the Mongols from the East. The Inquisition took place against the backdrop of the Ottoman threat and the Wars of Religion, just as the September Massacres and the Reign of Terror in revolutionary France were motivated by fears of foreign invasion.

Lord Acton accurately predicted that the liberal nation-state would persecute ethnic and cultural "minorities," who have indeed taken the place of "heretics." In Iraq, Pakistan, and Lebanon, traditional Sunni/ Shii animosity has been aggravated by nationalism and the problems of the postcolonial state. In the past Sunni Muslims were always loath to call their coreligionists "apostates," because they believed that God alone knew what was in a person's heart. But the practice of takfir has become common in our own day, when Muslims once again fear foreign enemies. When Muslims attack churches and synagogues today, they are not driven to do so by Islam. The Quran commands Muslims to respect the faith of "the people of the book."[1] One of the most frequently quoted jihad verses justifies warfare by stating: "If God did not repel some people by means of others, many monasteries, churches, synagogues, and mosques, where God's name is much invoked, would have been destroyed."[2] This new aggression toward religious minorities in the nation-state is largely the result of political tensions arising from Western imperialism (associated with Christianity) and the Palestinian problem.[3]

It is simply not true that "religion" is always aggressive. Sometimes it has actually put a brake on violence. In the ninth century BCE, Indian ritualists extracted all violence from the liturgy and created the ideal of ahimsa, "nonviolence." The medieval Peace and Truce of God forced knights to stop terrorizing the poor and outlawed violence from Wednesday to Sunday each week. Most dramatically, after the Bar Kokhba war, the rabbis reinterpreted the scriptures so effectively that Jews refrained from political aggression for a millennium. Such successes have been rare. Because of the inherent violence of the states in which we live, the best that prophets and sages have been able to do is provide an alternative. The Buddhist sangha had no political power, but it became a vibrant presence in ancient India and even influenced emperors. Ashoka published the ideals of ahimsa, tolerance, kindness, and respect in the extraordinary inscriptions he published throughout the empire. Confucians kept the ideal of humanity (*ren*) alive in the government of imperial China until the revolution. For centuries, the egalitarian code of the Shariah was a countercultural challenge to the Abbasid aristocracy; the caliphs acknowledged that it was God's law, even though they could not rule by it.

Other sages and mystics developed spiritual practices to help people control their aggression and develop a reverence for all human beings. In India, renouncers practiced the disciplines of yoga and ahimsa to eradicate egotistic machismo. Others cultivated the ideals of anatta ("no self") and kenosis ("self-emptying") to control the "me first" impulses that so often lead to violence; they sought an "equanimity" that would make it impossible for one to see oneself as superior to anybody else, taught that every single person has sacred potential, and asserted that people should even love their enemies. Prophets and psalmists insisted that a city could not be "holy" if the ruling class did not care for the poor and dispossessed. Priests urged their compatriots to draw on the memory of their own past suffering to assuage the pain of others, instead of using it to justify harassment and persecution. They all insisted in one way or another that if people did not treat all others as they would wish to be treated themselves and develop a "concern for everybody," society was doomed. If the colonial powers had observed the Golden Rule in their colonies, we would not be having so many political problems today.

One of the most ubiquitous religious practices was the cult of community. In the premodern world, religion was a communal rather than a private pursuit. People achieved enlightenment and salvation by learning to live harmoniously together. Instead of distancing themselves from their fellow humans as the warriors did, sages, prophets, and mystics helped people cultivate a relationship with and responsibility for those they would not ordinarily find congenial. They devised meditations that deliberately extended their benevolence to the ends of the earth; wished all beings happiness; taught their compatriots to revere the holiness of every single person; and resolved to find practical ways of assuaging the world's suffering. Neuroscientists have discovered that Buddhist monks who have practiced this compassionate meditation assiduously have physically enhanced those centers of the brain that spark our empathy. Jains cultivated an outstanding vision of the community of all creatures. Muslims achieved the surrender of *islam* by taking responsibility for one another and sharing what they had with those in need. In Paul's churches, rich and poor were instructed to sit at the same table and eat the same food. Cluniac monks made lay Christians live together like monks during a pilgrimage, rich and poor sharing the same hardships. The Eucharist was not a solitary communion with Christ but a rite that bonded the political community.

From a very early date, prophets and poets helped people to contemplate the tragedy of life and face up to the damage they did to others. In ancient Sumeria the *Atrahasis* could not find a solution to the social injustice on which their civilization depended, but this popular tale made people aware of it. Gilgamesh had to come face-to-face with the horror of death, which drained warfare of spurious glamour and nobility. The Prophets of Israel compelled rulers to take responsibility for the suffering they inflicted on the poor and lambasted them for their war crimes. The Priestly authors of the Hebrew Bible lived in a violent society and could not abjure warfare but believed that warriors were contaminated by their violence, even if the campaign had been endorsed by God. That was why David was not allowed to build Yahweh's temple. The Aryans loved warfare and revered their warriors; fighting and raiding were essential to the pastoral economy; but the warrior always carried a taint. Chinese strategists admitted that the military way of life was a "way of deception" and must be segregated from civilian life. They drew attention to the uncomfortable fact that even an idealistic state nurtured at its heart an institution dedicated to killing, lying, and treachery.

In the West secularism is now a part of our identity. It has been beneficial—not least because an intimate association with government can badly compromise a faith tradition. But it has had its own violence. Revolutionary France was secularized by coercion, extortion, and bloodshed; for the first time it mobilized the whole of society for war; and its secularism seemed propelled by an aggression toward religion that is still shared by many Europeans today. The United States did not stigmatize faith in the same way, and religion has flourished there. There was an aggression in early modern thought, which failed to apply the concept of human rights to the indigenous peoples of the Americas or to African slaves. In the developing world secularization has been experienced as lethal, hostile, and invasive. There have been massacres in sacred shrines; clerics have been tortured, imprisoned, and assassinated; madrassa students shot down and humiliated; and the clerical establishment systematically deprived of resources, dignity, and status.

Hence secularization has sometimes damaged religion. Even in the relatively benign atmosphere of the United States, Protestant fundamentalists became xenophobic and fearful of modernity. The horrors of Nasser's prison polarized the vision of Sayyid Qutb; his former liberalism was transformed into a paranoid vision that saw enemies everywhere. Khomeini too frequently spoke of conspiracies of Jews, Christians, and imperialists. The Deobandis, bruised by the British abolition of the Moghul Empire, created a rigid, rule-bound form of Islam and gave us the Taliban travesty, a noxious combination of Deobandi rigidity, tribal chauvinism, and the aggression of the traumatized war orphan. In the Indian subcontinent and the Middle East, the alien ideology of nationalism transformed traditional religious symbols and myths and gave them a violent dimension. But the relationship between modernity and religion has not been wholly antagonistic. Some movements, such as the two Great Awakenings and the Muslim Brotherhood, have actually helped people to embrace modern ideals and institutions in a more familiar idiom.

Modern religious violence is not an alien growth but is part of the modern scene. We have created an interconnected world. It is true that we are dangerously polarized, but we are also linked together more closely than ever before. When shares fall in one region, markets plummet all around the globe. What happens in Palestine or Iraq today can have repercussions tomorrow in New York, London, or Madrid. We are connected electronically so that images of suffering and devastation in a remote Syrian village or an Iraqi prison are instantly beamed around the world. We all face the possibility of environmental or nuclear catastrophe. But our perceptions have not caught up with the realities of our situation, so that in the First World we still tend to put ourselves in a special privileged category. Our policies have helped to create widespread rage and frustration, and in the West we bear some responsibility for the suffering in the Muslim world that Bin Laden was able to exploit. "Am I my brother's guardian?" The answer must surely be yes.

War, it has been said, is caused "by our inability to see relationships.

Our relationship with our economic and historical situation. Our relationship with our fellow-men. And above all our relationship to nothingness. To death."[4] We need ideologies today, religious or secular, that help people to face up to the intractable dilemmas of our current "economic and historical situation" as the prophets did in the past. Even though we no longer have to contend with the oppressive injustice of the agrarian empire, there is still massive inequality and an unfair imbalance of power. But the dispossessed are no longer helpless peasants; they have found ways of fighting back. If we want a viable world, we have to take responsibility for the pain of others and learn to listen to narratives that challenge our sense of ourselves. All this requires the "surrender," selflessness, and compassion that have been just as important in the history of religion as crusades and jihads.

We all wrestle—in secular or religious ways—with "nothingness," the void at the heart of modern culture. Ever since Zoroaster, religious movements that tried to address the violence of their time have absorbed some of its aggression. Protestant fundamentalism came into being in the United States when evangelical Christians pondered the unprecedented slaughter of the First World War. Their apocalyptic vision was simply a religious version of the secular "future war" genre that had developed in Europe. Religious fundamentalists and extremists have used the language of faith to express fears that also afflict secularists. We have seen that some of the cruelest and most self-destructive of these movements have been in part a response to the Holocaust or the nuclear threat. Groups such as Shukri Mustafa's Society in Sadat's Egypt can hold up a distorted mirror image of the structural violence of contemporary culture. Secularists as well as religious people have resorted to the suicide attack, which in some ways reflects the death wish in modern culture. Religious and secularists have shared the same enthusiasms. Kookism was clearly a religious form of secular nationalism and was able to work closely with the Israeli secular right. The Muslims who flocked to join the jihad against the Soviet Union were certainly reviving the classical Islamic practice of "volunteering," but they also experienced the impulse that prompted hundreds of Europeans to leave the safety of home and fight in the Spanish Civil War (1936–39) and Jews to hasten from the diaspora to support Israel on the eve of the Six-Day War.

When we confront the violence of our time, it is natural to harden our hearts to the global pain and deprivation that makes us feel uncomfortable, depressed, and frustrated. Yet we must find ways of contemplating these distressing facts of modern life, or we will lose the best part of our humanity. Somehow we have to find ways of doing what religion—at its best—has done for centuries: build a sense of global community, cultivate a sense of reverence and "equanimity" for all, and take responsibility for the suffering we see in the world. We are all, religious and secularist alike, responsible for the current predicament of the world. There is no state, however idealistic and however great its achievements, that has not incurred the taint of the warrior. It is a stain on the international community that Mamana Bibi's son can say: "Quite simply, nobody seems to care." The scapegoat ritual was an attempt to sever the community's relationship with its misdeeds; it cannot be a solution for us today.

Acknowledgments

This book is dedicated to Jane Garrett, my friend as well as my editor at Knopf for twenty years. From the very beginning, your encouragement and enthusiasm gave me the strength to persevere with the daily jihad of writing; it was a privilege and a joy to work with you.

I am also blessed with my editors George Andreou and Jorg Hensgen, whose stringent, meticulous work on the manuscript helped me to push the book into another dimension, for which I am sincerely grateful. My thanks also to all the people who have worked on the book with such skill and expertise—at The Bodley Head: Stuart Williams (editor), Beth Humphries (copy editor), Joe Pickering (publicist), James Jones (jacket designer), Mary Chamberlain (proofreader), and Katherine Ailes (assistant editor); at Knopf: Roméo Enriquez (production manager), Ellen Feldman (production editor), Kim Thornton (publicist), Oliver Munday (jacket designer), Cassandra Pappas (text designer), Janet Biehl (copy editor), and Terezia Cicelova (editorial assistant); and at Knopf Canada: Louise Dennys (editor) and Sheila Kaye (publicist). Many of you I have never met, but be assured I appreciate all you do for me.

As always, I must thank my agents Felicity Bryan, Peter Ginsberg, and Andrew Nurnberg for their tireless support, loyalty, and, above all, their continued faith in me; this time, I really could not have managed without you. Thanks too to Michele Topham, Jackie Head, and Carole Robinson in Felicity Bryan's office for helping me so cheerfully through the day-to-day crises of a writer's life, from bookkeeping to computer meltdowns. And my sincere gratitude to Nancy Roberts, my assistant, for dealing so patiently with my correspondence and for her adamantine firmness in ensuring that I have time and space to write.

A big thank-you to Sally Cockburn, whose paintings helped me to understand what my book was, in part, about. And, finally, thanks to Eve, Gary, Stacey, and Amy Mott, and Michelle Stevenson at My Ideal Dog, for looking after Poppy so devotedly during her last years and enabling me to do my work. This book is also in loving memory of Gary, who always saw to the heart of things and would, I think, have approved its contents.

Notes

INTRODUCTION

1. Leviticus 16:21–22. Unless otherwise stated, all biblical quotations—in both the Hebrew Bible and the New Testament—are from *The Jerusalem Bible* (London, 1966).

2. René Girard, *Violence and the Sacred,* trans. Patrick Gregory (Baltimore, 1977), p. 251.

3. Stanislav Andreski, *Military Organization in Society* (Berkeley, Los Angeles, and London, 1968); Robert L. O'Connell, *Ride of the Second Horseman: The Birth and Death of War* (New York and Oxford, 1995), pp. 6–13, 106–10, 128–29; O'Connell, *Of Arms and Men: A History of War, Weapons and Aggression* (New York and Oxford, 1989), pp. 22–25; John Keegan, *A History of Warfare* (London and New York, 1993), pp. 223–29; Bruce Lincoln, "War and Warriors: An Overview," in *Death, War, and Sacrifice: Studies in Ideology and Practice* (Chicago and London, 1991), pp. 138–40; Johan Huizinga, *Homo Ludens: A Study of the Play Element in Culture* (Boston, 1955 ed.), pp. 89–104; Mark Juergensmeyer, *Terror in the Mind of God: The Global Rise of Religious Violence* (Berkeley, Los Angeles, and London, 2001), p. 90; Malise Ruthven, *A Fury for God: The Islamist Attack on America* (London, 2002), p. 101; James A. Aho, *Religious Mythology and the Art of War: Comparative Religious Symbolisms of Military Violence* (Westport, CT, 1981), pp. xi–xiii, 4–35; Richard English, *Terrorism: How to Respond* (Oxford and New York, 2009), pp. 27–55.

4. Thomas A. Idinopulos and Brian C. Wilson, eds., *What Is Religion? Origins, Definitions, and Explanations* (Leiden, 1998); Wilfred Cantwell Smith, *The Meaning and End of Religion: A New Approach to the Religious Traditions of Mankind* (New York, 1962); Talal Asad, "The Construction of Religion as an Anthropological Category," in *Genealogies of Religion: Discipline and Reasons of Power in Christianity and Islam* (Baltimore and London, 1993); Derek Peterson and Darren Walhof, eds., *The Invention of Religion: Rethinking Belief in Politics and History* (New Brunswick, NJ, and London, 2002); Timothy Fitzgerald, ed., *Religion and the Secular: Historical and Colonial Formations* (London and Oakville, CT, 2007); Arthur L. Greil and David G. Bromley, eds., *Defining Religion: Investigating the Boundaries Between the Sacred and Secular* (Oxford, 2003); Daniel Dubuisson, *The Western Construction of Religion: Myths, Knowledge and Ideology,* trans. William Sayers (Baltimore, 2003); William T. Cavanaugh, *The Myth of Religious Violence* (Oxford, 2009).

5. Dubuisson, *Western Construction of Religion,* p. 168.

6. H. J. Rose, "Religion, Terms Relating to," in M. Carey, ed., *The Oxford Classical Dictionary* (Oxford, 1949).

7. Smith, *Meaning and End of Religion,* pp. 50–68.

8. Louis Jacobs, ed., *The Jewish Religion: A Companion* (Oxford, 1995), p. 418.

9. Smith, *Meaning and End of Religion,* pp. 23–25, 29–31, 33.

10. Cavanaugh, *Myth of Religious Violence,* pp. 72–85.

11. Mircea Eliade, *The Myth of Eternal Return, or, Cosmos and History,* trans. Willard R. Trask (Princeton, NJ, 1991), pp. 1–34.

12. Ibid., pp. 32–34; Karl Jaspers, *The Origin and Goal of History,* trans. Michael Bullock (London, 1953), p. 40.

13. Paul Gilbert, *The Compassionate Mind: A New Approach to Life's Challenges* (London, 2009).

14. P. Broca, "Anatomie comparée des circonvolutions cérébrales: le grand lobe limbique," *Revue d'anthropologie* 1 (1868).

15. Gilbert, *Compassionate Mind,* pp. 170–71.

16. Mencius, *The Book of Mencius,* 2A:6.

17. Walter Burkert, *Homo Necans: The Anthropology of Greek Sacrificial Ritual,* trans. Peter Bing (Berkeley, Los Angeles, and London, 1983), pp. 16–22.

18. Mircea Eliade, *A History of Religious Ideas,* trans. Willard R. Trask, 3 vols. (Chicago and London, 1978, 1982, 1985), 1:7–8, 24; Joseph Campbell, *Historical Atlas of World Mythologies,* 2 vols. (New York, 1988), 1:48–49; Joseph Campbell with Bill Moyers, *The Power of Myth* (New York, 1988), pp. 70–72, 85–87.

19. André LeRoi-Gourhan, *Treasures of Prehistoric Art,* trans. Norbert Guterman (New York, 1967), p. 112.

20. Jill Cook, *The Swimming Reindeer* (London, 2010).

21. Neil MacGregor, *A History of the Word in 100 Objects* (London and New York, 2001), pp. 22, 24.

22. J. Ortega y Gasset, *Meditations on Hunting* (New York, 1985), p. 3.

23. Walter Burkert, *Structure and History in Greek Mythology and Ritual* (Berkeley, Los Angeles, and London, 1980), pp. 54–56; Burkert, *Homo Necans,* pp. 42–45.

24. O'Connell, *Ride of Second Horseman,* p. 33.

25. Chris Hedges, *War Is a Force That Gives Us Meaning* (New York, 2003), p. 10.

26. Theodore Nadelson, *Trained to Kill: Soldiers at War* (Baltimore, 2005), pp. 64, 68–69.

27. Hedges, *War Is a Force,* p. 3.

28. Irenöus Eibl-Eibesfeldt, *Human Ethology* (New York, 1989), p. 405.

29. Lt. Col. Dave Grossman, *On Killing: The Psychological Cost of Learning to Kill in War and Society,* rev. ed. (New York, 2009), pp. 3–4.

30. Joanna Bourke, *An Intimate History of Killing: Face to Face Killing in Twentieth-Century Warfare* (New York, 1999), p. 67.

31. Peter Jay, *Road to Riches, or The Wealth of Man* (London, 2000), pp. 35–36.

32. K. J. Wenke, *Patterns of Prehistory: Humankind's First Three Million Years* (New York, 1961), p. 130; Keegan, *History of Warfare,* pp. 120–21; O'Connell, *Ride of Second Horseman,* p. 35.

33. M. H. Fried, *The Evolution of Political Society: An Essay in Political Anthropology* (New York, 1967), pp. 101–2; Clark McCauley, "Conference Overview," in Jonathan Haas, ed., *The Anthropology of War* (Cambridge, UK, 1990), p. 11.

34. Gerhard E. Lenski, *Power and Privilege: A Theory of Social Stratification* (Chapel Hill, NC, and London, 1966), pp. 189–90.

35. O'Connell, *Ride of Second Horseman,* pp. 57–58.

36. J. L. Angel, "Paleoecology, Pleodeography and Health," in S. Polgar, ed., *Population, Ecology, and Social Evolution* (The Hague, 1975); David Rindos, *The Origins of Agriculture: An Evolutionary Perspective* (Orlando, FL, 1984), pp. 186–87.

37. E. O. James, *The Ancient Gods: The History and Diffusion of Religion in the Ancient Near East and the Eastern Mediterranean* (London, 1960), p. 89; S. H. Hooke, *Middle Eastern Mythology: From the Assyrians to the Hebrews* (Harmondsworth, UK, 1963), p. 83.

38. Kathleen Kenyon, *Digging Up Jericho: The Results of the Jericho Excavations, 1953–1956* (New York, 1957).

39. Jacob Bronowski, *The Ascent of Man* (Boston, 1973), pp. 86–88; James Mellaart, "Early Urban Communities in the Near East, 9000 to 3400 BCE," in P. R. S. Moorey, ed., *The Origins of Civilisation* (Oxford, 1979), pp. 22–25; P. Dorell, "The Uniqueness of Jericho," in P. R. S. Moorey and P. J. Parr, eds., *Archaeology in the Levant: Essays for Kathleen Kenyon* (Warminster, UK, 1978).

40. Robert Eisen, *The Peace and Violence of Judaism: From the Bible to Modern Zionism* (Oxford, 2011), p. 12.

41. World Council of Churches, *Violence, Nonviolence and the Struggle for Social Justice* (Geneva, 1972), p. 6.

42. Lenski, *Power and Privilege,* pp. 105–14; O'Connell, *Ride of Second Horseman,* p. 28; E. O. Wilson, *On Human Nature* (Cambridge, MA, 1978), p. 140; Margaret Ehrenberg, *Women in Prehistory* (London, 1989), p. 38.

43. A. R. Radcliffe, *The Andaman Islanders* (New York, 1948), pp. 43, 177.

44. John H. Kautsky, *The Politics of Aristocratic Empires,* 2nd ed. (New Brunswick, NJ, and London, 1997), pp. 374, 177.

45. Keegan, *History of Warfare,* pp. 384–86; John Haldon, *Warfare, State and Society in the Byzantine World, 565–1204* (London and New York, 2005), pp. 10–11.

46. Bruce Lincoln, "The Role of Religion in Achaemenian Imperialism," in Nicole Brisch, ed., *Religion and Power: Divine Kingship in the Ancient World and Beyond* (Chicago, 2008).

47. Cavanaugh, *Myth of Religious Violence.*

I · FARMERS AND HERDSMEN

1. *The Epic of Gilgamesh,* Standard Version, tablet 1:38. Unless otherwise stated, all quotations are from *Gilgamesh: A New English Version,* trans. Stephen Mitchell (New York, London, Toronto, and Sydney, 2004).

2. *Gilgamesh* 1:18–20.

3. *Gilgamesh* 1:29–34, Mitchell's emphasis.

4. The earliest extant texts date from the late third millennium; the Old Babylonian Epic combined these in a single work (c. 1700 BCE). Sin-Leqi's poem (c. 1200 BCE) is the standard version on which most modern translations are based.

5. *Gilgamesh,* Standard Version, tablet 1:67–69; *The Epic of Gilgamesh: The Babylonian Epic Poem in Akkadian and Sumerian,* trans. Andrew George (London, 1999).

6. *Epic of Gilgamesh,* George translation, p. xlvi.

7. John Keegan, *A History of Warfare* (London and New York, 1993), pp. 126–30; Robert L. O'Connell, *Ride of the Second Horseman: The Birth and Death of War* (New York and Oxford, 1995), pp. 88–89.

8. R. M. Adams, *Heartlands of Cities: Surveys of Ancient Settlements and Land Use on the Central Floodplains of the Euphrates* (Chicago, 1981), pp. 60, 244; William H. McNeill, *Plagues and People* (London, 1994), p. 47.

9. McNeill, *Plagues and People,* pp. 54–55.

10. Gerhard E. Lenski, *Power and Privilege: A Theory of Social Stratification* (Chapel Hill, NC, and London, 1966), p. 228.

11. A. L. Oppenheim, *Ancient Mesopotamia: Portrait of a Dead Civilization* (Chicago, 1977), pp. 82–83; O'Connell, *Ride of Second Horseman,* pp. 93–95.

12. Samuel N. Kramer, *Sumerian Mythology: A Study of the Spiritual and Literary Achievement of the Third Millennium BC* (Philadelphia, 1944), pp. 118, 119.

13. Norman K. Gottwald, *The Politics of Ancient Israel* (Louisville, KY, 2001), pp. 118–19.

14. O'Connell, *Ride of Second Horseman,* pp. 91–92.

15. Georges Dumézil, *The Destiny of the Warrior,* trans. Alf Hiltebeitel (Chicago and London, 1969), p. 3.

16. Thorkild Jacobsen, "The Cosmos as State," in H. and H. A. Frankfort, eds., *The Intellectual Adventure of Ancient Man: An Essay on Speculative Thought in the Ancient Near East* (Chicago, 1946), pp. 148–51.

17. *Gilgamesh,* Standard Version, tablet 1:48.

18. I have discussed this more fully in *A Short History of Myth* (London, 2005).

19. Jacobsen, "Cosmos as State," pp. 145–48, 186–97; *Epic of Gilgamesh,* George translation, pp. xxxvii–xxxviii.

20. Jacobsen, "Cosmos as State," pp. 186–91; Tammi J. Schneider, *An Introduction to Ancient Mesopotamian Religion* (Grand Rapids, MI, and Cambridge, UK, 2011), pp. 66–79; George, *Epic of Gilgamesh,* pp. xxxviii–xxxix.

21. Schneider, *Ancient Mesopotamian Religion,* p. 5; Jacobsen, "Cosmos as State," p. 203.

22. John H. Kautsky, *The Politics of Aristocratic Empires,* 2nd ed. (New Brunswick, NJ, and London, 1997), pp. 15–16, 107.

23. Thomas Merton, *Faith and Violence* (Notre Dame, IN, 1968), pp. 7–8.

24. Walter Benjamin, "Theses on the Philosophy of History," in Benjamin, *Illuminations* (London, 1999), p. 248.

25. Max Weber, *The Theory of Social and Economic Organization,* trans. A. M. Henderson and Talcott Parsons (New York, 1947), pp. 341–48.

26. *Gilgamesh,* Standard Version, tablet 1:80, 82–90.

27. *Atrahasis* 1:i, in *Myths from Mesopotamia: Creation, the Flood, Gilgamesh, and Others,* trans. Stephanie Dalley (Oxford and New York, 1989), p. 10.

28. *Atrahasis* 1:iii, p. 12.

29. *Atrahasis* 1:iii, p. 14.

30. *Atrahasis* 2:iii, p. 23.

31. *Atrahasis* 3:vii, p. 28.

32. W. G. Lambert and A. R. Millard, *Atra-Hasis: The Babylonian Story of the Flood* (Oxford, 1969), pp. 31–39.

33. Schneider, *Ancient Mesopotamian Religion,* p. 45.

34. Keegan, *History of Warfare,* p. 128.

35. *Epic of Gilgamesh,* Standard Version, tablet 2:109–110, George translation.

36. *Epic of Gilgamesh,* tablet 1:220–23, George translation.

37. Ibid., Yale Tablet, 18, George translation.

38. O'Connell, *Ride of Second Horseman,* pp. 96–97.

39. A. L. Oppenheim, "Trade in the Ancient Near East," *International Congress of Economic History* 5 (1976).

40. Kautsky, *Politics of Aristocratic Empires,* p. 178.

41. Thorstein Veblen, *The Theory of the Leisure Class: An Economic Study of Institutions* (Boston, 1973), pp. 41, 45, 30; my emphasis.

42. *Gilgamesh,* Yale Tablet, 97; Standard Version, tablet 3:54.

43. Kautsky, *Politics of Aristocratic Empires,* pp. 170–72, 346.

44. *Gilgamesh,* Standard Version, tablet 2:233, Yale Tablet, 149–50.

45. *Gilgamesh,* 185–87; Mitchell's emphasis.

46. *Gilgamesh,* Standard Version, tablet 3:44.

47. Chris Hedges, *War Is a Force That Give Us Meaning* (New York, 2003), p. 21.

48. *Gilgamesh,* Yale Tablet, line 269.

49. *Gilgamesh,* Standard Version, tablet 11:322–26.

50. R. L. D. Cribb, *Nomads and Archaeology* (Cambridge, UK, 1999), pp. 18, 136, 215.

51. O'Connell, *Ride of Second Horseman,* pp. 67–68.

52. K. C. Chang, *The Archaeology of Ancient China* (New Haven, CT, 1968), pp. 152–54.

53. O'Connell, *Ride of Second Horseman*, pp. 77–78.

54. Ibid.

55. Tacitus, *Germania*, 14, quoted in Kautsky, *Politics of Aristocratic Empires*, p. 178.

56. Veblen, *Theory of Leisure Class*, p. 45.

57. Bruce Lincoln, "Indo-European Religions: An Introduction," in Lincoln, *Death, War, and Sacrifice: Studies in Ideology and Practice* (Chicago and London, 1991), pp. 1–10.

58. Mary Boyce, "Priests, Cattle and Men," *Bulletin of the School of Oriental and African Studies* 50, no. 3 (1998).

59. For example, *Yasna* 30.7c, 32, 49:4b, 50:7a, 30:106, 44:4d, 51:96; Bruce Lincoln, "Warriors and Non-Herdsmen; A Response to Mary Boyce," *Death, War, and Sacrifice*, pp. 147–60.

60. Lincoln, "Indo-European Religions," pp. 10–13.

61. Ibid., p. 12.

62. Bruce Lincoln, "War and Warriors: An Overview," in *Death, War, and Sacrifice*, pp. 138–40.

63. Homer, *Iliad*, 12:310–15, in *The Iliad of Homer*, trans. Richard Lattimore (Chicago and London, 1951). All quotes from the *Iliad* are from this translation.

64. Lincoln, "War and Warriors," p. 143.

65. Georges Dumézil, *The Destiny of the Warrior*, trans. Alf Hiltebeitel (Chicago and London, 1969), pp. 64–74.

66. *Iliad*, 20:490–94.

67. *Iliad*, 20:495–503; Seth L. Schein, *The Mortal Hero: An Introduction to Homer's Iliad* (Berkeley, Los Angeles, and London, 1984), pp. 145–46.

68. Lincoln, "Indo-European Religions," p. 4.

69. Dumézil, *Destiny of Warrior*, pp. 106–7.

70. *Iliad*, 4:492–88.

71. Homer, *Odyssey*, 11:500 in *Homer: The Odyssey*, trans. Walter Shewring (Oxford and New York, 1980).

72. James Mellaart, *Neolithic of the Near East* (New York, 1976), pp. 119, 167, 206–7; O'Connell, *Ride of Second Horseman*, pp. 74–81.

73. J. N. Postgate, *Early Mesopotamia: Society and Economy at the Dawn of History* (London, 1992), p. 251.

74. O'Connell, *Ride of Second Horseman*, pp. 132–42.

75. Keegan, *History of Warfare*, pp. 130–31.

76. John Romer, *People of the Nile: Everyday Life in Ancient Egypt* (New York, 1982), p. 115.

77. Keegan, *History of Warfare*, pp. 133–35.

78. Yigal Yadin, *The Art of Warfare in Biblical Lands*, 2 vols. (New York, 1963), 1:134–35; Robert McAdams, *The Evolution of Urban Society: Early Mesopotamia and Prehispanic Mexico* (New York, 1973), p. 149.

79. Kramer, *Sumerian Mythology*, pp. 123, 120.

80. Kautsky, *Politics of Aristocratic Empires*, p. 108. See Carlo M. Cipolla, *Before the Industrial Revolution: European Society and Economy, 1000–1700* (New York, 1976), pp. 129–30, 151.

81. Robert L. O'Connell, *Of Arms and Men: A History of War, Weapons, and Aggression* (New York and Oxford, 1989), p. 38; O'Connell, *Ride of Second Horseman*, pp. 100–101; William H. McNeill, *The Pursuit of Power: Technology, Armed Force, and Society Since A.D. 1000* (Chicago, 1982), pp. 2–3; Schneider, *Ancient Mesopotamian*

Religion, pp. 22–23; Oppenheim, *Ancient Mesopotamia,* pp. 153–54; Gwendolyn Leick, *Mesopotamia: The Invention of the City* (London, 2001), pp. 85–108.

82. Joseph A. Schumpeter, *Imperialism and Social Classes: Two Essays* (New York, 1955), p. 25; Perry Anderson, *Lineages of the Absolutist State* (London, 1974), p. 32.

83. Anderson, *Lineages,* p. 31; Anderson's emphasis.

84. Kautsky, *Politics of Aristocratic Empires,* pp. 148–52.

85. Marc Bloch, *Feudal Society* (Chicago, 1961), p. 298.

86. Leick, *Mesopotamia,* pp. 95, 100. The "Lower" and "Upper Seas" were, respectively, the Persian Gulf and the Mediterranean.

87. J. B. Pritchard, ed., *Ancient Near Eastern Texts Relating to the Old Testament* (Princeton, NJ, 1969), p. 164.

88. F. C. Fensham, "Widows, Orphans and the Poor in Ancient Eastern Legal and Wisdom Literature," *Journal of Near Eastern Studies* 21 (1962).

89. Pritchard, *Ancient Near Eastern Texts,* p. 178, my emphasis.

90. Marshall G. S. Hodgson, *The Venture of Islam: Conscience and History in a World Civilization* (Chicago and London, 1974), pp. 1:108–10.

91. Schneider, *Ancient Mesopotamian Religion,* pp. 105–6. The meaning and derivation of *akitu* is unknown; see Jacobsen, "Cosmos as State," p. 169.

92. Nancy K. Sandars, ed. and trans., "The Babylonian Creation Hymn," in Sandars, *Poems of Heaven and Hell from Ancient Mesopotamia* (London, 1971), pp. 44–60.

93. Jonathan Z. Smith, "A Pearl of Great Price and a Cargo of Yams: A Study in Situational Incongruity," in *Imagining Religion,* pp. 90–96; Mircea Eliade, *A History of Religious Ideas,* trans. Willard R. Trask, 3 vols. (Chicago, 1978), 1:72–76; Sandars, "Babylonian Creation Hymn," pp. 47–51.

94. Smith, "Pearl of Great Price," p. 91.

95. Sandars, "Babylonian Creation Hymn," section I, p. 73.

96. Ibid., pp. 73, 79.

97. O'Connell, *Ride of Second Horseman,* pp. 141–42.

98. Leick, *Mesopotamia,* pp. 198–216.

99. A. K. Grayson, *Assyrian Royal Inscriptions,* 2 vols. (Wiesbaden, 1972, 1976), 1:80–81.

100. H. W. F. Saggs, *The Might That Was Assyria* (London, 1984), pp. 48–49; I. M. Diakonoff, *Ancient Mesopotamia: Socio-Economic History* (Moscow, 1969), pp. 221–22.

101. Grayson, *Assyrian Royal Inscriptions,* pp. 123–24.

102. Saggs, *Might That Was Assyria,* pp. 62, 61.

103. *Ludlul Bel Nemeqi,* in Jacobsen, "Cosmos as State," pp. 212–14.

104. Yasna 46. Norman Cohn, *Cosmos, Chaos and the World to Come: The Ancient Roots of Apocalyptic Faith* (New Haven, CT, and London, 1993), p. 77; Mary Boyce, *Zoroastrians: Their Religious Beliefs and Practices,* 2nd ed. (London and New York), p. xliii; Peter Clark, *Zoroastrians: An Introduction to an Ancient Faith* (Brighton and Portland, OR, 1998), p. 19.

105. Yasna 30.

106. Boyce, *Zoroastrians,* pp. 23–24.

107. Lincoln, "Warriors and Non-Herdsmen," p. 153.

108. Yasna 44.

109. Lincoln, "Warriors and Non-Herdsmen," p. 158.

2 · INDIA: THE NOBLE PATH

1. Jarrod L. Whitaker, *Strong Arms and Drinking Strength: Masculinity, Violence, and the Body in Ancient India* (Oxford, 2011), pp. 152–53.

2. Rig Veda 3:32:1–4, 9–11.

3. Edwin Bryant, *The Quest for the Origins of Vedic Culture: The Indo-Aryan*

Debate (Oxford and New York, 2001); Colin Renfrew, *The Puzzle of Indo-European Origins* (London, 1987); Romila Thapar, *Early India: From the Origins to AD 1300* (Berkeley and Los Angeles, 2002), pp. 105–7.

4. Whitaker, *Strong Arms,* pp. 3–5; Wendy Doniger, *The Hindus: An Alternative History* (Oxford, 2009), pp. 111–13.

5. Louis Renou, *Religions of Ancient India* (London, 1953), p. 20; Michael Witzel, "Vedas and Upanishads," in Gavin Flood, ed., *The Blackwell Companion to Hinduism* (Oxford, 2003), pp. 70–71; J. C. Heesterman, "Ritual, Revelation, and the Axial Age," in S. N. Eisenstadt, ed., *The Origins and Diversity of Axial Age Civilizations* (Albany, NY, 1986), p. 398.

6. Heesterman, "Ritual, Revelation," pp. 396–98; *The Inner Conflict of Tradition: Essays on Indian Ritual, Kingship and Society* (Chicago and London, 1985), p. 206; John Keay, *India: A History* (London, 2000), pp. 31–33; Thapar, *Early India,* pp. 126–30.

7. Rig Veda 1:32:5, *The Rig Veda,* trans. Ralph T. H. Griffith (London, 1992).

8. Shatapatha Brahmana (SB), 6.8.1.1, in J. C. Heesterman, *The Broken World of Sacrifice: An Essay in Ancient Indian Religion* (Chicago and London, 1993), p. 123.

9. Rig Veda 8:16:1, 8:95:6, 10:38:4.

10. Whitaker, *Strong Arms,* pp. 3–5, 16–23; Catherine Bell, *Ritual Theory, Ritual Practice* (New York, 1992), pp. 180–81, 221.

11. Renou, *Religions of Ancient India,* p. 6; Witzel, "Vedas and Upanishads," p. 73.

12. Whitaker, *Strong Arms,* pp. 115–17.

13. Rig Veda 2:22:4.

14. Rig Veda 3:31, 10:62:2.

15. Witzel, "Vedas and Upanishads," p. 72.

16. Doniger, *Hindus,* p. 114.

17. Heesterman, "Ritual, Revelation," p. 403.

18. SB 7:1:1:1–4, in Mircea Eliade, *The Myth of the Eternal Return: Cosmos and History,* trans. Willard R. Trask (Princeton, NJ, 1974), pp. 10–11.

19. Maitrayani Samhita 4:2:1:23:2, in Heesterman, *Broken World,* pp. 23–24, 134–37.

20. SB 2:2:2:8–10; Heesterman, *Broken World,* p. 24.

21. Georges Dumézil, *The Destiny of the Warrior,* trans. Alf Hiltebeitel (Chicago and London, 1970), pp. 76–78.

22. John H. Kautsky, *The Political Consequences of Modernization* (New Brunswick, NJ, and London, 1997), pp. 25–26.

23. Whitaker, *Strong Arms,* p. 158.

24. Louis Renou, "Sur la notion de 'brahman,'" *Journal Asiatique* 237 (1949); Jan Gonda, *Change and Continuity in Indian Religion* (The Hague, 1965), p. 200.

25. Rig Veda 1:164:46. Garatman was the Sun.

26. Rig Veda 10:129:6–7.

27. Jan Gonda, *The Vision of the Vedic Poets* (The Hague, 1963), p. 18.

28. Renou, *Religions of Ancient India,* pp. 220–25; R. C. Zaehner, *Hinduism* (London, New York, and Toronto, 1962), pp. 219–25.

29. Rig Veda 10:90.

30. Rig Veda 10:90:11–14, Griffiths translation, modified.

31. Bruce Lincoln, "Indo-European Religions: An Introduction," in Lincoln, *Death, War, and Sacrifice: Studies in Ideology and Practice* (Chicago and London, 1991), p. 8.

32. Bruce Lincoln, "Sacrificial Ideology and Indo-European Society," in Lincoln, *Death, War, and Sacrifice,* p. 173.

33. Thapar, *Early India,* p. 123.

34. Lincoln, "Sacrificial Ideology," pp. 174–75.

35. Doniger, *Hindus,* pp. 143–47.

36. Reinard Bendix, *Kings or People: Power and the Mandate to Rule* (Berkeley, CA, 1977), p. 228.

37. Max Weber, *The Religion of India: The Sociology of Hinduism and Buddhism,* trans and ed. Hans H. Gerth and Don Martindale (Glencoe, IL, 1951), p. 65.

38. Alfred Vagts, *History of Militarism: Civilian and Military,* rev. ed. (New York, 1959), p. 42.

39. Pancavimsha Brahmana (PB) 7:7:9–10, cited in Weber, *The Religion of India,* p. 62.

40. SB 6:8:14; Heesterman "Ritual, Revelation," p. 402.

41. Heesterman, *Inner Conflict of Tradition,* pp. 68, 84–85.

42. Rig Veda I.132:20–21, Griffiths translation.

43. Taittiriya Samhita (TS) 6.4.8.1, in Heesterman, *Inner Conflict of Tradition,* p. 209.

44. Taittiriya Brahmana (TB) 3:7:7:14, in Heesterman, *Broken World,* p. 34.

45. Witzel, "Vedas and Upanisads," p. 82.

46. TB 10:6:5:8, in Heesterman, *Broken World,* p. 34.

47. Zaehner, *Hinduism,* pp. 59–60; Renou, *Religions of Ancient India,* p. 18; Witzel, "Vedas and Upanisads," p. 81; Brian K. Smith, *Reflections on Resemblance, Ritual, and Religion* (Oxford and New York, 1989), pp. 30–34, 72–81.

48. Jonathan Z. Smith, "The Bare Facts of Ritual," in Smith, *Imagining Religion: From Babylon to Jonestown* (Chicago and London, 1982), p. 63.

49. Doniger, *Hindus,* pp. 137–42; Gavin Flood, *An Introduction to Hinduism* (Oxford, 2003), pp. 80–81.

50. Thapar, *Early India,* pp. 150–52.

51. *The Laws of Manu,* 7:16–22, trans. George Buhler (Delhi, 1962).

52. Thapar, *Early India,* pp. 147–49; Doniger, *Hindus,* pp. 165–66.

53. Thapar, *Early India,* p. 138.

54. Hermann Kulke, "The Historical Background of India's Axial Age," in Eisenstadt, *Origins and Diversity,* p. 385.

55. Thapar, *Early India,* p. 154.

56. Gautama Dharmasutra 16:46; Richard Gombrich, *Theravada Buddhism: A Social History from Ancient Benares to Modern Colombo* (London and New York, 1988), p. 55.

57. Gombrich, *Theravada Buddhism,* pp. 58–59; William M. McNeill, *Plagues and Peoples* (Garden City, NY, 1976), p. 60; *The Samnyasa Upanisads: Hindu Scriptures on Asceticism and Renunciation,* ed. and trans. Patrick Olivelle (New York and Oxford, 1992), p. 34; Doniger, *Hindus,* p. 171.

58. Thomas J. Hopkins, *The Hindu Religious Tradition* (Belmont, CA, 1971), pp. 50–51; Doniger, *Hindus,* p. 165.

59. Chandogya Upanishad (CU) 5:10:7. Quotations from the *Upanishads* are from *Upanisads,* trans. Patrick Olivelle (Oxford and New York, 1996). Brhadaranyaka Upanishad (BU) 4:4:23–35; Thapur, *Early India,* p. 130.

60. Olivelle, *Samnyasa Upanisads,* pp. 37–38.

61. Ibid., p. xxix; Witzel, "Vedas and Upanisads," pp. 85–86.

62. BU 1:4:6.

63. BU 1:4:10.

64. BU 4:4:5–7.

65. BU 4:4:23–35.

66. CU 8:7–12.

67. CU 6:11.

68. CU 6:12.

69. CU 6:13.

70. CU 6:10.

71. Thapar, *Early India*, p. 132.

72. Flood, *Introduction to Hinduism*, p. 91; Patrick Olivelle, "The Renouncer Tradition," in Flood, *Blackwell Companion to Hinduism*, p. 271.

73. Steven Collins, *Selfless Persons: Imagery and Thought in Theravada Buddhism* (Cambridge, UK, 1982), p. 64; Paul Dundas, *The Jains*, 2nd ed. (London and New York, 2002), p. 64.

74. Manara Gryha Sutra 1:1:6, in Heesterman, *Broken World*, pp. 164–74; Gonda, *Change and Continuity*, pp. 228–35, 285–94.

75. Gonda, *Change and Continuity*, pp. 380–84; Olivelle, "Renouncer Tradition," pp. 281–82.

76. Digha Nikaya, in *Samnyasa Upanisads*, trans. Olivelle, p. 43.

77. Naradaparivrajaka Upanisad 143, ibid., pp. 108, 185.

78. A. Ghosh, *The City in Early Historical India* (Simla, 1973), p. 55; *Samnyasa Upanisads*, trans. Olivelle, pp. 45–46.

79. Mircea Eliade, *Yoga: Immortality and Freedom*, trans. Willard R. Trask (London, 1958), pp. 59–62.

80. Patanjali, *Yoga Sutras* 2:42, ibid., p. 52.

81. Dundas, *Jains*, pp. 28–30.

82. Ibid., pp. 106–7.

83. Acaranga Sutra (AS) 1.4.1.1–2, ibid., pp. 41–42.

84. AS 1:2:3, ibid.

85. Avashyaksutra 32, ibid., p. 171.

86. Western scholars once thought that the Buddha was born c. 563 BCE, but recent scholarship indicates that he lived about a century later. Heinz Berchant, "The Date of the Buddha Reconsidered," *Indologia Taurinensin* 10 (n.d.).

87. Majjhima Nikaya (MN) 38. Unless otherwise stated, all quotations from the Buddhist scriptures are my own versions of the texts cited.

88. I have described the Buddha's spiritual method more fully in *Buddha* (New York, 2001). See also Richard F. Gombrich, *How Buddhism Began: The Conditioned Genesis of the Early Teachings* (London and Atlantic Highlands, NJ, 1996); Michael Carrithers, *The Buddha* (Oxford and New York, 1993); Karl Jaspers, *The Great Philosophers: The Foundations*, ed. Hannah Arendt, trans. Ralph Manheim (London, 1962), pp. 99–105; Trevor Ling, *The Buddha: Buddhist Civilization in India and Ceylon* (London, 1973).

89. Edward Conze, *Buddhism: Its Essence and Development* (Oxford, 1951), p. 102; Hermann Oldenberg, *Buddha: His Life, His Doctrine, His Order*, trans. William Hoeg (London, 1882), pp. 299–302.

90. Sutta Nipata (SN) 118, my translation.

91. Vinaya, *Mahavagga* 1:ii, in Ling, *The Buddha*, p. 134.

92. Ibid. 1:211.

93. AG 1:27; SN 700, in Bhikkhu Nānamoli, ed., *The Life of the Buddha, According to the Pali Canon* (Kandy, Sri Lanka, 1992), p. 282.

94. MN 89, ibid.

95. Thapar, *Early India*, pp. 174–98.

96. Patrick Olivelle, ed., *Asoka: In History and Historical Memory* (Delhi, 2009), p. 1.

97. Major Rock Edict 13, in *Asoka and the Decline of the Mauryas*, trans. Romila Thapar (Oxford, 1961), pp. 255–56.

98. Ibid.

99. Olivelle, *Asoka*, p. 1.

100. Pillar Edict VII, in Thapar, *Asoka*, p. 255.

101. Major Rock Edict 12, ibid., p. 255.

102. Major Rock Edict 11, ibid., p. 254.

103. Ananda K. Coomaraswamy and Sister Nivedita, *Myths of the Hindus and Buddhists* (New York, 1967), p. 118.

104. Shruti Kapila and Faisal Devji, eds., *Political Thought in Action: The Bhagavad Gita and Modern India* (Cambridge, UK, 2013).

105. Doniger, *Hindus*, pp. 262–64.

106. Thapar, *Early India*, p. 207.

107. *Mahabharata* 7:70:44, in *The Mahabharata, Volume 3: Book 4: The Book of Virata; Book 5: The Book of the Effort,* trans. and ed. J. A. B. van Buitenen (Chicago and London, 1978).

108. *Mahabharata* 5:70:46–66, ibid.

109. *Mahabharata* 7:165:63, ibid.

110. *Mahabharata* 9:60:59–63, in *The Mahabharata: An Abridged Translation,* trans. and ed. John D. Smith (London, 2009).

111. *Mahabharata* 10:8:39, ibid.

112. *Mahabharata* 10:10:14, ibid.

113. *Mahabharata* 12:15, in Doniger, *Hindus*, p. 270.

114. *Mahabharata* 17:3, ibid.

115. *Bhagavad-Gita* 1:33–34, 36–37. All quotations are from *The Bhagavad-Gita: Krishna's Counsel in Time of War,* trans. Barbara Stoller Milller (New York, Toronto, and London, 1986).

116. *Bhagavad-Gita* 2:9.

117. *Bhagavad-Gita* 4:20.

118. *Bhagavad-Gita* 9:9.

119. *Bhagavad-Gita* 11:32–33.

120. *Bhagavad-Gita* 11:55.

3 · CHINA: WARRIORS AND GENTLEMEN

1. *Liezi jishi* 2, in Mark Edward Lewis, *Sanctioned Violence in Early China* (Albany, NY, 1990), pp. 200, 167–72.

2. Ibid., pp. 176–79.

3. Marcel Granet, *Chinese Civilization,* trans. Kathleen Innes and Mabel Brailsford (London and New York, 1951), pp. 11–12; Granet, *The Religion of the Chinese People,* trans. and ed. Maurice Freedman (Oxford, 1975), pp. 66–68.

4. *Taijong yulan* 79, in Lewis, *Sanctioned Violence,* p. 203.

5. Ibid., pp. 203, 201.

6. Granet, *Chinese Civilization,* pp. 11–16; Henri Maspero, *China in Antiquity,* trans. Frank A Kiermannn Jr., 2nd ed. (Folkestone, 1978), pp. 115–19.

7. John King Fairbank and Merle Goldman, *China: A New History,* 2nd ed. (Cambridge, MA, and London, 2006), p. 34.

8. Jacques Gernet, *A History of Chinese Civilization,* trans. J. R. Foster and Charles Hartman, 2nd ed. (Cambridge, UK, and New York, 1996), pp. 39–40.

9. Ibid., pp. 41–50; Jacques Gernet, *Ancient China: From the Beginnings to the Empire,* trans. Raymond Rudorff (London, 1968), pp. 37–65; William Theodore de Bary and Irene Bloom, eds. and trans., *Sources of Chinese Tradition: From Earliest Times to 1600,* 2nd ed.(New York, 1999), pp. 3–25; D. Howard Smith, *Chinese Religions* (London, 1968), pp. 1–11.

10. Gernet, *History of Chinese Civilization,* pp. 45–46; Gernet, *Ancient China,* pp. 50–53; Granet, *Religion of the Chinese People,* pp. 37–54.

11. *The Book of Songs,* 35, 167, 185.

12. Sima Qian, *Records of a Master Historian,* 1:56:79, cited in Granet, *Chinese Civilization,* p. 12.

13. Gernet, *History of Chinese Civilization,* p. 49.

14. Marshall G. S. Hodgson, *The Venture of Islam: Conscience and History in a World Civilization,* 3 vols. (Chicago and London, 1974), 1:281–82.

15. Lewis, *Sanctioned Violence,* pp. 15–27; Fairbank and Goldman, *China,* pp. 49–50.

16. Fairbank and Goldman, *China,* p. 45.

17. K. C. Chang, *Art, Myth, and Ritual: The Path to Political Authority in Ancient China* (Cambridge, MA, 1985), pp. 95–100; Fairbank and Goldman, *China,* pp. 42–44.

18. Walter Burkert, *Homo Necans: The Anthropology of Ancient Greek Sacrificial Ritual and Myth,* trans. Walter Bing (Berkeley, CA, 1983), p. 47.

19. David N. Keightley, "The Late Shang State: When, Where, What?" in Keightley, ed., *The Origins of Chinese Civilization* (Berkeley, CA, 1983), pp. 256–59.

20. Michael J. Puett, *To Become a God: Cosmology, Sacrifice, and Self-Divinization in Early China* (Cambridge, MA, and London, 2002), pp. 32–76.

21. Oracle 23, in *Sources of Chinese Tradition,* trans. De Bary and Bloom, p. 12.

22. Lewis, *Sanctioned Violence,* pp. 26–27.

23. *The Book of Mozi* 3.25, cited in Gernet, *Ancient China,* p. 65.

24. *Classic of Documents,* "The Shao Announcement," in *Sources of Chinese Tradition,* trans. De Bary and Bloom, pp. 35–37.

25. H. G. Creel, *Confucius: The Man and the Myth* (London, 1951), pp. 19–25; Benjamin I. Schwarz, *The World of Thought in Ancient China* (Cambridge, MA, and London, 1985), pp. 57–59; remarks by Jacques Gernet in Jean-Pierre Vernant, *Myth and Society in Ancient Greece,* trans. Janet Lloyd, 3rd ed. (New York, 1996), pp. 80–90.

26. Gernet, *Ancient China,* pp. 71–75.

27. Granet, *Chinese Civilization,* pp. 97–100.

28. Fung Yu-lan, *A Short History of Chinese Philosophy,* trans. Derk Bodde (New York, 1978), pp. 32–37.

29. *Classic of Documents,* "The Canon of Yao and the Canon of Shun," in De Bary and Bloom, *Sources of Chinese Tradition,* p. 29.

30. *Record of Rites* 2.263, in *The Li Ki,* trans. James Legge (Oxford, 1885), p. 900.

31. *Record of Rites* 2.359.

32. Granet, *Chinese Civilization,* pp. 297–308.

33. *Record of Rites* 1:215.

34. Granet, *Chinese Civilization,* pp. 310–43.

35. Gernet, *Ancient China,* p. 75.

36. Granet, *Chinese Civilization,* pp. 261–84; Gernet, *History of Chinese Civilization,* pp. 261–79; Gernet, *Ancient China,* p. 75; Holmes Welch, *The Parting of the Way: Lao Tzu and the Taoist Movement* (London, 1958), p. 18.

37. *Zuozhuan* ("The Commentary of Mr. Zuo") 1:320, in *The Ch'un Ts'ew and the Tso Chuen,* trans. James Legge, 2nd ed. (Hong Kong, 1960).

38. *Zuozhuan* 1:635.

39. *Zuozhuan* 2:234.

40. *Zuozhuan* 1:627.

41. James A. Aho, *Religious Mythology and the Art of War: Comparative Religious Symbolism of Military Violence* (Westport, CT, 1981), pp. 110–11.

42. *Spring and Autumn Annals* 10:17:4.

43. *Spring and Autumn Annals,* 1:9:6.

44. Herbert Fingarette, *Confucius: The Secular as Sacred* (New York, 1972).

45. Schwartz, *World of Thought,* p. 62; Fung, *Short History,* p. 12.

46. William Theodore de Bary, *The Trouble with Confucianism* (Cambridge, MA, and London, 1996), pp. 24–33.

47. *Analects* 12:3 in *The Analects of Confucius,* trans. and ed. Arthur Waley (New York, 1992).

48. *Analects* 15:24.

49. *Analects* 4:15, 15:23.

50. *Analects* 6:30, in Edward Slingerland, trans., *Confucius: Analects, with Selections from Traditional Commentaries* (Indianapolis, IN, and Cambridge, UK, 2003).

51. Ibid., Waley translation.

52. De Bary, *Trouble with Confucianism*, p. 30.

53. Schwartz, *World of Thought*, pp. 155, 157–58.

54. *Analects* 12:1, translation suggested by Schwartz, ibid., p. 77.

55. Ibid., Slingerland translation.

56. *Analects* 5:4.

57. Fingarette, *Confucius*, pp. 1–17, 46–79.

58. *Analects* 12:3.

59. *Analects* 7:30.

60. Tu Wei-ming, *Confucian Thought: Selfhood as Creative Transformation* (Albany, NY, 1985), pp. 115–16.

61. Ibid., pp. 57–58; Huston Smith, *The World's Religions: Our Great Wisdom Traditions* (San Francisco, 1991), pp. 180–81.

62. *Analects* 13:30.

63. Don J. Wyatt, "Confucian Ethical Action and the Boundaries of Peace and War," in Andrew R. Murphy, ed., *The Blackwell Companion to Religion and Violence* (Chichester, UK, 2011).

64. *Analects* 12:7, Slingerland translation.

65. *Analects* 12:7.

66. *Analects* 16:2.

67. *Analects* 2:3.

68. *The Book of Mencius* 3:A:4, in *Mencius*, trans. D. C. Lau (London, 1975).

69. Xinzhong Yao, *An Introduction to Confucianism* (Cambridge, UK, 2000), p. 28.

70. *Mencius* 7:B:4.

71. *Mencius* 7:B:4.

72. *Mencius* 7:B:2; Wyatt, "Confucian Ethical Action," pp. 240–44.

73. *Mencius* 2:A:1.

74. A. C. Graham, *Later Mohist Logic, Ethics, and Science* (Hong Kong, 1978), p. 4; Gernet, *Ancient China*, pp. 116–17.

75. *The Book of Mozi* 3:16, cited in Fung, *Short History*, p. 55.

76. *Mozi* 15:11–15, in *Mo-Tzu: Basic Writings*, trans. and ed. B. Watson (New York, 1963).

77. A. C. Graham, *Disputers of the Tao: Philosophical Argument in Ancient China* (La Salle, IL, 1989), p. 41.

78. *Mozi* 15.

79. Graham, *Later Mohist Logic*, p. 250.

80. Lewis, *Sanctioned Violence*, pp. 56–61.

81. *Zuozhuan* 2:30.

82. *Zuozhuan*, p. 254.

83. *Zuozhuan*, p. 243.

84. *Zuozhuan*, pp. 97–118; John Keegan, *A History of Warfare* (London and New York, 1993), pp. 202–8; Robert L. O'Connell, *Ride of the Second Horseman: The Birth and Death of War* (New York and Oxford, 1989), pp. 171–73; R. D. Sawyer, *The Military Classics of Ancient China* (Boulder, CO, 1993).

85. Sun Tzu, *The Art of War: Complete Texts and Commentaries*, trans. Thomas Cleary (Boston and London, 1988), p. 56.

86. *Art of War* 3.

87. Selections from the *Sunzi*, in *Sources of Chinese Tradition*, trans. De Bary and Bloom, p. 217.

88. *Art of War*, Cleary translation, pp. 81–83.

89. *Art of War,* Cleary translation, p. 86.

90. *Sunzi,* 5, De Bary and Bloom translation.

91. Fairbank and Goldman, *China,* pp. 53–54.

92. Graham, *Disputers of the Tao,* pp. 172–203; Schwartz, *World of Thought,* pp. 215–36; Fung, *Short History,* pp. 104–17.

93. Graham, *Disputers of the Tao,* pp. 170–213; Schwartz, *World of Thought,* pp. 186–215; Max Kaltenmark, *Lao Tzu and Taoism,* trans. Roger Greaves (Stanford, CA, 1969), pp. 93–103.

94. *Daodejing* 37, in *Lao Tzu: Tao Te Ching,* trans. D. C. Lau (London, 1963).

95. *Daodejing* 16, Lau translation.

96. *Daodejing* 76, Lau translation.

97. *Daodejing* 6, Lau translation.

98. *Daodejing* 31, in *Lao Tzu,* Greaves translation, p. 56.

99. *Daodejing* 68, in *Lao Tzu,* Greaves translation, p. 56.

100. *Daodejing* 22, in *Sources of Chinese Tradition,* trans. De Bary and Bloom.

101. *Shang Jun Shu,* cited in Lewis, *Sanctioned Violence,* p. 64.

102. Schwartz, *World of Thought,* pp. 321–23.

103. Lewis, *Sanctioned Violence,* pp. 61–65.

104. Graham, *Disputers of the Tao,* pp. 207–76; Schwartz, *World of Thought,* pp. 321–43; Fung, *Short History,* pp. 155–65; Julia Ching, *Mysticism and Kingship in China: The Heart of Chinese Wisdom* (Cambridge, UK, 1997), pp. 236–41.

105. *Shang Jun Shu,* cited in Mark Elvin, "Was There a Transcendental Breakthrough in China?" in Eisenstadt, *Origins and Diversity of the Axial Civilizations,* p. 352.

106. *Shang Jun Shu,* cited in Graham, *Disputers of the Tao,* p. 290.

107. *Shang Jun Shu* 15:72, in *Hsun-Tzu: Basic Writings,* ed. and trans. Burton Watson (New York, 1963).

108. *Shang Jun Shu* 15:72.

109. *The Book of Xunzi* 10, cited in Graham, *Disputers of the Tao,* p. 238.

110. *Hanfeizi* 5, in *Han Fei Tzu: Basic Writings,* ed. and trans. Burton Watson (New York, 1964).

111. *Hanfeizi* 5.

112. Ching, *Mysticism and Kingship,* p. 171.

113. *Xunzi* 21:34–38, in *Xunzi: Basic Writings,* trans. Burton Watson (New York, 2003).

114. Fairbank and Goldman, *China,* p. 56; Derk Bodde, "Feudalism in China," in Rushton Coulbourn, ed., *Feudalism in History* (Hamden, CT, 1965), p. 69.

115. Sima Qian, *Records of the Grand Historian* 6:239.

116. Sima Qian, *Records of the Grand Historian,* 6:87, cited in Fung, *Short History,* p. 204.

117. Lewis, *Sanctioned Violence,* pp. 99–101.

118. Sima Qian, *Records of the Grand Historian,* cited ibid., p. 141.

119. Schwartz, *World of Thought,* pp. 237–53.

120. Lewis, *Sanctioned Violence,* pp. 145–57; Derk Bodde, *Festivals in Classical China: New Year and Other Annual Observances During the Han Dynasty, 206 B.C.– A.D. 220* (Princeton, NJ, 1975).

121. Cited in Lewis, *Sanctioned Violence,* p. 147.

122. Sima Qian, *Records of the Grand Historian* 8.1, cited in Fung, *Short History,* p. 215.

123. Fung, *Short History,* pp. 205–16; Graham, *Disputers of the Tao,* pp. 313–77; Schwartz, *World of Thought,* pp. 383–406.

124. Fairbank and Goldman, *China,* pp. 67–71.

125. Joseph R. Levenson and Franz Schurmann, *China: An Interpretive History: From the Beginnings to the Fall of Han* (Berkeley, Los Angeles, and London, 1969), p. 94.

126. De Bary, *Trouble with Confucianism,* pp. 48–49.

127. *Yan tie lun* 19, in *Sources of Chinese Tradition,* trans. De Bary and Bloom, p. 223.

128. Hu Shih, "Confucianism," in *Encyclopaedia of Social Science* (1930–35) 4:198–201; Ching, *Mysticism and Kingship,* p. 85.

129. De Bary, *Trouble with Confucianism,* p. 49; Fairbank and Goldman, *China,* p. 63.

4 · THE HEBREW DILEMMA

1. Genesis 2:5–3.24. Unless otherwise stated, all biblical quotations are taken from *The Jerusalem Bible* (London, 1966).

2. Genesis 3:17–19.

3. Genesis 4:10–11, in *The Five Books of Moses,* trans. Everett Fox (New York, 1990).

4. Genesis 4:17–22.

5. Genesis 4:9.

6. Genesis 12:1–3.

7. Israel Finkelstein and Neil Asher, *The Bible Unearthed: Archaeology's New Vision of Ancient Israel and the Origins of Its Sacred Texts* (New York and London, 2001), pp. 103–7; William G. Dever, *What Did the Biblical Writers Know and When Did They Know It? What Archaeology Can Tell Us About the Reality of Ancient Israel* (Grand Rapids, MI, and Cambridge, UK, 2001), pp. 110–18.

8. George W. Mendenhall, *The Tenth Generation: The Origins of Biblical Tradition* (Baltimore and London, 1973); P. M. Lemche, *Early Israel: Anthropological and Historical Studies on the Israelite Society Before the Monarchy* (Leiden, 1985); D. C. Hopkins, *The Highlands of Canaan* (Sheffield, UK, 1985); James D. Martin, "Israel as a Tribal Society," in R. E. Clements, ed., *The World of Ancient Israel: Sociological, Anthropological and Political Perspectives* (Cambridge, UK, 1989); H. G. M. Williamson, "The Concept of Israel in Transition," in Clements, *World of Ancient Israel,* pp. 94–114.

9. Finkelstein and Asher, *Bible Unearthed,* pp. 89–92.

10. John H. Kautsky, *The Politics of Aristocratic Empires,* 2nd ed. (New Brunswick, NJ, and London, 1997), p. 275; Karl A. Wittfogel, *Oriental Despotism: A Comparative Study of Total Power* (New Haven, CT, 1957), pp. 331–32.

11. Joshua 9:15; Exodus 6:15; Judges 1:16, 4:11; I Samuel 27:10. Frank Moore Cross, *Canaanite Myth and Hebrew Epic: Essays in the History of the Religion of Israel* (Cambridge, MA, and London, 1973), pp. 49–50.

12. Cross, *Canaanite Myth,* p. 69; Peter Machinist, "Distinctiveness in Ancient Israel," in Mordechai Cogan and Israel Ephal, eds., *Studies in Assyrian History and Ancient Near Eastern Historiography* (Jerusalem, 1991).

13. This theme has been explored in more detail by Yoram Hazony, *The Philosophy of Hebrew Scripture* (Cambridge, UK, 2012), pp. 103–60.

14. Norman Gottwald, *The Hebrew Bible in Its Social World and in Ours* (Atlanta, 1993), pp. 115, 163.

15. Leviticus 25:23–28, 25:35–55; Deuteronomy 24:19–22; Gottwald, *Hebrew Bible,* p. 162.

16. I have described this process in *A History of God: The 4,000-Year Quest of Judaism, Christianity, and Islam* (London and New York, 1993).

17. Psalms 73:3, 73:8, 82:8, 95:3, 96:4ff, 97:7; Isaiah 51:9ff; Job 26:12, 40:25–31.

18. Genesis 11:1–9.

19. Genesis 11:9.

20. Genesis 12:3. Strictly speaking, Yahweh called Abraham from Harran in modern Iraq; but his father, Terah, had left Ur but only got as far as Haran. Yahweh himself back-

dates the call to Abraham, taking responsibility for the entire migration, telling Abraham: "I . . . brought you out of Ur of the Chaldeans" (Genesis 15:7).

21. Hazony, *Philosophy of Hebrew Scripture,* p. 121.

22. Ibid., pp. 122–26.

23. Genesis 12:10.

24. Genesis 26:16–22; cf. 36:6–8.

25. Genesis 41:57–42:3.

26. Genesis 37:5–7.

27. Genesis 37:8, Fox translation.

28. Genesis 37:10, Fox translation.

29. Genesis 41:51, Fox translation.

30. Genesis 41:48–49.

31. Genesis 47:13–14, 47:20–21.

32. Genesis 50:4–9. After Jacob's death, the brothers were permitted to take his body back to Canaan, accompanied by "a very large retinue" of chariots and cavalry, while their children and possessions were held hostage in Egypt.

33. Genesis 12:15, 20:2, 26:17–18, 14:11–12, 34:1–2; Hazony, *Philosophy of Hebrew Scripture,* pp. 111–13, 143.

34. Genesis 14:21–25.

35. Genesis 18:1–8, 19:1–9.

36. Genesis 18:22–32.

37. Genesis 49:7.

38. Genesis 49:8–12, 44:18–34.

39. Exodus 1:11, 1:14.

40. Exodus 2:11.

41. Hazony, *Philosophy of Hebrew Scripture,* pp. 143–44.

42. Exodus 24:9–11.

43. Exodus 31:18.

44. Exodus 24:9–31:18; William M. Schniedewind, *How the Bible Became a Book: The Textualization of Ancient Israel* (Cambridge, UK, 2004), pp. 121–34.

45. E.g., Judges 1; 3:1–6; Ezra 9:1–2.

46. Regina Schwartz, *The Curse of Cain: The Violent Legacy of Monotheism* (Chicago, 1997); Hector Avalos, *Fighting Words: The Origins of Religious Violence* (Amherst, NY, 2005).

47. Mark S. Smith, *The Early History of God: Yahweh and the Other Deities in Ancient Israel* (New York and London, 1990); Smith, *The Origins of Biblical Monotheism: Israel's Polytheistic Background and the Ugaritic Texts* (New York and London, 2001).

48. Joshua 24; S. David Sperling, "Joshua 24 Re-examined," *Hebrew Union College Annual* 58 (1987); S. David Sperling, *The Original Torah: The Political Intent of the Bible's Writers* (New York and London, 1998), pp. 68–72; John Bowker, *The Religious Imagination and the Sense of God* (Oxford, 1978), pp. 58–68.

49. Exodus 20:3, Fox translation.

50. Susan Niditch, *War in the Hebrew Bible: A Study of the Ethics of Violence* (New York and Oxford, 1993), pp. 28–36, 41–62, 152.

51. Compare a similar deal in Numbers 21:2.

52. Joshua 6:20.

53. Joshua 8:25.

54. Joshua 8:28.

55. Lauren A. Monroe, *Josiah's Reform and the Dynamics of Defilement; Israelite Rites of Violence and the Making of a Biblical Text* (Oxford, 2011), pp. 45–76.

56. *Mesha Stele* 15–17, in Kent P. Jackson, "The Language of the Mesha Inscription," in Andrew Dearman, ed., *Studies in the Mesha Inscription and Moab* (Atlanta, 1989),

p. 98; Norman K. Gottwald, *The Politics of Ancient Israel* (Louisville, KY, 2001), p. 194; cf. 2 Kings 3:4–27.

57. *Mesha Stele* 17.

58. H. Hoffner, "History and the Historians of the Ancient Near East: The Hittites," *Orientalia* 49 (1980); Niditch, *War in the Hebrew Bible*, p. 51.

59. Judges 21:25.

60. Judges 11:29–40.

61. Judges 18.

62. Judges 19.

63. Judges 20–21.

64. I Samuel 8:5.

65. I Samuel 11:18.

66. Gottwald, *Politics of Ancient Israel*, pp. 177–79.

67. Niditch, *War in the Hebrew Bible*, pp. 90–105.

68. I Samuel 17:1–13; Quincy Wright, *A Study of Warfare*, 2 vols. (Chicago, 1942), 1:401–15.

69. 2 Samuel 2:23.

70. 2 Samuel 5:6.

71. I Chronicles 22:8–9.

72. Gosta W. Ahlstrom, *The History of Ancient Palestine* (Minneapolis, 1993), pp. 504–5.

73. I Kings 7:15–26.

74. Richard J. Clifford, *The Cosmic Mountain in Canaan and the Old Testament* (Cambridge, MA, 1972), passim; Ben C. Ollenburger, *Zion, City of the Great King: A Theological Symbol of the Jerusalem Cult* (Sheffield, UK, 1987), pp. 14–16; Margaret Barker, *The Gate of Heaven: The History and Symbolism of the Temple in Jerusalem* (London, 1991), p. 64; Hans-Joachim Kraus, *Worship in Israel: A Cultic History of the Old Testament* (Oxford, 1966), pp. 201–4.

75. I Kings 9:3; David Ussishkin, "King Solomon's Palaces," *Biblical Archaeologist* 36 (1973).

76. I Kings 10:26–29.

77. I Kings 9:3, 5:4–6.

78. I Kings 4:1–5:1.

79. I Kings 5:27–32, which contradicts I Kings 9:20–21. The Deuteronomist authors were eager to blame Solomon's idolatry for the catastrophe, because of their reform.

80. I Kings 11:1–13.

81. I Kings 12:4.

82. I Kings 12:17–19.

83. Psalms 2:7–8, 110:12–14.

84. Psalm 110:5–6.

85. Andrew Mein, *Ezekiel and the Ethics of Exile* (Oxford and New York, 2001), pp. 20–38.

86. Amos 2:6.

87. Amos 3:10.

88. Amos 7:17; 9:7–8.

89. Amos 3:11–15.

90. Amos 1:2–2:5.

91. Isaiah 1:16–18.

92. Gottwald, *Politics of Ancient Israel*, pp. 210–12.

93. Finkelstein and Asher, *Bible Unearthed*, pp. 263–64.

94. Ibid., pp. 264–73.

95. 2 Kings 21:2–7, 23:10–11.

96. Psalms 68:17; Ahlstrom, *History of Palestine*, p. 734.

97. Schniedewind, *How the Bible Became a Book,* pp. 91–117; Calum M. Carmichael, *The Laws of Deuteronomy* (Eugene, OR, 1974); Bernard M. Levinson, *Deuteronomy and the Hermeneutics of Legal Innovation* (Oxford, 1997); Moshe Weinfeld, *Deuteronomy and the Deuteronomic School* (Oxford, 1972); Joshua Berman, *Biblical Revolutions: The Transformation of Social and Political Thought in the Ancient Near East* (New York and Oxford, 2008).

98. 2 Kings 22:8.

99. Exodus 24:3,7; Schniedewind, *How the Bible Became a Book,* pp. 121–26.

100. Exodus 24:4–8. This passage was inserted into the older traditions by the reformers; it is the only other place in the Bible where the phrase *sefer torah* is found.

101. Deuteronomy 6:4.

102. Deuteronomy 7:1–4.

103. Deuteronomy 28:64, 68.

104. 2 Kings 22:11–13.

105. 2 Kings 23:5.

106. Jeremiah 44:15–19; Ezekiel 8.

107. 2 Kings 23:4–20

108. Levinson, *Deuteronomy and Hermeneutics,* pp. 148–49.

109. Deuteronomy 7:22–26.

110. Deuteronomy 13:8–9, 12.

111. Niditch, *War in the Hebrew Bible,* pp. 65, 77.

112. I Kings 13:1–2; 2 Kings 23:15–18; 2 Kings 23:25.

113. 2 Kings 24:16. These numbers are disputed.

114. Ezekiel 3:15; Schniedewind, *How the Bible Became a Book,* p. 152.

115. Mein, *Ezekiel,* pp. 66–74.

116. Anshan is called Elam in the Hebrew sources.

117. Garth Fowden, *Empire to Commonwealth: Consequences of Monotheism in Late Antiquity* (Princeton, NJ, 1993), p. 19.

118. Cyrus Cylinder 18. Quotations from the Cyrus Cylinder are taken from the translation by Irving L. Finkel in John Curtis, *The Cyrus Cylinder and Ancient Persia: A New Beginning for the Middle East* (London, 2013), p. 42.

119. Bruce Lincoln, *Religion, Empire, and Torture: The Case of Achaemenian Persia, with a Postscript on Abu Graib* (Chicago and London, 2007), pp. 36–40.

120. Cyrus Cylinder 12, 15, 17, p. 42. Shuanna is another name for Babylon.

121. Isaiah 45:1.

122. Isaiah 45:1, 2, 4.

123. Isaiah 40:4–5.

124. Flavius Josephus, *The Antiquities of the Jews,* trans. William Whiston (Marston Gale, UK, n.d.), 11.8.

125. Cyrus Cylinder 16, p. 42.

126. Cyrus Cylinder 28–30, p. 43.

127. Lincoln, *Religion, Empire, and Torture,* p. ix.

128. Ibid., pp. 16, 95.

129. Bruce Lincoln, "The Role of Religion in Achaemenian Imperialism," in Nicole Brisch, ed., *Religion and Power: Divine Kingship in the Ancient World and Beyond* (Chicago, 2008), p. 223.

130. Clarisse Herrenschmidt, "Désignations de l'empire et concepts politiques de Darius Ier d'après inscriptions en vieux perse," *Studia Iranica* 5 (1976); Marijan Molé, *Culte, mythe, et cosmologie dans l'Iran ancien* (Paris, 1963).

131. Darius, First Inscription at Naqsh-i Rustum (DNa) 1, cited in Lincoln, *Religion, Empire, and Torture,* p. 52.

132. Ibid., pp. 55–56.

133. DNa 4, cited ibid., p. 71.

134. Darius, Fourth Inscription at Persepolis, cited ibid., p. 10.

135. Ibid., pp. 26–28.

136. Ibid., pp. 73–81; Darius, Inscription 19 at Susa, cited ibid., p. 73.

137. Cross, *Canaanite Myth,* pp. 293–323; Mary Douglas, *Leviticus as Literature* (Oxford and New York, 1999); Douglas, *In the Wilderness: The Doctrine of Defilement in the Book of Numbers* (Oxford and New York, 2001), pp. 58–100; Niditch, *War in the Hebrew Bible,* pp. 78–89, 97–99, 132–53.

138. Leviticus 25.

139. Leviticus 19:34.

140. Douglas, *Leviticus as Literature,* pp. 42–44.

141. Genesis 32:33.

142. Numbers 20:14.

143. Genesis 1:31.

144. Nehemiah 4:11–12.

145. Numbers 31.

146. Numbers 31:19–20.

147. 2 Chronicles 28:10–11.

148. 2 Chronicles 28:15.

149. Isaiah 46:1.

150. Zechariah 14:12.

151. Zechariah 14:16. See also Micah 4:1–5, 5; Haggai 1:6–9.

152. Isaiah 60:1–10.

153. Isaiah 60:11–14.

5 · JESUS: NOT OF THIS WORLD?

1. Luke 2:1.

2. Robert L. O'Connell, *Of Arms and Men: A History of War, Weapons, and Aggression* (New York and Oxford, 1989), p. 81.

3. E. N. Luttwak, *The Grand Strategy of the Roman Empire* (Baltimore, 1976), pp. 25–26, 41–42, 46–47; Susan P. Mattern, *Rome and the Enemy: Imperial Strategy in the Principate* (Berkeley, CA, 1999), pp. xii, 222.

4. O'Connell, *Arms and Men,* pp. 69–81; John Keegan, *A History of Warfare* (London and New York, 1993), pp. 263–71.

5. W. Harris, *War and Imperialism in Republican Rome* (Oxford, 1979), pp. 56, 51.

6. Tacitus, *Agricola,* 30, Loeb Classical Library translation.

7. Harris, *War and Imperialism,* p. 51.

8. Martin Hengel, *Judaism and Hellenism: Studies in Their Encounter in Palestine During the Early Hellenistic Period,* trans. John Bowden, 2 vols. (London, 1974), 1:294–300; Elias J. Bickerman, *From Ezra to the Last of the Maccabees* (New York, 1962), pp. 286–89; *The Jews in the Greek Age* (Cambridge, MA, and London, 1990), pp. 294–96; Reuven Firestone, *Holy War in Judaism: The Rise and Fall of a Controversial Idea* (Oxford and New York, 2012), pp. 26–40.

9. Daniel 10–12.

10. Daniel 7:13–14.

11. Richard A. Horsley, "The Historical Context of Q," in Richard A. Horsley and Jonathan A. Draper, eds., *Whoever Hears You Hears Me: Prophets, Performance, and Tradition in Q* (Harrisburg, PA, 1999), pp. 51–54.

12. Gerhard E. Lenski, *Power and Privilege: A Theory of Social Stratification* (Chapel Hill, NC, and London, 1966), pp. 243–48.

13. John H. Kautsky, *The Politics of Aristocratic Empires,* 2nd ed. (New Brunswick, NJ, and London, 1997), p. 81.

14. Horsley, "Historical Context of Q," p. 154.

15. Josephus, *The Life,* 10–12, trans. H. St. J. Thackeray (Cambridge, MA, 1926); Alan Mason, "Was Josephus a Pharisee?: A Re-Examination of *Life* 10–12," *Journal of Jewish Studies* 40 (1989); Alan F. Segal, *Paul the Convert: The Apostolate and Apostasy of Saul the Pharisee* (New Haven, CT, and London, 1990), pp. 81–82.

16. Josephus, *The Jewish War,* trans. G. A. Williamson (Harmondsworth, UK, 1967), 6:51–55.

17. Josephus, *The Antiquities of the Jews (AJ)* 17:157, cited in Richard A. Horsley, *Jesus and the Spiral of Violence: Popular Jewish Resistance in Roman Palestine* (New York, 1987), p. 76.

18. Josephus, *The Jewish War (JW)* 1:650.

19. *JW* 2:3.

20. *JW* 2:11–13.

21. *JW* 2:57, cited in Horsley, *Spiral of Violence,* p. 53.

22. *JW* 2:66–75.

23. John Dominic Crossan, *God and Empire: Jesus Against Rome, Then and Now* (San Francisco, 2007), pp. 91–94.

24. *AJ* 18:4–9, cited in Horsley, *Spiral of Violence,* p. 81; *JW* 2:117.

25. *JW* 2:169–74.

26. Philo, *On the Embassy to Gaius,* trans. E. H. Colson (Cambridge, MA, 1962), pp. 223–24.

27. *AJ* 18:292, cited in Horsley, *Spiral of Violence,* p. 111.

28. *AJ* 18:284, cited ibid.

29. *JW* 2.260.

30. *JW* 261–62.

31. *AJ* 18:36–38, cited in Horsley, "Historical Context of Q," p. 58.

32. John Dominic Crossan, *Jesus: A Revolutionary Biography* (New York, 1994), pp. 26–28.

33. A. N. Sherwin-White, *Roman Law and Roman Society in the New Testament* (Oxford, 1963), p. 139. Matthew 18:22–33, 20:1–15; Luke 16:1–13; Mark 12:1–9.

34. Matthew 2:16.

35. Matthew 14:3–12.

36. Matthew 10:17–18.

37. Marcus Borg, *Jesus: Uncovering the Life, Teachings, and Relevance of a Religious Revolutionary* (San Francisco, 2006), pp. 67–68.

38. Matthew 4:1–11; Mark 12–13; Luke 4:1–13.

39. Luke 10:17–18.

40. M. Lewis, *Ecstatic Religion: An Anthropological Study of Spirit Possession and Shamanism* (Baltimore, 1971), pp. 31, 32, 35, 127.

41. Mark 5:1–17; Crossan, *Jesus,* pp. 99–106.

42. Luke 13:31–33.

43. Matthew 21:1–11; Mark, 11:1–11; Luke 19:28–38.

44. Matthew 21:12–13.

45. Horsley, *Spiral of Violence,* pp. 286–89; Sean Frayne, *Galilee: From Alexander the Great to Hadrian, 323 BCE to 135 CE: A Study of Second Temple Judaism* (Notre Dame, IN, 1980), pp. 283–86.

46. Matthew 5:39, 44.

47. Matthew 26:63.

48. Luke 6:20–24.

49. Matthew 12:1–23.

50. Luke 13:13.

51. Luke 9:23–24.

52. Luke 1:51–54.

53. Mark 12:13–17; Horsley, *Spiral of Violence,* pp. 306–16.

54. F. F. Bruce, "Render to Caesar," in F. Bammel and C. F. D. Moule, eds., *Jesus and the Politics of His Day* (Cambridge, UK, 1981), p. 258.

55. Mark 12:38–40.

56. Horsley, *Spiral of Violence,* pp. 167–68.

57. A. E. Harvey, *Strenuous Commands: The Ethic of Jesus* (London and Philadelphia, 1990), pp. 162, 209.

58. Luke 14:14, 23–24; Crossan, *Jesus,* pp. 74–82.

59. Luke 6:20–21; translation amended in Crossan, *Jesus,* p. 68. The gospel does not use the Greek *penes* ("poor"), describing people making a bare living, but *ptochos,* "destitute, beggars."

60. Crossan, *Jesus,* pp. 68–70.

61. Luke 6:24–25.

62. Matthew 20:16.

63. Matthew 6:11–13.

64. Gerd Theissen, *The First Followers of Jesus: A Sociological Analysis of the Earliest Christians,* trans. John Bowden (London, 1978), pp. 8–14.

65. Mark 1:14–15, my translation.

66. Matthew 9:36.

67. Warren Carter, "Construction of Violence and Identities in Matthew's Gospel," in Shelly Matthews and E. Leigh Gibson, eds., *Violence in the New Testament* (New York and London, 2005), pp. 93–94.

68. John Pairman Brown, "Techniques of Imperial Control: The Background of the Gospel Event," in Norman Gottwald, ed., *The Bible of Liberation: Political and Social Hermeneutics* (Maryknoll, NY, 1983), pp. 357–77; Gerd Theissen, *The Miracle Stories: Early Christian Tradition* (Philadelphia, 1982), pp. 231–44; Warren Carter, *Matthew and the Margins: A Socio-Political and Religious Reading* (Sheffield, UK, 2000), pp. 17–29, 36–43, 123–27, 196–98.

69. Matthew 6:10.

70. Luke 6:28–30.

71. Luke 6:31–38.

72. Acts 2:23, 32–35; Philippians 2:9.

73. Matthew 10:5–6.

74. James B. Rives, *Religion in the Roman Empire* (Oxford, 2007), pp. 13–20, 104–14.

75. Jonathan Z. Smith, "Fences and Neighbours: Some Contours of Early Judaism," in Smith, *Imagining Religion: From Babylon to Jonestown* (Chicago and London, 1982), pp. 1–18; John W. Marshall, "Collateral Damage: Jesus and Jezebel in the Jewish War," in Matthews and Gibson, *Violence in the New Testament,* pp. 38–39; Julia Galambush, *The Reluctant Parting: How the New Testament's Jewish Writers Created a Christian Book* (San Francisco, 2005), pp. 291–92.

76. Acts of the Apostles 5:54–42.

77. Acts of the Apostles, 13:44, 14:19, 17:10–15.

78. I Corinthians 11:2–15.

79. I Corinthians 14:21–25.

80. Romans 13:1–2, 4.

81. Romans 13:6.

82. I Corinthians 7:31.

83. Acts of the Apostles 4:32, 34.

84. I Corinthians 12:12–27.

85. Luke 24:13–32.

86. Philippians 2:3–5.

87. Philippians 2:6–11, in *The English Revised Bible* (Oxford and Cambridge, UK, 1989).

88. Philippians 2:2–4.

89. I John 1.

90. I John 7:42–47.

91. I John 2:18–19.

92. Tacitus, *History*, 1:11, cited in Marshall, "Collateral Damage," pp. 37–38.

93. Reuven Firestone, *Holy War in Judaism: The Fall and Rise of a Controversial Idea* (Oxford and New York, 2012), pp. 46–47.

94. Michael S. Berger, "Taming the Beast: Rabbinic Pacification of Second Century Jewish Nationalism," in James K. Wellman, Jr., ed., *Belief and Bloodshed: Religion and Violence Across Time and Tradition* (Lanham, MD, 2007), pp. 54–55.

95. Jerusalem Talmud (J), Taanit 4.5 and Lamentations Rabbah 2.4, cited in C. G. Montefiore and H. Loewe, eds., *A Rabbinic Anthology* (New York, 1974).

96. Dio Cassius, *History* 69.12; Mireille Hadas-Lebel, *Jerusalem Against Rome*, trans. Robyn Freshat (Leuven, 2006), pp. 398–409.

97. Berger, "Taming the Beast," pp. 50–52.

98. B. Berakhot 58a; Shabbat 34a; Baba Batra 75a; Sanhedrin 100a; Firestone, *Holy War*, p. 73.

99. Firestone, *Holy War*, pp. 52–61.

100. Berger, "Taming the Beast," p. 48.

101. Avot de Rabbi Nathan B.31, cited in Robert Eisen, *The Peace and Violence of Judaism: From the Bible to Modern Zionism* (Oxford, 2011), p. 86.

102. B. Pesahim 118a, cited ibid.

103. Ibid.; Hadas-Lebel, *Jerusalem Against Rome*, pp. 265–95.

104. Mekhilta de Rabbi Yishmael 13; B. Avodah Zarah 18a, in Montefiore and Loewe, *Rabbinic Anthology*.

105. B. Shabbat 336b; B. Berakhot 58a, ibid.

106. Wilfred Cantwell Smith, *What Is Scripture? A Comparative Approach* (London, 1993), p. 290; Gerald L. Bruns, "Midrash and Allegory: The Beginnings of Scriptural Interpretation," in Robert Alter and Frank Kermode, eds., *A Literary Guide to the Bible* (London 1987), pp. 629–30; Nahum S. Glatzer, "The Concept of Peace in Classical Judaism," *Essays on Jewish Thought* (University, AL, 1978), pp. 37–38; Eisen, *Peace and Violence*, p. 90.

107. Michael Fishbane, *Garments of Torah: Essays in Biblical Hermeneutics* (Bloomington and Indianapolis, 1989), pp. 22–32.

108. B. Shabbat 63a; B. Sanhedrin 82a; B. Shabbat 133b; Tanhuman 10; Eisen, *Peace and Violence*, pp. 88–89; Reuven Kimelman, "Non-violence in the Talmud," *Judaism* 17 (1968).

109. Avot de Rabbi Nathan A. 23, cited in Eisen, *Peace and Violence*, p. 88.

110. Mishnah (M), Avot 4:1, in Montefiore and Loewe, *Rabbinic Anthology*.

111. Eisen, *Peace and Violence*, p. 89.

112. B. Berakhot 4a; Megillah 3a; Tamua 16a.

113. Exodus 14; B. Megillah 10b, in Montefiore and Loewe, *Rabbinic Anthology*.

114. M. Sotah 8:7; M. Yadayin 4:4; Tosefta Kiddushim 5:4; Firestone, *Holy War*, p. 74.

115. J. Sotah 8.1.

116. Song of Songs 2:7, 3:5, 8:4; B. Ketubot 110b–111a; Song of Songs Rabbah 2:7.

117. Firestone, *Holy War*, pp. 74–75.

118. Aviezer Ravitsky, *Messianism, Zionism, and Jewish Religious Radicalism*, trans. Michael Swirsky and Jonathan Chapman (Chicago, 1997), pp. 211–34.

119. Peter Brown, *The World of Late Antiquity, AD 150–750* (London, 1989), pp. 20–24; Brown, *The Rise of Western Christendom: Triumph and Diversity, AD 200–1000* (Oxford and Malden, MA, 1996), pp. 18–19.

120. Brown, *World of Late Antiquity*, pp. 24–27.

121. Peter Brown, *The Making of Late Antiquity* (Cambridge, MA, and London, 1978), p. 48; Brown, *Rise of Western Christendom,* pp. 19–20.

122. Revelation 3:21; Tacitus, *Annals* 15:44. Tacitus, however, was writing decades after the event, and it seems unlikely that at this early date Christians were recognized as a distinct body. Candida R. Moss, *The Myth of Persecution: How Early Christians Invented a Story of Martyrdom* (New York, 2013), pp. 138–39.

123. Tertullian, *Apology* 20, cited in Moss, *Myth of Persecution,* p. 128.

124. W. H. C. Frend, *Martyrdom and Persecution in the Early Church: A Study of the Conflict from the Maccabees to Donatus* (Oxford, 1965), p. 331.

125. Jonathan Z. Smith, "The Temple and the Magician," in Smith, *Map Is Not Territory: Studies in the History of Religions* (Chicago and London, 1978), p. 187; Peter Brown, "The Rise of the Holy Man in Late Antiquity," *Journal of Roman Studies* 61 (1971).

126. Rives, *Religion in the Roman Empire,* pp. 207–8.

127. Ibid., pp. 68, 82.

128. Moss, *Myth of Persecution,* pp. 127–62; G. E. M. de Ste. Croix, "Why Were the Early Christians Persecuted?" in Ste. Croix, *Christian Persecution, Martyrdom, and Orthodoxy,* ed. Michael Whitby and Joseph Streeter (Oxford, 2006).

129. James B. Rives, "The Decree of Decius and the Religion of Empire," *Journal of Roman Studies* 89 (1999); Robin Lane Fox, *Pagans and Christians* (New York, 1987), pp. 455–56.

130. B. Baba Metziah 59b, Montefiore and Loewe, *Rabbinic Anthology.*

131. *Collatio Legum Romanarum et Mosaicarum* 15:3, cited in Brown, *Rise of Western Christendom,* p. 22.

132. Ramsay MacMullen, *The Second Church: Popular Christianity A.D. 200–400* (Atlanta, 2009). Christians had traditionally worshipped in private houses. Churches like the offending basilica were a recent innovation.

133. Moss, *Myth of Persecution,* pp. 154–58.

134. Candida R. Moss, *The Other Christs: Imitating Jesus in Ancient Christian Ideologies of Martyrdom* (Oxford, 2010).

135. Victricius, *De Laude Sanctorum* 10:452 B, cited in Peter Brown, *The Cult of the Saints: Its Rise and Function in Latin Christianity* (Chicago, 1981), p. 79.

136. *Decretum Gelasianum,* cited ibid.

137. *The Martyrs of Lyons* 1:4, in *The Acts of the Christian Martyrs,* trans. H. Musurillo (Oxford, 1972).

138. Perpetua, *Passio,* 9, in Peter Dronke, ed. and trans., *Women Writers of the Middle Ages: A Critical Study of Texts from Perpetua (†203) to Marguerite Porete (†1310)* (Cambridge, UK, 1984), p. 4.

139. Perpetua, *Passio,* 10, cited.

140. Frend, *Martyrdom and Persecution,* p. 15.

141. Brown, *World of Late Antiquity,* pp. 82–84.

142. Origen, *Contra Celsum* 2:30, trans. Henry Chadwick (Cambridge, UK, 1980).

143. Cyprian, *Letters* 40:1, 48:4.

144. Cyprian, *Letters* 30:2; Brown, *Making of Late Antiquity,* pp. 79–80.

145. Lactantius, *Divine Institutions,* in *Lactantius: Works,* trans. William Fletcher, (Edinburgh, 1971), p. 366.

146. Ibid., p. 427.

147. Ibid., p. 328.

6 · BYZANTIUM: THE TRAGEDY OF EMPIRE

1. Garth Fowden, *Empire to Commonwealth: Consequences of Monotheism in Late Antiquity* (Princeton, NJ, 1993), pp. 13–16, 34.

2. Eusebius, *In Praise of Constantine: A Historical Study and New Translation of Eusebius' Tricennial Orations,* trans. H. A. Drake (Berkeley and Los Angeles, 1976), p. 89.

3. Aziz Al-Azmeh, *Muslim Kingship: Power and the Sacred in Muslim, Christian, and Pagan Polities* (London and New York, 1997), pp. 27–33.

4. Michael Gaddis, *There Is No Crime for Those Who Have Christ: Religious Violence in the Christian Roman Empire* (Berkeley, Los Angeles, and London, 2005), p. 88.

5. Eusebius, *Life of Constantine* 1:5, 1:24, 2:19, trans. and ed. Averil and Stuart G. Hall (Oxford, 1999).

6. Eusebius, *Life of Constantine,* 4:8–13; Fowden, *Empire to Commonwealth,* pp. 93–94.

7. Al-Azmeh, *Muslim Kingship,* pp. 43–46.

8. Matthew 28:19.

9. John Haldon, *Warfare, State, and Society in the Byzantine World, 565–1204* (London and New York, 2005), pp. 16–19.

10. Fowden, *Empire to Commonwealth,* pp. 93–94; Gaddis, *There Is No Crime,* pp. 62–63.

11. Eusebius, *Life of Constantine* 4:61.

12. Eusebius, *Life of Constantine* 4:62, cited in Gaddis, *There Is No Crime,* pp. 63–64.

13. Gaddis, *There Is No Crime,* pp. 51–59.

14. Eusebius, *Life of Constantine* 4.24.

15. Constantine, *Letter to Aelafius, Vicor of Africa,* in *Optatus: Against the Donatists,* trans. Mark Edwards (Liverpool, UK, 1988), appendix 3.

16. The Donatists argued that Caecilian had been ordained by Felix of Apthungi, who had apostatized during the persecution of Diocletian. Their protest was an act of piety to the memory of the martyrs.

17. Gaddis, *There Is No Crime,* pp. 51–58.

18. Constantine, in *Optatus,* appendix 9, cited in Gaddis, *There Is No Crime,* p. 57.

19. Richard Lim, *Public Disputation, Power, and Social Order in Late Antiquity* (Berkeley, CA, 1995).

20. Peter Brown, *The World of Late Antiquity, AD 150–750* (London, 1989 ed.), pp. 86–89.

21. James B. Rives, *Religion in the Roman Empire* (Oxford, 2007), pp. 13–20.

22. Genesis 18:1–17; Exodus 33:18–23, 34:6–9; Joshua 5:13–15.

23. Jaroslav Pelikan, *The Christian Tradition: A History of the Development of Doctrine,* vol. 1: *The Emergence of the Catholic Tradition* (Chicago and London, 1971), p. 145.

24. Eusebius, *Demonstratio Evangelium (Proof of the Gospel)* (Kindle ed., 2010), 5–6, Preface 1–2.

25. Peter Brown, *The Body and Society: Men, Women, and Sexual Renunciation in Early Christianity* (London and Boston, 1988), p. 236.

26. Athanasius, *On the Incarnation,* cited in Andrew Louth, *The Origins of the Christian Mystical Tradition: From Plato to Denys* (Oxford, 1981), p. 78.

27. John Meyndorff, *Byzantine Theology: Historical Trends and Doctrinal Themes* (New York and London, 1975), p. 78.

28. Brown, *World of Late Antiquity,* p. 90.

29. Evelyne Patlagean, *Pauvreté économique et pauvreté sociale à Byzance, 4ᵉ–7ᵉ siècles* (Paris, 1977), pp. 78–84.

30. Matthew 6:25.

31. Matthew 4:20; Acts 4:35.

32. Matthew 19:21.

33. Athanasius, *Vita Antonii* 3.2, in *The Life of Antony and the Letter to Marcellinus,* trans. R. C. Gregg (New York, 1980).

34. David Caner, *Wandering, Begging Monks: Spiritual Authority and the Promotion of Monasticism in Late Antiquity* (Berkeley, Los Angeles, and London, 2002), p. 25.

35. 2 Thessalonians 3:6–12.

36. Athanasius, *Vita,* 50:4–6.

37. H. I. Bell, V. Martin, E. G. Turner, and D. van Berchem, *The Abinnaeus Archive* (Oxford, 1962), pp. 77, 108.

38. A. E. Boak and H. C. Harvey, *The Archive of Aurelius Isidore* (Ann Arbor, MI, 1960), pp. 295–96.

39. Brown, *Making of Late Antiquity,* pp. 82–86.

40. Matthew 6:34.

41. Brown, *Body and Society,* pp. 218–21.

42. Evagrius Ponticus, *Praktikos* 9, in *Evagrius Ponticus: The Praktikos and Chapters on Prayer,* trans. J. E. Bamberger (Kalamazoo, MI, 1978).

43. Olympios 2, 313d–316a, *Sayings of the Desert Fathers,* in J. P. Migne, ed., *Patrologia Gracca (PG)* (Paris, 1800–1875).

44. Brown, *Making of Late Antiquity,* pp. 88–90.

45. Poemen 78, PG 65. 352cd, in *Sayings of the Desert Fathers.*

46. Ibid., 60; PG 65:332a.

47. Douglas Burton-Christie, *The Word in the Desert: Scripture and the Quest for Holiness in Early Christian Monasticism* (New York and Oxford, 1993), pp. 261–83.

48. Brown, *Body and Society,* p. 215; *World of Late Antiquity,* p. 98.

49. Athanasius, *Vita,* pp. 92–93.

50. Macarius 32; PG 65:273d, in *Sayings of the Desert Fathers.*

51. Brown, *World of Late Antiquity,* pp. 93–94.

52. Gaddis, *There Is No Crime,* p. 278.

53. Hilary of Poitiers, *Against Valerius and Ursacius* 1:2:6, in *Hilary of Poitiers: Conflicts of Conscience and Law in the Fourth-Century Church,* trans. Lionel R. Wickham (Liverpool, UK, 1997).

54. Athanasius, *History of the Arians* 81, in *Nicene and Post Nicene Fathers (NPNF),* trans. and ed. Alexander Roberts and James Donaldson, 14 vols. (Edinburgh, 1885).

55. Athanasius, *Apology Before Constantius* 33, NPNF.

56. Genesis 14:18–20.

57. Gaddis, *There Is No Crime,* pp. 89–97.

58. Ibid., p. 93.

59. Socrates, *History of the Church,* 3:15, NPNF.

60. Gaddis, *There Is No Crime,* pp. 93–94; cf. Mark Juergensmeyer, *Terror in the Mind of God: The Global Rise of Religious Violence* (Berkeley, CA, 2000), pp. 190–218.

61. Harold A. Drake, *Constantine and the Bishops: The Politics of Intolerance* (Baltimore, 2000), pp. 431–36.

62. Brown, *Power and Persuasion,* pp. 34–70.

63. G. W. Bowerstock, *Hellenism in Late Antiquity* (Ann Arbor, MI, 1990), pp. 2–5, 35–40, 72–81; Brown, *Power and Persuasion,* pp. 134–45.

64. Gregory of Nazianzus, Oration 6.6, PG 35:728, cited in Brown, *Power and Persuasion,* p. 50.

65. Brown, *Power and Persuasion,* pp. 123–26.

66. Raimundo Panikkar, *The Trinity and the Religious Experience of Man* (Maryknoll, NY 1973), pp. 46–67.

67. Gaddis, *There Is No Crime,* pp. 251–82.

68. Eusebius, *The History of the Church,* 6:43, 5–10.

69. Palladius, *Dialogue on the Life of John Chrysostom,* 20.561–71, trans. Robert T. Meyer (New York, 1985).

70. Gaddis, *There Is No Crime,* p. 16.

71. Hilary of Poitiers, *Against Valerius and Ursacius,* 1:2:6.

72. Patlagean, *Pauvreté économique,* pp. 178–81, 301–40.

73. Peter Garnsey, *Famine and Food Shortage in the Greco-Roman World* (Cambridge, UK, 1988), pp. 257–68.

74. E. W. Brooks, *The Sixth Book of the Select Letter of Severus, Patriarch of Antioch,* 1.9 (London, 1903), cited in Brown, *Power and Persuasion,* p. 148; Brown, *World of Late Antiquity,* p. 110.

75. Sozomen, *History of the Church,* 6:33:2, *NPNF.*

76. Gaddis, *There Is No Crime,* pp. 242–50.

77. Caner, *Wandering, Begging Monks,* pp. 125–49. Cf. I Thessalonians 5:17.

78. Gaddis, *There Is No Crime,* pp. 94–97.

79. Libanius, Oration 30:8–9, in *Libanius: Select Orations,* ed. and trans. A. F. Norman, 2 vols. (Cambridge, MA, 1969, 1977).

80. Gaddis, *There Is No Crime,* p. 249.

81. Ambrose, Epistle 41, cited ibid., pp. 191–96.

82. Ramsay MacMullen, *Christianizing the Roman Empire, AD 100–400* (New Haven, CT, and London, 1984), p. 99.

83. Rufinus, *History of the Church* 11.22, in *The Church History of Rufinus of Aquileia,* trans. Philip R. Amidon (Oxford, 1997).

84. Gaddis, *There Is No Crime,* p. 250.

85. Ibid., pp. 99–100.

86. MacMullen, *Christianizing the Roman Empire,* p. 119.

87. Augustine, Letters, 93:5:17, *NPNF.*

88. Augustine, *The City of God,* 18:54, in MacMullen, *Christianizing the Roman Empire,* p. 100.

89. Peter Brown, "Religious Dissent in the Later Roman Empire: The Case of North Africa," *History* 46 (1961); Brown, "Religious Coercion in the Later Roman Empire: The Case of North Africa," *History* 48 (1963); Gaddis, *There Is No Crime,* p. 133.

90. Augustine, Letter 47:5, *NPNF.*

91. Augustine, *Against Festus,* 22:74, *NPNF.*

92. Augustine, Letter 93:6, *NPNF.*

93. Augustine, *One the Free Choice of the Will,* 9:1:5, trans. Thomas Williams (Indianapolis, 1993).

94. Brown, *Rise of Western Christendom,* pp. 7–8.

95. Gaddis, *There Is No Crime,* pp. 283–89.

96. Nestorius, *Bazaar of Heracleides,* trans. G. R. Driver and Leonard Hodgson (Oxford, 1925), pp. 199–200.

97. Socrates, *Historia Ecclesiastica* 7:32, *NPNF.*

98. Palladius, *Dialogue on the Life of John Chrysostom,* 20:579.

99. Gaddis, *There Is No Crime,* pp. 292–310.

100. *Letter of Theodosius to Bausama,* May 14, 449, cited ibid., p. 298.

101. Acts of the Council of Chalcedon, cited ibid., p. 156n.

102. Nestorius, *Bazaar of Heracleides,* pp. 482–83.

103. Gaddis, *There Is No Crime,* pp. 310–27.

104. John Meyendorff, "The Role of Christ, I: Christ as Saviour in the East," in Jill Raitt, Bernard McGinn, and John Meyendorff, eds., *Christian Spirituality: High Middle Ages and Reformation* (New York, 1987), pp. 236–37.

105. Meyendorff, *Byzantine Theology,* pp. 213–15.

106. Brown, *World of Late Antiquity,* pp. 166–68.

107. Khosrow I, cited ibid., p. 166.

108. Brown, *World of Late Antiquity,* pp. 160–65; Brown, *Rise of Western Christendom,* pp. 173–74.

109. Maximus, *Ambigua* 42, cited in Meyendorff, *Byzantine Theology,* p. 164.

110. Maximus, Letter 2: On Love, 401D.

111. Maximus, *Centuries on Love* 1:61, cited in Andrew Lowth, *Maximus the Confessor* (London, 1996), pp. 39–40; Matthew 5:44; I Timothy 2:4.

112. Meyndorff, *Byzantine Theology,* pp. 212–22.

7 · THE MUSLIM DILEMMA

1. I have discussed the career of Muhammad and the history of Arabia in more detail in *Muhammad: A Prophet for Our Time* (London and New York, 2006).

2. Muhammad A. Bamyeh, *The Social Origins of Islam: Mind, Economy, Discourse* (Minneapolis, 1999), pp. 11–12.

3. Toshihiko Izutsu, *Ethico-Religious Concepts in the Qur'an* (Montreal and Kingston, ON, 2002), pp. 29, 46.

4. R. A. Nicholson, *A Literary History of the Arabs* (Cambridge, UK, 1953), pp. 83, 28–45.

5. Bamyeh, *Social Origins of Islam,* p. 38.

6. Genesis 16, 17:25, 21:8–21.

7. Quran 5:69, 88:17–20.

8. Quran 3:84–85.

9. W. Montgomery Watt, *Muhammad at Mecca* (Oxford, 1953), p. 68.

10. Quran 90:13–17.

11. Izutsu, *Ethico-Religious Concepts,* p. 28.

12. Ibid., pp. 68–69; Quran 14:47, 39:37, 15:79, 30:47, 44:16.

13. Quran 25:63, in *The Message of the Quran,* trans. Muhammad Asad (Gibraltar, 1980).

14. W. Montgomery Watt, *Muhammad's Mecca: History of the Quran* (Edinburgh, 1988), p. 25.

15. W. Montgomery Watt, *Muhammad at Medina* (Oxford, 1956), pp. 173–231.

16. Ibn Ishaq, *Sirat Rasul Allah,* in *The Life of Muhammad,* trans. and ed. A. Guillaume (London, 1955), p. 232.

17. Watt, *Muhammad at Medina,* pp. 6–8; Bamyeh, *Social Origins of Islam,* pp. 198–99; Marshall G. S. Hodgson, *The Venture of Islam: Conscience and History in a World Civilization,* 3 vols. (Chicago and London, 1974), pp. 1:75–76.

18. Quran 29:46.

19. Michael Bonner, *Jihad in Islamic History* (Princeton, NJ, and Oxford, 2006), p. 193.

20. Martin Lings, *Muhammad: His Life Based on the Earliest Sources* (London, 1983), pp. 247–55; Tor Andrae, *Muhammad: The Man and His Faith,* trans. Theophil Menzel (London, 1936), pp. 215–15; Watt, *Muhammad at Medina,* pp. 46–59; Bamyeh, *Social Origins of Islam,* pp. 222–27.

21. Quran 48:26, cited in Izutsu, *Ethico-Religious Concepts,* p. 31.

22. Ibn Ishaq, *Sirat Rasul Allah,* 751, cited in Guillaume, *Life of Muhammad.* Cf. Quran 110.

23. Paul L. Heck, "*Jihad* Revisited," *Journal of Religious Ethics* 32, no.1 (2004); Bonner, *Jihad in Islamic History,* pp. 21–22.

24. Bonner, *Jihad in Islamic History,* p. 25; Reuven Firestone, *Jihad: The Origin of Holy War in Islam* (Oxford and New York, 1999), pp. 42–45.

25. Quran 16:135–28.

26. Quran 22:39–41, 2:194, 2:197.

27. Quran 9:5.

28. Quran 8:61.

29. Quran 9:29.

30. Firestone, *Jihad,* pp. 49–50.

31. Quran 15:94–95, 16:135.

32. Quran 2:190, 22:39–45.

33. Quran 2:191, 2:217.

34. Quran 2:191, 9:5, 9:29.

35. Firestone, *Jihad*, pp. 50–65.

36. Quran 2:216, Asad translation.

37. Quran 9:38–39, in *The Qur'an: A New Translation*, trans. M. A. S. Abdel Haleem (Oxford, 2004).

38. Quran 9:43, ibid.

39. Quran 9:73–74, 63:1–3.

40. Quran 2:109, Abdel Haleem translation; cf. 50:59.

41. Quran 5:16, ibid.

42. Firestone, *Jihad*, pp. 73, 157.

43. Quran 9:5, Abdel Haleem translation.

44. Quran 2:193, in Firestone, *Jihad*, p. 85.

45. Garth Fowden, *Empire to Commonwealth: Consequences of Monotheism in Late Antiquity* (Princeton, NJ, 1993), pp. 140–42.

46. John Keegan, *A History of Warfare* (London and New York, 1993), pp. 195–96.

47. Peter Brown, *The World of Late Antiquity, AD 150–750* (London, 1989), p. 193.

48. Hadith reported by Muthir al Ghiram, Shams ad-Din Suyuti, and al Walid ibn Muslim, cited in Guy Le Strange, *Palestine Under the Moslems: A Description of Syria and the Holy Land from AD 650 to 1500* (London, 1890), pp. 139–43; Tabari, *Tarikh ar-Rasul wa'l Muluk*, 1:2405; Moshe Gil, *A History of Palestine, 634–1099*, trans. Ethel Broido (Cambridge, UK, 1992), pp. 70–72, 143–48, 636–38.

49. "Book of Commandments," quoted in Gil, *History of Palestine*, p. 71.

50. Michael the Syrian, *History* 3.226, quoted in Joshua Prawer, *The Latin Kingdom in Jerusalem: European Colonialism in the Middle Ages* (London, 1972), p. 216.

51. Peter Brown, *The Rise of Western Christendom: Triumph and Diversity, AD 200–1000* (Oxford and Malden, MA, 1996), p. 185; Bonner, *Jihad in Islamic History*, p. 56.

52. Bonner, *Jihad in Islamic History*, pp. 64–89; 168–69.

53. David Cook, *Understanding Jihad* (Berkeley, Los Angeles, and London, 2005), pp. 22–24.

54. Ibid., pp. 13–19; Bonner, *Jihad in Islamic History*, pp. 46–54; Firestone, *Jihad*, pp. 93–99.

55. Jan Wensinck, *Concordance et indices de la tradition musulmane*, 5 vols. (Leiden, 1992), 1:994, 5:298.

56. Al-Hindi, *Kanz* (Beirut, 1989), 4:P:282 n. 10,500; Cook, *Understanding Jihad*, p. 18.

57. Ibn Abi Asim, *Jihad* (Medina, 1986), 1:140–41 n. 11.

58. Wensinck, *Concordance*, p. 2:212; Suliman Bashear, "Apocalyptic and Other Materials on Early Muslim–Byzantine Wars," *Journal of the Royal Asiatic Society*, ser. 3, vol. 1, no. 2 (1991).

59. Wensinck, *Concordance*, p. 4:344; Bonner, *Jihad in Islamic History*, p. 51.

60. Wensinck, *Concordance*, 2:312.

61. Cook, *Understanding Jihad*, pp. 23–25.

62. Ibn al-Mubarak, *Kitab al-Jihad* (Beirut, 1971), pp. 89–90 n. 105; Cook, *Understanding Jihad*, p. 23.

63. Abu Daud, *Sunan* III, p. 4 n. 2484, in Cook, *Understanding Jihad*.

64. Quran 3:157, 3:167.

65. Muhammad b. Isa al-Tirmidhi, *Al-jami al-sahih*, ed. Abd al-Wahhab Abd al-Latif, 5 vols. (Beirut, n.d), 3:106, cited in David Cook, "Jihad and Martyrdom in Islamic History," in Andrew R. Murphy, ed., *The Blackwell Companion to Religion and Violence* (Chichester, UK, 2011), pp. 283–84.

66. Ibn al-Mubarak, *Jihad,* pp. 63–64 n. 64, cited in Cook, *Understanding Jihad,* p. 26.

67. Bonner, *Jihad in Islamic History,* pp. 119–20.

68. Ibid., pp. 125–26; Hodgson, *Venture of Islam,* 1:216; John L. Esposito, *Unholy War: Terror in the Name of Islam* (Oxford, 2002), pp. 41–42.

69. Al-Azmeh, *Muslim Kingship,* pp. 68–69. The Umayyads learned this lore from the Lakhmid Arab dynasty, who had been clients of Persia. Timothy H. Parsons, *The Rule of Empires: Those Who Built Them, Those Who Endured Them, and Why They Always Fail* (Oxford, 2010), pp. 79–80.

70. Brown, *World of Late Antiquity,* pp. 201–2.

71. Michael Bonner, *Aristocratic Violence and Holy War: Studies in the Jihad and the Arab-Byzantine Frontier* (New Haven, CT, 1996), pp. 99–106.

72. Abu Nuwas, *Diwan,* 452, 641, cited in Bonner, *Jihad in Islamic History,* p. 129.

73. Ibid., pp. 127–31.

74. Ibid., pp. 99–110.

75. Peter Partner, *God of Battles: Holy Wars of Christianity and Islam* (London, 1997), p. 51.

76. Ibn al-Mubarak, *Jihad,* p. 143 n. 141; Al Bayhagi, *Zuhd* (Beirut, n.d.), p. 165 n. 273, cited in Cook, *Understanding Jihad,* p. 35.

77. Parsons, *Rule of Empires,* p. 77; Bonner, *Jihad in Islamic History,* p. 89; Hodgson, *Venture of Islam,* 1:305.

78. Al-Azmeh, *Muslim Kingship,* p. 239; Hodgson, *Venture of Islam,* pp. 444–45.

79. Hodgson, *Venture of Islam,* pp. 315–54.

80. Ibid., p. 317; Bonner, *Jihad in Islamic History,* pp. 92–93; Cook, *Understanding Jihad,* p. 21.

81. Hodgson, *Venture of Islam,* p. 323.

82. Sunni Muslims form the majority, basing their lives on the *sunnah,* or "customary practice," of the Prophet.

83. It was called the Fatimid Empire because, like all Shiis, Ismails revere Fatima, the Prophet's daughter, the wife of Ali, and the mother of Husain.

84. Bernard Lewis, *The Assassins* (London, 1967); Edwin Burman, *The Assassins: Holy Killers of Islam* (London, 1987).

8 · CRUSADE AND JIHAD

1. H. E. J. Cowdrey, "Pope Gregory VII's 'Crusading' Plans of 1074," in B. Z. Kedar, H. E. Mayer, and R. C. Smail, eds., *Outremer* (Jerusalem, 1982).

2. Jonathan Riley-Smith, *The First Crusade and the Idea of Crusading* (London, 1986), pp. 17–22.

3. Joseph R. Strager, "Feudalism in Western Europe," in Rushton Coulborn, ed., *Feudalism in History* (Hamden, CT, 1965), p. 21; Michael Gaddis, *There Is No Crime for Those Who Have Christ: Religious Violence in the Christian Roman Empire* (Berkeley, Los Angeles, and London, 2005), pp. 334–35; John Keegan, *A History of Warfare* (London and New York, 1993), pp. 283, 289.

4. Peter Brown, *The World of Late Antiquity, AD 150–750* (London, 1989), p. 134.

5. J. M. Wallace-Hadrill, *The Frankish Church* (Oxford, 1983), pp. 187, 245.

6. Peter Brown, *The Rise of Western Christendom: Triumph and Diversity, AD 200–1000* (Oxford and Malden, MA, 1996), pp. 254–57.

7. Ibid., pp. 276–302.

8. Einard, "Life of Charlemagne," in *Two Lives of Charlemagne,* trans. Lewis Thorpe (Harmondsworth, UK, 1969), p. 67.

9. Karl F. Morrison, *Tradition and Authority in the Western Church, 300–1140* (Princeton, NJ, 1969), p. 378.

10. Rosamund McKitterick, *The Frankish Kingdoms Under the Carolingians, 751–987* (London and New York, 1983), p. 62.

11. Brown, *World of Late Antiquity*, pp. 134–35.

12. Alcuin, Letter 174, cited in R. W. Southern, *Western Society and the Church in the Middle Ages* (New York, 1990), p. 2:32.

13. This letter was actually written for him by Alcuin. Epistle 93 in Wallace-Hadrill, *Frankish Church*, p. 186.

14. Brown, *Rise of Western Christendom*, p. 281.

15. Talal Asad, "On Discipline and Humility in Medieval Christian Monasticism," in *Genealogies of Religion, Discipline and Reasons of Power in Christianity and Islam* (Baltimore and London, 1993), p. 148.

16. Ibid., pp. 130–34.

17. Southern, *Western Society and the Church*, pp. 217–24.

18. Georges Duby, "The Origins of a System of Social Classification," in Duby, *The Chivalrous Society*, trans. Cynthia Postan (London, 1977), p. 91.

19. Georges Duby, "The Origins of Knighthood," in *The Chivalrous Society*, p. 165.

20. Foundation Charter of King Edgar for New Minster, Winchester, in Southern, *Western Society and the Church*, pp., 224–25.

21. Ordericus Vitalis, *Historia Ecclesiastica*, in Southern, *Western Society and the Church*, p. 225.

22. Brown, *Rise of Western Christendom*, p. 301.

23. Georges Duby, *The Three Orders: Feudal Society Imagined*, trans. Arthur Goldhammer (London, 1980), p. 151; Riley-Smith, *First Crusade*, p. 3.

24. Marc Bloch, *Feudal Society*, trans. L. A. Manyon (London, 1961), pp. 296, 298.

25. Georges Duby, *The Early Growth of the European Economy: Warriors and Peasants from the Seventh to the Twelfth Century*, trans. Howard B. Clarke (Ithaca, NY, 1974), p. 49.

26. Duby, "Origins of System of Social Classification," pp. 91–92.

27. The first extant formulations of this system have been found in a poem by Adalbéron of Laon (c. 1028–30) and *Gesta episcoporum cameracensium* by Bishop Gerard of Cambrai, c. 1025; but there may have been earlier versions. George Duby, "Origins of Knighthood," p. 165.

28. Bishop Merbad of Rennes, cited in J. P. Migne, ed., *Patrologia Latina* (Paris 1844–64), vol. 1971, pp. 1483–34; Baldric of Bol, in *Patrologia Latina*, vol. 162, pp. 1058–59: R. I. Moore, *The Formation of a Persecuting Society: Power and Deviance in Western Europe, 950–1250* (Oxford, 1987), p. 102.

29. Maurice Keen, *Chivalry* (New Haven, CT, and London, 1984), pp. 46–47.

30. Thomas Head and Richard Landes, eds., *The Peace of God: Social Justice and Religious Response in France Around the Year 1000* (Ithaca, NY, 1992); Tomaz Mastnak, *Crusading Peace: Christendom, the Muslim World, and Western Political Order* (Berkeley, Los Angeles, and London, 2002), pp. 1–18; Duby, *Chivalrous Society*, pp. 126–31; H. E. J. Cowdrey, "The Peace and the Truce of God in the Eleventh Century," *Past and Present* 46 (1970).

31. James Westfall Thompson, *Economic and Social History of the Middle Ages* (New York, 1928), p. 668.

32. The Council of Narbonne (1054), in Duby, *Chivalrous Society*, p. 132.

33. Glaber, *Historiarum* V:i:25, cited in Mastnak, *Crusading Peace*, p. 11.

34. Duby, "Origins of Knighthood," p. 169.

35. P. A. Sigal, "Et les marcheurs de Dieu prirent leurs armes," *L'histoire* 47 (1982); Riley-Smith, *First Crusade*, p. 10.

36. Riley-Smith, *First Crusade*, pp. 7–8.

37. Ibid., pp. 17–27.

38. Urban, Letter to the Counts of Catalonia, cited ibid., p. 20.

39. Matthew 19:29.

40. Mastnak, *Crusading Peace,* pp. 130–36.

41. Sigal, "Et les marcheurs de Dieu," p. 23; Riley-Smith, *First Crusade,* p. 23.

42. Riley-Smith, *First Crusade,* pp. 48–49.

43. "Chronicle of Rabbi Eliezer bar Nathan," in *The Jews and the Crusaders: The Hebrew Chronicles of the First and Second Crusades,* trans. and ed. Shlomo Eidelberg (London, 1977), p. 80.

44. Guibert of Nogent, *De Vita Sua* II:1, cited in *Monodies and On the Relics of the Saints: The Autobiography and a Manifesto of a French Monk from the Time of the Crusades,* trans. and ed. Joseph McAlhany and Jay Rubinstein (London, 2011), p. 97.

45. Henri Pirenne, *Economic and Social History of Medieval Europe,* trans. I. E. Clegg (New York, 1956), pp. 7, 10–12.

46. John H. Kautzky, *The Political Consequences of Modernization* (New York, London, Sydney, and Toronto, 1972), p. 48.

47. Georges Duby, "The Transformation of the Aristocracy," in *Chivalrous Society,* p. 82.

48. Norman Cohn, *Pursuit of the Millennium: Revolutionary Millenarians and Mystical Anarchists of the Middle Ages* (London, 1984), pp. 68–70.

49. Duby, "The Juventus," in *Chivalrous Society,* pp. 112–21.

50. Cohn, *Pursuit of the Millennium,* p. 63.

51. Riley-Smith, *First Crusade,* p. 46.

52. Ralph of Caen, *Gesta Tancredi, Recueil des historiens des croisades,* ed. Académie des Inscriptions et Belles-Lettres (1841–1900) [*RHC*], 3, cited in Riley-Smith, *First Crusade,* p. 36.

53. E. O. Blake, "The Formation of the 'Crusade Idea,'" *Journal of Ecclesiastical History* 21, no. 1 (1970); Mastnak, *Crusading Peace,* pp. 56–57.

54. *The Deeds of the Franks and the Other Pilgrims to Jerusalem,* trans. Rosalind Hill (London, 1962), p. 27.

55. Fulcher of Chartres, *A History of the Expedition to Jerusalem, 1098–1127,* trans. and ed. Frances Rita Ryan (Knoxville, TN, 1969), p. 96.

56. Riley-Smith, *First Crusade,* p. 91.

57. Ibid., pp. 84–85, 117.

58. John Fowles, *The Magus,* rev. ed. (London, 1997), p. 413.

59. Mastnak, *Crusading Peace,* p. 66.

60. *Deeds of the Franks,* p. 91.

61. Raymond in *The First Crusade: The Accounts of Eyewitnesses and Participants,* ed. and trans. August C. Krey (Princeton, NJ, and London, 1921), p. 266.

62. Fulcher, *History of the Expedition,* p. 102.

63. Raymond in Krey, *First Crusade,* p. 266.

64. Robert the Monk, *Historia Iherosolimitana, RHC,* 3, p. 741.

65. Fulcher, *History of the Expedition,* pp. 66–67; Robert the Monk, *Historia,* p. 725; Riley-Smith, *First Crusade,* p. 143.

66. Keegan, *History of Warfare,* p. 295.

67. Bernard, *In Praise of the New Knighthood,* 2:3, 2, 1, cited in *In Praise of the New Knighthood: A Treatise on the Knights Templar and the Holy Places of Jerusalem,* trans. M. Conrad Greenia, OCSO (Collegeville, MN, 2008).

68. Ibid., 3:5.

69. Amin Maalouf, *The Crusades Through Arab Eyes,* trans. Jon Rothschild (London, 1984), pp. 38–39. The figures quoted by Ibn al-Athir are clearly exaggerated, since the city's population at this time was no more than ten thousand.

70. Michael Bonner, *Jihad in Islamic History* (Princeton, NJ, and Oxford, 2006), pp. 137–38.

71. Izz ad-Din ibn al-Athir, *The Perfect History* X.92, in *Arab Historians of the Crusades,* trans. and ed. Francesco Gabrieli (London, Melbourne, and Henley, 1978).

72. Carole Hillenbrand, *The Crusades: Islamic Perspectives* (Edinburgh, 1999), pp. 75–81.

73. Maalouf, *Crusades Through Arab Eyes,* pp. 2–3.

74. Bonner, *Jihad in Islamic History,* pp. 139–40; Emmanuel Sivan, "Genèse de contre-croisade: un traité damasquin de début du XIIe siècle," *Journal Asiatique* 254 (1966).

75. R. A. Nicholson, *The Mystics of Islam* (London, 1963), p. 105.

76. Ibn al-Qalanisi, *History of Damascus* 173, in Gabrieli, *Arab Historians of the Crusades.*

77. Kamal ad-Din, *The Cream of the Milk in the History of Aleppo,* 2:187–90, ibid.

78. Maalouf, *Crusades Through Arab Eyes,* p. 147.

79. Imad ad-Din al-Isfahani, *Zubat al-nuores,* in Hillebrand, *Crusades,* p. 113.

80. All quotations are from Ibn al-Athir, *Perfect History,* 11:264–67, in Gabrieli, *Arab Historians of the Crusades.*

81. Baha ad-Din, *Sultanly Anecdotes,* ibid., p. 100.

82. Ibn al-Athir, *Perfect History,* ibid., pp. 141–42.

83. Ibn al-Athir, *Perfect History,* in Maalouf, *Crusades Through Arab Eyes,* pp. 205–6.

84. Christopher J. Tyerman, "Sed nihil fecit? The Last Capetians and the Recovery of the Holy Land," in J. Gillingham and J. C. Holt, eds., *War and Government in the Middle Ages: Essays in Honor of J. O. Prestwich* (Totowa, NJ, 1984); Norman Housley, *The Later Crusades, 1274–1580: From Lyons to Alcazar* (Oxford, 1992), pp. 12–30; Mastnak, *Crusading Peace,* pp. 139–40.

85. Two contrasting views are given in R. W. Southern, *The Making of the Middle Ages* (New Haven, CT, and London, 1953), pp. 56–62, and Steven Runciman, *A History of the Crusades,* 3 vols. (Cambridge, UK, 1954), 2:474–77.

86. Hillenbrand, *Crusades,* pp. 249–50.

87. David Abulafia, *Frederick II: A Medieval Emperor* (New York and Oxford, 1992), pp. 197–98.

88. John Esposito, *Unholy War: Terror in the Name of Islam* (Oxford, 2002), pp. 43–46; David Cook, *Understanding Jihad* (Berkeley, Los Angeles, and London, 2005), pp. 63–66; Bonner, *Jihad in Islamic History,* pp. 143–44; Marshall G. S. Hodgson, *The Venture of Islam, Conscience and History in a World Civilization,* 3 vols. (Chicago and London, 1974), 2:468–71; Natana J. Delong-Bas, *Wahhabi Islam: From Revival and Reform to Global Jihad* (Cairo, 2005), pp. 247–55; Hillenbrand, *Crusades,* pp. 241–43.

89. Moore, *Formation of Persecuting Society,* pp. 26–43.

90. H. G. Richardson, *The English Jewry Under the Angevin Kings* (London, 1960), p. 8; John H. Mundy, *Liberty and Political Power in Toulouse* (New York, 1954), p. 325.

91. Moshe Gil, *A History of Palestine, 634–1099,* trans. Ethel Broido (Cambridge, UK, 1992), pp. 370–80; F. E. Peters, *The Distant Shrine: The Islamic Centuries in Jerusalem* (New York, 1993), pp. 73–74, 92–96. The Greeks called the Anastasis that enshrined Christ's Tomb the Church of the Resurrection; the Crusaders would rename it the Church of the Holy Sepulcher.

92. Cohn, *Pursuit of the Millennium,* pp. 76–78, 80, 86–87.

93. Ibid., pp. 87–88.

94. Moore, *Formation of Persecuting Society,* pp. 105–6.

95. Ibid., pp. 84–85; Richardson, *English Jewry,* pp. 50–63.

96. Peter Abelard, *Dialogus* 51, in *A Dialogue of a Philosopher with a Jew and a Christian,* trans. P. J. Payer (Toronto, 1979), p. 33.

97. M. Montgomery Watt, *The Influence of Islam on Medieval Europe* (Edinburgh, 1972), pp. 74–86.

98. Duby, "Introduction," in *Chivalrous Society,* pp. 9–11.

99. Jonathan and Louise Riley-Smith, *The Crusades: Idea and Reality, 1095–1274* (London, 1981), pp. 78–79.

100. Ibid., pp. 83, 85.

101. Zoé Oldenbourg, *Le Bûcher de Montségur* (Paris, 1959), pp. 115–16.

102. Ibid., p. 89.

103. G. D. Mansi, *Sacrorum Consiliorum nova et amplissima collectio* (Paris and Leipzig, 1903), 21:843, in Moore, *Formation of Persecuting Society,* p. 111.

104. Norman Cohn, *Warrant for Genocide* (London, 1967), p. 12.

105. Peter the Venerable, *Summary of the Whole Heresy of the Diabolic Sect of the Saracens,* in Norman Daniel, *Islam and the West: The Making of an Image* (Edinburgh, 1960), p. 124.

106. Benjamin Kedar, *Crusade and Mission: European Approaches to the Muslims* (Princeton, NJ, 1984), p. 101.

107. Moore, *Formation of Persecuting Society,* pp. 60–67.

108. Ibid., pp. 102, 110–11.

109. Carl Erdmann, *The Origin of the Idea of Crusade,* trans. Marshall W. Baldwin and Walter Goffart (Princeton, NJ, 1977), p. 19.

110. *King Arthur's Death: The Middle English Stanzaic Morte d'Arthur and the Alliterative Morte d'Arthur,* ed. and trans. Larry Benson (Kalamazoo, MI, 1994), line 247.

111. *The Song of Roland,* line 2196, all trans. Dorothy L. Sayers (Harmondsworth, UK, 1957).

112. Ibid., lines 2240, 2361.

113. Ibid., lines 1881–82.

114. Keen, *Chivalry,* pp. 60–63.

115. *The Quest of the Holy Grail,* trans. and ed. P. M. Matarasso (Harmondsworth, UK, 1969), pp. 119–20.

116. Franco Cardini, "The Warrior and Knight," in Jacques LeGoff, ed., *The Medieval World: The History of European Society,* trans. Lydia G. Cochrane (London, 1987), p. 95.

117. Raoul de Hodenc, *"Le roman des eles" and Anonymous, "ordene de chevalerie":* *Two Early Old French Didactic Poems,* ed. Keith Busby (Philadelphia, 1983), p. 175.

118. Richard W. Kaeuper, *Holy Warriors: The Religious Ideology of Chivalry* (Philadelphia, 2009), pp. 53–57.

119. *History of William Marshal,* trans. and ed. A. T. Holden, S. Gregory, and David Crouch, 2 vols. (London, 2002–6), lines 16,853–63.

120. Kaeuper, *Holy Warriors,* pp. 38–49.

121. Henry of Lancaster, "Book of Holy Remedies," in E. J. Arnould, ed., *Le Livre de Seyntz Medicines: The Unpublished Devotional Treatises of Henry of Lancaster* (Oxford, 1940), p. 4.

122. Kaeuper, *Holy Warriors,* p. 194.

123. Ibid., pp. 176–77.

124. Mastnak, *Crusading Peace,* pp. 233–39.

125. Malcolm Barber, *The New Knighthood: A History of the Order of the Temple* (Cambridge, UK, 1994), pp. 280–313; Norman Cohn, *Europe's Inner Demons; The Demonization of Christians in Medieval Christendom* (London, 1975), pp. 79–101.

126. Brian Tierney, *The Crisis of Church and State, 1050–1300* (Toronto, 1988), p. 172; J. H. Shennon, *The Origins of the Modern European State 1450–1725* (London, 1974); Quentin Skinner, *The Foundations of Modern Political Thought,* 2 vols. (Cambridge, UK, 1978), 1:xxiii; A. Fall, *Medieval and Renaissance Origins: Historiographical Debates and Demonstrations* (London, 1991), p. 120.

127. Mastnak, *Crusading Peace,* pp. 244–46.

128. J. N. Hillgarth, *Ramon Lull and Lullism in Fourteenth-Century France* (Oxford, 1971), pp. 107–11, 120.

129. Christopher J. Tyerman, *England and the Crusades, 1095–1588* (Chicago, 1988), pp. 324–43; William T. Cavanaugh, *Migrations of the Holy: God, State, and the Political Meanings of the Church* (Grand Rapids, MI, 2011).

130. John Barnie, *War in Medieval English Society: Social Values in the Hundred Years War, 1337–99* (Ithaca, NY, 1974), pp. 102–3.

131. Mastnak, *Crusading Peace,* pp. 248–51; Thomas J. Renna, "Kingship in the *Disputatio inter clericum et militem,*" *Speculum* 48 (1973).

132. Ernst K. Kantorowicz, "*Pro Patria Mori* in Medieval Political Thought," *American Historical Review* 56, no. 3 (1951): 244, 256.

9 · THE ARRIVAL OF "RELIGION"

1. Felipe Fernández-Armesto, *1492: The Year the Four Corners of the Earth Collided* (New York, 2009), pp. 9–11, 52.

2. Marshall G. S. Hodgson, *The Venture of Islam: Conscience and History in a World Civilization,* 3 vols. (Chicago and London, 1974), 3:14–15, 2:334–60.

3. John H. Kautsky, *The Politics of the Aristocratic Empires,* 2nd ed. (New Brunswick, NJ, and London, 1997), p. 146.

4. Perry Anderson, *Lineages of the Absolutist State* (London, 1974), p. 505.

5. Fernández-Armesto, *1492,* pp. 2–4.

6. Timothy H. Parsons, *The Rule of Empires: Those Who Built Them, Those Who Endured Them, and Why They Always Fail* (Oxford, 2010), p. 117; Peter Jay, *Road to Riches, or The Wealth of Man* (London, 2000), pp. 147.

7. Jay, *Road to Riches,* pp. 151, 152–53.

8. Henry Kamen, *Empire: How Spain Became a World Power, 1492–1763* (New York, 2003), p. 83.

9. Howard Zinn, *A People's History of the United States: From 1492 to the Present,* 2nd ed. (London and New York, 1996), p. 11.

10. Massimo Livi Bacci, *A Concise History of World Population* (Oxford, 1997), pp. 56–59.

11. Parsons, *Rule of Empires,* pp. 121, 117.

12. Jay, *Road to Riches,* p. 150.

13. Mark Levene, *Genocide in the Age of the Nation-State: The Rise of the West and the Coming of Genocide* (London and New York, 2005), pp. 15–29.

14. Cajetan, *On Aquinas' Secunda Scundae,* q. 66, art. 8, quoted in Richard Tuck, *The Rights of War and Peace: Political Thought and the International Order from Grotius to Kant* (Oxford, 1999), p. 70.

15. Francisco de Vitoria, *Political Writings,* ed. Anthony Pagden and Jeremy Lawrence (Cambridge, UK, 1991), pp. 225–26.

16. Thomas More, *Utopia,* ed. George M. Logan and Robert M. Adams (Cambridge, UK, 1989), pp. 89–90, 58.

17. Tuck, *Rights of War and Peace,* p. 15. Max Weber made the same point in 1906; cf. *From Max Weber,* trans. and ed. H. H. Gerth and C. Wright Mills (London, 1948), pp. 71–72.

18. The Tacitus passage is quoted in Grotius's *The Rights of War and Peace, in Three Books* (London, 1738), 2:2:17, and in Tuck, *Rights of War and Peace,* pp. 47–48.

19. Aristotle, *Politics* 1256.b.22, in *The Basic Works of Aristotle,* ed. Richard McKeon (New York, 1941).

20. Henry Kamen, *The Spanish Inquisition: An Historical Revision* (London, 1997), pp. 45, 68, 137.

21. Paul Johnson, *A History of the Jews* (London, 1987), pp. 225–29.

22. Haim Beinart, *Conversos on Trial: The Inquisition in Ciudad Real* (Jerusalem, 1981), pp. 3–6.

23. Norman Roth, *Conversos, Inquisition, and the Expulsion of Jews from Spain* (Madison, WI, 1995), pp. 283–84, 19.

24. Fernández-Armesto, *1492*, pp. 94–96.

25. Johnson, *History of Jews*, p. 229; Yirmiyahu Yovel, *Spinoza and Other Heretics*, vol. 1: *The Marrano of Reason* (Princeton, NJ, 1989), pp. 17–18.

26. Johnson, *History of Jews*, pp. 225–29.

27. Kamen, *Spanish Inquisition*, pp. 57–59; E. William Monter, *Frontiers of Heresy: The Spanish Inquisition from the Basque Lands to Sicily* (Cambridge, UK, 1990), p. 53.

28. Kamen, *Spanish Inquisition*, p. 69.

29. Robin Briggs, "Embattled Faiths: Religion and Natural Philosophy," in Euan Cameron, ed., *Early Modern Europe: An Oxford History* (Oxford, 1999), pp. 197–205.

30. Jay, *Road to Riches*, pp. 160–63.

31. Henri Pirenne, *Medieval Cities: Their Origins and the Revival of Trade* (Princeton, NJ, 1946), pp. 168–212; Bert F. Hoselitz, *Sociological Aspects of Economic Growth* (New York, 1960), pp. 163–72.

32. Norman Cohn, *Pursuit of the Millennium: Revolutionary Millenarians and Mystical Anarchists of the Middle Ages* (London, 1984 ed.), pp. 107–16.

33. Euan Cameron, "The Power of the Word: Renaissance and Reformation," in Cameron, *Early Modern Europe*, pp. 87–90.

34. Richard Marius, *Martin Luther: The Christian Between God and Death* (Cambridge, MA, and London, 1999), pp. 73–74, 214–15, 486–87.

35. Joshua Mitchell, *Not by Reason Alone: History and Identity in Early Modern Political Thought* (Chicago, 1993), pp. 23–30.

36. Martin Luther, "Temporal Authority: To What Extent It Should Be Obeyed," trans. J. J. Schindel, rev. Walther I. Brandt, in J. M. Porter, ed., *Luther: Selected Political Writings* (hereafter *SPW*) (Eugene, OR, 2003), pp. 54, 55, 56.

37. Martin Luther, "Whether Soldiers, Too, Can Be Saved," trans. Charles M. Jacobs, rev. Robert C. Schultz, in *SPW*, p. 108.

38. J. W. Allen, *A History of Political Thought in the Sixteenth Century* (London, 1928), p. 16; Sheldon S. Wolin, *Politics and Vision: Continuity and Innovation in Western Political Thought* (Boston, 1960), p. 164.

39. Cohn, *Pursuit of Millennium*, pp. 245–50.

40. Martin Luther, "Admonition to Peace: A Reply to the Twelve Articles of the Peasants in Swabia" (1525), trans. J. J. Schindel, rev. Walther I. Brandt, in *SPW*, pp. 72, 78, 82.

41. Martin Luther, "Against the Robbing and Murdering Hordes of Peasants" (1525), trans. Charles M. Jacobs, rev. Robert C. Schultz, in *SPW*, p. 86.

42. Steven Ozment, *The Reformation of the Cities: The Appeal of Protestantism to Sixteenth-Century Germany and Switzerland* (New Haven, CT, 1975), pp. 10–11, 123–25, 148–50.

43. Charles A. McDaniel Jr., "Violent Yearnings for the Kingdom of God: Münster's Militant Anabaptism," in James K. Wellman, ed. *Belief and Bloodshed: Religion and Violence Across Time and Tradition* (Lanham, MD, 2007), p. 74. The social danger persisted, even though in the last days of Anabaptist Münster, its leader Jan of Leyden set himself up as king and introduced a pseudo-imperial court and a reign of terror.

44. Cohn, *Pursuit of Millennium*, pp. 255–79.

45. I have discussed this at length in *The Case for God* (London and New York, 2009). See also Wilfred Cantwell Smith, *The Meaning and End of Religion: A New Approach to the Religious Traditions of Mankind* (New York, 1962); Smith, *Belief in History* (Charlottesville, VA, 1985); Smith, *Faith and Belief* (Princeton, NJ, 1987).

46. William T. Cavanaugh, *The Myth of Religious Violence* (Oxford, 2009), pp. 72–74.

47. Thomas More, *A Dialogue Concerning Heresies*, ed. Thomas M. C. Lawlor (New Haven, CT, 1981), p. 416.

48. François André Isambert, ed., *Recueil général des anciennes lois françaises depuis l'an 420 jusqu'à la Révolution de 1789* (Paris, 1821–33), 12:819.

49. Brad S. Gregory, *Salvation at Stake: Christian Martyrdom in Early Modern Europe* (Cambridge, MA, and London, 1999), p. 201.

50. Raymond A. Mentzer, *Heresy Proceedings in Languedoc, 1500–1560* (Philadelphia, 1984), p. 172.

51. Philip Spierenberg, *The Spectacle of Suffering: Executions and the Evolution of Repression: From a Pre-Industrial Metropolis to the European Experience* (Cambridge, UK, 1984); Lionello Puppi, *Torment in Art: Pain, Violence, and Martyrdom* (New York, 1991), pp. 11–69.

52. Gregory, *Salvation at Stake,* pp. 77–79.

53. David Nicholls, "The Theatre of Martyrdom in the French Reformation," *Past and Present* no. 121 (1998); Susan Brigdon, *London and the Reformation* (Oxford, 1989), p. 607; Mentzer, *Heresy Proceedings,* p. 71.

54. Gregory, *Salvation at Stake,* pp. 80–81.

55. Deuteronomy 13:1–3, 5, 6–11, quoted by Johannes Eck, *Handbook of Commonplaces* (1525), and by Calvin to justify his execution of Michael Servetus, who denied the doctrine of the Trinity.

56. Gregory, *Salvation at Stake,* pp. 84–87, 111, 154, 261–69.

57. William Allen, *Apologie of the English College* (Douai, 1581); Gregory, *Salvation at Stake,* p. 283.

58. Gregory, *Salvation at Stake,* pp. 285–86.

59. Kamen, *Spanish Inquisition,* pp. 204–13, 203, 98.

60. Ibid., pp. 223–45.

61. Cavanaugh, *Myth of Religious Violence,* p. 122.

62. J. V. Poliskensky, *War and Society in Europe, 1618–1848* (Cambridge, UK, 1978), pp. 77, 154, 217.

63. Cavanaugh, *Myth of Religious Violence,* pp. 142–55.

64. Richard S. Dunn, *The Age of Religious Wars, 1559–1689* (New York, 1970), p. 6; James D. Tracy, *Charles V, Impresario of War: Campaign Strategy, International Finance, and Domestic Politics* (Cambridge, UK, 2002), pp. 45–47, 306.

65. Wim Blockmans, *Emperor Charles V, 1500–1558* (London and New York, 2002), pp. 95, 110; William Maltby, *The Reign of Charles V* (New York, 2002), pp. 112–13.

66. Tracy, *Charles V,* p. 307; Blockmans, *Charles V,* p. 47.

67. Klaus Jaitner, "The Pope and the Struggle for Power during the Sixteenth and Seventeenth Centuries," in Klaus Bussman and Heinz Schilling, eds., *War and Peace in Europe,* 3 vols. (Münster, 1998), 1:62.

68. Maltby, *Reign of Charles V,* p. 62; Tracy, *Charles V,* pp. 209–15.

69. Tracy, *Charles V,* pp. 32–34, 46.

70. Maltby, *Reign of Charles V,* pp. 62–62.

71. Cavanaugh, *Myth of Religious Violence,* p. 164.

72. Dunn, *Age of Religious Wars,* pp. 49, 50–51.

73. Steven Gunn, "War, Religion, and the State," in Cameron, *Early Modern Europe,* p. 244.

74. Cavanaugh, *Myth of Religious Violence,* pp. 145–47, 153–58.

75. James Westfall Thompson, *The Wars of Religion in France, 1559–1576: The Huguenots, Catherine de Medici, Philip II,* 2nd ed. (New York, 1957); Lucien Romier, "A Dissident Nobility Under the Cloak of Religion," in J. H. M. Salmon, ed., *The French Wars of Religion: How Important Were Religious Factors?* (Lexington, MA, 1967); Henri Hauser, "Political Anarchy and Social Discontent," cited in Salmon, *French Wars.*

76. Natalie Zemon Davis, "The Rites of Violence: Religious Riot in Sixteenth-Century France," *Past and Present* 59 (1973).

77. Mack P. Holt, "Putting Religion Back into the Wars of Religion," *French Historical Studies* 18, no. 2 (Autumn 1993); John Bossy, "Unrethinking the Sixteenth-Century Wars of Religion," in Thomas Kselman, ed., *Belief in History: Innovative Approaches in European and American Religion* (Notre Dame, IN, 1991); Denis Crouzet, *Les guerriers de Dieu: La violence au temps des troubles de religion* (Seyssel, 1990); Barbara Diefendorf, *Beneath the Cross: Catholics and Huguenots in Sixteenth-Century Paris* (New York, 1991). Some scholars have argued that Davis was herself incorrect to describe the conflict as "essentially" religious, because religion still permeated all human activities; see Cavanaugh, *Myth of Religious Violence,* pp. 159–60.

78. Mack P. Holt, *The French Wars of Religion, 1562–1629* (Cambridge, UK, 1995), pp. 17–18.

79. Bossy, "Unrethinking the Sixteenth-Century Wars of Religion," pp. 278–80.

80. Virginia Reinberg, "Liturgy and Laity in Late Medieval and Reformation France," *Sixteenth Century Journal* 23 (Autumn 1992).

81. Holt, *French Wars of Religion,* pp. 18–21.

82. Ibid., pp. 50–51.

83. J. H. M. Salmon, *Society in Crisis: France in the Sixteenth Century* (New York, 1975), p. 198; Henry Heller, *Iron and Blood: Civil Wars in Sixteenth-Century France* (Montreal, 1991), p. 63.

84. Holt, *French Wars of Religion,* p. 99; Salmon, *Society in Crisis,* pp. 176, 197.

85. Salmon, *Society in Crisis,* pp. 204–5.

86. Holt, *French Wars of Religion.* pp. 50–51.

87. Heller, *Iron and Blood,* pp. 209–11, 126.

88. Holt, *French Wars of Religion,* pp. 156–57; Salmon, *Society in Crisis,* pp. 282–91.

89. Holt, *French Wars of Religion,* pp. 3–4, 126, 168–69; Cavanaugh, *Myth of Religious Violence,* pp. 173–74.

90. Cavanaugh, *Myth of Religious Violence,* pp. 147–50.

91. Geoffrey Parker, *The Thirty Years' War* (London, 1984), pp. 29–33, 59–64.

92. Ibid., p. 195.

93. Dunn, *Age of Religious Wars,* pp. 71–72.

94. William H. McNeill, *Pursuit of Power: Technology, Armed Force, and Society Since AD 1000* (Chicago, 1982), pp. 120–23; Robert L. O'Connell, *Of Arms and Men: A History of War, Weapons, and Aggression* (New York and Oxford, 1999), pp. 143–44.

95. Ibid., pp. 121–23.

96. Parker, *Thirty Years' War,* pp. 127–28.

97. Jeremy Black, "Warfare, Crisis and Absolutism," in Cameron, *Early Modern Europe,* p. 211.

98. Parker, *Thirty Years' War,* pp. 142, 216–17.

99. Cavanaugh, *Myth of Religious Violence,* p. 159; John Bossy, *Christianity in the West, 1400–1700* (Oxford, 1985), pp. 170–71.

100. Andrew R. Murphy, "Cromwell, Mather and the Rhetoric of Puritan Violence," in Andrew R. Murphy, ed., *The Blackwell Companion to Religion and Violence* (Chichester, UK, 2011), pp. 528–34.

101. Thomas Carlyle, ed., *Oliver Cromwell's Letters and Speeches,* 3 vols. (New York, 1871), 1:154, 2:153–54.

102. Cavanaugh, *Myth of Religious Violence,* p. 172.

103. Ann Hughes, *The Causes of the English Civil War* (London, 1998), pp. 25, 10–25, 58–59, 90–97, 89, 85.

104. Cavanaugh, *Myth of Religious Violence,* pp. 160–72.

105. Parker, *Thirty Years' War,* p. 172.

106. Jan N. Brenner, "Secularization: Notes Toward the Genealogy," in Henk de Vries, ed., *Religion: Beyond a Concept* (New York, 2008), p. 433.

107. Heinz Schilling, "War and Peace at the Emergence of Modernity: Europe Between

State Belligerence, Religious Wars, and the Desire for Peace in 1648," in Bussman and Schilling, *War and Peace in Europe*, p. 14.

108. Thomas Ertman, *Birth of the Leviathan: Building States and Regimes in Early Modern Europe* (Cambridge, UK, 1997), p. 4.

109. Salmon, *Society in Crisis*, p. 13.

110. Cavanaugh, *Myth of Religious Violence,* pp. 72–85; Russell T. McCutcheon, "The Category 'Religion' and the Politics of Tolerance," in Arthur L. Greil and David G. Bromley, eds., *Defining Religion: Investigating the Boundaries Between the Sacred and the Secular* (Oxford, 2003), pp. 146–52; Derek Peterson and Darren Walhof, "Rethinking Religion," in Peterson and Walhof, *The Invention of Religion*, pp. 3–9; David E. Gunn, "Religion, Law and Violence," in Murphy, *Blackwell Companion,* pp. 105–7.

111. Edward, Lord Herbert, *De Veritate*, trans. Meyrick H. Carre (Bristol, UK, 1937), pp. 303, 298.

112. Edward, Lord Herbert, *De Religio Laici,* trans. and ed. Harold L. Hutcheson (New Haven, CT, 1944), p. 127.

113. Thomas Hobbes, *Behemoth; or, The Long Parliament,* ed. Frederick Tönnies (Chicago, 1990), pp. 55, 95.

114. Thomas Hobbes, *On the Citizen,* ed. Richard Tuck and Michael Silverthorne (Cambridge, UK, 1998), 3.26; Thomas Hobbes, *Leviathan,* ed. Richard Tuck (Cambridge, UK, 1991), p. 223.

115. Hobbes, *Leviathan*, pp. 315, 431–34.

116. John Locke, *A Letter Concerning Toleration* (Indianapolis, 1955), pp. 31, 27.

117. Ibid., p. 17.

118. Ibid., p. 15.

119. John Locke, "Second Treatise," 5:24, 5:120–21, 5:3, in *Two Treatises of Government,* ed. Peter Laslett (Cambridge, UK, 1988).

120. Hugo Grotius, *Rights of War and Peace, in Three Books* 2:2:17; 2:20:40 (London, 1738), cited in Tuck, *Rights of War and Peace,* pp. 103–4.

121. Hobbes, *On the Citizen,* p. 30.

122. John Donne, *Sermons of John Donne,* ed. George R. Potter and Evelyn M. Simpson (Berkeley, 1959), 4:274.

10 · THE TRIUMPH OF THE SECULAR

1. Thomas Morton, "New English Canaan" (1634–35), and John Cotton, "God's Promise to His Plantations" (1630), in Alan Heimert and Andrew Delbanco, eds., *The Puritans in America: A Narrative Anthology* (Cambridge, MA, 1985), pp. 49–50.

2. Kevin Phillips, *The Cousins' Wars: Religious Politics and the Triumph of Anglo-America* (New York, 1999), pp. 3–32; Carla Garden Pesteria, *Protestant Empire: Religion and the Making of the British Atlantic World* (Philadelphia, 2004), pp. 503–15; Clement Fatoric, "The Anti-Catholic Roots of Liberal and Republican Conception of Freedom in English Political Thought," *Journal of the History of Ideas* 66 (January 2005).

3. John Winthrop, "A Model of Christian Charity," in Heimert and Delbanco, *Puritans in America,* p. 91.

4. John Winthrop, "Reasons to Be Considered for . . . the Intended Plantation in New England" (1629), ibid., p. 71.

5. Winthrop, "Model of Christian Charity," p. 82.

6. Cotton, "God's Promise to His Plantations," p. 77.

7. Robert Cushman, "Reasons and Considerations Touching the Lawfulness of Removing out of England into the Parts of America," in Heimert and Delbanco, *Puritans in America,* pp. 43–44.

8. Perry Miller, "The Puritan State and Puritan Society," in *Errand into the Wilderness* (Cambridge, MA, and London, 1956), pp. 148–49.

9. John Smith, "A True Relation," in Edwin Arber and A. C. Bradley, eds., *John Smith: Works* (Edinburgh, 1910), p. 957.

10. Perry Miller, "Religion and Society in the Early Literature of Virginia," in *Errand*, pp. 104–5.

11. William Crashaw, *A Sermon Preached in London Before the Right Honourable Lord Werre, Lord Gouernour and Captaine Generall of Virginea* (London, 1610), in Miller, *Errand*, pp. 111, 138, 101.

12. David S. Lovejoy, *Religious Enthusiasm in the New World: Heresy to Revolution* (Cambridge, MA, and London, 1985), pp. 11–13; Louis B. Wright, *Religion and Empire: The Alliance Between Piety and Commerce in English Expansion, 1558–1625* (Chapel Hill, NC, 1943); Miller, "Religion and Society," pp. 105–8.

13. Purchas, *Hakluytus Posthumous, or Purchas His Pilgrim*, 3 vols. (Glasgow, 1905–6), 1:1–45.

14. "A True Declaration of the Estate of the Colonie in Virginia" (1610), in Peter Force, ed., *Tracts* (New York, 1844), 3:5–6.

15. Miller, "Religion and Society," pp. 116–17.

16. Howard Zinn, *A People's History of the United States: From 1492 to the Present*, 2nd ed. (London and New York, 1996), pp. 12, 13.

17. Andrew Preston, *Sword of the Spirit, Shield of Faith: Religion in American War and Diplomacy* (New York and Toronto, 2012), pp. 15–17.

18. Purchas, *Hakluytus Posthumous* 1:41–45, 138–39.

19. Preston, *Sword of the Spirit*, pp. 31–38.

20. Bradford, *History of the Plymouth Plantation*, in Zinn, *People's History*, p. 15.

21. Ronald Dale Kerr, "Why Should You Be So Furious? The Violence of the Pequot War," *Journal of American History* 85 (December 1998).

22. Preston, *Sword of the Spirit*, pp. 41–45; Andrew R. Murphy, "Cromwell, Mather and the Rhetoric of Puritan Violence," in Murphy, ed., *The Blackwell Companion to Religion and Violence* (Chichester, UK, 2011), pp. 525–35.

23. Miller, "Puritan State," pp. 150–51.

24. Sherwood Eliot Wirt, ed., *Spiritual Awakening: Classic Writings of the Eighteenth-Century Devotios to Inspire and Help the Twentieth-Century Reader* (Tring, UK, 1988), p. 110.

25. Alan Heimert, *Religion and the American Mind: From the Great Awakening to Revolution* (Cambridge, MA, 1968), p. 43.

26. Miller, "Puritan State," p. 150.

27. Solomon Stoddard, "An Examination of the Power of the Fraternity" (1715), in Heimert and Delbanco, *Puritans in America*, p. 388.

28. Perry Miller, "Jonathan Edwards and the Great Awakening," in *Errand*, pp. 162–66.

29. Ibid., p. 165.

30. Ruth H. Bloch, *Visionary Republic: Millennial Themes in American Thought, 1756–1800* (Cambridge, UK, 1985), pp. 14–15.

31. The original draft of the Declaration listed the self-evident rights as "life, liberty and property"; only later was that amended to "the pursuit of happiness."

32. Jon Butler, *Awash in a Sea of Faith: Christianizing the American People* (Cambridge, MA, 1990), p. 198.

33. Bloch, *Visionary Republic*, pp. 81–88.

34. Timothy Dwight, *A Valedictory Address to the Young Gentlemen Who Commenced Bachelors of Arts, July 27, 1776* (New Haven, CT, 1776), p. 14.

35. Lovejoy, *Religious Enthusiasm in New World*, p. 226.

36. Thomas Paine, *Common Sense and the Crisis* (New York, 1975), p. 59.

37. Bloch, *Visionary Republic*, pp. 55, 60–63, 29, 31.

38. Edwin S. Gaustad, *Faith of Our Fathers: Religion and the New Nation* (San Francisco, 1987), p. 38.

39. James Madison to William Bradford, April 1, 1774, in William T. Hutchinson and William M. E. Rachal, eds., *The Papers of James Madison,* 17 vols. (Chicago, 1962–91), 1:212–13.

40. James Madison, "Memorial and Remonstrance" (1785), in Gaustad, *Faith of Our Fathers,* p. 145.

41. Jefferson, *Statute for Establishing Religious Freedom* (1786), in Gaustad, *Faith of Our Fathers,* p. 150.

42. Henry S. Stout, "Rhetoric and Reality in the Early Republic: The Case of the Federalist Clergy," in Mark A. Noll, ed., *Religion and American Politics: From the Colonial Period to the 1980s* (Oxford and New York, 1990), pp. 65–66, 75.

43. Nathan O. Hatch, *The Democratization of American Christianity* (New Haven, CT, and London, 1989), pp. 22, 25–129.

44. John F. Wilson, "Religion, Government and Power in the New American Nation," in Noll, *Religion and American Politics.*

45. Gaustad, *Faith of Our Fathers,* p. 44.

46. Perry Miller, *Roger Williams: His Contribution to the American Tradition,* 2nd ed. (New York, 1962), p. 192.

47. Miller, "Puritan State," p. 146.

48. Thomas Jefferson to William Baldwin, January 19, 1810, in Dickenson W. Adams, ed., *Jefferson's Extracts from the Gospels* (Princeton, NJ, 1983), p. 345; Jefferson to Charles Clay, January 29, 1816, ibid., p. 364.

49. Hatch, *Democratization of American Christianity,* pp. 68–157.

50. Daniel Walker Howe, "Religion and Politics in the Antebellum North," in Noll, *Religion and American Politics,* pp. 132–33; George M. Marsden, "Religion, Politics, and the Search for an American Consensus," ibid., pp. 382–83.

51. Mark A. Noll, "The Rise and Long Life of the Protestant Enlightenment in America," in William M. Shea and Peter A. Huff, eds., *Knowledge and Belief in America: Enlightenment Traditions and Modern Religious Thought* (New York, 1995); cf. D. W. Bebbington, *Evangelicalism in Modern Britain: A History from the 1730s to the 1980s* (London, 1989), p. 74; Michael Gauvreau, *The Evangelical Century: College and Creed in English Canada from the Great Revival to the Great Depression* (Kingston, ON, and Montreal, 1991), pp. 13–56.

52. Alexis de Tocqueville, *Democracy in America,* ed. and trans. Harvey Claflin Mansfield and Delba Winthrop (Chicago, 2000), p. 43; Tocqueville's emphasis.

53. Henry F. May, *The Enlightenment in America* (New York, 1976); Mark A. Noll, *America's God: From Jonathan Edwards to Abraham Lincoln* (Oxford and New York, 2002), pp. 93–95.

54. Mark A. Noll, *The Civil War as a Theological Crisis* (Chapel Hill, NC, 2006), pp. 24–25.

55. John M. Murrin, "A Roof Without Walls: The Dilemma of American National Identity" in Richard Beeman, Stephen Botein, and Edward E. Carter II, eds., *Beyond Confederation: Origins of the Constitution and American Identity* (Chapel Hill, NC, 1987), pp. 344–47.

56. Noll, *Civil War,* pp. 25–28.

57. Claude E. Welch, Jr., *Political Modernization* (Belmont, CA, 1971), pp. 2–6.

58. John H. Kautsky, *The Political Consequences of Modernization* (New York, London, Sydney, and Toronto, 1972), pp. 45–47.

59. T. C. W. Blanning, "Epilogue: The Old Order Transformed," in Euan Cameron, *Early Modern Europe: An Oxford History* (Oxford, 1999), pp. 345–60; Michael Burleigh, *Earthly Powers: The Clash of Religion and Politics from the French Revolution to the Great War* (New York, 1995), pp. 48–66.

60. M. G. Hutt, "The Role of the Cures in the Estates General of 1789," *Journal of Ecclesiastical History* 6 (1955).

61. George Lefebvre, *The Great Fear of 1789,* trans. R. R. Farmer and Joan White (Princeton, NJ, 1973).

62. Philip G. Dwyer, *Talleyrand* (London, 2002), p. 24.

63. Ibid., pp. 61–62.

64. Mark A. Noll, *The Old Religion in a New World: The History of North American Christianity* (Grand Rapids, MI, 2002), pp. 82–83; Gertrude Himmelfarb, *The Roads to Modernity* (New York, 2004), pp. 18–19.

65. Burleigh, *Earthly Powers,* pp. 96–101; Claude Petitfrère, "The Origins of the Civil War in the Vendée," *French History* 2 (1988): 99–100.

66. Instructions from the Committee of Public Safety (1794), cited in Burleigh, *Earthly Powers,* p. 100.

67. Reynald Secher, *Le génocide franco-français: La Vendée-vengée* (Paris, 1986), pp. 158–59.

68. Jonathan North, "General Hocte and Counterinsurgency," *Journal of Military History* 67 (2003).

69. Mircea Eliade, *Patterns in Comparative Religion,* trans. Rosemary Sheed (London, 1958), p. 11.

70. Burleigh, *Earthly Powers,* pp. 79–80, 76.

71. Jules Michelet, *Historical View of the French Revolution from Its Earliest Indications to the Flight of the King in 1791,* trans. C. Cooks (London, 1888), p. 393.

72. Burleigh, *Earthly Powers,* p. 81.

73. Boyd C. Schafer, *Nationalism, Myth and Reality* (New York, 1952), p. 142.

74. Alexis de Tocqueville, *The Old Regime and the French Revolution,* ed. François Furet and Françoise Melonio (Chicago, 1998), 1:101.

75. Jean-Jacques Rousseau, *Politics and the Arts, Letter to M. D'Alembert on the Theatre,* trans. Allan Bloom (Ithaca, NY, 1960), p. 126.

76. Jean-Jacques Rousseau, *The Social Contract and Other Later Political Writings,* ed. Victor Gourevitch (Cambridge, UK, 1997), pp. 150–51.

77. Donald Greer, *The Incidence of Terror in the French Revolution* (Gloucester, MA, 1935).

78. John Keegan, *A History of Warfare* (London and New York, 1993), pp. 348–59; Robert L. O'Connell, *Of Arms and Men: A History of Weapons and Aggression* (New York and Oxford, 1989), pp. 174–88; William H. McNeill, *The Pursuit of Power: Technology, Armed Force, and Society Since AD 1000* (Chicago, 1984), pp. 185–215.

79. Russell Weigley, *The Age of Battles: The Quest for Decisive Warfare from Breitenfeld to Waterloo* (Bloomington, IN, 1991), O'Connell, *Of Arms and Men,* pp. 148–50.

80. John U. Neff, *War and Human Progress: An Essay on the Rise of Industrial Civilization* (New York, 1950), pp. 204–5; Theodore Ropp, *War in the Modern World* (Durham, NC, 1959), pp. 25–26.

81. Keegan, *History of Warfare,* p. 344; O'Connell, *Arms and Men,* pp. 157–66; McNeill, *Pursuit of Power,* p. 172.

82. Quoted in McNeill, *Pursuit of Power,* p. 192.

83. Keegan, *History of Warfare,* pp. 350, 351–52.

84. O'Connell, *Arms and Men,* p. 185.

85. George Annesley, *The Rise of Modern Egypt: A Century and a Half of Egyptian History* (Durham, UK, 1997), p. 7.

86. *Nicholas Turc: Chronique d'Égypte, 1798–1804,* ed. and trans. Gaston Wait (Cairo, 1950), p. 78.

87. Peter Jay, *Road to Riches, or The Wealth of Man* (London, 2000), pp. 205–36; Gerhard E. Lenski, *Power and Privilege: A Theory of Social Stratification* (Chapel Hill, NC, and London, 1966), pp. 297–392; Marshall G. S. Hodgson, *The Venture of Islam,*

Conscience and History in a World Civilization, 3 vols. (Chicago and London, 1974), 3:195–201.

88. Hodgson, *Venture of Islam,* 3:194.

89. John H. Kautsky, *The Politics of Aristocratic Empires,* 2nd ed. (New Brunswick, NJ, and London, 1997), p. 349. Even fascist governments were coalitions.

90. Hodgson, *Venture of Islam,* 3:199–201; G. W. F. Hegel, *Elements of the Philosophy of Right,* ed. Allen W. Wood, trans. H. B. Nisbet (Cambridge, UK, 1991), paragraphs 246, 248.

91. John H. Kautsky, *The Political Consequences of Modernization* (New York, London, Sydney, and Toronto, 1972), pp. 60–61.

92. Hodgson, *Venture of Islam,* 3:208; Bassam Tibi, *The Crisis of Political Islam: A Pre-Industrial Culture in the Scientific-Technological Age* (Salt Lake City, UT, 1988), pp. 1–25.

93. Hodgson, *Venture of Islam,* 3:210–12.

94. O'Connell, *Of Arms and Men,* p. 235; Percival Spear, *India* (Ann Arbor, MI, 1961), p. 270.

95. Daniel Gold, "Organized Hinduisms: From Vedic Truth to Hindu Nation," in Martin E. Marty and R. Scott Appleby, eds., *Fundamentalisms Observed* (Chicago and London, 1991), pp. 534–37.

96. Wilfred Cantwell Smith, *The Meaning and End of Religion: A New Approach to the Religious Traditions of Mankind* (New York, 1964), pp. 61–62.

97. Patwant Singh, *The Sikhs* (New York, 1999).

98. Guru Garth Sahib, 1136, cited ibid., p. 18.

99. John Clark Archer, *The Sikhs in Relation to Hindus, Christians, and Ahmadiyas* (Princeton, NJ, 1946), p. 170.

100. T. N. Madan, "Fundamentalism and the Sikh Religious Tradition," in Marty and Appleby, *Fundamentalisms,* p. 602.

101. Kenneth W. Jones, "The Arya Samaj in British India, 1875–1947," in Robert D. Baird, ed., *Religion in Modern India* (Delhi, 1981), pp. 50–52.

102. Madan, "Fundamentalism and the Sikh Religious Tradition," p. 605.

103. Ibid., pp. 603–6.

104. Harjot S. Oberoi, "From Ritual to Counter Ritual: Rethinking the Hindu-Sikh Question, 1884–1015," in Joseph T. O'Connell, ed., *Sikh History and Religion in the Twentieth Century* (Toronto, 1988), pp. 136–40.

105. N. Gould Barrier, "Sikhs and Punjab Politics," ibid.

106. Madan, "Fundamentalism and the Sikh Religious Tradition," p. 617.

107. Mumtaz Ahmad, "Islamic Fundamentalism in South Asia: The Jama'at-i-Islami and the Tablighi Jamaat," in Marty and Appleby, *Fundamentalisms,* p. 460.

108. O'Connell, *Arms and Men,* pp. 231–35, 191, 233.

109. G. W. Stevans, *With Kitchener to Khartoum* (London, 1898), p. 300.

110. Sir John Ardagh, speech, June 22, 1899, in *The Proceedings of the Hague Peace Conference* (London, 1920), pp. 286–87.

111. Elbridge Colby, "How to Fight Savage Tribes," *American Journal of International Law* 21, no. 2 (1927); author's emphasis.

112. Ernest Gellner, *Nations and Nationalism: New Perspectives on the Past* (Oxford, 1983), passim.

113. Anthony Giddens, *The Nation-State and Violence* (Berkeley, CA, 1987), p. 89.

114. Ibid., pp. 85–89; William T. Cavanaugh, *Migrations of the Holy: God, State, and the Political Meaning of the Church* (Grand Rapids, MI, 2011), pp. 18–19.

115. Benedict Anderson, *Imagined Communities: Reflections on the Origin and Spread of Nationalism* (London and New York, 2003).

116. Mark Levene, *Genocide in the Age of the Nation-State,* vol. 3: *The Rise of the West and the Coming of Genocide* (London and New York, 2005), pp. 26–27, 112–20;

David Stannard, *American Holocaust: The Conquest of the New World* (New York and Oxford, 1992), p. 120; Ward Churchill, *A Little Matter of Genocide, Holocaust, and Denial in the Americas, 1492 to the Present* (San Francisco, 1997), p. 150; Anthony F. C. Wallace, *Jefferson and the Indians: The Tragic Fate of the First Americans* (Cambridge, MA, 1999).

117. Norman Cantor, *The Sacred Chain: A History of the Jews* (London, 1995), pp. 236–37.

118. John Stuart Mill, *Utilitarianism, Liberty, and Representational Government* (London, 1910), pp. 363–64.

119. Quoted in Antony Smith, *Myths and Memories of the Nation* (Oxford, 1999), p. 33.

120. Cited in Levene, *Genocide*, pp. 150–51. Cf. C. A. Macartney, *National States and National Minorities* (London, 1934), p. 17.

121. Bruce Lincoln, *Holy Terrors: Thinking About Religion After September 11*, 2nd ed. (Chicago and London, 2006), pp. 62–63.

122. Johann Gottlieb Fichte, "What a People Is, and What Is Love of Fatherland," in Fichte, *Addresses to the German Nation*, ed. and trans. Gregory Moore (Cambridge, UK, 2008), p. 105.

123. Zinn, *People's History*, pp. 23–58; Basil Davidson, *The African Slave Trade* (Boston, 1961); Stanley Elkins, *Slavery: A Problem of American Institutional and Intellectual Life* (Chicago, 1796); Edmund S. Morgan, *American Slavery, American Freedom: The Ordeal of Colonial Virginia* (New York, 1975).

124. Leviticus 25:45–46; Genesis 9:25–27, 17:12; Deuteronomy 20:10–11; I Corinthians 7:21; Romans 13:1,7; Colossians 3:22, 4:1; I Timothy 6:1–2; Philemon.

125. Rev. J. H. Thornwell, "Our National Sins," in *Fast Day Sermons or The Pulpit on the State of the Country*, ed. anonymous (1890; reprint Charleston, SC, 2009 ed.), p. 48.

126. Rev. Henry Ward Beecher, "Peace, Be Still," ibid., p. 276.

127. Rev. Henry J. Van Dyke, "The Character and Influence of Abolitionism," ibid., p. 137.

128. Tayler Lewis, "Patriarchal and Jewish Servitude: No Argument for American Slavery" ibid., p. 180.

129. Noll, *Civil War*, pp. 1–8.

130. Ibid., pp. 19–22; Mark A. Noll, "The Rise and Long Life of the Protestant Enlightenment in America," in William M. Shea and Peter A. Huff, eds., *Knowledge and Belief in America: Enlightenment Trends and Modern Thought* (New York, 1995), pp. 84–124; Henry F. May, *The Enlightenment in America* (New York, 1976), passim.

131. James M. McPherson, *For Cause and Comrades: Why Men Fought in the Civil War* (New York, 1997), p. 63; McPherson, "Afterword," in Randall M. Miller, Harry S. Stout, and Charles Reagan Wilson, eds., *Religion and the American Civil War* (New York, 1998), p. 412.

132. McPherson, *For Cause and Comrades*, pp. 52–79.

133. Henry Ward Beecher, "Abraham Lincoln," in Beecher, *Patriotic Addresses in America and England, from 1850 to 1885 . . .* (New York, 1887), p. 711.

134. Horace Bushnell, "Our Obligations to the Dead," in Bushnell, *Building Eras in Religion* (New York, 1881), pp. 328–29.

135. O'Connell, *Arms and Men*, pp. 189–96.

136. Grady McWhiney and Perry D. Jamieson, *Attack and Die: The Civil War, Military Tactics, and Southern Heritage* (Montgomery, AL, 1982), pp. 4–7.

137. Bruce Cotton, *Grant Takes Command* (Boston, 1968), p. 262.

138. O'Connell, *Arms and Men*, pp. 198–99.

139. Noll, *Civil War*, pp. 90–92.

140. Alister McGrath, *The Twilight of Atheism: The Rise and Fall of Disbelief in the Modern World* (London and New York, 2006), pp. 52–55, 60–66.

141. James R. Moore, "Geologists and Interpreters of Genesis in the Nineteenth Century," in David C. Lindberg and Ronald L. Numbers, eds., *God and Nature: Historical Essays on the Encounter Between Christianity and Science* (New York, 1986), pp. 341–43.

142. Noll, *Civil War*, pp. 159–62.

143. Richard Maxwell Brown, *Strain of Violence: Historical Studies of American Violence and Vigilantism* (New York, 1975), pp. 217–18.

144. O'Connell, *Arms and Men*, pp. 202–10; McNeill, *Pursuit of Power*, pp. 242–55.

145. I. F. Clarke, *Voices Prophesying War: Future Wars 1763–3749*, rev. ed. (Oxford and New York, 1992), pp. 37–88.

146. Paul Johnson, *A History of the Jews* (London, 1987), p. 365.

147. Zygmunt Bauman, *Modernity and the Holocaust* (Ithaca, NY, 1989), pp. 40–77.

148. Amos Elon, *The Israelis: Founders and Sons*, 2nd ed.(London, 1981), pp. 112, 338.

149. Eric J. Leed, *No Man's Land: Combat and Identity in World War I* (Cambridge, UK, 1979), pp. 39–72.

150. Stefan Zweig, *The World of Yesterday*, trans. Anthea Bell (New York, 1945), p. 224.

151. Leed, *No Man's Land*, p. 55.

152. Ibid., p. 47; Zweig, *World of Yesterday*, p. 24.

153. Quoted in H. Hafkesbrink, *Unknown Germany: An Inner Chronicle of the First World War Based on Letters and Diaries* (New Haven, CT, 1948), p. 37.

154. Rudolf G. Binding, *Erlebtes Leben* (Frankfurt, 1928), p. 237, cited in Leed, *No Man's Land*, p. 43.

155. Carl Zuckmayer, *Pro Domo* (Stockholm, 1938), pp. 34–35.

156. Franz Schauwecker, *The Fiery Way*, trans. Thonald Holland (London and Toronto, 1929), p. 29.

157. Quoted in Carl E. Schorske, *German Social Democracy, 1905–1917: The Development of the Great Schism* (Cambridge, MA, 1955), p. 390.

158. Leed, *No Man's Land*, p. 29.

159. Philipp Witkop, ed., *Kriegsbriefe gefallener Studenten* (Munich, 1936), p. 100, cited ibid.

160. T. E. Lawrence, *The Mint* (New York, 1963), p. 32.

161. Simone de Beauvoir, *Memoirs of a Dutiful Daughter* (New York, 1974), p. 180.

162. Emilio Lussu, *Sardinian Brigade* (New York, 1939), p. 167.

11 · RELIGION FIGHTS BACK

1. I have explained this at length in *The Battle for God: A History of Fundamentalism* (London and New York, 2000).

2. John Calvin, Commentary on Genesis 1:6, in *The Commentaries of John Calvin on the Old Testament*, 30 vols. (Westminster, UK, 1643–48), 1:86. For a fuller account of the traditional nonliteral interpretation of scripture in both Judaism and Christianity, see my *The Bible: The Biography* (London and New York, 2007).

3. Charles Hodge, *What Is Darwinism?* (Princeton, NJ, 1874), p. 142.

4. 2 Thessalonians 2:3–12; Revelation 16:15; Paul Boyer, *When Time Shall Be No More: Prophecy Belief in American Culture* (Cambridge, MA, 1992), p. 192; George M. Marsden, *Fundamentalism and American Culture* (Oxford, 2006), pp. 154–55.

5. Marsden, *Fundamentalism and American Culture*, pp. 90–92; Robert C. Fuller, *Naming the Antichrist: The History of an American Obsession* (Oxford, 1995), p. 119.

6. Marsden, *Fundamentalism and American Culture*, pp. 184–89; R. Laurence Moore, *Religious Outsiders and the Making of Americans* (Oxford and New York, 1986), pp. 160–63; Ronald L. Numbers, *The Creationists: The Evolution of Scientific Creationism* (Berkeley, Los Angeles, and London, 1992), pp. 41–44, 48–50; Ferenc Mor-

ton Szasz, *The Divided Mind of Protestant America, 1880–1930* (University, AL, 1982), pp. 117–35.

7. Marsden, *Fundamentalism and American Culture,* pp. 187–88.

8. Aurobindo Ghose, *Essays on the Gita* (Pondicherry, 1972), p. 39.

9. Louis Fischer, ed., *The Essential Gandhi* (New York, 1962), p. 193.

10. Mahatma Gandhi, "My Mission," *Young India,* April 3, 1924, in Judith M. Brown, ed., *Mahatma Gandhi: Essential Writings* (Oxford and New York, 2008), p. 5.

11. Mahatma Gandhi, "Farewell," *An Autobiography,* ibid., p. 65.

12. Kenneth W. Jones, "The Arya Samaj in British India, 1875–1947" in Robert D. Baird, ed., *Religion in Modern India* (Delhi, 1981), pp. 44–45.

13. Radhey Shyam Pareek, *Contribution of Arya Samaj in the Making of Modern India, 1875–1947* (New Delhi, 1973), pp. 325–26.

14. Daniel Gold, "Organized Hinduisms: From Vedic Truth to Hindu Nation," in Martin E. Marty and R. Scott Appleby, eds., *Fundamentalisms Observed* (Chicago and London, 1991), pp. 533–42.

15. Vinayak Damdar Savarkar, *Hindutva* (Bombay, 1969), p. 1.

16. Gold, "Organized Hinduisms," pp. 575–80.

17. M. S. Golwalkar, *We or Our Nationhood Defined* (Nagpur, 1939), pp. 47–48, 35.

18. Sudhir Kakar, *The Colors of Violence: Cultural Identities, Religion, and Conflict* (Chicago and London, 1996), pp. 31, 38.

19. Gold, "Organized Hinduisms," pp. 531–32; Sushil Srivastava, "The Ayodhya Controversy: A Third Dimension," *Probe India,* January 1988.

20. Sayyid Abul Ala Mawdudi, *The Islamic Way of Life* (Lahore, 1979), p. 37.

21. Charles T. Adams, "Mawdudi and the Islamic State," in John Esposito, ed., *Voices of Resurgent Islam* (New York and Oxford, 1983); Youssef M. Choueiri, *Islamic Fundamentalism: The Story of Islamist Movements* (London and New York, 2010), pp. 94–139.

22. Mumtaz Ahmad, "Islamic Fundamentalism in South Asia," in Marty and Appleby, *Fundamentalisms,* pp. 487–500.

23. Abul Ala Mawdudi, *Tafhim-al-Qur'an,* in Mustansire Mir, "Some Features of Mawdudi's Tafhim al-Quran," *American Journal of Islamic Social Sciences* 2, no. 2 (1985): 242.

24. *Introducing the Jamaat-e Islami Hind,* in Ahmad, "Islamic Fundamentalism in South Asia," pp. 505–6.

25. Ibid., pp. 500–501.

26. Khurshid Ahmad and Zafar Ushaq Ansari, *Islamic Perspectives* (Leicester, UK, 1979), pp. 378–81.

27. Abul Ala Mawdudi, "Islamic Government," *Asia* 20 (September 1981): 9.

28. Rafiuddin Ahmed, "Redefining Muslim Identity in South Asia: The Transformation of the Jama'at-i-Islami," in Martin E. Marty and R. Scott Appleby, *Accounting for Fundamentalisms: The Dynamic Character of Movements* (Chicago and London, 1994), p. 683.

29. The Ahmadis were said to be heretical because their founder, M. G. Ahmad (d. 1908), had claimed to be a prophet.

30. Ahmad, "Islamic Fundamentalism in South Asia," pp. 587–89.

31. Abul Ala Mawdudi, "How to Establish Islamic Order in the Country," *Universal Message,* May 1983, pp. 9–10.

32. Marshall G. S. Hodgson, *The Venture of Islam: Conscience and History in a World Civilization,* 3 vols. (Chicago and London, 1974), 3:218–19.

33. George Annesley, *The Rise of Modern Egypt: A Century and a Half of Egyptian History* (Durham, UK, 1997), pp. 62, 51–56.

34. Hodgson, *Venture of Islam,* 3:71.

35. Nikki R. Keddie, *Roots of Revolution: An Interpretive History of Modern Iran* (New Haven, CT, and London, 1981), pp. 72–73, 82.

36. John Kautsky, *The Political Consequences of Modernization* (New York, London, Sydney, and Toronto, 1972), pp. 146–47.

37. Bruce Lincoln, *Holy Terrors: Thinking About Religion After September 11*, 2nd ed. (Chicago and London, 2006), pp. 63–65.

38. Daniel Crecelius, "Non-Ideological Responses of the Ulema to Modernization," in Nikki R. Keddie, ed., *Scholars, Saints, and Sufis: Muslim Religious Institutions in the Middle East Since 1500* (Berkeley, Los Angeles, and London, 1972), pp. 181–82.

39. Gilles Kepel, *Jihad: The Trail of Political Islam*, trans. Anthony F. Roberts, 4th ed. (London, 2009), p. 53.

40. Alastair Crooke, *Resistance: The Essence of the Islamist Revolution* (London, 2009), pp. 54–58.

41. Bobby Sayyid, *A Fundamental Fear: Eurocentrism and the Emergence of Islamism* (London, 1997), p. 57.

42. Hodgson, *Venture of Islam*, 3:262.

43. Donald Bloxham, *The Great Game of Genocide: Imperialism, Nationalism, and the Destruction of the Ottoman Armenians* (Oxford, 2007), p. 59.

44. Quoted in Joanna Bourke, "Barbarisation vs. Civilisation in Time of War," in George Kassimeris, ed., *The Barbarisation of Warfare* (London, 2006), p. 29.

45. Moojan Momen, *An Introduction to Shii Islam: The History and Doctrines of Twelver Shiism* (New Haven, CT, and London, 1985), p. 251; Keddie, *Roots of Revolution*, pp. 93–94.

46. Azar Tabari, "The Role of Shii Clergy in Modern Iranian Politics," in Nikki R. Keddie, ed., *Religion and Politics in Iran: Shiism from Quietism to Revolution* (New Haven, CT, and London, 1983), p. 63.

47. Shahrough Akhavi, *Religion and Politics in Contemporary Islam: Clergy-State Relations in the Pahlavi Period* (Albany, NY, 1980), pp. 58–59.

48. Majid Fakhry, *History of Islamic Philosophy* (New York, 1970), pp. 376–81; Bassam Tibi, *Arab Nationalism: A Critical Inquiry*, trans. Marion Farouk Slugett and Peter Slugett, 2nd ed. (London, 1990), pp. 90–93; Albert Hourani, *Arabic Thought in the Liberal Age, 1798–1939* (Cambridge, UK, 1983), pp. 130–61; Hodgson, *Venture of Islam*, 3:274–76.

49. Evelyn Baring, Lord Cromer, *Modern Egypt*, 2 vols. (New York, 1908), 2:184.

50. Hourani, *Arabic Thought in the Liberal Age*, pp. 224, 230, 240–43.

51. John Esposito, "Islam and Muslim Politics," in Esposito, *Voices of Resurgent Islam*, p. 10; Richard P. Mitchell, *The Society of Muslim Brothers* (New York and Oxford, 1969), passim.

52. Mitchell, *Society of Muslim Brothers*, p. 8. The story and speech may be apocryphal, but it expresses the spirit of the early Brotherhood.

53. Ibid., pp. 9–13, 328.

54. Anwar Sadat, *Revolt on the Nile* (New York, 1957), pp. 142–43.

55. Mitchell, *Society of Muslim Brothers*, pp. 205–6, 302.

56. John O. Voll, "Fundamentalisms in the Sunni Arab World: Egypt and the Sudan," in Marty and Appleby, *Fundamentalisms*, pp. 369–74; Yvonne Haddad, "Sayyid Qutb," in Esposito, *Voices of Resurgent Islam*; Choueiri, *Islamic Fundamentalism*, pp. 96–151.

57. Qutb, *Fi Zilal al-Quran*, 2:924–25.

58. Harold Fisch, *The Zionist Revolution: A New Perspective* (Tel Aviv and London, 1968), pp. 77, 87.

59. Theodor Herzl, *The Complete Diaries of Theodor Herzl*, ed. R. Patai, 2 vols. (London and New York, 1960), 2:793–94.

60. Mircea Eliade, *The Sacred and the Profane*, trans. Willard J. Trask (New York, 1959), p. 21.

61. Meir Ben Dov, *The Western Wall* (Jerusalem, 1983), pp. 146, 148, 146.

62. Meron Benvenisti, *Jerusalem: The Torn City* (Jerusalem, 1975), p. 84.

63. Ibid., p. 119.

64. Psalm 72.4.

65. Michael Rosenak, "Jewish Fundamentalism in Israeli Education," in Martin E. Marty and R. Scott Appleby, eds., *Fundamentalisms and Society* (Chicago and London, 1993), p. 392.

66. Gideon Aran, "The Father, the Son and the Holy Land," in R. Scott Appleby, ed., *Spokesmen for the Despised: Fundamentalist Leaders of the Middle East* (Chicago, 1997), pp. 310, 311.

67. Interview with *Maariv* (14 Nisan 572 [1963]), cited in Aviezer Ravitzky, *Messianism, Zionism, and Jewish Religious Radicalism,* trans. Michael Swirsky and Jonathan Chipman (Chicago and London, 1993), p. 85.

68. Ian S. Lustick, *For the Land and the Lord: Jewish Fundamentalism in Israel* (New York, 1988), p. 85; Aran, "Father, Son, and Holy Land," p. 310.

69. Samuel C. Heilman, "Guides of the Faithful, Contemporary Religious Zionist Rabbis," in Appleby, *Spokesmen for the Despised,* p. 357.

70. Ehud Sprinzak, "Three Models of Religious Violence: The Case of Jewish Fundamentalism in Israel," in Martin E. Marty and R. Scott Appleby, eds., *Fundamentalism and the State* (Chicago and London, 1993), p. 472.

71. Gideon Aran, "Jewish Zionist Fundamentalism: The Bloc of the Faithful in Israel," in Marty and Appleby, *Fundamentalisms Observed,* p. 290.

72. Ibid., p. 280.

73. Ibid., p. 308.

74. Keddie, *Roots of Revolution,* pp. 160–80.

75. Mehrzad Borujerdi, *Iranian Intellectuals and the West: The Tormented Triumph of Nativism* (Syracuse, NY, 1996), p. 26; Choueiri, *Islamic Fundamentalism,* p. 156.

76. Michael J. Fischer, "Imam Khomeini: Four Levels of Understanding," in Esposito, *Voices of Resurgent Islam,* p. 157.

77. Keddie, *Roots of Revolution,* pp. 154–56.

78. Ibid., pp. 158–59; Momen, *Introduction to Shii Islam,* p. 254; Hamid Algar, "The Oppositional Role of the Ulema in Twentieth Century Iran," in Keddie, *Scholars, Saints and Sufis,* p. 248.

79. Willem M. Floor, "The Revolutionary Character of the Ulama: Wishful Thinking or Reality," in Nikki R. Keddie, ed., *Religion and Politics in Iran: Shiism from Quietism to Revolution* (New Haven, CT, and London, 1983), appendix, p. 97.

80. Hamid Algar, "The Fusion of the Mystical and the Political in the Personality and Life of Imam Khomeini," lecture delivered at the School of Oriental and African Studies, London, June 9, 1998.

81. John XXIII, *Mater et Magistra,* "Christianity and Social Progress" in Claudia Carlen, ed., *The Papal Encyclicals, 1740–1981,* 5 vols. (Falls Church, VA, 1981), 5:63–64.

82. Camilo Torres, "Latin America: Lands of Violence," in J. Gerassi, ed., *Revolutionary Priest: The Complete Writings and Messages of Camilo Torres* (New York, 1971), pp. 422–23.

83. Thia Cooper, "Liberation Theology and the Spiral of Violence," in Andrew R. Murphy, ed., *The Blackwell Companion to Religion and Violence* (Chichester, UK, 2011), pp. 543–55.

84. Andrew Preston, *Sword of the Spirit, Shield of Faith: Religion in American War and Diplomacy* (New York, 2012), pp. 502–25.

85. Martin Luther King, Jr., *Strength to Love* (Philadelphia, 1963), p. 50.

86. Keddie, *Roots of Revolution,* pp. 282–83; Mehntad Borujerdi, *Islamic Intellectuals and the West: The Tormented Triumph of Nativism* (Syracuse, NY, 1996), pp. 29–42.

87. Akhavi, *Religion and Politics in Contemporary Iran,* pp. 129–31.

88. Algar, "Oppositional Role of the Ulema," p. 251.

89. Keddie, *Roots of Revolution,* pp. 215–59; Sharough Akhavi, "Shariati's Social

Thought," in Keddie, *Religion and Politics in Iran;* Abdulaziz Sachedina, "Ali Shariati, Ideologue of the Islamic Revolution," in Esposito, *Voices of Resurgent Islam;* Michael J. Fischer, *Iran: From Religious Dispute to Revolution* (Cambridge, MA, and London, 1980), pp. 154–67; Borujerdi, *Iranian Intellectuals,* pp. 106–15.

90. Sayeed Ruhollah Khomeini, *Islam and Revolution,* trans. and ed. Hamid Algar (Berkeley, CA, 1981), p. 28.

91. Keddie, *Roots of Revolution,* p. 242; Fischer, *Iran,* p. 193.

92. Gary Sick, *All Fall Down: America's Fateful Encounter with Iran* (London, 1985), p. 30.

93. Keddie, *Roots of Revolution,* p. 243.

94. Fischer, *Iran,* p. 195.

95. Momen, *Introduction to Shii Islam,* p. 288.

96. Fischer, *Iran,* p. 184.

97. Momen, *Introduction to Shii Islam,* p. 288.

98. Fischer, *Iran,* pp. 198–99.

99. Ibid., p. 199; Sick, *All Fall Down,* p. 51; Keddie, *Roots of Revolution,* p. 250. The government claimed that only 120 demonstrators died and 2,000 were injured; others claimed between 500 and 1,000 dead.

100. Fischer, *Iran,* p. 204.

101. Ibid., p. 205. Keddie, *Roots of Revolution,* pp. 252–53, believes that only one million took part.

102. Amir Taheri, *The Spirit of Allah: Khomeini and the Islamic Revolution* (London, 1985), p. 227.

103. Baqir Moin, *Khomeini: Life of the Ayatollah* (London, 1999), pp. 227–28.

104. Daniel Brumberg, "Khomeini's Legacy: Islamic Rule and Islamic Social Justice," in Appleby, *Spokesmen for the Despised.*

105. Joos R. Hiltermann, *A Poisonous Affair: America, Iraq and the Gassing of Halabja* (Cambridge, UK, 2007), pp. 22–36.

106. Homa Katouzian, "Shiism and Islamic Economics: Sadr and Bani Sadr," in Keddie, *Religion and Politics in Iran,* pp. 161–62.

107. Michael J. Fischer, "Imam Khomeini: Four Levels of Understanding," in Esposito, *Voices of Resurgent Islam,* p. 171.

108. Sick, *All Fall Down,* p. 165.

109. Hannah Arendt, *On Revolution* (New York, 1963), p. 18.

110. Kautsky, *Political Consequences of Modernization,* pp. 60–127.

111. William O. Beeman, "Images of the Great Satan: Representations of the United States in the Iranian Revolution," in Keddie, *Religion and Politics in Iran,* p. 215.

12 · HOLY TERROR

1. Rebecca Moore, "Narratives of Persecution, Suffering, and Martyrdom: Violence in the People's Temple and Jonestown," in James R. Lewis, ed., *Violence and New Religious Movements* (Oxford, 2011); Moore, "American as Cherry Pie: The People's Temple and Violence," in Catherine Wessinger, ed., *Millennialism, Persecution, and Violence: Historical Circumstances* (Syracuse, NY, 1986); Wessinger, *How the Millennium Comes Violently: Jonestown to Heaven's Gate* (New York, 2000); Mary Maaga, *Hearing the Voices of Jonestown* (Syracuse, NY, 1998).

2. Moore, "Narratives of Persecution," p. 102.

3. Ibid., p. 103.

4. Huey Newton, *Revolutionary Suicide* (New York, 1973).

5. Moore, "Narratives of Persecution," pp. 106, 108, 110.

6. George Steiner, *In Bluebeard's Castle: Some Notes Towards the Redefinition of Culture* (New Haven, CT, 1971), p. 32.

7. Zygmunt Bauman, *Modernity and the Holocaust* (Ithaca, NY, 1989), pp. 77–92.

8. Joanna Bourke, "Barbarisation vs. Civilisation in Time of War," in George Kassimeris, ed., *The Barbarisation of Warfare* (London, 2006), p. 26.

9. Amir Taheri, *The Spirit of Allah: Khomeini and the Islamic Revolution* (London, 1985), p. 85.

10. Michael Barkun, *Religion and the Racist Right: The Origins of the Christian Identity Movement* (Chapel Hill, NC, 1994).

11. Ibid., pp. 107, 109. There may be as few as 50,000 members.

12. Barkun, *Religion and the Racist Right,* p. 213

13. William T. Cavanaugh, *The Myth of Religious Violence* (Oxford, 2009), pp. 34–35.

14. C. Gearty, "Introduction," in C. Gearty, ed., *Terrorism* (Aldershot, UK, 1996), p. xi.

15. C. Gearty, "What Is Terror?," ibid., p. 495; A. Guelke, *The Age of Terrorism and the International Political System* (London, 2008), p. 7.

16. Richard English, *Terrorism: How to Respond* (Oxford, 2009), pp. 19–20.

17. A. H. Kydd and B. F. Walter, "The Stratagems of Terrorism," *International Security* 31, no. 1 (Summer 2006).

18. P. Wilkinson, *Terrorism Versus Democracy: The Liberal State Response* (London, 2001), pp. 19, 41; Mark Juergensmeyer, *Terror in the Mind of God: The Global Rise of Religious Violence* (Berkeley, CA, 2001), p. 5; J. Horgan, *The Psychology of Terrorism* (London, 2005), p. 12; English, *Terrorism,* p. 6.

19. Hugo Slim, "Why Protect Civilians? Innocence, Immunity and Enmity in War," *International Affairs* 79, no. 3 (2003).

20. B. Hoffman, *Inside Terrorism* (London, 1998), p. 14; C. C. Harmon, *Terrorism Today* (London, 2008), p. 7; D. J. Whittaker, ed., *The Terrorist Reader* (London, 2001), p. 9.

21. Harmon, *Terrorism Today,* p. 160.

22. Martha Crenshaw, "Reflections on the Effects of Terrorism," in Crenshaw, ed., *Terrorism, Legitimacy, and Power: The Consequences of Political Violence* (Middletown, CT, 1983), p. 25.

23. Richard Dawkins, *The God Delusion* (London, 2007), p. 132.

24. Cavanaugh, *Myth of Religious Violence,* pp. 24–54.

25. Muhammad Heikal, *Autumn of Fury: The Assassination of Sadat* (London, 1984), pp. 94–96.

26. Gilles Kepel, *The Prophet and Pharaoh: Muslim Extremism in Egypt,* trans. Jon Rothschild (London, 1985), p. 85.

27. Fedwa El-Guindy, "The Killing of Sadat and After: A Current Assessment of Egypt's Islamic Movement," *Middle East Insight* 2 (January/February 1982).

28. Kepel, *Prophet and Pharaoh,* pp. 70–102.

29. Ibid., pp. 152–59.

30. Heikal, *Autumn of Fury,* pp. 118–19.

31. Patrick D. Gaffney, *The Prophet's Pulpit: Islamic Preaching in Contemporary Egypt* (Berkeley, Los Angeles, and London, 1994), pp. 97–101, 141–42.

32. Johannes J. G. Jansen, *The Neglected Duty: The Creed of Sadat's Assassins and Islamic Resurgence in the Middle East* (New York and London, 1988), pp. 49–88, 169.

33. Ibid., p. 166.

34. Wilfred Cantwell Smith, *Islam in Modern History* (Princeton, NJ, and London, 1957), p. 241.

35. Ibid., pp. 90, 198, 201–2.

36. English, *Terrorism,* p. 51.

37. Abdulaziz A. Sachedina, "Activist Shi'ism in Iran, Iraq and Lebanon," in Martin E. Marty and R. Scott Appleby, eds., *Fundamentalisms Observed* (Chicago and London, 1991), pp. 404–5.

38. Alastair Crooke, *Resistance: The Essence of the Islamist Revolution* (London, 2009), p. 173.

39. Martin Kramer, "Hizbullah: The Calculus of Jihad," in Martin E. Marty and R. Scott Appleby, eds., *Fundamentalisms and the State* (Chicago and London, 1993), pp. 540–41.

40. Sheikh Muhammad Fadl Allah, *Al-Islam wa Muntiq al Quwwa* (Beirut, 1976), in Crooke, *Resistance*, p. 173.

41. Kramer, "Hizbullah," p. 542.

42. Sachedina, "Activist Shi'ism," p. 448.

43. Interview with Fadl Allah, *Kayhan*, November 14, 1985; Kramer, "Hizbullah," p. 551.

44. Fadl Allah, speech, *Al-Nahar*, May 14, 1985; Kramer, "Hizbullah," p. 550.

45. Kramer, "Hizbullah," pp. 548–49; Ariel Meroni, "The Readiness to Kill or Die: Suicide Terrorism in the Middle East," in Walter Reich, ed., *The Origins of Terrorism* (Cambridge, UK, 1990), pp. 204–5.

46. Crooke, *Resistance*, pp. 175–76.

47. Fadl Allah, interview, *Al-Shira*, March 18, 1985; Kramer, "Hizbullah," pp. 552–53.

48. Fadl Allah, interview, *La Repubblica*, August 28, 1989; Kramer, "Hizbullah," p. 552.

49. Crooke, *Resistance*, pp. 175–82.

50. Ibid., pp. 183–87.

51. Robert Pape, *Dying to Win: The Strategic Logic of Suicide Terrorism* (New York, 2005), pp. xiii, 22.

52. Ehud Sprinzak, *The Ascendance of Israel's Far Right* (Oxford and New York, 1991), p. 97. In the event, only two of the targeted mayors were wounded.

53. Ibid., pp. 94–95.

54. Ibid., p. 96; Aviezar Ravitsky, *Messianism, Zionism, and Jewish Religious Radicalism,* trans. Michael Swirsky and Jonathan Chipman (Chicago and London, 1993), pp. 133–34.

55. Sprinzak, *Ascendance*, pp. 97–98.

56. Gideon Aran, "Jewish Zionist Fundamentalism," in Marty and Appleby, *Fundamentalisms Observed*, pp. 267–68.

57. Mekhilta on Exodus 20:13; M. Pirke Aboth 6:6; B. Horayot 13a; B. Sanhedrin 4:5.

58. Sprinzak, *Ascendance*, pp. 121, 220.

59. Amartya Sen, *Identity and Violence: The Illusion of Destiny* (London and New York, 2006).

60. Raphael Mergui and Philippe Simonnot, *Israel's Ayatollahs: Meir Kahane and the Far Right in Israel* (London, 1987), p. 45.

61. Tom Segev, *The Seventh Million: The Israelis and the Holocaust,* trans. Haim Watzman (New York, 1991), pp. 515–17.

62. Sprinzak, *Ascendance*, p. 221.

63. Ehud Sprinzak, "Three Models of Religious Violence: The Case of Jewish Fundamentalism in Israel," in Marty and Appleby, *Fundamentalisms and the State*, pp. 479, 480.

64. Ellen Posman, "History, Humiliation, and Religious Violence," in Andrew R. Murphy, ed., *The Blackwell Companion to Religion and Violence* (Chichester, UK, 2011), pp. 336–37, 339.

65. Sudhir Kakar, *The Colors of Violence: Cultural Identities, Religion, and Conflict* (Chicago and London, 1996), p. 15.

66. Daniel Gold, "Organized Hinduisms: From Vedic Truth to Hindu Nation," in Marty and Appleby, *Fundamentalisms Observed*, pp. 532, 572–73.

67. Kakar, *Colors of Violence*, pp. 48–51.

68. Paul R. Brass, *Communal Riots in Post-Independence India* (Seattle, 2003), pp. 66–67.

69. Kakar, *Colors of Violence,* pp. 154–57, 158.

70. David Cook, *Understanding Jihad* (Berkeley, Los Angeles, and London, 2005), p. 114.

71. Beverley Milton-Edwards, *Islamic Politics in Palestine* (London and New York, 1996), pp. 73–116, 118.

72. Cook, *Understanding Jihad,* p. 114.

73. Samuel C. Heilman, "Guides of the Faithful: Contemporary Religious Zionist Rabbis," in R. Scott Appleby, ed., *Spokesmen for the Despised: Fundamentalist Leaders in the Middle East* (Chicago, 1997), pp. 352–53, 354.

74. Glenn E. Robinson, *Building a Palestinian State: The Incomplete Revolution* (Bloomington, IN, 1997); Jeroen Gunning, "Rethinking Religion and Violence in the Middle East," in Murphy, *Blackwell Companion,* p. 519.

75. Gunning, "Rethinking Religion and Violence," pp. 518–19.

76. Milton-Edwards, *Islamic Politics,* p. 148.

77. Anne Marie Oliver and Paul F. Steinberg, *The Road to Martyrs' Square: A Journey to the World of the Suicide Bomber* (Oxford, 2005), p. 71.

78. Cook, *Understanding Jihad,* p. 116.

79. *The Covenant of the Islamic Resistance Movement,* sec. 1, cited in John L. Esposito, *Unholy War: Terror in the Name of Islam* (Oxford, 2002), p. 96.

80. Cook, *Understanding Jihad,* p. 116.

81. *Covenant,* Section 1, in Esposito, *Unholy War,* p. 96.

82. Talal Asad, *On Suicide Bombing: The Wellek Lectures* (New York, 2007), pp. 46–47.

83. Dr. Abdul Aziz Reutizi, in Anthony Shehad, *Legacy of the Prophet: Despots, Democrats, and the New Politics of Islam* (Boulder, CO, 2001), p. 124.

84. Esposito, *Unholy War,* pp. 97–98.

85. Bernard Lewis, "The Roots of Muslim Rage," *Atlantic Monthly* (September 2, 1990); Bruce Hoffman, *Inside Terrorism* (New York, 2006).

86. Gunner, "Rethinking Religion and Violence," p. 516.

87. Asad, *Suicide Bombing,* p. 50.

88. Pape, *Dying to Win,* p. 130. These figures differ slightly from those quoted earlier from another survey, but both arrive at the same general conclusion.

89. Robert Pape, "Dying to Kill Us," *New York Times,* September 22, 2003.

90. May Jayyusi, "Subjectivity and Public Witness: An Analysis of Islamic Militance in Palestine," unpublished paper (2004), quoted in Asad, *Suicide Bombing.*

91. Gunning, "Rethinking Religion and Violence," pp. 518–19.

92. Oliver and Steinberg, *Road to Martyr's Square,* p. 120.

93. Ibid., pp. 101–2; Gunning, "Rethinking Religion and Violence," pp. 518–19.

94. Oliver and Steinberg, *Road to Martyr's Square,* p. 31.

95. Roxanne Euben, "Killing (for) Politics: Jihad, Martyrdom, Political Action," *Political Theory* 30 (2002): 9, 49.

96. Judges 16:23–31.

97. John Milton, *Samson Agonistes,* lines 1710–11.

98. Ibid., lines 1721–24.

99. Ibid., lines 1754–55.

100. Asad, *Suicide Bombing,* pp. 74–75.

101. Ibid., p. 63.

102. Bourke, "Barbarisation vs. Civilisation," p. 21.

103. Jacqueline Rose, "Deadly Embrace," *London Review of Books* 26, no. 21 (November 4, 2004).

13 · GLOBAL JIHAD

1. Jason Burke, *Al-Qaeda* (London, 2003), pp. 72–75; Thomas Hegghammer, *Jihad in Saudi Arabia: Violence and Pan-Islamism Since 1979* (Cambridge, UK, 2010), pp. 7–8, 40–42; Gilles Kepel, *Jihad: The Trail of Political Islam*, trans. Anthony F. Roberts, 4th ed. (London, 2009), pp. 144–47; Lawrence Wright, *The Looming Tower: Al-Qaeda's Road to 9/11* (New York, 2006), pp. 95–101; David Cook, *Understanding Jihad* (Berkeley, Los Angeles, and London, 2005), pp. 128–31.

2. Abdullah Azzam, "The Last Will of 'Abdallah Yusuf' Azzam, Who Is Poor unto His Lord," dictated April 20, 1986, at www.alribat.com, September 27, 2001; trans. amended by Cook, *Understanding Jihad*, p. 130.

3. Burke, *Al-Qaeda*, p. 75.

4. Andrew Preston, *Sword of the Spirit, Shield of Faith: Religion in American War and Diplomacy* (New York and Toronto, 2012), p. 585.

5. Kepel, *Jihad*, pp. 137–40, 147–49; Burke, *Al-Qaeda*, pp. 58–62; Hegghammer, *Jihad in Saudi Arabia*, pp. 58–60.

6. Abdullah Azzam, "Martyrs: The Building Blocks of Nations," in Cook, *Understanding Jihad*, p. 129.

7. Ibid.

8. Ibid.

9. Azzam, "Last Will of 'Abdullah Yusuf' Azzam," p. 130.

10. Abdullah Yusuf Azzam, *Join the Caravan* (Birmingham, UK, n.d.).

11. Wright, *Looming Tower*, pp. 96, 130.

12. Hegghammer, *Jihad in Saudi Arabia*. pp. 8–37, 229–33.

13. Natana J. DeLong-Bas, *Wahhabi Islam: From Revival and Reform to Global Jihad* (Cairo, 2005), pp. 35, 194–96, 203–11, 221–24.

14. Hamid Algar, *Wahhabism: A Critical Essay* (Oneonta, NY, 2002).

15. DeLong-Bas, *Wahhabi Islam*, pp. 247–56; Cook, *Understanding Jihad*, p. 74.

16. Kepel, *Jihad*, pp. 57–59, 69–86; Burke, *Al-Qaeda*, pp. 56–60; John Esposito, *Unholy War: Terror in the Name of Islam* (Oxford, 2002), pp. 106–10.

17. Kepel, *Jihad*, pp. 71, 70.

18. Hegghammer, *Jihad in Saudi Arabia*, pp. 19–24.

19. Ibid., pp. 60–64.

20. *Al-Quds al-Arabi*, March, 20, 2005, quoted ibid., p. 61.

21. Ibid., pp. 61–62.

22. Ibid., p. 64.

23. Michael A. Sells, *The Bridge Betrayed: Religion and Genocide in Bosnia* (Berkeley and Los Angeles, 1996), pp. 154, 9, 29–52, 1–3.

24. Ibid., pp. 72–79, 117.

25. Chris Hedges, *War Is a Force That Gives Us Meaning* (New York, 2003), p. 9.

26. *New York Times*, October 18, 1995; Sells, *Bridge Betrayed*, p. 10.

27. S. Burg, "The International Community and the Yugoslav Crisis," in Milton Eshman and Shibley Telhami, eds., *International Organization of Ethnic Conflict* (Ithaca, NY, 1994); David Rieff, *Slaughterhouse: Bosnia and the Failure of the West* (New York, 1995).

28. Thomas L. Friedman, "Allies," *New York Times*, June 7, 1995.

29. Cook, *Understanding Jihad*, pp. 119–21.

30. Mahmoun Fandy, *Saudi Arabia and the Politics of Dissent* (New York, 1999), p. 183.

31. Kepel, *Jihad*, pp. 223–26.

32. Cook, *Understanding Islam*, pp. 135–36; Marc Sageman, *Leaderless Jihad: Terror Networks in the Twenty-First Century* (Philadelphia, 2008), pp. 44–46; Burke, *Al-Qaeda*, pp. 118–35.

33. Hegghammer, *Jihad in Saudi Arabia*, pp. 229–30.

34. Burke, *Al-Qaeda,* pp. 7–8.

35. Esposito, *Unholy War,* pp. 14, 6, 8.

36. Kepel, *Jihad,* pp. 13–14.

37. Burke, *Al-Qaeda,* pp. 161–64; DeLong-Bas, *Wahhabi Islam,* pp. 276–77.

38. Esposito, *Unholy War,* pp. 21–22; Burke, *Al-Qaeda,* pp. 175–76.

39. Hegghammer, *Jihad in Saudi Arabia,* pp. 102–3.

40. Osama bin Laden, "Hunting the Enemy," in Esposito, *Unholy War,* p. 24.

41. Burke, *Al-Qaeda,* p. 163.

42. Hegghammer, *Jihad in Saudi Arabia,* pp. 133–41.

43. Matthew Purdy and Lowell Bergman, "Where the Trail Led: Between Evidence and Suspicion; Unclear Danger: Inside the Lackawanna Terror Case," *New York Times,* October 12, 2003.

44. Cook, *Understanding Jihad,* p. 150; Sageman, *Leaderless Jihad,* p. 81.

45. Cook, *Understanding Jihad,* pp. 136–41.

46. Abu Daud, *Sunan* (Beirut, 1988), 4:108 n. 4297, ibid., p. 137.

47. Quran 2:249; Burke, *Al-Qaeda,* pp. 24–25.

48. Quran 2:194; communiqué from Qaidat al-Jihad, April 24, 2002; Cook, *Understanding Jihad,* p. 178.

49. Sageman, *Leaderless Jihad,* pp. 81–82.

50. Marc Sageman, *Understanding Terror Networks* (Philadelphia, 2004), pp. 103–8.

51. Sageman, *Leaderless Jihad,* pp. 59–60.

52. Ibid., pp. 28, 57.

53. Timothy McDermott, *Perfect Soldiers: The 9/11 Hijackers: Who They Were, Why They Did It* (New York, 2005), p. 65.

54. Fraser Egerton, *Jihad in the West: The Rise of Militant Salafism* (Cambridge, UK, 2011), pp. 155–56.

55. Sageman, *Understanding Terror Networks,* p. 105.

56. Anthony Giddens, *The Consequences of Modernity* (Cambridge, UK, 1991), p. 53.

57. Bin Laden, "Hunting the Enemy," p. 23.

58. Andrew Sullivan, "This *Is* a Religious War," *New York Times Magazine,* October 7, 2001.

59. Cavanaugh, *Myth of Religious Violence,* p. 204.

60. Emmanuel Sivan, "The Crusades Described by Modern Arab Historiography," *Asian and African Studies* 8 (1972).

61. Hegghammer, *Jihad in Saudi Arabia,* pp. 104–5.

62. Two other copies were found: one in the car used by one of the hijackers before he boarded American Airlines Flight 77 in Washington, the other at the crash site of United Airlines Flight 93 in Pennsylvania.

63. The translated text is found in Bruce Lincoln, Appendix A, "Final Instructions to the Hijackers of September, 11, Found in the Luggage of Muhammad Atta and Two Other Copies," in *Holy Terrors: Thinking About Religion After September 11,* 2nd ed. (Chicago, 2006). See, for example, para. 10, p. 98; para. 24, p. 100; para. 30, p. 101.

64. "Final Instructions," para. 1, p. 97.

65. In Cook, *Understanding Jihad,* 6, p. 196; Lincoln, *Holy Terrors,* p. 97.

66. Lincoln, *Holy Terrors,* pp. 98, 200, 201.

67. Cook, *Understanding Jihad,* p. 234 no. 37.

68. Quran 3:173–74, trans. M. A. S. Abdel Haleem (Oxford, 2004).

69. Cook, *Understanding Jihad,* p. 198.

70. Ibid., p. 201.

71. Louis Atiyat Allah, "Moments Before the Crash, by the Lord of the 19" (January 22, 2003), in Cook, *Understanding Jihad,* pp. 203, 207.

72. "Osama bin Laden, Videotaped Address, October 7, 2001," appendix C in Lincoln, *Holy Terrors,* p.106.

73. Hamid Mir, "Osama Claims He Has Nukes. If US Uses N. Arms It Will Get the Same Response," *Dawn,* Internet ed., November 10, 2001.

74. Lincoln, *Holy Terrors,* pp. 106–7.

75. "George W. Bush, Address to the Nation, October 7, 2001," Appendix B, ibid., p. 104.

76. Remarks by the president at the Islamic Center of Washington, D.C., September 17, 2001, http://usinfo.state.gov/islam/s091701b.htm.

77. Lincoln, *Holy Terrors,* p. 104.

78. Paul Rogers, "The Global War on Terror and Its Impact on the Conduct of War," in George Kassimeris, ed., *The Barbarisation of Warfare* (London, 2006), p. 188.

79. Cook, *Understanding Jihad,* p. 157. Cook comments: "Sadly, in the light of the revelations at the Abu Ghraib prison in the spring of 2004, this description is not as implausible as it should have been."

80. Anthony Dworkin, "The Laws of War in the Age of Asymmetric Conflict," in Kassimeris, *Barbarisation of Warfare,* pp. 220, 233.

81. Joanna Bourke, "Barbarisation vs. Civilisation in Time of War," in Kassimeris, *Barbarisation of Warfare,* p. 37.

82. Dworkin, "Laws of War," p. 220.

83. Rogers, "Global War on Terror," p. 192.

84. *Guardian,* Datablog, April 12, 2013. The United Nations began to report statistics of civilian deaths in 2007.

85. Sageman, *Leaderless Jihad,* pp. 136–37.

86. White House Press Release, "President Discusses the Future of Iraq," February 26, 2003.

87. White House Press Release, "President Bush Saluting Veterans at White House Ceremony," November 11, 2002.

88. Timothy H. Parsons, *The Rule of Empires: Those Who Built Them, Those Who Endured Them, and Why They Always Fail* (Oxford, 2010), pp. 423–50.

89. Bruce Lincoln, *Religion, Empire, and Torture: The Case of Achaemenian Persia, with a Postscript on Abu Ghraib* (Chicago and London, 2007), pp. 97–99.

90. Ibid., pp. 97–98.

91. Luke 4:18–19.

92. Lincoln, *Religion, Empire, and Torture,* pp. 101–7.

93. Susan Sontag, "What Have We Done?" *Guardian,* May 24, 2005.

94. Lincoln, *Religion, Empire and Torture,* pp. 101–2.

95. Parsons, *Rule of Empires,* pp. 423–34.

96. Bashir, Friday Prayers, Umm al-Oura, Baghdad, June 11, 2004, quoted in Edward Coy, "Iraqis Put Contempt for Troops on Display," *Washington Post,* June 12, 2004; Kassimeris, "Barbarisation of Warfare," in Kassimeris, *Barbarisation of Warfare,* p. 16.

97. Rogers, "Global War on Terror," pp. 193–94.

98. Dworkin, "Laws of War," p. 253.

99. Sageman, *Leaderless Jihad,* pp. 139–42.

100. Ibid., pp. 31–32.

101. Michael Bonner, *Jihad in Islamic History* (Princeton, NJ, and Oxford, 2006), p. 164.

102. Sageman, *Leaderless Jihad,* pp. 156–57, 159.

103. John L. Esposito and Dahlia Mogahed, *Who Speaks for Islam? What a Billion Muslims Really Think; Based on Gallup's World Poll—The Largest Study of Its Kind* (New York, 2007), pp. 69–70.

104. Cited in Joos R. Hiltermann, *A Poisonous Affair: America, Iraq, and the Gassing of Halabja* (Cambridge, UK, 2007), p. 243.

105. Naureen Shah, "Time for the Truth About 'Targeted Killings,'" *Guardian,* October 22, 2013.

106. Rafiq ur Rehman, "Please Tell Me, Mr President, Why a US Drone Assassinated My Mother," *Guardian,* October 25, 2013.

AFTERWORD

1. Quran 29:46, to cite just one example.
2. Quran 22:40; trans. M. A. S. Abdel Haleem (Oxford, 2004).
3. It is also due to the prevalence of Wahhabi ideas that have been promoted throughout the Muslim world with the tacit agreement of the United States.
4. John Fowles, *The Magus,* rev. ed. (London, 1987), p. 413.

Bibliography

Abdel Haleem, M. A. S. trans. *The Qur'an: A New Translation*. Oxford and New York, 2004.

Abelard, Peter. *A Dialogue of a Philosopher with a Jew and a Christian*. Trans. P. J. Payer. Toronto, 1979.

Abulafia, David. *Frederick II: A Medieval Emperor*. New York and Oxford, 1992.

Adams, Charles. "Mawdudi and the Islamic State." In John L. Esposito, ed., *Voices of Resurgent Islam*. New York and Oxford, 1983.

Adams, Dickenson W., ed. *Jefferson's Extracts from the Gospels*. Princeton, NJ, 1983.

Adams, R. M. *Heartlands of Cities: Surveys on Ancient Settlements and Land Use on the Central Floodplains of the Euphrates*. Chicago, 1981.

Agamben, Giorgio. *The Kingdom and the Glory: For a Theological Genealogy of Economy and Government*. Trans. Lorenzo Chiesa with Matteo Mandarini. Stanford, CA, 2011.

———. *State of Exception*. Trans. Kevin Attell. Chicago and London, 2005.

Ahlstrom, Gosta W. *The History of Ancient Palestine*. Minneapolis, 1993.

Ahmad, Kharshid, and Zafar Ushaq. *Islamic Perspectives*. Leicester, UK, 1979.

Ahmad, Mumtaz. "Islamic Fundamentalism in South Asia: The Jamaat-i-Islami and the Tablighi Jamaat." In Martin E. Marty and R. Scott Appleby, eds., *Fundamentalisms Observed*. Chicago and London, 1991.

Ahmed, Rafiuddin. "Redefining Muslim Identity in South Asia: The Transformation of the Jamaat-i-Islami." In Martin E. Marty and R. Scott Appleby, eds., *Accounting for Fundamentalisms: The Dynamic Character of Movements*. Chicago and London, 1994.

Aho, James A. *Religious Mythology and the Art of War: Comparative Religious Symbolisms of Military Violence*. Westport, CT, 1981.

Akhavi, Shahrough. *Religion and Politics in Contemporary Iran: Clergy-State Relations in the Pahlavi Period*. Albany, NY, 1980.

———. "Shariati's Social Thought." In Nikki R. Keddie, ed. *Religion and Politics in Iran: Shiism from Quietism to Revolution*. New Haven, CT, and London, 1983.

Al-Azmeh, Aziz. *Islams and Modernities*. 3rd ed. London and New York, 2009.

———. *Muslim Kingship: Power and the Sacred in Muslim Christian and Pagan Politics*. London and New York, 1997.

Algar, Hamid. "The Oppositional Role of the Ulema in Twentieth-Century Iran." In Nikki R. Keddie, ed., *Scholars, Saints and Sufis: Muslim Religious Institutions in the Middle East Since 1500*. Berkeley, Los Angeles, and London, 1972.

——. *Religion and State in Iran, 1785–1906.* Berkeley, CA,1984.

——. *Wahhabism: A Critical Essay.* Oneonta, NY, 2002.

Allah, Louis Atiyat. "Moments Before the Crash, By the Lord of the 19." In David Cook, *Understanding Jihad.* Berkeley, Los Angeles, and London, 2005.

Allen, J. W. *A History of Political Thought in the Sixteenth Century.* London, 1928.

Allen, William. *Apologie of the English College.* Douai, 1581.

Alter, Robert, and Frank Kermode, eds. *A Literary Guide to the Bible.* London, 1987.

Anderson, Benedict. *Imagined Communities: Reflections on the Origin and Spread of Nationalism.* London and New York, 2003.

Anderson, Perry. *Lineages of the Absolutist State.* London, 1974.

——. *Passages from Antiquity to Feudalism.* London, 1974.

Andrae, Tor. *Muhammad: The Man and His Faith.* Trans. Theophil Menzel. London, 1936.

Andreski, Stanislav. *Military Organization and Society.* Berkeley, Los Angeles, and London, 1968.

Angel, J. L. "Paleoecology, Paleogeography and Health." In S. Polgar, ed., *Population, Ecology, and Social Evolution.* The Hague, 1975.

Annesley, George. *The Rise of Modern Egypt: A Century and a Half of Egyptian History.* Durham, UK, 1997.

Anonymous. "Final Instructions to the Hijackers of September 11." In Bruce Lincoln, *Holy Terrors: Thinking About Religion After September 11.* 2nd ed. Chicago and London, 2006.

Anonymous, ed. *Fast Day Sermons, or The Pulpit on the State of the Country.* Charleston, SC, 2009 ed.

Appleby, R. Scott. *The Ambivalence of the Sacred: Religion, Violence and Reconciliation.* Lanham, MD, 2000.

——, ed. *Spokesmen of the Despised: Fundamentalist Leaders of the Middle East.* Chicago, 1997.

Aran, Gideon. "The Father, the Son and the Holy Land: The Spiritual Authorities of Jewish-Zionist Fundamentalism in Israel." In R. Scott Appleby, ed., *Spokesmen of the Despised: Fundamentalist Leaders of the Middle East.* Chicago, 1997.

——. "Jewish Zionist Fundamentalism." In Marty E. Marty and R. Scott Appleby, eds., *Fundamentalisms Observed.* Chicago and London, 1991.

——. "The Roots of Gush Emunim." *Studies in Contemporary Jewry* 2 (1986).

Ardagh, Sir John. Speech in *The Proceedings of the Hague Peace Conference.* London, 1920.

Arendt, Hannah. *On Revolution.* London, 1963.

——. *On Violence.* San Diego, 1970.

——. *The Origins of Totalitarianism.* San Diego, 1979.

Aristotle. *The Basic Works of Aristotle.* Ed. Richard McKeon. New York, 1941.

Asad, Muhammad, trans. *The Message of the Qur'an.* Gibraltar, 1980.

Asad, Talal. *Formations of the Secular: Christianity, Islam, Modernity.* Stanford, CA, 2003.

——. *Genealogies of Religion: Discipline and Reasons of Power in Christianity and Islam.* Baltimore and London, 1993.

——. *On Suicide Bombing: The Wellek Lectures.* New York, 2007.

Athanasius. "Life of Antony." In R. C. Gregg, trans., *The Life of Anthony and the Letter to Marcellinus.* New York, 1980.

Augustine, Aurelius. *On the Free Choice of the Will.* Trans. Thomas Williams. Indianapolis, 1993.

Avalos, Hector. *Fighting Words: The Origins of Religious Violence.* Amherst, NY, 2005.

Azzam, Abdullah Yusuf. *The Defence of Muslim Lands.* Birmingham, UK, n.d.

——. *Join the Caravan.* Birmingham, UK, n.d.

————. "The Last Will of Abdullah Yusuf Azzam, Who Is Poor Unto His Lord." Birmingham, UK, n.d.

Bachrach, David S. *Religion and the Conduct of War, c. 300–1215*. Woodbridge, UK, 2003.

Baer, Yitzhak. *A History of the Jews in Christian Spain*. 2 vols. Philadelphia, 1966.

Bainton, Ronald H. *Christian Attitudes Toward War and Peace*. Nashville and New York, 1960.

Baird, Robert D., ed. *Religion in Modern India*. Delhi, 1981.

Bammel, F., and C. F. D. Moule, eds. *Jesus and the Politics of His Day*. Cambridge, UK, 1981.

Bamyeh, Mohammed A. *The Social Origins of Islam: Mind, Economy, Discourse*. Minneapolis, 1999.

Barber, Malcolm. *The New Knighthood: A History of the Order of the Templars*. Cambridge, UK, 1995.

Barber, Richard. *The Knight and Chivalry*. New York, 1970.

Baring, Evelyn, Lord Cromer. *Modern Egypt*. 2 vols. New York, 1908.

Barker, Margaret. *The Gate of Heaven: The History and Symbolism of the Temple in Jerusalem*. London, 1991.

Barkun, Michael. *Religion and the Racist Right: The Origins of the Christian Identity Movement*. Chapel Hill, NC, 1996.

Barnie, John. *War in Medieval English Society: Social Values and the Hundred Years War, 1337–99*. Ithaca, NY, 1974.

Bary, Wm. Theodore de. *The Trouble with Confucianism*. Cambridge, MA, and London, 1996.

————, and Irene Bloom, eds. *Sources of Chinese Tradition, from Earliest Times to 1600*. 2nd ed. New York, 1999.

Bashear, Suliman, "Apocalyptic and Other Materials on Early Muslim-Byzantine Wars." *Journal of the Royal Asiatic Society*, 3rd ser., vol. 1, no. 2 (1991).

Bauman, Zygmunt. *Modernity and the Holocaust*. Cambridge, UK, 1992.

Beauvoir, Simone de. *Memoirs of a Dutiful Daughter*. New York, 1974.

Bebbington, D. W. *Evangelicalism in Modern Britain: A History from the 1730s to the 1980s*. London, 1989.

Beecher, Henry W. *Patriotic Addresses*. New York, 1887.

Beeman, Richard, Stephen Botein, and Edward E. Carter III, eds. *Beyond Confederation: Origins of the Constitution in American Identity*. Chapel Hill, NC, 1987.

Beeman, William. "Images of the Great Satan: Representations of the United States in the Iranian Revolution." In Nikki R. Keddie, ed., *Religion and Politics in Iran: Shiism from Quietism to Revolution*. New Haven, CT, and London, 1983.

Behr, John. *Irenaeus of Lyons: Identifying Christianity*. Oxford, 2013.

Beinart, Haim. *Conversos on Trial: The Inquisition in Ciudad Real*. Jerusalem, 1981.

Bell, Catherine. *Ritual Theory, Ritual Practice*. New York, 1992.

Bell, H. I., V. Martin, E. G. Turner, and D. Van Burchem. *The Abinnaeus Archive*. Oxford, 1962.

Bendix, Reinard. *Kings or People: Power and the Mandate to Rule*. Berkeley, CA, 1977.

Ben Dov, Meir. *The Western Wall*. Jerusalem, 1983.

Benson, Larry, ed. and trans. *King Arthur's Death: The Middle English Stanzaic Morte d'Arthur and the Alliterative Morte d'Arthur*. Kalamazoo, MI, 1994.

Benvenisti, Meron. *Jerusalem: The Torn City*. Jerusalem, 1975.

Berchant, Heinz. "The Date of the Buddha Reconsidered." *Indologia Taurinensen* 10 (n.d.).

Berger, Michael S. "Taming the Beast: Rabbinic Pacification of Second-Century Jewish Nationalism." In James K. Wellman Jr., ed., *Belief and Bloodshed: Religion and Violence Across Time and Tradition*. Lanham, MD, 2007.

Berger, Peter. *The Sacred Canopy: Elements of Sociological Theory*. New York, 1967.

Berman, Joshua. *Biblical Revolutions: The Transformation of Social and Political Thought in the Ancient Near East*. New York and Oxford, 2008.

Berman, Paul. *Terror and Liberalism*. New York, 2003.

Bernard of Clairvaux. *In Praise of the New Knighthood: A Treatise on the Knights Templar and the Holy Places of Jerusalem*. Trans. M. Conrad Greenia OCSO. Introduction by Malcolm Barber. Collegeville, MN, 2008.

Black, Jeremy. "Warfare, Crisis and Absolutism." In Euan Cameron, ed., *Early Modern Europe: An Oxford History*. Oxford, 1999.

Blake, E. O. "The Formation of the Crusade Idea." *Journal of Ecclesiastical History* 21, no. 1 (1970).

Blanning, T. C. "Epilogue: The Old Order Transformed." In Euan Cameron, ed., *Early Modern Europe: An Oxford History*. Oxford, 1999.

Bloch, Marc. *Feudal Society*. Trans. L. A. Manyon. London, 1961.

Bloch, Ruth H. *Visionary Republic: Millennial Themes in American Thought, 1756–1800*. Cambridge, UK, 1985.

Bloxham, David. *The Great Game of Genocide: Imperialism, Nationalism and the Destruction of the Ottoman Armenians*. Oxford, 2007.

Bickerman, Elias J. *From Ezra to the Last of the Maccabees*. New York, 1962.

Blockmans, Wim. *Emperor Charles V, 1500–1558*. London and New York, 2002.

Boak, A. E., and H. C. Harvey. *The Archive of Aurelius Isidore*. Ann Arbor, MI, 1960.

Bodde, Derk. *Festivals in Classical China and Other Annual Observances During the Han Dynasty, 206 B.C.–A.D. 220*. Princeton, NJ, 1975.

———. "Feudalism in China." In Rushton Coulborn, ed., *Feudalism in History*. Hamden, CT, 1965.

Bonner, Michael. *Aristocratic Violence and the Holy War: Studies in Jihad and the Arab-Byzantine Frontier*. New Haven, CT, 1996.

———. *Jihad in Islamic History*. Princeton, NJ, and Oxford, 2006.

Bonney, Richard. *Jihad: From Qur'an to Bin Laden*. New York, 2004.

Borg, Marcus. *Jesus: Uncovering the Life, Teachings, and Relevance of a Religious Revolutionary*. New York, 2006.

Borowitz, Albert. *Terrorism for Self-Glorification: The Herostratos Syndrome*. Kent, OH, 2005.

Borujerdi, Mehrzad. *Iranian Intellectuals and the West: The Tormented Triumph of Nativism*. Syracuse, NY, 1996.

Bossy, John. *Christianity in the West, 1400–1700*. Oxford, 1985.

———. "Unrethinking the Wars of Religion." In Thomas Kselman, ed., *Belief in History: Innovative Approaches to European and American Religion*. Notre Dame, IN, 1991.

Bourke, Joanna. "Barbarisation vs. Civilisation in Time of War." In George Kassimeris, ed., *The Barbarisation of Warfare*. London, 2006.

———. *An Intimate History of Killing: Face to Face Killing in Twentieth-Century Warfare*. New York, 1999.

Boustan, Ra'anau S., Alex P. Jassen, and Calvin J. Roetzal, eds. *Violence, Scripture and Textual Practice in Early Judaism and Christianity*. Leiden, 2010.

Bowerstock, G. W. *Hellenism in Late Antiquity*. Ann Arbor, MI, 1990.

Bowker, John. *The Religious Imagination and the Sense of God*. Oxford, 1978.

Boyce, Mary. "Priests, Cattle and Men." *Bulletin of the School of Oriental and African Studies* 50, no. 3 (1998).

———. *Zoroastrians: Their Religious Beliefs and Practices*. 2nd ed. London and New York, 2001.

Boyer, Paul. *When Time Shall Be No More: Prophecy Belief in Modern American Culture*. Cambridge, MA, 1992.

Brace, F. F. "Render to Caesar." In F. Bammel and C. F. D. Moule, eds., *Jesus and the Politics of His Day*. Cambridge, UK, 1981.

Brass, Paul R. *Communal Riots in Post-Independence India*. Seattle, 2003.

Brenner, Jan N. "Secularization: Notes Toward the Genealogy." In Henk De Vries, ed., *Religion Beyond a Concept*. New York, 2008.

Brigdon, Susan. *London and the Reformation*. Oxford, 1989.

Briggs, Robin. "Embattled Faiths: Religion and Natural Philosophy." In Euan Cameron ed., *Early Modern Europe: An Oxford History*. Oxford, 1999.

Brisch, Nicole, ed. *Religion and Power: Divine Kingship in the Ancient World and Beyond*. Chicago, 2008.

Brodie, Bernard, and Fawn Brodie. *From Crossbow to H-Bomb*. Bloomington, IN, 1972.

Bronowski, Jacob. *The Ascent of Man*. Boston, 1973.

Brooks, E. W., trans. *The Sixth Book of the Select Letter of Severus, Patriarch of Antioch*. London, 1903.

Brown, John Pairman. "Techniques of Imperial Control: Background of the Gospel Event." In Normal Gottwald, ed., *The Bible of Liberation: Political and Social Hermeneutics*. Maryknoll, NY, 1985.

Brown, Judith M., ed. *Mahatma Gandhi: Essential Writings*. London and New York, 2008.

Brown, Peter. *Authority and the Sacred: Aspects of the Christianization of the Roman World*. Cambridge, UK, 1995.

———. *The Body and Society: Men, Women and Sexual Renunciation in Early Christianity*. London and Boston, 1988.

———. *The Cult of the Saints: Its Rise and Function in Latin Christianity*. Chicago and London, 1981.

———. *The Making of Late Antiquity*. Cambridge, MA, and London, 1973.

———. *Poverty and Leadership in the Later Roman Empire*. Hanover, NH, and London, 2002.

———. *Power and Persuasion in Late Antiquity: Towards a Christian Empire*. Madison, WI, and London, 1992.

———. "Religious Coercion in the Later Roman Empire: The Case of North Africa." *History* 48 (1961).

———. "Religious Dissent in the Later Roman Empire: The Case of North Africa." *History* 46 (1961).

———. "The Rise of the Holy Man in Late Antiquity." *Journal of Roman Studies* 61 (1971).

———. *The Rise of Western Christendom: Triumph and Diversity, AD 200–1000*. Oxford and Malden, MA, 1996.

———. *Society and the Holy in Late Antiquity*. Berkeley, Los Angeles, and London, 1982.

———. *The World of Late Antiquity, AD 150–750*. London, 1971, 1989.

Brown, Richard Maxwell. *Strains of Violence: Historical Studies of American Violence and Vigilantism*. New York, 1975.

Brumberg, Daniel. "Khomeini's Legacy: Islamic Rule and Islamic Social Justice." In R. Scott Appleby, ed., *Spokesmen for the Despised: Fundamentalist Leaders of the Middle East*. Chicago, 1997.

Bruns, Gerald L. "Midrash and Allegory: The Beginnings of Scriptural Interpretation." In Robert Alter and Frank Kermode, eds., *A Literary Guide to the Bible*. London, 1987.

Bryant, Edwin. *The Quest for the Origins of Vedic Culture: The Indo-Aryan Debate*. Oxford and New York, 2001.

Bryce, T. *The Kingdom of the Hittites*. Oxford, 1998.

Burg, S. "The International Community and the Yugoslav Crisis," in Milton Eshman and Shibley Telhami, eds., *International Organization of Ethnic Conflict*. Ithaca, NY, 1994.

Burke, Jason. *Al-Qaeda*. London, 2003.

Burke, Victor Lee. *The Clash of Civilizations: War-Making & State Formation in Europe.* Cambridge, UK, 1997.

Burkert, Walter. *Homo Necans: The Anthropology of Ancient Greek Sacrificial Ritual and Myth.* Trans. Walter Bing. Berkeley, Los Angeles, and London, 1983.

———. *Structure and History in Greek Mythology and Ritual.* Berkeley, Los Angeles, and London, 1980.

Burleigh, Michael. *Earthly Powers: Religion and Politics in Europe from the Enlightenment to the Great War.* London, New York, Toronto, and Sydney, 2005.

Burman, Edward. *The Assassins: Holy Killers of Islam.* London, 1987.

Burton-Christie, Douglas. *The Word in the Desert: Scripture and the Quest for Holiness in Early Christian Monasticism.* New York and Oxford, 1993.

Busby, Keith, trans. *Raoul de Hodence: Le Roman des eles: The Anonymous Ordere de Cevalerie.* Philadelphia, 1983.

Bushnell, Howard. *Building Eras in Religion.* New York, 1981.

Bussmann, Klaus, and Heinz Schilling, eds. *War and Peace in Europe.* 3 vols. Münster, 1998.

Butler, Jon. *Awash in a Sea of Faith: Christianizing the American People.* Cambridge, MA, and London, 1990.

Butzer, Karl W. *Early Hydraulic Civilization in Egypt: A Study in Cultural Ecology.* Chicago, 1976.

———. *Environment and Archaeology: An Ecological Approach to Prehistory.* Chicago, 1971.

Calvin, John. *The Commentaries of John Calvin on the Old Testament.* 30 vols. Westminster, UK, 1643–48.

Cameron, Euan, ed. *Early Modern Europe: An Oxford History.* Oxford, 1999.

———. "The Power of the Word: Renaissance and Reformation." In Cameron, *Early Modern Europe.*

Campbell, Joseph. *Historical Atlas of World Mythologies.* 2 vols. New York, 1988.

———, with Bill Moyers. *The Power of Myth.* New York, 1988.

Caner, Daniel. *Wandering, Begging Monks: Spiritual Authority and the Promotion of Monasticism in Late Antiquity.* Berkeley, Los Angeles, and London, 2002.

Cantor, Norman. *The Sacred Chain: A History of the Jews.* New York, 1994; London, 1995.

Cardini, Franco. "The Warrior and the Knight." In James Le Goff, ed., *The Medieval World,* trans. Lydia C. Cochrane. London, 1990.

Carlen, Claudia, ed. *The Papal Encyclicals, 1740–1981.* 5 vols. Falls Church, VA, 1981.

Carlyle, Thomas, ed. *Oliver Cromwell's Letters and Speeches.* 3 vols. New York, 1871.

Carmichael, Calum M. *The Laws of Deuteronomy.* Eugene, OR, 1974.

———. *The Spirit of Biblical Law.* Athens, GA, 1996.

Carrasco, David. *City of Sacrifice: The Aztec Empire and the Role of Violence in Civilization.* Boston, 1999.

Carrithers, Michael. *The Buddha.* Oxford and New York, 1983.

Carter, Warren. "Construction of Violence and Identities in Matthew's Gospel." In Shelly Matthews and E. Leigh Gibson, eds., *Violence in the New Testament.* New York and London, 2005.

———. *Matthew and the Margins: A Socio-Political and Religious Reading.* Sheffield, UK, 2000.

Cavanaugh, William T. *Migrations of the Holy: God, State and the Political Meaning of the Church.* Grand Rapids, MI, 2011.

———. *The Myth of Religious Violence.* Oxford, 2009.

Chang, Kwang-chih. *Archaeology of Ancient China.* New Haven, CT, 1968.

———. *Art, Myth and Ritual: The Path to Political Authority in Ancient China.* Cambridge, MA, 1985.

———. *Shang Civilization.* New Haven, CT, 1980.

Childs, John. *Armies and Warfare in Europe, 1648–1789.* Manchester, UK, 1985.

Ching, Julia. *Mysticism and Kingship in China: The Heart of Chinese Wisdom.* Cambridge, UK, 1997.

Choueiri, Youssef M. *Islamic Fundamentalism.* London, 1970.

Churchill, Ward. *A Little Matter of Genocide: Holocaust and Denial in the Americas, 1492 to the Present.* San Francisco, 1997.

Cipolla, Carlo M. *Before the Industrial Revolution: European Society and Economy, 1000–1700.* New York, 1976.

Clark, Peter. *Zoroastrianism: An Introduction to an Ancient Faith.* Brighton, UK, and Portland, OR, 1998.

Clarke, I. F. *Voices Prophesying War: Future Wars, 1763–3749.* 2nd ed. Oxford and New York, 1992.

Clements, R. E., ed. *The World of Ancient Israel: Sociological, Anthropological and Political Perspectives.* Cambridge, UK, 1989.

Clifford, Richard J. *The Cosmic Mountain in Canaan and the Old Testament.* Cambridge, MA, 1972.

Cogan, Mordechai, and Israel Ephal, eds. *Studies in Assyrian History and Ancient Near Eastern Historiography.* Jerusalem, 1991.

Cohen, Mark Nathan. *The Food Crisis in Prehistory.* New Haven, CT, 1978.

Cohn, Norman. *Cosmos, Chaos and the World to Come: The Ancient Roots of Apocalyptic Faith.* New Haven, CT, and London, 1993.

———. *Europe's Inner Demons: The Demonization of Christians in the Middle Ages.* London, 1975.

———. *The Pursuit of the Millennium: Revolutionary Millenarians and Mystical Anarchists in the Middle Ages.* London, 1984 ed.

———. *Warrant for Genocide.* London, 1967.

Colby, Elbridge. "How to Fight Savage Tribes." *American Journal of International Law* 21, no. 2 (1927).

Collins, Steven. *Selfless Persons: Imagery and Thought in Theravada Buddhism.* Cambridge, UK, 1982.

Contamine, Philippe. *War in the Middle Ages.* Trans. Michael Jones. Oxford, 1984.

Conze, Edward. *Buddhism: Its Essence and Development.* Oxford, 1981.

———. *Buddhist Meditation.* London, 1956.

Cook, David. "Jihad and Martyrdom in Islamic History." In Andrew R. Murphy, ed., *The Blackwell Companion to Religion and Violence.* Chichester, UK, 2011.

———. *Understanding Jihad.* Berkeley, Los Angeles, and London, 2005.

Cook, Jill. *The Swimming Reindeer.* London, 2010.

Coomaraswamy, Ananda, and Sister Nivedita. *Myths of the Hindus and Buddhists.* London, 1967.

Cooper, Thia. "Liberation Theology and the Spiral of Violence." In Andrew R. Murphy, ed., *The Blackwell Companion to Religion and Violence.* Chichester, UK, 2011.

Coote, Robert, and Keith E. Whitelam. *The Emergence of Early Israel in Historical Perspective.* Sheffield, 1987.

Cotton, Bruce. *Grant Takes Command.* Boston, 1968.

Coulborn, Rushton, ed. *Feudalism in History.* Hamden, CT, 1965.

Cowdrey. H. E. J. "The Peace and Truce of God in the Eleventh Century." *Past and Present* 46 (1970).

———. "Pope Gregory VII's 'Crusading' Plans of 1074." In B. Z. Kedar, H. E. Mayer, and R. C. Smail, eds., *Outremer.* Jerusalem, 1982.

Crecelius, Daniel, "Nonideological Responses of the Egyptian Ulema to Modernization." In Nikki R. Keddie, ed., *Scholars, Saints and Sufis: Muslim Religious Institutions in the Middle East Since 1500.* Berkeley, Los Angeles, and London, 1972.

Creel, H. G. *Confucius: The Man and the Myth.* London, 1951.

Crenshaw, Martha, ed. "Reflections on the Effects of Terrorism." In Crenshaw, *Terrorism, Legitimacy, and Power.*

——. *Terrorism, Legitimacy, and Power: The Consequences of Political Violence.* Middletown, CT, 1983.

Cribb, Roger. *Nomads and Archaeology.* Cambridge, UK, 1999.

Crooke, Alastair. *Resistance: The Essence of the Islamist Revolution.* London, 2009.

Cross, Frank Moore. *Canaanite Myth and Hebrew Epic: Essays in the History of the Religion of Israel.* Cambridge, MA, and London, 1973.

Crossan, John Dominic. *God and Empire: Jesus Against Rome, Then and Now.* New York, 2007.

——. *Jesus: A Revolutionary Biography.* New York, 1994.

Crouzet, Denis. *Les guerriers de Dieu: La violence au temps des troubles de religion.* Seyssel, 1990.

Crusemann, Frank. *The Torah: Theology and Social History of Old Testament Law.* Trans. Allen W. Mahnke. Minneapolis, 1996.

Curtis, John. *The Cyrus Cylinder and Ancient Persia: A New Beginning for the Middle East.* London, 2013.

Dalley, Stephanie, trans. and ed. *Myths from Mesopotamia: Creation, The Flood, Gilgamesh, and Others.* Oxford and New York, 1989.

Daniel, Norman. *The Arabs and Medieval Europe.* London and Beirut, 1975.

——. *Islam and the West: The Making of an Image.* 2nd ed. Oxford, 1993.

Davidson, Basil. *The African Slave Trade.* Boston, 1961.

Davis, Natalie Zemon. "The Rites of Violence: Religious Riot in Sixteenth-Century France," *Past and Present* 59 (1973).

Dawkins, Richard. *The God Delusion.* London, 2007.

Dearman, Andrew, ed. *Studies in the Mesha Inscription and Moab.* Atlanta, 1989.

DeLong-Bas, Natana J. *Wahhabi Islam: From Revival and Reform to Global Jihad.* Cairo, 2005.

Dever, William G. *What Did the Biblical Writers Know and When Did They Know It? What Archaeology Can Tell Us About the Reality of Ancient Israel.* Grand Rapids, MI, and Cambridge, UK, 2001.

Diakonoff, I. M. *Ancient Mesopotamia: Socio-Economic History.* Moscow, 1969.

Diefendort, Barbara. *Beneath the Cross: Catholics and Huguenots in Sixteenth-Century Paris.* New York, 1991.

Doniger, Wendy. *The Hindus: An Alternative History.* Oxford, 2009.

Donne, John. *Sermons of John Donne.* Ed. George R. Potter and Evelyn M. Simpson. Berkeley, CA, 1959.

Donner, F. *The Early Islamic Conquests.* Princeton, NJ, 1980.

——. "The Origins of the Islamic State." *Journal of the American Oriental Society* 106 (1986).

Dorrell, P. "The Uniqueness of Jericho." In P. R. S. Moorey and P. J. Parr, eds., *Archaeology in the Levant: Essays for Kathleen Kenyon.* Warminster, UK, 1978.

Douglas, Mary. *In the Wilderness: The Doctrine of Defilement in the Book of Numbers.* Oxford and New York, 2001.

——. *Leviticus as Literature.* Oxford and New York, 1999.

Drake, Harold A. *Constantine and the Bishops: The Politics of Intolerance.* Baltimore, 2000.

——. *In Praise of Constantine: A Historical Study and New Translation of Eusebius' Tricennial Orations.* London and New York, 1997.

Dronke, Peter, ed. and trans. *Women Writers of the Middle Ages: A Critical Study of Texts from Perpetua († 203) to Marguerite Porete († 1310).* Cambridge, MA, 1984.

Dubuisson, Daniel. *The Western Construction of Religion: Myths, Knowledge, and Ideology.* Trans. William Sayers. Baltimore, 2003.

Duby, Georges. *The Chivalrous Society*. London, 1977.
————. *The Early Growth of the European Economy: Warriors and Peasants from the Seventh to the Twelfth Century*. Trans. H. B. Clarke. Ithaca, NY, 1974.
————. *The Knight, the Lady and the Priest*. Harmondsworth, UK, 1983.
————. *The Three Orders: Feudal Society Imagined*. London, 1980.
Dumezil, Georges. *The Destiny of the Warrior*. Trans. Alf Hiltebeitel. Chicago and London, 1969.
Dumont, Louis. "World Renunciation in Indian Religions." *Contributions to Indian Sociology* 4 (1960).
Dundas, Paul. *The Jains*. London and New York, 2002.
Dunn, Richard. *The Age of Religious Wars, 1559–1689*. New York, 1970.
Durkheim, Émile. *The Elementary Forms of the Religious Life*. Trans. Joseph Swain. Glencoe, IL, 1915.
Dutton, P. E. *Carolingian Civilization*. Peterborough, ON, 1993.
Dwight, Timothy. *A Valedictory Address to the Young Gentlemen Who Commenced Bachelor of Arts, July 27, 1776*. New Haven, CT, 1776.
Dworkin, Anthony. "The Laws of War in the Age of Asymmetric Conflict." In George Kassimeris, ed., *The Barbarization of Warfare*. London, 2006.
Dwyer, Philip G. *Talleyrand*. London, 2002.
Eberhard, W. *A History of China*. London, 1977.
Edbury, Peter W., ed. *Crusade and Settlement*. Cardiff, 1985.
Edwards, Mark, trans. *Optatus: Against the Donatists*. Liverpool, UK, 1997.
Egerton, Frazer. *Jihad in the West: The Rise of Militant Salafism*. Cambridge, UK, 2011.
Ehrenberg, Margaret. *Women in Prehistory*. London, 1989.
Ehrenreich, Barbara. *Blood Rites: Origins and History of the Passions of War*. New York, 1997.
Eibl-Eibesfeldt, Irenöus. *The Biology of Peace and War: Man, Animals and Aggression*. New York, 1979.
————. *Human Ethology*. New York, 1989.
Eidelberg, Shlomo, trans. and ed. *The Jews and the Crusaders: The Hebrew Chronicles of the First and Second Crusades*. London, 1977.
Eisen, Robert. *The Peace and Violence of Judaism: From the Bible to Modern Zionism*. Oxford, 2011.
Eisenstadt, S. N., ed. *The Origins and Diversity of Axial Age Civilizations*. Albany, NY, 1986.
El-Guindy, Fedwa. "The Killing of Sadat and After: A Current Assessment of Egypt's Islamist Movement." *Middle East Insight* 2 (January/February 1982).
Eliade, Mircea. *A History of Religious Ideas*. 3 vols. Trans. Willard R. Trask. Chicago and London, 1978, 1982, 1985.
————. *The Myth of the Eternal Return, or, Cosmos and History*. Trans. Willard R. Trask. Princeton, NJ, 1991.
————. *Patterns in Comparative Religion*. Trans. Rosemary Sheed. London, 1958.
————. *The Sacred and the Profane: The Nature of Religion*. Trans. Willard R. Trask. San Diego, New York, and London, 1957.
————. *Yoga: Immortality and Freedom*. Trans. Willard R. Trask. London, 1958.
Elisseeff, N. *Nur al-Din: Un grand prince musulman de Syrie au temps des Croisades*. 3 vols. Damascus, 1967.
Elkins, Stanley. *Slavery: A Problem of American Institutional and Intellectual Life*. Chicago, 1976.
Elon, Amos. *The Israelis: Founders and Sons*. 2nd ed. London, 1981.
Elvin, Mark. "Was There a Transcendental Breakthrough in China?" In S. N. Eisenstadt, ed., *The Origins and Diversity of Axial Age Civilizations*. Albany, NY, 1986.
English, Richard. *Terrorism: How to Respond*. Oxford and New York, 2009.

Epsztein, Léon. *Social Justice in the Ancient Near East and the People of the Bible*. Trans. John Bowden. London, 1986.

Erdmann, Carl. *The Origin of the Idea of Crusade*. Trans. Marshall W. Baldwin and Walter Goffart. Princeton, NJ, 1977.

Ertman, Thomas. *Birth of the Leviathan: Building States and Regimes in Early Modern Europe*. Cambridge, UK, 1997.

Eshman, Milton, and Shibley Telhami, eds. *International Organization of Ethnic Conflict*. Ithaca, NY, 1994.

Esposito, John L. "Islam and Muslim Politics." In Esposito, *Voices of Resurgent Islam*.

———. *Unholy War: Terror in the Name of Islam*. New York and Oxford, 2002.

———, ed. *Voices of Resurgent Islam*. New York and Oxford, 1983.

———, and John J. Donohue, eds. *Islam in Transition: Muslim Perspectives*. New York, 1982.

———, and Dahlia Mogahed. *Who Speaks for Islam? What a Billion Muslims Really Think*. New York, 2007.

Euben, Roxanne. "Killing (for) Politics: Jihad, Martyrdom, Political Action." *Political Theory* 30 (2002).

Eusebius. *Life of Constantine*. Trans. Averil Cameron and Stuart G. Hall. Oxford, 1999.

Fakhry, Majid. *A History of Islamic Philosophy*. New York and London, 1970.

Fairbank, John King, and Merle Goldman. *China: A New History*. 2nd ed. Cambridge, MA, and London, 2006.

Fall, A. *Medieval and Renaissance Origins: Historiographical Debates and Demonstrations*. London, 1991.

Fandy, Mahmoun. *Saudi Arabia and the Politics of Dissent*. New York, 1999.

Fatoric, Clement. "The Anti-Catholic Roots of Liberal and Republican Conception of Freedom in English Political Thought." *Journal of the History of Ideas* 66 (January 2005).

Fensham, F. C. "Widows, Orphans and the Poor in Ancient Eastern Legal and Wisdom Literature." *Journal of Near Eastern Studies* 21 (1962).

Ferguson, Niall. *Colossus: The Price of America's Empire*. New York, 2004.

———. *Empire: How Britain Made the Modern World*. London, 2003.

———. "An Empire in Denial: The Limits of U.S. Imperialism." *Harvard International Review* 25 (Fall 2003).

Fernández-Armesto, Felipe. *1492: The Year the Four Corners of the Earth Collided*. New York, 2009.

Fichte, Johann Gottlieb. *Addresses to the German Nation*. Trans. and ed. Gregory Moore. Cambridge, UK, 2008.

Fingarette, Herbert. *Confucius: The Secular as Sacred*. New York, 1972.

Finkelstein, Israel, and Neil Asher Silberman. *The Bible Unearthed: Archaeology's New Vision of Ancient Israel and the Origin of Its Sacred Texts*. New York, 2001.

Finley, M. I., ed. *Studies in Ancient Society*. London and Boston, 1974.

Finn, Melissa. *Al-Qaeda and Sacrifice: Martyrdom, War and Politics*. London, 2012.

Firestone, Reuven. *Holy War in Judaism: The Fall and Rise of a Controversial Idea*. Oxford and New York, 2012.

———. *Jihad: The Origin of the Holy War in Islam*. Oxford and New York, 1999.

Fisch, Harold. *The Zionist Revolution: A New Perspective*. Tel Aviv and London, 1978.

Fischer, Louis, ed. *The Essential Gandhi*. New York, 1962.

Fischer, Michael J. "Imam Khomeini: Four Levels of Understanding." In John L. Esposito, ed., *Voices of Resurgent Islam*. New York and Oxford, 1980.

———. *Iran: From Religious Dispute to Revolution*. Cambridge, MA, and London, 1980.

Fishbane, Michael. *The Garments of Torah: Essays in Biblical Hermeneutics*. Bloomington and Indianapolis, 1989.

Fitzgerald, Timothy. *The Ideology of Religious Studies*. Oxford, 2000.

————, ed. *Religion and the Secular: Historical and Colonial Formations.* London and Oakville, CT, 2007.

Flood, Gavin. *An Introduction to Hinduism.* Cambridge, UK, and New York, 1996.

————, ed. *The Blackwell Companion to Hinduism.* Oxford, 2003.

Floor, Willem M. "The Revolutionary Character of the Ulema: Wishful Thinking or Reality?" In Nikki R. Keddie, ed., *Religion and Politics in Islam: Shiism from Quietism to Revolution.* New Haven, CT, and London, 1983.

Force, Peter. *Tracts.* New York, 1844.

Fossier, Robert, ed. *The Middle Ages.* 2 vols. Trans. Janet Sondheimer. Cambridge, UK, 1989.

Fowden, Garth. *Empire to Commonwealth: Consequences of Monotheism in Late Antiquity.* Princeton, NJ, 1993.

Fowles, John. *The Magus, Revised Edition.* London, 1997.

Fox, Everett, trans. *The Five Books of Moses.* New York, 1990.

Francisco de Vitoria. *Political Writings.* Ed. Anthony Pagden and Jeremy Lawrence. Cambridge, UK, 1991.

Frankfort, H., and H. A. Frankfort, eds. *The Intellectual Adventure of Ancient Man: An Essay on Speculative Thought in the Ancient Near East.* Chicago, 1946.

Frayne, Sean. *Galilee: From Alexander the Great to Hadrian, 323 BCE–135 CE: A Study of Second Temple Judaism.* Notre Dame, IN, 1980.

Frend, W. H. C. *Martyrdom and Persecution in the Early Church: A Study of a Conflict from the Maccabees to Donatus.* Oxford, 1965.

Fried, M. H. *The Evolution of Political Society: An Essay in Political Anthropology.* New York, 1967.

Fulcher of Chartres. *A History of the Expedition to Jerusalem, 1098–1127.* Trans. and ed. Frances Rita Ryan. Knoxville, TN, 1969.

Fuller, Robert C. *Naming the Antichrist: The History of an American Obsession.* Oxford and New York, 1995.

Fung, Yu Lan. *A Short History of Chinese Philosophy.* Ed. and trans. Derk Bodde. New York, 1976.

Gabrieli, Francesco, ed. and trans. *Arab Historians of the Crusades.* Trans. from the Italian by E. J. Costello. London, 1969.

Gaddis, Michael. *There Is No Crime for Those Who Have Christ: Religious Violence in the Christian Roman Empire.* Berkeley, Los Angeles, and London, 2005.

Gaffney, Patrick D. *The Prophet's Pulpit: Islamic Preaching in Contemporary Egypt.* Berkeley, Los Angeles, and London, 1994.

Galambush, Julia. *The Reluctant Parting: How the New Testament Jewish Writers Created a Christian Book.* San Francisco, 2005.

Garlan, Yvon. *War in the Ancient World: A Social History.* London, 1975.

Garnsey, Peter. *Famine and Food Shortage in the Greco-Roman World.* Cambridge, UK, 1988.

Gaustad, Edwin S. *Faith of Our Fathers: Religion and the New Nation.* San Francisco, 1987.

Gauvreau, Michael. "Between Awakening and Enlightenment." In *The Evangelical Century: College and Creed in English Canada from the Great Revival to the Great Depression.* Kingston, ON, and Montreal, 1991.

Gearty, C. *Terrorism.* Aldershot, UK, 1996.

Gellner, Ernst. *Nations and Nationalism (New Perspectives on the Past).* 2nd ed., with an introduction by John Breuilly. Oxford, 2006.

Gentili, Alberico. *The Rights of War and Peace, in Three Books.* London, 1738.

Geoffroi de Charny. *The Book of Chivalry of Geoffroi de Charny: Text, Context and Translation.* Trans. Richard W. Kaeuper and Elspeth Huxley. Philadelphia, 1996.

George, Andrew. *The Epic of Gilgamesh: The Babylonian Epic Poem and Other Texts in Akkadian and Sumerian.* London and New York, 1999.

Gerassi, J., ed. *Revolutionary Priest: The Complete Writings and Messages of Camilo Torres*. New York, 1971.

Gernet, Jacques. *Ancient China: From the Beginnings to the Empire*. Trans. Raymond Rudorff. London, 1968.

———. *A History of Chinese Civilization*. 2nd ed. Ed. and trans. J. R. Foster and Charles Hartman. Cambridge, UK, and New York, 1996.

Gerth, H. H., and C. Wright Mills, eds. *From Max Weber*. London, 1948.

Ghose, Aurobindo. *Essays on the Gita*. Pondichery, 1972.

Ghosh, A. *The City in Early Historical India*. Simla, 1973.

Giddens, Anthony. *The Consequences of Modernity*. Cambridge, UK, 1991.

———. *The Nation-State and Violence*. Berkeley, CA, 1987.

Gil, Moshe. *A History of Palestine, 634–1099*. Trans. Ethel Broido. Cambridge, UK, 1992.

Gilbert, Paul. *The Compassionate Mind: A New Approach to Life's Challenges*. London, 2009.

Gillingham, J., and J. C. Holt, eds. *War and Government in the Middle Ages: Essays in Honour of J. O. Prestwich*. Woodbridge, UK, and Totowa, NJ, 1984.

Girard, Rene. *Violence and the Sacred*. Trans. Patrick Gregory. Baltimore, 1977.

Glatzer, Nahum. "The Concept of Peace in Classical Judaism." In *Essays on Jewish Thought*. University, AL, 1978.

Gold, Daniel. "Organized Hinduisms: From Vedic Truth to Hindu Nation." In Martin E. Marty and R. Scott Appleby, eds. *Fundamentalisms Observed*. Chicago and London, 1991.

Golwalkar, M. S. *We or Our Nationhood Defined*. Nagpur, 1939.

Gombrich, Richard F. *How Buddhism Began: The Conditioned Genesis of the Early Teachings*. London and Atlantic Highlands, NJ, 1996.

———. *Theravada Buddhism: A Social History from Ancient Benares to Modern Colombo*. London and New York, 1988.

Gonda, Jan. *Change and Continuity in Indian Tradition*. The Hague, 1965.

———. *The Vision of the Vedic Poets*. The Hague, 1963.

Gottwald, Norman K. *The Hebrew Bible: A Brief Socio-Literary Introduction*. Minneapolis, 2009.

———. *The Hebrew Bible in Its Social World and in Ours*. Atlanta, 1993.

———. *The Politics of Ancient Israel*. Louisville, KY, 2001.

———. *The Tribes of Yahweh*. Maryknoll, NY, 1979.

———, ed. *The Bible of Liberation: Political and Social Hermeneutics*. Maryknoll, NY, 1983.

Graham, A. C. *Disputers of the Tao: Philosophical Argument in Ancient China*. La Salle, IL, 1989.

———. *Early Mohist Logic, Ethics and Science*. Hong Kong, 1978.

Granet, Marcel. *Chinese Civilization*. Trans. Kathleen Innes and Mabel Brailsford. London and New York, 1951.

———. *Festivals and Songs of Ancient China*. Trans. E. D. Edwards. London, 1932.

———. *The Religion of the Chinese People*. Trans. and ed. Maurice Freedman. Oxford, 1975.

Grayson, A. K. *Assyrian Royal Inscriptions*. 2 vols. Wiesbaden, 1972.

Gregory, Brad S. *Salvation at Stake: Christian Martyrdom in Early Modern Europe*. Cambridge, MA, and London, 1999.

Greer, Donald. *The Incidence of Terror in the French Revolution*. Gloucester, MA, 1935.

Greil, Arthur L., and David G. Bromley, eds. *Defining Religion: Investigating the Boundaries Between the Sacred and the Secular*. Oxford, 2003.

Griffith, Ralph T. H., trans. *The Rig Veda*. Rpt. New York, 1992.

Grossman, Lt. Col. David. *On Killing: The Psychological Cost of Learning to Kill in War and Society*. Rev. ed. New York, 2009.

Grotius, Hugo. *Rights of War and Peace: In Ten Books*. London, 1738.

Guelke, A. *The Age of Terrorism and the International Political System*. London, 2008.

Guibert of Nogent. *Monodies and On the Relics of Saints: The Autobiography and a Manifesto of a French Monk from the Time of the Crusades*. Ed. and trans. Joseph McAlhany and Jay Rubenstein. London and New York, 2011.

Guillaume, A., trans. and ed. *The Life of Muhammad: A Translation of Ishaq's Sirat Rasul Allah*. London, 1955.

Gunn, David E. "Religion, Law and Violence." In Andrew R. Murphy, ed., *The Blackwell Companion to Religion and Violence*. Chichester, UK, 2011.

Gunn, Steven. "War, Religion and the State." In Euan Cameron, ed., *Early Modern Europe: An Oxford History*. Oxford, 1999.

Gunning, Jeroen. "Rethinking Religion and Violence in the Middle East." In Andrew R. Murphy, ed., *The Blackwell Companion to Religion and Violence*. Chichester, UK, 2011.

Hadas-Lebel, Mireille. *Jerusalem Against Rome*. Trans. Robyn Freshunt. Leuven, 2006.

Haddad, Yvonne K. "Sayyid Qutb: Ideologue of Islamic Revival." In John L. Esposito, ed., *Voices of Resurgent Islam*. New York and Oxford, 1980.

Hafkesbrink, Hanna. *Unknown Germany: An Inner Chronicle of the First World War Based on Letters and Diaries*. New Haven, CT, 1948.

Haldon, John. *Warfare, State and Society in the Byzantine World, 565–1204*. London and New York, 2005.

Harmon, C. C. *Terrorism Today*. London, 2008.

Harris, J., ed. *The Anthropology of War*. Cambridge, UK, 1990.

Harris, Marvin. *Cannibals and Kings: The Origins of Cultures*. New York, 1977.

———. *Our Kind: Who We Are, Where We Come From, and Where We Are Going*. New York, 1989.

Harris, William. *War and Imperialism in Republican Rome*. Oxford, 1979.

Harvey, A. E. *Strenuous Commands: The Ethic of Jesus*. London and Philadelphia, 1990.

Hassig, Ross. *War and Society in Ancient Mesopotamia*. Berkeley, CA, 1992.

Hatch, Nathan O. *The Democratization of American Christianity*. New Haven, CT, 1989.

———. *The Sacred Cause of Liberty: Republican Thought and the Millennium in Revolutionary New England*. New Haven, CT, 1977.

Hauser, Henri. "Political Anarchy and Social Discontent." In J. H. M. Salmon, ed., *The French Wars of Religion: How Important Were Religious Factors?* Lexington, MA, 1967.

Hayes, Carlton J. H. *Essays on Nationalism*. New York, 1926.

———. *Nationalism: A Religion*. New York, 1960.

Hazony, Yoram. *The Philosophy of Hebrew Scripture*. Cambridge, UK, 2012.

Head, Thomas, and Richard Landes, eds. *The Peace of God: Social Violence and Religious Response in France Around the Year 1000*. Ithaca, NY, 1992.

Heck, Paul, L. "*Jihad* Revisited." *Journal of Religious Ethics* 32, no. 1 (2004).

Hedges, Chris. *War Is a Force That Gives Us Meaning*. New York, 2003.

Heesterman, J. C. *The Broken World of Sacrifice: An Essay in Ancient Indian Religion*. Chicago and London, 1993.

———. *The Inner Conflict of Tradition: Essays on Indian Ritual, Kingship and Society*. Chicago and London, 1985.

———. "Ritual, Revelation and the Axial Age." In S. N. Eisenstadt, ed., *The Origins and Diversity of Axial Age Civilizations*. Albany, NY, 1986.

Hegel, G. W. F. *Elements of the Philosophy of Right*. Ed. Allen W. Wood. Trans. H. B. Nisbet. Cambridge, UK, 1991.

Hegghammer, Thomas. *Jihad in Saudi Arabia: Violence and Pan-Islamism Since 1979*. Cambridge, UK, 2010.

Heikal, Mohamed. *Autumn of Fury: The Assassination of Sadat*. London, 1984.

Heilman, Samuel. "Guides of the Faithful: Contemporary Religious Zionist Rabbis." In R. Scott Appleby, ed., *Spokesmen for the Despised: Fundamentalist Leaders of the Middle East*. Chicago, 1997.

Heimart, Alan. *Religion and the American Mind: From the Great Awakening to the Revolution* Cambridge, MA, 1968.

———, and Andrew Delbanco, eds. *The Puritans in America: A Narrative Anthology*. Cambridge, MA, and London, 1985.

Heller, Henry. *Iron and Blood: Civil Wars in Sixteenth-Century France*. Montreal, 1991.

Hengel, Martin. *Judaism and Hellenism: Studies in Their Encounter in Palestine During the Early Hellenistic Period*. 2 vols. Trans. John Bowden. London, 1974.

Henry of Lancaster. *Le Livre de Seyntz Medicines: The Unpublished Treatises of Henry of Lancaster*. Trans. A. J. Arnold. Oxford, 1940.

Herbert, Edward, Lord. *De Religio Laici*. Trans. and ed. Harold L. Hutcheson. New Haven, CT, 1944.

———. *De Veritate*. Trans. Mayrick H. Carre. Bristol, UK, 1937.

Herrenschmidt, Clarisse. "Designations de l'empire et concepts politiques de Darius Ier d'après inscriptions en vieux perse." *Studia Iranica* 5 (1976).

Herzl, Theodor. *The Complete Diaries of Theodor Herzl*. 2 vols. Ed. R. Patai. London and New York, 1960.

Hill, Rosalind, trans. *The Deeds of the Franks and Other Pilgrims to Jerusalem*. London, 1962.

Hillenbrand, Carole. *The Crusades: Islamic Perspectives*. Edinburgh, 1999.

Hillgarth, J. N. *Ramon Lull and Lullism in Fourteenth-Century France*. Oxford, 1971.

Hiltebeitel, Alf. *The Ritual of Battle: Krishna in the Mahabharata*. Ithaca and London, 1976.

Hiltermann, Joos R. *A Poisonous Affair: America, Iraq and the Gassing of Halabja*. Cambridge, UK, 2007.

Himmelfarb, Gertrude. *The Roads to Modernity*. New York, 2001.

Hobbes, Thomas. *Behemoth; or, The Long Parliament*. Ed. Frederick Tönnies. Chicago, 1990.

———. *Leviathan*. Ed. Richard Tuck. Cambridge, UK, 1991.

———. *On the Citizen*. Ed. Richard Tuck and Michael Silverthorne. Cambridge, UK, 1998.

Hobsbaum, E. J. *Bandits*. Rev. ed. New York, 1985.

———. *Primitive Rebels*. New York, 1965.

Hodge, Charles. *What Is Darwinism?* Princeton, NJ, 1874.

Hodgson, Marshall G. S. *The Venture of Islam: Conscience and History in a World Civilization*. 3 vols. Chicago and London, 1974.

Hoffman, Bruce. *Inside Terrorism*. London, 1998.

Hoffner, H. "History and the Historians of the Ancient Near East: The Hittites," *Orientalia* 49 (1980).

Holt, Mack P. *The French Wars of Religion, 1562–1629*. Cambridge, UK, 1995.

———. "Putting Religion Back into the Wars of Religion." *French Historical Studies* 18, no. 2 (Autumn 1973).

Holt, P. M. *The Age of the Crusades*. London, 1986.

Homer. *The Iliad of Homer*. Trans. Richard Lattimore. Chicago and London, 1951.

———. *The Odyssey*. Trans. Walter Shewring with an introduction by G. S. Kirk. Oxford, 1980.

Hooke, S. H. *Middle Eastern Mythology: From the Assyrians to the Hebrews*. Harmondsworth, UK, 1963.

Hopkins, D. C. *The Highlands of Canaan*. Sheffield, UK, 1985.

Hopkins, Thomas J. *The Hindu Religious Traditions*. Belmont, CA, 1971.

Horgan, J. *The Psychology of Terrorism*. London, 2005.

Horsley, Richard A. "The Historical Context of Q." In Horsley and Draper, *Whoever Hears You Hears Me*.

———. *Jesus and the Spiral of Violence: Popular Jewish Resistance in Roman Palestine*. Minneapolis, 1993 ed.

———, with Jonathan A. Draper. *Whoever Hears You Hears Me: Prophets, Performance, and Tradition in Q*. Harrisburg, PA, 1999.

Hoselitz, Bert F. *Sociological Aspects of Economic Growth*. New York, 1960.

Hourani, Albert. *Arabic Thought in the Liberal Age, 1798–1939*. Oxford, 1962.

Housely, Norman. "Crusades Against Christians: Their Origin and Early Development." In Peter W. Edbury, ed. *Crusade and Settlement*. Cardiff, 1985.

———. *The Later Crusades, 1274–1558: From Lyons to Alcazar*. Oxford, 1992.

Howard, Michael. *The Invention of Peace: Reflections on War and International Order*. New Haven, CT, 2000.

Howe, Daniel Walker. "Religion and Politics in the Antebellum North." In Mark A. Noll, ed., *Religion and American Politics: From the Colonial Period to the 1980s*. Oxford and New York, 1990.

Hsu, C. Y., and K. M. Lindoff. *Western Chou Civilization*. New Haven, CT, 1988.

Hubert, Henry, and Marcel Mauss. *Sacrifice: Its Nature and Functions*. Trans. D. Halls. Chicago, 1964.

Hughes, Anne. *The Causes of the English Civil War*. London, 1998.

Huizinga, Johan. *Homo Ludens: A Study of the Play Element in Culture*. Boston, 1955 ed.

Humble, Richard. *Warfare in the Ancient World*. London, 1980.

Hutchinson, William T., and William M. E. Raphael, eds. *The Papers of James Madison*. 17 vols. Chicago, 1962–91.

Hutt, M. G. "The Role of the Cures in the Estates General of 1789." *Journal of Ecclesiastical History* 6 (1955).

Ibrahim, Raymond, ed. and trans. *The Al-Qaeda Reader*. New York, 2007.

Idinopulos, Thomas A., and Brian C. Wilson, eds. *What Is Religion? Origins, Definitions, and Explanations*. Leiden, 1998.

Isambert, François André, ed. *Recueil général des anciennes lois françaises depuis l'an 420 jusqu'à la Révolution de 1789*, vol. 12. Paris, n.d.

Izutsu, Toshihiko. *Ethico-Religious Concepts in the Qur'an*. Montreal and Kingston, ON, 2002.

Jackson, Kent P. "The Language of the Mesha Inscription." In Andrew Dearman ed., *Studies in the Mesha Inscription and Moab*. Atlanta, NY, 1989.

Jacobi, Hermann, trans. *Jaina Sutras*. New York, 1968.

Jacobs, Louis, ed. *The Jewish Religion: A Companion*. Oxford, 1995.

Jacobsen, Thorkold. "The Cosmic State." In H. and H. A. Frankfort, eds., *The Intellectual Adventure of Ancient Man: An Essay on Speculative Thought in the Near East*. Chicago, 1946.

Jaitner, J. "The Pope and the Struggle for Power During the Sixteenth and Seventeenth Centuries." In Klaus Bussman and Heinz Schilling, eds., *War and Peace in Europe*. 3 vols. Münster, 1998.

James, E. O. *The Ancient Gods: The History and Diffusion of Religion in the Ancient Near East and the Eastern Mediterranean*. London, 1960.

Jansen, Johannes J. G., trans. and ed. *The Neglected Duty*. New York, 1986.

Jaspers, Karl. *The Great Philosophers: The Foundations*. Ed. Hannah Arendt. Trans. Ralph Manheim. London, 1962.

———. *The Origin and Goal of History*. Trans. Michael Bullock. London, 1953.

Jay, Peter. *Road to Riches, or The Wealth of Man*. London, 2000.

Jayussi, May. "Subjectivity and Public Witness: An Analysis of Islamic Militance in Palestine." Unpublished paper, 2004.

Jeremias, J. *Jerusalem in the Time of Jesus*. London and Philadelphia, 1969.
———. *The Lord's Prayer*. Philadelphia, 1973.
John XXIII, Pope (Angelo Giuseppe Roncalli). *Mater et Magistra* and *Pacem in Terris*. In Claudia Carlen, ed., *The Papal Encyclicals, 1740–1981*. 5 vols. Falls Church, VA, 1981.
Johnson, Paul. *A History of the Jews*. London, 1987.
Jones, A. H. M. *The Later Roman Empire*. 2 vols. Oxford, 1964.
Jones, Kenneth W. "The Arya Samaj in British India." In Robert D. Baird, ed., *Religion in Modern India*. Delhi, 1981.
Josephus, Flavius. *The Antiquities of the Jews*. Trans. William Whiston. Marston Gale, UK, n.d.
———. *The Jewish War*. Trans. G. A. Williamson. Harmondsworth, UK, 1967.
Juergensmeyer, Mark. *Global Rebellion: Religious Challenges to the Secular State from Christian Militias to Al-Qaeda*. Berkeley, CA, 2008.
———. *The New Cold War? Religious Nationalism Confronts the Secular State*. Berkeley, CA, 1993.
———. *Terror in the Mind of God: The Global Rise of Religious Violence*. Berkeley, Los Angeles, and London, 2001.
———, ed. *Violence and the Sacred in the Modern World*. London, 1992.
Kaeuper, Richard W. *Holy Warrior: The Religious Ideology of Chivalry*. Philadelphia, 2009.
Kahane, Meir. *Listen World, Listen Jew*. Tucson, 1978.
Kakar, Sudhir. *The Colors of Violence: Cultural Identities, Religion, and Conflict*. Chicago and London, 1996.
Kaltenmark, Max. *Lao-Tzu and Taoism*. Trans. Roger Greaves. Stanford, CA, 1969.
Kamen, Henry. *Empire: How Spain Became a World Power, 1492–1763*. New York, 2003.
———. *The Spanish Inquisition: An Historical Revision*. London, 1997.
Kant, Immanuel. *Critique of Pure Reason*. Trans. Norman Kemp Smith. London, 1993.
———. *Lectures on Ethics*. Trans. Lewis Infield. Ed. Lewis White Beck. New York, 1963.
Kantorowicz, K. "*Pro Patria Mori* in Medieval Political Thought." *American Historical Review* 56, no. 3 (1951).
Kapila, Shruti, and Faisal Devji, eds. *Political Thought in Action: The Bhagavad Gita and Modern India*. Cambridge, UK, 2013.
Kassimeris, George, ed. *The Barbarisation of Warfare*. London, 2006.
Kautsky, John H. *The Political Consequences of Modernization*. New York, London, Sydney, and Toronto, 1972.
———. *The Politics of Aristocratic Empires*. 2nd ed. New Brunswick, NJ, and London, 1997.
Keay, John. *India: A History*. London, 2000.
Kedar, Benjamin Z. *Crusade and Mission: European Approaches Toward Muslims*. Princeton, NJ, 1984.
———, H. E. Mayer, and R. C. Smail, eds. *Outremer: Studies in the History of the Crusading Kingdom of Jerusalem*. Jerusalem, 1982.
Keddie, Nikki R. *Roots of Revolution: An Interpretive History of Modern Iran*. New Haven, CT, and London, 1981.
———, ed. *Religion and Politics in Iran: Shiism from Quietism to Revolution*. New Haven, CT, and London, 1983.
———. *Scholars, Saints and Sufis: Muslim Religious Institutions in the Middle East Since 1500*. Berkeley, Los Angeles, and London, 1972.
Keegan, John. *The Face of Battle*. London, 1976.
———. *A History of Warfare*. London and New York, 1993.
Keen, Maurice. *Chivalry*. New Haven, CT, and London, 1984.
Keightley, David N., ed. *The Origins of Chinese Civilization*. Berkeley, CA, 1983.

Kenyon, Kathleen. *Digging Up Jericho: The Results of the Jericho Excavations, 1953–56.* New York, 1957.

Kepel, Gilles. *Beyond Terror and Martyrdom: The Future of the Middle East.* Trans. Pascale Ghazaleh. Cambridge, MA, and London, 2008.

———. *Jihad: The Trail of Political Islam.* Trans. Anthony F. Roberts. 4th ed. London, 2009.

———. *The Prophet and Pharaoh: Muslim Extremism in Egypt.* Trans. Jon Rothschild. London, 1985.

———, and Jean-Pierre Milleli, eds. *Al-Qaeda in Its Own Words.* Trans. Pascale Ghazaleh. Cambridge, MA, 2008.

Kerr, Ronald Dale. "'Why Should You Be So Furious?': The Violence of the Pequot War." *Journal of American History* 85, no. 3 (December 1998).

Kertzer, David I. *Ritual, Politics and Power.* New Haven, CT, and London, 1988.

Khomeini, Sayeed Ruhollah. *Islam and Revolution.* Trans. and ed. Hamid Algar. Berkeley, CA, 1981.

Khrosrokhavar, Farhad. *Suicide Bombers: Allah's New Martyrs.* Trans. David Macey. London, 2005.

Kierman, Frank A., Jr., and John K. Fairbank, eds. *Chinese Ways in Warfare.* Cambridge, MA, 1974.

Kimball, Charles. *When Religion Becomes Evil.* San Francisco, 2002.

Kimelman, K. "Non-violence in the Talmud." *Judaism* 17 (1968).

King, Martin Luther, Jr. *Strength to Love.* Philadelphia, 1963.

Kramer, Martin. "Hizbullah: The Calculus of Jihad." In Martin E. Marty and R. Scott Appleby, eds., *Fundamentalisms and the State: Rethinking Polities, Economies and Militance.* Chicago and London, 1993.

Kramer, Samuel N. *History Begins at Sumer.* Philadelphia, 1981.

———. *Sumerian Mythology: A Study of the Spiritual and Literary Achievement of the Third Millennium BC.* Philadelphia, 1944.

Krauss, Hans-Joachim. *Worship in Israel: A Cultic History of the Old Testament.* Oxford, 1966.

Kreister, Fritz. *Four Weeks in the Trenches: The War Story of a Violinist.* Boston and New York, 1915.

Krey, August C., ed. and trans. *The First Crusade: The Accounts of Eye-Witnesses and Participants.* Princeton, NJ, and London, 1921.

Kritzeck, James. *Peter the Venerable and Islam.* Princeton, NJ, 1964.

Kselman, Thomas, ed. *Belief in History: Innovative Approaches to European and American Religion.* Notre Dame, IN, 1991.

Kulke, Hermann. "The Historical Background of India's Axial Age." In S. N. Eisenstadt, ed., *The Origins and Diversity of Axial Age Civilizations.* Albany, NY, 1986.

Kydd, A. H., and B. F. Walter. "The Stratagems of Terrorism." *International Security* 31, no. 1 (Summer 2006).

Lactantius. *Lactantius: Works.* Trans. William Fletcher. Edinburgh, 1971.

Lal, Deepak. *In Praise of Empires: Globalization and Order.* New York, 2004.

Lambert, W. G., and A. R. Millard, trans. and eds. *The Atra-Hasis: The Babylonian Story of the Flood.* Oxford, 1969.

Lane Fox, Robin. *Pagans and Christians.* London, 1986.

Lau, D. C., trans. and ed. *Mencius.* London, 1970.

———. *Tao Te Ching.* London, 1963.

Lawrence, T. E. *The Mint.* New York, 1963.

Lea, H. C. *A History of the Inquisition of the Middle Ages.* Philadelphia, 1866.

Leed, Eric J. *No Man's Land: Combat and Identity in World War I.* Cambridge, UK, 1979.

Lefeburem, Leo D. *Revelation, the Religions and Violence.* Maryknoll, NY, 2000.

Lefebvre, Genge. The Great Fear of 1789. Trans. R. R. Farmer and Joan White. Princeton, NJ, 1973.

Legge, J., trans. The Ch'un Ts'ew and the Tso Chuen. 2nd ed. Hong Kong, 1960.

———. The Li Ki. Oxford, 1885.

Le Goff, Jacques, ed. The Medieval World. Trans. Lydia C. Cochrane. London, 1990.

Leick, Gwendolyn. Mesopotamia: The Invention of the City. London, 2001.

Lemche, Niels P. Early Israel: Anthropological and Historical Studies on the Israelite Society Before the Monarchy. Leiden, 1985.

Lenski, Gerhard E. Power and Privilege: A Theory of Social Stratification. Chapel Hill, NC, and London, 1966.

LeRoi-Gourhan, Andre. Treasures of Prehistoric Art. Trans. Norbert Guterman. New York, 1967.

Le Strange, Guy. Palestine Under the Moslems: A Description of Syria and the Holy Land from AD 650 to 1500. London, 1890.

Levine, Lee I., ed. The Galilee in Late Antiquity. New York and Jerusalem, 1992.

Levene, Mark. Genocide in the Age of the Nation-State: The Rise of the West and the Coming of Genocide. London and New York, 2005.

Levenson, Joseph R., and Franz Schurmann. China: An Interpretive History: From the Beginnings to the Fall of Han. Berkeley, Los Angeles, and London, 1969.

Levinson, Bernard M. Deuteronomy and the Hermeneutics of Legal Innovation. Oxford and New York, 1998.

Lewis, Bernard. The Assassins. London, 1967.

———. "The Roots of Muslim Rage." Atlantic Monthly, September 1, 1990.

Lewis, James R., ed. Violence and New Religious Movements. Oxford, 2011.

Lewis, M. Ecstatic Religion: An Anthropological Study of Spirit Possession and Shamanism. Baltimore, 1971.

Lewis, Mark Edward. Sanctioned Violence in Early China. Albany, NY, 1990.

Libanius. Select Orations. Trans. A. F. Norman. 2 vols. Cambridge, MA, 1969, 1970.

Lim, Richard. Public Disputation, Power, and Social Order in Late Antiquity. Berkeley, CA, 1995.

Lincoln, Bruce. Death, War, and Sacrifice: Studies in Ideology and Practice. Chicago and London, 1991.

———. Holy Terrors: Thinking About Religion After September 11. 2nd ed. Chicago and London, 2006.

———. Religion, Empire, and Torture: The Case of Achaemenian Persia, with a Postscript on Abu Graib. Chicago and London, 2007.

———. "The Role of Religion in Achmenean Inscriptions." In Nicole Brisch, ed., Religion and Power: Divine Kingship in the Ancient World and Beyond. Chicago, 2008.

Lindberg, David, and Ronald L. Numbers, eds. God and Nature: Historical Essays on the Encounter Between Christianity and Science. Berkeley, Los Angeles, and London, 1986.

Ling, Trevor. The Buddha: Buddhist Civilization in India and Ceylon. London, 1973.

Lings, Martin. Muhammad: His Life Based on the Earliest Sources. London, 1983.

Livvi-Bacci, Massimo. A Concise History of World Population. Oxford, 1997.

Locke, John. Essays on the Law of Nature. Ed. W. van Leyden. Oxford, 1970.

———. A Letter Concerning Toleration. Indianapolis, 1955.

———. Political Writings. Ed. David Wootton. London, 1993.

———. Two Treatises of Government. Ed. Peter Laslett. Cambridge, UK, 1988.

Lovejoy, David S. Religious Enthusiasm in the New World: Heresy to Revolution. Cambridge, MA, and London, 1985.

Lowth, Andrew. Maximus the Confessor. London, 1996.

———. The Origins of Christian Mysticism: From Plato to Denys. London, 1975.

Lussu, Emilio. Sardinian Brigade. New York, 1939.

Luther, Martin. *Luther: Selected Political Writings.* Ed. J. M. Porter. Philadelphia, 1974.

Luttwak, Edward N. *The Grand Strategy of the Roman Empire.* Baltimore, 1976.

Lyons, M. C., and D. E. P. Jackson. *Saladin: The Politics of the Holy War.* Cambridge, UK, 1982.

Maaga, Mary. *Hearing the Voices of Jonestown.* Syracuse, NY, 1958.

Maalouf, Amin. *The Crusades Through Arab Eyes.* Trans. Jon Rothschild. London, 1984.

Macartney, C. A. *National States and National Minorities.* London, 1934.

MacGregor, Neil. *A History of the World in 100 Objects.* London and New York, 2010.

Machinist, Peter. "Distinctiveness in Ancient Israel." In Mordechai Cogan and Israel Ephal eds., *Studies in Assyrian History and Ancient Near Eastern Historiography.* Jerusalem, 1991.

MacMullen, Ramsey. *Christianity and Paganism in the Fourth to Eighth Centuries.* New Haven, CT, 1997.

———. *Christianizing the Roman Empire, AD 100–400.* New Haven, CT, 1984.

———. *The Second Church: Popular Christianity AD 200–400.* Atlanta, 2009.

Maltby, William. *The Reign of Charles V.* New York, 2002.

Marius, Richard. *Martin Luther: The Christian Between God and Death.* Cambridge, MA, and London, 1999.

Marsden, George. "Afterword." In Mark A. Noll, ed., *Religion and American Politics: From the Colonial Period to the 1980s.* Oxford and New York, 1990.

———. *Fundamentalism and American Culture: The Shaping of Twentieth-Century Evangelicalism, 1870–1925.* New York and Oxford, 1980.

Marshall, John W. "Collateral Damage: Jesus and Jezebel in the Jewish War." In Shelly Matthews and E. Leigh Gibson, eds., *Violence in the New Testament.* New York and London, 2005.

Martin, James D. "Israel as a Tribal Society." In R. E. Clements, ed., *The World of Ancient Israel: Sociological, Anthropological and Political Perspectives.* Cambridge, UK, 1989.

Marty, Martin E., and R. Scott Appleby, eds. *Accounting for Fundamentalisms: The Dynamic Character of Movements.* Chicago and London, 1994.

———. *Fundamentalisms and Society: Reclaiming the Sciences, the Family, and Education.* Chicago and London, 1993.

———. *Fundamentalisms and the State: Remaking Politics, Economies, and Militance.* Chicago and London, 1993.

———. *Fundamentalisms Comprehended.* Chicago and London, 1995.

———. *Fundamentalisms Observed.* Chicago and London, 1991.

Mason, S. N. "Was Josephus a Pharisee? A Re-Examination of *Life* 10–12." *Journal of Jewish Studies* 40 (1989).

Masparo, Henri. *China in Antiquity.* 2nd. ed. Trans. Frank A. Kiermann Jr. Folkestone, UK, 1978.

Masselman, George. *The Cradle of Colonialism.* New Haven, CT, 1963.

Mastnak, Tomaz. *Crusading Peace: Christendom, the Muslim World, and Western Political Order.* Berkeley, Los Angeles, and London, 2002.

Matarasso, P. M., trans. *The Quest of the Holy Grail.* Harmondsworth, UK, 1969.

Mattern, Susan. *Rome and the Enemy: Imperial Strategy in the Principate.* Berkeley, CA, 1999.

Matthews, Shelly, and E. Leigh Gibson, eds. *Violence in the New Testament.* New York and London, 2005.

Mawdudi, Abul Ala. "How to Establish Islamic Order in the Country." *Universal Message,* May 1983.

———. "Islamic Government." *Asia* 20 (September 1981).

———. *The Islamic Way of Life.* Lahore, 1979.

May, Henry F. *The Enlightenment in America*. New York, 1976.

Mayer, Hans Eberhard. *The Crusades*. Trans. J. Gillingham. 2nd ed. Oxford, 1993.

McCauley, Clark. "Conference Overview." In Jonathan Haas, ed., *The Anthropology of War*. Cambridge, UK, 1990.

McCutcheon, Russell. "The Category 'Religion' and the Politics of Tolerance." In Arthur L. Greil and David G. Bromley, eds., *Defining Religion: Investigating the Boundaries Between the Sacred and the Secular*. Oxford, 2003.

———. *Manufacturing Religion: The Discourse on Sui Generis Religion and the Politics of Nostalgia*. New York, 1997.

McDaniel, Charles A. "Violent Yearnings for the Kingdom of God: Munster's Militant Anabaptism." In James K. Wellman Jr., ed., *Belief and Bloodshed: Religion and Violence Across Time and Tradition*. Lanham, MD, 2007.

McDermott, Timothy. *Perfect Soldiers: The 9/11 Hijackers: Who They Were, Why They Did It*. New York, 2005.

McGinn, Bernard, and John Meyendorff, eds. *Christian Spirituality I: Origins to the Twelfth Century*. London, 1985.

McGrath, Alister. *The Twilight of Atheism: The Rise and Fall of Disbelief in the Modern World*. London and New York, 2006.

McKitterick, Rosamund. *The Frankish Kingdoms Under the Carolingians, 751–987*. London and New York, 1983.

McNeill, William H. *Plagues and People*. London, 1994.

———. *The Pursuit of Power: Technology, Armed Force and Society Since A.D. 1000*. Chicago, 1982.

McPherson, James M. *For Cause and Comrades: Why Men Fought in the Civil War*. New York, 1997.

McWhiney, Grady, and Perry D. Jamieson. *Attack or Die: The Civil War, Military Tactics and Southern Heritage*. Montgomery, AL, 1982.

Mein, Andrew. *Ezekiel and the Ethics of Exile*. Oxford and New York, 2001.

Mellaart, James. *Catal Huyuk: A Neolithic Town in Anatolia*. New York, 1967.

———. "Early Urban Communities in the Near East, 9000–3400 BCE." In P. R. S. Moorey, ed., *The Origins of Civilisation*. Oxford, 1979.

———. *The Neolithic of the Near East*. London, 1975.

Mendenhall, George W. *The Tenth Generation: The Origins of Biblical Tradition*. Baltimore, 1973.

Mentzer, Raymond A. *Heresy Proceedings in Languedoc, 1500–1560*. Philadelphia, 1984.

Mergui, Raphael, and Philippe Simonnot. *Israel's Ayatollahs: Meir Kahane and the Far Right in Israel*. London, 1987.

Meroni, Ariel. "The Readiness to Kill or Die: Suicide Terrorism in the Middle East." In Walter Reich, ed., *The Origins of Terrorism*. Cambridge, UK, 1990.

Michelet, Jules. *Historical View of the French Revolution from Its Earliest Indications to the Flight of the King in 1791*. Trans. C. Cooks. London, 1888.

Migne, J. P., ed. *Patrologia Latina*. Paris, 1844–67.

Mill, John Stuart. *Utilitarianism, Liberty, Representational Government*. London, 1990.

Miller, Perry. *Errand into the Wilderness*. Cambridge, MA, and London, 1956.

———. *Roger Williams: His Contribution to the American Tradition*. 2nd ed. New York, 1962.

Milton, John. *Major Works*. Ed. Stephen Orgel and Jonathan Goldberg. Oxford, 2008.

Milton-Edwards, Beverley. *Islamic Politics in Palestine*. London and New York, 1996.

Mir, Mustansire. "Some Features of Mawdudi's Tafhim al-Quran." *American Journal of Islamic Social Sciences* 2, no. 2 (1985).

Mitchell, Joshua. *Not by Reason Alone: Religion, History, and Identity in Early Modern Political Thought*. Chicago, 1993.

Mitchell, Richard P. *The Society of Muslim Brothers.* London, 1969.

Mitchell, Stephen. *Gilgamesh: A New English Version.* New York, London, Toronto, and Sydney, 2004.

Mohamedou, M. M. Ould. *Understanding al-Qaeda: The Transformation of War.* London, 2007.

Moin, Baqer. *Khomeini: Life of the Ayatollah.* London, 1999.

Molé, Marijan. *Culte, mythe, et cosmologie dans l'Iran ancien.* Paris, 1963.

Momen, Moojan. *An Introduction to Shii Islam: The History and Doctrines of Twelver Shiism.* New Haven, CT, and London, 1985.

Monroe, Lauren A. *Josiah's Reform and the Dynamics of Defilement: Israelite Rites of Violence and the Making of the Biblical Text.* Oxford, 2011.

Montagu, Ashley, ed. *Man and Aggression.* New York, 1973.

Montefiore, C. G., and H. Loewe, eds. *A Rabbinic Anthology.* New York, 1974.

Monter, William. *Frontiers of Heresy: The Spanish Inquisition from the Basque Lands to Sicily.* Cambridge, UK, 1990.

Moore, James R. "Geologists and the Interpreters of Genesis in the Nineteenth Century." In David Lindberg and Ronald L. Numbers, eds., *God and Nature: Historical Essays on the Encounter Between Christianity and Science.* Berkeley, Los Angeles, and London, 1986.

Moore, R. I. *The Formation of a Persecuting Society: Power and Deviance in Western Europe, 950–1250.* Oxford, 1987.

Moore, R. Laurence. *Religious Outsiders and the Making of Americans.* Oxford and New York, 1986.

Moore, Rebecca. "American as Cherry Pie: The People's Temple and Violence." In Catherine Wessinger, ed., *Millennialism, Persecution, and Violence: Historical Circumstances.* Syracuse, NY, 1986.

———. "Narratives of Persecution, Suffering, and Martyrdom in the People's Temple and Jonestown." In James R. Lewis, ed., *Violence and the New Religious Movements.* Oxford, 2011.

Moorey, P. R. S. *The Origins of Civilisation.* Oxford, 1979.

———, and P. J. Parr, eds. *Archaeology in the Levant: Essays for Kathleen Kenyon.* Warminster, UK, 1978.

More, Thomas. *A Dialogue Concerning Heresies.* Ed. Thomas M. C. Lawlor. New Haven, CT, 1981.

———. *Utopia.* Ed. George M. Logan and Robert M. Adams. Cambridge, UK, 1989.

Morgan, Edmund S. *American Slavery, American Freedom: The Ordeal of Colonial Virginia.* New York, 1975.

Morris, Christopher. *The Papal Monarchy: The Western Church from 1050 to 1250.* Oxford, 1991.

Morrison, Karl F. *Tradition and Authority in the Western Church, 300–1140.* Princeton, NJ, 1969.

Moss, Candida R. *The Myth of Persecution: How Early Christians Invented a Story of Martyrdom.* New York, 2013.

———. *The Other Christs: Imitating Jesus in Ancient Christian Ideologies of Martyrdom.* Oxford, 2010.

Murphy, Andrew R., ed. *The Blackwell Companion to Religion and Violence.* Chichester, UK, 2011.

———. "Cromwell, Mather and the Rhetoric of Puritan Violence." In Murphy, *The Blackwell Companion to Religion and Violence.*

Murrin, John M. "A Roof Without Walls: The Dilemma of National Identity." In Richard Beeman, Stephen Botein, and Edward E. Carter III, eds., *Beyond Confederation: Origins of the Constitution in American Identity.* Chapel Hill, NC, 1987.

Musurillo, H., trans. *The Acts of the Christian Martyrs.* Oxford, 1972.

Nadelson, Theodore. *Trained to Kill: Soldiers at War.* Baltimore, 2005.

Nānamoli, Bhikku, ed. *The Life of the Buddha, According to the Pali Canon.* Kandy, Sri Lanka, 1992.

Neff, John U. *War and Human Progress: An Essay on the Rise of Industrial Civilization.* New York, 1950.

Nestorius. *Bazaar of Heracleides.* Trans. G. R. Driver and Leonard Hodgson. Oxford, 1925.

Netanyahu, Benzion. *The Origins of the Inquisition in Fifteenth-Century Spain.* New York, 1995.

Neusner, Jacob. *From Politics to Piety.* Englewood Cliffs, NJ, 1973.

Newton, Huey. *Revolutionary Suicide.* New York, 1973.

Nicholls, David. "The Theatre of Martyrdom in the French Reformation." *Past and Present* 121 (1998).

Nicholson, R. A. *A Literary History of the Arabs.* Cambridge, UK, 1953.

———. *The Mystics of Islam.* London, 1963.

Niditch, Susan. *War in the Hebrew Bible: A Study in the Ethics of Violence.* New York and Oxford, 1993.

Noll, Mark A., *America's God: From Jonathan Edwards to Abraham Lincoln.* Oxford and New York, 2002.

———. *The Civil War as a Theological Crisis.* Chapel Hill, NC, 2006.

———. *The Old Religion in a New World: The History of American Christianity.* Grand Rapids, MI, 2002.

———. *Religion and American Politics: From the Colonial Period to the 1980s.* Oxford and New York, 1990.

———. "The Rise and Long Life of the Protestant Enlightenment in America." In William M. Shea and Peter A. Huff, eds., *Knowledge and Belief in America: Enlightenment Traditions and Modern Religious Thought.* New York, 1995.

North, Jonathan. "General Hochte and Counterinsurgency." *Journal of Military History* 62 (2003).

Numbers, Ronald L. *The Creationists: The Evolution of Scientific Creationism.* Berkeley, Los Angeles, and London, 1992.

O'Connell, Robert L. *Of Arms and Men: A History of War, Weapons and Aggression.* New York and Oxford, 1989.

———. *Ride of the Second Horseman: The Birth and Death of War.* New York and Oxford, 1995.

Oldenbourg, Zoé. *Le Bûcher de Montségur.* Paris, 1959.

Oldenburg, Hermann. *Buddha: His Life, His Doctrine, His Order.* Trans. William Hoey. London, 1982.

Olivelle, Patrick. "The Renouncer Tradition." In Gavin Flood, ed., *The Blackwell Companion to Hinduism.* Oxford, 2003.

———, ed. and trans. *Samnyasa Upanisads: Hindu Scriptures on Asceticism and Renunciation.* New York and Oxford, 1992.

———. *Upanisads.* New York and Oxford, 1996.

Oliver, Anne Marie, and Paul F. Steinberg. *The Road to Martyrs' Square: A Journey to the World of the Suicide Bomber.* Oxford, 2005.

Ollenburger, Ben C. *Zion, the City of the Great King: A Theological Symbol of the Jerusalem Cult.* Sheffield, UK, 1987.

Olmstead, A. T. *History of Assyria.* New York, 1923.

Oppenheim, A. L. *Ancient Mesopotamia: Portrait of a Dead Civilization.* Chicago, 1977.

———. "Trade in the Ancient Near East." *International Congress of Economic History* 5 (1976).

Origen. *Against Celsus.* Trans. Henry Chadwick. Cambridge, UK, 1980.

Ortega y Gasset, J. *Meditations on Hunting.* New York, 1985.

Ozment, Steven. *The Reformation of the Cities: The Appeal of Protestantism to Sixteenth-Century Germany and Switzerland*. New Haven, CT, 1975.

Paine, Thomas. *Common Sense and the Crisis*. New York, 1975.

Palladius, *Dialogue on the Life of John Chrysostom*. Trans. Robert T. Meyer. New York, 1985.

Pannikkar, Raimundo. *The Trinity and the Religious Experience of Man*. London and New York, 1973.

Pape, Robert. "Dying to Kill Us." *New York Times*, September 22, 2003.

———. *Dying to Win: The Strategic Logic of Suicide Terrorism*. New York, 2005.

———. "The Logic of Suicide Terrorism." Interview by Scott McConnell. *The American Conservative*, July 18, 2007.

Pareek, Radhey Shyam. *Contribution of Arya Samaj in the Making of Modern India, 1975–1947*. New Delhi, 1973.

Parker, Geoffrey, ed. *The Thirty Years' War*. London, 1984.

Parsons, Timothy H. *The Rule of Empires: Those Who Built Them, Those Who Endured Them, and Why They Always Fail*. Oxford, 2010.

Partner, Peter. *God of Battles: Holy Wars of Christianity and Islam*. London, 1997.

Patlagean, Evelyne. *Pauvreté économique et pauvreté sociale à Byzance, 4ᵉ–7ᵉ*. Paris, 1977.

Pelikan, Jaroslav. *The Christian Tradition: A History of the Development of Doctrine*. Vol. 1: *The Emergence of the Catholic Tradition*. Chicago and London, 1971.

Perrin, Norman. *Jesus and the Language of the Kingdom*. Philadelphia, 1976.

———. *Rediscovering the Teachings of Jesus*. New York, 1967.

Pesteria, Carla Garden. *Protestant Empire: Religion and the Making of the British Atlantic World*. Philadelphia, 2004.

Peters, F. E. *The Distant Shore: The Islamic Centuries in Jerusalem*. New York, 1993.

Peterson, Derek, and Darren Walhof, eds. *The Invention of Religion: Rethinking Belief in Politics and History*. New Brunswick, NJ, and London, 2002.

Petitfrère, Claude. "The Origins of the Civil War in the Vendée." *French History* 2 (1998).

Phillips, Keith. *The Cousins' Wars: Religious Politics and the Triumph of Anglo-America*. New York, 1999.

Pirenne, Henri. *Ecclesiastical and Social History of Europe*. New York, 1956.

———. *Medieval Cities: Their Origins and the Revival of Trade*. Princeton, NJ, 1946.

Polgar, S., ed. *Population, Ecology and Social Evolution*. The Hague, 1975.

Poliskensky, J. V. *War and Society in Europe, 1618–1848*. Cambridge, UK, 1978.

Posman, Ellen. "History, Humiliation and Religious Violence." In Andrew R. Murphy, ed., *The Blackwell Companion to Religion and Violence*. Chichester, UK, 2011.

Postgate, J. N. *Mesopotamian Society and Economics at the Dawn of History*. London, 1992.

Potter, David. *A History of France, 1460–1560: The Emergence of a Nation State*. London, 1995.

Prawer, Joshua. *The Latin Kingdom of Jerusalem: European Colonialism in the Middle Ages*. London, 1972.

Prescott, William H. *History of the Conquest of Mexico and Peru*. New York, 1936.

Preston, Andrew. *Sword of the Spirit, Shield of Faith: Religion in American War and Diplomacy*. New York and Toronto, 2012.

Pritchard, J. B., ed. *Ancient Near Eastern Texts Relating to the Old Testament*. Princeton, NJ, 1950.

Puett, Michael J. *To Become a God: Cosmology, Sacrifice and Self-Divination in Early China*. Cambridge, MA, and London, 2002.

Purchas, Samuel. *Hakluytus Posthumous or Purchas His Pilgrimes*. Glasgow, 1905–6.

Puppi, Lionello. *Torment in Art: Pain, Violence and Martyrdom*. New York, 1991.

Qutb, Sayed. *Milestones (Ma'alim fi'l-tareeq)*. Ed. and trans. A. B. al-Mehri. Birmingham, UK, 2006.

Radcliffe, A. R. *The Andaman Islanders*. New York, 1948.

Ravitsky, Aviezer. *Messianism, Zionism and Jewish Religious Radicalism*. Trans. Michael Swirsky and Jonathan Chapman. Chicago, 1996.

———. *The Roots of Kahanism: Consciousness and Political Reality*. Trans. Moshe Auman. Jerusalem, 1986.

Redfield, Robert. *Peasant Society and Culture: An Anthropological Approach to Civilization*. Chicago, 1956.

Reich, Walter, ed. *The Origins of Terrorism*. Cambridge, UK, 1990.

Reinberg, Virginia, "Liturgy and Laity in Late Medieval and Reformation France." *Sixteenth Century Journal* 23 (Autumn 1992).

Renfrew, Colin. *The Puzzle of Indo-European Origins*. London, 1987.

Renna, Thomas J. "Kingship in the *Disputatio inter clericum et militem*." *Speculum* 48 (1973).

Renou, Louis. *Religions of Ancient India*. London, 1953.

———. "Sur la notion de *brahman*." *Journal Asiatique* 23 (1949).

Richardson, H. G. *The English Jewry Under the Angevin Kings*. London, 1960.

Richardson, Louise. *What Terrorists Want: Understanding the Terrorist Threat*. London, 2006.

Rieff, David. *Slaughterhouse: Bosnia and the Failure of the West*. New York, 1995.

Riley-Smith, Jonathan. "Crusading as an Act of Love." *History* 65 (1980).

———. *The First Crusade and the Idea of Crusading*. London, 1986.

———. *The First Crusaders, 1095–1131*. Cambridge, UK, 1997.

———, and Louise Riley-Smith. *The Crusades: Idea and Reality, 1095–1274*. London, 1981.

Rindos, David. *The Origins of Agriculture: An Evolutionary Perspective*. Orlando, FL, 1984.

Rives, James B. "The Decree of Decius and the Religion of Empire." *Journal of Roman Studies* 89 (1999).

———. *Religion in the Roman Empire*. Oxford, 2007.

Roberts, Alexander, and James Donaldson, trans. *The Nicene and Post-Nicene Fathers*. 14 vols. Edinburgh, 1885.

Robert the Monk. *Historia Iherosolimitana*. Paris, 1846.

Robinson, Glenn E. *Building a Palestinian State: The Incomplete Revolution*. Bloomington, IN, 1997.

Robinson, I. S. "Gregory VII and the Soldiers of Christ." *Historia* 58 (1978).

Rogers, Paul. "The Global War on Terror and Its Impact on the Conduct of War." In George Kassimeris, ed., *The Barbarisation of Warfare*. London, 2006.

Romier, Lucien. "A Dissident Nobility Under the Cloak of Religion." In J. H. H. Salmon, ed., *The French Wars of Religion: How Important Were Religious Factors?* Lexington, MA, 1967.

Ropp, Theodore. *War in the Modern World*. Durham, NC, 1959.

Rose, Jacqueline. "Deadly Embrace." *London Review of Books* 26, no. 21 (November 4, 2004).

Rosenak, Michael. "Jewish Fundamentalism in Israeli Education." In Martin E. Marty and R. Scott Appleby, eds., *Fundamentalisms and Society: Reclaiming the Sciences, the Family and Education*. Chicago and London, 1993.

Roth, Norman. *Conversos, Inquisition and the Expulsion of Jews from Spain*. Madison, WI, 1995.

Rousseau, Jean-Jacques. *Political Writings*. Ed. C. E. Vaughan. Cambridge, UK, 1915.

———. *Politics and the Arts: Letter to M. D'Alembert on the Theatre*. Trans. Alan Bloom. Ithaca, NY, 1960.

———. *The Social Contract*. Trans. Willmoore Kendall. South Bend, IN, 1954.

————. *The Social Contract and Discourses*. Trans. and ed. G. D. H. Cole. Rev. J. H. Brumfitt and John C. Hall. London, 1973.

————. *The Social Contract and Other Later Political Writings*. Ed. Victor Gourevitch. Cambridge, UK, 1997.

Routledge, Bruce. *Moab in the Iron Age: Hegemony, Polity, Archaeology*. Philadelphia, 2004.

————. "The Politics of Mesha: Segmented Identities and State Formation in Iron Age Moab." *Journal of the Economic and Social History of the Orient* 43 (2000).

Rufinus. *The Church History of Rufinus of Aquileia*. Trans. Philip R. Amidon. Oxford, 1997.

Runciman, Steven. *A History of the Crusades*. 3 vols. London, 1965.

Ruthven, Malise. *A Fury for God: The Islamist Attack on America*. London, 2003.

Sachedina, Abdulaziz Abdulhussein. "Activist Shi'ism in Iran, Iraq and Lebanon." In Martin E. Marty and R. Scott Appleby, eds., *Fundamentalisms Observed*. Chicago and London, 1991.

————. "Ali Shariati: Ideologue of the Iranian Revolution." In John L. Esposito, ed., *Voices of Resurgent Islam*. New York and Oxford, 1980.

Sadat, Anwar. *Revolt on the Nile*. New York, 1957.

Sageman, Marc. *Leaderless Jihad: Terror Networks in the Twenty-First Century*. Philadelphia, 2008.

————. *Understanding Terror Networks*. Philadelphia, 2004.

Saggs, H. W. F. "Assyrian Warfare in the Sargonid Period." *Iraq* 25 (1963).

————. *The Might That Was Assyria*. London, 1984.

Sagi, Avi. "The Punishment of Amalek in Jewish Tradition: Coping with the Moral Problem." *Harvard Theological Review* 87, no. 3 (1994).

Salmon, J. H. M. *Society in Crisis: France in the Sixteenth Century*. New York, 1975.

————, ed. *The French Wars of Religion: How Important Were Religious Factors?* Lexington, MA, 1967.

Sanders, N. K., trans. and ed. *Poems of Heaven and Hell from Ancient Mesopotamia*. London, 1971.

Savarkar, Vinayak Damdas. *Hindutva*. Bombay, 1969.

Sawyer, R. D., ed. *The Seven Military Classics of Ancient China*. Boulder, CO, 1993.

Sayers, Dorothy L., trans. *The Song of Roland*. Harmondsworth, UK, 1957.

Sayyid, Bobby. *A Fundamental Fear: Eurocentrism and the Emergence of Islamism*. London, 1997.

Schafer, Boyd C. *Nationalism: Myth and Reality*. New York, 1952.

Schauwecker, Franz. *The Fiery Way*. London and Toronto, 1921.

Schein, Seth, L. *The Mortal Hero: An Introduction to Homer's* Iliad. Berkeley, Los Angeles, and London, 1984.

Schilling, Heinz. "War and Peace at the Emergence of Modernity: Europe Between State Belligerence, Religious Wars and the Desire for Peace in 1648." In Klaus Bussman and Heinz Schilling, eds., *War and Peace in Europe*. 3 vols. Münster, 1998.

Schneider, Tammi J. *An Introduction to Ancient Mesopotamian Religion*. Grand Rapids, MI, and Cambridge UK, 2011.

Schniedewind, William M. *How the Bible Became a Book: The Textualization of Ancient Israel*. Cambridge, UK, 2004.

Schorske, Carl E. *German Social Democracy, 1905–1917: The Development of the Great Schism*. Cambridge, MA, 1955.

Schumpeter, Joseph A. *Imperialism and Social Classes: Two Essays*. New York, 1955.

Schwartz, Benjamin I. *The World of Thought in Ancient China*. Cambridge, MA, 1985.

Schwartz, Regina. *The Curse of Cain: The Violent Legacy of Monotheism*. Chicago, 1997.

Secher, Reynauld. *La Génocide franco-français: La Vendée-vengee*. Paris, 1986.

Segev, Tom. *The Seventh Million: The Israelis and the Holocaust.* Trans. Haim Watzman. New York, 1991.

Segal, Alan F. *Paul the Convert: The Apostolate and Apostasy of Saul the Pharisee.* New Haven, CT, and London, 1990.

Selengut, Charles. *Sacred Fury: Understanding Religious Violence.* Walnut Creek, CA, 2003.

Sells, Michael A. *The Bridge Betrayed: Religion and Genocide in Bosnia.* Berkeley, Los Angeles, and London, 1996.

Sen, Amartya. *Identity and Violence: The Illusion of Destiny.* London, 2007.

Shea, William M., and Peter A. Huff, eds. *Knowledge and Belief in America: Enlightenment Traditions and Modern Religious Thought.* New York, 1995.

Shehad, Anthony. *Legacy of the Prophet: Despots, Democrats and the New Politics of Islam.* Boulder, CO, 2011.

Shennon, J. H. *The Origins of the Modern European State.* London, 1974.

Sherwin-White, A. N. *Roman Law and Roman Society in the New Testament.* Oxford, 1963.

Sick, Gary. *All Fall Down: America's Fateful Encounter with Iran.* London, 1985.

Sigal, P. A. "Et les marcheurs de Dieu prierent leurs armes." *L'Histoire* 47 (1982).

Sivan, Emmanuel. "The Crusades Described by Modern Arab Historiography." *Asian and African Studies* 8 (1972).

———. "Genèse de contre-croisade: Un traité damasquin de début du XIIe siècle." *Journal Asiatique* 254 (1966).

———. *L'Islam et la Croisade.* Paris, 1968.

Skinner, Quentin. *The Foundations of Modern Political Thought.* 2 vols. Cambridge, UK, 1978.

Slim, Hugo. "Why Protect Civilians? Innocence, Immunity and Enmity in War." *International Affairs* 79, no. 3 (2003).

Slingerland, Edward, trans. *Confucius: Analects, with Selections from Traditional Commentaries.* Indianapolis and Cambridge, UK, 2003.

Smith, Brian K. *Reflections on Resemblance, Ritual, and Religion.* Oxford and New York, 1989.

Smith, Howard D. *Chinese Religions.* London, 1968.

Smith, Huston. *The World's Religions: Our Great Wisdom Traditions.* San Francisco, 1991.

Smith, John. *John Smith: Works.* Ed. Edwin Arber and A. C. Bradley. Edinburgh, 1910.

Smith, John D., ed. and trans. *The Mahabharata: An Abridged Translation.* London, 2009.

Smith, Jonathan Z. *Imagining Religion: From Babylon to Jonestown.* Chicago and London, 1982.

———. *Map Is Not Territory: Studies in the History of Religions.* Chicago and London, 1978.

Smith, Mark S. *The Early History of God: Yahweh and the Other Deities in Ancient Israel.* New York and London, 1990.

———. *The Origins of Biblical Monotheism: Israel's Polytheistic Background and the Ugaritic Texts.* New York and London, 2001.

Smith, William Cantwell. *Belief in History.* Charlottesville, VA, 1985.

———. *Faith and Belief.* Princeton, NJ, 1987.

———. *Islam in Modern History.* Princeton, NJ, and London, 1957.

———. *The Meaning and End of Religion: A New Approach to the Religious Traditions of Mankind.* New York, 1962.

———. *What Is Scripture?: A Comparative Approach.* London, 1993.

Sontag, Susan. "What Have We Done?" *Guardian,* May 24, 2005.

Southern, R. W. *The Making of the Middle Ages.* London, 1967.

————. *Western Society and the Church in the Middle Ages.* Harmondsworth, UK, 1970.

————. *Western Views of Islam in the Middle Ages.* Cambridge, MA, 1962.

Sozomen. *The Ecclesiastical History of Sozomen.* Trans. Chester D. Harnaft. Grand Rapids, MI, 1989.

Spear, Percival. *India.* Ann Arbor, MI, 1961.

Sperling, S. David. "Joshua 24 Re-examined." *Hebrew Union College Annual* 58 (1987).

————. *The Original Torah: The Political Intent of the Bible's Writers.* New York and London, 1998.

Spierenberg, Peter. *The Spectacle of Suffering: Executions and the Evolution of Repression: From a Pre-Industrial Metropolis to the European Experience.* Cambridge, UK, 1984.

Sprinzak, Ehud. *The Ascendance of Israel's Radical Right.* New York, 1991.

————. "Three Models of Religious Violence: The Case of Jewish Fundamentalism in Israel." In Martin E. Marty and R. Scott Appleby, eds., *Fundamentalisms and the State: Remaking Polities, Economies and Militance.* Chicago and London, 1993.

Srivasta, Sushil. "The Ayodhya Controversy: A Third Dimension." *Probe India,* January 1998.

Stannard, David. *American Holocaust: The Conquest of the New World.* New York and Oxford, 1992.

Ste. Croix, G. E. M. de. "Why Were the Early Christians Persecuted?" In Michael Whitby and Joseph Street, eds., *Martyrdom and Orthodoxy.* New York, 1987.

Steiner, George. *In Bluebeard's Castle: Some Notes Towards the Redefinition of Culture.* New Haven, CT, 1971.

Stevans, G. W. *With Kitchener to Khartoum.* London, 1898.

Stout, Henry S. "Rhetoric and Reality in the Early Republic; the Case of the Federalist Clergy." In Mark A. Noll, ed., *Religion and American Politics: From the Colonial Period to the 1980s.* Oxford and New York, 1980.

Strayer, Joseph R. "Feudalism in Western Europe." In Rushton Coulborn ed., *Feudalism in History.* Hamden, CT, 1965.

————. *Medieval Statecraft and the Perspectives of History.* Princeton, NJ, 1971.

————. *On the Medieval Origin of the Modern State.* Princeton, NJ, 1970.

Strozier, Charles B., David M. Terman, and James W. Jones, eds. *The Fundamentalist Mindset.* Oxford, 2010.

Stuart, Henry S., and Charles Reagan Wolfson, eds. *Religion and the American Civil War.* New York, 1998.

Sullivan, Andrew. "This *Is* a Religious War." *New York Times Magazine,* October 7, 2001.

Sun Tzu. *The Art of War: Complete Texts and Commentaries.* Trans. Thomas Cleary. Boston and London, 1988.

Szasz, Ferenc. *The Divided Mind of Protestant America, 1880–1930.* University, AL, 1982.

Tabari, Azar. "The Role of the Shii Clergy in Modern Iranian Politics." In Nikki R. Keddie, ed., *Religion and Politics in Iran: Shiism from Quietism to Revolution.* New Haven, CT, and London, 1983.

Tacitus, Cornelius. *Agricola, Gemania, Dialogus.* Trans. M. Hutton and W. Peterson. Cambridge, MA, 1989.

Taheri, Amir. *The Spirit of Allah: Khomeini and the Islamic Revolution.* London, 1985.

Thapar, Romila. *Asoka and the Decline of the Mauryas.* Oxford, 1961.

————. *Early India: From the Origins to AD 1300.* Berkeley and Los Angeles, 2002.

Theissen, Gerd. *The First Followers of Jesus: A Sociological Analysis of the Earliest Christianity.* Trans. John Bowden. London, 1978.

————. *The Miracle Stories: Early Christian Tradition.* Philadelphia, 1982.

———. *The Social Setting of Pauline Christianity: Essays on Corinth.* Ed. and trans. John H. Schutz. Eugene, OR, 2004.

Thompson, James Westfall. *Economic and Social History of the Middle Ages.* New York, 1928.

———. *The Wars of Religion in France, 1559–1576: Huguenots, Catherine de Medici, Philip II.* 2nd ed. New York, 1957.

Tibi, Bassam. *The Crisis of Political Islam: A Pre-Industrial Culture in the Scientific-Technological Age.* Salt Lake City, 1988.

Tierny, Brian. *The Crisis of Church and State, 1050–1300.* Toronto, 1988.

Tilly, Charles, ed. *The Formation of National States in Western Europe.* Princeton, NJ, 1975.

Tocqueville, Alexis de. *Democracy in America.* Ed. and trans. Harvey Claflin Mansfield and Delba Winthrop. Chicago, 2000.

———. *The Old Regime and the French Revolution.* 2 vols. Ed. and trans. François Furet and Françoise Melonio. Chicago, 1988.

Tracy, James D. *Emperor Charles V, Impresario of War: Campaign Strategy, International Finance and Domestic Politics.* Cambridge, UK, 2002.

———, ed. *Luther and the Modern State in Germany.* Kirbville, MO, 1986.

Tu Wei-ming. *Confucian Thought: Selfhood as Creative Transformation.* Albany, NY, 1985.

Tuck, Richard. *The Rights of War and Peace: Political Thought and the International Order from Grotius to Kant.* Oxford, 1999.

Tyerman, Christopher J. *England and the Crusades, 1095–1588.* Chicago, 1988.

———. "Sed nihil fecit? The Last Captians and the Recovery of the Holy Land." In J. Gillingham and J. C. Holt, eds., *War and Government in the Middle Ages: Essays in Honour of J. D. Prestwich.* Woodbridge, UK, and Totowa, NJ, 1980.

Ur Rehman, Rafiq. "Please Tell Me, Mr President, Why a US Drone Assassinated My Mother." *Guardian,* October 25, 2013.

Ussishkin, David. "King Solomon's Palaces." *Biblical Archaeologist* 36 (1973).

Van Buitenen, J. A. B, ed. and trans. *The Mahabharata.* 3 vols. Chicago and London, 1973, 1975, 1978.

Veblen, Thorstein. *The Theory of the Leisure Class: An Economic Study of Institutions.* Boston, 1973.

Vernant, Jean-Pierre. *Myth and Society in Ancient Greece.* Trans. Janet Lloyd. 3rd ed. New York, 1996.

Vogts, Alfred. *A History of Militarism, Civilian and Military.* Rev. ed. New York, 1959.

Voll, John O. "Fundamentalism in the Sunni Arab World: Egypt and the Sudan." In Martin E. Marty and R. Scott Appleby, eds. *Fundamentalisms Observed.* Chicago and London, 1991.

Vries, Hent de, ed. *Religion Beyond a Concept.* New York, 2008.

Wait, Gaston, ed. and trans. *Nicholas Turc: Chronique d'Egypte, 1798–1804.* Cairo, 1950.

Waley, Arthur, trans. and ed. *The Analects of Confucius.* New York, 1992.

Wallace, Anthony F. C. *Jefferson and the Indians: The Tragic Fate of the First Americans.* Cambridge, MA, 1999.

Wallace-Hadrill, J. M. *The Barbarian West: The Early Middle Ages, AD 400–1000.* New York, 1962.

———. *Early Medieval History.* Oxford, 1975.

———. *The Frankish Church.* Oxford, 1983.

Watson, B., ed. and trans. *Han Fei Tzu: Basic Writings.* New York, 1964.

———. *Mo-Tzu: Basic Writings.* New York, 1963.

———. *Records of the Grand Historian of China.* New York, 1961

———. *Xunzi: Basic Writings.* New York, 2003.

Watt, W. Montgomery. *The Influence of Islam in Medieval Europe.* Edinburgh, 1972.

————. *Muhammad at Mecca*. Oxford, 1953.

————. *Muhammad at Medina*. Oxford, 1956.

————. *Muhammad's Mecca: History in the Qur'an*. Edinburgh, 1988.

Weber, Max. *The Protestant Ethic and the Spirit of Capitalism*. Trans. Talcott Parsons. New York, 1958.

————. *The Religion of China: Confucianism and Taoism*. Trans. Hans H. Gerth. Glencoe, IL, 1949.

————. *The Religion of India: The Sociology of Hinduism and Buddhism*. Trans. Hans H. Gerth and Don Martindale. Glencoe, IL, 1958.

————. *The Theory of Social and Economic Organization*. Trans. A. M. Henderson and Talcott Parsons. New York, 1947.

Wedgwood, C. W. *The Thirty Years War*. New Haven, CT, 1939.

Weigley, Russell F. *The Age of Battles: The Quest for Decisive Warfare from Breitenfeld to Waterloo*. Bloomington, IN, 1991.

Weinfeld, Moshe. *Deuteronomy and the Deuteronomic School*. Oxford, 1972.

Welch, Claude E., Jr. *Political Modernization*. Belmont, CA, 1967.

Welch, Holmes. *The Parting of the Way: Lao Tzu and the Taoist Movement*. London, 1958.

Wellman, James K., Jr., ed. *Belief and Bloodshed: Religion and Violence Across Time and Tradition*. Lanham, MD, 2007.

Wenke, K. J. *The Origins of Civilizations*. Oxford, 1979.

————. *Patterns of Prehistory: Humankind's First Three Million Years*. New York, 1961.

Wensinck, Jan. *Concordance et indices de la tradition musulmane*. 5 vols. Leiden, 1992.

Wessinger, Catherine. *How the Millennium Comes Violently: Jonestown to Heaven's Gate*. New York, 2000.

————, ed. *Millennialism, Persecution and Violence: Historical Circumstances*. Syracuse, NY, 1986.

Whitaker, Jarrod L. *Strong Arms and Drinking Strength: Masculinity, Violence and the Body in Ancient India*. Oxford, 2011.

Whittaker, D. H., ed. *The Terrorist Reader*. London, 2001.

Whitby, Michael, and Joseph Street, eds. *Martyrdom and Orthodoxy*. New York, 1987.

Wickham, Lionel R. *Hilary of Poitiers: Conflicts of Conscience and Law in the Fourth Century*. Liverpool, 1997.

Wilkinson, P. *Terrorism Versus Democracy: The Liberal State Response*. London, 2001.

Williamson, H. G. M. "The Concept of Israel in Transition." In E. E. Clements, ed., *The World of Ancient Israel: Sociological, Anthropological and Political Perspectives*. Cambridge, UK, 1989.

Wilson, E. O. *On Human Nature*. Cambridge, MA, 1978.

Wilson, John F. "Religion, Government and Power in the New American Nation." In Mark A. Noll, ed., *Religion and American Politics, from the Colonial Period to the 1980s*. Oxford and New York, 1990.

Wirt, Sherwood Eliot, ed. *Spiritual Awakening: Classic Writings of the Eighteenth-Century Devotions to Inspire and Help the Twentieth-Century Reader*. Tring, UK, 1988.

Wittfogel, Karl A. *Oriental Despotism: A Comparative Study of Total Power*. New Haven, CT, 1957.

Witzel, Michael. "Vedas and Upanisads." In Gavin Flood, ed., *The Blackwell Companion to Hinduism*. Oxford, 2003.

World Council of Churches. *Violence, Nonviolence and the Struggle for Social Justice*. Geneva, 1972.

Wright, Lawrence. *The Looming Tower: Al-Qaeda's Road to 9/11*. New York, 2006.

Wright, Louis B. *Religion and Empire: The Alliance Between Piety and Commerce in the English Expansion, 1558–1625*. Chapel Hill, NC, 1943.

Wright, Quincy. *A Study of War.* 2nd ed. Chicago, 1965.

Wyatt, Don J. "Confucian Ethical Action and the Boundaries of Peace and War." In Andre R. Murphy, ed., *The Blackwell Companion to Religion and Violence.* Chichester, UK, 2011.

Yadin, Yigal. *The Art of Warfare in Biblical Lands: In Light of Archaeological Study.* 2 vols. New York, 1963.

Yao, Xinzhong. *An Introduction to Confucianism.* Cambridge, UK, 2000.

Yovel, Yirmanyahu. *Spinoza and Other Heretics.* 2 vols.: I. *The Marrano of Reason;* II. *Adventures of Immanence.* Princeton, NJ, 1989.

Zaehner, R. C. *Hinduism.* London, New York, and Toronto, 1962.

Zinn, Howard. *A People's History of the United States, from 1492 to the Present.* 2nd ed. London and New York, 1996.

Zuckmayer, Carl. *Pro Domo.* Stockholm, 1938.

Zweig, Stefan. *The World of Yesterday: An Autobiography.* Trans. Anthea Bell. New York, 1945.

Index

Abbasids, 194–5, 197–200, 221, 349, 397
Abd al-Aziz University, 367
Abd al-Malik, 194
Abd al-Nasser, Gemal, 316–17, 321–3, 345, 399
Abdu, Muhammad, 319
Abel, 104, 392
abolitionists, 294–5
Abraham, 104, 107, 108, 156, 180, 326, 418–19n20
Abrahamic faiths, 16, 226; see also Christianity; Islam; Judaism
absolute monarchies, 71, 194; Chinese, 81, 98, 99; European, 241, 246, 256, 257, 259, 276; Muslim, 195, 233, 394; Persian, 174–5, 193
absolutism, 198, 244, 293; religious, 45, 62, 106, 123, 168, 192, 243, 263 (see also fundamentalism); royal, see absolute monarchies
Abu Bakr (first caliph), 187
Abu Ghraib prison, 389, 457n79
Achaemenid dynasty, 120
Achilles, 34, 35
Acre, 220
Acton, John Emerich Edward Dalberg, Lord, 293, 298, 326, 396
Acts of the Martyrs, 149, 152
Adadnirari I, King of Assyria, 42
Adalbéron, bishop of Laon, 433n27
Adam, 103–4, 125, 263, 264
Adams, John, 270–2
Adams, Sam, 270
Adebolajo, Michael, 390
Adebolawe, Michael, 390
Advani, L. K., 358
Aelia Capitolina (Jerusalem), 145

Afghanistan, 337; al-Qaeda in, 378–81; ancient, 29, 42, 69, 120; Arab Islamist supporters of, see Arab-Afghans; Soviet invasion and occupation of, 366–9, 372; Taliban control of, 377, 378; United States war against, 385–7
Africa, 170, 178; Islam in, 370; slave trade to Americas from, 235, 294, 399; see also specific nations and regions
African Americans, 298, 331, 338, 356
Afula (Israel), 362
Agni (sacred fire), 48, 50–2, 61
Agnicayana, 50, 55
agrarian civilizations, 12–14, 26–7; see also specific empires, kingdoms, regions and states
ahadith, 189–90, 196, 216, 218, 219, 334, 362, 364
Ahmadis, 313, 448n29
Ahura Mazda, 122
Ai, 110–11
Ain Jalut, Battle of, 221
Ajatashatru, King of Magadha, 68
Ajax, 34
Ajivaka school, 69
Akbar, Moghul Emperor, 287
Akitu ritual, 39–40, 43, 120
Akiva, Rabbi, 145
Akkadian Empire, 37–8, 120
al-Bahri, Nasir, 371, 372
al-Banna, Hassan, 319–21
al-Dukhayyil, Feisal, 380
al-Fazari, Abu Ishaq, 196
al-Hakim, Abu Ali Mansur Tariqu, Fatimid emperor, 223
al-Haqq, Zia, 314

A NOTE ON THE TYPE

The text of this book was set in Sabon, a typeface designed by Jan Tschichold (1902–1974), the well-known German typographer. Based loosely on the original designs by Claude Garamond (c. 1480–1561), Sabon is unique in that it was explicitly designed for hot metal composition on both the Monotype and Linotype machines as well as for filmsetting. Designed in 1966 in Frankfurt, Sabon was named for the famous Lyons punch cutter Jacques Sabon, who is thought to have brought some of Garamond's matrices to Frankfurt.

Typeset by Scribe,
Philadelphia, Pennsylvania

Printed and bound by Berryville Graphics,
Berryville, Virginia

Designed by Cassandra J. Pappas